ENGLISH FOR THE COLLEGE BOARDS
-1995-

PREPARING FOR THE
SCHOLASTIC ASSESSMENT TEST

SAT I: REASONING TEST—VERBAL

HENRY I. CHRIST

Dedicated to serving

AMSCO

our nation's youth

Amsco School Publications, Inc.
315 Hudson Street / New York, N.Y. 10013

Henry I. Christ has had a long and distinguished career as writer, editor, teacher, and supervisor. A specialist in language, literature, and composition, he has written more than a hundred textbooks in the field of English, including many published by Amsco. For nearly ten years, he was the editor of the teachers' magazine *High Points*. He has been active in professional organizations and has held office at the local, state, and national levels. A frequent speaker at English conventions and workshops throughout the United States, he has also lectured on educational television and frequently participated in curriculum development and evaluation.

Marie E. Christ has worked with Henry I. Christ as a partner throughout his writing career. She has provided many practical suggestions and usable materials. As always, her good judgment, common sense, and hard work played a major role in the development and preparation of this book.

Grateful acknowledgment is made to **Dr. Stephen Sparacio,** Baldwin Public Schools, Baldwin, New York, for his helpful suggestions on the manuscript.

When ordering this book, please specify:
either **R 615 W** or ENGLISH FOR THE COLLEGE BOARDS

ISBN 1-56765-016-3
NYC Item 56765-016-2

Printed in the United States of America

1 2 3 4 5 6 7 8 9 10   00 99 98 97 96 95 94

CONTENTS

SECTION IV: CLUES FROM ANALOGIES   146

DIVISION B READING COMPREHENSION   181

SECTION I: DRAWING GENERALIZATIONS AND FINDING THE MAIN IDEA   184

SECTION II: DRAWING INFERENCES   197

SECTION III: FINDING DETAILS   210

ACKNOWLEDGMENTS

Grateful acknowledgment is made to the following sources for permission to reprint copyrighted materials. Every effort has been made to obtain permission to use previously published material. Any errors or omissions are unintentional.

Page 246: From *Art and Ardor*, by Cynthia Ozick, by permission of Alfred A. Knopf, Inc.

Page 248: From "The Long Loneliness," *The Star Thrower*, by Loren Eisely, by permission of Times Books, a Division of Random House, Inc.

Page 265: Excerpted from *Look Homeward, Angel*. Copyright 1929 Charles Scribner's Sons: copyright renewed 1957 Edward C. Aswell, Administrator C.T.A. Estate of Thomas Wolfe and/or Fred W. Wolfe. Reprinted with permission of Charles Scribner's Sons.

Page 266: From *The Works of Robert Louis Stevenson in One Volume*, R. L. Stevenson.

Page 268: From "A Cup of Tea," from *The Dove's Nest*, by Katherine Mansfield.

Page 271: From *The Great Railway Bazaar* by Paul Theroux. Copyright © 1975 by Paul Theroux. Reprinted by permission of Houghton Mifflin Co. All rights reserved.

Page 273: From *David Copperfield* by Charles Dickens.

Page 275: "Starlight," from *Floating* by Marian Thurm. Copyright © 1978, 1979, 1981, 1982, 1983, 1984 by Marian Thurm. Used by permission of Viking Penguin, a division of Penguin Books USA Inc.

Page 314: "The Mission of Jane," from *The Selected Short Stories of Edith Wharton*, edited by R. W. B. Lewis (New York: Schribner's, 1992).

Page 323: Excerpt from *Pilgrim at Tinker Creek*, by Annie Dillard. Copyright © 1974 by Annie Dillard. Reprinted by permission of HarperCollins Publishers Inc.

Page 330: From "How 'Bigger' Was Born," pages 232–233 in Ducas *Great Documents in Black American History* (Praeger Publishers, 1970), an imprint of Greenwood Publishing Group, Inc., Westport, CT. Reprinted with permission.

Page 334: From *Under the Sea Wind* by Rachel Carson. Copyright © 1941 by Rachel Carson. Renewed 1969 by Roger Christie. Reprinted by permission of Oxford University Press, Inc.

Page 336: From "Microbiological Mining" by Carole L. Brierley, in *Scientific American*, August 1982, page 44, by permission of Scientific American, Inc.

Page 338: Excerpted with permission, from "The Five Layers of Ambiguity," BYTE Magazine, January 1993. © McGraw-Hill, Inc., New York, NY. All rights reserved.

Page 342: From *The Birth of Britain*, by Winston Churchill, copyright 1956, by permission of Dodd, Mead & Company, Inc. (U.S. rights) and McClelland & Stewart Ltd. (Canadian rights).

Page 343: From "The King of Ragtime," by Brian McGinty, May 1984, *American History, Illustrated*, reprinted courtesy of Historical Times, Inc., 1984.

Page 344: From "Let's Stop Farming the System," by Rexford A. Resler, May 1984, *American Forests*, by permission of American Forestry Association, Washington, D.C.

Page 344: From "The Metropolitan Museum of Art Bulletin," Winter 1981–82, page 58, copyright © 1982, The Metropolitan Museum of Art, by permission of The Metropolitan Museum of Art, New York.

Page 345: From *Innocents Abroad*, by Mark Twain.

Page 346: From "Structuralism in Reverse" by J. Randall Curtis, reprinted from *Et cetera*, Vol. 40, No. 4, by permission of the International Society for General Semantics.

Page 348: From *Teaching a Stone to Talk: Expeditions and Encounters*, by Annie Dillard, copyright 1982 by Annie Dillard, reprinted by permission of HarperCollins Publishers, Inc.

Page 355: "The Pocketbook Game" by Alice Childress from *Like One of the Family*. Copyright © 1956. Renewed 1984 by Alice Childress. Used by permission of Flora Roberts, Inc.

Page 356: Excerpted from "A biologist Whose Heresy Redraws Earth's Tree of Life," by Jeanne McDermott. From *Smithsonian*, August, 1989.

Page 366: Excerpts from *Civilisation* by Kenneth Clark. Copyright 1969 by Kenneth Clark. Reprinted by permission of HarperCollins Publishers Inc.

Page 372: From "Sophisticated Man Is Not Superstitious?" from *The Prevalence of Nonsense* by Ashley Montague and Edward Darling. Copyright © 1967 by M. F. Ashley Montague and Edward Darling. Reprinted by permission of HarperCollins Publishers, Inc.

Page 374: Excerpt from "Of Course" from *The Lottery* by Shirley Jackson. Copyright © 1949 by Shirley Jackson. Copyright renewed © 1976, 1977 by Laurence Hyman, Barry Hyman, Mrs. Sarah Webster and Mrs. Joanne

Schnurer. Reprinted by permission of Farrar, Straus and Giroux, Inc.

Page 391: Excerpted from the Introduction, by Anita Brookner, to *The Stories of Edith Wharton*. Reprinted by permission of Simon & Schuster, London.

Page 400: Excerpted from *Skinwalkers* by Tony Hillerman. Copyright © 1987 by Tony Hillerman. Reprinted by permission of HarperCollins Publishers Inc.

Page 406: Excerpted from *Gothic Europe* by Sacheverell Sitwell. Reprinted by permission of George Weidenfeld & Nicolson Ltd., London.

Page 408: "The Appalachian Trail" reprinted, by permission, from *Black Tulips* (Turnstone Press, 1991), © Bruce Eason.

Page 414: From Bernard Lewis, *History Remembered, Recovered, Invented*. Copyright © 1975 by Princeton University Press. Reprinted by permission of Princeton University Press.

Page 425: From *Extraterrestrial Civilizations*, by Isaac Asimov; copyright © 1979 by Isaac Asimov. Used by permission of Crown Publishers, Inc.

Page 427: Excerpted from *Shakespeare's Imagery*, by Caroline Spurgeon. Copyright © 1935 by Cambridge University Press. Reprinted by permission of Cambridge University Press, New York.

Page 433: Excerpt from "The Comforts of Home" from *Everything that Rises Must Converge* by Flannery O'Connor. Copyright © 1965 by the Estate of Mary Flannery O'Connor. Copyright © 1960 by Regina O'Connor. Copyright renewed © 1988 by Regina O'Connor. Reprinted by permission of Farrar, Straus and Giroux, Inc.

SAT questions selected from 6 SATs. College Entrance Examination Board, 1982. Reprinted by permission of Educational Testing Service, the copyright owners of the sample questions.

Permission to reprint the above material does not constitute review or endorsement by Educational Testing Service or the College Board of this publication as a whole or of any other testing information it may contain.

Introduction

Preparing to Take the Scholastic Assessment Test (SAT)

You are consulting this book because you are planning to take the SAT. You may be wondering how to go about preparing for the test or hoping that some magic formula may be found here for obtaining a high score.

When Pharaoh Ptolemy I asked the philosopher Euclid whether there might be some easy way to learn geometry, Euclid is reported to have told him, "There is no royal road to geometry."

Nor is there a royal road to success on the SAT. What can you do? How can you prepare for so formidable a challenge? With so little time and so much at stake, how should you go about preparing for the SAT? Can any book provide the crucial help you need for this task?

Even if you have little time to prepare, there are some steps to take. You have not lived your life in a scholastic and cultural vacuum. You have been developing many skills throughout your life. Suggestions later in this introduction (pages 5–6) consider some of the short-term and long-term steps you may take.

English for the College Boards accepts the point of view that a crash course in amassing knowledge is impractical preparation. What *is* practical, however, is learning how to use the resources you already have and to develop certain key concepts and insights that will be helpful when you sit down to take the SAT.

English for the College Boards is NOT a cram course. It is, instead, a program with specific major goals:

1. To develop critical reading and critical thinking skills.
2. To explain test strategy in general and the SAT strategy in particular.
3. To demonstrate how you can put this strategy to good use.
4. To show you how to reach into your experiences for insights and answers.
5. To provide certain organizing principles that will help you to handle SAT questions.
6. To supply key information, like a detailed study of contexts and roots, that will repay a hundred times over the time you spend on mastery.
7. To build language power, not merely amass bits of knowledge.
8. To be useful beyond the SAT, providing a source book and reference volume for the years ahead.

Doing well on the SAT is one goal. Doing well in later life is another. *English for the College Boards* has been planned to help you with both. Cram courses have limited value beyond the demands of the present. A full program for the years ahead is much to be preferred.

The Old and the New

For many years prior to 1994, the format of the SAT remained unchanged. The new SAT places a greater emphasis upon *using* knowledge and skills rather than on *having* them. The new SAT is an enhanced reasoning test. The changes are reflected in the content and distribution of items.

QUESTIONS

	Old SAT	New SAT
Antonyms	25	None
Analogies	20	19
Sentence Completions	15	19
Reading	25	40
Total	85	78

Reading passages are longer and the questions more challenging.

Does the reduction in questions mean that the new SAT is easier than the old? Not at all. Because it places greater emphasis on reading skills, it is extremely challenging. Though memory may play a significant role in some analogies or sentence completions, reading passages call for on-the-spot analysis unaided by any previous memorization. Indeed, since reading answers must be based solely on the reading passages, previous knowledge or biases may be a hindrance.

This new revision of *English for the College Boards* is designed to meet the challenges of the new SAT.

How Does This Book Help?

1. It has as its major goal the building of language power, not the amassing of bits of knowledge—soon to be forgotten.
2. It analyzes in detail the three kinds of questions on the SAT verbal sections and provides detailed explanations of strategy.
3. It provides an extensive study of analogies; for example, the discussion breaks down the various types of analogies, explains each type, and provides examples and drill.
4. It provides direct and specific help in handling questions involving vocabulary power. It develops strategies that will help you to approach new and unfamiliar words intelligently.
5. It stresses important matters like figurative language and allusions. It reviews and amplifies the subject matter, with abundant examples.
6. It provides extensive help in the area of roots, prefixes, and suffixes, with sample words, reviews, applications, and summaries.
7. The structure of the book is pedagogically sound. It is a self-teaching text. Trial tests, examples, explanations, reviews, and summaries de-

velop sound strategies for approaching SAT questions. A glance at the contents will give some idea of the book's teaching strategy.

8. The diagnostic tests and the facsimile tests have cross-references to text pages where help can be found in answering the questions.

How Is the Book Organized?

The book is organized into four major *divisions:*

Division A: Vocabulary
Division B: Reading Comprehension
Division C: Facsimile Tests
Division D: Answers

Divisions A and B are subdivided into *sections* and *subsections,* specializing in the specific concepts and skills needed for the SAT. Each subsection follows a sound procedure.

1. The topic is introduced and explained.
2. A *Trial Test* gives immediate practice in trying out the skill. Answers and analysis of the Trial Test provide further help.
3. A typical SAT question is introduced—called *Problem* in the text.
4. The problem is analyzed and a *Strategy* outlined to solve it.
5. *Review* provides additional drill and application.
6. A *Summary* pulls together the teaching points and reviews the information.

Answers and analyses for the *Trial Tests,* all diagnostic tests, and *Facsimile Tests 1, 2,* and *3* appear on pages 443–478.

How Is Each Kind of Question Handled?

Sentence Completions. As the phrase *sentence-completion* implies, you will meet sentences with gaps to be filled. Choosing the right answer depends upon your understanding of the total context, a concept fully developed in *English for the College Boards*.

There are two different types of sentence completion questions. The first type is a straightforward vocabulary-in-context question. The second type combines vocabulary and reasoning. Understanding the sentence is as important as knowing the vocabulary.

Analogies (Word Relationships). Analogies pick up certain key likenesses in otherwise dissimilar things. We might say that a blank page is to a writer as a canvas is to an artist. Though the artist and the writer are different in many respects, both work on a physical medium: a page or canvas. The analogy question in the SAT challenges you to find similar relationships in other dissimilar objects.

Familiarity with the form of the analogy question is essential for success in answering correctly. Though superficially formidable, the analogy question yields to common sense. Once the relationship of the first pair in the question is discerned, the relationship in the second pair becomes much easier. One device for solving the analogy puzzle is to put the analogy into statement form. *English for the College Boards* shows you how to remove some of the mystery by setting up a simple statement. It also breaks analogy questions into 25 different types. Numerous examples and accompanying analyses will help you master this demanding format. (See page 146.)

In one form or another, vocabulary plays a major role throughout the SAT. *English for the College Boards* provides ample assistance in mastering the basics.

Reading Comprehension Questions. Always an important part of the SAT, reading now accounts for more than half of the questions and certainly more than half of the time. This is a crucial area meriting a great deal of pretest attention. The new reading test also tests vocabulary words as they are used in the passage. Since reading depends upon vocabulary—which is essential for all SAT questions—this entire book provides preparation for the reading test.

The new reading passages run from 400–550 words to 700–850 words. They include materials from the humanities, social sciences, natural sciences, and narratives. They concentrate more on the ability to make inferences than on the simpler identification of details. In addition, a *pair* of passages requires students to draw comparisons, point out contrasts, identify supporting elements. See page 183 for a further discussion of the SAT reading test.

Extensive drill in the newer type of reading question will be found in these pages:

265–313 Sections VII and VIII
314–341 Practice Tests
342–348 Reading Diagnostic Tests
349–439 Facsimile Tests

Though not every subject appeals to every person, the passages in this book, like those on the SAT, have been chosen because of their general interest. You will find them interesting as well as challenging.

To prepare for the test, take the reading tests in the book. Study the analyses. Read books, newspapers, and magazines that include complex ideas. Look for reading material that challenges you to think. When you read a passage, look for those specific words that contradict or support each choice.

Again, the procedure is sound.

1. The topic is introduced and explained.
2. A reading passage and *Trial Test* enable you to try your skill.
3. Another reading passage (a *Problem*) is presented.
4. A detailed analysis (a *Strategy*) explains the skills tested in the problem.
5. *Review* provides still another passage. The test accompanying this passage tests skills just taught and reviews other skills taught earlier in the section.
6. A *Summary* pulls the main points together.

Short-Term Preparation for the SAT

Can anything be done at a late date to help you do well on the SAT? It's never too late to do something.

1. Concentrate on learning how the test works.
2. Follow the advice beginning with "long-term preparation" below.
3. Review the *Contents* pages of this book. Are there areas you consider yourself particularly weak in? Concentrate most of your time in these areas.
4. Read the introduction to each section (e.g., Section I, page 14) and go over *Problem* and *Strategy* (e.g., page 15) whenever possible. These will provide information in capsule form.
5. Read the summary of each section (e.g., page 20).
6. Take *Facsimile Test 1* (page 353) to find out what your special strengths and weaknesses are. Study the answers and analyses (pages 464–468). Take as many of these as you can for practice.
7. Focus on weaknesses in the time you have.

Long-Term Preparation for the SAT

Long-term preparation is the ideal way to face the SAT. Getting a good education is the best way to prepare for a Power Test.

1. Try to broaden your reading. Choose some challenging books as well as entertaining ones. Figure out what the author means. Read between the lines.
2. Keep a vocabulary notebook or better yet a card file. List new words that challenge you. Don't interrupt your reading to look up every word, or you'll soon be discouraged. Make a brief note of the word's context and read on. Look up meanings later.
3. Tackle this book systematically. If you are in a class studying this text, your teacher will assign sections or suggest work to be done on your own. Amsco School Publications supplies to teachers suggested syllabi for getting maximum advantage from this book.
4. If you are not using this book in class, you will find it a self-teaching text. The majority of questions are answered and analyzed in the book itself.
5. Set up a schedule, perhaps several hours a week at specified times.
6. Concentrate first on your areas of greatest weakness, but don't saturate yourself to the point of irritation. Occasionally work in other areas. Enjoy your strengths.
7. If you have enough time to proceed throughout the book, you will find cumulative reviews that refresh your memory about areas you've visited.

8. Several months before the SAT, begin trying your hand at the facsimile tests. Pinpoint areas that still need attention while you still have time to do something constructive.
9. Don't put off the bulk of your study till the last minute. Cramming can be self-defeating.

Getting Ready to Take the Test

1. Set up a schedule of preparation with some time devoted each day to the project.
2. Don't cram. Probably not a single last-minute fact will help on the exam.
3. Before the test, review key strategies as outlined in the *Introduction*. Go over the types of questions asked on the SAT. Be sure you are familiar with the test's structure. Take another look at the *Facsimile Tests* (pages 349–439) just to see how questions may be arranged.
4. Keep yourself in good physical condition. The test is a nervous and physical drain.
5. Try to relax, especially the day before. Get a good night's sleep.
6. Become familiar with the way in which answers are recorded.
7. Arrive in plenty of time. Leave time for possible emergencies: traffic jams, flat tires, uncertain directions.

At the Test

1. Have a watch with you to gauge your allotment of time. Don't spend too much time on any one question. If you are stumped, go on to the next question. If you have time, go back for another look; since you may write on the test booklet, check a question you want to go back to. In a multiple-choice question, put a line through answers you've ruled out, so that you don't have to go back over those rejected answers on a rerun. Use the booklet in any constructive way you can. Use it as scratch paper, if you like.
2. Timing is an individual matter. If you are especially strong in analogies, you may sail through these, taking a quarter of time another might take. One rough bit of advice is to allot, on average, about 30–40 seconds for a shorter question and 70–75 for a reading question, including the time spent for reading the passage. Thus, the time allotment is about twice as much for reading questions as for the others.
3. Take the shorter questions first. Run through these, nailing down as many as possible. If you are stumped on one, check it on the question booklet and move on. If you have time, go back, but don't use up too much time on any one question. You will probably discover that the sentence completions and analogies are arranged in the order of difficulty.
4. Read the directions carefully and follow them, noting the time allotted for the section you are tackling.

5. Since you will be penalized a fraction for incorrect answers, don't guess if you have absolutely *no* clue. If, however, you can definitely eliminate one wrong answer, you should probably guess among the others. You have raised the possible percentage a bit. An educated guess is wise, but not a know-nothing stab. See the example ("When Guessing Helps") below.

6. Check your answer sheet to make sure that you are putting your answers in the right places. If you skip a question, be sure you skip a space on your answer sheet. Don't find yourself at the end with three additional spaces after you think you have put all answers in the right spots.

7. Keep moving, but don't rush. Haste can truly make waste. Occasionally take a deep relaxing breath. If you have devices for calming yourself down, use them. Don't panic.

8. Always look for the *best* answer. Some reading questions have several *possible* answers. You must choose the best. Although first impressions are frequently the right ones, these first impressions may prompt you to choose the first "right" answer that you come to. Snap judgments may be wrong. Always check *all* the alternatives before you answer a question.

9. Think positively. Keep cool. Don't suddenly become defeatist. Remember that there is no such thing as a failing mark. There is no magic number that you must reach to "pass." You may omit a number of answers and still do well. The average score is approximately 420 of 800. Thus if you answer a bit more than half the questions correctly, you'll be better than average. Give yourself the best chance. Do the best that you can with the resources you have. That's all you can be expected to do.

Good luck!

Postscript: When Guessing Helps

The following example demonstrates the strategy of guessing. Three students take the following test item. Who should guess?

EXAMPLE
Though ostensibly a put-down in its good-natured ribbing, the average "Celebrity Roast" turns out to be more of a _____ in reality.
(A) critique
(B) masquerade
(C) eulogy
(D) debacle
(E) calamity

Student A hasn't the faintest idea. All answers look equally good. A should *not* guess.

Student B notices that because of *though*, the blank requires a word contrasted with *put-down*. B thus eliminates (E) altogether, but isn't too sure of the others. Even with one answer definitely eliminated B *should* guess.

Student C isn't sure of the answer but he does recall that *eu* appears in the word *euphemism*, just met in an English class. Realizing that *eu*, meaning "good," "well," may be the opposite of *put-down*, C should guess. The guess is a sound one. Though *eulogy*, a "speech of praise," is often delivered at a funeral, it is also appropriate in other contexts, as here.

A Note on Entering Answers

For convenience in machine scoring, the SAT supplies ovals to be blacked in. Here is a typical format.

EXAMPLE

Martha's Vineyard, once a sleepy vacation spot for _____ visitors, has now become a _____ mecca for hordes of sun-worshiping tourists.
  (A) myriad . . quiet
  (B) impoverished . . weary
  (C) discriminating . . bustling
  (D) impetuous . . depressing
  (E) curious . . pensive   Ⓐ Ⓑ ● Ⓓ Ⓔ

This method, efficient for quick scoring, is unsuitable for the drill and analysis offered in *English for the College Boards*. Instead, this book uses a slightly different format.

EXAMPLE

Martha's Vineyard, once a sleepy vacation spot for _____ visitors, has now become a _____ mecca for hordes of sun-worshiping tourists.
  (A) myriad . . quiet
  (B) impoverished . . weary
  (C) discriminating . . bustling
  (D) impetuous . . depressing
  (E) curious . . pensive

                                                          C

Division A
Vocabulary

Remember . . . When Preparing for the SAT

■ Rely upon your built-in knowledge of words, the experiences you have already had with language. *English for the College Boards* will show you how to use this built-in knowledge and how to expand your current vocabulary.

■ Do not rely on studying long lists of difficult words. Unless you use the words soon afterward, you will probably forget them. Besides, the word lists you study may not contain any of the words on the test you will take.

■ Master the skills of test-taking. This book will show you how.

The Sentence-Completion Segment

The next several pages will increase your vocabulary skills and help prepare you for the sentence-completion questions on the SAT. A knowledge of vocabulary is basic to success on these questions, but reasoning ability is also called for. The following pages will consider both vocabulary and reasoning ability.

Directions for the Sentence-Completion Segment

On the SAT, the directions for sentence-completion tests have the following wording.

Each sentence below has one or two blanks, each blank indicating that something has been omitted. Beneath the sentence are five lettered words or sets of words labeled A through E. Choose the word or set of words that, when inserted in the sentence, best fits the meaning of the sentence as a whole.

Example:

Spiders, considered by many to be a _____, kill a hundred times their number in insects and help maintain the balance of nature.
  (A) freak   (D) champion
  (B) bête-noire   (E) vertebrate
  (C) curiosity

ⒶⒷ̇ⒸⒹⒺ

The ovals in the box above are the marking devices used by the SAT. See page 8 for an explanation of the method used in this book.

Vocabulary-Based Test Items

In the new SAT, there are two basic types of sentence-completion items: those that call principally for your familiarity with key test words and those "logic-based" questions that test your reasoning ability as well.

1. The dancer in the skeleton costume struck a(n) _____ note at the masked ball.
   - (A) benign
   - (B) omnipotent
   - (C) macabre
   - (D) lackluster
   - (E) vacuous

A sentence of this sort presents few clues to the meaning of the omitted word. You may have a good idea of the probable effect of the costume on the other dancers, but you still need some knowledge of vocabulary. *Benign* (A), meaning "kindly," doesn't fit. *Omnipotent* (B), "all powerful," is absurd. It is unlikely that a dramatic skeleton outfit would qualify as *lackluster* (D), "dull." *Vacuous* (E), "stupid," makes little sense. Under certain conditions, perhaps with intended irony, some of the four rejected alternatives might fit, but the SAT requires you to choose the *best*, most sensible word. *Macabre* (C), meaning "gruesome" or "ghastly," sensibly completes the sense of the sentence.

2. When awakened suddenly from a deep sleep, Gordon tended to be _____ and his reply _____.
   - (A) merciless . . roguish
   - (B) pompous . . punctilious
   - (C) uneasy . . dilatory
   - (D) brusque . . laconic
   - (E) grateful . . chivalrous

Sometimes the vocabulary-based question has two blanks, as in this example. The sentence here is not complicated or difficult, but knowing the meanings of the suggested alternatives is quite important. Try reading the sentence to yourself, substituting the suggested alternatives for the blanks.

(A) When awakened suddenly from a deep sleep, Gordon tended to be merciless and his reply roguish.

It's conceivable that Gordon might be angry enough to be *merciless,* but then his reply would not be *roguish*.

(B) When awakened suddenly from a deep sleep, Gordon tended to be pompous and his reply punctilious.

This is a sentence in which neither word in the pair makes sense.

(C) When awakened suddenly from a deep sleep, Gordon tended to be uneasy and his reply dilatory.

These words could be stretched to make an offbeat kind of sense, but would this be the best answer?

(D) When awakened suddenly from a deep sleep, Gordon tended to be brusque and his reply laconic.

Now we have it. Both words make sense, aptly suggesting an irritated ex-sleeper! But we haven't checked the last pair.

(E) When awakened suddenly from a deep sleep, Gordon tended to be grateful and his reply chivalrous.

As in (C), this answer has a kind of sense in a special, perhaps humorous, situation, but when matched with (D), it is obviously inferior.

Logic-Based Test Items

Though long sentences look forbidding, they are sometimes easier to handle than shorter ones. If you keep your wits about you, you will often find that the extra words provide more clues.

3. After twelve days of fruitless debate, the jury reached an unbreakable _____ and had to be dismissed by the judge.
   (A) contract
   (B) conviction
   (C) acquittal
   (D) annulment
   (E) impasse

The sentence provides the needed clues if you follow the reasoning. *Twelve days* is a long time for deliberations. The phrase suggests disagreement in the jury room. *Fruitless debate* states without qualification that nothing has been accomplished. *Unbreakable* carries along the sense of inaction. *Dismissed by the judge* provides the clinching information. The jury was deadlocked, unable to reach a verdict.

Even if the word *impasse* is unfamiliar to you, the sentence tells you that (E) is the correct choice if only by a strategy of elimination. Each of the other words suggests some kind of decision, a possibility ruled out by the original sentence.

(E) After twelve days of fruitless debate, the jury reached an unbreakable impasse and had to be dismissed by the judge.

Now the sentence makes sense.

4. Murray cultivated a(n) _____ personality, but his charming manner toward those he considered his equals contrasted with his _____ behavior toward all others.
   (A) gracious . . condescending
   (B) delightful . . sociable
   (C) debonair . . affable
   (D) unnatural . . vicious
   (E) indifferent . . complicated

Sometimes this type of sentence-completion question also has two blanks, as in the example above.

(A) Murray cultivated a gracious personality, but his charming manner toward those he considered his equals contrasted with his condescending behavior toward all others.

This sentence works. *But* tells us that Murray's charm was superficial. The first word in the pair is positive in connotation; the second, negative. Important words like *but* are discussed on page 39. The transitional function words are essential to the structure of the sentence.

For one reason or another, the other possible answers do not work. In (B) the second word, *sociable,* makes no sense when preceded by *but.* Both alternatives in (C) are positive, a distortion of the sense of the sentence. Both alternatives in (D) are negative, equally unsuitable answers. Neither word in the (E) pair makes much sense.

Note that though the sentence is rather long, its structure becomes readily apparent upon examination. It consists of three clauses: two coordinate clauses and one subordinate clause.
   Coordinate:
   "Murray . . personality"
   "But . . others"

   Subordinate:
   "(that) he . . equals

The subordinate (adjective) clause is nestled inside the second coordinate clause.

When you read a sentence with comprehension, you do not consciously identify clauses and phrases. Your knowledge of English sentence structure, acquired from childhood on, helps you to analyze a sentence quite unconsciously and to put sequences in order.

This introduction to the sentence-completion segment of the SAT is intended to suggest the general types of questions presented. In the following pages, you will have many opportunities to try your skill at handling sentence completion items.

Section I: Context Clues

How did you learn that a **lane** is a narrow road, that a **platter** is a kind of dish, and that a **glove** is a hand covering? You probably never looked these words up in a dictionary. You learned them through experience, through hearing the words in a certain situation, a *context*.

"Here, put on these **gloves** when you go out. It's cold outside."

You learned the word **glove** without having it defined for you. Nearly all common words are learned through the context of experience. Even words like **hope, love, friendship,** and **justice** are mastered in much the same way.

Here is another example.

"That's not **fair**."

If you hear that expression applied to certain situations, you soon decide what is **fair** and what is **unfair**.

You have learned new words in your reading, too. Consider this sentence.

"The sailors caught a dozen **pompano** and made a beach fire for a fish fry at sunset."

Even if you had never seen the word **pompano** before, you would know, from the context, that the pompano is a fish. The words surrounding **pompano**, the word's context, provide all the clues you need.

Each time you use a word in a new context, you sharpen your understanding of the word. One reading will often provide enough clues to learn a new word. The image created will also help you remember the word.

How will learning to use context clues help you in taking the SAT? One section of the test, the sentence-completion question, relies heavily on context clues for deriving the correct answer, but context helps elsewhere as well. First, let's sample a few easier sentences to familiarize you with the context clues in action and to analyze techniques for handling words. Next you will examine some actual test questions.

Context Clue 1: The Entire Sentence

This clue is a common one, but it sometimes requires some thought and ingenuity to make an intelligent guess with word meanings.

A. The **incessant** traffic noise outside my hotel window, though not loud, gave me scarcely a moment's sleep throughout the night.

What kind of noise would keep someone from sleeping? A loud noise would present a problem, but the sentence specifically says "not loud." What other quality of noise would interfere with sleep? Some kind of persistent noise. Is the noise in the quoted sentence occasional, or steady and continuous? "Gave me scarcely a moment's sleep" suggests that the noise is steady. It never stops. If the sentence had said the noise "interrupted my sleep," we might infer that the sound comes and goes. But the sentence tells us the noise "gave me scarcely a moment's sleep."

Obviously, **incessant** means "never stopping." As you will see later, the spelling of **incessant** provides some other clues to meaning, clues that help you nail down the meaning.

    B. As a result of the new owner's surprisingly **indolent** ways, the formerly flourishing farm sank into neglect and failure.

What ways would cause a farm to sink into "neglect and failure"? Certainly not careful, energetic, or efficient ways. A neglected farm is not worked enough. If it is not worked enough, the owner must be either lazy or physically unable to do the work. What is the best guess here? The word "surprisingly" suggests that everyone expected the new owner to do a good job. Apparently, the owner was not ill or physically incapacitated in any way. Therefore, he or she must be lazy. **Indolent** means "lazy."

Problem

    Bill Cosby showed a keen understanding of family life, providing a(n) _____ role model for other parents to use.

    (A) embarrassing   (D) dogmatic
    (B) confused   (E) positive
    (C) superficial

Strategy.   The expression *keen understanding of family life* suggests that Cosby's influence would be a good one. Such awareness immediately eliminates the negative (A), (B), and (C). Both (D) and (E) are possible, but the tone of *keen understanding* does not suit (D), but it does suit (E).

    (E) Bill Cosby showed a keen understanding of family life, providing a positive role model for other parents to use.

Trial Test

Take the following short test to make sure you understand this kind of context clue. Write the letter of the word or words that have the same meaning as the boldfaced word.

After the flood the policyholders took some comfort in knowing that they would be **compensated** for their losses.
  (A) charged   (D) called
  (B) forgiven   (E) repaid
  (C) prepared   E

If the policyholders were comforted, then the correct choice is (E).

1. Through the binoculars we could **discern** two hikers on the ridge of Mt. Jefferson.
   (A) call to   (D) report
   (B) see clearly   (E) wave to
   (C) photograph
                                1 ___

2. Because the plan seemed **feasible,** the explorers put it into operation.
   (A) detailed   (D) workable
   (B) exciting   (E) common-
   (C) premeditated   place

                                2 ___

3. After the **cessation** of hostilities, an unaccustomed calm settled over the city.
   (A) stopping   (D) description
   (B) expansion   (E) denunciation
   (C) eruption
                                3 ___

4. The medication **assuaged** the pain and permitted Charles a few hours of sleep.
   (A) localized   (D) recalled
   (B) varied   (E) lessened
   (C) inflamed
                                4 ___

5. Bonnie made a **grimace** when she sipped the vinegar instead of the cider.
   (A) curtsy
   (B) prepared speech
   (C) distorted face
   (D) backbend
   (E) agitated dance step

                                5 ___

6. In the tennis tournament, Jeanne slapped a hard volley to the corner, and Linda quickly **retaliated** with a smash down the line.
   (A) struck   (D) found ex-
       quietly   cuses
   (B) exclaimed   (E) returned like
       bitterly   for like
   (C) objected
       strenuously   6 ___

7. Mel couldn't conceal his **chagrin** when he tripped awkwardly in front of Betty.
   (A) embar-   (D) expression
       rassment   (E) curiosity
   (B) sense of
       humor   7 ___
   (C) delight

8. The March robin has always been the traditional **harbinger** of spring.
   (A) bird   (D) friend
   (B) forerunner   (E) latecomer
   (C) lover
                                8 ___

9. Pru worked **assiduously** throughout the night and completed her term report in time for morning class.
   (A) cheerfully   (D) industriously
   (B) thoughtlessly (E) prayerfully
   (C) frequently
                                9 ___

10. In a relatively brief career, Jesse James **perpetrated** many crimes.
   (A) committed   (D) permitted
   (B) solved   (E) witnessed
   (C) reported
                                10 ___

Now examine an actual test question. The question requires the applicant to select the word or set of words that *best* completes the sentence.

Problem

Susan did not resent the arduous work, for she believed that every _____ that demands thought, attention, and independent judgment _____ the quality of daily life.

    (A) task . . heightens
    (B) profession . . belittles
    (C) hobby . . undercuts
    (D) folly . . exalts
    (E) diversion . . disrupts

Strategy. Here is a helpful first step. Finish the sentence with *your own words* before looking at the answers suggested. Taking this first step gives you some feeling for the structure of the completed sentence and helps with judging possible alternatives. Then evaluate the alternatives provided.

If you are unfamiliar with a word in the sentence, examine the context and make an intelligent guess. If, for example, you don't know the word *arduous*, you will find a lot of help in the context, or the other words, in the sentence. The sentence suggests that arduous work might be resented, for a special point is made of the fact that Susan did <u>not</u> resent it. What kind of work might be resented? A good guess is *hard work*. *Arduous* probably means "hard to do." But even if you did not determine the meaning of *arduous* exactly, you could still figure out that arduous work might be considered unpleasant. This judgment would assist in choosing the correct answer.

How do the various alternatives fit?

Choice (*A*) Try out the first pair.

> Susan did not resent the arduous work, for she believed that every *task* that demands thought, attention, and independent judgment *heightens* the quality of daily life.

Task is obviously a good choice, for it is clearly related to "work" in the preceding clause. How does *heightens* also fit into the scheme? Sometimes in questions of this kind the first alternative may work, but the second one may not. Or the reverse may be true. If *heightens* is an unfamiliar word to you, the word within it is a clue. The word *height* is associated with intensity. The height of indignation, for example, is an intense form of indignation. *Heightens* probably means "make more intense." Does the word make sense in the completed sentence? Obviously it does. A demanding task improves the quality of everyday living.

Notice that now the entire sentence makes sense. Susan did not resent hard work because she realized that challenging tasks make living richer. These two words (*task* and *heightens*) fit admirably well. But the directions say to select the words that <u>best</u> complete the sentence. Perhaps there are other words that do an even better job.

Choice (*B*)   If you insert *profession* and *belittles,* you run into problems. *Profession* isn't as good a word as *task,* but it does make sense. However, what of *belittles*? *Belittles* destroys the meaning of the sentence. *Belittle,* clearly meaning "make little," makes nonsense of Susan's attitude. Choice (*B*) then is incorrect.

Choice (*C*)   If you insert *hobby* into the first blank, you have a barely possible answer but not so good an answer as that in (*A*). The required word should involve arduous work. A task certainly involves arduous work, as does a profession. A *hobby* might involve arduous work, but *hobby* is a leisure-time activity. Go on to *undercuts.* This presents the same problem as *belittles* in (*B*). Even if you are not precisely sure of the meaning of *undercut* ("to make less effective"), you can still be sure the idea is negative. The barely possible *hobby* and the unsuitable *undercuts* make this a poor choice.

Choice (*D*)   If you insert *folly* into the first blank, you run into trouble immediately. *Folly* runs counter to the idea of work. Susan accepts work but not folly. Besides, *folly* doesn't demand "thought, attention, and independent judgment." You can reject this choice immediately, but just to be sure, you ought to try out the second word in the second blank. If you know that *exalts* means "raise up," "glorify," you have verified your guess that (*D*) is incorrect. If you do not know the meaning of *exalts,* you have still rejected (*D*) because *folly* doesn't make sense. Thus far no alternative is as good as (*A*).

Choice (*E*)   The first choice in (*E*) is *diversion,* a hard word. You can guess at the meaning by looking at the little word within the bigger one and noting related words (divert, diverse, diversity). A strategy for handling this skill is discussed later (page 66). Fortunately, however, you don't have to waste too much time, for if one alternative in the pair is incorrect, the answer is incorrect. Look at *disrupts. Disrupts* (meaning "breaks up, disturbs") is a fairly common word, but even if it is unfamiliar to you, you can guess that a word beginning with *dis* may well be a negative word. *Dislike, displease,* and *disloyal* are all negative words. The context of the entire sentence requires a positive word here. Why else would Susan not resent the arduous work? A *diversion* that disturbs or lessens the quality of everyday life would <u>not</u> be Susan's choice.

The preceding analysis shows certain things.

1. You don't have to know every word to get the answer correct.
2. By a process of elimination, you can often find the best answer. Quite often it is enough to guess intelligently at only one of the choices.
3. The context of the sentence AS A WHOLE is the crucial element in the answer. Just ask: "What words make best sense when inserted into the blanks?"

Although we have taken a lot of time to analyze each choice carefully, you will not need to spend as much time in deciding upon your answer. Trying out all alternatives rapidly and in succession often gives the applicant a feeling for the sentence as a whole. Quite often the correct answer will jump from the page. At other times, a little more careful evaluation will be necessary.

Review

Write the letter of the word or words that have the same meaning as the boldfaced word.

1. The group of **ornithologists** went on lengthy bird-watching hikes.
   - (A) dental specialists
   - (B) spellers
   - (C) bird experts
   - (D) story collectors
   - (E) bone doctors

   1 ___

2. A victim is doomed because there is no known **antidote** for the rare snakebite.
   - (A) amusing story
   - (B) appetizer
   - (C) old furniture
   - (D) remedy
   - (E) deer

   2 ___

3. The audience was shrieking with laughter, but no one could discover the reason for such **levity**.
   - (A) frivolity
   - (B) tax
   - (C) riverbank
   - (D) floating in air
   - (E) controlling device

   3 ___

4. No one knew the reason for the sudden, **prodigious** increase in real estate values in so short a time.
   - (A) small
   - (B) enormous
   - (C) average
   - (D) disappointing
   - (E) expected

   4 ___

5. The play *Blithe Spirit* is about a nonthreatening, fun-loving ghost.
   - (A) ghostly
   - (B) athletic
   - (C) deteriorated
   - (D) cheerful
   - (E) flexible

   5 ___

6. Totally absorbed in the computer program, the students were **oblivious to** the hallway noises.
   - (A) unaware of
   - (B) antagonistic toward
   - (C) concerned about
   - (D) absorbed in
   - (E) distracted by

   6 ___

7. Because of the **plethora** of jobs and housing in the area, everyone was well off.
   - (A) curse
   - (B) plentiful supply
   - (C) lack
   - (D) lung disease
   - (E) feeling of well-being

   7 ___

8. The press club did a hilarious **parody** of the President's address, called "The State of the Household."
   - (A) talking bird
   - (B) abnormal distrust
   - (C) contradictory statement
   - (D) one-celled creature
   - (E) humorous imitation

   8 ___

9. At its **apogee** the satellite reached its maximum distance of 480 miles from earth.
   - (A) words of regret
   - (B) attack
   - (C) farthest point
   - (D) lack of interest
   - (E) window opening

   9 ___

10. The job is too much responsibility for a **callow** youngster, hardly out of school.
    - (A) thick-skinned
    - (B) immature
    - (C) lily-like
    - (D) rich in food energy
    - (E) experienced

    10 ___

SUMMARY

Context Clue 1: The Entire Sentence

When you deal with the problem in an SAT question, there are strategies to use. Often the entire sentence provides clues to the meaning of a word in that sentence.

1. Complete the sentence with *your own words* before looking at the choices.
2. Then go ahead and work with the choices provided.
3. If you are not familiar with a word, examine the word's context. Then make an intelligent choice.

Context Clue 2: Pairing

Problem

The 13th-century carved ivory and bronze portrait busts of Benin in West Africa are _____ designed and competently modeled.

    (A) irregularly   (D) strangely
    (B) skillfully   (E) fortunately
    (C) properly

Strategy. This example emphasizes the importance of getting the *best* answer, not just an acceptable answer. (A) and (E) seem out of the running and may be rejected at once, but the others can fit and still make sense. Obviously the conjunction *and* is intended to link equivalent items. Which word is closest in association to *competently*? The answer is (B) *skillfully*. *Properly* (C) makes a judgment without much meaning. What is a "properly" carved ivory? *Strangely* (D) is certainly a possibility, but without additional context, the reader must stick with (B). In answering sentence-completion questions, check whether a pair of words suggests the meaning.

  (B) The 13th-century carved ivory and bronze portrait busts of Benin in West Africa are skillfully designed and competently modeled.

Since writers often repeat themselves slightly to make a point, watch out for paired words. If you don't know the first word, you'll probably know the second.

Pauline was an **ardent,** enthusiastic collector of old Roman coins.

Since the words *ardent* and *enthusiastic* are paired and obviously descriptive of the same person, you have good reason to believe they are related. *Enthusiastic*, a common word, provides a substantial clue to the less common word *ardent*.

Trial Test

Take the following trial test to make sure you understand this type of context clue. Write the letter of your answer in the space at the right.

Benedict Arnold at last was **perfidious,** faithless to the ideals he once professed.
(A) fastidious   (D) egotistical
(B) talented   (E) treacherous
(C) relentless
                                    E

"Faithless" makes clear that **perfidious** means *treacherous* (*E*).

1. Perry has a colorful, **flamboyant** style of dress that sets him apart.
   (A) drab   (D) happy
   (B) showy   (E) irritating
   (C) conservative
                                    1 __

2. The audience's **acclamation** gratified the soloist, who liked the obvious approval of her performance.
   (A) interest   (D) applause
   (B) participation   (E) coolness
   (C) evaluation
                                    2 __

3. Scrooge's actions were mean and **despicable.**
   (A) aware
   (B) unpredictable
   (C) generous
   (D) desperate
   (E) unkind
                                    3 __

4. The lawyer **demurred,** disapproving the suggested settlement.
   (A) objected   (D) orated
   (B) chuckled   (E) sat down
   (C) consented
                                    4 __

5. It is not unusual for a young child to live in **reveries** and daydreams.
   (A) nurseries   (D) prayers
   (B) realities   (E) misgivings
   (C) fantasies
                                    5 __

6. The treasurer's reports were always **concise** and to the point.
   (A) elaborate
   (B) uninformative
   (C) funny
   (D) brief
   (E) labored
                                    6 __

7. The mountain climb proved too **arduous** and difficult for the inexperienced members of the party.
   (A) monotonous   (D) chilly
   (B) strenuous   (E) rocky
   (C) unexpected
                                    7 __

8. To **malign** someone, to tell an evil lie about him, might lay the speaker open to charges of slander.
   (A) wrong   (D) irritate
   (B) advertise   (E) discuss
   (C) report
                                    8 __

9. The inhabitants of the besieged city endured **privation** and hardship unknown in peacetime.
   (A) fury   (D) experiences
   (B) want   (E) repetition
   (C) excitement
                                    9 __

10. Ever since he failed the math test, Greg has been **morose** and ill-tempered.
    (A) excitable   (D) speechless
    (B) resigned   (E) gloomy
    (C) vicious
                                    10 __

Problem

Ms. Wilton urged patience and _____ in dealing with the protesters rather than the unyielding attitude the administration had adopted.

    (A) obstinacy   (D) compromise
    (B) desperation   (E) retaliation
    (C) arrogance

Strategy. Here "patience" is obviously being paired with the word needed in the blank. How does each of the alternatives fit as a possible member of the pair?

Choice (*A*) *Obstinacy* doesn't fit the blank too well. *Obstinacy* (remember the adjective *obstinate*) means "stubbornness." Stubbornness does not go well with patience.

Choice (*B*) *Desperation* is a poor match as well. *Desperation* (remember *desperate*), like *obstinacy*, does not go well with patience.

Choice (*C*) *Arrogance* clashes with patience. Arrogant persons are rarely patient, for they want their way—immediately.

Choice (*D*) *Compromise* is a good match. Patient people are not overbearing or in a hurry. They are willing to take time, to see other sides, to make adjustments in their own viewpoints. *Compromise* seems like the answer, but make sure by looking at the last possibility.

Choice (*E*) *Retaliation* conflicts directly with patience. To *retaliate,* to "strike back," may come after patience has been exhausted, but it does not match patience.

Compromise (*D*) is obviously the right answer. Notice that this sentence also provides other clues. The sentence as a whole calls for a positive word in the blank.

As you work with context clues, you will often find several in one sentence, all helping you to learn the unfamiliar word.

Review

Write the letter of the word or words that have the same meaning as the boldfaced word.

1. The combination of high inflation and low employment was a **paradox,** a pairing of opposite conditions.
    (A) heavenly place
    (B) example
    (C) established custom
    (D) contradiction
    (E) illustrative story

1 ___

2. The Delmarva Peninsula **comprises,** or includes, parts of three states: Delaware, Maryland, and Virginia.
    (A) agrees to
    (B) contains
    (C) obeys; follows
    (D) promises
    (E) understands

2 ___

3. With the sandals, gym shorts, and cap, the white shirt and tie were indeed **incongruous,** hopelessly out of place.
(A) without ability
(B) without a name
(C) inappropriate
(D) disrespectful
(E) colorful

3 ___

4. One warning of an earthquake is a display of uncommon, **unwonted** behavior of animals.
(A) brilliant   (D) irreverent
(B) unusual   (E) colorful
(C) angered

4 ___

5. The news of the fare increase was received with **vituperation** and abusive remarks.
(A) a sense of humor
(B) a healthful food element
(C) bitter scolding
(D) surgery
(E) approval

5 ___

6. There was an unspoken, **tacit** agreement that all expenses would be shared.
(A) diplomatic   (D) touching
(B) silent; under-   (E) debatable
    stood
(C) maneu-
    verable

6 ___

7. Money had not been a problem for Gale since she came into the bequest, or **legacy,** from her aunt.
(A) old tale   (D) lawsuit
(B) inheritance   (E) readable
(C) veterans'   writing
    group

7 ___

8. It isn't worth all the trouble to get a measly, **paltry** 20-cent refund.
(A) small   (D) trembling
(B) pale   (E) warm
(C) unexpected

8 ___

9. The house in the expensive new neighborhood seemed showy and **ostentatious.**
(A) swinging to   (D) pretentious;
    and fro   done to at-
(B) banished;   tract at-
    shut out   tention
(C) modest   (E) absorbent

9 ___

10. After the business failed, the owner was **destitute,** without a penny to his name.
(A) very sad   (D) dried out
(B) deserted   (E) like a tyrant
(C) very poor

10 ___

SUMMARY

Context Clue 2: Pairing

1. Be on the lookout for paired words or ideas. (Writers often repeat themselves to make a point.)
2. If you don't know one of the words or ideas, you may know the other.

Context Clue 3: Direct Explanation

Problem

All our farm animals had been _____ by the year 2000 B.C.; but since that time no new animals have been added to the farmer's work force.

(A) described   (D) noticed
(B) domesticated   (E) captured
(C) painted

Strategy. The sentence here deals with the practical uses of animals, as the last two words disclose. Therefore the best answer is (B) *domesticated*. The other answers make some kind of sense, but not one of these answers is relevant to the second clause: "but . . force."

(B) All our farm animals had been domesticated by the year 2000 B.C., but since that time no new animals have been added to the farmer's work force.

Surprisingly often, a tricky word will actually be explained in the same sentence in which it appears.

Greg was so **avaricious** he refused to spend money even for necessities and almost starved among his collection of gold coins.

The sentence provides the explanation of **avaricious.** Someone who hoards money unwisely, who refuses to spend even for necessities, is "greedy to the point of sickness." There you have the definition of avaricious.

Sometimes an appositive provides the direct explanation you need.

Hedonism, the pursuit of pleasure at all costs, may lead to misery.

The appositive phrase, "the pursuit of pleasure at all costs," clearly tells the meaning of **hedonism.** It defines the word in context.

Sometimes a participial phrase provides helpful clues to the meaning of a word.

Gazelles are **herbivorous,** eating only grasses and other vegetation.

The participial phrase, "eating only grasses and other vegetation," tells the meaning of **herbivorous.** It, too, defines the word in context.

Trial Test

Take the following trial test to make sure you understand this type of context clue. Underline the word or words that explain the boldfaced word. Write the letter of your answer in the space at the right.

Jud's remarks served to **exacerbate** the problem, making a solution more remote than ever.
(A) slightly ease
(B) make worse
(C) clearly reveal
(D) cleverly explain
(E) repeat

B

"Making a solution more remote than ever" explains **exacerbate.** The correct answer is *make worse (B).*

1. Jody lived a **sedentary** life, rarely engaging in exercise or even leaving the house for a walk along the colorful streets near his home.
(A) lively
(B) varied
(C) puzzling
(D) inactive
(E) interesting

1 ___

2. Each wave of frantic buying and selling in the stock market tends to **subside,** or settle down, after a short time.
(A) calm down
(B) whirl about
(C) stir up
(D) explode
(E) recover

2 ___

3. In carpentry, Chuck is a model of **ineptitude,** hitting a finger with a hammer and sawing a crooked line.
(A) humor
(B) clumsiness
(C) failure to plan
(D) surprise
(E) discontent

3 ___

4. A 20-degree day can feel like ten below zero, depending on the wind **velocity,** the speed at which it is blowing.
(A) heat
(B) unpredictability
(C) agreement
(D) good fortune
(E) rapidity

4 ___

5. Among the high-risk group are fairly inactive adults with a **predilection,** or taste, for cholesterol-rich foods.
(A) amusement
(B) necessity
(C) accuracy
(D) preference
(E) portion

5 ___

6. Senator Fogg launched into his usual **harangue,** an endless lecture on the frightful conditions everywhere.
(A) long, ranting speech
(B) exclamation of pleasure
(C) humorous comment
(D) obvious lie
(E) dessert

6 ___

7. When they heard the Prime Minister's proposals, the members were **derisive,** hooting and howling their displeasure.
(A) violent
(B) scornful
(C) joyous
(D) silent
(E) secure

7 ___

8. A portion of the sign **protrudes** beyond the corner of the building, presenting an obstacle for every passerby.
(A) becomes visible
(B) is being constructed
(C) twists
(D) sticks out
(E) reappears

8 ___

9. The assassination of the Archduke Ferdinand **precluded** a peaceful solution, making unavoidable the mass slaughter of World War I.
(A) foretold
(B) unfolded
(C) prevented
(D) presented
(E) suggested

9 ___

10. Mr. Allen was **parsimonious** by nature, miserly and thrifty to the point of excess.
(A) thoughtful
(B) clever
(C) stingy
(D) small
(E) suspicious

10 ___

Problem

Meteors become _____ only after
they enter the atmosphere, for it is then
that they begin to burn and leave their
luminous trails.

    (A) incandescent   (D) reflective
    (B) invisible   (E) elemental
    (C) illusionary

Strategy. Quite often, a clause beginning with "for" (meaning "because" or "since") actually explains the point of the previous clause.

I screamed, for the pain was intense.

Similarly, in the test sentence, the "for" clause says specifically that meteors "burn and leave luminous trails." If the word "luminous" is new to you, you have the word *illuminate* to fall back on. Also, when something burns, it is usually bright.

Choice *(A) Incandescent* is probably a familiar word to you because of the incandescent electric light bulb. This seems like a good answer because the "for" clause has just told you that the meteors burn and leave bright trails. Just to be sure check the other alternatives.

Choice *(B) Invisible* is clearly inappropriate. If the meteors burn brightly, they cannot be invisible.

Choice *(C) Illusionary* suggests trickery or deception, from the word *illusion*. But there's nothing tricky or deceptive about the meteor's bright trail.

Choice *(D) Reflective* doesn't make sense in the sentence. *Reflective* means "thoughtful," a meaning without relevance here.

Choice *(E) Elemental* is wide of the mark. The word has obviously nothing to do with brightness.

Note that the sense of the entire sentence is also a clue to meaning here. Having more than one clue to fall back on guarantees accuracy.

Quite often a subordinate clause actually explains the point of the main clause.

The Congressional committee sought to investigate **covert actions,** which had been concealed illegally from the American public.

This time the "which" clause explains that **covert actions** deal with illegal concealment.

Review

Write the letter for the word or words that have the same meaning as the boldfaced word in each sentence.

1. Some citizens continue to live in **abject** poverty, with no way to escape from it.
(A) conforming (D) forgiven
(B) hopeless (E) attention-
(C) sudden   getting

1 —

2. "Waste not, want not" is an old **maxim,** a tried and true bit of advice.
(A) wise saying (D) woman in
(B) greatest   charge
   amount (E) grown-up
(C) person who   person
   knows
   everything   2 —

3. In combat, a large tent may house an **infirmary,** a hospital for the injured.
(A) shaky place (D) illness
(B) kind of tent (E) endless dis-
(C) treatment   tance
   place   3 —

4. Only a trained eye can **discern,** or tell the difference between, a high and low quality diamond.
(A) disagree (D) control; train
(B) recognize (E) throw away
(C) rule out   4 —

5. The entire school was run by a small, **arrogant** group, who lorded it over the rest of the students.
(A) well-spoken (D) romantic
(B) aromatic (E) disorderly
(C) haughty;
   scornful   5 —

6. Wherever the terrorist went, he was a **firebrand,** who stirred up the people to revolt and strike.
(A) good speaker (D) newscaster
(B) messenger (E) troublemaker
(C) friend   6 —

7. In the 14th century, the Black Death was **rampant** in Europe, raging unchecked through the crowded cities.
(A) unrestrained (D) unforced
(B) unfortunate (E) unpopular
(C) unexpected   7 —

8. John Paul entered with his hat **askew,** for it perched at an impossible angle on his head.
(A) colorful (D) crooked
(B) upside down (E) untouched
(C) reversed   8 —

9. The counsel for the defense took strong exception to the prosecutor's **derogatory** comments, which humiliated the defendant and prejudiced the case against him.
(A) unfavorable and disparaging
(B) generous but sarcastic
(C) fierce and cruel
(D) unexpected and partial
(E) thoughtless and indefinite

9 —

10. A book jacket often gives a **synopsis** of the plot, summarizing the major events.
(A) grammatical (D) artificiality
   system (E) simulta-
(B) condensation   neous event
(C) combination

10 —

SUMMARY
Context Clue 3: Direct Explanation

For help with this kind of context clue, look for:

1. An appositive: an explanatory word or phrase set off by a comma or a pair of commas.
2. A participial phrase explaining the meaning of the key word.
3. An explanation beginning with *for*, meaning "because" or "since."
4. An explanation provided by a subordinate clause.

Context Clue 4: Comparison

Problem

The ruins of Pompeii reveal a city as _____ as any pleasant resort city in the modern world.

- (A) tragic
- (B) flamboyant
- (C) poorly run
- (D) polluted
- (E) comfortable

Strategy. The comparison tells all. Pompeii is compared with a modern pleasant resort city. *Pleasant* suggests that the basis of comparison is positive, not negative. Thus (C) and (D) should be eliminated. Pompeii is certainly a tragic memory, but *tragic* (A) conflicts with *pleasant*. *Flamboyant* (B) is nowhere suggested. The remaining alternative, (E), makes sense.

(E) The ruins of Pompeii reveal a city as comfortable as any pleasant resort city in the modern world.

Sometimes a sentence will reveal the meaning of an unfamiliar word by including a helpful comparison.

In attacking the problem, Sandy was as **diligent** as a bee gathering honey.

A characteristic of a "bee gathering honey" is single-minded devotion to the task. The comparison tells us Sandy was hard-working and industrious.

Trial Test

Take the following trial test to make sure you understand this type of context clue. Write the letter of your answer in the space at the right.

After the hostage was **liberated** he felt as free as a bird.
- (A) embarrassed
- (B) let go
- (C) educated
- (D) changed
- (E) understood

B

"As free as a bird" tells how a hostage that is "liberated" will feel if he is *let go. (B)*

1. Dundee often displays the **irascibility** of a wasp whose nest has been disturbed.
   - (A) subtle charm
   - (B) cowardly behavior
   - (C) quickness to anger
   - (D) inventive genius
   - (E) sweetness

   1 __

2. With the subtlety of a hammer smashing an eggshell, Frank **bludgeoned** everyone to agree.
   - (A) asked
   - (B) elected
   - (C) calmed
   - (D) destroyed
   - (E) bullied

   2 __

ENGLISH FOR THE COLLEGE BOARDS

3. The interior of the building was as **murky** as winter twilight with an overcast sky.
   - (A) brilliant
   - (B) cold
   - (C) gloomy
   - (D) colorful
   - (E) odorous

   3 ——

4. Pete's **incessant** interruptions had all the qualities of endless drops from a leaky faucet.
   - (A) irrelevant
   - (B) sharp
   - (C) continuing
   - (D) exaggerated
   - (E) ill-tempered

   4 ——

5. When the dinner bell is sounded, Carl moves with the **alacrity** of a startled lizard.
   - (A) quick motion
   - (B) intelligence
   - (C) grace
   - (D) resource-fulness
   - (E) body language

   5 ——

6. Jan's costume was as **incongruous** as an evening dress at a picnic.
   - (A) dazzling
   - (B) pleasing
   - (C) unsuitable
   - (D) indecisive
   - (E) unavailing

   6 ——

7. Maz's retorts had all the **caustic** charm of a corrosive acid.
   - (A) biting
   - (B) witty
   - (C) delightful
   - (D) bewildering
   - (E) immortal

   7 ——

8. The moped's tracks in the sand were as **sinuous** as a snake's trail.
   - (A) unpleasant
   - (B) intriguing
   - (C) easily read
   - (D) loathsome
   - (E) winding

   8 ——

9. The senator's **tirade** in Congress was like a mother's scolding of a naughty son.
   - (A) stay
   - (B) denunciation
   - (C) filibuster
   - (D) absenteeism
   - (E) explanation

   9 ——

10. After two weeks I was as **ravenous** as a tiger on a starvation diet.
    - (A) angry
    - (B) upset
    - (C) hungry
    - (D) prepared
    - (E) blissful

    10 ——

Problem

Just as congestion plagues every important highway, so it ——— the streets of every city.
- (A) delimits
- (B) delays
- (C) clogs
- (D) obviates
- (E) destroys

Strategy. The comparison with *as* helps determine the answer to this question. The sentence compares congestion on the rural highways and on the city streets. The second clause must follow the sense of the first clause. The word *plague* is obviously negative. It tells us that congestion slows traffic on highways. The second clause must suggest that congestion slows traffic on city streets. Look at the choices.

Choice *(A) Delimits* has nothing to do with "congestion" in a physical sense. It means "fix the limits of," but the meaning has little to do with the sentence.

Choice *(B) Delays* has the right suggestion. Traffic does cause delays. But streets are not delayed. "Delaying the streets of every city" doesn't make sense.

Choice (C) *Clogs* strikes the right note at once. *Congestion* suggests clogging. This alternative fits perfectly.

Choice (D) *Obviates* has the right negative tone, but it doesn't fit into the sentence. We can *clog* streets; we cannot *obviate* ("get rid of") them.

Choice (E) *Destroys* is hopelessly overstated. *Congestion* doesn't destroy the streets. It may destroy the peace of mind of the drivers, but it doesn't destroy the streets. The correct answer, *clogs (C)*, was suggested by the comparison in the two clauses.

Review

Write the letter of the word or words that have the same meaning as the boldfaced word in each sentence.

1. Melissa served the luncheon with the **dexterity** of a professional magician.
   (A) clumsiness   (D) foolishness
   (B) skillfulness   (E) forgetfulness
   (C) slowness
   1 ___

2. The chain-reaction accident on the freeway threw everyone into a state of **consternation,** like the frenzied activity of ants when a shovel is thrust into an ant colony.
   (A) utter con-   (D) incom-
        fusion   petence
   (B) total calm   (E) preservation
   (C) seeing stars
   2 ___

3. If the transit authority raises fares any more, the public will become as **restive** as a crowd waiting for a fight to break out.
   (A) relaxed   (D) completely
   (B) highly   restored
        amused   (E) restless
   (C) supportive
   3 ___

4. On the hot, hazy afternoon, we felt as **torpid** as a cat snoozing in the sun.
   (A) hot   (D) punished
   (B) energetic   (E) injured
   (C) sluggish
   4 ___

5. With the **impartiality** of a computer following its program, a competent judge makes a decision based on clear-cut evidence and facts.
   (A) impatience
   (B) fairness; not favoring either side
   (C) disorderliness
   (D) slowness
   (E) joyfulness
   5 ___

6. The shop windows filled with merchandise were as **tantalizing** to us as rich, tasty foods are to a dieter.
   (A) confusing   (D) tempting
   (B) actual   (E) disgusting
   (C) meddling
   6 ___

7. Old Mr. Scaggs is as **parsimonious** as a miser counting his pennies.
   (A) generous   (D) happy
   (B) exact   (E) outgoing
   (C) stingy
   7 ___

8. The speaker's opening remarks were as **trite** as a third-rate verse on a flowery greeting card.
   (A) literate   (D) ordinary
   (B) splendid   (E) memorable
   (C) moving
   8 ___

9. Craig's abruptly quitting the committee was an **impetuous** act, like a child throwing a tantrum.
   (A) thoughtful; careful
   (B) profitable
   (C) foolish; rash
   (D) mature
   (E) tiresome; boring

   9 ___

10. The Hollidays' response to the invitation was as **tentative** as a cat's sniffing of some unfamiliar food.
    (A) keyed up
    (B) hesitant; uncertain
    (C) soft
    (D) decisive; sure
    (E) fast; quick

    10 ___

SUMMARY

Context Clue 4: Comparison

1. Comparisons can suggest meanings. If you don't know a word, you will probably know the compared word or meaning.
2. "As" or "like" often begins a comparison.

Context Clue 5: Contrast

Problem

At the time of the Revolutionary War, Philadelphia was a well-populated metropolis, not an unimportant _____.
   (A) community
   (B) capital
   (C) diocese
   (D) backwater
   (E) resort

Strategy. The negative *not* (40) controls the answer. The blank is contrasted with *well-populated metropolis*. The word most obviously contrasted is *backwater* (D). Note that for one reason or another the other alternatives are faulty. *Community* (A) is rather general; it doesn't contrast particularly with *metropolis*. *Capital* (B) clashes with *unimportant*. *Diocese* (C) is a religious term, not parallel with *metropolis*. *Resort* is a possibility, but it is not so perfectly suited as *backwater*. The advice is worth repeating: choose the *best* answer, not just a *possible* answer.

(D) At the time of the Revolutionary War, Philadelphia was a well-populated metropolis, not an unimportant backwater.

Another form of comparison—what might be called a *negative comparison*—is contrast. Contrast frequently provides a clue to meaning.

The actions of the speaker served to **nullify** the effect of the suggestion, not to support it.

The contrast beginning with *not* tells what the key word **nullify** is not. *Support* is opposed to **nullify.** The speaker obviously did his best to oppose the suggestion.

Though the firecracker looked **innocuous,** it contained enough powder to shatter a small building.

The contrast suggested by *though* tells us **innocuous** means "innocent, not dangerous."

Trial Test

Take the following trial test to make sure you understand this type of context clue. Write the letter of your answer in the space at the right.

At one moment Prue seems to be sunk in **melancholy;** the next moment she changes and becomes bright and cheerful.

  (A) gloom   (D) argument
  (B) wit   (E) sleep
  (C) fierce dis-
     cussion   **A**

"Bright" and "cheerful" contrast with **melancholy.** The contrast makes clear that **melancholy** means *gloom (A).*

---

1. The relationship between the twins was **discordant,** not harmonious.
  (A) careless   (D) curious
  (B) conflicting   (E) interesting
  (C) musical   1 ___

2. Carla did not make a **unilateral** decision; instead, she invited all participants to share in decision making.
  (A) one-sided   (D) universally
  (B) foolish   disapproved
  (C) single   (E) ill-consid-
               ered
                  2 ___

3. Hayes made a **ludicrous** suggestion, but the other members took the proposal seriously.
  (A) meaty   (D) solemn
  (B) vigorous   (E) pleasant
  (C) laughable   3 ___

4. When Miss Webster gets hold of an idea, she is **tenacious,** never weak and changing.
  (A) offensive   (D) adaptable
  (B) fickle   (E) persistent
  (C) friendly   4 ___

5. At times, Mr. Collins is **penurious;** at others, generous.
  (A) penny-wise   (D) contributory
  (B) stingy   (E) weary
  (C) helpful   5 ___

6. Jeremy is not **infallible;** he makes many errors.
  (A) always right   (D) optimistic
  (B) sometimes   (E) never arbi-
     uncertain   trary
  (C) generally
     persuasive   6 ___

7. In this uncertain weather, the bees may be either active or **dormant.**
   (A) irritable
   (B) quiet
   (C) frivolous
   (D) indecisive
   (E) unprofitable

   7 ___

8. Too often, fame is **ephemeral,** not lasting.
   (A) livelong
   (B) lively
   (C) short-lived
   (D) living
   (E) lifelike

   8 ___

9. Joella's efforts with a clarinet range from **cacophony** to a blissful blending of sounds.
   (A) ingenuity
   (B) improvi-
       sation
   (C) symphony
   (D) harsh sounds
   (E) surprise

   9 ___

10. Midge's explanation did not **placate** her partner; it angered him.
    (A) interest
    (B) trick
    (C) arouse
    (D) eliminate
    (E) soothe

    10 ___

Problem

Alice was annoyed that, although Edgar accepted the _____ of her argument, he would not _____ that her conclusion was correct.

(A) logic . .
    concede
(B) absurdity . .
    require
(C) sequence . .
    predict
(D) existence . .
    preclude
(E) feasibility . .
    dispute

Strategy. The contrast suggested by the *although* clause is the key to answer this question. The contrast is between acceptance and rejection. Edgar accepted some aspect of Alice's argument, but he obviously rejected her conclusion. Sometimes it is easy to overlook important little words. The key word *not* plays an important part in the analysis.

Choice *(A)* Try the sentence, substituting the alternatives suggested. Alice was annoyed that, although Edgar accepted the *logic* of her argument, he would not *concede* that her conclusion was correct.

That sounds good! Every now and then, the first choice seems the best. The contrast now makes sense. Edgar accepted the logic of Alice's argument, but he wouldn't accept her conclusion. This lack of consistency might well annoy someone! The contrast between acceptance and rejection is clear if we substitute the two words suggested. But examine the remaining choices.

Choice *(B)* The first alternative, *absurdity,* tends to discredit this pair. One is unlikely to accept *absurdity.* The second alternative, *require,* doesn't make sense.

Choice *(C)* The first alternative, *sequence,* is a possibility, though not nearly as good a choice as *logic* in *(A).* The second alternative, *predict,* is clearly inadequate. Why would Edgar make a prediction? The alternatives are clearly not as good as those in *(A).*

Choice *(D) Existence* is a weak alternative, but *preclude* is even more unlikely.

Choice *(E) Dispute* is the clue to this answer. If Edgar did not dispute the conclusion, Alice would not have been annoyed.

The correct answer, *(A)*, was indicated by the contrast suggested by the two clauses.

Review

Write the letter of the word or words that have the same meaning as the boldfaced word in each sentence.

1. In a pressroom, the roar of machinery is **perpetual,** but the rumbling is easier to bear than an occasional sudden burst of sound.
   (A) brief   (D) harmful
   (B) constant   (E) puzzling
   (C) periodic
                              1 ___

2. They say that Robin Hood took from the **affluent** and gave to the poor.
   (A) flowing   (D) rich
   (B) sick   (E) soaked
   (C) engaged
                              2 ___

3. An organization that prevents cruelty to animals is a **benevolent** organization.
   (A) kindly   (D) neutral
   (B) unkind   (E) large
   (C) neglectful
                              3 ___

4. Jennifer has an unusual **aptitude** for playing the piano, but a total inability to play any other instrument.
   (A) viewpoint   (D) talent
   (B) height   (E) enjoyment
   (C) appreciation
                              4 ___

5. Although everyday folklore says that dogs and cats dislike one another, many of them are clearly **affectionate** toward one another.
   (A) sweet   (D) candied
   (B) catching   (E) harmful
   (C) loving
                              5 ___

6. The owner of the famous restaurant greeted every guest **cordially;** there was nothing unpleasant or unfriendly about the place.
   (A) coldly   (D) hastily
   (B) huffily   (E) indifferently
   (C) warmly
                              6 ___

7. Although the salespersons seemed honest, their "promises" about the product were **deceptive.**
   (A) misleading   (D) true
   (B) straight-   (E) clear
       forward
   (C) deep; pene-   7 ___
       trating

8. A cat can be loving and gentle, but it can attack an enemy with astonishing strength and **ferocity.**
   (A) speed   (D) viciousness
   (B) honesty   (E) intelligence
   (C) perfection
                              8 ___

9. Even though the picnic lunch was **sufficient,** everyone could have eaten more.
   (A) bountiful   (D) healthful
   (B) adequate   (E) unbearable
   (C) delicious
                              9 ___

10. Although you might not call Harvey **obese,** you wouldn't nominate him for the Thin Man award, either.
    (A) skinny   (D) athletic
    (B) jolly   (E) healthy
    (C) fat
                              10 ___

Context Clue 6: Sequence

Problem

Hitler's Nazi party began as a small, ruthless minority, took control of the government, and then _____ every method, legal or illegal, to extend its power and control the populace.

(A) disclosed
(B) disavowed
(C) exploited
(D) commandeered
(E) promised

Strategy. There is a sequence of events reported in the sentence: *began, took control*, and the blank. *Disclosed* (A) is unlikely, especially with the inclusion of *illegal* and *ruthless. Disavowed* (B) runs counter to the sense of the sentence. *Commandeered* (D) is too obvious a word for a clever, ruthless group. Besides, it is usually used for physical objects. *Promised* (E) *illegal methods* would not be a likely strategy. Only *exploited* (C) captures the essential meaning of the sentence.

(C) Hitler's Nazi party began as a small, ruthless minority, took control of the government, and then exploited every method, legal or illegal, to extend its power and control the populace.

Sometimes the way in which items are arranged in a sentence provides a clue to meaning. In the Gettysburg Address, Abraham Lincoln said, "We cannot dedicate—we cannot consecrate—we cannot hallow—this ground." The sequence of items clearly indicates a rise in intensity. *Dedicate* is a strong word to honor the ground where the soldiers are buried. *Consecrate* is stronger. *Hallow* is stronger still.

The article I read is weak, tasteless, really **insipid.**

The grouping of adjectives suggests a progression from the mild word *weak* to the stronger word **insipid.**

Trial Test

Take the following trial test to make sure you understand this type of context clue. Write the letter of your answer in the space at the right.

The Halloween costume looked eerie and strange enough by day; at night it was positively **grotesque.**

  (A) handsome   (D) fantastic
  (B) well made   (E) commonplace
  (C) timely

                          D

The phrasing shows a sequence from *eerie* and *strange* to **grotesque. Grotesque** is apparently a stronger word than *eerie* and *strange*. **Grotesque** means *fantastic (D).*

---

1. When facing a math problem, Grover is slow, even **obtuse.**
  (A) witty   (D) dull
  (B) secure   (E) well-rounded
  (C) thorough

                     1 ___

2. Leora's creative style requires that she first **improvise** freely and later revise carefully.
  (A) write slowly   (D) copy slavishly
  (B) read intensively   (E) carry homeward
  (C) compose offhand

                     2 ___

3. The prices of articles at the fair were much too high, ranging from steep to **exorbitant.**
  (A) modest   (D) surprising
  (B) reasonable   (E) low
  (C) excessive

                     3 ___

4. At the party, Lon's behavior was at first merely irritating, but later it became **obnoxious.**
  (A) offensive   (D) positive
  (B) funny   (E) serious
  (C) cruel

                     4 ___

5. Climbing on the lower slopes of Everest was challenging, but crossing ice fields on the upper slopes was truly **arduous.**
  (A) satisfying   (D) improbable
  (B) strenuous   (E) simple
  (C) comical

                     5 ___

6. The characters in Dina's novel were more than dull; they were **stereotyped.**
  (A) composed in haste   (D) copied from another novel
  (B) tried beforehand   (E) stamped from a mold
  (C) painted from life

                     6 ___

7. The inconveniences most travelers consider merely **irksome** Sam finds unbearable.
  (A) annoying   (D) inevitable
  (B) expected   (E) preventable
  (C) enjoyable

                     7 ___

8. The visual effects in the average horror movie are no longer mildly frightening; they must be **gruesome.**
  (A) unpleasant   (D) hideous
  (B) interesting   (E) colorful
  (C) bitter

                     8 ___

9. The approaches to the Grand Canyon are magnificent, but the Canyon itself is **unparalleled.**
  (A) unexpected   (D) speechless
  (B) incomparable   (E) incomprehensible
  (C) deep

                     9 ___

10. My day started wild and gradually became more and more **frenetic.**
  (A) even   (D) normal
  (B) frantic   (E) independent
  (C) picturesque

                    10 ___

Problem

In order to make the best use of
available human resources, we must
first _____ and then _____ human
talents.

    (A) educate . .
        equalize
    (B) decompose . .
        rebuild
    (C) revitalize . .
        discern

    (D) discover . .
        develop
    (E) produce . .
        accrue

Strategy. The sequence suggested by "first" and "and then" is the key to this question. Obviously the second alternative is an outgrowth of the first. This is how the alternatives work.

Choice *(A) Educate* seems like a fairly good alternative until we notice that "talents" is probably the object of the verb. We don't educate "talents." We educate *people*. The second alternative, *equalize,* is impractical and out of keeping with the suggestion "to make the best use of available human resources."

Choice *(B)* Why would anyone wish to *decompose,* break down, human talents? What would be the point of breaking them down only to rebuild them? This pair is unsatisfactory.

Choice *(C) Revitalize* sounds acceptable, but *discern* is inappropriate. We want to do more than look at human talents after we've revitalized them.

Choice *(D)* The sequence here makes sense. We first *discover* the talents and then *develop* them. Steps 1 and 2 are logical and reasonable.

Choice *(E)* We don't *produce* human talents. We *discover* and *develop* them. Some students might choose *accrue* because they don't know its meaning and think it just might be the right answer. The word means "to grow," but it doesn't take an object. Besides, the first alternative, *produce,* is clearly incorrect.

Since *(D)* is so obviously correct, none of the other alternatives make a strong showing. It is wise to check them anyway, even if rapidly. Here, the sequence is the clue to meaning.

Review

Write the letter for the word or words that have the same meaning as the boldfaced word in each sentence.

1. A back injury is not just painful; it can be **excruciating.**
    (A) left out
    (B) unpleasant
    (C) extremely
        painful
    (D) forgiven;
        pardoned
    (E) rejected

1 __

2. Taking inventory is a difficult, **onerous** task.
    (A) one of a kind
    (B) ongoing;
        continuous
    (C) all-knowing
    (D) burden-
        some; op-
        pressive
    (E) unrepeated

2 __

3. Scott may be lazy, but his brother is downright **lethargic**.
   (A) leathery; tough
   (B) very strong
   (C) extremely sluggish
   (D) very heavy
   (E) deadly
   3 ___

4. The officials were stubbornly against changing any rules, but they were **adamantly** opposed to easing the entrance requirements.
   (A) moderately
   (B) addictively
   (C) increasingly
   (D) unyieldingly
   (E) confusedly
   4 ___

5. The members of the reducing clinic ranged in size from plump to **corpulent**.
   (A) very fat
   (B) incorporated
   (C) correctable
   (D) proven
   (E) very certain
   5 ___

6. During the long hike, the youngsters quickly became hungry and eventually became **ravenous**.
   (A) unstrung
   (B) very hungry
   (C) very beautiful
   (D) eaten up
   (E) destroyed
   6 ___

7. A heavy, gas-guzzling sedan may be outdated, but a horse and buggy is **archaic**.
   (A) very cold
   (B) no longer used
   (C) very difficult
   (D) very enthusiastic
   (E) more recent
   7 ___

8. First the accused asked the judge for a light sentence; then he **implored** him to be set free.
   (A) detested completely
   (B) suggested indirectly
   (C) punished severely
   (D) pleaded urgently
   (E) placed firmly
   8 ___

9. Forgetting to thank the participants was a bad mistake, but leaving their names out of the program was an **egregious** one.
   (A) self-centered
   (B) equalizing
   (C) conceited
   (D) sociable; outgoing
   (E) outrageous
   9 ___

10. Most of the committee meetings were private ones, but one was so **clandestine** it was never revealed to the public.
    (A) very secretive
    (B) very quiet
    (C) very noisy
    (D) very unpleasant
    (E) very clear
    10 ___

SUMMARY

Context Clue 6: Sequence

Words arranged in sequence show an increase in intensity. If you know just one of the words, you can figure out the rest.

Context Clue 7: Function Words

Problem

_____ Julius Caesar who said, "I came, I saw, I conquered," Romeo might have said of Juliet, "I came, I saw, I was conquered."

(A) With

(B) Following

(C) Admiring

(D) Unlike

(E) Besides

Strategy. This sentence highlights the importance of a connecting word, a preposition. Since the supposed Romeo quotation is critically different from the Julius Caesar quotation, the blank must demonstrate this difference. Only *Unlike* (D) qualifies. (A) and (B) run counter to the meaning. (C) is remotely possible, but not so good as (D). *Besides* (E) expresses a relationship not suggested in the sentence.

(D) Unlike Julius Caesar who said, "I came, I saw, I conquered," Romeo might have said of Juliet, "I came, I saw, I was conquered."

In English, nouns and verbs are heavyweight words. They carry the burden of meaning in most sentences. Even a simple sentence like "Wasps sting" shows how important nouns and verbs can be. Just two words tell volumes.

Adjectives and adverbs are also strong content words, as they describe, limit, and qualify the powerful nouns and verbs. "Angry wasps sting mercilessly" paints a strong picture.

Because these four content words (nouns, verbs, adjectives, and adverbs) are so overpowering, we sometimes overlook other important words, like prepositions and conjunctions, words that show connections and relationships. These other words provide the glue that holds the content words together. Without the important *function words,* as they are sometimes called, sentences would not hang together.

After Claude had skied, he put his skis **in** the rack **near** the front door **and** went **inside** the lodge.

In the preceding sentence, the content words provide most of the essential information, but they do not tell when and where. Words like **after, in, near, and,** and **inside** are needed to convey the message.

Often the meaning of a sentence hangs on a simple word like **not, but,** or **then.**

The following sampling of these function words will suggest the extent of their influence in creating sentences.

CAUSE-EFFECT: **as, because, for, if, since, so that, yet**

DEGREE: **somewhat, too, very**

PLACE: **above, along, across, around, at, behind, beside, below, beyond** (and many others)

OPPOSITE DIRECTION: **although, but, however, nevertheless, otherwise, unless**

SAME DIRECTION: **and, also, as well, besides**

TIME: **after, before, during, meanwhile, then, when, while, till, until**

NUMBERS: **few, less, many, more, some, one** (and other numerals)

NEGATIVE: **no, not, nobody, no one, neither**

Buddy's room was **chaotic.** It did have a certain informal charm.

These two sentences provide very little help in suggesting the meaning of **chaotic.** In the context provided, **chaotic** might mean almost anything favorable, from "masculine" to "beautiful." We cannot make an intelligent guess.

Notice what happens when two seemingly unimportant words, **somewhat** and **but,** are inserted into the sentence.

> Buddy's room was **somewhat chaotic, but** it did have a certain informal charm.

Now the meaning of **chaotic** can be guessed at. The word **but** suggests that the room's charm is unexpected. Therefore **chaotic** must be a negative word, but **somewhat** softens the blow. The room is not **chaotic;** it is **somewhat chaotic.**

If, in spite of everything, the room has "a certain informal charm," we might reasonably guess that **chaotic** means "upset, disordered." *Informal* becomes an important clue to the meaning of **chaotic,** but the two words **but** and **somewhat** put us on the right track.

Function words are crucially important. Review the importance of **rather than** in the test question for Context Clue #2 (page 22) and the importance of **first** and **and then** in the test question for Context Clue #6 (page 37).

Trial Test

Take the following trial test to make sure you understand this type of context clue. Write the letter of your answer on the line at the right.

Her knowledge and **expertise** in the field of computer science qualified her for the job.
- (A) beauty
- (B) wealth
- (C) specialized skill
- (D) acting ability
- (E) dress

__C__

You should have noticed the function word *and*, which shows that knowledge is related to expertise. *Expertise* must mean *specialized skill, (C)*, since the other choices are not in the same direction as knowledge.

---

1. Because the father was **domineering,** the children rebelled and left home.
   - (A) weak but pleasant
   - (B) indifferent
   - (C) wittily charming
   - (D) humorously fanciful
   - (E) strongly controlling

   1 ___

2. If there is further **diminution** of club funds, we'll have to increase next year's dues.
   - (A) advertising
   - (B) decrease
   - (C) expansion
   - (D) spread
   - (E) theft

   2 ___

3. A long drought threatened the community water supply, but a series of heavy rains **replenished** much of the water in the reservoir.
   (A) drained
   (B) polluted
   (C) dissipated
   (D) refilled
   (E) wasted
   3 ___

4. Because Ted is so **gullible,** his friends like to tell him wild stories and exaggerated anecdotes.
   (A) funny
   (B) agreeable
   (C) believing
   (D) birdlike
   (E) excitable
   4 ___

5. The editor replaced many tired words and expressions in an attempt to make the report sound less **hackneyed.**
   (A) commonplace
   (B) vivid
   (C) critical
   (D) unsound
   (E) grim
   5 ___

6. I'll be left in a **quandary** unless you give me more help in choosing the right course.
   (A) time of decision
   (B) trick of fate
   (C) expression of hope
   (D) state of uncertainty
   (E) call for action
   6 ___

7. Although Barbara is **meticulous** in matters of personal grooming, she is careless in keeping her checkbook account.
   (A) somewhat slovenly
   (B) too cowardly
   (C) very careful
   (D) occasionally gentle
   (E) rather casual
   7 ___

8. Since she had been caught in a heavy downpour, Beth looked **disheveled** when she came into the house.
   (A) angry
   (B) puzzled
   (C) untidy
   (D) adorned
   (E) tired
   8 ___

9. Until the roof leaked rainwater onto the dirt floor of the barn, we had been able to keep the stables **immaculate.**
   (A) spotless
   (B) wide open
   (C) dressy
   (D) locked
   (E) colorful
   9 ___

10. If I cannot **rectify** my mistake, I'll resign as club president.
    (A) explain
    (B) correct
    (C) conceal
    (D) clarify
    (E) magnify
    10 ___

Problem

Because even the briefest period of idleness bored and exasperated her, she worked _____ at some project or activity.
   (A) constantly
   (B) reluctantly
   (C) occasionally
   (D) cynically
   (E) languidly

Strategy. "Because" is the key to the answer. Cause and effect are at work. The way in which she works at a project or activity is a result of her boredom and exasperation.

Choice *(A) Constantly* seems to fit the sentence well. The "because" clause tells us she cannot stand even the briefest period of idleness. Therefore, when she works, she'll avoid even a brief period of idleness—in short, *constantly,* all the time.

Choice *(B) Reluctantly* is directly opposed to the sense of the sentence. If she is bored by idleness, she won't be reluctant to work. She'll be eager to do so.

Choice *(C) Occasionally* does consider the time problem, but boredom at even brief periods of idleness suggests occasional work will not be enough.

Choice *(D) Cynically* suggests an attitude, a bitter attitude, but there is nothing in the sentence to suggest such an attitude. She won't overcome her boredom by being cynical.

Choice *(E) Languidly* also suggests an attitude and a manner of weakness, sluggishness. But she is a dynamo of activity, as the *because* clause suggests.

Constantly is clearly the best answer, indeed the only answer possible.

Review

Write the letter of the word or words that have the same meaning as the boldfaced word in each sentence.

1. We wished the day of surprises would go on forever, but such pleasures are usually **ephemeral.**
   (A) pleasurable   (D) surprising
   (B) lasting   (E) elated
   (C) short-lived

   1 ___

2. Although the topic was **abstruse,** Stephanie was able to write about it simply and clearly.
   (A) easy to understand
   (B) hard to understand
   (C) blunt; insensitive
   (D) very simple
   (E) badly treated

   2 ___

3. No one thought their intentions were **bellicose** until their troops stormed the city.
   (A) peaceful   (D) beautiful
   (B) stormy   (E) warlike
   (C) heavy

   3 ___

4. After the **sardonic** reviews in the news media, nobody bothered to see the movie.
   (A) fishy   (D) praising
   (B) scornful   (E) neutral
   (C) positive

   4 ___

5. Because of the **salubrious** food and climate at the resort, everyone felt wonderful after staying there.
   (A) sloppy   (D) healthful
   (B) salty   (E) unpleasant
   (C) moist

   5 ___

6. Even though the professor is **erudite** in his subject, he doesn't know the first thing about everyday matters like balancing a checkbook or driving a car.
   (A) uninformed   (D) scholarly
   (B) rude   (E) impractical
   (C) incorrect

   6 ___

7. Because the fashion show displayed only the **quintessence** of the new styles, only the best designers could participate.
   (A) finest   (D) hint
   (B) worst   (E) selection
   (C) fifth

   7 ___

8. The youngsters had only a **nebulous** understanding of the opera, but they did enjoy the lavish staging and costumes.
   (A) complete   (D) marvelous
   (B) vague   (E) necessary
   (C) lavish

   8 ___

9. Because Stan is so **gregarious,** he always seems to be in the center of activity, surrounded by people.
(A) very deceitful
(B) growing
(C) sociable
(D) tall
(E) outrageous

9 ___

10. After Lincoln **emancipated** the slaves, many of them still stayed with their former masters.
(A) underfed
(B) mistreated
(C) set free
(D) imprisoned
(E) employed

10 ___

SUMMARY

Context Clue 7: Function Words

1. Nouns, verbs, adjectives, and adverbs are heavyweight words, giving basic meanings.
2. Function words (**because, somewhat, above, although,** etc.) change, intensify, and redirect the basic meanings.
3. Often the meaning of a sentence depends on one function word.

Context Clues: Review Test

The sentences below provide context clues to word meanings. From the group of words below, select a word to replace each boldface word. Write the word on the line at the right.

deceit	hateful	overelaborate	soaked
equivalent	made poor	peculiarities	timid
excessive	nobody	pierced	turned aside
fortress	noisy speech	poisonous	wearing away
harsh	overcrowding	punishment	yellowish

1. Because of her own high standards of morality, Marilyn spurned the *duplicity* of her comrades.

1. _____

2. The trader had a virtual monopoly on salt, and he charged *exorbitant* prices for it.

2. _____

3. From a *nonentity,* Jackson rose to the highest honor America can grant.

3. _____

4. He feared *retribution* for his evil deeds.

4. _____

5. The terms were *tantamount* to complete surrender.

5. _____

6. They stormed the *citadel* with arrows.

6. _____

7. There was such *congestion* in the halls that members could scarcely move.

7. _____

8. The tax plan of the nobles *impoverished* the peasantry, draining away all wealth.

8. _____

9. Soil *erosion* stripped the topsoil from some of our richest land.

9. _____

10. Far from being *diffident,* she has boldly stepped into the limelight.

10. _____

11. The tips of the shoes were *perforated,* the holes being at regular intervals.

11. _____

12. To the newcomer, the Northeast winters were *rigorous* and severe.

12. _____

13. After long confinement in the dungeon, he emerged with thin frame and *sallow* complexion.

13. _____

14. She rushed into the house from the storm, her clothing thoroughly *saturated.*

14. _____

15. The mob growled menacingly as they listened to the speaker's unrestrained *harangue.*

15. _____

16. The theft from the poor widow made the crime even more *heinous.*

16. _____

17. The escaping fumes were not *noxious* but actually beneficial to the animals in the laboratory.

17. _____

18. Despite Thomson's odd *quirks,* people are very fond of him.

18. _____

19. The carved ceiling was too *ornate,* displeasing in its lack of simplicity.

19. _____

20. Jonathan never once *deviated* from the course he had set for himself early in life.

20. _____

Context Clues: Summary

Review these context clues from time to time. If you understand how context helps you learn new words, you'll do better on the vocabulary sections of the SAT. You'll also do better on the reading sections. As a special bonus, you'll become a more efficient general reader and student.

Clue 1   The Entire Sentence
Use your own words first to make an intelligent guess with word meanings; then examine the whole sentence as a context clue.
The first **tremor** of the earthquake rattled the dishes and bounced the pots together.

Clue 2   Pairing
If you don't know one word in a pair, you may know the other.
Jefferson is so **dogmatic** and opinionated, no one cares to discuss anything with him.

Clue 3   Direct Explanation

The test sentence may give an explanation directly, in an appositive, in a participial phrase, in an explanation beginning with **for,** or in one provided by a subordinate clause.

Pittsburgh is at the **confluence** of the Allegheny and Monongahela rivers, where the two flow together to form the Ohio.

Clue 4   Comparison

The compared word or meaning can be a clue; **as** or **like** are clue words.

When Doreen has a task to do, she is as **assiduous** as a bee on a nectar-gathering expedition.

Clue 5   Contrast

A contrast, or a *negative* comparison, tells what something is *not:* some contrast words—**not, although, though, never, instead, but, either. . .or.**

Paul felt he was a **nonentity,** not a person of real importance.

Clue 6   Sequence

Words in sequence show an increase in intensity; if you know one of the words, you can figure out the rest.

At the beginning Curren worried about Becker's serves, but they became even harder, more accurate, and **formidable** as the match went on.

Clue 7   Function Words

Often the meaning of a sentence depends on one function word. (See pages 39–40 for a sampling of function words.)

When the stranger struck the first awful blow, Tom **retaliated** with all his might.

Section II: Word Clues

Word Clue 1: Connotation and Denotation

Problem

Many people daydream of owning a
modest _____ someday in the woods or
at the seashore.
- (A) abode
- (B) aerie
- (C) cabin
- (D) hovel
- (E) shack

Strategy. All alternatives identify a kind of dwelling, but the task is to select the most suitable. *Abode* (A) is too general. *Aerie* (B) suggests a dwelling in a high place, perhaps on a peak, unlikely at the seashore. (D) and (E) have negative connotations. Daydreamers have more positive hopes. *Cabin* (C) fits the slot best.

(C) Many people daydream of owning a modest cabin someday in the woods or at the seashore.

"I'd like you to meet my mommy."
"I'd like you to meet my mother."

"Mommy" and "mother" mean the same person, but the words seem quite different. An adult talks freely about his or her "mother" but rarely uses the word "mommy" outside the home. "Mommy" seems to belong to an earlier period of life. It is a word used by younger children or by adults in the company of small children. It has an altogether different tone from "mother."

Words have many meanings, but all these meanings can usually be divided into two broad types: (1) dictionary meanings and (2) suggested meanings. The first kind of meaning is called *denotation;* the second is called *connotation.* The denotations (dictionary meaning) of "mommy" and "mother" are pretty much the same. The connotations (suggested meanings), however, are quite different. "Mother" is more formal, more general, more applicable to many situations, even to other living creatures. "Mommy" has the flavor of childhood and expresses a certain tone and meaning.

The world of childhood is filled with words that have very special connotations, words like *choo-choo, ducky,* and *kitty.* Childhood words make especially good illustrations of connotation because they are so dramatically different from more adult words like *train, duck,* and *cat.* Sometimes words are rich in connotations for one individual and not another. *Snake* has a very negative connotation for the average camper and a very positive connotation for a naturalist.

No two words are exactly alike. As we shall see later, no two words—even close synonyms—are exactly the same, but many pairs of words are fairly close in meaning. Their denotations are similar, but their connotations may be further apart. *Vision* and *sight* have similar denotations and are listed as synonyms. But they may have widely different connotations.

"That movie star is a vision."
"That movie star is a sight."

If you have a feeling for connotation as well as denotation, you'll do better in all portions of the verbal part of the SAT.

Dan and Merle are friendly (adversaries, antagonists, foes, rivals) for the affections of the new student in class.

All four words suggest that Dan and Merle are competing. The trick is to select the word with the most appropriate *tone.* The sentence says the competition is friendly. The strongly negative connotation of *adversaries, antagonists,* and *foes* is too powerful for friendship. *Rival* is more neutral. *Friendly rivalry* is more likely than *friendly antagonism.*

The spectators were gripped by sudden (consternation, dismay, dread, panic) and stampeded when the cry of "Fire!" was raised.

All four words suggest both fear and upset. The choice becomes a matter of connotation. *Consternation, dismay,* and *dread* are less overpowering than *panic. Dismay* and *dread* suggest long-term worry or concern. *Consternation* suggests fear that leads to inactivity. *Panic,* on the other hand, suggests wild, uncontrolled action.

As a word is used, and as a connotation becomes more widespread, the connotation may become part of the dictionary definition. The word *appease* was once a fairly neutral word. It meant simply "to quiet, to satisfy." In the expression "to appease one's appetite," the word is still neutral. But just before and during World War II, the word *appeasement* came to mean "giving in to the demands of a hostile power." It became a very negative word, and the growing negative connotation eventually became included in the dictionary definition.

Trial Test

Take the following trial test to make sure you understand this type of word clue. Write the letter for the word that best completes the meaning in each sentence.

The new nations of Africa were _____ of their rights and their hard-won independence.
  (A) suspicious   (D) unconcerned
  (B) jealous   (E) weary
  (C) fearful
                                    _B_

Since *jealous* suggests a desire to hold onto what one has, *(B)* is the correct answer.

1. The ex-champion's muscles became _____ from lack of exercise.
  (A) delicate   (D) limp
  (B) flabby   (E) loose
  (C) flimsy
                                    1 ___

2. The photographer specialized in _____ camera shots.
  (A) frank   (D) plain
  (B) open   (E) blunt
  (C) candid
                                    2 ___

3. The characters in this novel are _____ and bear no intentional resemblance to actual people.
  (A) fabulous   (D) imagined
  (B) mythical   (E) fictitious
  (C) legendary
                                    3 ___

4. A mild _____ blew in out of the west.
  (A) breeze   (D) tornado
  (B) blast   (E) gale
  (C) tempest
                                    4 ___

5. Medieval monks spent a great deal of time _____ ancient manuscripts.
  (A) imitating   (D) copying
  (B) mocking   (E) matching
  (C) aping
                                    5 ___

6. When the four racing cars crashed, the spectators were stricken by sudden _____ and ran in all directions.
  (A) dismay   (D) dread
  (B) panic   (E) anxiety
  (C) conster-
      nation
                                    6 ___

7. The owner was unreasonable because he expected nothing short of _____ in his employees.
  (A) merit   (D) quality
  (B) excellence   (E) perfection
  (C) virtue
                                    7 ___

8. Although she had been away for years, when Sheila approached her house, everything suddenly seemed to become _____.
  (A) confidential   (D) exciting
  (B) intimate   (E) common-
  (C) familiar   place
                                    8 ___

9. After a week in the desert without food and very little water, the returning hiker looked _____.
  (A) haggard   (D) weary
  (B) wan   (E) thin
  (C) weak
                                    9 ___

10. Three blocks of houses were burned in one great _____.
  (A) blaze   (D) burning
  (B) fire   (E) conflagration
  (C) combustion
                                    10 ___

Problem

It would be _____ for any serious candidate to _____ such an influential constituency.
  (A) profitable . .   (D) selfish . .
      snub   overrate
  (B) illogical . .   (E) immaterial . .
      appease   recognize
  (C) foolish . .
      offend

Strategy.   If you have studied Context Clues (Section I), you already have many approaches to try in answering the question. The sentence as a whole eliminates alternatives *(A)*, *(D)*, and *(E)*. They don't make sense. Only choices *(B)* and *(C)* seem possible. They provide similar words as first choices: *illogical* and *foolish*. The second choices, *appease* and *offend*, will help you to choose the right answer, *(C)*. But suppose you don't know the second words. You can still work with *illogical* and *foolish*. Both obviously mean something like "unwise," but *illogical* suggests reasoning. *Foolish* does not. The sentence deals with actions, not with reasons. Therefore *foolish* seems a better choice. Substitute the suggested answers to see how they fit.

> It would be **foolish** for any serious candidate to **offend** such an influential constituency.

They fit perfectly. In sentences of this type, the SAT question will often give similar words as alternatives to be chosen. In this test question, *snub* and *offend*, as well as *illogical* and *foolish*, are similar. Our strategy has two steps: (1) first, use context clues for unfamiliar words; (2) then, if this plan doesn't help, examine the connotations of similar words.

Problem

> He had a delightfully indulgent way of showing his _____ for his friends; these actions in themselves _____ a kind heart.
>
> (A) respect . .   (D) intolerance . .
>   contradicted   denoted
> (B) concern . .   (E) fondness . .
>   deprecated   betokened
> (C) disdain . .
>   established

Strategy.   You can immediately discard the negative alternatives *disdain* and *intolerance*, for the sentence as a whole has positive expressions like "delightfully indulgent," "friends," and "kind heart." *Concern* is a possibility, but *deprecated* is negative. *Respect* and *fondness* are both positive words and somewhat related. Pairs like this occur to make the question more challenging. Thus at first glance, either *(A)* or *(E)* seems to be a good possibility. If you know the second words, *contradicted* and *betokened,* you're home free, of course. *Contradicted* is a negative word, out of keeping with the positive words already mentioned. But if you know neither word, you can still make an educated guess by weighing the connotations of *respect* and *fondness*.

Both *respect* and *fondness* suggest positive attitudes. *Respect* is more a matter of the intellect. *Fondness* is more a matter of the emotions. Which tone is more suitable here? The key words "kind heart" tip the scales toward the emotions. It's a kind heart that develops *fondness*. So *fondness* is the better word. Incidentally, words like *betokened* can also be guessed at by looking at the smaller word within the larger word (pages 65–67).

Review

Write the letter for the word that makes best sense in each sentence.

1. Garment sizes for the gowns were petite, small, medium, and _____.
   (A) jumbo   (D) large
   (B) fat   (E) bloated
   (C) overweight

   1 ___

2. Some wrinkle-free fabrics are made of _____ fibers.
   (A) fake   (D) synthetic
   (B) phony   (E) counterfeit
   (C) unreal

   2 ___

3. The moisturizing cream is supposed to make the complexion _____.
   (A) limp   (D) mushy
   (B) wet   (E) slippery
   (C) soft

   3 ___

4. Many mobile homes are surprisingly _____.
   (A) palatial   (D) cavernous
   (B) roomy   (E) enormous
   (C) immense

   4 ___

5. The rude audience's idle _____ was annoying.
   (A) discourse   (D) debate
   (B) chatter   (E) speech
   (C) discussion

   5 ___

6. The constant urban problem is _____ streets and parkways.
   (A) infested   (D) congealed
   (B) overflowing (E) stuffed
   (C) congested

   6 ___

7. Buying defective merchandise hurriedly is a bit _____.
   (A) rash   (D) slothful
   (B) foolish   (E) tiresome
   (C) insane

   7 ___

8. The important executive _____ into the room.
   (A) strode   (D) fell
   (B) trudged   (E) stumbled
   (C) wandered

   8 ___

9. Millions of viewers _____ the championship game.
   (A) ogled   (D) noticed
   (B) glanced at   (E) watched
   (C) stared at

   9 ___

10. Homeowners must _____ their property from theft.
    (A) barricade   (D) protect
    (B) militarize (E) isolate
    (C) arm

    10 ___

SUMMARY

Word Clue 1: Connotation and Denotation

No two words are exactly alike. Words have many meanings, but all meanings can usually be divided into two types: dictionary meanings called *denotation* and suggested meanings called *connotation*.

House and *home* are sometimes used interchangeably, but *home* has far richer connotations than *house*. "There's no place like a house" is not quite the same as "There's no place like home."

Recognizing connotation is especially helpful in answering reading comprehension questions on the SAT.

Word Clue 2: Figurative Language

Problem

He was suddenly thrown into a fit of despair, his faith in himself infirm, his self-confidence _____.

    (A) shattered   (D) inflated
    (B) soaring   (E) delayed
    (C) unassailable

Strategy. As it happens, all the alternatives provided are examples of figurative language. They are all metaphors. *Shattered* suggests breakage. *Soaring* suggests flight. *Unassailable* suggests conflict. *Inflated* suggests increase. *Delayed* suggests obstruction. Which implied comparison is most suitable here?

Two clues help: "fit of despair" and "infirm faith." Someone who is in despair and of infirm faith has lost his self-confidence. Which figurative meaning suggests the loss? *Shattered* fits. Self-confidence might well crumble and be lost. Quickly check the others to be sure.

Soaring and *unassailable* do not fit at all. They are positive words and suggest the wrong picture. *Inflated* also suggests an improvement in self-confidence, the opposite of the meaning we need. *Delayed* is a milder word than *shattered*. It suggests that self-confidence is slightly affected, but despair suggests something more drastic. *(A) Shattered,* the correct answer, uses a physical picture to make the point more strongly.

> March comes in like a *lion* and goes out like a *lamb*.
> When Ellen heard the news, her eyes *danced* and her smile *sparkled*.

In the sample sentences, March does not really resemble a lamb or a lion. Ellen's eyes don't actually dance, nor does her smile sparkle. These examples of "it is what it isn't" are good illustrations of *figurative language,* or *figures of speech.*

SIMILE

The March sentence provides an example of **simile** (SIM uh lee), the comparison of unlike things by using *like* or *as*. Some similes like *white as snow* and *sweet as sugar* have long since worn out their usefulness, and are avoided by careful speakers and writers. However, other phrases startle us by their freshness and appropriateness: *as lonesome as a bell buoy at sea.*

METAPHOR

In the Ellen sentence, *danced* and *sparkled* are examples of **metaphor** (MET uh for), comparisons without *like* or *as*. Metaphor is the poetry of everyday life. We can speak scarcely a sentence without using metaphor, either obvious or concealed. Action metaphors are everywhere, as we *run up* a bill, *skirt* a topic, *win* approval, *hold down* a job, *catch* a cold, *kill* time, *flock* to a new idea, *find* a solution, or *go over* an answer. We may call a person a *rock,* a *tower of strength,* or a *chameleon.* We talk of an *arm* of the sea, the *eye* of a hurricane, the *teeth* of a gale, a *shoulder* of a mountain, or an *elbow* of land. Flowers are often gems of metaphor: *lady's slipper, baby's breath, buttercup, larkspur, Queen Anne's lace, snow-on-the-mountain, jewelweed.* The English language is incredibly rich in metaphor. Metaphors often appear in sentence completion and reading comprehension questions.

Though simile and metaphor are most familiar, there are other kinds of figurative language.

PERSONIFICATION

Personification (per SAHN uh fi KAY shun) gives some human traits to things not human. *Duty* calls. *Truth* cries out. *War* stalks the land. *Joy* flees the house. *Happiness* grows. *Justice* is sometimes blind. *Democracy* encourages citizen participation in government. *Violins* cry, and *trombones* wail. Personification is usually easy to identify.

METONYMY

Metonymy (met ON uh me) substitutes one word for another closely associated with it. If we say, "The kettle is boiling," we're using metonymy. The kettle itself isn't boiling; it's the water inside. "Kettle" is used to represent water. Other examples of metonymy follow.

The *pen is mightier than the sword.*
     (pen = writing; sword = force and violence)
I like the new *dish* you cooked.
     (dish = food in the dish)
No man can live by *bread* alone.
     (bread = food and the physical needs for survival)

SYNECDOCHE

Synecdoche (sin ECK duh kee) also relies on association. Synecdoche substitutes a part for the whole or the whole for a part. If we talk about hired *hands,* we really mean *laborers.* If we take a *head* count, we are really counting *people.* If a store sign says, "Now Hiring Smiling Faces," the owner is looking for new employees, not just faces.

HYPERBOLE

Hyperbole (high PURR buh lee) is exaggeration for effect. When someone says, "I ran a thousand miles before breakfast," *thousand miles* is certainly exaggerated! Occasional hyperbole is effective, but some speakers overuse this device. "I was absolutely *famished.* I drank *gallons* of water and gulped down a *ton* of hamburgers." Like all strong statements, hyperbole is most effective in small doses.

UNDERSTATEMENT

Understatement, the opposite of hyperbole, may also be used for emphasis.

> This dessert *isn't bad* at all! "It's excellent."
> After staying awake for 36 hours, I was a *little tired.* "I was exhausted."

IRONY

Irony is intentionally using words to say one thing and imply something quite the opposite. Suppose you take a clock apart and can't get it back together again. You might then say, "I guess I'm just a *skilled mechanic,*" and mean the opposite. *Skilled mechanic* is an example of irony. Satire and sarcasm belong to the irony family.

REVIEW OF FIGURATIVE LANGUAGE

A single expression may combine two or more figures of speech. Personification is closely related to metaphor. "Truth may whisper and falsehood shout." *Truth* and *falsehood* are personified. *Whisper* and *shout* are metaphors. No person or thing is actually whispering or shouting. "Buddy laughed till he burst" is certainly hyperbole. *Burst* is also a metaphor.

If you become sensitive to figurative language, you will be better able to handle the vocabulary and reading questions on the SAT. You'll also enrich all your reading and listening.

Notice how the same action may be reported differently. A clumsy young man enters a room, trips over a rug, breaks a priceless lamp, and pours coffee over an expensive sofa. He is unhurt, however. What are some reactions an observer might make?

> You're *like a bull in a china shop!* (Simile)
> You're a clumsy *clown!* (Metaphor)
> *Destruction* enters our quiet room! (Personification)
> Oh, mighty *toe!* (Synecdoche)
> You've just ruined *everything* in this room! (Hyperbole)
> You had a *bit of a fall,* didn't you? (Understatement)
> My, but you're an *agile* person! (Irony)

Trial Test

Write the letter for the name of the figurative language in boldface in each of the following sentences.

(A) Simile   (C) Personification   (E) Hyperbole   (G) Irony
(B) Metaphor   (D) Synecdoche   (F) Understatement   (H) Metonymy

> When I broke the expensive butter dish,
> I **died** of embarrassment.
>
>   _E_
>
> _Died_ is an exaggeration. This is an example of hyperbole _(E)_.

1. Jean stepped back from the rattlesnake in the path **like a mouse jumping away from a cat.**　　1 ____

2. The **eyes** of the potato are really buds.　　2 ____

3. Isn't all this rainy weather, with its hordes of mosquitoes, **a lot of fun!**　　3 ____

4. Mr. Acton **hit the roof** when he saw the dent in his new car.　　4 ____

5. We call our dog **"the nose"** because he can smell food a mile away.　　5 ____

6. **Gloom** makes few friends.　　6 ____

7. In reading the passage. I **stumbled** over the first word.　　7 ____

8. It was as cold as the **north side of a January gravestone by starlight.**　　8 ____

9. My six weeks in the hospital caused me a **bit of inconvenience.**　　9 ____

10. **Love** conquers all.　　10 ____

Problem

Ballet is known to be _____; once you go, you are likely to find yourself going again and again, loving the performances more each time.

  (A) addictive   (D) anticlimactic
  (B) erratic   (E) interminable
  (C) expendable

Strategy. Once again, figurative language is the key to the correct answer. _Addictive_ is a word used originally for physical bondage to a habit. Drug addiction, for example, suggests a powerful need involving slavery to narcotics. But addiction, through metaphor, has acquired much wider uses. People say they're addicted to jogging, to square dancing, to tennis, or a host of other activities. Though addiction to jogging is quite different from addiction to drugs, there are enough points of similarity to make the comparison effective, especially the compulsive need to participate almost daily.

The sentence provides several clues, as is so often the case. "Going again and again" emphasizes the repetition. "Loving the performances" suggests the joy. Alternatives _(B)_ to _(E)_ are too negative or have the wrong tone for the sentence. Only _(A)_, with its appropriate figurative meaning, is suitable as an answer.

Review

Write the letter for the name of the figurative language in boldface in each sentence.

  (A) Simile   (C) Personification   (E) Hyperbole   (G) Irony
  (B) Metaphor   (D) Synecdoche   (F) Understatement   (H) Metonymy

1. The entire **theater burst into laughter.**   1 ___

2. When she stumbled over the doorsill and fell flat, she earned the title **Miss Graceful.**   2 ___

3. Suddenly the child was **as quiet as a mouse.**   3 ___

4. Late as usual, Dexter had **an alibi that was a mile long.**   4 ___

5. The flight across the ocean was **as smooth as silk.**   5 ___

6. The old **house told** us of happier days.   6 ___

7. The humid, 100-degree day was **not especially refreshing.**   7 ___

8. The command was given: **"All hands on deck."**   8 ___

9. Her delicate **laughter rippled** through the air.   9 ___

10. They talked and talked, while **ten thousand people were waiting** to use the phone.   10 ___

SUMMARY

Word Clue 2: Figurative Language

SIMILE: comparison with **like** or **as**
Gray-haired Saturn, **quiet as a stone.** (John Keats)

METAPHOR: implied comparison
I felt a **cleavage** in my mind. (Emily Dickinson)

PERSONIFICATION: representing an object or idea as a person
Love laughs at locksmiths. (George Colman)

METONYMY: use of a word for another closely associated word
This hairy meteor did announce
The fall of **sceptres** and of **crowns.** (Samuel Butler)

SYNECDOCHE: use of the part for the whole, or the reverse
We dispatch you for bearers of this greeting to old **Norway.**
(William Shakespeare)

HYPERBOLE: exaggeration for effect
At every word a reputation **dies.** (Alexander Pope)

UNDERSTATEMENT: emphasis by saying less than is meant
The report of my death was **an exaggeration.** (Mark Twain)

IRONY: saying one thing and implying the opposite
Stick close to your desks and never go to sea,
And you all may be **Rulers of the Queen's Navee.** (W. S. Gilbert)

    Mastering the types of figurative language will help you to answer many of the vocabulary test items on the SAT.

Word Clue 3: Synonym Discrimination

Are you happy at this moment? How would you describe your happiness? Are you *cheerful, contented, elated, exuberant, joyful, jubilant, pleased, satisfied?* The English language supplies synonyms by the dozens. We have so many words with similar meanings because English has roots in many languages. Greek, Latin, Celtic, Anglo-Saxon, German, French, Italian—the roll call sounds like a list of the world's languages, dead and living.

Two main streams, the native Anglo-Saxon and Norman, came together when the Normans under William the Conqueror overran England. But before and since, English has borrowed from Latin, Greek, and other sources, to provide enrichment unparalleled in the world's languages. New coinages and borrowings occur today, enriching the treasure of English.

Notice how many degrees of happiness are suggested in the opening group of synonyms. *Happy* is a general word including many degrees of feeling. Some of the other words are more specific. *Elated, exuberant,* and *jubilant* suggest greater joy than *happy. Contented, pleased,* and *satisfied* suggest a moderate degree of happiness. *Cheerful* puts more emphasis on the obvious display of happiness. A person might be *happy* and not show anything. But a *cheerful* person makes an impression.

Although synonyms have generally similar meanings, no two words are interchangeable in all situations. Denotations and connotations vary enough to make every word slightly different from any other word. Synonyms may be as close as *pardon* and *excuse,* and still be different. We may say, "Pardon me" or "Excuse me" and the words seem interchangeable. But a prison inmate may be *pardoned,* not *excused.*

Look at another group of synonyms. *Gleam, glitter, glow, shimmer,* and *sparkle* all refer to light, but each word has a specific application of its own. A beacon may *gleam* in the wilderness but not *glitter* or *shimmer.* Certain metals may *glitter* with reflected light but not *gleam.* Embers may *glow* after a fire has died down but not *sparkle.* Beautiful eyes may *sparkle* but not *glow.* Water may *shimmer* in moonlight but not *gleam.* And so it goes for all groups of synonyms. Subtle differences determine suitability for a given context.

> The lawyer brought on a surprise witness in an attempt to aid the almost hopeless cause of his (client, customer, patient, patron).

All four words apply to a person who pays others for a service, but we use the word *client* with "lawyer." A doctor has a *patient.* A store has a *customer.* A theater has a *patron.*

> The landlord went to court to get an order to (dismiss, eliminate, evict, expel) the tenant from the apartment.

All four words have something to do with getting rid of something or someone. The word used for the removal of a tenant from occupancy is **evict.**

Problem

A truly _____ historian of science,
Meyer neither _____ the abilities of the
scientists she presents nor condescends to
them.

- (A) unbiased . . scrutinizes
- (B) objective . . inflates
- (C) impressiona- ble . . pa- tronizes
- (D) reverent . . admires
- (E) analytic . . evaluates

Strategy. Answer *(E)* is incorrect. If the historian is *analytic,* she will not fail to *evaluate.* Answer *(D)* is incorrect. If the historian is *reverent,* she will not fail to *admire.* Answer *(C)* is incorrect. If the historian is *impressionable,* the answer *patronizes* does not fit. It has nothing to do with being impressionable or not being impressionable.

Answers *(A)* and *(B)* have words somewhat similar in meaning: *unbiased* and *objective.* When this situation occurs, look closely at the second alternative: *scrutinizes* or *inflates.* This time, the two function words, *neither* and *nor* suggest a comparison. We already know that the historian doesn't condescend to the scientists. If she doesn't condescend, then she also doesn't inflate their abilities.

Substitute the correct alternatives and look at the sentence again.

A truly **objective** historian of science, Meyer neither **inflates** the abilities of the scientists she presents nor condescends to them.

You might be led astray by thinking *unbiased* fits reasonably well in the first blank. The historian *is* probably *unbiased,* but *objective* is better. It has just the right meaning to fit here: ''impersonal'' and ''fair.'' The clincher is the second alternative, *inflates.* It's opposed to ''condescends'' and keyed to **objective.**

Trial Test

Write the letter for the word that is most appropriate in each sentence.

The thirsty travelers thought they saw a pond of water in the shimmering sand, but the pond proved to be a _____.
- (A) daydream
- (B) mistake
- (C) vision
- (D) mirage
- (E) fantasy

D

All alternatives suggest that the travelers were deceived, but the specific word for a trick-of-the-eye in the desert is *mirage (D).*

1. Young Mozart _____ concertos, sonatas, and symphonies before he was 13.
- (A) constructed
- (B) composed
- (C) created
- (D) prepared
- (E) produced

1 ___

2. When planning her landscaping, Anne decided upon a(n) _____ bed along the driveway.
- (A) eternal
- (B) everlasting
- (C) perpetual
- (D) perennial
- (E) fadeless

2 ___

3. Citizens who fail to cooperate with law agencies _____ justice.
   (A) counteract   (D) curb
   (B) obstruct   (E) inhibit
   (C) repress

   3 ___

4. Very little food is needed to _____ Owen's appetite.
   (A) glut   (D) satisfy
   (B) cloy   (E) gorge
   (C) cram

   4 ___

5. The boss sent around a brief _____ reminding employees of the changed office hours.
   (A) catalog
   (B) enumeration
   (C) memorandum
   (D) inscription
   (E) register

   5 ___

6. Yvonne's _____ athletic ability almost guarantees her success as a tennis player.
   (A) native   (D) ingrained
   (B) inbred   (E) indis-
   (C) internal   pensable

   6 ___

7. Upon arising, Norm follows a rigid _____ each morning.
   (A) habit   (D) fashion
   (B) routine   (E) practice
   (C) custom

   7 ___

8. The two roads _____ in the outskirts of Springfield.
   (A) mingled   (D) merged
   (B) mixed   (E) fused
   (C) intertwined

   8 ___

9. The _____ edition of Shakespeare's plays exactly reproduces the look of the First Folio.
   (A) facsimile   (D) copy
   (B) duplicate   (E) imitation
   (C) sample

   9 ___

10. Sandra's _____ mannerisms are charming, not unpleasant.
    (A) impudent   (D) haughty
    (B) defiant   (E) overbearing
    (C) pert

    10 ___

Problem

He angrily _____ Plato as more consistently _____ than any other philosopher on all questions involving physical science, politics, ethics, or education.
   (A) approved . .   (D) quoted . .
        debatable   brilliant
   (B) defended . .   (E) derided . .
        refuted   acceptable
   (C) condemned . .
        wrong

Strategy. The answers have two sets of similar words: *condemned* and *derided, approved* and *defended.* You will have to make a further analysis to find the correct answer.

Some answers can be rejected because they contradict themselves.

Answer *(A)* is incorrect. If he *approved* Plato, Plato would not be consistently *debatable.*

Answer *(B)* is incorrect. If he *defended* Plato, Plato would not be consistently *refuted*.

Answer *(D)* is incorrect. He wouldn't be *quoting* Plato "angrily" if Plato were more *brilliant* than any other philosopher.

Answer *(E)* is incorrect. If he *derided* Plato "angrily," he would not consider Plato *acceptable*.

Answer *(C)* fits perfectly. He angrily *condemned* Plato because he considered Plato so *wrong*. Both parts fit. Note that both *derided* and *condemned* are similarly negative. *Condemned* wins out because of the second alternative, *wrong*.

Sometimes close pairs like *condemned* and *derided* can lead you astray. In situations like these, the answer is usually found elsewhere, especially in the second alternative.

Review

A. Following each sentence are three word choices in parentheses. Write the words in the spaces where they make best sense in the sentence.

1. The _____ hadn't done any

   real _____ to the body tissues,

   though the _____ was considerable. (damage, pain, wound)

2. She was _____ though perhaps

   not _____. Her every motion

   was _____. (beautiful, graceful, pretty)

3. He _____ his goal in life when

   he _____ the 440-yard race. The

   coaches all agreed that he had _____ the victory. (attained, earned, won)

4. His costume was so _____ and his

   manner of speaking so _____ that all of us considered him ex-

   tremely _____. (comical, witty, grotesque)

5. Good, _____ food, prepared

   under _____ conditions, is influential

   in keeping us _____. (healthy, sanitary, wholesome)

6. Charles renounced the _____ of the French nobility he hated, and adopted

   the _____ of Darnay to conceal his

   real _____ of Evremonde. (name, pseudonym, title)

7. In a(n) _____ Ford, like the knights

   of _____ times, the _____ suitor for the hand of the town widow rode forth. (antiquated, elderly, olden)

8. The circus people considered it a

   great _____ for the aerialists to at-

   tempt their daring _____ at

   every _____. (achievement, feat, performance)

9. A petty _____ led to a long and bit-

   ter _____ that brought _____ to the little town. (feud, quarrel, strife)

10. The _____ whistles and the _____

    crowd made for a _____ celebration. (boisterous, loud, shrill)

B. Many of our commonest words often have a number of colorful and discriminating synonyms. From the list of words below select a word to fill a blank in each of the following sentences.

distinguished   peered   stared
gazed   recognized   surveyed
glowered   scanned
observed   scrutinized

1. The travelers _____ in the distance the familiar towers of home.

2. The art dealer _____ the painting for any traces of retouching.

3. The angry knight _____ at his opponent before the battle.

4. The visitors _____ at the famous painting for a long time in admiration.

5. Deep in thought, she _____ unseeingly out of the window.

6. Her eye _____ the magazine hurriedly.

7. The small boy _____ eagerly through the knothole in an effort to see the baseball game.

8. He _____ the changes in society without alarm.

9. At that distance, her eye just _____ the climbers on the ridge.

10. From her viewpoint on top of Mt. Washington, she _____ the entire countryside around.

SUMMARY

Word Clue 3: Synonym Discrimination

Synonyms are words of similar meaning, but no two words are always interchangeable. When you meet synonyms that need to be discriminated, consider connotation (page 46). Try the words out in sentences of your own to see where a word fits or doesn't fit.

If you cannot see the difference between *inability* and *disability,* for example, try them out in a sentence. "Pete may have had a physical disability, but this meant no inability to play golf." If you interchange the words, the sentence doesn't work.

Synonym discrimination is especially helpful in sentence completion, analogy, and reading comprehension questions on the SAT.

Word Clue 4: Associated Words

Problem

Aunt Ellen's specialized skills included weaving, knitting, embroidering, needle-point, and _____.

(A) cooking   (D) crocheting
(B) refinishing   (E) sculpting
(C) painting

Strategy. It's obvious that all five answers might reasonably be assigned to Aunt Ellen, but in the context of grouping, the best answer is *crocheting* (D), another needlework skill.

(D) Aunt Ellen's specialized skills include weaving, knitting, embroidering, needlepoint, and crocheting.

When your life experience expands, so does your vocabulary. If you become interested in watching football, you soon learn what these words mean: *clipping, cornerback, pass interference, blitz, bomb,* and *touchback.* You know where the *end zone* is and what the *hash marks* are used for. You discover that a *goal line stand* is not a wooden structure, a *nose guard* is not part of a helmet, and a *quarterback sack* is not a kind of bag. Once you become interested in any new subject, you soon learn a great many new words.

Reading a book about the sea introduces you to words like *tiller, forecastle, boom, tack, jib, port,* and *starboard.* If you join a theater group, you learn what *upstage, downstage,* and *stage left* mean. If you collect coins, you meet *numismatist, mint, obverse,* and *uncirculated.* Carpentry brings you into contact with *awl, veneer, gimlet,* and *keyhole saw.*

The more activities you engage in, the larger your vocabulary. The more you read, the more you increase your word resources.

Association sometimes helps in answering questions on the SAT, as in the following sentence-completion exercise.

Problem

Before leaving for his favorite painting spot, Mitsui took along brush, canvases, easel, spatula, and _____.

(A) pliers   (D) sweater
(B) dictionary   (E) mask
(C) palette

Strategy. Our painter might conceivably take any one of the items for one reason or another, but in the context of this sentence, the best answer is palette (C), a crucial element in the painter's carrying case.

(C) Before leaving for his favorite painting spot, Mitsui took along brush, canvases, easel, spatula, and palette.

Trial Test

Write the letter for the word in each of the following groups that is *not* ordinarily associated with the others.

(A) cracked   (D) mended
(B) broken   (E) split
(C) chipped

                D

All alternatives suggest a breaking, but *(D)* emphasizes repair and is not as closely associated with the others.

---

1. (A) song   (D) hymn
   (B) rhapsody   (E) chant
   (C) struggle
             1 ___

2. (A) dwell   (D) support
   (B) lodge   (E) occupy
   (C) reside
             2 ___

3. (A) dye   (D) paint
   (B) stain   (E) sketch
   (C) tint
             3 ___

4. (A) aid   (D) comply
   (B) heed   (E) obey
   (C) mind
             4 ___

5. (A) medley   (D) ballad
   (B) mixture   (E) blend
   (C) hodgepodge
             5 ___

6. (A) impetuous   (D) bold
   (B) brash   (E) impulsive
   (C) nervous
             6 ___

7. (A) root   (D) bark
   (B) leaf   (E) violet
   (C) stem
             7 ___

8. (A) differ   (D) dissent
   (B) argue   (E) debate
   (C) agree
             8 ___

9. (A) majesty   (D) greatness
   (B) queen   (E) splendor
   (C) grandeur
             9 ___

10. (A) flinch   (D) recoil
    (B) cringe   (E) shrink
    (C) scratch
              10 ___

Problem

A sense of the absurd and a keen awareness of pretense developed Sharon's skill in satire, caricature, lampoon, and _____.

    (A) eulogy
    (B) commentary
    (C) broadside
    (D) dissertation
    (E) parody

Strategy. The grouping of *satire, caricature,* and *lampoon* suggests that the answer is probably associated in meaning with all three. All three suggest the sharp humor in revealing human weakness. Like these three, the answer should poke fun for comic effect. (A), high praise, is opposed in meaning to the three. (B) and (D) are neutral. There is a broader, less devious attack in *broadside* (C). Only *parody* (E), a humorous imitation of a writer or composer's skill, fills the slot satisfactorily.

Review

A. Write the letter for the word in each of the groups that is *not* ordinarily associated with the others.

1. (A) plain (D) wealthy
   (B) ordinary (E) common
   (C) simple
   1 ___

2. (A) house (D) cabin
   (B) apartment (E) tent
   (C) car
   2 ___

3. (A) mystery (D) solution
   (B) puzzle (E) riddle
   (C) problem
   3 ___

4. (A) party (D) banquet
   (B) feast (E) champi-
   (C) picnic onship
   4 ___

5. (A) dollar (D) lira
   (B) franc (E) finance
   (C) peso
   5 ___

6. (A) probable (D) presumable
   (B) likely (E) amusing
   (C) hopeful
   6 ___

7. (A) song (D) anthem
   (B) ballad (E) story
   (C) hymn
   7 ___

8. (A) cabinet (D) cupboard
   (B) chair (E) pantry
   (C) closet
   8 ___

9. (A) beautiful (D) pretty
   (B) gorgeous (E) friendly
   (C) handsome
   9 ___

10. (A) theater (D) arena
    (B) stadium (E) skyscraper
    (C) auditorium
    10 ___

B. Write the letter for the word that *best* fits the meaning of the sentence as a whole.

1. Mountain men of the Old West, skilled in the challenges and dangers of the rugged terrain, often acted as _____ for wagon trains through the mountain passes.
   (A) foils (D) challengers
   (B) pathfinders (E) comrades
   (C) arbiters
   1 ___

2. Many of the imaginative dreams of the past, decried as being too _____, have proved to be practical solutions for today's problems.
   (A) negative (D) visionary
   (B) utilitarian (E) common-
   (C) vulgar place
   2 ___

3. Kenneth Branagh's bleak and dour version of Shakespeare's *Henry V* is more _____ than the brighter film of Laurence Olivier.
   (A) popular   (D) placid
   (B) tantalizing   (E) austere
   (C) vital

   3 ___

4. The craggy summit of Mt. Adams can be reached only by a rugged trail passing over _____ rocks.
   (A) jagged   (D) beckoning
   (B) gray   (E) uniform
   (C) delicate

   4 ___

5. When Harris heard the enthusiastic praise for him at his testimonial, he could scarcely believe the _____ was intended for him.
   (A) analysis   (D) criticism
   (B) digression   (E) evocation
   (C) eulogy

   5 ___

SUMMARY

Word Clue 4: Associated Words

1. In general, you learn a cluster of words in a group, not just one word in isolation.

2. If you can associate a group of words on a test question, you can often answer the question correctly even if you are not sure of the *specific* meaning of a word. For example, if you know only that a *parody* is some kind of literary work, you can disregard all word choices that have nothing to do with literature.

3. Rely on free association to recall related words. A group of words somehow associated with a test word will often provide the clues you need. The SAT takes words from every area of life; so, the more words you know, the better you will be able to make word associations.

Word Clue 5: Words Within Words

Problem

Despite the separatist movements all around the world, most Americans wish to keep our nation _____.
- (A) undisheartened
- (B) prosperous
- (C) indivisible
- (D) modern
- (E) unindemnified

Strategy. Longer words may be easy if broken down into their smaller parts. The clue to the best alternative is the mention of separatist movements preceded by the negative *despite*. The answer requires the idea of *not* being separated or divided. *Indivisible* (C) ("not able to be divided") is clearly the answer. Did you remember that the phrase "one nation indivisible" appears in the Pledge of Allegiance to the Flag? Sometimes bits of information come in handy when answering an SAT question.

(C) Despite the separatist movements all around the world, most Americans wish to keep our nation indivisible.

Which is probably a harder word, *foible* or *incomprehensibility?* Your first impulse might be to point to the longer word, but if you think about it a moment, you realize that *foible* is actually harder, even though it is much shorter. The length of a word may not be related to difficulty.

Problem

To some readers, the _____ of the essayist's prose was too great a barrier to understanding the message, no matter how significant.
- (A) incomprehensibility
- (B) triviality
- (C) intrepidity
- (D) backwardness
- (E) inadvertency

Strategy. The key word in the sentence is *understanding*. The answer must mean the opposite. *Incomprehensibility* (A) qualifies. At first glance, *incomprehensibility* is an overpowering word. Yet hidden inside is a common word: *comprehend*. You almost certainly know that *comprehend* means "understand." You therefore have the key to the whole question. The prefix *in* frequently means "not." The suffix *ible* means "able." Thus *incomprehensibility* suggests the quality of "not being understandable."

(A) To some readers, the incomprehensibility of the essayist's prose was too great a barrier to understanding the message, no matter how significant.

Trial Test

Write the number of each word in column A next to its opposite, or antonym, in column B.

A		B
1. disorganization	____	hope
2. inconclusive	____	clearness
3. disillusionment	____	efficiency
4. unpalatable	____	certain
5. miscalculation	____	normality
6. incoherence	____	tasty
7. improvident	____	understanding
8. commensurate	____	unequal
9. eccentricity	____	criticism
10. endearment	____	thrifty

Problem

Although the candidate's staff urged her
to take a strong stand on the housing bill,
she remained _____.
   (A) obliging   (D) staunch
   (B) noncommittal   (E) entrenched
   (C) involved

Strategy.   *Although* suggests that the missing word is opposed to *a strong stand*. Inside the larger word *noncommittal* is the common word *commit*. We may commit ourselves to an action, a philosophy, or an idea. If we are *noncommittal,* we refuse to promise, pledge, or participate. Clearly, *noncommittal* is the best answer here, though other alternatives make some kind of sense.

In later sections you will deal with etymology. This is the study of word origins: prefixes, roots, and suffixes. A study of etymology will give you a powerful weapon for analyzing a word and studying its parts. But don't overlook the strategy outlined in this section. It sometimes works when etymology fails. The root of the word *unpalatable,* for example, is not a common one. It does not appear in lists of common roots. Yet you do know the word *palate,* meaning *the roof of the mouth*. You also know that palate has something to do with *taste,* as in the expression *tickle the palate*. You can guess that *unpalatable* is not *tasty*. Look for the smaller word within the larger.

Review

Write the number of each word in column A next to its antonym, or opposite in column B.

A	B
1. liabilities	___ pliable
2. obstinate	___ kindly
3. inconsequential	___ wealthy
4. incredible	___ conflict
5. malevolent	___ important
6. indolent	___ mature
7. impoverished	___ energetic
8. cooperation	___ assets
9. vendor	___ believable
10. infantile	___ buyer

SUMMARY

Word Clue 5: Words Within Words

1. Long words are sometimes easier to define than short ones.
2. Many long words contain within them familiar elements that provide a key to the meaning.
3. Sometimes you may guess at a completely unfamiliar long word by finding the short word within it. For example, within *noncommittal* is the known word *commit*. This word clue will help you to analyze long words that appear on the SAT.

Word Clue 6: Allusions

Problem

Sonny had a(n) _____ appetite; he was known far and wide for his enormous consumption of any food set before him.

    (A) mediocre   (D) gargantuan

    (B) inconsiderable   (E) discriminating

    (C) sultry

Strategy.   If you are familiar with the word *gargantuan,* you may stop there. In literature, Gargantua was a giant king noted for his huge size and phenomenal appetite. *Gargantuan* (D) clearly fills the bill. Even if you do not know the allusion to Gargantua, you may still, however, find the answer by elimination. *Mediocre* (A) and *inconsiderable* (B) contradict *enormous.* *Sultry* (C) is irrelevant. *Discriminating* (E) must be rejected because Sonny ate "any food set before him."

> (D) Sonny had a gargantuan appetite; he was known far and wide for his enormous consumption of any food set before him.

An **allusion** is a reference to a literary or historical person, place, or event.

> In lifting the fallen tree trunk from the injured boy, the police officer showed *herculean* strength.
> Karate is one of the best-known of the Japanese *martial* arts.

If you are unfamiliar with *herculean,* you notice that the sentence suggests that it means "powerful." The lifting achievement is obviously out of the ordinary. *Herculean* comes from *Hercules,* the Greek hero noted for his feats of strength. The concealed allusion, or reference to Hercules, in the word enriches understanding and adds drama to the sentence.

If you know what "karate" means, you can guess that *martial* has to do with discipline, fighting, and war. If you are not sure, however, you have an allusion concealed within *martial:* the word *Mars. Mars* is the name of the fourth planet of the solar system and also of the god of war. Knowing the origin of *martial* enriches the meaning and makes it easier to remember.

TYPES OF ALLUSIONS

CONCEALED ALLUSIONS: *Spartan* attitude, *stentorian* voice, *pasteurized* milk, *cashmere* sweater, *iridescent* colors, *mercurial* disposition—all have allusions concealed within them.

Spartans were noted for discipline, courage, moderation, and thrift. A *Spartan* attitude is characterized by discipline and bravery.

Stentor was a Greek herald during the Trojan War. His voice was as loud as that of fifty men all shouting together. *Stentorian* then means "very loud."

Louis Pasteur, a French scientist, pioneered in the study of microbes and the harm they could do. *Pasteurizing* is a method of killing harmful microbes by heat. (It doesn't have anything to do with a "pasture.")

Cashmere comes from Kashmir, a district of India noted for the fine wool made from Kashmir goats.

Iris was the goddess of the rainbow. *Iridescent* colors are brilliant, shifting like the colors of the rainbow.

Mercury, messenger of the gods and god of speed and travel, moved about rapidly. *Mercurial* suggests changeability, fickleness.

WORDS FROM NAMES: Some words have come from names without change; for example, *boycott, derrick, diesel, macadam, ohm, volt, watt,* and *maverick.*

Boycott arises from Captain Charles Boycott, an English agent in Ireland. The Irish peasants, under Charles Parnell's leadership, refused to work for Boycott or do any business with him. Thus the word *boycott* came to mean a refusal to buy, sell, or have anything to do with a person, a company, or a product. Ironically, Boycott was the victim of the strategy, not its organizer!

Derrick is named for Thomas Derrick, a London hangman. A derrick, an apparatus for lifting heavy objects, looked like a gallows to the first persons using the name.

A *diesel* motor or vehicle is named for the German engineer who invented this kind of engine, Rudolph Diesel.

Macadam is named for John Loudon McAdam. Even as a child, McAdam constructed miniature road systems in his backyard. He pioneered the type of pavement that even today is common around the world.

Ohm, volt, and *watt* are all named for pioneers in the field of electricity and mechanics: Georg Simon Ohm, Alessandro Volta, and James Watt.

Maverick was named for Samuel August Maverick, a fiery Texas rancher who did not brand his cattle. *Maverick* has the primary meaning of "an unbranded calf" and the secondary meaning of a "fiery independent person." *Maverick* cattle do not stay with their group. *Mavericks* in politics can't be tied down to a rigid doctrine or party line.

Now see how you can use allusions to figure out definitions in trial test items.

Trial Test

Select the alternative that best defines the word in capital letters. The explanation of the allusion appears in parentheses.

BLARNEY:
  (A) clever flattery (D) down-to-
  (B) skin disease   earth
  (C) plea for funds   reporting
                        (E) repetition

                                    A

(Blarney Castle in Ireland has a famous stone. The person who kisses it is supposed to gain great skill in giving compliments and charming people.) Great skill in giving compliments is allied to clever flattery. The answer is *(A)*.

1. BEDLAM:
   (A) noise and confusion
   (B) calm and serenity
   (C) thoughtfulness and
       reflection
   (D) joy and contentment
   (E) time and tide

                                    1 ___

(Bedlam was the name of a London hospital for the insane. The full name of the hospital was once *St. Mary of Bethlehem.*)

2. MARTINET:
   (A) small bird
   (B) musical instrument
   (C) strict disciplinarian
   (D) long poem
   (E) piece of furniture

   2 ____

   (Jean Martinet was a French general during the reign of Louis XIV. Martinet built the first modern army in Europe.)

3. MACHIAVELLIAN:
   (A) forthright
   (B) reliable
   (C) vital
   (D) sound
   (E) crafty

   3 ____

   (Niccolo Machiavelli was an Italian writer who believed a ruler should use any means, honorable or deceitful, to maintain a strong government.)

4. QUIXOTIC:
   (A) brave
   (B) fearful
   (C) slow
   (D) contemptible
   (E) impractical

   4 ____

   (Don Quixote, hero of Cervantes' novel, was a foolish dreamer who resolved to remake the world by impossible knightly feats.)

5. ACHILLES' HEEL:
   (A) funny bone
   (B) source of weakness
   (C) article of clothing
   (D) unpleasant person
   (E) ailment

   5 ____

   (In Greek mythology, the mother of the hero Achilles dipped him, while a baby, into the River Styx to render him safe from injury. She held him by his heel, which was thus not protected.)

6. BERSERK:
   (A) speaking thoughtfully
   (B) sleeping restlessly
   (C) running evenly
   (D) planning craftily
   (E) raging violently

   6 ____

   (Berserkers were wild warriors, who in battle howled, growled, bit their shields, and foamed at the mouth.)

7. HOBSON'S CHOICE:
   (A) dilemma
   (B) no alternative
   (C) cream of the crop
   (D) strong preference
   (E) argument

   7 ____

   (Thomas Hobson, stablekeeper, let out his horses in strict rotation, not by rider's choice.)

8. MEANDER:
   (A) talk rapidly
   (B) shout loudly
   (C) wander aimlessly
   (D) walk steadily
   (E) run competitively

   8 ____

   (The Meander was a river in Asia Minor noted for its twists and turns.)

9. MESMERISM:
   (A) philosophical disagreement
   (B) hypnotic fascination
   (C) dull repetition
   (D) commonplace wisdom
   (E) unchecked evil

   9 ____

   (Franz Anton Mesmer was an Austrian physician who believed that his hands had miraculous healing powers, "animal magnetism.")

10. PROTEAN:
    (A) violently cruel
    (B) very nutritious
    (C) carefully selected
    (D) extremely changeable
    (E) attractive and appealing

    10 ____

    (Proteus was a sea god, who was able to change his shape at will.)

Problem

Among the staid and sober employees of Grissom's law firm, Jared's erratic behavior seemed more and more _____.

(A) slothful
(B) quixotic
(C) somber
(D) preprogramed
(E) congenial

Strategy. If you recognize *quixotic* as deriving from the comical, unpredictable figure of Don Quixote, you have found the answer, (B). Again, even if you don't recognize the allusion, you can find the answer by eliminating the wrong answers. Mention of *staid* and *sober* is meant to contrast with *erratic* and the blank. The answer cannot be *slothful* (A), *preprogramed* (D), or *congenial* (E). Similarly, *somber* (C) is too close to *staid* and *sober*.

(B) Among the staid and sober employees of Grissom's law firm, Jared's erratic behavior seemed more and more quixotic.

Review

Write the letter of the alternative that best defines the word in capital letters.

1. BANTAM:
   (A) small, combative person
   (B) sports referee
   (C) reluctant scholar
   (D) volunteer soldier
   (E) welcoming host

   1 ___

2. BIGOT:
   (A) ambidextrous athlete
   (B) intolerant person
   (C) obvious pretender
   (D) marriage broker
   (E) charitable giver

   2 ___

3. CABAL:
   (A) oriental vegetable
   (B) term used in cricket
   (C) unintentional deception
   (D) Scottish folk dance
   (E) secret group

   3 ___

4. CHAUVINISM:
   (A) petty thievery
   (B) attitude of superiority
   (C) nonterminal disease
   (D) English political party
   (E) excessive meekness

   4 ___

5. CUPIDITY:
   (A) curiosity
   (B) amiability
   (C) rage
   (D) greed
   (E) loveliness

   5 ___

6. EXODUS:
   (A) departure
   (B) sermon
   (C) preacher
   (D) assault
   (E) moving stairway

   6 ___

7. GIBBERISH:
   (A) exotic spice
   (B) high-flown idea
   (C) instability
   (D) meaningless language
   (E) term used in sailing

   7 ___

8. HOCUS-POCUS:
   (A) disease resembling influenza
   (B) Austrian card game
   (C) popular song
   (D) art of composing limericks
   (E) sleight of hand

   8 ___

9. JOVIAL:
   (A) loud
   (B) well-intentioned
   (C) good-humored
   (D) complimentary
   (E) reserved in manner

   9 ___

10. LILLIPUTIAN:
   (A) rugged individualist
   (B) cult member
   (C) undersized person
   (D) skilled athlete
   (E) environmentalist

   10 ___

SUMMARY

Word Clue 6: Allusions

1. Some words are taken with little change from names of actual people: *cardigan, mackintosh, raglan, silhouette, zeppelin.*
2. Others use names of actual people, but with some change in form: *dunce, galvanize, nicotine, philippic, saxophone, teddy bear.*
3. Still others use words based on characters in legends and myths: *aurora, cereal, janitor, jovial, saturnine, titanic, vulcanize.*
4. Some words are taken from place names: *china, currant, italic type, morocco leather, peach, sardonic, spruce.*
5. Many words have interesting stories to tell: *blarney, Cassandra, donnybrook, Frankenstein, hector, Job's comforter, Pandora's box, pooh-bah, utopian.*

You may wish to refer to the following books to help you with allusions:
   Robert Hendrickson, *Human Words*
   Nancy Caldwell Sorel, *Word People*
   Willard Espy, *O Thou Improper, Thou Uncommon Noun*

Word Clues: Review Test

The sentences that follow provide clues to meanings. Write the letter of the word that makes best sense in each sentence.

1. The _____ of the sandy soil caused the beachside buildings to be unsafe.
   (A) beauty   (D) age
   (B) instability   (E) length
   (C) height

   1 ___

2. Because of his _____ disposition, you can never predict what he will do.
   (A) sound   (D) mercurial
   (B) Spartan   (E) herculean
   (C) stentorian

   2 ___

3. Use Renewo shampoo to give your hair its natural _____.
   (A) shininess   (D) color
   (B) lustre   (E) strength
   (C) reflection

   3 ___

4. The clever politician was as _____ as an eel.
   (A) quick   (D) slippery
   (B) sharp   (E) smart
   (C) shiny

   4 ___

5. The reason for the special traffic lights and turning lanes is to _____ traffic flow, not impede it.
   (A) facilitate   (D) delay
   (B) decrease   (E) hamper
   (C) hinder

   5 ___

6. The winner's eyes were _____ with excitement.
   (A) reflecting   (D) charged
   (B) sparkling   (E) transparent
   (C) fiery

   6 ___

7. The government's _____ in enforcing the new law encourages lawlessness.
   (A) promptness   (D) prudence
   (B) cruelty   (E) carelessness
   (C) kindness

   7 ___

8. The religious service ended with a _____ of praise and joy.
   (A) tune   (D) ballad
   (B) melody   (E) hymn
   (C) book

   8 ___

9. It is natural and _____ for a cat to keep itself clean.
   (A) internal   (D) learned
   (B) external   (E) accepted
   (C) instinctive

   9 ___

10. The hand-rubbed finish on the custom-built furniture was as _____ as satin.
    (A) slippery   (D) smooth
    (B) slick   (E) soft
    (C) shiny

    10 ___

Word Clues: Summary

Review these word clues from time to time. If you understand how word clues help you learn new words, you will do better on the vocabulary and reading sections of the SAT.

Clue 1   Connotation and Denotation
Connotation is the tone and meaning acquired by use.
Denotation is the dictionary definition.
Although we often use the terms porpoise and dolphin *interchangeably*, careful marine biologists observe the *distinctions between* the two.

Clue 2   Figurative Language
Simile: comparing by using *like* or *as*
The clean sheets looked *as white as snow*.

Metaphor: implying a comparison of two different things without using *like* or *as*

The lazy person could not *hold down a job*.

Personification: representing an object as a person

The *truth cries* out for justice.

Metonymy: using a word for another closely associated word

She prepared a new *dish* for dinner.

Synecdoche: using the part for the whole, or the reverse

The show featured fifty *dancing feet*.

Hyperbole: exaggerating for effect

I was *scared to death*.

Understatement: emphasizing by saying less than is meant

After the marathon I was a *little tired*.

Irony: saying one thing and implying the opposite

I love this as much as *going to the dentist*.

Clue 3 **Synonyms:** discriminating between words of similar meaning

The unpleasant boss was *haughty* and *overbearing*.

Clue 4 **Associated Words:** using related words you already know

For my term paper I read ballads, sonnets, and many haiku.

Clue 5 **Words Within Words:** looking for the familiar smaller words in larger words

She tried hard, but her efforts were *ineffectual* (effect).

Clue 6 **Allusions:** using a reference to a literary or historical person, place, or event.

Her *mercurial* (Mercury) personality made her unfit for the management position.

Section III: Clues from Etymology

Etymology Clue 1: Latin Prefixes

Problem

Although the oak is a _____ tree, losing its leaves every year, some dead leaves persist through the winter, awaiting the impulses of spring to set them free.

(A) statuesque
(B) regressive
(C) monochromatic

(D) deciduous
(E) provocative

Strategy. Some familiarity with Latin prefixes, suffixes, and stems can help in questions like this. As the sentence states, deciduous trees lose their leaves every year. The root *cid* (from *cad*) means "fall." The prefix *de* means "down." Thus *deciduous* means "falling down." If you don't know the Latin elements, try the elimination process. *Statuesque* (A) has nothing to do with losing leaves. *Monochromatic* (C), "of one color," is equally off the topic. *Regressive* (B) and *provocative* (E) are not ordinarily applied to trees. Mastering the important Latin and Greek root words can pay dividends on tests and in reading comprehension.

(D) Although the oak is a deciduous tree, losing its leaves every year, some dead leaves persist through the winter, awaiting the impulses of spring to set them free.

Would you like the key to thousands of words? According to Dr. James I. Brown of the University of Minnesota, the following 14 words will help you master 100,000 words.

aspect	intermittent	oversufficient
detain	mistranscribe	precept
epilogue	monograph	reproduction
indisposed	nonextended	uncomplicated
insist	offer	

Epilogue and *monograph* are of Greek origin and will be treated in Etymology Clue 4, page 103. All the others contain basic Latin prefixes and roots, which will be treated here in clues 1–3. Several of the prefixes are Anglo-Saxon.

How is it possible for so few words to provide clues to the meanings of so many other words? English, like many other languages, builds words by putting elements together. We call these elements *prefixes, roots,* and *suffixes*. Here are some examples.

PREFIX: beginning word part
                *dis*like   *re*port   *de*part

ROOT: main word part
                dis*like*   re*port*   de*part*

SUFFIX: ending word part
                dislik*ing*   report*er*   depart*ure*

Some words, like *aspect* and *insist,* contain prefixes and roots. Other words, like *victor* and *nutrition,* contain roots and suffixes. Some words contain prefixes, roots, and suffixes; for example, *reproduction* and *uncomplicated.* Some words contain only roots; such as, *course* and *pose.*

Where Our Words Come From

In the richness of its resources, English is different from most languages. There are four major streams in English: Greek, Latin, French (ultimately derived from Latin), and Anglo-Saxon. All four provide thousands of words for us to choose from. Synonyms abound in many possibilities. See how some synonyms of *mark,* all from a different source, enrich our language.

mark—from Anglo-Saxon. *Mark* is a general word suggesting a token, impression, feature.

signature—from Latin (modified). *Signature* is the special *mark,* usually handwritten, to identify a person.

imprimatur—from Latin (unchanged). *Imprimatur* is a *mark* of approval signifying that a book has been accepted for publication.

criterion—from Greek. *Criterion* suggests a *mark,* a test, a standard for judging.

vestige—from French (and ultimately Latin). *Vestige* suggests a small *mark,* a remnant of something that has disappeared.

graffiti—from Italian (and ultimately from Latin and Greek). *Graffiti* is a plural word designating *marks* that appear where they don't belong; for example, scribbling on public walls.

An average synonym dictionary suggests scores of other synonyms for *mark;* for example, *badge, blemish, blot, boundary, brand, characteristic, disfigurement,* and so on through the alphabet. These words have diverse origins. All contribute to the English treasure house and make distinctions finer and more subtle in English.

You have noticed that a number of words above, listed from other languages, ultimately come from Latin or Greek. *Vestige* and *graffiti,* for example, come through French and Italian, but their ultimate source is Latin. French, however, is a far richer source than Italian.

We have labeled French as one of the four great sources of English, even though it is basically derived from Latin. When William the Conqueror settled in England after the Battle of Hastings in 1066, he brought Norman (French) noblemen, ladies, customs, settlers, and language with him. We thus have pairs like *house* (Anglo-Saxon) and *mansion* (French) to enrich our language.

Many SAT questions, especially the analogy questions, rely on such words and word pairs for their answer choices.

Get the Dictionary Habit

To increase your vocabulary, get the dictionary habit. Look up words to find their derivations. Notice how the following excerpt from *Webster's New World Dictionary* tells the fascinating story of *volume*. Why should a word meaning *turn* be used to describe a flat book today? The meaning is there. *Volumes* were originally scrolls—rolled-up papers.

> **vol•ume** (väl′yoom, -yəm) *n.* [ME. < MFr. < L. *volumen*, a roll, scroll, hence a book written on a parchment < *volulus*, pp. of *volvere*, to roll: see WALK] **1** orig., a roll of parchment, a scroll, etc. **2** *a)* a collection of written, typewritten, or printed sheets bound together; book *b)* any of the separate books making up a matched set or a complete work **3** a set of the issues of a periodical over a fixed period of time, usually a year **4** the amount of space occupied in three dimensions; cubic contents or cubic magnitude **5** *a)* a quantity, bulk, mass, or amount *b)* a large quantity **6** the degree, strength, or loudness of sound **7** *Music* fullness of tone —*SYN.* see BULK[1]—**speak volumes** to be very expressive or meaningful* —**vol′-umed** *adj.*

Following a trail through the dictionary is like playing a video game—without the need for special equipment. The quest can be fascinating and the rewards great. If you get the dictionary habit now, you'll have a lifetime of fun and growth. If, for example, you find *scroll* associated with *volume*, look up *scroll*. You'll find that *scroll* is related to the English *roll*. The dictionary suggests that you look up *escrow*, another related word. *Escrow* introduces you to another expression: *in escrow*, a phrase you should know in adult life. And so it goes if you use your dictionary often.

It has been estimated that 65% of the words in the dictionary come from Latin or Greek. Learning the basic Latin and Greek prefixes and roots is an excellent way to extend your vocabulary.

Common Latin Prefixes

In the following lists, the first column gives the prefix. The second column gives the basic meaning of the prefix. The third column gives a word or words showing the use of the prefix in a word. The fourth column explains how the prefix keeps some of its original meaning, even though the word may have come a long way from its introduction into English. This explanation often serves as a definition of the word, as well, though its major purpose is to show how a word acquires meanings.

---

* With permission. From *Webster's New World Dictionary,* Third College Edition. Copyright © 1988 by Simon & Schuster, Inc.

Prefix	Meaning	Example	Explanation
a, ab	away, from	avert	turn *away*
		abnormal	deviating *from* normal
ac, ad, a	to, toward	access	coming *toward*
		advance	move *toward*
ambi	both	ambidextrous	skilled with *both* hands
ante	before	antecedent	coming *before*
circum	around	circumnavigate	sail *around*
com, con	with	compare	make equal *with*, regard as similar
contra	against	contradict	say *against*
de	down, from, away	depose	put *down*
dis, di	apart, from, not	disenfranchise	*not* allow to vote
		digress	move *apart*
e, ex	out of	evict	cast *out*
		exit	go *out*
extra	beyond, additional	extraordinary	*beyond* the ordinary
in	into	insert	put *into*
in	not	inimical	*not* friendly
inter	between,	intervene	come *between*
intra,	within,	intramural	*within* a school
intro	in, into	introduction	*into* a book
medi	middle	medieval	pertaining to the *Middle* Ages
non	not	nonproductive	*not* productive
ob	against, toward	obstruct	build *against,* hinder
pen	almost	peninsula	*almost* an island
per	through, thoroughly	pernicious	*thoroughly* evil
		pervade	move *through*
post	after	postpone	put *after*
pre	before	prearrange	arrange *before*
prim, prin	first	principal	*first* teacher, leader
pro	forward, before	proceed	go *forward*
re	back, again	remit	send *back*
		reread	read *again*
retro	back, backward	retrograde	*backward* motion
se	aside, apart	secede	pull *apart*
sub	under	submarine	*under* the sea
super, supr	above, beyond	superhuman	*beyond* the human
		supreme	*above* all others
trans	across	transmigrate	move *across*
ultra	beyond, extremely	ultramodern	*beyond* the modern
vice	in place of	vice-president	*in place of* the president

A few prefixes change the last letter to match the first letter of the root word. Thus **ad** becomes **af** *(affect)*, **ag** *(aggression)*, **al** *(alliteration)*, **an** *(annex)*, **ap** *(apply)*, **ar** *(arrest)*, and **at** *(attend)*. **Sub** becomes **suc** *(succumb)*, **suf** *(suffer)*, **sug** *(suggest)*, and **sup** *(supplant)*. **In** becomes **il** *(illegal)*, **im** *(immature)*, and **ir** *(irregular)*.

A word of caution about roots, prefixes, and word meanings: words change in use. Word meanings sometimes depart from the original strict meanings. *Extravagant,* for example, according to its root and prefix means "wandering beyond." The word has, however, acquired a wider, more figurative sense. *Extravagant* purchases, for example, "wander beyond" the normal and wise. *Extravagant* yarns "wander beyond" the reasonable. Once you know the roots, you will find these extended meanings especially interesting.

Try to use your new information in answering the following sentence-completion item.

Problem

Driving with a valid driver's license
is _____ for operating a motor vehicle,
but boating regulations are too lenient.

    (A) suggested   (D) frequent
    (B) archaic   (E) mandatory
    (C) debated

Strategy. Since states demand the issuance of a driver's license, the answer should contain the thought of requirement. Only *mandatory* carries the idea of "command," from the root *mand.*

(E) Driving with a valid driver's license is mandatory for operating a motor vehicle, but boating regulations are too lenient.

Trial Test

Take the following trial test for practice in using Latin prefixes. Fill in the blank in each sentence by writing a Latin prefix from the list on page 78. The word in italics is a clue to the needed prefix. The number in parentheses tells the number of letters needed to complete each word.

> As I went *back* in imagination to my childhood home, the old cottage seemed huge in **retro**spect. (5)

The italicized word *back* tells you the prefix **retro** should be inserted. *Retrospect* means "looking backward."

1. Most of the words in the description

   are _____fluous, for they go far *beyond* what is needed to make an effective picture. (5)

2. I feel _____valent toward Jennifer, for I find her *both* charming and annoying at times. (4)

3. A(n) _____mortem is an examination made *after* death to determine the cause of death. (4)

4. Doug gave his _____ry opinion and spoke vehemently *against* the proposal. (6)

5. Because he could *not* function in the game, the fullback was put on

   the _____abled list. (3)

6. A(n) _____patriate is a person who goes *out* of his country to settle elsewhere. (2)

7. The artist gave a(n) _____spective show and enabled her fans to look *back* at her illustrious past. (5)

8. Marie Antoinette had a(n) _____ cluded villa, *apart* from the bustle of the palace. (2)

9. A(n) _____ errant social group is one that deviates *from* the normal. (2)

10. That _____ diluvian idea of yours must have originated *before* the flood! (4)

Problem

Although the agreement was finally signed in October, under the terms of the pact, payments of lost wages would be _____ to April, the time the original contract _____.

(A) retroactive . . expired
(B) charged . . began
(C) referred . . expanded
(D) conducive . . germinated
(E) applied . . deteriorated

Strategy. The prefix **retro,** meaning "back," provides the key to this answer. *Retroactive* suggests going back into the past, usually to a period before another event. Here the contract was signed in October, but the pact pretended it had been signed in April, with full benefits beginning at that time. The only choice that makes sense is *(A)*. Wages are paid as though the new agreement immediately followed the expiration of the old.

None of the alternatives makes good sense when preceding the words "to April."

Latin Prefixes Denoting Number

Prefix	Meaning	Example	Explanation
bi	two	**bi**ennial	every *two* years
cent	hundred	**cent**imeter	*hundredth* of a meter
dec	ten	**dec**imal	system of *tens*
duo, du	two	**du**et	performance by *two*
duodec	twelve	**duodec**imal	system of *twelves*
mill	thousand	**mill**enium	a *thousand* years
multi	many	**multi**tude	*many* persons
nona	nine	**nona**genarian	*ninety*-year-old
novem	nine	**novem**ber	*ninth* month (originally)
oct	eight	**oct**et	group of *eight*
omni	all	**omni**scient	*all*-knowing
quadr	four	**quadr**ilateral	*four*-sided
quinqu, quint	five	**quinqu**ennial	every *five* years
		quintuplets	multiple birth of *five*
semi	half	**semi**circle	*half* a circle
sept	seven	**Sept**ember	*seventh* month (originally)
sex	six	**sex**tet	group of *six*
tri	three	**tri**ple	*three* times
uni	one	**un**animous	of *one* mind

Problem

In an election decided by majority or plurality, the vote need not be _____.

(A) counted   (D) unbiased
(B) total   (E) impartial
(C) unanimous

Strategy. Again, the Latin provides some help. *Uni* means "one" and appears in words like *union, united,* and *unified. Anim* means "mind." *Unanimous* is "of *one* mind . . . one vote." (A) and (B) suggest a faulty procedure. (D) and (E) suggest a misuse of the voting process.

(C) In an election decided by majority or plurality, the vote need not be unanimous.

Trial Test

Fill in the blank in each sentence by writing a Latin number prefix from the list on page 80. The word in italics is a clue to the needed prefix. The number in parentheses tells the number of letters needed to complete each word.

> The setting sun made a perfect **semi**circle, as only *half* was visible on the horizon. (4)

The italicized word *half* tells us the prefix *semi* should be inserted.

1. Some colleges have a(n) _____mestral organization, dividing the school year into *three* parts. (3)

2. A(n) _____ave is the *eighth* full tone above a given tone, having twice as many vibrations a second. (3)

3. Brock's plans are _____farious, having *many* angles and procedures. (5)

4. In a(n) _____nary system, *two* suns revolve about each other. (2)

5. Our town is celebrating its _____centennial, having been in existence *half* a hundred years. (4)

6. A truly _____que specimen is *one* of a kind. (3)

7. Superman was not _____ potent, for he could not overcome *all* obstacles. (4)

8. A(n) _____angle is a *three*-sided figure. (3)

9. In the _____igrade, or Celsius, thermometer, the difference between the boiling point and the freezing point is divided into *100* degrees. (4)

10. A(n) _____ipede may seem to have a *thousand* legs, but the actual number is between 100 and 200. (4)

Problem

Raccoons are survivors because of their flexibility, adaptability, and _____ appetite.

(A) innovative   (D) ill-proportioned
(B) finicky   (E) delicate
(C) omnivorous

Strategy. You may remember *carnivore,* "meat-eating animal," and *herbivore,* "vegetation-eating animal." The prefix *omni,* "all," suggests that an omnivore eats both flesh and vegetation. *Omnivorous* is the preferred word in this context.

Review

Fill in the blank in each sentence by writing the Latin prefix that makes best sense. The word in italics is a clue. The number in parentheses tells the number of letters needed.

1. A good _____ator takes a *middle* position, favoring neither one side nor the other. (4)

2. A(n) _____opus is so named because it has *eight* arms. (3)

3. Walt's _____terminable speeches seem *not* to have a purpose or an end. (2)

4. When a seller offers a used car, he is often shocked to learn how much normal _____preciation has brought *down* the price of the car. (2)

5. A group of *five* musicians is called a(n) _____et. (5)

6. An idea that is said to correspond *with* another is _____gruent with that idea. (3)

7. The _____urban bus service ran *between* towns. (5)

8. _____historic events took place *before* the invention of writing. (3)

9. The bottle held only a(n) _____iliter, or one-*tenth* of a liter, of liquid. (3)

10. If you're going *to* Walt Disney World, buy your ticket of _____mission at the main gate. (2)

11. By _____polation Helen went *beyond* present statistics and estimated the probable population of Grimesdale by the year 2000. (5)

12. A(n) _____spect person looks *around* carefully before taking action. (6)

13. A(n) _____el is a formal fight between *two* persons. (2)

14. Our _____genitors, those who came *before* us, have left for us a valuable heritage of art and wisdom. (3)

15. For my taste the Cortland apple is _____lative, far *above* other apples in flavor and texture. (5)

16. The Patriots stated once *again* what they believed in and _____affirmed their allegiance to the cause of freedom. (2)

17. A presidential election is always a(n) _____ennial event, occurring every *four* years. (5)

18. A layer of _____cutaneous fat, *under* the outer layer of skin, provides insulation against the cold. (3)

19. Tiny _____mitters, powered by solar batteries, send messages *across* millions of miles of space. (5)

20. Because the chairperson had been delayed, the _____-chairperson acted *in place of* the chairperson and opened the meeting. (4)

SUMMARY

Etymology Clue 1: Latin Prefixes

1. Etymology, the study of word origins, is extremely helpful in figuring out the meaning of new and unknown words.
2. A great many English words begin with common Latin prefixes and number prefixes. If you know the prefix, you have a good chance of figuring out the whole word.
3. A few prefixes change the last letter to match the first letter of the root word:

sub—suc (succumb)	**sub**—sug (suggest)
sub—suf (suffer)	**sub**—sup (supplant)

Etymology Clue 2: Latin Roots——Verbs

Note how a knowledge of roots helps with a sentence-completion item.

Problem

Pittsburgh is situated at the _____ of two rivers, the Allegheny and the Mononga-hela, thus forming the Ohio.
(A) confluence   (D) cascades
(B) watershed   (E) divergence
(C) rapids

Strategy.   The sentence suggests that two rivers join at Pittsburgh. *Confluence* (A) means "flowing together." *Flu* means "flow" and appears in words like *fluid, affluent,* and *influenza. Con* is a prefix meaning "together." (B), (C) and (D) do not address the major point of joining. (E) suggests the opposite. *Verg* means "turn" or "bend," but *di* means "away." Thus *divergence* is opposed to *confluence*.

(A) Pittsburgh is situated at the confluence of two rivers, the Allegheny and the Monongahela, thus forming the Ohio.

Now we come to the longest list in our study of word elements: Latin roots. Though the lists seem overwhelmingly long, do not lose heart. You already *know* most of these roots because you see them every day in familiar words. You already know, for example, that *victory* involves *conquering* a person, a group, an obstacle. You may not have put that meaning into so many words before, but your knowledge gives you an advantage in working with the root **vinc-vict,** meaning "conquer." When you meet *invincible,* you know it means "unconquerable."

When you go over the lists that follow, associate a word with each root, preferably a word you already know. Doing so will expand your vocabulary enormously and also help you meet many new words with confidence.

Latin Roots

The lists of Latin roots here are by no means all the roots used in English words, but they include most of the important and helpful ones. Don't forget, even if you meet a word with a root not included in the lists, you can often guess at the meaning of the word by thinking of other words with the same root.

To make the lists more manageable, the words have been arbitrarily divided into two large categories: those derived from Latin nouns and adjectives and those derived from Latin verbs. Some words are borderline. *Labor,* for example, comes from a Latin noun which is related to a Latin verb. The lists 1, 2, and 3 are for convenience, so that you can work with a small number of roots at one time. A trial test follows each list.

Roots from Latin Verbs—1

Root	Meaning	Example	Explanation
ag, act	do, act, drive	**ag**ile	*act*ive
am, ami	love	**ami**able	good-natured (originally *lov*able)
arbit	judge	**arbit**rate	*judge* between
aud	hear	**aud**ible	able to be *heard*
cad, cas, cid	fall	**cad**ence	*fall* of the voice in speaking
		coin**cid**ence	a *falling* together of events
can, cant, chant	sing	**cant**or	*sing*er
cap, capt, cip, cept	take	**cap**ture	*take* by force
ced, cess, cede, ceed	go	pro**ceed**	*go* forward
		re**cede**	*go* back
cern, cert	perceive, separate	dis**cern**	recognize as *separate,* see clearly
cis, cid, caed	kill, cut	sui**cid**e	*kill*ing of oneself
		in**cis**ion	*cut*ting into
clam, claim	cry out, shout	ex**claim**	*cry* out
		pro**clam**ation	*cry*ing forth
clud, claus, clus	shut, close	se**clud**ed	*shut* away
cogn	know	re**cogn**ize	*know* by some detail
col, cult	till, inhabit	agri**cult**ure	*till*ing the fields

Root	Meaning	Example	Explanation
cred	believe	**cred**ible	*believ*able
cresc, crease	grow	in**crease**	*grow* in size
curr, curs	run	in**curs**ion	*run*ning in, invasion
da, dat, don	give	**don**ation	*gift*
dic, dict	say	**dic**tate	*say* aloud
doc	teach	**doc**trine	*teach*ing
dorm	sleep	**dorm**ant	*sleep*ing, inactive
duc, duct	lead	ab**duct**	*lead* away, kidnap
err	wander	**err**ant	*wander*ing
fac, fec, fic, fy	do, make	magni**fy**	*make* large
		factory	place where things are *made*
fer, lat	carry	re**fer**	*carry* back
		trans**late**	*carry* across
flect, flex	bend	**flex**ible	easily *bent*
flu, flux	flow	**flu**id	something that *flows*
		in**flux**	a *flowing* in
frang, fract, frag, fring	break	**fract**ure	*break*
		fragment	*broken* piece
fug	flee	**fug**itive	one who *flees*
fund, fus	pour	in**fus**ion	*pour*ing in
gen	cause, bear, produce	con**gen**ital	*born* with
ger, gest	carry	belli**ger**ent	one who *carries* war to another

Trial Test

Fill in the blank in each sentence by writing a Latin root from the preceding list. The word in italics is the clue to the needed root. The number in parentheses tells the number of letters needed.

Mark was too **cred**ulous, *believ*ing everything he heard. (4)

The italicized *believ* tells us the root **cred** should be inserted.

1. A(n) _____ent moon soon after sunset tells us the moon is waxing, or *grow*ing. (5)

2. To prevent someone from *know*ing you, you might travel in _____ito. (4)

3. To *say* in advance is to pre_____. (4)

4. Our play group has a bene_____tor who has *done* many good things for us. (3)

5. He was charged with an in_____ion because he had *broken* the law about parking in restricted areas. (5)

6. Marcia is _____ent in French: her speech *flows* so effortlessly. (3)

7. The _____ry *carried* us across New York Harbor and back. (3)

8. Wally was in _____ed to wear the clown costume and was even *led* to performing a humorous routine. (3)

9. The _____itories could *sleep* a dozen people in a pinch. (4)

10. The sports fans at the airport *shouted* when the plane landed and _____ored for a brief speech by the triumphant coach. (4)

11. When we decided to sell the house, we arranged for a real estate _____ent to *act* for us. (2)

12. When we opened the crowded closet, a pro_____ion of odds and ends *poured* forth. (3)

13. The _____erator *produced* enough current for a small village. (3)

14. Brett *ran* his eye over the manuscript, but his _____ory glance provided no clue to the importance of the contents. (4)

15. If you *go* beyond our budgeted expenditures and ex_____ the amount allotted to costumes, you'll put us in the red before we start. (4)

16. The witch doctor pronounced the in_____ation in a *sing*song voice. (4)

17. Ralph Waldo Emerson preached the _____trine of self-reliance and so *taught* his contemporaries to believe in themselves. (3)

18. Several wealthy _____ors *gave* sufficient funds to build a new rectory. (3)

19. Re_____ees were *flee*ing the city under attack. (3)

20. The *kill*ing of a brother is called fratri_____e. (3)

Roots from Latin Verbs—2

Root	Meaning	Example	Explanation
grad, gress	walk	pro**gress**	a *walk* forward
hab, hib	hold	**hab**it	something that *holds* us
her, hes	stick	co**her**e	*stick* together
		ad**hes**ive	something that *sticks* to something else
it	go	ex**it**	*go* out
jac, ject	throw	re**ject**	*throw* back
jud	judge	pre**jud**ice	a *judg*ing in advance
jung, junct, jug	join	**junct**ion	a *join*ing
jur	swear	**jur**or	one *sworn* to give a just verdict
leg, lect	choose, gather, read	il**leg**ible	not *read*able
		col**lect**	*gather* together
loqu, locut,	speak, talk	**loqu**acious	*talk*ative
mand	entrust, command	**mand**ate	a land *entrust*ed to another country
merg, mers	dip, plunge	sub**merg**e	*dip* below water
mit, miss	send	trans**mit**	*send* across
mon, monit	warn	ad**mon**ition	mild *warn*ing
mov, mot	move	**mot**or	something that *moves*
mut	change	**mut**able	*change*able

Root	Meaning	Example	Explanation
nasc, nat	born	**nat**ive	one *born* in a country
neg	deny	**neg**ative	*deny* truth of
ora	speak, pray	**ora**tor	*speak*er
orn	decorate	ad**orn**	*decorate*
pat, pass	suffer	**pat**ient	one who *suffers,* who receives care
pel, puls	drive	re**pel**	*drive* back
		com**puls**ion	*driv*ing force
pet	seek	centri**pet**al	*seek*ing the center
plac	please	im**plac**able	unable to be *please*d
plaud, plus, plod, plos	clap, strike	ap**plaud**	*clap*
plic, plex, ply	fold	com**plic**ated	involved (*folded* in on itself)
pon, pos	place, put	post**pon**e	*place* after
port	carry	im**port**	*carry* in
prehend, prehens, pris	seize	com**prehend**	*seize* (as an idea)
press	press, print	im**press**ion	something *press*ed or *print*ed on
prob	prove	**prob**ation	a period of test, of *prov*ing someone can perform as expected
pugn	fight	**pugn**acious	ready to *fight*
quir, ques, quis	seek	in**quis**itive	*seek*ing information
rid, ris	laugh	**rid**iculous	*laugh*able

Trial Test

Fill in the blank in each sentence by writing a Latin root from the preceding list. The word in italics is the clue to the needed root. The number in parentheses tells the number of letters needed.

1. Cheryl *sent* the re_____tance to the power company. (3)

2. In grammar, a con_____ion *joins* two elements together. (5)

3. Who will be chosen to ad_____icate the lawsuit, *judg*ing whether the plaintiff's case will prevail? (3)

4. Pauline in_____ed a few witty remarks, *throwing* them in casually at intervals. (4)

5. Humans are planti_____e creatures, for they *walk* on the soles of their feet. (4)

6. *Place* this envelope in the de_____it box. (3)

7. A(n) _____tionnaire is designed to *seek* information. (4)

8. Geraldine uses a(n) _____manteau for *carry*ing documents and letters. (4)

9. The minister *read* the Bible verse from the _____ern. (4)

10. Some col_____ial expressions are suitable for *speak*ing but not for writing. (4)

11. The judge re_____ed the prisoner to a detention home, *entrusting* him to a pair of sheriff's deputies. (4)

12. Sheila im_____ed the dusty jacket in warm soapy water, *dip*ping it again and again until the stains were removed. (4)

13. The governor *changed* his mind and com_____ed the condemned man's sentence to life imprisonment. (3)

14. The re_____ent industrial life of many New England cities proves that a re*birth* of vigor is not impossible. (4)

15. A(n) _____ligent driver may *deny* others the right to life. (3)

16. The police officers ap_____ed the smuggler and *seized* his cargo. (7)

17. The hero of Cotter's novel is *driven* by unpredictable im_____es. (4)

18. Naturally, Isabelle enjoyed the *clap*ping of the audience and the _____its of the critics. (5)

19. A com_____ent person is *pleased* with himself and quite smug. (4)

20. The _____ition *seeks* to bring to the notice of the authorities the dangerous intersection of Fifth and Main streets. (3)

Roots from Latin Verbs—3

Root	Meaning	Example	Explanation
rog	ask	inter**rog**ate	*ask*
rump, rupt	break	**rupt**ure	*break*
sal, salt, sult	lcap	**sal**ient	*leap*ing out
sci	know	con**sci**ous	able to *know*
scrib, script	write	in**scrib**e	*write* in
		in**script**ion	*writ*ing in
seg, sect	cut	bi**sect**	*cut* in two
sed, sess	sit	**sess**ion	a *sit*ting
sens, sent	feel	**sens**ation	*feel*ing
sequ, secu	follow	**sequ**el	work that *follows* another
solv, solut	loosen	**solv**ent	something that *loosens*
spec, spect	see	**spec**tacles	device for *seeing*
spir	breathe	re**spir**atory	pertaining to *breath*ing
sta, sist, stit	stand	**sta**ble	able to *stand*
string, strict	bind	**string**ent	*bind*ing
stru, struct	build	de**struct**ion	opposite of *building*
tang, tact	touch	**tang**ible	able to be *touch*ed
tent, tin, tain	hold	**ten**acious	*hold*ing on
tend, tens, tent	stretch	ex**tend**	*stretch* out
torqu, tort	twist	dis**tort**ed	*twist*ed
trah, tract	draw	at**tract**ion	something that *draws*
trib	share, pay	**trib**ute	something *paid*
trud, trus	thrust	in**trud**e	*thrust* in
turb	agitate	dis**turb**	*agitate*
vad, vas	go	in**vad**e	*go* in
ven, vent	come	con**ven**e	*come* together

Root	Meaning	Example	Explanation
verg	lean, turn	con**verg**e	*turn* together
vert, vers	turn	re**vers**e	*turn* back
vid, vis	see	**vis**ible	able to be *seen*
vinc, vict	conquer	con**vinc**e	*conquer* (in a discussion)
viv, vict	live	re**viv**e	bring back to *life*
voc, vok	call	**voc**ation	*call*ing
vol	wish, will	in**vol**untary	against the *will*
volv, volut	turn	re**volv**e	*turn* around

Trial Test

Fill in the blank in each sentence by writing a Latin root from the preceding list. The word in italics is the clue to the needed root. The number in parentheses tells the number of letters needed.

1. The entertainer was able to *twist* his body into the strangest con_____ions. (4)

2. The boa con_____or *binds* and crushes its foe. (6)

3. The car *stand*ing in the garage will remain _____tionary until you replace the battery. (3)

4. Tele_____ion enables us to *see* events happening far away. (3)

5. The strong armies of Genghis Khan were in_____ible, *conquer*ing every force in their path. (4)

6. Ancient Egyptian _____es *wrote* on stone, messages that still survive. (5)

7. _____entary people *sit* too much, avoiding exercise. (3)

8. Although English royalty could not *hold* onto real power, it has re_____ed the pomp and glitter of centuries ago. (4)

9. Fred dreaded dis_____ing the frog in biology class, but after the first *cut* he became fascinated by the complexity of his subject. (4)

10. The cor_____ administration *broke* every moral and legal guideline in running the city. (4)

11. _____ion *stretches* mind and body almost to the breaking point. (4)

12. The purpose of the in_____ion was to *see* if the regulations had been followed. (5)

13. Some of our actions have important con_____ences that *follow* us all our days. (4)

14. The con_____ions of the brain show twists, *turns,* and folds on the surface. (5)

15. The storm *agitated* the formerly calm lake and caused dangerous _____ulence for small boats. (4)

16. Bene_____ent actions arise from feelings of good*will* toward others. (3)

17. To re_____e a license is to *call* it back and cancel it. (3)

18. A di_____ent point of view *turns* from the average. (4)

19. To inter_____e in a dispute is to *come* between the two parties in an attempt to settle the argument. (3)

20. The plastic models are formed by ex_____ion, that is, by *thrust*ing the plastic through small holes to provide the desired shape. (4)

Problem

Though deceptively smooth in some areas, the Colorado River can become a _____, raging torrent in others.

    (A) disagreeable   (D) distorted
    (B) turbulent   (E) circuitous
    (C) quiescent

Strategy.   Though all alternatives may be applied to some river somewhere, only one word fits the sentence: *turbulent*. *Turbulent* (B) contains the Latin root verb *turb* "agitate." *Turbulent* means "agitated," "stormy," "violent." The pairing with *raging* and the contrast with *smooth* identifies (B) as the answer. (A) is too mild. (C) is opposed in meaning. (D) and (E) are unsuitable adjectives for a raging torrent.

    (B) Though deceptively smooth in some areas, the Colorado River can become a turbulent, raging torrent in others.

Review

Fill in the blank in each sentence by writing a Latin root from the three preceding lists. The word in italics is the clue to the needed root. The number in parentheses tells the number of letters needed.

1. The critic de_____ed the novel's purpose and *laugh*ed at the intended motivation of the central character. (3)

2. Humane societies protest _____isection, research operations performed on *living* animals. (3)

3. Huge skyscrapers are *built* by specialized con_____ion contractors. (6)

4. Gail is so _____ulous she'll *believe* anything. (4)

5. The _____cle at Delphi *spoke* words that could be taken in many ways. (3)

6. We need an impartial _____er to *judge* the merits of the case. (5)

7. The letter expressed the ap_____ation of the council and *proved* that government was responsible for public needs. (4)

8. Daryl fancies he is omni_____ent, *know*ing everything about everything. (3)

9. The re_____e *shut* himself away from all society. (4)

10. The slightest sound on stage can be *heard* all through the _____itorium. (3)

11. The keynote *speaker* delivered a lengthy _____tion. (3)

12. A manu_____tured article was once, by word origin, *made* by hand. (3)

13. Many elements of Victorian houses were purely _____amental, added for *decoration*, not function. (3)

14. The ex_____ it *held* many items of interest to the visitor. (3)

15. Are insects _____ient creatures that *feel* some kind of primitive emotions, like fear? (4)

16. The _____or *drew* the plow through the moist soil. (5)

17. Before the jet aircraft had been per-
fected, airplanes were *driven* by one or
more pro_____lers. (3)

18. The spy inter_____ed the message
and *took* it to the enemy contact. (4)

19. The referee ad_____ished the boxer,
*warn*ing him that another foul would
cost him the match. (3)

20. Some families are _____ile, *touch*ing
and hugging each other on greetings
and farewells. (4)

SUMMARY

Etymology Clue 2: Latin Roots——Verbs

1. Because English contains more words from Latin than from any other
language, Latin roots, as well as prefixes, can help you figure out meanings—and SAT answers.
2. Just one root can lead to several words:

   port ("carry")—import, deport, report, portable

Etymology Clue 3: Latin Roots—— Nouns and Adjectives

Latin verbs have provided a solid list of roots to help you in attacking
new words. Latin nouns and adjectives also supply information you can use
to master new and unfamiliar words. Spend time on these lists as you prepare
for the SAT.

Roots from Latin Nouns and Adjectives—1

Root	Meaning	Example	Explanation
al, alter, altr	other	alien	person from *another* land
		altruism	concern for *others*
anim	life, mind	animated	*live*ly
		unanimous	of one *mind*
ann, enn	year	annual	*year*ly
		millennium	period of a thousand *years*
apt, ept	suitable, appropriate	aptitude	*suitabi*lity for a task
		inept	not *suitable*, unfit
aqu	water	aqueous	*water*y

Root	Meaning	Example	Explanation
arm	arm, weapon	**arm**ament	*weapon*ry
art	art, craft, skill	**art**isan	a person skilled in a *craft*
bell	beautiful	em**bell**ish	make *beautiful*
bene, bon	good	**bene**factor	one who does *good*
brev	short	ab**brev**iate	*shorten*
cand	white, glowing	in**cand**escent	*glow*ing
capit	head	**capit**al	chief* *(head)* city
centr	center	ec**centr**ic	off *center*
civ, cit	city, citizen	**civ**ic	dealing with problems of the *city*
cor	heart	**cor**dial	sincere, from the *heart*
corp	body	**corp**oreal	*bodi*ly
crux, cruc	cross	**cruc**iform	*cross*-shaped
culp	blame, fault	**culp**able	deserving *blame*
cur	care	pedi**cur**e	foot *care*
dent	tooth	**dent**al	pertaining to *teeth*
dia, di	day	**di**urnal	*dai*ly
digit	finger	**digit**al	pertaining to *finger*
dom	house, home	**dom**icile	*house*
domin	master	**domin**ate	rule as a *master*
dur	hard, lasting	**dur**able	*lasting*
ego	I, self	**ego**centric	centered on the *self*
equ	horse	**equ**ine	pertaining to the *horse*
equ	equal	ine**qu**ality	condition of being *unequal*
ev	age, time	co**ev**al	of the same *age*
felic	happy	**felic**ity	*happi*ness
ferv	boil, bubble	**ferv**ent	*boil*ing, ardent
fid	faith	**fid**elity	*faith*fulness
fil	son	**fil**ial	pertaining to a *son*

*Here's another example of the incredible richness of English. *Chief,* meaning head, comes to us through the French; the French word itself comes from the Latin *capit.* When English borrows the same word twice, the borrowings are called *doublets.* See pages 141–142.

Trial Test

Fill the blank in each sentence by writing a Latin root from the previous list. The word in italics is the clue to the needed root. The number in parentheses tells the number of letters needed.

The **cur**ator of a museum is a person who takes *care* of the exhibits. The italicized word *care* tells you to use the root **cur**. The *curator* takes care of the museum.

---

1. The presti _____ator was a superb magician, as he demonstrated trick after trick with nimble *fingers*. (5)

2. _____ity in writing suggests that the writer take the *shortest* path to his goal, avoiding all unnecessary words. (4)

3. Objects without *life* are in _____ate. (4)

4. A name *other* than your own is a(n) _____ias. (2)

5. The important testimony of the key witness ex_____ated the defendant, removing any *blame* from his actions. (4)

6. A(n) _____uity is an amount of money paid every *year*. (3)

7. A substance _____eficial to the health is *good* for you. (3)

8. A(n) _____ifrice is a powder for cleaning *teeth*. (4)

9. A(n) _____tist uses the pronoun *I* almost exclusively. (3)

10. At the horse show riders demonstrated _____estrian skills. (3)

11. A con_____ant is a close friend, someone we put *faith* in. (3)

12. A(n) _____ilian is a *citizen* not in the armed forces. (3)

13. Dis_____d, or disagreement, is a metaphor suggesting that two *hearts* are not beating together. (3)

14. A(n) _____ulent, obese person has just too much *body!* (4)

15. A per _____a distribution is literally according to each *head,* that is, equally to each individual. (5)

16. _____ifugal force flees the *center*. (5)

17. A(n) _____ry is meant to be kept faithfully, every *day*. (3)

18. An ef_____escent liquid *bubbles* and *boils*. (4)

19. A(n) _____ivalent payment is *equal* in value. (3)

20. Scrooge was a(n) _____eering boss, seeking to show himself the *master* in every situation involving his employees. (5)

21. Perkins has a medi_____al attitude toward labor, a point of view lifted straight out of the Middle *Ages*. (2)

22. A(n) _____arium is a *watery* wonderland, with fish as the principal inhabitants. (3)

23. The _____ator of a museum is a person who takes *care* of the exhibits. (3)

24. The victors dis_____ed the losers, taking away all *weapons* and tools of war. (3)

25. A *cross*-shaped object is _____iform. (4)

Problem

Without thought of personal gain, Irene Russell proved to be _____ as she put her personal fortune at risk to help stem the financial panic.

(A) altruistic   (D) egocentric
(B) felicitous   (E) durable
(C) culpable

Strategy. The key to the answer is the pair of opening phrases. Irene Russell had nothing to gain personally from her actions, so they had to be *unselfish*, devoted to others. *Altruistic* (A) from the Latin *alter* "other," satisfies the requirement. *Altruistic* means "unselfish," "concerned for others." *Felicitous* (B), "pleasant," "suitable," makes little sense. Equally inappropriate are *culpable* (C), "blameworthy," and *durable* (E), "lasting." *Egocentric* (D), "self-centeredness," actually runs counter to the sense of the sentence and must be rejected.

(A) Without thought of personal gain, Irene Russell proved to be altruistic as she put her personal fortune at risk to help stem the financial panic.

Roots from Latin Nouns and Adjectives—2

Root	Meaning	Example	Explanation
fin	end	**fin**ally	at the *end*
firm	strong	in**firm**	not *strong*
flor	flower	**flor**al	pertaining to *flowers*
foli	leaf	**foli**age	*leaves*
form	form, shape	de**form**ation	change in *form* (for the worse)
fort	strong	**fort**ify	make *strong*
fum	smoke	**fum**es	*smoke*
grat	free, thankful, pleased	**grat**itude	expression of *thanks*
grav	heavy	ag**grav**ate	make worse, *heavier*
greg	flock	con**greg**ation	*flock*ing together
herb	grass	**herb**ivorous	*grass*-eating
ign	fire	**ign**ite	set on *fire*
labor	work	**labor**atory	place to *work* in
leg	law	**leg**al	pertaining to *law*
lev	light	al**lev**iate	*light*en
liber	free	**liber**ate	*free*
libr	book	**libr**ary	storehouse of *books*
liter	letter	al**liter**ation	beginning with same *letter*
loc	place	**loc**ation	*place*
lud, lus	play, game	pre**lud**e	before the *game*, introduction
		col**lus**ion	conspiracy (a *play*ing together)
magn	great	**magn**ify	make *great*
mal	evil	**mal**efactor	one who does *evil*
man	hand	**man**ual	by *hand*
mar	sea	sub**mar**ine	beneath the *sea*
mater, matr	mother	**matr**iarch	rule by *mother*
maxim	largest	**maxim**ize	make *largest*
ment	mind	**ment**al	pertaining to *mind*
min	less, little, small	**min**imum	*least* amount
miser	wretched	**miser**able	*wretched*
mor	custom	**mor**es	*customs*
mort	death	im**mort**al	*death*less
nav, naut	ship, sail	**nav**al	pertaining to *ships*

Trial Test

Fill in the blank in each sentence by writing a Latin root from the previous list. The word in italics is the clue to the needed root. The number in parentheses tells the number of letters needed to complete the word.

1. An unfortunate person not in his right *mind* is de_____ed. (4)

2. The famous Rodgers and Hammerstein col_____ated on many musicals, *work*ing together as an effective team. (5)

3. _____eous rock had its origins in *fire* in the earth's early history. (3)

4. _____islators make *laws;* judges test them. (3)

5. Serious debates can be *light*ened by a touch of _____ity. (3)

6. _____itime regulations have developed from the unwritten laws of the *sea.* (3)

7. _____animity is a *great*ness of spirit reflected in good and generous actions. (4)

8. A(n) _____icure is care of the *hands;* pedicure, of the feet. (3)

9. It is hard for a human mind to conceive of in_____ity, space without *end.* (3)

10. One's *strong* point is called his _____e. (4)

11. A dis_____ated bone is out of its proper *place.* (3)

12. To _____ign someone is to say *evil* things about him. (3)

13. The female stickleback doesn't have _____nal instincts; the male fish acts as *mother* and father. (5)

14. In the battle off Cape Trafalgar, Admiral Nelson received a(n) _____al wound, but he won victory even in *death.* (4)

15. The strict laws were _____alized, *free*ing the citizens from many unnecessary regulations. (5)

16. _____ity on the moon is so much less than on earth that we'd feel much less *heavy.* (4)

17. People who like to *flock* together are _____arious. (4)

18. Keep that _____icide away from the *grass* or you'll kill it. (4)

19. Vince _____imized his injury, making it seem *less* than it really was. (3)

20. To interpret the law too _____ally may emphasize the *letter* of the law at the expense of its spirit. (5)

21. On the _____ly rations allotted them, the serfs lived a *wretched* life. (5)

22. The exterminators used a deadly *smoke* in _____igating the house and ridding it of pests. (3)

23. Because his speech was excellent, the speaker was given a _____uity to express the *thanks* of the audience. (4)

24. The _____ist sold a beautiful bouquet of *flowers* for Mother's Day. (4)

25. Some chemicals de_____ate trees, stripping them of *leaves* and often killing the trees. (4)

Problem

Acid rain may have helped cause the trees on Mt. Mitchell to be _____, gaunt skeletons in midsummer.

(A) herbaceous   (D) cohesive

(B) succulent   (E) defoliated

(C) incinerated

Strategy. If trees are "gaunt skeletons in midsummer," they must have lost their leaves unnaturally. The Latin root *foli* "leaf," is firmly embedded in (E) *defoliated,* "stripped of leaves." When you meet this kind of sentence, you'll find clues but you'll still need to know the meaning of the key word. Having some knowledge of basic Latin and Greek roots is always helpful.

(E) Acid rain may have helped cause the trees on Mt. Mitchell to be defoliated, gaunt skeletons in midsummer.

Roots from Latin Nouns and Adjectives—3

Root	Meaning	Example	Explanation
noc, nox	night	**noc**turnal	pertaining to *night*
norm	rule, standard	ab**norm**al	away from the *standard*
nov	new	**nov**elty	*new*ness
numer	number	e**numer**ate	list by *number*
ocul	eye	bin**ocul**ars	fieldglasses for two *eyes*
oper	work	co**oper**ate	*work* together
optim	best	**optim**al	*best*
pac	peace	**pac**ify	make *peace*ful
par	equal	**par**ity	*equal*ity
pater, patr	father	**pater**nal	pertaining to *father*
ped	foot	**ped**estal	*foot* of a column
plus, plur	more	**plur**ality	*more* than any other candidate
popul	people	**popul**ation	*people* of a country
prim, prin	first	**prim**ary	*first*
reg, rig	rule, straight, right	**reg**ent	*ruler* for another
salut	health	**salut**ary	*health*y
sanct	holy	**sanct**uary	*holy* place
sign	sign	**sign**al	*sign* giving warning
sol	alone	**sol**itary	*alone*
somn	sleep	in**somn**ia	*sleep*lessness
son	sound	re**son**ance	reinforcement of a *sound*
temp	time	**temp**orary	for the *time* being
tenu	thin	at**tenu**ate	*thin* out
term, termin	end, limit	**term**inal	*end* of a bus or train line
terr	earth	**terr**estrial	pertaining to *earth*
test	witness	**test**ify	bear *witness*
umbr	shade	**umbr**ella	screen to provide *shade*
urb	city	**urb**an	pertaining to *city*

Root	Meaning	Example	Explanation
vac	empty	**vac**uum	*empty* space
ver	true	**ver**acious	*truth*ful
verb	word	**verb**al	in *words*
via	way	**via**	by *way* of
voc, vok	call	con**vok**e	*call* together
vulg	common	**vulg**arity	*common*ness

Trial Test

Fill in the blank in each sentence with a Latin root from the preceding list. Use the word in italics as a clue. The number in parentheses tells the number of letters needed.

1. Patrick was filled with *new* ideas, but not all his in_____ations proved practical. (3)

2. The equi_____es are the two periods each year when days and *nights* are equally long. (3)

3. Cervantes was a con_____orary of Shakespeare, living at the same *time* though in a different country. (4)

4. Perry's feet are e_____ous, requiring shoes far beyond the *standard* sizes. (4)

5. The government de_____ated the cities, forcing the *people* to go out into the countryside and face death by starvation. (5)

6. The new _____ime *ruled* with heartless disregard of human rights. (3)

7. The _____a donna is the *first* lady of the opera. (4)

8. The driver's license was *call*ed back and re_____ed for a year. (3)

9. To dis_____age someone is to make him lower in rank, not *equal*. (3)

10. A grain sur_____ means we have *more* than we need for domestic consumption. (4)

11. *Foot*paths over bridges usually delight _____estrians, but many bridges provide only for motor traffic. (3)

12. Vera refused the chance to sing _____o, for she dreaded standing *alone* before a crowded auditorium. (3)

13. On a very clear night the stars seem in_____able, but the *number* of visible stars is tiny compared with the number of stars beyond the range of sight. (5)

14. _____ambulists may walk in their *sleep,* but they usually get back to bed safely. (4)

15. Some modern composers combine *sounds* in harsh and unusual ways, seeking creative dis_____ance rather than harmony. (3)

16. A(n) _____ist considers this the *best* of all possible worlds. (5)

17. A city in the Australian Outback is sub_____anean, below the surface of the *earth* with its scorching heat. (4)

18. During the eclipse of the moon, the moon passed first into the pen_____a, the area of partial *shadow* caused by the earth's position between the sun and moon. (4)

19. _____anity, supposedly a quality of sophisticated *city* dwellers, is no longer a local quality. (3)

20. The Webers _____ated the house, *empty*ing it of all their possessions. (3)

21. The star _____ated her contract with the studio, *end*ing all contacts with one stroke of the pen. (6)

22. Many *holy* places are _____ified by the unselfish deeds of men and women in the past. (5)

23. A mon_____ar is a telescope with a single *eye*piece. (4)

24. The officer _____ified the witness's account and found he had given a *true* report. (3)

25. There's too much _____iage in your composition. Cut out half those *words*. (4)

Review

Fill the blank in each sentence by supplying a Latin root from one of the three preceding lists. The word in italics is the clue to the needed root. The number in parentheses tells the number of letters needed.

1. The Buffalo team was _____ly coached by Marv Levy, who provided *suitable* leadership all the way to the Super Bowl. (3)

2. When a smaller organization af_____iates itself with a larger one, the result is almost a parent-*son* relationship. (3)

3. The card _____itated the pair on their marriage and wished *happiness* for many years to come. (5)

4. _____estic skills are especially helpful for the running of a *home*. (3)

5. Though times were *hard*, the citizens of London en_____ed the terrors of the London blitz. (3)

6. Because of her *beauty*, Scarlett O'Hara was the _____e of the ball. (4)

7. The _____ifacts of a lost civilization reveal the *crafts* and skills of those who lived before us. (3)

8. The filament of an in_____escent bulb *glows*. (4)

9. _____ality encourages following the right *customs* and behavior of a group. (3)

10. The con_____ation of a building suggests the arrangement of the *forms* and shapes that make up the structure. (4)

11. Even after the crew sighted land, the *ship* had to sail many _____ical miles before reaching the dock. (4)

12. An optical il_____ion is a trick of the eye, a *game* of perception. (3)

13. To con_____ an agreement is to make a *strong* commitment to carry it out. (4)

14. The _____um score was achieved by the candidate who had the *greatest* interest in words and vocabulary building. (5)

15. A(n) _____arism is an expression that is frowned upon as *common* and substandard. (4)

16. Before you can properly _____ate a motor vehicle, you must learn how to *work* the brakes. (4)

17. A person's _____ature is a distinctive *sign* to distinguish the writer from others. (4)

18. A(n) _____duct is a span carrying a *roadway* across a valley or a highway. (3)

19. Though named the _____ific, or "*peace*ful" ocean, this largest of all seas can be turbulent and remorseless. (3)

20. By derivation, a(n) _____ation was originally an expression of good will and good *health*. (5)

Which Word Parts Are Most Important?

Return for a moment to the 14 key words on page 75 at the beginning of this section. Which Latin prefixes and roots does Dr. Brown consider most important?

LATIN PREFIXES

ad, a	to	**a**spect
con, com	together	un**com**plicated
de	from	**de**tain
dis	apart from	in**dis**posed
ex	out of	non**ex**tended
in	not	**in**disposed
in	into	**in**sist
inter	between	**inter**mittent
non	not	**non**extended
ob, of	against, towards	**of**fer
pre	before	**pre**cept
pro	forward	re**pro**duction
sub, suf	under	over**suf**ficient*
re	back, again	**re**production
trans	across	mis**trans**cribe

Oversufficient is a good example of how words change through the years. "How," you may ask, "is it possible for a prefix meaning 'over' and a prefix meaning 'under' (**sub**) to appear in the same word?" *Sufficient* originally derived from **sub** and **fac.** How has it reached its present meaning? If you have *sufficient* funds, you have built a foundation *under* your position ("do under"). Thus *sufficient has come to mean "as much as is needed."* *Oversufficient* provides *more* than is necessary. The Anglo-Saxon prefix **over** has retained its common meaning, but the Latin prefix **sub** has lost its literal meaning and become part of a total concept. A word like *oversufficient* that uses elements from two different sources is sometimes called a *hybrid word*.

LATIN ROOTS

cept	take	pre**cept**
duct	lead	repro**duct**ion
fer	carry	of**fer**
fic	do, make	oversuf**fic**ient
mit	send	inter**mit**tent
plic	fold	uncom**plic**ated
pos	place, put	indis**pos**ed
scrib	write	mistran**scrib**e
sist	stand	in**sist**
spec	see	a**spec**t
tain	hold	de**tain**
tend	stretch	nonex**tend**ed

The remaining elements will be treated in the next two chapters, but for completeness they are included here also.

ANGLO-SAXON PREFIXES

mis	bad, badly	**mis**transcribe
over	above, too much	**over**sufficient
un	not	**un**complicated

GREEK PREFIXES

| epi | on, after | **epi**logue |
| mono | one | **mono**graph |

GREEK ROOTS

| graph | write | mono**graph** |
| log | word | epi**logue** |

Although some of the words have moved away from their original meanings, the core of meaning in each word is still apparent. *Aspect* obviously has something to do with *seeing*. *Detain* has something to do with *holding*. *Epilogue* has something to do with *words*. And so on through the remaining words. The elements of these words lead to thousands of others.

Problem

What makes the modern period in art _____ is that this time, in most categories, the older _____ has not been replaced by something equally substantial, accessible and satisfying.

   (A) exacting . . efficiency
   (B) ideal . . illusiveness
   (C) unique . . ignorance
   (D) unprecedented . . reality
   (E) worthless . . depravity

Strategy. This is a difficult question, but if you have been building power for the SAT, you have several ways to attack it.

1. Some students prefer to try out all the alternatives as a first step to see which "sound right" or "possible." This tactic sometimes allows you to reject one or more alternatives immediately. Usually you'll need to go on to the next step.

2. In sentence-completion activities always look for context clues. You know that smaller key words like *not, thus, like,* and *though* are always important, but there are longer key words, too. In this question the word "replaced" obviously carries a lot of weight. If the "older . . . has not been replaced by something satisfying,'' then you may assume that there is something unusual on the art scene this time.

3. Are there any words that suggest that this situation is unusual? *Exacting (A)*, *ideal (B)*, and *worthless (E)* don't seem to fit. *Unique (C)* is a possibility. What of *unprecedented (D)?*

4. Our familiarity with prefixes and roots comes in handy here. We recognize **un** (''not''), **pre** (''before''), and **ced** (''go''). If something is *unprecedented,* nothing like it has gone before. *Unprecedented* is clearly a possibility.

5. Check the second half of the *(C)* and *(D)* pairs. The word paired with *unique* is *ignorance*. *Ignorance* would not be *substantial* or *satisfying*. *Ignorance* is clearly incorrect, so we can discard *(C)* as an answer. The word paired with *unprecedented* is *reality*. This fits. The correct answer is *(D)*. This is how the completed sentence looks.

> What makes the modern period in art **unprecedented** is that this time, in most categories, the older **reality** has not been replaced by something equally substantial, accessible and satisfying.

This detailed analysis reviews some of the skills you have been acquiring. As you become more and more familiar with this type of question, however, you will speed up your work. You will find your own shortcuts and draw upon your own special strengths.

Review

A. Use context and etymology to figure out the answers. Write the letter for the word or word pair that best completes the meaning.

1. The fox's raid on the chicken coop was like a _____ _____ into an unprotected harbor.
   (A) lion's . . rush
   (B) sailor's . . navigation
   (C) pirate's . . foray
   (D) rower's . . sally
   (E) pilot's . . approach

   1 __

2. June's bursts of energy are _____; she is actually an expert in _____.
   (A) sporadic . . placidity
   (B) overpowering . . relaxation
   (C) unexpected . . karate
   (D) infrequent . . motivation
   (E) illuminating . . electronics

   2 __

3. That error is fortunately not _____; it can be corrected if we retrace our steps and follow correct procedures.
   (A) relevant   (D) advertised
   (B) irremediable   (E) com-
   (C) hopeful   promising

   3 __

4. The departing guest thanked her host _____; still the cautious host _____ avoided extending a second invitation.
   (A) reservedly . . somehow
   (B) reflectively . . angrily
   (C) engagingly . . unconsciously
   (D) tactlessly . . righteously
   (E) effusively . . pointedly

   4 __

5. Although Timothy much preferred to _____ during the summer months, his father insisted _____ that Timothy get a job.
   (A) work . . tentatively
   (B) vegetate . . vehemently
   (C) travel . . vaguely
   (D) compete . . unintentionally
   (E) read . . carelessly

   5 ___

6. The purpose of the roller coaster is to provide _____ thrills, to stimulate a sense of extreme _____, yet frighten people safely.
   (A) vicarious . . vertigo
   (B) inhuman . . illness
   (C) casual . . indifference
   (D) humdrum . . enthusiasm
   (E) unimaginative . . terror

   6 ___

7. Seeking to magnify their own glories at the expense of earlier rulers, later pharaohs _____ from tombs and monuments the names of their illustrious _____.
   (A) humiliated . . contemporaries
   (B) deciphered . . progeny
   (C) obliterated . . predecessors
   (D) plagiarized . . scribes
   (E) reconnoitered . . generals

   7 ___

8. According to many therapists, the true function of a(n) _____ is to _____ energies and revive the spirit.
   (A) chore . . humble
   (B) anecdote . . dramatize
   (C) avocation . . regenerate
   (D) diatribe . . shrivel
   (E) confrontation . . dissipate

   8 ___

9. Despite his reputation for hard-heartedness, the sergeant showed _____ to the injured recruit, binding his injury and speaking encouraging words to the young soldier.
   (A) merit   (D) indignation
   (B) compassion   (E) firmness
   (C) casualness

   9 ___

10. Some economists feel that a(n) _____ distribution of all wealth would find great _____ in actual holdings less than a year later.
    (A) average . . equalization
    (B) scheduled . . disappointment
    (C) circumspect . . felicity
    (D) equitable . . discrepancies
    (E) unanticipated . . diminution

    10 ___

B. Build your own vocabulary. Put together words of your own by taking prefixes from column A and combining them with roots from the two B columns.

A (PREFIXES)	B (ROOTS)	
a, ab	act	pel
ad, ac, af, ag, al, am, at	cede	pone
ante	claim	port
com, cof, col, com, con	credit	pose
contra	cur	prehend
de	date	rupt
dis, di	dict	scribe
ex, e	duct	sect
extra	fect	sense
in	fer	solve

A (PREFIXES)	B (ROOTS)	
inter	flux	spect
non	form	strict
ob, o, oc	gress	sult
per	ject	tain
post	junct	tract
pre	late	vene
pro	mand	verge
sub, suc, suf, sup, sus	merge	vert
super	mit	vise
trans	mute	volve

_____   _____   _____

_____   _____   _____

_____   _____   _____

_____   _____   _____

_____   _____   _____

SUMMARY

Etymology Clue 3: Latin Roots——Nouns and Adjectives

1. English contains more words from Latin than from any other language.
2. Words are often built block by block. If you know what each block (word part) originally meant, you can probably figure out today's meaning—the one used in SAT questions.
3. The best strategy is to know the root and prefix. The second best strategy is to think of other words having the same elements.

Etymology Clue 4: Greek Prefixes and Roots

Though words derived from Greek prefixes and roots often look difficult, their meanings are sometimes easier to guess than words from other sources. First, the commonly used Greek roots are fewer in number than those from Latin. Secondly, the building blocks are often easier to see. A word like Dr. Brown's *monograph* (page 75), for example, is delightfully simple, once you know the elements **mono** and **graph.** Both elements have so many word-cousins, from *monotone* to *monotheism,* from *telegraph* to *biography.* The prefix **mono** clearly means "one" in those *mono* words. The root **graph** clearly means "write" in those *graph* words. A monograph is an article written about one special subject.

Words from Greek and Latin differ from each other in another way, too. Words from Latin usually have *one* root and one or more prefixes, but Greek often combines *two* roots. *Biography,* for example, combines two roots: **bio** and **graph.** We'll have more to say about this kind of combination later.

Before you begin studying lists of Greek prefixes and roots, try an experiment. You probably know more about word origins than you think you do. Take the following test and prove to yourself that you can often derive the meanings of prefixes and roots on your own.

Trial Test

In each of the following ten groups, one root is common to all four words. You already know at least three of the four words in every group. Think of the meanings of the words you know, and try to determine the meaning of the root. You will find the answer among the words following the root. Write the letter for the meaning of the word.

---

telegraph, autograph, biography, graphic
GRAPH:
  (A) distance   (C) friendship
  (B) writing   (D) pictures

$$\underline{\quad B \quad}$$

Since the words all have to do with writing, the correct answer is (B). The meaning of the root **graph** is *writing.*

---

1. phonograph, telephone, radiophone, euphony
PHON:
  (A) light   (C) sound
  (B) heat   (D) water

1 ___

2. automatic, autograph, automobile, autocrat
AUTO:
  (A) ruler   (C) only
  (B) self   (D) written

2 ___

3. monotone, monopoly, monarchy, monogram
MONO:
  (A) busy   (C) two
  (B) loud   (D) one

3 ___

4. democrat, aristocrat, autocrat, bureaucrat
CRAT:
  (A) person   (C) wealth
  (B) rule   (D) nature

4 ___

5. synonym, antonym, homonym, patronymic
ONYM:
  (A) name   (C) father
  (B) opposite   (D) same

5 ___

6. bicycle, cyclone, cycle, encyclopedia
CYCL:
  (A) storm   (C) play
  (B) circle   (D) two

6 ___

7. centimeter, meter, metric, perimeter
   METER:
   (A) coin   (C) 100
   (B) instrument   (D) measure

   7 ___

8. biology, biography, autobiography, amphibian
   BIO:
   (A) book   (C) science
   (B) life   (D) water

   8 ___

9. antislavery, antitoxin, antidote, antipathy
   ANTI:
   (A) related   (C) against
   (B) before   (D) afterward

   9 ___

10. microscope, microphotograph, microbe, microcosm
    MICRO:
    (A) small   (C) germ
    (B) picture   (D) telescope

    10 ___

Greek Prefixes

Prefix	Meaning	Example	Explanation
a, an	no, not	atypical	*not* typical
		anarchy	condition of *no* government
amphi	around, both	amphibian	on *both* land and sea
ana	up, again, back	analysis	examination of details (a loosening *up*)
anti	against	antiseptic	*against* infection
apo	away from, off	apostle	messenger sent *from* one place to another
auto	self	automatic	running by *itself*
cata	down	cataclysm	a washing *down*, a flood
dys	bad, badly	dyspepsia	*bad* digestion
dia	across, through	diameter	a measure *across* a circle
ec, ex	out of	exodus	a going *out*
en	in, into	engender	bring *into* being, cause
endo	inside	endomorph	a crystal *inside* another
epi	upon, after	epitaph	inscription placed *upon* a tomb
eu	well, good, pleasant	eulogy	a speaking *well*, praise
hyper	above, beyond	hyperbole	speech *beyond* truth, exaggeration
hypo	under, below	hypothermia	body heat *below* normal
iso	equal	isotherm	line to show *equal* heat
mega, megal	great	megalomania	personality disorder of assumed *great*ness
meta	after, beyond, over	metamorphosis	change*over* into another form
micro	small	micrometer	tool for making *small* measurements
mis	hatred of	misanthropic	*hating* mankind
neo	new	neologism	*new* word
pan, panto	all	panchromatic	sensitive to light of *all* colors
para	beside	paraphrase	a speaking *beside*, a rewording
peri	around	perimeter	measure *around*
poly	many	polysyllabic	having *many* syllables
pro	before	prophet	one who predicts the future (speaks *before*hand)

Prefix	Meaning	Example	Explanation
pseudo	false	**pseudo**science	*false* science
sym, syn	together	**sym**phony	a sounding *together*
		synagogue	a place for bringing people *together*

We have already called your attention to the fact that words sometimes travel far from their origins. Words introduced into the language long ago often have figurative meanings, but usually the basic meaning is still there. Ordinarily the more recently a word has come into the language, the closer the word is to its basic elements. The recent word *astrophysics,* for example, deals with the nature (**physi**) of the stars (**astro**).

Even though they seem simple, Greek prefixes are a little more difficult than Greek roots, because the prefixes have more meanings than the roots. A prefix like **meta,** for example, has many meanings ("along with," "after," "between," "among," "beyond," "over").

The word *metaphysics* has an interesting history. *Physics,* with its root **physi,** means "nature," "natural." When Aristotle was gathering his thoughts about nature and life, he came to those dealing with things *beyond* science, things that cannot be explained by experiment. He called these ideas *metaphysics* because they came *after* or beyond the *physics.*

Trial Test

Fill the blank in each sentence by writing a Greek prefix from the preceding list. The word in italics is a clue to the needed prefix. The number in parentheses tells the number of letters needed.

> When two organisms live *together* with mutual benefit, this unique arrangement is called _____biosis. (3) The italicized word *together* tells you the prefix **sym** should be inserted.

1. Although at times Pierce pretended to be a *hater* of women, he was not really a(n) _____ogynist. (3)

2. By definition, the two legs of a(n) _____sceles triangle are *equal.* (3)

3. Bert used a(n) _____phone and *great*ly increased the range of his voice. (4)

4. A(n) _____lyst may speed up or slow *down* the rate of a chemical reaction. (4)

5. A(n) _____cracy is a government in which one person, by him*self,* holds absolute power. (4)

6. The critics of astrology call it a(n) _____science, *false*ly assuming the mantle of a true science. (6)

7. Bennett was a true _____glot, writing and speaking *many* languages fluently. (4)

8. The _____eroid barometer, unlike the mercury barometer, uses *no* liquid. (2)

9. A(n) _____biotic works *against* the growth of harmful bacteria. (4)

10. _____trophy is the growth of an organ far *beyond* its normal size. (5)

11. Most colleges and universities now use many _____professionals to work *beside* fully licensed teachers and help with many education projects. (4)

12. A(n) _____scope enables a viewer to look *around* a corner. (4)

13. Despite its *small* size, _____film can store pages of material in a single frame. (5)

14. The _____phytes, all *new* members of the church, came to the altar in a group. (3)

15. Old-time medicine men used to offer their concoctions as _____aceas, guaranteed to cure *all* ailments from headache to pneumonia. (3)

16. In _____grams words are mixed *up* and then put *back* into different forms. (3)

17. In the Greek _____theater the seats curled *around* the stage. (5)

18. Pruitt _____chronized his watch with Helen's, making sure his time agreed *with* hers. (3)

19. _____thermia is a dangerous condition in which the body temperature falls far *below* normal. (4)

20. It is human nature to use _____phemisms, expressions that make unpleasant subjects sound neutral or *pleasant*. (2)

Problem

John Dickson Carr chose the _____ *Carter Dickson* at the publisher's request, so that there'd not be too many mystery novels with the same author's name.

(A) symbiosis   (D) pseudonym
(B) paradigm   (E) fabrication
(C) counterfeit

Strategy. *Pseudo,* "false," combines with *nym,* "name," to suggest a "false name," in this sentence a pen name. *Counterfeit* and *fabrication* have negative connotations and may be rejected. *Symbiosis* and *paradigm* are unrelated and unsuitable.

Greek Number Prefixes

Prefix	Meaning	Example	Explanation
hemi	half	**hemi**sphere	*half* a sphere
mono	one	**mono**tone	*one* tone
proto	first	**proto**type	*first* kind
di	two	**di**lemma	*two* choices (both bad!)
tri	three	**tri**cycle	*three*-wheeler
tetra	four	**tetra**meter	having *four* poetic feet
penta	five	**penta**gon	*five*-sided figure
hexa	six	**hexa**gonal	having *six* sides
hepta	seven	**hepta**meter	having *seven* poetic feet
octa	eight	**octa**ve	*eighth* tone above a given tone
deca	ten	**deca**logue	the *Ten* Commandments
hect	hundred	**hect**ograph	machine for making a *hundred* (*many*) copies
kilo	thousand	**kilo**gram	a *thousand* grams

Greek number prefixes occur in a great many English words. The field of mathematics, for example, relies heavily upon Greek prefixes (as in *trigonometry* or *pentagon*), but these little elements appear in other English words, as well, such as *protozoan* and *monologue*. If you know the number prefix, you can usually figure out the right SAT answer.

Note how efficiently English borrows from both Latin and Greek. The Latin prefix for *thousand,* **mille,** appears in *millimeter* (a *thousandth* of a meter). The Greek prefix for *thousand,* **kilo,** appears in *kilometer* (a *thousand* meters). Neither prefix is wasted. Scientists keep drawing upon Greek for new words to express new ideas. A **milli**second, for example, is a *thousandth* of a second. But suppose you want a word to express a billionth of a second? The Greek word for dwarf is **nano.** A billionth of a second is a **nano**second ("a very small second"!).

Trial Test

Fill the blank in each sentence with a Greek number prefix from the list. The word in italics is a clue to the needed prefix. The number in parentheses tells the number of letters needed.

> A small child needs the *three* wheels on a **tri**cycle to provide balance. (3) The italicized word *three* tells you that *tri* is the correct Greek number prefix.

1. A(n) _____meter, which is *1000* meters, is approximately five-eighths of a mile. (4)

2. In the _____thlon each contestant takes part in *five* events. (5)

3. Jim spoke in _____syllables, allowing himself only *one* syllable at a time. (4)

4. _____gonometry, literally the measure of *three* angles, deals with the relationships of triangles. (3)

5. A(n) _____hedron is a solid figure with *four* triangular faces. (5)

6. _____zoans, one-celled animals, may resemble the *first* form of life on earth. (5)

7. In linguistics, a(n) _____phthong, combines *two* vowel sounds into one continuous sound. (2)

8. To win the _____thlon, a contestant need not win all *ten* events; he must, however, have the highest average over all. (4)

9. The great epics of Greece and Rome were written in dactylic _____meter, with *six* beats to every line. (4)

10. The unusual old building has a(n) _____gonal shape, with *eight* equal sides. (4)

Problem

Hester foolishly put a red filter over the lens and found that all her slides were _____, though she had used a good color film.

(A) endomorphic
(B) monochromatic
(C) prototypical
(D) hyperbolic
(E) foreshortened

Strategy. A red filter with color film will result in all-red slides, slides of *one color*. The Greek root *mono*, "one," assures us that *monochromatic* (B) means "of *one* color." The other alternatives may distract if you don't know the root *mono*.

> (B) Hester foolishly put a red filter over the lens and found that all her slides were monochromatic, though she had used a good color film.

Review

Fill the blank in each sentence with a Greek prefix from the two preceding lists. The word in italics is a clue to the needed prefix. The number in parentheses tells the number of letters needed.

1. Pain on *half* the head or body carries the medical name of _____algia. (4). The root *alg* (pain) appears in *neuralgia, nostalgia, analgesic,* and similar words.

2. A(n) _____ergetic person puts much exertion *into* work or play. (2)

3. A slanting straight line *across* a square is called a(n) _____gonal. (3)

4. _____crine glands are nestled *inside* the body and produce secretions carried in the bloodstream. (4)

5. In _____phor, meaning is conveyed indirectly, *beyond* the literal meaning. (4)

6. In 1880, the _____ograph was invented to provide copies, a *hundred* or even more. (4)

7. Utopia is an imaginary place where life is perfect; the word "_____topia" was invented in 1950 to suggest a place where the opposite is true, where good has been replaced by *bad*. (3)

8. A(n) _____gram is prepared *before* a play or concert. (3)

9. Because the Roman emperor Julian fell *away* from the Christian religion, he is known in history as "Julian the _____state." (3)

10. The _____logue of a book or play appears *after* the main presentation. (3)

Greek Roots—1

Now we come to one of the most helpful word groups in the study of etymology—Greek roots. Many of these are different from Latin roots because they may appear anywhere in a word—at the beginning, middle, or end. **Lith,** meaning "stone," may appear at the beginning in *lithography* and at the end in *monolith*. In some ways, Greek roots are more fun to combine because they combine so freely and in so many ways. **Meter,** meaning "measure," appears first in *metronome* and last in *diameter*. It also appears in the middle in *symmetrical*.

All the Greek roots are important and worth studying, but if you wish to concentrate upon some basic ones, study the starred (*) items first. These will be especially helpful as you prepare for the SAT. These Greek roots are also divided into two lists for your convenience.

Root	Meaning	Example	Explanation
alg	pain	neur**alg**ia	nerve *pain*
anthrop, andro	man	**anthrop**ology	study of *man*kind
		android	robot like a *man*
arch	chief, rule	**arch**bishop	*chief* bishop
		mon**arch**y	*rule* of one person
bar	weight, pressure	**bar**ometer	measure of *pressure*
bibli	book	**bibli**ophile	one who loves *books*
chiro	hand	**chiro**podist	*hand* and foot specialist
chrom	color	**chrom**atic	highly *color*ed
*chron	time	ana**chron**istic	out of proper *time*
cosm	universe	micro**cosm**	*universe* in little
crat, crac	rule	demo**crac**y	*rule* by the people
crypt	hidden	**crypt**ic	having *hidden* meaning
*cycl	circle	**cycl**one	storm that whirls in a *circle*
*dem	people	**dem**agogue	a rabble-rousing leader of *people*
derm	skin	hypo**derm**ic	beneath the *skin*
dos, dot	give	anti**dot**e	something *given* to counteract a poison
dyn, dynam	energy, power	**dynam**ite	*power*ful explosive
erg, urg	work	metall**urg**y	metal *work*ing
gam	marriage	poly**gam**y	many *marriages*
*ge, geo	earth	**geo**physics	dealing with the physics of the *earth*
gen	birth, cause, kind, race, origin	homo**gen**ize	make uniform, of the same *kind*
*gram, graph	writing	autobio**graph**y	*writing* about one's own life
		mono**graph**	*writing* about a particular subject
heli	sun	**heli**otrope	flower that turns toward the *sun*
hem	blood	**hem**orrhage	unchecked flow of *blood*
*hetero	different, other	**hetero**geneous	of a *different* kind
*homo	same	**homo**geneous	of the *same* kind
hydr	water	de**hydr**ation	loss of *water*
iatr	healing	psych**iatr**ist	one who *heals* the mind
lith	stone	mono**lith**	single large block of *stone*
*log	word, study	geo**log**y	study of the *earth*

Trial Test

Fill the blank in each sentence with a Greek root from the preceding list.
The word in italics is a clue to the needed root. The number in parentheses
tells the number of letters needed.

ENGLISH FOR THE COLLEGE BOARDS

A bi**gam**ist has two *marriages* in force at the same time. (3) The italicized word *marriage*, tells you the Greek root **gam** should be used. One who has two marriages in force at the same time is a *bigamist*.

1. _____olysis is a chemical reaction in which a compound reacts with the ions of *water*. (4)

2. Copernicus upset the _____centric theory of the earth, pointing out that the *earth* is not the center of the universe. (3)

3. _____atitis is an inflammation of the *skin*. (4)

4. Ronny has _____ophobia; he has a morbid fear of *work!* (3)

5. An olig_____y is the *rule* of a few people. (4)

6. On a weather map iso_____s are lines of equal *pressure*. (3)

7. Eva is a(n) _____o of *energy*. (5)

8. The presence of _____um on the *sun* was first discovered during a solar eclipse in 1868, and the name reflects its origin. (4)

9. A(n) _____orama is a series of connected pictures in a *circular* room, often showing a landscape. (4)

10. Have you listed in your _____ography all *books* referred to? (5)

11. A basic treatment in _____practic is manipulation of the spine by the trained *hands* of the doctor. (5)

12. The *pain* of being separated from his friends and family gave the college student an acute case of nost_____ia. (3)

13. _____oid apes are so called because of their *man*like appearance and mannerisms. (7)

14. Ted usually adopts _____dox positions, *different* from those of his peers. (6)

15. At first _____ography used flat *stones* to reproduce a design on paper; later metal plates were introduced. (4)

16. People send *written* messages over distances via the tele_____. (5)

17. A(n) _____nym has the *same* pronunciation as another word but different meaning. (4)

18. _____atic aberration in a lens causes a margin of *colors* to appear around the edges of the image. (5)

19. An epi_____ic is a disease afflicting vast numbers of *people*. (3)

20. Ger_____ics deals with the *healing* of old people's ailments. (4)

21. A(n) _____ic ailment keeps coming back *time* and time again. (5)

22. A pluto_____ seeks the power to *rule* because of his wealth. (4)

23. In a(n) _____ogram the meaning is *hidden,* concealed in code or cipher. (5)

24. A bi_____ist has two *marriages* still in force at the same time. (3)

25. _____oglobin is the red coloring in the *blood*. (3)

Problem

_____ are spelled the same, but have different meanings and pronunciations.

(A) Antonyms   (D) Heteronyms
(B) Synonyms   (E) Aphorisms
(C) Epigrams

Strategy. You probably already know *antonyms* and *synonyms* but must look elsewhere for the answer. The word *different* provides the clue that the answer must emphasize difference. The Greek root *hetero*, "different," points to the answer *heteronym*.

Greek Roots—2

As before, study the starred (*) items first.

Root	Meaning	Example	Explanation
*meter, metr	measure	baro**meter**	*measure* of air pressure
morph	form, shape	a**morph**ous	*form*less
neur	nerve	**neur**itis	inflammation of *nerves*
nom, nomy	law, order, custom	astro**nom**er	one who studies the *order* of the stars
onym, onoma	name	an**onym**ous	*name*less
ortho	straight	**ortho**dontia	teeth *straight*ening
path	suffering, feeling	a**path**y	lack of *feeling*
phan, phen	show, appear	**phen**omenon	something *apparent* to the senses
*phil	love	**phil**anthropist	*lover* of mankind
phor, pher	carry, bear	sema**phor**	apparatus for signaling, for *bear*ing messages
*phos, phot	light	**phot**ography	producing images by use of *light*
pod	foot	**pod**iatrist	*foot* doctor
poli	city	metro**poli**s	main *city*
psych	mind	**psych**ology	study of the *mind*
pyr	fire	**pyr**otechnics	*fire*works
scop	see	tele**scop**e	device for *see*ing at a distance
soph	wise	**soph**isticated	worldly-*wise*
tax, tac	arrangement	**tac**tics	*arrang*ing forces in battle
techn	art, skill	**techn**ique	method of using *skills*
*tele	from afar	**tele**metry	measuring *from afar*
the, theo	god	**the**ist	believer in *God*
therm	heat	**therm**ostat	device for regulating *heat*
thes, thet	place, put	anti**thes**is	a *plac*ing against, contrast of thought
tom	cut	a**tom**	substance that cannot be *cut* or split (now proved wrong)
top	place	**top**ography	description of a *place*
trop	turn	**trop**ism	tendency to *turn* in response to a stimulus
typ	model, impression	**typ**ical	like a *model*
zo	animal	**zo**ology	study of *animals*

More about Greek Roots

A root like **therm** is easy to find in English words. It always means "heat." Some roots, however, travel a little farther afield. Like Latin roots, they sometimes have figurative meanings. The extremely useful root **graph,** for example, appears in a great many words. You notice the meaning of *writing* instantly in a word like *graphology,* the study of handwriting. But notice the figurative meanings in *phonograph* and *photograph. Photography,* by derivation, is "light written down." *Phonograph* is "sound written down." Here the concept of *writing* is much broader than usual. There's a poetic image in "written sound."

Fortunately, the words with figurative meanings have been in the language a long time. You certainly know *phonograph* and *photograph* anyway. But if you meet a new word like *thermograph,* you can reasonably guess it's a device for recording heat, or temperature. Even though the meanings are sometimes figurative, the core of meaning is usually clear.

Trial Test

Fill the blank in each sentence with a root from the preceding list of Greek roots. The word in italics is a clue to the needed root. The number in parentheses tells the number of letters needed.

1. In a syn_____is is ideas are *put* together to form a whole. (4)

2. Maurya is a pan_____ist and believes that *God* is manifest in everything, everywhere. (3)

3. The _____diac was so named because it was considered the zone of the *animals:* the ram, the lion, the bull, and others. (2)

4. In a tonsillec_____y the surgeon removes the tonsils by deft *cut*ting. (3)

5. The _____on is the structural and functional unit of the *nervous* system. (4)

6. Meta_____ic rock has been changed in *form* by heat, pressure, or chemical action. (5)

7. An acr_____ is a *name* formed by using the first letters of a series of words; for example, NATO for *N*orth *A*tlantic *T*reaty *O*rganization. (4)

8. _____pedics is a branch of surgery whose goal is the *straight*ening of deformed parts of the body, especially in children. (5)

9. According to legend, Dido prepared a(n) _____e for herself, planning to cast herself upon the *fire* as the ships of Aeneas disappeared in the distance. (3)

10. _____ology is a *love* of learning. (4)

11. _____istry is a misleading but clever argument that gives the impression of being *wise.* (4)

12. A kaleido_____e is a specially designed tube for *see*ing beautiful forms and shapes. (4)

13. _____onomy is the science of the *arrangement* of animals and plants in orders, families, genera, and other groupings. (3)

14. A gastro_____ is a mollusk that has one large *foot* associated with its stomach. (3)

15. _____pathy, communication at a *distance* without using the normal sensory channels, is an attractive, if unproven, possibility. (4)

16. That plant is photo_____ic, *turn*ing to any light source for energy. (4)

17. The arche_____e is the original *model* from which all others of the same kind are made. (3)

18. Through the dia_____ous curtain on the stage, two shadowy figures suddenly *appeared*. (4)

19. Em_____y is the ability to share another's *feelings* by putting oneself in the other's place. (4)

20. An am_____ *measures* the strength of an electric current in amperes. (5)

Review

Fill the blank in each sentence with a Greek prefix or root. The word in italics is a clue to the needed prefix or root. The number in parentheses tells the number of letters needed.

1. Study of the nature, origin, and structure of the *universe* is known

   as _____ology. (4)

2. The _____esis of an idea suggests the *origin,* or *birth,* of the concept. (3)

3. Paleonto_____y is the *study* of fossils and the life forms of previous ages. (3)

4. By derivation, an anec_____e was originally not *given* out, not published. It has lost that specialized meaning. (3)

5. By derivation, eco_____ics is the *ordering* and organization of a household. (3)

6. _____iatry is the science that attempts to treat disorders of the *mind.* (5)

7. _____ology is a scientific application of *arts* and *skills* to achieve practical purposes. (5)

8. On the weather map, lines of equal *heat* are called iso_____s. (5)

9. _____ology is the study of a particular *place* or region. (3)

10. Since *city*-states were equivalent to nations in ancient Greece, the art or science of government was called "_____tics." (4)

11. In many seas, _____phorescence, caused by swarms of small organisms, produces flashes of silvery *light* in the water. (4)

12. By derivation, eco_____y means *study* of the home—an appropriate word, for all the earth is our home. (3)

13. Thermo_____ics deals with the *power* of heat. (5)

14. The _____ic of Cancer is the imaginary line on the earth's surface where the sun seems to *turn* southward at the solstice. (4)

15. A mono_____atic painting consists of one *color* or hue. (5)

16. Students who read very *badly* may be suffering from _____lexia. (3)

17. Maureen loved to _____gnosticate events, suggesting their outline *before* they happened. (3)

18. A(n) _____phyte lives *upon* another plant but does not deprive the host plant of food. (3)

19. Sharon is a(n) _____lectic designer, picking *out* what she likes from many different periods and still making a harmonious total design. (2)

20. At _____gee the moon is farthest *away* from the earth. (3)

Greek prefixes and roots play a role in the following sentence-completion item.

Problem

The latest edition of the dictionary defines several thousand _____ and refines the definitions of some older words.

(A) synonyms   (D) homophones
(B) antonyms   (E) polymorphs
(C) neologisms

Strategy. The second half of the sentence contrasts *older* with something else, probably *newer*. If we insert new words into the slot, we make sense, but *new words* is not provided. A substitute is. A knowledge of the Greek prefix *neo*, "new," and the Greek root *log*, "word," provides a readymade answer. A *neologism* is a "new word."

(C) The latest edition of the dictionary defines several thousand neologisms and refines the definitions of some older words.

Review

Build your own vocabulary. Put together words of your own by taking elements from column A and combining them with elements from column B. You may use any element more than once.

A	B	
auto	algia	_____
chiro	cracy	
cosmo	graph(y)	_____
demo	logy	
geo	meter	_____
micro	nomic	
neur	phone	_____
photo	podist	
tele	politan	_____
theo	scope	
		_____
		_____

SUMMARY

Etymology Clue 4: Greek Prefixes and Roots

1. The Greek language is an important source of English words.
2. When scientists create new words for new concept and substances, they borrow freely from Greek. You are not likely to meet some of these technical creations, like *microencapsulate* and *neuroendocrinology,* but you will meet a great many others like *psychedelic* and *Xerox.*
3. Though words change in use, even words with figurative meanings can be guessed at by figuring out their basic elements. *Hydraulic* is derived from **hydr,** the root for *water.* The word has been expanded to mean other liquids: *hydraulic* brakes use *oil.* But if you know **hydr,** you can guess at the meaning of related words like *hydraulic* and *hydrometer.*
4. Some coinages, like *polyunsaturates* and *megavitamins,* borrow from both Latin and Greek.

Etymology Clue 5: Anglo-Saxon Prefixes and Roots

You will feel at home with this section. You use Anglo-Saxon prefixes and roots in everyday English words you already know. As we have already seen, William the Conqueror overran England in 1066. He brought his own French language with him, but French did not replace the native English, or Anglo-Saxon. Instead of fighting English, it joined with it.

The French nobility lorded it over the Anglo-Saxon peasantry. Some words from French show this master-servant relationship: *dame, peer, prince, treasurer, minister, mayor, baron,* and *noble.* The French upper classes enjoyed the fruits of Anglo-Saxon labor. The Anglo-Saxon *calf* was *veal (veau)* to the French nobility. And so we have both words, one for the living animal and one for the meat of the animal. *Bull* and *beef, sheep* and *mutton, pig* and *pork* all show this relationship.

French enriched the language with new words from the law: *plaintiff, jury, attorney, indictment, felon, bail, decree,* and *prison.* French provided religious words like *sermon, sacrament, prayer, parson, friar,* and *chaplain.* French provided words for clothing: *apparel, gown, embroidery, cape, cloak, frock.* French provided words for medicine: *surgeon, remedy, ointment, jaundice, pulse.* These are topics and words that often come up in SAT questions, especially the sentence-completion type.

We use some of these French words every day. Others, like *hauberk, barbican,* and *portcullis,* are fairly specialized and rarely used. This borrowing from French is, of course, also a borrowing from Latin secondhand. The double borrowing has enriched our language with doublets (page 141).

Anglo-Saxon Is Alive and Well

Despite the power of the new French language, Anglo-Saxon stubbornly held its own. A word count of conversation today would show that we use Anglo-Saxon words most of the time. Here's a typical brief dialogue of greeting:

> "How are you, John? I haven't seen you in months. How's everything?"
>
> "Great! Did you hear the news? Joan and I are getting married next week. We're planning to live here, in the city."

This is the language of our everyday life. The Anglo-Saxon words have never given up. In this dialogue there are a few words of French origin: *news, married,* and *city.* All the rest are Anglo-Saxon.

Occasionally, as time went on, a French word replaced the Anglo-Saxon. The briefer *news,* for example, has replaced the lengthier Anglo-Saxon *tidings.* When both words have survived and are frequently used, they usually take on somewhat different meanings. *Marriage* (from French) usually refers to the *state* of being married. *Wedding* (from Anglo-Saxon) usually refers to the *ceremony.* In general, however, the nuts-and-bolts words of English—the pronouns, the being verbs, the basic words for things around us—are Anglo-Saxon.

The first words we learn as children are mostly Anglo-Saxon words; for example, *mother, father, sister, dog, cat, love, like, good, see, home, house,* etc. Consequently, because they are associated with things we knew as children, they tend to arouse emotional responses in us.

At the end of Charles Dickens' *A Tale of Two Cities,* Sidney Carton muses on his way to the guillotine. His last thoughts are dramatic and famous:

> "It is a far, far better thing I do, than I have ever done; it is a far, far better rest I go to than I have ever known."

Under the stress of great emotion—of happiness, grief, or anger—we tend to use Anglo-Saxon words which remain the backbone of English.

Scandinavian Words

Before the Normans took over, Viking raiders invaded again and again. They brought many Scandinavian words into the mainstream of English; for example, *sky, skin, skill,* and *whisk.* The *sk* sound is typically Scandinavian and so we have both *shirt* (Anglo-Saxon) and *skirt* (Scandinavian).

Trial Test

In the following sentences the boldfaced words are all of Scandinavian origin. In each sentence write the letter for the word that is closest in meaning to the boldfaced word.

1. Suddenly there was a **rift** in the clouds.
   (A) crack
   (B) trap
   (C) storm
   (D) bright spot
   (E) drift

   1 ___

2. He found the **snare** where he'd left it.
   (A) tuba
   (B) trap
   (C) rope
   (D) knife
   (E) bite of food

   2 ___

3. Imitation **down** is made from milkweed.
   (A) seed
   (B) feathers
   (C) mats
   (D) flour
   (E) milky beverage

   3 ___

4. He was large in **girth.**
   (A) stature
   (B) heart
   (C) circumference
   (D) size of hand
   (E) head

   4 ___

5. The Spartans were **rugged** people.
   (A) sea-going
   (B) sickly
   (C) curious
   (D) hardy
   (E) unusual

   5 ___

6. The ruthless dictator's followers were recruited from the **dregs** of society.
   (A) worthless section
   (B) wealthiest people
   (C) pillars
   (D) businessmen
   (E) farmers

   6 ___

7. The day was **muggy.**
   (A) hot and dry
   (B) cold and dry
   (C) cold and moist
   (D) warm and moist
   (E) warm and dry

   7 ___

8. Hasn't he an unusual **gait?**
   (A) way of walking
   (B) door
   (C) manner of speaking
   (D) half-door
   (E) reading ability

   8 ___

9. Ichabod despised the **swains** who sought the hand of Katrina Van Tassel.
   (A) old men
   (B) young suitors
   (C) wealthy land-owners
   (D) members of the nobility
   (E) rivals

   9 ___

10. They **ransacked** the house.
    (A) burnt
    (B) sold
    (C) plundered
    (D) bought at a sale
    (E) painted

    10 ___

The Scandinavian words were thoroughly absorbed into English at the time of the Norman Conquest. For our purposes no further distinctions need be made between Scandinavian and Anglo-Saxon.

Anglo-Saxon Prefixes

Prefix	Meaning	Example	Explanation
be	completely	**be**draggled	*completely* soiled
by	near	**by**stander	one who stands *near*
for	not	**for**bid	*not* allow
fore	before, front	**fore**going	going *before*
mis	bad, badly, wrong, wrongly	**mis**take	take *wrongly*
in	in	**in**come	money that comes *in*
off	off, from	**off**set	set *off*
out	beyond	**out**law	*beyond* the law
on	on	**on**looker	one who looks *on*
over	too much, over	**over**pay	pay *too much*
		oversee	watch *over*
un	not	**un**happy	*not* happy
under	below, against	**under**pay	pay *below* reasonable amount
up	up	**up**heaval	a heaving *up*
with	against	**with**stand	stand *against*

Some words from Anglo-Saxon, like words from other sources, have acquired figurative meanings in use. *Understand,* for example, by derivation means "stand under." Now it means "get the meaning of." We can only guess how the current meaning came into being. Fortunately, the word has been used in the current sense for so long a time, it is an easy word. Ordinarily, the more figurative the meaning, the longer the word has been in the language and the more likely you are to know and use it.

Some Anglo-Saxon words almost exactly translate words of French or Latin derivation. *Dejected,* for example, is exactly parallel to the Anglo-Saxon *downcast.* Both *dejected* and *downcast* have evolved figurative meanings. *Downcast* does not require physical action; we don't throw or cast anything down. The word, like *dejected,* has become purely figurative.

Anglo-Saxon roots and prefixes rarely cause difficulty, but occasionally knowledge of a prefix can help, as in this sentence-completion item.

Problem

With all the charts and graphs provided, it is difficult to _____ the aims and goals of the new legislation.

(A) comprehend
(B) misconceive
(C) negotiate
(D) espouse
(E) paraphrase

Strategy. Sometimes a seemingly simple challenge is deceptive. In one context or another, each of the preceding alternatives would be acceptable. Again, you must ask, "Which is the *best* alternative in the limited context provided?" *Charts* and *graphs* are provided for clarification. Thus, the word *difficult* suggests an opposing idea. That idea is contained in *misconceive* (B), "fail to understand." The Anglo-Saxon prefix *mis,* "wrongly," reverses the meaning of *conceive,* as it does in the more familiar word *misunderstand.*

(B) With all the charts and graphs provided it is difficult to misconceive the aims and goals of the new legislation.

Trial Test

Fill the blank in each sentence by writing an Anglo-Saxon prefix from the previous list. The word in italics is a clue to the needed prefix. The number in parentheses tells the number of letters.

The director's choice was *wrong*. Denny is **mis**cast as the lead in the school play. (3)

The italicized word *wrong* tells us to insert the prefix **mis.**

---

1. When Yvonne is _____ mused, she is so *completely* plunged in thought, she doesn't see or hear anything. (2)

2. We've cooked the chicken *too much;* it's _____ done. (4)

3. That _____ landish costume goes *beyond* any reasonable one I've ever seen! (3)

4. Looking back is easy; looking at the years in *front* of us is hard. Hindsight is 20–20, but _____ sight is not so certain! (4)

5. It takes a wise person to _____ bear saying, "I told you so," for it is hard *not* to gloat. (3)

6. Young children are _____ inhibited, *not* yet restrained by adult standards of decorum. (2)

7. _____ beat personalities differ *from* normal people in their unusual reactions to ordinary events. (3)

8. Many Americans are still _____ nourished, with diets *below* minimum standards for good health. (5)

9. A thousand shoppers descended *on* the store, and the ensuing _____ rush was like a riot. (2)

10. When teacher salaries were _____ graded, the average salary went *up* 10%. (2)

No Roots?

At this point you would expect a list of Anglo-Saxon roots, like the ones for Greek and Latin. Such a list would contain a paradox: It would be both too long—and too easy! You already know most Anglo-Saxon roots. They are the word elements you used as a child.

Here's proof. There are two kinds of English verbs: weak verbs and strong verbs. Weak verbs add *ed* for the past tense and the past participle. Examples of weak verbs are *talk, talked,* (have, has, had) *talked* and *help, helped,* (have, etc.) *helped.* Strong verbs change in other ways in the past tense and the past participle. Examples of strong verbs are *go, went,* (have, etc.) *gone* and *sing, sang,* (have, etc.) *sung.* Verbs from French and other languages tend to be weak verbs; for example, *nominate* and *sympathize.* The strong verbs are Anglo-Saxon.

Here's a list of strong verbs in English. *You already know them.* You may have trouble with forms of the tenses, but you know the meaning of every word in the list. There is no need to list the Anglo-Saxon roots.

arise	draw	grind	shine	sting
beat	drink	grow	sink	stride
behold	eat	hold	sit	strike
bind	fall	know	slay	swing
bite	fight	lie	slide	take
blow	find	ring	speak	tear
break	fly	rise	spin	throw
choose	freeze	run	spring	weave
cling	get	see	stand	win
come	give	shake	steal	write

You may meet an Anglo-Saxon word in a sentence-completion test.

Problem

The _____ of all the disagreement was the call for a new election.
(A) undergirding   (D) overreach
(B) foreclosure   (E) upshot
(C) rancor

Strategy.   The *upshot* was once the final shot in an archery match. Thus it came to mean "conclusion." The familiar prefix *up* and common root *shot* tell us we have a word of Anglo-Saxon origin here.

Review

Write the letter for the antonym of each capitalized word.

1. UNWARRANTED:
   (A) not sold   (D) scrutinized
   (B) garbled   (E) pressured
   (C) suitable
                                      1 __

2. OFFSPRING:
   (A) cousin   (D) sire
   (B) sibling   (E) infant
   (C) aunt
                                      2 __

3. MISGIVING:
   (A) assurance   (D) gift
   (B) theft   (E) greed
   (C) reluctance
                                      3 __

4. FORBEARANCE:
   (A) impatience   (D) refusal
   (B) allowance   (E) breakdown
   (C) leniency
                                      4 __

5. OUTGROWTH:
   (A) cause   (D) result
   (B) appendage   (E) rock ledge
   (C) drop in
        profits   5 ___

6. OVERINDULGE:
   (A) scan   (D) fast
   (B) press   (E) clamor
   (C) strike   6 ___

7. WITHDRAWAL:
   (A) retreat   (D) attainment
   (B) deposit   (E) decrease
   (C) authorization   7 ___

8. UNDERTAKE:
   (A) give up   (D) carry on
   (B) pursue   (E) disclose
   (C) disgrace   8 ___

9. BEWITCHMENT:
   (A) embar-
        rassment   (D) conversion
   (B) disen-   (E) betrayal
        chantment   9 ___
   (C) sorcery

10. UPLIFT:
    (A) redesign   (D) discard
    (B) depart   (E) debase
    (C) prevail   10 ___

Compound Words

The Anglo-Saxons loved to build compound words, just as modern German does. (They are related languages.) For our modern word *traveler,* they had *earth-walker.* The *king* was a *ring-giver.* A *successor* was an *after-comer.* A *lamp* was a *light-vessel.* The *sea* was the *whale-road. Geometry* was *earth-craft.* A *boat* was *sea-wood.* Many compounds were poetically beautiful, like *day-red* for *dawn.*

Many of the old compounds were dropped. Some, like *ring-finger,* are still with us. Some compounds have been combined to make a single word. *Walrus,* for example, was a *whale-horse.*

Modern English still creates new compound words. Words like *counter-culture* and *cost-efficient* are fairly recent additions. A living language never stops changing.

Try your hand at creating compounds from Anglo-Saxon word elements.

B. Match words from column A and words from column B to form present-day compound words. Write the compound words on the lines below. Example:

basket ball. *Basket* plus *ball* equals *basketball.*

	A		B
back	rail	ache	mill
dress	saw	band	road
eye	sea	beam	rocket
foot	sky	boat	sickness
gate	snow	book	sight
gold	sun	fish	step
hand	tooth	ground	storm
home	water	less	stroke
life	work	maker	way
moon	wrist	man	works

_____   _____

_____   _____

_____   _____

_____   _____

_____   _____

_____   _____

_____   _____

_____   _____

SUMMARY

Etymology Clue 5: Anglo-Saxon Words

1. Words from Anglo-Saxon predominate in most writing and nearly all conversation.
2. Words for basic human actions and for commonplace objects tend to be of Anglo-Saxon origin. In times of great emotion, people tend to call upon Anglo-Saxon words.
3. Words long in use often have figurative meanings, but the central meanings of the words tends to be recognizable.
4. Anglo-Saxon words are particularly useful in making compound words.

Etymology Clue 6: Suffixes

Suffixes are crucial little word elements. They make the difference between *hopeful* and *hopeless*, *journalist* and *journalese*, *elective* and *election*, *thirteen* and *thirty*. They make verbs of adjectives: *short, shorten*. They make adverbs of adjectives: *sweet, sweetly*.

Suffixes provide clues to the part of speech. Typical noun suffixes include **dom, ness, ship, ion,** and **tude.** Typical adjective suffixes include **ish, less, y, esque,** and **ose.** Typical verb suffixes include **fy, ize,** and **ate.**

Although English derives suffixes from Latin, Greek, and Anglo-Saxon, suffixes were not treated in those sections of the book. A major reason is that English tends to make all kinds of combinations, using Latin roots with old Anglo-Saxon suffixes (*gratefully*) and Anglo-Saxon roots with old Latin suffixes (*breakable*). A word like *hypothetically* has a Greek prefix **hypo** and Greek root **thes.** The Latin suffix **al** combines with the Anglo-Saxon suffix **ly,** and we have a word from three different sources—Greek, Latin, and Anglo-Saxon. When English creates new words, all languages are fair game. There is little practical point in classifying suffixes as of Latin, Greek, or Anglo-Saxon origin.

Suffixes You Already Know

You can instantly recognize many suffixes, like **less** and **able.** You already know the meaning of most suffixes. You can guess, for example, that *happiness* is the "state of being happy" and that **ness** means "state of." You can often identify the meaning of unfamiliar words with suffixes by recalling other words you already know that have the same suffix.

Suppose you come upon the word *quiescent*. You recognize the word *quiet* but what of the suffix, **escent?** Think of other words with the same suffix: *adolescent* and *convalescent*. Both suggest a *state of becoming: becoming* an adult and *becoming* well. The suffix **escent** does mean "becoming." *Quiescent* suggests the process of *becoming* quiet. You would never call the ancient stillness of an Egyptian tomb *quiescent*. It is not *becoming* quiet. It has been quiet for a long time.

If you come upon the word *senescent,* you have something to build upon. You have already decided that the **escent** suffix means "becoming," but what of the root, **sene.** You think of words like *senior, seniority, senile,* and *senility*. These have to do with age. Even *senate* and *senator* originally suggested the older, more experienced, wiser heads in government. You may reasonably decide that *senescent* means "becoming older," "aging." Suffixes help to make fine distinctions.

Some suffixes are so rich and helpful they deserve your special attention. **Fy,** meaning "make," is such a suffix.

ENGLISH FOR THE COLLEGE BOARDS

Review the meanings of these **fy** words.

amplify	magnify	satisfy
clarify	mortify	simplify
codify	ossify	solidify
deify	pacify	stultify
dignify	petrify	testify
horrify	rectify	unify
identify	revivify	verify
indemnify	sanctify	vilify

The concept of *making* is apparent in all these words, even though in some words the meaning is more figurative than literal. *Mortify*, for example, by derivation means "make dead." Isn't that rather strange? Not at all. Speakers of English are prone to exaggeration. Think of a typical exclamation: "I was so mortified I thought I'd die!"

Suffixes Suggest Meaning

Suffixes go beyond denotation. They may also be clues to connotation. The **ish** suffix, for example, is a popular one. Often it has a negative connotation. Think of *boyish, babyish, childish, mannish, foolish, boorish, kittenish, cleverish,* and *clownish*. Contrast the neutral *childlike* with the negative *childish*. The **ster** suffix also tends to have a negative connotation, as in words like *trickster, mobster, gangster, prankster, gamester, huckster,* and *rhymester*. An occasional **ster** may be an exception. *Punster* may have had a mildly negative tone at one time, but now it seems almost affectionate. *Youngster* is a fairly neutral word, but for some people it seems patronizing. Still, the **ster** suffix is a good clue to negative words.

Some suffixes suggest affection. The suffix **y**, for example, appears in words like *kitty, aunty, Johnny, Elly,* and *sissy* (for sister). Some suffixes suggest science and learning: **ics** in *economics, hydroponics, harmonics, astrophysics,* and *electronics*.

Some suffixes have sudden bursts of popularity. **Ette**, meaning "small," has been widely used in recent years to suggest compactness and charm. Most people would shun a *small kitchen*, but they're proud of a *kitchenette*. Words like *luncheonette, launderette,* and *statuette* are perfectly acceptable. One small grocery store proudly called itself a *superette!* The **ama** suffix, originally from *orama* meaning "to see," started with *cyclorama*, then made its way to *launderama*.

A living language has vitality, vigor, and the capacity for change. Suffixes play a role in that change.

Become familiar with the following lists of suffixes. Knowing suffixes will help you on the SAT. The suffixes here are in two sections for convenience.

Suffixes—1

Suffix	Meaning	Example	Explanation
able, ible	able to	manage**able**	*able to* be managed
		collaps**ible**	*able to* be collapsed
ac, ic	related to	cardi**ac**	*related to* the heart
		dramat**ic**	*related to* drama
aceous, scious	having quality of	ver**acious**	*having quality of* truth, true
age	state, quality, act	shrink**age**	*state of* shrinking
al, ical	related to, like	nav**al**	*related to* ships
		crit**ical**	*related to* criticism
an, ian	related to, one who	urb**an**	*related to* the city
		magic**ian**	*one who* works with magic
ana	information about	Americ**ana**	*information about* America
ance, ence	state, quality	resist**ance**	*state of* resisting
ancy, ency	act	despond**ency**	*state of* being downcast
ant, ent	one who, that which	particip**ant**	*one who* takes part
		tang**ent**	*that which* touches
ar	like, related to, one who	circul**ar**	*like* a circle
		li**ar**	*one who* lies
ary, arium	place where	gran**ary**	*place where* grain is stored
		sanit**arium**	*place where* people go to regain health
ard, art	one who (usually negative)	bragg**art**	*one who* boasts
ate	make, act,	dehyd**rate**	*make* waterless
	one who	advo**cate**	*one who* pleads another's cause
	having quality of	mode**rate**	*having quality of* reasonableness
cle	small	parti**cle**	*small* element
craft	skill, practice of	witch**craft**	*practice of* being a witch
dom	state, quality	wis**dom**	*state* of being wise
ee	one who	employ**ee**	*one who* is employed
eer	one who	auction**eer**	*one who* auctions
el, le	little, small	parc**el**	*small* bundle
en	make	hard**en**	*make* hard
en	having quality	wood**en**	*having quality* of wood
er, or	one who, that which	sail**or**	*one who* sails
		wash**er**	*that which* washes
ern	related to	east**ern**	*related to* east
ery, erie	place where	hatch**ery**	*place where* fish are hatched
		menag**erie**	*place where* animals are displayed
ery, ry	state of, quality, act of	drudg**ery**	*state of* hard, dull work
		bigot**ry**	*state of or act of* prejudice
escent	becoming	obsol**escent**	*becoming* obsolete
ese	like, related to	Chin**ese**	*related to* China
esque	in the manner of	Whitman**esque**	*in the manner of* Whitman
ess*	feminine	act**ress**	*female* actor*

Suffix	Meaning	Example	Explanation
et, ette	little, small	ring**let**	*little* ring
fic, fy	making, make	honori**fic**	*making* or conferring honor
		simpli**fy**	*make* simple
fold	times	ten**fold**	ten *times*
ful	having quality of	care**ful**	*having quality of* care
hood	state of, quality of	child**hood**	*state of* being a child
		false**hood**	*quality of* falseness
ics	science, system	linguist**ics**	*science* of languages
ice	act of, time of	serv**ice**	*act of* serving
id	related to	flu**id**	*related to* a liquid

*This suffix has been under attack as being sexist. Opponents argue that *actor* refers to both sexes. Words like *steward* and *stewardess,* they say, should give way to *flight attendant.* The suffix is included here for completeness, but you may wish to think about your own use of it.

Trial Test

Each of the words in column A contains a suffix from the preceding list. Each suffix is in boldface. Write the number for each word from column A next to its meaning in column B. Clues in column B are in *italics*. Note how suffixes can help to sharpen meaning.

A	B
1. avi**ary**	___ *make* systematic, arrange
2. benefac**tor**	___ *small*est speck
	___ *science* of production, distribution,
3. bliss**ful**	and consumption of wealth
4. cod**ify**	___ *place where* birds are kept
5. incorrig**ible**	___ *having quality of* happiness
6. econom**ics**	___ manual *skill*
7. handi**craft**	___ *related to* light, clear
8. luc**id**	___ *one who* does good deeds
9. parti**cle**	___ *in the manner of* a statue
10. sculptur**esque**	___ *not able to* be reformed

Familiarity with suffixes sometimes helps define a partially familiar word.

Problem

Proof of bad faith may be used as a reason to _____ the agreement.

(A) nullify   (D) temper

(B) celebrate   (E) consider

(C) advertise

Strategy. The context suggests that the agreement is in trouble. *Nullify,* "to make null," satisfies the meaning. You have probably met *null* in the expression *null and void,* meaning "not binding." *Nullify* thus suggests "not binding." Even if you have not heard *null and void,* you have probably heard the word *annul,* meaning "cancel." Or perhaps you've heard the word *annulment,* the "dissolution of a marriage."

The *fy* suffix is one of the most useful of all, as in words like *magnify, petrify,* and *horrify.*

Suffixes—2

Suffix	Meaning	Example	Explanation
ie, y	small	doggie	*small* dog
		kitty	*small* kitten
ine	like, related to	feline	*like* a cat
ion	state, quality, act of	suspicion	*act of* suspecting
ish	like, related to	boorish	*like* a boor
isk	small	asterisk	*small* star
ism	state of, quality, act	egotism	*state of* being self-centered
ist	one who	dentist	*one who* works with teeth
ite	one who	favorite	*one who* is favored
itis	inflammation	neuritis	*inflammation* of nerves
ity	state, quality, act	nobility	*quality* of being noble
ize	make, act	tranquilize	*make* quiet
ive	one who, that which	captive	*one who* has been taken
ive	having power	creative	*having power* to create
kin	little, small	manikin	*little* man
less	without	homeless	*without* a home
let	little	booklet	*little* book
like	like	apelike	*like* an ape
ly	having quality of	friendly	*having quality of* a friend
ly	in the manner of (adverb suffix)	hurriedly	*in a* hurried *manner*
ment	state of, quality, act	excitement	*state of* being excited
mony	state of, quality, that which	matrimony	*state of* being married
or	one who, that which	donor	*one who* gives
ory, orium	place where	factory	*place where* things are made
		auditorium	*place where* one can hear
ory	like, having quality of	regulatory	*having quality of* controlling
ose	having quality of	bellicose	*having quality of* quarrelsomeness
osis	state, condition, action	hypnosis	*state* resembling sleep
	abnormal or diseased condition	tuberculosis	*diseased condition* of lungs
ous	having quality of	famous	*having quality of* fame
ship	state of, quality of	ownership	*state of* being an owner
some	having quality of, full of	worrisome	*having quality of* worry

Suffix	Meaning	Example	Explanation
ster	one who	prank**ster**	*one who* plays pranks
th	state, quality, that which	tru**th**	*state of* being true
tude	state, quality of, act of	multi**tude**	*state of* being numerous
ty	state of, quality of, that which	safe**ty**	*state of* being safe
ure	state of, quality of, act, that which	rupt**ure**	*state of* being broken
ward, wards	in direction of	home**ward**	*in direction of* home
wise	in the manner of, in a certain direction	clock**wise**	*in the direction* a clock rotates
y	having quality of, somewhat, tending to, suggestive of	hast**y** yellow**y** drows**y** willow**y**	*having quality of* haste *somewhat* yellow *tending to* drowse *suggestive of* a willow, gracefully slender

Trial Test

Each of the words in column A contains a suffix from the preceding list. Each suffix is in boldface. Write the number for each word from column A next to its meaning in column B. Clues in column B are in *italics*. Note how suffixes can help to sharpen meaning.

A	B
1. altru**ism**	____ *having quality of* being annoying
2. cura**tor**	____ *inflammation* of the stomach
3. cut**let**	____ *little* slice
4. equ**ine**	____ *one who* is in charge of a museum or a library
5. eulog**ize**	____ *make* a speech of praise
6. gastr**itis**	____ *in the manner of* a greedy person
7. glutton**ously**	____ *place where* people work and experiment
8. laborat**ory**	____ *like* a horse
9. psych**osis**	____ *diseased condition* of the mind
10. vexat**ious**	____ *quality of* unselfishness

Try your skill at another sentence-completion question.

Problem

The _____ of the health-insurance
problem can be gauged by the number and
variety of plans and solutions offered.

    (A) analysis   (D) demographics
    (B) amplitude   (E) sturdiness
    (C) interest

Strategy. You are familiar with the word *ample,* "generous, large." The prefix *tude,* "state of," combines with *ample* to produce *amplitude,* the answer best associated with "number and variety."

Review

1. The long, _____ speech of the undistinguished candidate put most of the audience to sleep.
   - (A) trenchant
   - (B) narrative
   - (C) somnolent
   - (D) confidential
   - (E) consequential

2. Though usually easygoing and tolerant of different viewpoints, the voters in New Jersey showed a strong _____ toward increased taxation without accompanying spending cuts.
   - (A) inquiry
   - (B) antipathy
   - (C) attitude
   - (D) approbation
   - (E) disenfranchisement

3. At the beginning of his first term, Franklin D. Roosevelt was severely criticized for the introduction of new and revolutionary programs, but he remained _____ throughout.
   - (A) imperturbable
   - (B) antagonistic
   - (C) indeterminate
   - (D) unconventional
   - (E) undignified

4. Andy Warhol, commenting upon the _____ nature of fame, once said that everyone can be a celebrity for fifteen minutes.
   - (A) indomitable
   - (B) repetitive
   - (C) dormant
   - (D) fanatical
   - (E) transient

5. At one time, United Parcel Service required the _____ of every package to sign for acceptance, but nowadays packages are often left at the doorstep.
   - (A) dispatcher
   - (B) identifier
   - (C) recipient
   - (D) owner
   - (E) proprietor

6. In an Agatha Christie mystery, Miss Marple early on suspected the identity of the murderer, but her proof was _____.
   - (A) invulnerable
   - (B) inconclusive
   - (C) fallacious
   - (D) uninspiring
   - (E) unintelligible

7. Carol Burnett won a judgment against a national magazine on the charge of _____ of character.
   - (A) disclosure
   - (B) defamation
   - (C) inflammation
   - (D) incongruity
   - (E) restitution

8. Harold is able to hold two divergent points of view at the same time without realizing their _____.
   - (A) incomprehensibility
   - (B) spontaneity
   - (C) variability
   - (D) incompatibility
   - (E) symmetricality

9. Although I find the sauna _____, Marie enjoys it and can stay inside for ten minutes at a time.
   - (A) enervating
   - (B) volatile
   - (C) propitious
   - (D) luminous
   - (E) winsome

10. The President's proposals were _____ to the leaders of his own party, and he had to retreat.
    - (A) tolerable
    - (B) nurturing
    - (C) unpalatable
    - (D) analogous
    - (E) proliferating

SUMMARY

Etymology Clue 6: Suffixes

1. Suffixes provide important clues to the part of speech, word meanings, and word history.
2. English uses suffixes without regard for word origins. Anglo-Saxon and Latin suffixes are often used together.
3. You can find the meaning of most suffixes: think of other words containing the suffix. Then decide what meaning all the words have in common.
4. Suffixes sometimes suggest connotation as well as denotation.

   Suffixes can help you with SAT questions, especially when you need to know the part of speech.

Etymology Clue 7: Foreign Words in English

Think of a typical American **barbecue.** In addition to the meat, there might be baked **potato,** baked **yam,** sliced **tomato,** all served with **lemonade, ginger** ale, iced **tea,** or iced **coffee.** Of course the inevitable bottle of **ketchup** would be on hand for the feast. For dessert there might be **orange sherbet.** Some guests might prefer **chocolate** ice cream, made from **cocoa.** In season, **apricots** and **avocados** might be welcome additions. **Bananas** would almost certainly be available.

Notice how much we depend upon foreign borrowings. Every one of the boldfaced words originally came from lands all around the world.

barbecue—American Indian	orange—Persian
potato—American Indian	sherbet—Arabic
yam—African	chocolate—Mexican
tomato—Mexican	cocoa—Mexican
lemon—Persian	apricots—Arabic
ginger—Indian	avocados—Mexican
tea—Chinese	bananas—African
coffee—Arabic	syrup—Arabic
ketchup—Malayan-Chinese	sugar—Arabic

These are just a few of the food words borrowed from other languages. Sometimes the borrowings provide a clue to the special contribution of a particular language. From Hebrew, for example, we get words like **amen, cherub, hallelujah, Jehovah, jubilee, Pharisee, sabbath,** and **shibboleth.** These words suggest our indebtedness to the ancient Hebrews for many religious terms.

Trial Test

A. Below are listed groups of words from various other languages. Decide from what language each group of words came and match each group with the proper language from the list below. What do you think was a major contribution of each nation?

> **arcade, balcony, colonnade, corridor, portico**
>
> Language: Contribution:
> *Italian*   *architecture*
>
> These are all of Italian origin. Since all have something to do with parts of buildings, we can safely assume that Italian contributions to architecture have been considerable.

Languages

African	French
American	German
American Indian	Italian
Arabic	Persian
Dutch	Spanish

1. hominy, maize, pecan, succotash, squash
   Language: _____   Contribution: _____

2. beret, cambric, chapeau, cretonne
   Language: _____   Contribution: _____

3. deck, dock, hoist, jib, skipper, sloop
   Language: _____   Contribution: _____

4. bismuth, cobalt, Fahrenheit, gneiss, quartz, shale, zinc
   Language: _____   Contribution: _____

5. alchemy, algebra, chemistry, cipher, zenith, zero
   Language: _____   Contribution: _____

6. adobe, bronco, canyon, corral, lariat
   Language: _____   Contribution: _____

7. jasmine, lemon, lilac, orange, peach, tulip
   Language: _____   Contribution: _____

8. andante, aria, opera, piano, soprano
   Language: _____   Contribution: _____

9. chimpanzee, gnu, gorilla, ibis, quagga
   Language: _____   Contribution: _____

10. carborundum, cellophane, kodak, listerine, thermos, victrola
    Language: _____   Contribution: _____

B. The words in column A have all been based upon the names of places in other lands. Look up the origin and the meaning of each word in column A. Then write each word's number next to its country of origin in column B.

	A		B
1.	astrachan	___	China
2.	bayonet	___	England
3.	calico	___	England and Scotland
4.	cantaloupe	___	France
5.	cheviot	___	Germany
6.	coach	___	Hungary
7.	damask	___	India
8.	frankfurter	___	Italy
9.	muslin	___	Mesopotamia
10.	oolong	___	Mexico
11.	peach	___	Morocco
12.	polka	___	Persia
13.	tabasco	___	Poland
14.	tangerine	___	Russia
15.	worsted	___	Syria

Word History

Among the ancient Greeks, citizens of Laconia, or Sparta, had the reputation of speaking directly, wasting no words. This characteristic has given us the word **laconic. Laconic** means "brief," "to the point." Many qualities or products of various places have given us new words. The American favorite, **hamburger,** is named after the city of Hamburg. **Italic** type originated in Italy. **Copper** took its name from Cyprus, as did **spaniel** from Spain. **China, turkey, cologne,** and **morocco** (leather) are self-explanatory.

Words from sources other than Latin, Greek, or Anglo-Saxon appear occasionally in the word sections of the SAT and the reading sections. The best preparation for this section is also the best preparation for extending your vocabulary in general. Become word curious. When you meet an interesting new word, look up the definition, of course, but also check its history.

Note the interesting history behind the word **bizarre.**

> **bi·zarre** (bi zär') *adj.* [Fr. < It. *bizarro;*
> angry, fierce, strange < Sp. *bizarro,* bold,
> knightly < Basque *bizar,* a beard] **1.** odd in
> manner, appearance, etc.; grotesque; queer;
> eccentric **2.** marked by extreme contrasts
> and incongruities of color, design, or style
> **3.** unexpected and unbelievable; fantastic [a
> *bizarre* sequence of events]—**SYN.** see FAN-
> TASTIC—**bi·zarre'ly** *adv.*—**bi·zarre'ness** *n.**

Bizarre originally came from Basque *bizar,* meaning "beard." The Spaniards borrowed the word as *bizarro* to mean "bold, knightly." Knights, we may assume, were *bearded.* The Italians then borrowed the word with the same spelling to mean "angry, fierce." Knightly battles were not gentle struggles! Then English borrowed the same word as **bizarre** to mean "odd," "eccentric." Reading the history makes an impression. (Note that the similar-sounding word, *bazaar,* is completely unrelated. *Bazaar* comes from the Persian *bazar,* meaning "market.")

Karate comes from two Japanese words: *kara* meaning "empty," "open" and *te* meaning "hand." **Karate** literally means "open hand." A demonstration of karate clearly shows how the word originated, as thrusts are made with hands open.

Sometimes a colorful borrowed word appears in a sentence-completion item.

Problem

When contrasted with the staid and
sober Charles Darnay, Charles Dickens's
Sidney Carton seemed almost _____.
    (A) austere   (D) flamboyant
    (B) formidable   (E) perspicacious
    (C) dour

Strategy. *Contrasted* tells us that the blank must have a word opposed in meaning to *staid* and *sober.* On this basis alone, (A) and (C) fail to qualify. *Formidable* (B) and *perspicacious* (E) are neither synonyms nor antonyms of *staid* and *sober,* thus disqualifying them as answers. *Flamboyant* (D) suggests a "dramatic display," a residue of its French ancestry. We can even discern the word *flame* within it.

(D) When contrasted with the staid and sober Charles Darnay, Charles
     Dickens's Sidney Carton seemed almost flamboyant.

Review

A. After each of the following words, the origin of the word is given, along with its original meaning. Read the clues and write the letter for the answer which most closely explains the test word.

KOWTOW (from the Chinese meaning "knock head"):
    (A) find unexpectedly
    (B) respect excessively
    (C) support enthusiastically
    (D) understand poorly
    (E) reject suddenly

                      B

Since the original meaning suggests a person touching his head to the floor in submission, alternative *(B), respect excessively,* is the correct answer.

1. CHECKMATE (from the Persian "The king is dead."):
    (A) delay intentionally
    (B) replace secretly
    (C) marry in haste
    (D) support financially
    (E) defeat completely

                        1 ___

2. PUNDIT (from Hindi "learned person"):
    (A) authority   (D) police officer
    (B) mayor   (E) humorist
    (C) enthusiast

                        2 ___

3. UKASE (from the Russian "to order"):
   (A) container for bottles
   (B) kind of instrument
   (C) voting irregularity
   (D) official decree
   (E) all-purpose cement

   3 ___

4. AMOK (from the Malay "fighting furiously"):
   (A) sympathetic
   (B) at a standstill
   (C) in a rage
   (D) wearily accepting
   (E) quietly responsible

   4 ___

5. NADIR (from the Arabic "opposite the highest point"):
   (A) kind of telescope
   (B) sunspot
   (C) good fortune
   (D) tropical fruit
   (E) time of dejection

   5 ___

6. MOGUL (from Persian "Mongol conqueror"):
   (A) superb athlete
   (B) member of endangered species
   (C) powerful person
   (D) falsehood
   (E) bill of sale

   6 ___

7. GARBLE (from Arabic "sieve"):
   (A) close
   (B) mix up
   (C) win at chess
   (D) wander aimlessly
   (E) find fault

   7 ___

8. RUCKSACK (from German "back" plus "sack"):
   (A) potato sack
   (B) handbag
   (C) pocketbook
   (D) hiker's pack
   (E) wallet

   8 ___

9. ARGOSY (from Italian "vessel from Ragusa"):
   (A) merchant ship
   (B) newly published book
   (C) fan magazine
   (D) financial wizard
   (E) tall tale

   9 ___

10. MANDARIN (from Portuguese "minister of state"):
    (A) skilled chef
    (B) member of elite group
    (C) fruit punch
    (D) stringed instrument
    (E) mythological monster

    10 ___

B. Words from foreign sources are everywhere in English. They are found in every field of activity, every subject, at every level of difficulty. How many words in the following test are familiar to you? For each item, write the letter for the answer that best defines the test word. If you don't know a word, look it up.

1. WAINSCOT is a
   (A) ceremonial car
   (B) kind of celluloid
   (C) formal dinner
   (D) roofing material
   (E) woodwork

   1 ___

2. QUININE is a
   (A) tropical disease
   (B) medicine
   (C) kind of dance
   (D) paint ingredient
   (E) beef tea

   2 ___

3. A CATAMARAN is a(n)
   (A) tiger-like animal
   (B) insect
   (C) Malayan hut
   (D) kind of boat
   (E) cure for malaria

   3 ___

4. FANFARE involves
   (A) display
   (B) the use of a fan
   (C) charging admission
   (D) baseball
   (E) jealousy

   4 ___

5. CURRY is a
   (A) carriage
   (B) harness
   (C) pack animal
   (D) seasoning
   (E) comb
   5 ___

6. TURQUOISE is a kind of
   (A) fowl
   (B) plant
   (C) color
   (D) powder
   (E) French dish
   6 ___

7. FAHRENHEIT and CELSIUS are words dealing with
   (A) severity of earthquakes
   (B) degrees of heat
   (C) electronic calculations
   (D) atmospheric pressure
   (E) relative humidity
   7 ___

8. A SHIBBOLETH is a
   (A) monster
   (B) password
   (C) proclamation
   (D) flower
   (E) game
   8 ___

9. A SERAPH is a(n)
   (A) kind of printing
   (B) old woman
   (C) medicine
   (D) angel
   (E) mounted soldier
   9 ___

10. A FEZ is a kind of
    (A) fish
    (B) mythical animal
    (C) cap
    (D) coat
    (E) worship
    10 ___

11. A TABOO is a
    (A) mark
    (B) prince
    (C) restriction
    (D) narrative
    (E) permit
    11 ___

12. AZIMUTH is a term used in
    (A) painting
    (B) music
    (C) navigation
    (D) handicraft
    (E) the study of minerals
    12 ___

13. A MAZURKA is a kind of
    (A) broiled chicken
    (B) dance
    (C) vehicle
    (D) herb
    (E) building
    13 ___

14. A FREEBOOTER is a
    (A) football player
    (B) member of a soccer team
    (C) fighter for freedom
    (D) pirate
    (E) weaver
    14 ___

15. A JUGGERNAUT is something that
    (A) plays a tune
    (B) crushes
    (C) works automatically
    (D) takes care of gardens
    (E) can perform acrobatic stunts
    15 ___

16. An ALPACA is a(n)
    (A) ballad
    (B) artificial fabric
    (C) light jacket
    (D) animal
    (E) special kind of stew
    16 ___

17. A JAGUAR is a(n)
    (A) medicinal root
    (B) animal
    (C) bird
    (D) savage
    (E) knife
    17 ___

18. A BAZAAR is a
    (A) cloak
    (B) strange tale
    (C) protest
    (D) musical instrument
    (E) fair
    18 ___

19. The ZENITH is
    (A) on the horizon
    (B) below one's feet
    (C) at a 45-degree angle
    (D) above one's head
    (E) at the equator
    19 ___

20. A PARIAH is a(n)
    (A) staunch friend
    (B) outcast
    (C) religious fanatic
    (D) oriental singer
    (E) weak-willed person
    20 ___

SUMMARY

Etymology Clue 7: Foreign Words in English

1. English has borrowed extensively from almost every language and culture it has come in contact with.
2. Borrowing has enriched the language by providing words for new objects and new ideas.
3. Finding the stories in foreign loan words enriches the study of vocabulary and impresses new words on the memory.
4. The borrowing goes both ways. English words also appear in almost every language in the original or changed form.

Studying foreign words in English and word histories will help you to prepare for the SAT.

Etymology Clue 8: The Growth of English

Think of expressions like *space shuttle, launch window, computer chip,* and *video game.* A few years ago these expressions did not exist because the things they name did not exist. We need new words and expressions to name new processes and substances. Unfortunately, as our problems increase, we need new expressions for these, too: *hazardous waste, endangered species,* and *acid rain.*

Sometimes, as in the examples above, new expressions merely combine older words to create wholly new concepts. Sometimes, however, we need a wholly new word. When inflation strained the resources of a stagnant economy, we coined the new word *stagflation.* Words like *microprocessing* and *transistorize* show that we still have the ability to create new words from old roots.

The best way to learn new words is to listen carefully and read widely. Current newspapers and magazines are filled with new words and expressions. Words and expressions like *quark, jet lag, personal computer, word processor, laser,* and *burnout* have become commonplace in modern communication.

Because words enter the language at so rapid a rate, it is impossible to prepare an up-to-date book on new words, or *neologisms,* as they are called. Dictionaries of new words are out of date before publication day. If there is a knowledge explosion, there is also a language explosion. New words will not play a key role in the SAT, but it is always a good idea to keep up to date.

When you work with roots, be aware of the tendency of language to change. The root of *common* suggests "shared by all." But the word has acquired a negative connotation of "inferiority," even "coarseness." Similarly, *vulgar* once meant "general," "popular," "belonging to the great mass of people." Now a certain snobbishness in language has sent the word downhill to mean "coarse," "crude," "boorish."

Uphill In Meaning

Words can go up the social scale, too. A *knight* was once a "servant." A *marshal* was a "groom," a "horse servant." A *constable* was the "chief groom." A *chamberlain,* now a high official, was once just a "servant." A *steward* was the "guardian of the sty." *Chivalry* was just another word for "cavalry." Even *fame* once meant only "something spoken about someone." Now it suggests "a good reputation."

Narrower In Meaning

While some words are going up or down the social scale, others are changing in different ways. Specialization has changed *meat* from "any solid food" to the "flesh of animals." A *ballad* was once just a "song." Now it's a rather special kind of song. *Corn* was once any "grain." Now in America it refers to the plant the Indians called "maize." *Ghost* once meant just "spirit." Now it is usually applied to an "apparition" said to haunt houses. In fact, *apparition* itself once meant just "appearance."

Downhill In Meaning

Enormity suggests one way in which words change—for the worse. Once it meant merely "something unusual." Now it suggests "unusual in evil." Similarly, *boor* once meant merely "farmer." *Knave* meant just "boy." *Homely* meant "simple," and *sullen* meant "alone." A *villain* was a "farm servant," and a *hussy* was just a "housewife." *Servile* meant "not free." Now it suggests "cringing," "unnecessarily submissive." A *busybody* was just a "busy person," and a *hypocrite* was just an "actor."

Broader In Meaning

English often extends word meanings. A *journey* was originally a "trip of one day's duration." Now it means a "trip of any length." *Front* once meant merely "forehead." *Paper* was a substance made from "papyrus." Now paper can be made from many substances. A *scene* was once just "part of a theater stage." We still use it in that sense, but think of all the broader uses of the term, as in *the modern scene*. *Hazard* was once a "game of dice." Now it means a "chance occurrence" and, by extension, a "risk," a "danger."

Figurative In Meaning

One of the most common changes in English is figurative use of a word. *Deliberate* literally means "put on the scales." *Dilapidate* means "throw stones." A *pedigree* literally means a "crane's foot." If you look at a pedigree, or family tree (another figurative expression), you can see that foot! Pages 51–55 have already considered the importance of figurative language. The sections on roots have urged you to look for figurative meanings in many common words.

However, language grows and changes in other ways, too. If you know about these changes, you will have a better background for handling some of the questions on the SAT.

Sometimes deceptive changes in meaning can prove puzzling on sentence-completion items.

Problem

The extent of the evil and the _____ of Joseph Stalin's actions became generally known in Russia during the Nikita Khrushchev era.

(A) beneficence (D) enormity
(B) quality (E) minimization
(C) revelation

Strategy. *Enormity* (D) once meant "something out of the normal." Then it became associated with evil, as in the sentence above. Through possible misuse or misunderstanding, the word is acquiring the sense of *large size*, of *enormousness*. Whichever definition is chosen, (D) is the correct choice here. Both (A) and (E) run counter to the meaning of the sentence as suggested in "the extent of the evil." (B) is too neutral. (Remember always to choose the *best* answer.) (C) is redundant: "the revelation . . . became known."

(D) The extent of the evil and the enormity of Joseph Stalin's actions became generally known in Russia during the Nikita Khrushchev era.

Trial Test

In each sentence, write the word in parentheses that most suitably completes the meaning of the sentence.

The ending of the musical *Carousel* is so (poignant, pungent), it often brings a tear to every eye in the audience.

In this sentence *poignant* means "emotionally touching," "evoking pity." *Pungent* would be too strong. *Pungent* may be piercing to the mind; *poignant* to the emotions. *Pungent* can apply to taste. *Poignant* cannot.

1. An (abbreviated, abridged) dictionary keeps the most important words and omits infrequently used words.

   1 _____

2. Jim's speech was interesting, but his ideas were too (tenuous, thin) for a practical program.

   2 _____

3. When Caroline brought out the Ping-Pong balls, the kittens became unusually (fresh, frisky) in playing with them.

   3 _____

4. After a morning in the garden. Don's complexion became (florid, flowery) from the heat.

   4 _____

5. Because of a disagreement, the two families (separated, severed) all ties that had once joined them.

   5 _____

6. Though Billy Dawn in *Born Yesterday* at first seemed (naive, native), she gradually developed a shrewd awareness of Brock's dishonesty.

   6 _____

7. From an early age, Teddy showed an (aptitude, attitude) for things mechanical.

   7 _____

8. Once Patty becomes interested in a subject, she (jealously, zealously) learns all she can about it.

   8 _____

9. By three, Jennifer could already (compute, count) from 1 to 10.

   9 _____

10. Pollen granules are (born, borne) on the wind.

   10 _____

Problem

The petty _____ of some persons in charge of others is often traceable to a basic _____ in their lives.
  (A) cheerfulness . . melancholy
  (B) talkativeness . . charm
  (C) vigor . . misunderstanding
  (D) provincialism . . awareness
  (E) tyranny . . insecurity

Strategy. Analyze the possibilities. *(A)* contains a contradiction. *Cheerfulness* cannot logically be traced to *melancholy*. Although it might be argued that such an answer is not impossible, you are not asked to choose just a possible answer. You must choose the best answer. If a clue word like *although* had been included, things might be different. Notice the difference the following wording makes.

Although some persons in charge of others display *cheerfulness,* they may be concealing a basic *melancholy* in their lives.

Talkativeness and *charm* are negatively related, if at all. We can reject *(B)*. *Vigor* and *misunderstanding* are not related. Misunderstanding would not logically lead to vigor. Reject *(C)*. *(D)* also contains a contradiction. People who are *open and aware* are not likely to be *provincial*.

A process of elimination leaves you with *(E)*. Do these answers fit? Yes, tyranny can arise from a feeling of insecurity. Those who feel insecure may try to generate security by being oppressive to others. *(E)* is correct.

Tyranny is a word that has gone downhill. A *tyrant* was once just a "ruler" in ancient Greece. Then, since rulers often abuse their powers, the word *tyrant* came to mean an "unjust, oppressive ruler." For the purpose of this question it is not necessary to know that *tyranny* has gone downhill, as long as you know its present meaning. But knowing a little about the history of a word makes it much easier to remember. Now that you know something about the origin of *tyranny,* you are unlikely to forget it.

Doublets

One of the most fruitful sources of the growth of English is borrowing. As we have already noted, English may borrow the same word twice or even more. This multiple borrowing enriches our language, increases the number of synonyms, and makes for finer discriminations in speaking and writing.

Both **potion** and **poison** come from the Latin word meaning "drink." These doublets have acquired different meanings. A **poison** is a deadly **potion. Loyal** and **legal** both come from the Latin *lex* meaning "law." **Loyal,** which reached English through French, has acquired a different meaning from **legal.** Similarly, **frail** has acquired a meaning slightly different from its doublet **fragile.** An ill person may become **frail** but not **fragile.**

Doublets may come from different languages. Here's a sampling.

Anglo-Saxon and Latin	eatable, edible
Anglo-Saxon and French	bench, bank
Anglo-Saxon and Scandinavian	shriek, screech
Anglo-Saxon and Dutch	slide, sled
Latin and French	concept, conceit
French and Italian	study, studio
French and Spanish	army, armada
Greek and French	cathedral, chair

Doublets may come from the same language, though at different periods.

Earlier and Later French	castle, chateau
Earlier and Later Latin	camp, campus

Doublets may come from various changes within English itself.

Loss of a Syllable	despite, spite
Change of Vowel	cloths, clothes
Change of Consonant	stitch, stick
Word Shortening	van, caravan
Spelling Variation	flour, flower

Words borrowed three times are called *triplets*.

French, Italian, Spanish   place, piazza, plaza

Some words have been borrowed four times and now appear in four different forms, each with a different meaning: **stack, stake, steak, stock.** Some words have been borrowed five times and appear in five different forms: **discus, disk, dish, desk, dais.**

Why are doublets important in a vocabulary-building program? They provide associated words and synonyms. When you take a test, you must be able to discriminate meanings.

Review

In each of the following sentences, doublets appear in parentheses. Write the word that most suitably completes the meaning of the sentence.

1. As a storyteller Maud is without a (pair, peer) in our club.

    1 _____

2. What seems like (concept, conceit) in Rod is really shyness.

    2 _____

3. With her new hairdo, Fran looks like a (spirit, sprite) from elfdom.

    3 _____

4. When Henry Ford started, his friends were critical of the risky (adventure, venture) he was engaged in.

    4 _____

5. Until Cynthia becomes 18, her uncle remains her legal (guardian, warden).

    5 _____

6. The sign in the window said, "We buy old furniture; we sell (antics, antiques)."

    6 _____

7. You'll need a(n) (example, sample) of your wallpaper if you want to buy a matching bedspread.

    7 _____

8. Making sure all five kittens had a good home was a (human, humane) action.

    8 _____

9. Mr. Hathaway (dealt, doled) out his son's allowance as if he were mortgaging the family homestead for the money.

    9 _____

10. Despite his advanced age, George Bernard Shaw remained surprisingly (hale, whole) and vigorous.

    10 _____

11. Because of her rigorous diet, Madge has become too (tenuous, thin).

    11 _____

12. Mr. Mackenzie has a rugged, (florid, flowery) complexion.

    12 _____

13. How did our ancestors (thrash, thresh) grain in generations past?

    13 _____

14. *Etc.* is an (abbreviation, abridgment) of *et cetera*.

    14 _____

15. When do (male, masculine) chickens begin to develop the characteristic comb?

    15 _____

16. When asked to explain his absence, Mark gave a (feeble, foible) excuse.

    16 _____

17. In certain groups, shunning encourages members to (snob, snub) other members who have strayed from the fold.

17 _____

18. If the Forty-Niners win Sunday, they'll (clench, clinch) the division title.

18 _____

19. When the linebacker tackled the quarterback later, there was a (scuffle, shuffle) on the field.

19 _____

20. (Calibers, Calipers) are adjustable measuring instruments.

20 _____

SUMMARY

Etymology Clue 8: The Growth of English

1. As a living language, English adds new words constantly.
2. Some words are needed for technological advances and setbacks. Others are needed for new customs, fashions, and life-styles.
3. Some new expressions merely combine old words in new ways, but some actually create new words.
4. Most new words are constructed by putting together the building blocks of prefixes, roots, and suffixes.
5. Not only are new words created; words change. Some words go downhill; some, up. Some words become narrower in meaning; some, broader. Figurative use of existing words extends the possibilities of English.
6. Some words are borrowed twice, three times, or even more. These multiple borrowings enrich English with new synonyms and new concepts.

If you know how the language grows and changes, you will have a better background for verbal SAT questions.

Clues from Etymology: Review Test

Write the letter for the pair of words that best completes the meaning of the sentence as a whole.

1. Television's _____ appetite for novelty _____ material at an ever-increasing rate.
   (A) insatiable . . devours
   (B) devious . . expands
   (C) indiscriminate . . creates
   (D) well-known . . resolves
   (E) amiable . . displays

1 ___

2. Thor Heyerdahl, on the *Ra* papyrus boat, discovered floating _____ of oil in the mid-Atlantic, pointing to the continuing _____ of the seas.
   (A) cans . . commerce
   (B) mounds . . beautification
   (C) globs . . pollution
   (D) glimpses . . mining
   (E) tankers . . revival

2 ___

3. Alice Neel is an artist whose art and life are _____, one feeding the other to the mutual _____ of both.
   (A) exceptional . . surprise
   (B) intertwined . . enrichment
   (C) old-fashioned . . depiction
   (D) separated . . benefit
   (E) contemporary . . appeal

   3 ___

4. For a true _____, democracy encourages _____ opinions as well as those that support the existing state of affairs.
   (A) inference . . complementary
   (B) mandate . . conforming
   (C) elimination . . haphazard
   (D) juxtaposition . . straightforward
   (E) consensus . . heterodox

   4 ___

5. Nature films on television frequently inject a powerful plea for regulations limiting the _____ of natural areas and the inevitable _____ of wildlife.
   (A) closure . . hunting
   (B) opening . . improvement
   (C) depiction . . expansion
   (D) exploitation . . destruction
   (E) mapping . . census

   5 ___

6. Settlers from the Northeast sometimes find it difficult to _____ themselves to the low humidity and _____ beauty of the American Southwest.
   (A) transport . . luxurious
   (B) invite . . unexpected
   (C) adjust . . dank
   (D) will . . contrary
   (E) acclimate . . austere

   6 ___

7. Mike McElroy, eminent scientist and _____ professor of chemistry at Harvard, has _____ interests that carry him from the atmosphere of planets to the origins of life.
   (A) dapper . . planetary
   (B) prestigious . . wide-ranging
   (C) retiring . . enjoyable
   (D) emaciated . . biased
   (E) susceptible . . meager

   7 ___

8. Charles made a _____ bid to mend the broken relationship, but Laura _____ refused to open his letter.
   (A) hopeless . . cheerfully
   (B) tentative . . disdainfully
   (C) lighthearted . . resentfully
   (D) fanatical . . casually
   (E) pointless . . modestly

   8 ___

9. A Washington group teaches children how to _____ with handicapped children by working with puppets that show various kinds of physical _____.
   (A) converse . . activities
   (B) compete . . variations
   (C) walk . . characteristics
   (D) win . . aids
   (E) interact . . disability

   9 ___

10. As video games become more and more _____, the players become more _____ in their search for new challenges.
    (A) sophisticated . . discriminating
    (B) garish . . alert
    (C) metallic . . vigorous
    (D) alike . . idiotic
    (E) timely . . defiant

    10 ___

ENGLISH FOR THE COLLEGE BOARDS

Clues from Etymology: Summary

Review these clues from etymology from time to time. If you understand how etymology helps you learn new words, you'll do better on the SAT vocabulary test.

Clue 1 Latin Prefixes
Many English words begin with common Latin prefixes and number prefixes. Study these examples.
   advance, **ex**it, **prin**cipal, **deci**mal, **tri**ple

Clue 2 Latin Roots—Verbs
English has more words from Latin than from any other language. One root can appear in several words.
   re**fer**, con**fer**ence, trans**fer**, in**fer**red

Clue 3 Latin Roots—Nouns and Adjectives
If you know the root and prefix, you can figure out the meaning. If not, think of other words with the same elements. Then make a good guess.
   bene**fac**tor, **ben**ediction, **fac**tory

Clue 4 Greek Prefixes and Roots
As with Latin, you can figure out words with Greek origins if you know the prefixes and roots. If not, think of similar words and make a guess.
   autocratic, **auto**biography, demo**crat**ic

Clue 5 Anglo-Saxon Prefixes and Roots
Anglo-Saxon words are the everyday words. You already know the prefixes and roots because you use them all the time.

Clue 6 Suffixes
Suffixes are the third building block (after prefixes and roots). They give important clues to a word's part of speech, its meaning, and its history.
   ampl**ify**, manage**able**, moder**ate**

Clue 7 Foreign Words in English
English is a great borrower. Find the stories in borrowed words to learn and remember them.
   coach, tangerine, muslin, polka

Clue 8 The Growth of English
English keeps making new words, usually by putting together prefixes, roots, and suffixes. Words keep changing in meaning—uphill and down, broader and narrower.

Section IV: Clues from Analogies

You have undoubtedly noticed the *log* root in *analogy*. *Log* originally meant "word," but like words in English, the Greek word *logos* took on other meanings. Because words are crucial to thought, *log* was associated with thinking, as in *logic*. Then, since thinking involves weighing choices, *log* took on the additional meaning of "ratio" and "proportion." In fact, *analogy* comes from a Greek compound meaning "proportion," "in proper ratio."

In its simplest form, an analogy is like a mathematical equation.

$$2 : 4 :: 4 : 8$$

The equation says, "Two is to four as four is to eight." Four is twice two. In the same way, eight is twice four.

The SAT verbal sections use words, not numbers, to express relationships. The trick is to uncover what the word relationship is. Put an SAT-type question into equation form.

$$\text{swimming} : \text{water} :: \text{flying} : \text{air}$$

This equation says, "*Swimming* is to *water* as *flying* is to *air*." The relationship is clear. Water is the medium for swimming just as air is the medium for flying.

The order of words in each pair may be reversed, but the order in the answer must correspond to the order in the question. The previous analogy might have been stated in a different order:

$$\text{water} : \text{swimming} :: \text{air} : \text{flying}$$

How To Do Analogies

To become familiar with the *form* of the analogy, or word relationship, questions, take the following test. For this warm-up activity, the relationships are related words or opposed words.

Directions: Each question below consists of a related pair of words or phrases, followed by five lettered pairs of words or phrases, labeled A through E. Select the lettered pair that *best* expresses a relationship similar to that expressed in the original pair.

EXAMPLE:
YAWN : BOREDOM :: (A) dream : sleep
(B) anger : madness (C) smile : amusement
(D) face : expression (E) impatience : rebellion   Ⓐ Ⓑ ● Ⓓ Ⓔ

Trial Test

Write the letter for the word pair that best completes the analogy.

REPROOF : APPLAUSE :: _____
- (A) harmony : controversy
- (B) ignorance : indifference
- (C) prejudice : mischief
- (D) support : foundation
- (E) nourishment : nutrition

_____A_____

Since **applause** is an antonym of **reproof,** look for a pair of antonyms. The only pair of antonyms is *(A)*. The others are synonyms or unrelated. If the test words had been synonyms, then you'd look for synonyms in the answers.

1. EXHAUST : FATIGUE :: _____
   - (A) utensil : implement
   - (B) plunge : swim
   - (C) exertion : slumber
   - (D) confederation : officer
   - (E) generosity : greed

2. FRANKNESS : TRICKERY :: _____
   - (A) radical : tasty
   - (B) bankruptcy : insolvency
   - (C) benefit : harm
   - (D) memory : recollection
   - (E) mercy : commentary

3. AFFIRM : DENY :: _____
   - (A) converse : declare
   - (B) follow : pursue
   - (C) check : inhibit
   - (D) endeavor : attempt
   - (E) prosper : fail

4. MISFORTUNE : TRIBULATION ::
   - (A) affliction : sanitation
   - (B) fluid : food
   - (C) repute : uncertainty
   - (D) suggestion : denunciation
   - (E) injustice : unfairness

25 TYPES OF ANALOGIES

You may find up to 25 types of analogies in the SAT. For convenience, we will take up these types in groups of five, beginning with antonyms.

Clues from Analogies: 1–5

Clue
1. Word : Opposed Word
2. Word : Related Word
3. Part : Whole, or Whole : Part
4. Cause : Effect
5. Container : Something Contained

Problem 1. Word : Opposed Word

STRAIGHTFORWARD : LIAR :: _____
- (A) brilliant : genius
- (B) dreary : onlooker
- (C) popular : outcast
- (D) generous : friend
- (E) sympathetic : artisan

Strategy.   Though *antonym* is defined as "a word having a meaning opposite to that of another word," the relationship is not that of word and antonym. Pairs of antonyms are the same part of speech. They may be adjectives: *hot-cold*; nouns: *victory-defeat*; verbs: *find-lose*; or other parts of speech: *in-out*; *cheerfully-glumly*. This analogy uses *straightforward*, an adjective, and *liar*, a noun.

The idea of *brilliance* is associated with *genius,* not opposed to it. Eliminate *(A)*. The idea of *dreariness* does not seem to be related to *onlooker*. Eliminate *(B)*. The idea of *generosity* is more likely to be associated with *friend* than opposed to it. Eliminate *(D)*. The idea of *sympathy* does not seem to be associated with an *artisan* (a skilled worker). Eliminate *(E)*.

Elimination leaves us with *(C)*. If you are *popular,* you will not be an *outcast. Popular* and *outcast* are opposed in meaning in the same way as are **straightforward** and **liar.** *(C)* is the correct answer. You may find the answer immediately without eliminating the others, but the process of elimination just demonstrated is an extra check.

It helps to put the analogy in the form of a sentence. In the example just given, the sentence would look like this:

Statement: If you are *straightforward,* then you will not be a *liar.*

Now put the alternatives into the same form to see how they fit.

(A) If you are *brilliant,* then you will not be a *genius.*
(B) If you are *dreary,* then you will not be an *onlooker.*
(C) If you are *popular,* then you will not be an *outcast.*
(D) If you are *generous,* then you will not be a *friend.*
(E) If you are *sympathetic,* then you will not be an *artisan.*

Again *(C)* proves to be correct.

Sometimes it helps to turn the word pair around. For the question just given, we might have constructed this sentence: A **liar** is not **straightforward.**

Both statements say essentially the same thing. Feel free to put your statement into the form most helpful to you. Always be sure that you keep the *same word order* when you test your possibilities in the statement.

Sometimes an alternative way of devising the statement is helpful, though it is less simple than the suggestion given.

Statement: In the same way that a **liar** is not **straightforward,** so an *outcast* is not *popular.*

The disadvantage of this kind of statement is its length. Its advantage is that it focuses more directly on the relationship. It brings the correct alternative into the statement.

Look at a question from the SAT.

Problem

IMMEDIATELY : DELAY :: _____
- (A) voluntarily : motive
- (B) urgently : aid
- (C) continuously : effort
- (D) flawlessly : error
- (E) accidentally : injury

Strategy.   Once again the ideas are opposed, but the words are not antonyms. **Immediately** is an adverb and **delay** is a noun. (We can assume **delay**
is not a verb here because the alternatives seem to have nouns as second
words.) The ideas being contrasted are *immediate* action and *delayed* action.

Let's put the analogy into the form of a sentence.

Statement: If we act *immediately,* we'll not be subject to *delay.*

We can put the alternatives into the same form.

- *(A)* If we act *voluntarily,* we'll not be subject to *motive.*
- *(B)* If we act *urgently,* we'll not be subject to *aid.*
- *(C)* If we act *continuously,* we'll not be subject to *effort.*
- *(D)* If we act *flawlessly,* we'll not be subject to *error.*
- *(E)* If we act *accidentally,* we'll not be subject to *injury.*

Clearly the only alternative that makes sense is *(D).*

Some SAT questions, like this one, do not contain any difficult words.
The problem is just to work out the relationship between the two test words.
Sometimes, however, several words in the test are more challenging. Then
you should draw upon the skills you learned earlier in this book.

Suppose, for example, you meet a pair like this: EUPHONIOUS : DIS-
SONANT. A knowledge of common prefixes and roots is the key here. From
eu (well) and *phon* (sound) we have a word meaning "having a beautiful
sound," "harmonious." From *dis* ("apart") and *son* ("sound") we have a
word with an opposite meaning: "having a bad combination of sounds,"
"discordant." These words are obviously antonyms.

The type of idea-*opposition* in the test question above is a frequent device
in SAT analogy questions. Occasionally, however, idea-*similarity* appears in
test words. Examine an SAT question.

Problem 2. Word : Related Word

STRUT : OSTENTATIOUS :: _____
- (A) vacillate : modest
- (B) cringe : servile
- (C) flinch : indolent
- (D) waver : arrogant
- (E) sputter : fastidious

Strategy. This time the words are almost synonymous in meaning, not opposed. As in the previous examples, however, the words are of different parts of speech. **Strut** is a verb and **ostentatious** is an adjective. To **strut** is to "walk showily, in a self-important way." Peacocks **strut.** Cocky persons **strut.** Persons who wear too much jewelry are **ostentatious.** People who act in extravagant ways are **ostentatious.** Call upon your previous associations with these words to get a sense of their central meaning. Then put the words into sentence form.

Statement: Those who *strut* are *ostentatious.*

If you put all the alternatives into sentence form, only one makes sense.

Those who *cringe* are *servile.*

Alternatives *(A)*, *(C)*, and *(E)* have words apparently unrelated. Alternative *(D)* has opposed words. Those who waver are *not* likely to be arrogant. Alternative *(B)* is the correct answer.

One of the test words may be used figuratively. Study the following problem.

Problem

ADORN : EXAGGERATE :: _____
    (A) empower : diminish
    (B) replenish : reaffirm
    (C) furbish : absorb
    (D) soak : saturate
    (E) crochet : create

Strategy. **Adorn** and **exaggerate** are related, but how? The relationships in *(A)–(E)* are varied, but there is a pair of synonyms: *soak : saturate.* Could **adorn** and **exaggerate** be synonyms? Think of a sentence like the following:

Tom Sawyer loved to **adorn** his stories with fancy and imagination.

The word **adorn,** which basically means "add decorations to," has a figurative meaning. If we tell stories and *add decorations,* we **exaggerate.** The correct answer is *(D).* See "figurative language," pages 51–55.

Problem 3. Part : Whole, or Whole : Part

HUB : WHEEL :: _____
    (A) diameter : circle
    (B) apex : triangle
    (C) eye : hurricane
    (D) clasp : tie
    (E) top : desk

Strategy. The relationship between **hub** and **wheel** is that of the part to the whole. The relationship is a little more specific, though. What part of the wheel is the hub? The center. If we put the relationship into sentence form, it would look like this:

Statement: The *hub* is the center of the *wheel*.

Note that all the alternatives show the part-to-the-whole relationship, but only *(C)* has the exact relationship.

The *eye* is the center of the *hurricane*.

A hasty choice would be *(A)*, since *circle* and **wheel** are so closely related. But the diameter is not the center of the circle.

Some questions are solved merely by finding general relationships, like *part* : *whole*. If *eye* : *hurricane* did not appear on this question, you'd be able to take the general answer, *diameter* : *circle*. Often, however, you must find special relationships within the general relationships, as in this question. The hub is not just *part* of the wheel. It's the *center* of the wheel. The eye is not just *part* of the hurricane. It's the *center* of the hurricane.

Remember that all the terms in this question could have been inverted without changing the essential relationship.

WHEEL : HUB :: hurricane : eye

As we analyze other analogy questions, consider that the relationships might also be expressed in inverted form. It would not, however, be correct to choose the following relationship.

HUB : WHEEL :: hurricane : eye

It's all right to reverse both pairs, but *not just one*.

Problem 4. Cause : Effect

WINCE : PAIN :: _____
    (A) forget : confidence
    (B) tremble : fright
    (C) grovel : embarrassment
    (D) glower : anguish
    (E) growl : delight

Strategy. In this question from a past SAT, **wince** and **pain** are directly related by cause and effect. **Pain** is the cause and **wince** is the effect.

Now if we put the possible answers into statement form, only one makes sense.

Fright causes a person to *tremble*.

The question might have been harder. One of the possible answers for *(A)* might have been *laugh : joke*. This possible answer also shows a causal relationship. A *joke* causes a person to *laugh*. Answer *(B)* is still better, however, because *fright* and **pain** are both negative, while *joke* is positive.

Remember: The order of words in the question must correspond to the order of words in the answer. To *grovel* might cause *embarrassment,* but the order is reversed.

Problem 5. Container : Something Contained

VALUABLES : SAFE :: _____
(A) jewelry : gemstone
(B) water : droplet
(C) dessert : dish
(D) corn : granary
(E) fish : ocean

Strategy. This is a popular type of question, appearing in many forms. Here the container is **safe** and the thing contained, **valuables.** Put the relationship into statement form.

Statement: *Valuables* are stored in a *safe*.

Although *dessert* is served on a *dish,* it is not stored in a dish. We can reject *(C)*. Although *fish* live in the *ocean,* they are not stored in the ocean. Note that the relationship is one where the storing is done by people. People store valuables in a safe. The correct answer is clearly *(D)*. *Corn* is stored in a *granary*.

Review

1. Word : Opposed Word
2. Word : Related Word
3. Part : Whole, or Whole: Part
4. Cause : Effect
5. Container : Something Contained

The five analogy types appear in the following five questions, but in a different order. Try your skill. To get you started, a statement is provided for the first question.

ENGLISH FOR THE COLLEGE BOARDS

Write the letter for the word pair that best completes the analogy.

1. GROUCHY : COMPLAINER :: _____
   (A) dry : desert
   (B) flaky : teacup
   (C) pitiless : celebrity
   (D) comical : tragedian
   (E) barren : poetry

   Statement: **A complainer** tends to be **grouchy.**

2. DEFIANT : RESIGNATION :: _____
   (A) vigorous : health
   (B) humdrum : weakness
   (C) commonplace : situation
   (D) lovable : laughter
   (E) humble : arrogance

3. OPERATION : SCAR :: _____
   (A) fire : ashes
   (B) substitution : replacement
   (C) repetition : novelty
   (D) explosion : blast
   (E) landslide : tunnel

4. STEM : LEAF :: _____
   (A) dog : kennel
   (B) wall switch : lamp
   (C) landscaping : house
   (D) toe : foot
   (E) letter : stamp

5. HANGAR : AIRPLANE :: _____
   (A) waterfall : water
   (B) clock : numerals
   (C) book : novel
   (D) route : directions
   (E) terminal : bus

SUMMARY
Clues from Analogies: 1–5

Clue 1. Word : Opposed Word
   STRAIGHTFORWARD : LIAR :: popular : outcast

Clue 2. Word : Related Word
   STRUT : OSTENTATIOUS :: cringe : servile

Clue 3. Part : Whole, or Whole : Part
   HUB : WHEEL :: eye : hurricane

Clue 4. Cause : Effect
   WINCE : PAIN :: tremble : fright

Clue 5. Container : Something Contained
   VALUABLES : SAFE :: corn : granary

Clues from Analogies : 6–10

Clue
   6. Tool : Activity or Object
   7. Lesser : Greater Degree of Intensity

8. Smaller : Larger
9. General Term : Specific Term
10. Action : Object Acted Upon, or Result of Action

Problem 6. Tool : Activity or Object

RACKET : TENNIS :: _____
  (A) puck : hockey
  (B) rifle : duck
  (C) hammer : nail
  (D) ball : soccer
  (E) bat : baseball

Strategy.   Obviously this is a tool or implement and the activity or object it is used for. Put this analogy into statement form.

Statement: A *racket* is used in the activity of *tennis.*

Put the various possibilities into statement form.

  (A) A *puck* is used in the activity of *hockey.*
  (B) A *rifle* is used in the activity of *duck.*
  (C) A *hammer* is used in the activity of *nail.*
  (D) A *ball* is used in the activity of *soccer.*
  (E) A *bat* is used in the activity of *baseball.*

We can discard *(B)* and (C) immediately, but *(A)*, *(D)*, and *(E)* all seem possible. When such a situation occurs, you must refine the statement even more. What is the special relationship between **racket** and **tennis?** A **racket** is held in the hand. When we spot that special relationship, we discard *(A)* and *(D)*. We decide that *(E)* is correct. A *bat*, like a **racket,** is held in the hand.

We can state the special relationship like this.

A **racket,** held in the hand, is used in the activity of **tennis.**

Problem 7. Lesser : Greater Degree of Intensity

RIPPLE : TIDAL WAVE :: _____
  (A) breeze : hurricane
  (B) blizzard : avalanche
  (C) valley : earthquake
  (D) puddle : downpour
  (E) rock : waterfall

Strategy.   What is the relationship of **ripple** to **tidal wave?** Both are obviously waves of a kind. A ripple is a tiny wave. A tidal wave is an enormous wave. The two objects are similar, but they differ enormously in degree. Look at the statement.

If we try the statement with all the possibilities, only one makes sense: *(A)* breeze : hurricane. A breeze is a very minor form of a hurricane.

Though the other possibilities all show relationships, the relationships are not the same. A *puddle* is small compared with a *downpour,* but a puddle is not a small *form* of a downpour. It's the *result.* A *blizzard* may cause an *avalanche,* but a blizzard is not a small form of an avalanche. A *valley* may be created by an *earthquake* or afflicted by an earthquake, but the two are not related in intensity. *Rock* and *waterfall* are associated in space but not in degree.

Problem 8. Smaller : Larger

MILL : PENNY :: _____
(A) silver : quarter
(B) currency : nickel
(C) dime : dollar
(D) check : cash
(E) wallet : money

Strategy. A **mill** is a "thousandth of a cent." (Remember the number prefix *mill?* See page 80.) Though it is not an actual coin, it is used in various tax computations. The relationship, expressed in statement form, is simple.

Statement: A *mill* is a smaller percentage of a **penny.**

Silver is not a smaller percentage of a *quarter.* Silver is actually no longer used in a quarter. *Currency* is not a smaller percentage of a *nickel.* A nickel is currency. A *check* is not a smaller percentage of *cash.* A check is an alternative to cash. A *wallet* is not a smaller percentage of *money.* A wallet holds money. The only possible answer is *(C), dime : dollar.* A *dime* is a smaller percentage of a *dollar.*

Problem 9. General Term : Specific Term

TALK : WHISPER :: _____
(A) discover : deteriorate
(B) fly : tour
(C) listen : disagree
(D) walk : amble
(E) jump : marvel

Strategy. Both **talk** and **whisper** refer to the same basic activity, but one is a general term and one is specific. Put the relationship into statement form.

Statement: *Whispering* is a special kind of **talking.**

The only possibility is *(D), walk : amble. Ambling* is a special kind of *walking*.

Problem 10. Action : Object Acted Upon, or Result of Action

WEAVE : CLOTH :: _____
- (A) destroy : barricade
- (B) write : narrative
- (C) call : messenger
- (D) droop : trees
- (E) reduce : statue

Strategy. The simplest relationship is verb-object.

Statement: Someone *weaves cloth.*

The best answer is *(B), write : narrative.* Someone *writes* a *narrative.*

Both *(A)* and *(C)* make sense in the statement, but there is an important difference between these and the test pair. **Weaving cloth** is positive, constructive, creative. So is *writing a narrative.* There is, however, nothing particularly constructive in *destroying a barricade* or *calling a messenger.* Sometimes you have to take your statement a step further when you see how the various possibilities fit into the statement framework. If you wanted to revise the statement, it might look something like this.

Statement: Someone *weaves cloth* and performs a constructive action.

Let's look at another example: Action : Result.

Problem

ELECT : INAUGURATION :: _____
- (A) attempt : oblivion
- (B) grow : uncertainty
- (C) drill : hole
- (D) climb : tree
- (E) success : study

Strategy. The simplest relationship is action : result of action.

Statement: To *elect* a candidate results in an ***inauguration.***

The best answer is *(C),* drill : hole. To *drill* results in a *hole.*

Alternative *(E)* seems to make sense. To *study* results in *success.* Note, however, that the words in the alternative are reversed. Here the result is the first member of the pair. In the test pair, the result is the second member. In *(D),* the relationship is action: object acted upon. Both *(A)* and *(B)* are not related to the test pair.

Review

1. SING : ARIA :: _____
   (A) devour : pastry
   (B) recite : poem
   (C) win : encounter
   (D) approve : decision
   (E) allow : exception

2. BOOKLET : TOME :: _____
   (A) essay : biography
   (B) tree : shrub
   (C) lake : waterfall
   (D) friend : foe
   (E) kitten : cat

3. ANNOY : ENRAGE :: _____
   (A) annex : reject
   (B) erase : disapprove
   (C) disembark : enlist
   (D) emancipate : flatter
   (E) decorate : embellish

4. LAUGH : GUFFAW :: _____
   (A) look : scrutinize
   (B) lead : follow
   (C) discover : invent
   (D) drive : putt
   (E) missive : arrow

5. PLANE : CARPENTRY :: _____
   (A) beetle : gardening
   (B) tree : forestry
   (C) reel : fishing
   (D) house : painting
   (E) tiger : cage

SUMMARY

Clues from Analogies: 6–10

Clue 6. Tool : Activity or Object
RACKET : TENNIS :: bat : baseball

Clue 7. Lesser : Greater Degree of Intensity
RIPPLE : TIDAL WAVE :: breeze : hurricane

Clue 8. Smaller : Larger
MILL : PENNY :: dime : dollar

Clue 9. General Term : Specific Term
TALK : WHISPER :: walk : amble

Clue 10. Action : Object Acted Upon, or Result of Action
WEAVE : CLOTH :: write : narrative

Remember, if you think of analogies as challenging games rather than difficult types of verbal questions, you will have an easier time preparing for this part of the SAT.

Clues from Analogies: 11–15

Clue

11. Persons : What They Do or Act Upon, or How They Are Acted Upon
12. Persons : Quality or Condition Associated With
13. Person : Person, Subject, or Place Associated With
14. Person : Purpose
15. Person or Activity : Important Tool

In this group, someone is related to an activity, a quality, an instrument, a purpose, or a place. Look at some of these specifically.

Problem 11. Persons : What They Do or Act Upon, or How They Are Acted Upon

MAGICIAN : DELUDES :: _____
   (A) potentate : obeys
   (B) swimmer : relaxes
   (C) comedian : entertains
   (D) welder : rivets
   (E) acrobat : complains

Strategy.   Here someone is doing something to someone. The statement is simple.

> **Statement: The *magician deludes* an audience.**
>
> The only alternative that fits is *(C), comedian : entertains*. The *comedian entertains* an audience.
>
> Although the other possibilities show someone doing something, they lack the idea of an audience associated with *magician*. After you have decided upon the relationship and checked the other possible answers, you may have to make the relationship a little more specific.

The question above showed the relationship between the person, the **magician,** and the verb **deludes.** Sometimes a question will show the relationship between the person and an object.

LOGGER : TREES

The **logger** acts upon the *trees*. A correct pair would have to show a similar relationship—for example, *farmer : wheatfield*.

In questions of this type an *animal* might replace a *person:*

MOLE : LAWN

A mole certainly acts upon a lawn.

Sometimes the person is not doing the acting but is acted upon.

Problem

DEPOSED : RULER :: _____

    (A) checkmated : chess player
    (B) watchdog : bark
    (C) employee : discharged
    (D) manuscript : writer
    (E) surgeon : operates

Strategy. The simplest relationship is person : how acted upon.

> **Statement:** A *ruler* may be *deposed.*
>
>   Both *(A)* and *(C)* suggest the desired relationship. A *chess player* may be *checkmated.* An *employee* may be *discharged.* Note, however, that the words are reversed in alternative *(C),* eliminating this as a possibility. The remaining alternatives show a different relationship —person : what he or she does or acts upon.

Note that the original pairing suggests a negative result. The king ordinarily doesn't wish to be deposed. Suppose the test included this alternative:

(E) feted : celebrity

This is tricky; it shows the desired relationship. When a celebrity is feted, he or she is acted upon. But the relationship here is positive, not negative as in the test pair. Thus *(A)* would still clearly be the answer.

Problem 12. Person : Quality or Condition Associated With

PILGRIM : PIETY :: _____

    (A) explorer : curiosity
    (B) miser : poverty
    (C) gambler : winner
    (D) knight : beauty
    (E) monk : loneliness

Strategy. The relationship here is one of an essential quality. **Piety** is the central core of a **pilgrim.** The statement might look like this.

Statement: The essential quality of a pilgrim is piety.

Now analyze the answers. The essential quality of an *explorer* is indeed *curiosity.* *(A)* seems to be the correct answer, but try the others. *Poverty* is not the essential quality of a *miser,* though under certain circumstances a miser might be poor. Being a *winner* is, unfortunately, not an essential quality of a *gambler.* Losing may outweigh winning. *Beauty* is not the essential quality of a *knight.* Some monks may be lonely, but *loneliness* is not the essential quality of a *monk.* A monk usually chooses the monastery because he is able to be alone much of the time. *(A)* is indeed correct.

Don't be misled by similar words in the choices. In this question you might associate **pilgrim** and *monk,* since both have religious motivations. The relationship between **pilgrim** and **piety** on the one hand and between *monk* and *loneliness* on the other are not similar. Always look for relationships, not merely associations or shared meanings of a word in each pair.

The relationship may also show a *lack* of an associated quality or condition.

Problem

EGOIST : ALTRUISM :: _____
- (A) saint : virtue
- (B) courage : coward
- (C) moderator : tact
- (D) criminal : honesty
- (E) performer : skill

Strategy

> **Statement:** An *egoist lacks* the quality of **altruism.**
>
> Both *(B)* and *(D)* suggest the desired relationship. A *coward* lacks *courage.* A *criminal* lacks *honesty.* Note, however, that the words are reversed in *(B),* clearing the way for *(D)* as the correct answer. Both *(A)* and *(C)* are good examples of the relationship described above—person : associated quality. In *(E),* a performer may or may not display skill.

Problem 13. Person : Person, Subject, or Place Associated With

LABORATORY : TECHNICIAN :: _____
- (A) stream : trout
- (B) studio : sculptor
- (C) factory : ranger
- (D) discovery : scientist
- (E) play : musician

Strategy. The relationship is between a worker and the place he or she works in. The statement is simple.

> **Statement:** A *technician* works in a *laboratory.*
>
> Though a *trout* is indeed found in a *stream,* it does not work there. The correct answer is *(B), studio : sculptor.* A *sculptor* works in a *studio.*

Note that we have reversed the order of words in our statement. We might also have created this statement.

A *laboratory* is a place where a *technician* works.

The first statement is a little simpler. It doesn't matter whether or not we reverse the paired words. The important point is to test the possibilities in the same order.

A *studio* is a place where a *sculptor* works.

Let's look at another related example: Persons: What They Acquire.

Problem

HEIR : BEQUEST :: _____
- (A) books : bibliophile
- (B) child : measles
- (C) graduate : diploma
- (D) riveter : skyscraper
- (E) tractor : farmer

Strategy. Here the relationship is between a person and something positive acquired.

Statement: An *heir* acquires a *bequest*.

The best answer is *(C)*. Just as an heir acquires a bequest, so a *graduate* acquires a *diploma*. The acquisition is positive, not negative as in *(B)*. In *(A)* and *(E)*, the paired words are reversed. In *(D)*, a *riveter* may work on a *skyscraper*, but he or she doesn't acquire one.

Problem 14. Person : Purpose

ALCHEMIST : TRANSMUTATION :: _____
- (A) traitor : loyalty
- (B) proselytizer : conversion
- (C) scientist : equivocation
- (D) anarchist : tranquillity
- (E) astronomer : consternation

Strategy. Here the relationship is between a person and his or her major goal. An alchemist sought to transmute baser metals into gold. Here's the statement.

Statement: A major purpose of the *alchemist* was *transmutation*.

As we have already noted, some analogies present fairly easy words, with the major problem that of finding relationships. Other analogies, however, present more difficult words as here. In your own reading you probably have come across the word **alchemist.** If you have, you probably remember the two major goals of these forerunners of modern chemistry: finding the elixir (or lengthener) of life and transmuting (or changing) other metals into gold. If you cannot recall anything about alchemists, your best course is an educated guess, using whatever clues you can derive from the pairs of words provided.

Even if you don't know one or both of the original pair, you can deduce the answer just by studying the possible answers.

You know immediately that *loyalty* does not go with *traitor*. This is a negative association. You also know that *tranquillity* is not likely to go with *anarchist*. This is another negative association. If there are two negative pairs, the answer probably is *not* a negative pair. (Otherwise there might be a conflict between the two.) *Consternation* does not go with *astronomer*. (*Constellation* would be possible, but not *consternation*.) We now have three negative pairs.

Look further at the problem. *Equivocation* by derivation means "speaking equally." Equivocation is using terms with two or more possible meanings, being confusing. Scientists try to avoid being confusing. Thus *(C)* contains another negative pair. Negative elements are contained in all but *(B)*. Thus *(B)* would be a good guess. As it happens, those who proselytize do try to convert. Just as **alchemists** are interested in **transmutation,** so *proselytizers* are interested in *conversion*.

This detailed analysis shows that even seemingly hopeless situations sometimes yield to careful analysis. Don't spend an excessive amount of time on any one question, however. But if you do have time, don't give up without calling upon all your resources.

Problem 15. Person or Activity : Important Tool

GARDENER : HOE :: _____
- (A) welder : apron
- (B) halfback : helmet
- (C) astronomer : chart
- (D) woodsman : axe
- (E) weaver : saw

Strategy. The relationship between **hoe** and **gardener** is that between tool and worker. A glance at the other possibilities suggests we have to be more specific. We cannot just say, "A **gardener** uses a **hoe**." A *welder* uses an *apron*. A *halfback* uses a *helmet*. An *astronomer* uses a *chart*. We can, at any rate, immediately discard *(E)*. A *weaver* does not use a *saw*. But how shall we discriminate among the others? A **gardener** applies the **hoe** to the materials he or she works with. In the same way a *woodsman* applies the *axe* to the material he works with. Garden soil and wood are materials handled by hoe and axe. We can discard the other possibilities and word the sentence like this.

Statement: The *gardener* uses an important hand tool, the *hoe*.

Since *helmet, apron,* and *chart* are not tools in the same sense, we can be sure *(D)*, *woodsman : axe* is the correct answer.

Review

1. INTERN : HOSPITAL :: _____
   (A) farmer : factory
   (B) flight attendant : travel agency
   (C) teller : bank
   (D) navigator : classroom
   (E) author : theater

2. COMBATANT : VICTORY :: _____
   (A) programmer : computer
   (B) professor : travel
   (C) pyromaniac : surgery
   (D) penitent : forgiveness
   (E) photographer : silhouette

3. ANGLER : CASTS :: _____
   (A) golfer : drives
   (B) soprano : sings
   (C) entrepreneur : loses
   (D) economist : delays
   (E) contributor : peruses

4. CONDUCTOR : BATON :: _____
   (A) violin : bow
   (B) magician : wand
   (C) soldier : spectacles
   (D) globe-trotter : shoes
   (E) senator : representative

5. ROGUE : GUILE :: _____
   (A) dentist : drill
   (B) doctor : surgeon
   (C) philanthropist : generosity
   (D) denizen : cruelty
   (E) recluse : joy

SUMMARY

Clues from Analogies: 11–15

Clue 11. Persons : What They Do or Act Upon, or How They Are Acted Upon
   MAGICIAN : DELUDES :: comedian : entertains

Clue 12. Person : Quality or Condition Associated With
   PILGRIM : PIETY :: explorer : curiosity

Clue 13. Person : Person, Subject, or Place Associated With
   LABORATORY : TECHNICIAN :: studio : sculptor

Clue 14. Person : Purpose
   ALCHEMIST : TRANSMUTATION :: proselytizer : conversion

Clue 15. Person or Activity : Important Tool
   GARDENER : HOE :: woodsman : axe

Clues from Analogies: 16–20

Clue
16. Something : Associated Quality, or Essential Quality or Condition
17. Something : A Form or Degree of
18. Something : Something Affected by or Associated With
19. Something : Something Studied
20. Something : Unit of Measurement

In this group, relationships are expressed between something and something else: an activity, a quality, an instrument, a purpose, a place, a result. Examine some of these relationships.

The associated quality may be negative as well as positive. Note the following SAT question:

Problem 16. Something : Associated Quality, or Essential Quality or Condition

CIRCUMLOCUTORY : SPEECH :: _____
(A) humorous : joke
(B) meandering : path
(C) tactless : remark
(D) successful : attack
(E) logical : conclusion

Strategy. **Circumlocutory** is a quality associated with some speeches. Here the special relationship is the indirectness of the speech. All five choices show associated qualities, like a *humorous joke* or a *tactless remark*. Here the special quality is the wandering nature of the speech. Therefore *(B)*, *meandering : path* is correct. Just as some speeches wander, so some paths meander. Note that the associated word **circumlocutory** has a negative connotation. The associations may not always be positive. Look at another example.

Problem

OBSOLESCENCE : DISUSED :: _____
(A) diversity : varied
(B) obstinacy : voided
(C) disability : vigorous
(D) investigation : thorough
(E) distress : curious

Strategy. If **obsolescence** is an unfamiliar word, you can use the smaller word inside the word as a clue: *obsolete*. You may recall the suffix *escent* meaning *becoming*. **Obsolescence** is the "condition of becoming obsolete, out of date." The helpful prefix *dis*, meaning *not*, suggests that **disused** means "not being used."

We can summarize the relationship here in our usual statement.

Statement: In *obsolescence*, things are inevitably *disused*.

The first possibility, *(A)*, immediately pops out as an answer.

In *diversity*, things are inevitably *varied*.

Look at the other possibilities. The only one that must give us pause is *(D)*.

In *investigation*, things are inevitably *thorough*.

Being *disused* is an essential characteristic of *obsolescence*. Being *thorough* is not an essential characteristic of *investigation*. An investigation may be careless, sloppy, or superficial.

The correct answer, *(A)*, *diversity : varied*, best shows the relationship.

Problem

PUZZLING : MYSTERY :: _____
  (A) house : sturdy
  (B) flea-bitten : dog
  (C) leafy : tree
  (D) church : religious
  (E) impartial : arbitrator

Strategy. Here the relationship is between something and its essential (not merely associated) quality.

Statement: A *mystery* is essentially *puzzling*.

The reverse order eliminates *(A)* and *(D)* out of hand. The best answer is *(E)*. An *arbitrator* should be *impartial*. Not all dogs have fleas *(B)*. Not all trees have leaves *(C)*; some have needles.

Problem 17. Something : A Form or Degree of

DISAGREEMENT : ALTERCATION :: _____
  (A) distress : upset
  (B) equality : compensation
  (C) scheme : conspiracy
  (D) correspondence : envy
  (E) construction : blueprint

Strategy. An **altercation** is a form of **disagreement**. More specifically, it shows a greater degree of **disagreement**. An altercation is a heated, angry disagreement. The sentence might look like this.

Statement: An *altercation* is a more intense form of *disagreement*.

A *conspiracy* is a more intense form of *scheme*.

If we try the various possibilities, we find that *(C)* fits.

Distress is a more intense form of *upset,* but the words are reversed, so *(A), distress : upset,* is incorrect. Although *blueprint* and *construction (E)* are related, *blueprint* is a help in *construction.* It is not a more intense form of *construction.*

You may not know one of the words in the example pair. If there are no clues within the unfamiliar word, try to guess the meaning by examining the possible answers. There is little apparent relationship between the paired words in *(B)* and *(D)*. In *(E), blueprint* is used to guide *construction.* It is unlikely that an altercation (even if you don't know it) is used to *guide* argument. Eliminating *(B), (D),* and *(E)* reduces the possibilities to two and increases your chances of guessing right.

If you look at *(A)* and *(C),* you notice that one member in each pair is a more intense form of the other. **Disagreement** is negative, and so are *distress* and *scheme.* Both are good possibilities. Which shall you choose? Is **disagreement** a more intense form of **altercation,** Or is **altercation** a more intense form of **disagreement?** Since **disagreement** is a fairly mild word, **altercation** is probably a more intense form. Thus you could guess that *(C)* is the answer even if you're not exactly sure what **altercation** means.

If you have time, you'll find many unexpected clues in the way the analogies are arranged and paired.

Problem 18. Something : Something Affected by or Associated With

> PLOW : SOIL :: _____
>   (A) message : decipher
>   (B) grow : vegetables
>   (C) wear : clothes
>   (D) prune : fruit trees
>   (E) reach : solution

Strategy. Here something is being affected by an object. The **soil** is **plowed.** We can reject *(A)* because the words are reversed. We may *decipher* a *message.* We don't *message* a *decipher.* All the other possibilities seem to fit—on first check. We can *grow vegetables, wear clothes, prune fruit trees,* and *reach a solution.* Is there some special characteristic of plowing soil? Plowing involves cutting into the soil. *Pruning* involves cutting into branches of trees. The special relationship calls for *(D), prune : fruit trees.*

Statement: We *plow soil* by cutting into it.

166   **ENGLISH FOR THE COLLEGE BOARDS**

Problem

PARCHMENT : PAPER :: _____
  (A) dog : kennel
  (B) friend : acquaintance
  (C) quill : ballpoint pen
  (D) table : dining room
  (E) title page : book

Strategy. All five possibilities are associated in some way. The task is to find the right relationship. Parchment was used before paper and eventually gave way to paper for all but highly specialized uses. In the same way a quill gave way to a ballpoint pen. Thus, *(C),* quill : ballpoint pen, is correct.

There are several other analogy types that are linked with the associations suggested in Problem 18.

Sometimes the relationship is one of having or lacking.

Problem

FOOD : STARVATION :: _____
  (A) peace of mind : remorse
  (B) rejection : inquisitiveness
  (C) challenge : excitement
  (D) disease : immunity
  (E) sense of humor : laughter

Strategy. Here the relationship is between the lack of something and the result.

> **Statement:** If you don't have *food,* you experience *starvation.*
>
> The best answer is *(A).* If you don't have *peace of mind,* you experience *remorse.* Alternative *(D)* isn't bad, but the items are reversed. The other alternatives suggest the *having* rather than the *lack.*

Sometimes the relationship is one of goal and purpose.

Problem

BASKETBALL : BASKET :: _____
  (A) skier : skis
  (B) football : goal line
  (C) baseball : fly ball
  (D) racquet : tennis
  (E) marathon : runner

Strategy. Here the relationship is between something and the goal it is designed for.

Statement: The *goal* of **basketball** is finding the **basket.**

If we try out each alternative, only *(B)* makes sense: the goal of *football* is finding the *goal line.* The goal of the skier *(A)* is not skis. The goal of baseball *(C)* is not the fly ball. It may be caught. The remaining two are reversed, but even if put in the same order as the test pair, they do not qualify. The goal of tennis is not the racquet. The goal of the runner may or may not be the marathon.

Problem

AFTERTHOUGHT : IDEA :: _____
  (A) Labor Day : Thanksgiving
  (B) turkey : dessert
  (C) engagement : marriage
  (D) correspondence : telephone
  (E) solution : problem

Strategy.   Here the relationship is one of time.

Statement: *Idea* precedes *afterthought* OR *afterthought* follows *idea.*

All alternatives but one, *(D)*, suggest a time relationship. Only *(E)* has the pair in the same order as the test pair. A problem precedes its solution. The time order is reversed in *(A)*, *(B)*, and *(C)*.

Problem 19. Something : Something Studied

PSYCHOLOGY : PERSONALITY :: ____
  (A) physiology : philosophy
  (B) genetics : heredity
  (C) botany : animals
  (D) ecology : finance
  (E) oceanography : shipbuilding

Strategy.   The relationship is that between a science and the subject of study.

Statement: *Psychology* is the study of *personality.*

Substituting the possible answers we find that *(B)*, *genetics* : *heredity,* fits perfectly.

Genetics is the study of *heredity.*

Botany (C) is the study of plants, not *animals. Physiology (A)* is not related to *philosophy. Ecology (D)* has little direct relationship with *finance.* Shipbuilders *(E)* may help oceanographers by providing transportation, but the relationship stops at that point.

Problem 20. Something : Unit of Measurement

DISTANCE : KILOMETERS ::_____
- (A) emotion : laughter
- (B) duration : years
- (C) achievement : salary
- (D) light : brilliance
- (E) surgery : scalpel

Strategy. Our statement is simple.

> **Statement.** *Distance* is measured in units called *kilometers*.
>
> The best possibility is *(B)*, *duration : years*.
>
> *Duration* is measured in units called *years*.
>
> *Emotion (A)* and *laughter* are associated, but laughter is not a unit of measurement. *Brilliance (D)* is a quality of *light*, but again it is not a unit of measurement. *Scalpel (E)* is an instrument used in *surgery*, but it doesn't measure. To some people, *salary* may be a measure of *achievement*, but in any case salary is not a unit of measurement. If *dollars* had been provided instead of *salary*, you'd still have chosen *(B)*. *Years* is a universally accepted unit of elapsed time. Dollars is not a universally accepted unit of achievement.

Occasionally the suggestion of measurement may be expressed in ways other than units.

Problem

HEIGHT : MOUNTAIN :: _____
- (A) lake : purity
- (B) toxic waste : dispersal
- (C) depth : ocean
- (D) potatoes : weight
- (E) position : longitude

Strategy. Here the idea of measurement is present but the relationship is not suggested in units like miles, pounds, or degrees.

> **Statement:** One *measurement* of a *mountain* is its *height*.
>
> One *measurement* of an *ocean* is its *depth (C)*. Both *(D)* and *(E)* would be correct if in the right order. Both *(A)* and *(B)* have nothing to do with measurement.

Review

Clue 16. Something : Associated Quality
Clue 17. Something : Form or Degree of
Clue 18. Something : Something Affected by or Associated With
Clue 19. Something : Something Studied
Clue 20. Something : Unit of Measurement

The five analogy types appear in the following five questions. Try your skill. Write the letter for the pair that best completes each analogy.

1. CAPACITY : PECK :: _____
   (A) bushel : quart
   (B) size : nibble
   (C) pound : kilogram
   (D) volume : liquid
   (E) area : acre

2. EDIT : MANUSCRIPT :: _____
   (A) find : excuses
   (B) swallow : medication
   (C) revise : plans
   (D) scan : billboards
   (E) win : contest

3. CARTOGRAPHY : MAPS :: _____
   (A) ballistics : projectiles
   (B) hydraulics : sailboats
   (C) anatomy : surgeons
   (D) astronomy : physics
   (E) mineralogy : coins

4. DOLDRUMS : SLUGGISH :: _____
   (A) jollity : boring
   (B) elation : confusing
   (C) courage : fearless
   (D) assurance : blessed
   (E) compulsion : voluntary

5. HAPPINESS : ECSTASY :: _____
   (A) havoc : alertness
   (B) envy : boredom
   (C) valor : trust
   (D) depression : enthusiasm
   (E) fear : terror

SUMMARY

Clues from Analogies: 16–20

Clue 16. Something : Associated Quality
 OBSOLESCENCE : DISUSED :: diversity : varied

Clue 17. Something : A Form or Degree of
 DISAGREEMENT : ALTERCATION :: scheme : conspiracy

Clue 18. Something : Something Affected by or Associated With
 PLOW : SOIL :: prune : fruit trees

Clue 19. Something : Something Studied
 PSYCHOLOGY : PERSONALITY :: genetics : heredity

Clue 20. Something : Unit of Measurement
 DISTANCE : KILOMETERS :: duration : years

Analogy Clues 21–25 (Summarized)

The twenty analogy types provide a solid basis for attacking the analogy questions on the SAT. The strategies have shown you how to proceed and how to make the best of your abilities and background. Sometimes the relationships will be in slightly different form, but the skills developed in this chapter will enable you to meet them all with some confidence.

You may find additional examples, often variations of the 20 already presented.

Clue 21. RAM : EWE (gender—male : female)
Clue 22. ABDICATE : ABDICATION (part of speech—verb : noun)
Clue 23. SHEEP : LAMB (parent : offspring)
Clue 24. STITCH : TIME (elements of one proverb : elements of another proverb)
Clue 25. PHOENIX : IMMORTALITY (symbol : thing symbolized)

Review

The five analogy types just mentioned appear in the following five questions. Try your skill. Remember: after you have formed the statement for each test pair, be sure you try out the possibilities in the same order as in your statement.

Write the letter for the word pair that best completes each analogy.

1. MARE : COLT :: _____
   (A) lion : panther
   (B) cow : calf
   (C) cub : bear
   (D) egg : chicken
   (E) larva : butterfly

2. WIZARD : WITCH :: _____
   (A) countess : count
   (B) elk : moose
   (C) pickerel : pike
   (D) nephew : niece
   (E) grandfather : grandson

3. ATONE : ATONEMENT :: _____
   (A) firm : firmament
   (B) believe : adore
   (C) repeat : repetition
   (D) reconciliation : agreement
   (E) invigorate : renewal

4. PUMPKIN : HALLOWEEN :: _____
   (A) election : ballot box
   (B) roast beef : Wyoming
   (C) money : finance
   (D) turkey : Thanksgiving
   (E) puppy : child

5. LOOK : LEAP :: _____
   (A) smoke : fire
   (B) horse : cart
   (C) babes : toyland
   (D) try : succeed
   (E) invest : speculate

Clues from Analogies: Review Test

Write the letter for the word pair that best completes each analogy.

1. KITH : KIN :: _____
   (A) cousin : opponent
   (B) time : tide
   (C) neighbor : acquaintance
   (D) friend : enemy
   (E) buyer : seller

2. SMELL : FRAGRANT :: _____
   (A) touch : earsplitting
   (B) sound : tuneful
   (C) sight : slow
   (D) taste : musical
   (E) thought : fearful

3. VASE : FLOWERS :: _____
   (A) urn : barrel
   (B) apiary : bees
   (C) jar : glass
   (D) bowl : stove
   (E) kettle : handle

4. STING : SWELLING :: _____
   (A) wasp : anger
   (B) poison ivy : rash
   (C) flood : storm
   (D) thunder : lightning
   (E) infection : cut

5. BALLERINA : BALLET :: _____
   (A) carpenter : wrench
   (B) stage director : play
   (C) soprano : cantata
   (D) prima donna : marathon
   (E) photographer : film

6. GARRULOUS : TALKATIVE :: ____
   (A) placid : tranquil
   (B) noisy : considerate
   (C) wealthy : generous
   (D) complete : detailed
   (E) ethical : social

7. COOL : FRIGID :: _____
   (A) hot : lukewarm
   (B) fierce : gentle
   (C) vital : significant
   (D) unpleasant : contemptible
   (E) cold : north

8. PHARMACIST : PRESCRIPTION ::
   (A) diagnosis : doctor
   (B) baker : pastry
   (C) accountant : tax
   (D) veterinarian : horse
   (E) steeplejack : race

9. NEUTRON : ATOM :: _____
   (A) circus : performer
   (B) molecule : quark
   (C) drop : lake
   (D) puppy : wolfhound
   (E) earth : satellite

10. HERD : SHEEP :: _____
    (A) meadow : ox
    (B) eyrie : eagle
    (C) pack : wolf
    (D) covey : lion
    (E) school : hamsters

Clues from Analogies: Summary

1. An analogy is a comparison.
2. The analogy question on the SAT compares two sets of words.
3. The question, stated in the form of an incomplete equation, evaluates the relationship of two pairs of words.
4. The words in the second pair must show the same relationship to each other as the words in the first pair in the same order.
5. Relationships are many and varied. The best way to evaluate each relationship is to put it into statement form. Substitute possible answers to find the correct pair.

Analogies are important! 19 SAT questions are analogies.

Vocabulary Diagnostic Tests

Now you have an opportunity to practice the vocabulary skills and strategies you have been using. First take Test A. Allow yourself 30 minutes. Refer to the "Answers and Analysis" section on pages 449–452. Check your answers and go over the analysis for each of the 25 items. Note your incorrect answers. In the Answers and Analysis section you will find the page numbers in this book for additional help and strategy review.

Vocabulary Diagnostic Test A

Part 1

Each sentence below has one or two blanks, each blank indicating that something has been omitted. Beneath the sentence are five lettered words or sets of words labeled A through E. Choose the word or set of words that *best* fits the meaning of the sentence as a whole.

EXAMPLE

Although its publicity has been _____, the film itself is intelligent, well-acted, handsomely produced, and altogether _____.
  (A) tasteless . . respectable
  (B) extensive . . moderate
  (C) sophisticated . . spectacular
  (D) risque . . crude
  (E) perfect . . spectacular

● Ⓑ Ⓒ Ⓓ Ⓔ

---

1. A three-day blizzard seriously _____ the climbers, only a thousand feet from the summit of Mt. Everest.
  (A) motivated   (D) impaired
  (B) embittered   (E) revolted
  (C) impeded

  1 ___

2. When the sculptor picked up the clay, it was a(n) _____ mass, but under his _____ fingers, a statuette began to take shape.
  (A) sodden . . stubby
  (B) incredible . . tapering
  (C) manageable . . clumsy
  (D) shapely . . skilled
  (E) amorphous . . dextrous

  2 ___

3. Throughout the world there are Hitler and Mussolini _____ who would sweep democracy away and impose _____ rule on the people.
  (A) clones . . authoritarian
  (B) namesakes . . unified
  (C) associates . . constitutional
  (D) descendants . . popular
  (E) Germans . . monastic

  3 ___

4. In a 1993 speech, President Clinton proposed to "guarantee to every American _____ health benefits that could never be taken away."
   - (A) inexpensive
   - (B) helpful
   - (C) superlative
   - (D) comprehensive
   - (E) underfinanced

   4 ___

5. Tom Watson optimistically declared that cooler weather might _____ one of the major problems faced by the American team in golf's Ryder Cup.
   - (A) exacerbate
   - (B) alleviate
   - (C) promulgate
   - (D) subjugate
   - (E) innovate

   5 ___

6. When it is time to return home after achieving _____ in medicine, some students from Third World countries _____.
   - (A) miracles . . boast
   - (B) prominence . . experiment
   - (C) control . . question
   - (D) competence . . balk
   - (E) serenity . . quarrel

   6 ___

7. By the merest _____ Denning attempts to _____ the impressive philosophical structure outlined by his rival.
   - (A) quibble . . topple
   - (B) insinuation . . tout
   - (C) flattery . . rationalize
   - (D) hesitation . . justify
   - (E) exposition . . deplete

   7 ___

8. Like many modern athletes, _____ athletes in ancient Greek Olympic games _____ their success.
   - (A) harried . . envied
   - (B) triumphant . . exploited
   - (C) participating . . contemplated
   - (D) canny . . squandered
   - (E) lackluster . . belittled

   8 ___

9. For 240 challenging days a year Japanese children have a much more _____ schooling than do their American _____.
   - (A) diluted . . colleagues
   - (B) imaginative . . correspondents
   - (C) imitative . . associates
   - (D) spontaneous . . adherents
   - (E) intensive . . counterparts

   9 ___

10. _____ communication with a pet dog or cat is often excellent _____.
    - (A) Casual . . strategy
    - (B) Tactile . . therapy
    - (C) Verbal . . psychology
    - (D) Repetitive . . mimicry
    - (E) Intuitive . . discipline

    10 ___

11. Despite the director's _____ after the disastrous dress rehearsal, the opening night performance was a total success, with many curtain calls at its conclusion.
    - (A) excitement
    - (B) smugness
    - (C) apathy
    - (D) vigor
    - (E) foreboding

    11 ___

12. Hattie Caraway was the first woman elected to the Senate, an inspiration for those who would _____ her.
    - (A) emulate
    - (B) encourage
    - (C) interpret
    - (D) lionize
    - (E) discuss

    12 ___

13. Sequoyah, in a(n) _____ feat of scholarship, created for the Cherokee nation a written language consisting of 86 characters.
    - (A) comparable
    - (B) singular
    - (C) imitative
    - (D) unfettered
    - (E) dispassionate

    13 ___

14. Although Mandy _____ responsibility for the accident, the jury decided it was a clear case of _____ on her part.
(A) denied . . attentiveness
(B) disclaimed . . negligence
(C) accepted . . boredom
(D) assigned . . dexterity
(E) misinterpreted . . clairvoyance

14 ___

15. Unlike De Kooning, who _____ the perils of modern living, his artist _____, Gorky, Smith, and Pollock, died tragic deaths.
(A) belittled . . henchmen
(B) delineated . . characters
(C) survived . . peers
(D) accepted . . namesakes
(E) attacked . . kinsmen

15 ___

Part 2

Each question below consists of a related pair of words, followed by five lettered pairs of words labeled A through E. Select the lettered pair that *best* expresses a relationship similar to that expressed in the original pair.

YAWN : BOREDOM ::
(A) anger : madness
(B) dream : sleep
(C) smile : amusement
(D) face : expression
(E) impatience : rebellion

C

16. CANDID : HYPOCRITE ::
(A) insatiable : glutton
(B) curious : expert
(C) cheerful : scientist
(D) angelic : fiend
(E) competent : executive

16 ___

17. AQUARIUM : GUPPY ::
(A) terrarium : lion
(B) letter : file
(C) dog : kennel
(D) automobile : street
(E) safe : jewelry

17 ___

18. GOLF : PUTTER ::
(A) mallet : croquet
(B) javelin : track
(C) knitting : needle
(D) football : line judge
(E) cooking : onion

18 ___

19. POUND : KILOGRAM ::
(A) century : year
(B) foot : yard
(C) liter : quart
(D) centimeter : gram
(E) calorie : heat

19 ___

20. REFEREE : IMPARTIALITY ::
(A) chef : strength
(B) winner : regret
(C) counselor : understanding
(D) pessimist : certainty
(E) archer : arrows

20 ___

21. INSECT : BEETLE ::
(A) reptile : cobra
(B) porpoise : mammal
(C) mollusk : jellyfish
(D) frog : lizard
(E) falcon : condor

21 ___

22. CONFUSION : CHAOS ::
(A) poise : serenity
(B) happiness : indifference
(C) discord : conversation
(D) headache : noise
(E) recklessness : leadership

22 ___

23. INFECTION : ILLNESS ::
    (A) destruction : explosion
    (B) eclipse : disaster
    (C) bark : howl
    (D) sentimentality : ingenuity
    (E) cloudburst : flooding

                                        23 ___

24. FONDNESS : INFATUATION ::
    (A) rage : irritation
    (B) enjoyment : rapture
    (C) excitement : indifference
    (D) comical : original
    (E) backward : deceitful

                                        24 ___

25. COMPETES : ATHLETE ::
    (A) plants : meteorologist
    (B) plows : potter
    (C) repairs : aerialist
    (D) kills : matador
    (E) sews : manicurist

                                        25 ___

Now that you have taken Test A and have read the analysis of the correct answers (pages 449–452), try your skill at Test B. Again, correct answers will be analyzed for you (pages 453–456), with cross-references to the pages that cover the skills being tested.

Taking both tests may provide help in revealing areas where you are particularly strong as well as areas where you need special attention.

Vocabulary Diagnostic Test B

Part 1

Each sentence below has one or two blanks, each blank indicating that something has been omitted. Beneath the sentence are five lettered words or sets of words labeled A through E. Choose the word or set of words that best fits the meaning of the sentence as a whole.

EXAMPLE

Although its publicity has been _____, the film itself is intelligent, well-acted, handsomely produced, and altogether _____.
    (A) tasteless . . respectable
    (B) extensive . . moderate
    (C) sophisticated . . amateur
    (D) risqué . . crude
    (E) perfect . . spectacular   ● Ⓑ Ⓒ Ⓓ Ⓔ

---

1. During the initial stages of his first term, President Lyndon Johnson, in a search for party harmony, gently _____ the Kennedy aides, while demonstrating his own personal style.
   (A) disregarded (D) cajoled
   (B) intimidated (E) distracted
   (C) irritated

   1 ___

2. In discussing the shuttle's flight, the director of NASA said that "all the _____ leading to take off—two months' delay to be exact—paid off at the end."
   (A) tribulations (D) experimentation
   (B) jubilation
   (C) sabotage (E) achievements

   2 ___

3. Quilting expert Georgia Bonesteel _____ lap quilting as _____ modern American lifestyles.
   (A) debunks . . related to
   (B) downplays . . in keeping with
   (C) studies . . opposed to
   (D) describes . . contrary to
   (E) espouses . . compatible with

   3 ___

4. _____, some of the passengers killed in the crash had chosen train travel because of a fear of flying.
   (A) Wistfully (D) Realistically
   (B) Ironically (E) Contradictorily
   (C) Prematurely

   4 ___

5. The First Ten Amendments, known as the Bill of Rights, were added to the Constitution because many of the Founding Fathers felt that the rights had not been made _____ enough in the Constitution itself.
   (A) responsible (D) suggestive
   (B) contemporary (E) uncomplicated
   (C) explicit

   5 ___

6. Americans have been accused of being _____, wasteful of their _____ resources.
   (A) indigent . . plentiful
   (B) unconventional . . natural
   (C) disillusioned . . subterranean
   (D) profligate . . irreplaceable
   (E) uncooperative . . aquatic

   6 ___

7. Though *abnormality* is a frightening word, some _____ from normal are _____, not harmful.
   (A) quotations . . curious
   (B) abstractions . . medicinal
   (C) deviations . . benign
   (D) condensations . . concise
   (E) fluctuations . . provocative

   7 ___

8. Nowhere else in the United States, during the next decade, are as many _____ species facing possible _____ as in the Hawaiian Islands.
   (A) exotic . . misinterpretation
   (B) desert . . scrutiny
   (C) poisonous . . mismanagement
   (D) alpine . . stabilization
   (E) native . . extinction

   8 ___

9. The radio signals were _____, with _____ static that scrambled the message.
   (A) intermittent . . disruptive
   (B) melodic . . harmonious
   (C) unanticipated . . frivolous
   (D) clear . . isolated
   (E) unbroken . . raucous

   9 ___

10. _____ changes in the basic swimming strokes have created new world records and made _____ many previous swimming techniques.
    (A) Unexpected . . ridiculous
    (B) Subtle . . obsolete
    (C) Extreme . . significant
    (D) Mechanical . . dramatic
    (E) Trivial . . valuable

    10 ___

11. Jean Henri Fabre shifted the _____ of science from dead laboratory specimens to _____, living creatures in the field.
    (A) emphasis . . stodgy
    (B) scrutiny . . vibrant
    (C) mediocrity . . nameless
    (D) nomenclature . . unobserved
    (E) carelessness . . active

    11 ___

12. The exhibit of American flower painting shows an _____ diversity from the _____ realism of Severin Roesen to the abstract design of Georgia O'Keeffe.
    (A) expected . . shoddy
    (B) unpretentious . . breezy
    (C) unbroken . . critical
    (D) exalted . . unattractive
    (E) incredible . . literal

    12 ___

13. Although the chance of discovering _____ intelligence may be slim, the SETI program continues to _____ sounds from outer space.
    (A) superior . . transfer
    (B) extraterrestrial . . monitor
    (C) UFO . . disregard
    (D) galactic . . broadcast
    (E) inhuman . . clarify

    13 ___

14. In light of the almost _____ possibilities available, simple coincidence is neither mysterious nor _____.
    (A) incomprehensible . . ridiculous
    (B) demonstrable . . expected
    (C) inconsequential . . purposeful
    (D) limitless . . miraculous
    (E) invariable . . substantial

    14 ___

15. Like a meteor on an August night, the rock star _____ across stages throughout the land and then _____ into oblivion.
    (A) blazed . . faded
    (B) ran . . dashed
    (C) flew . . collapsed
    (D) marched . . hobbled
    (E) promenaded . . fell

    15 ___

Part 2

Each question below consists of a related pair of words or phrases, followed by five lettered pairs of words or phrases labeled A through E. Select the lettered pair that *best* expresses a relationship similar to that expressed in the original pair.

YAWN : BOREDOM ::
  (A) anger : madness
  (B) dream : sleep
  (C) smile : amusement
  (D) face : expression
  (E) impatience : rebellion

    C

16. GARDENER : TROWEL ::
    (A) aviator : signal
    (B) skater : net
    (C) amateur : tennis
    (D) angler : rod
    (E) chef : dairy

    16 ___

17. FILAMENT : BULB ::
    (A) stamen : flower
    (B) tree : bark
    (C) blanket : warmth
    (D) novel : character
    (E) message : telephone

    17 ___

18. MILLIGRAM : WEIGHT ::
    (A) capacity : liter
    (B) acre : area
    (C) heat : calorie
    (D) ecstasy : happiness
    (E) meter : foot

    18 ___

19. ASTRONAUT : SHUTTLE ::
    (A) garage : mechanic
    (B) museum : botanist
    (C) cook : galley
    (D) canary : kennel
    (E) senator : White House

    19 ___

20. CHISEL : MARBLE ::
    (A) burn : field
    (B) grow : asparagus
    (C) read : article
    (D) buy : newspaper
    (E) mold : clay

    20 ___

21. EULOGIZE : COMPLIMENTARY ::
    (A) circumvent : weepy
    (B) reconcile : impatient
    (C) garnish : devious
    (D) gawk : noisy
    (E) economize : prudent

    21 ___

22. GUIDES : MENTOR ::
    (A) memorizes : felon
    (B) repeats : prophet
    (C) opines : ascetic
    (D) deceives : impostor
    (E) triumphs : recipient

    22 ___

23. CORRAL : MUSTANG ::
    (A) train : tiger
    (B) cage : antelope
    (C) paint : camel
    (D) spring : trap
    (E) herd : sheep

    23 ___

24. RAINBOW : HOPE ::
    (A) flag : patriotism
    (B) sustenance : food
    (C) Halloween : skeleton
    (D) graduation : diploma
    (E) crown : wealth

    24 ___

25. GENETICS : HEREDITY ::
    (A) seismology : earthquakes
    (B) aerodynamics : air pollution
    (C) volcanoes : vulcanology
    (D) meteorology : asteroids
    (E) metaphysics : subatomic particles

    25 ___

Division B
Reading Comprehension

A Strategy for the Reading Tests

■ Now that you have mastered many of the skills of vocabulary building, you will find yourself ready for the reading tests. Begin to read each selection with calm confidence, for that is half the battle. If you consider each selection as a puzzle and as fun, you'll be more relaxed.

■ After you have read a selection, first look for the main idea. The test questions actually help you here, for they always provide five possibilities, one of which is the best. If you use the suggestions given in the text, you'll usually be able to spot the best answer.

■ Test questions usually fit into one of three broad categories: language, details, and inference. Even finding the title requires drawing inferences.

■ "Language in Action" builds directly on Part A and should be, for you, an extension of the work you've already been doing in this text.

■ "Finding Details" is fairly cut and dried. The answers are right there, in the passages themselves, and can be identified.

■ "Drawing Inferences" is a broad and challenging skill. It requires you to read between the lines as you draw inferences, predict what happens next, provide applications, and infer tones and attitudes. Though this kind of question is challenging, it can be more fun than merely picking out details. It leads to a disciplined approach that eliminates guesswork.

■ Review page 4.

Section I: Drawing Generalizations and Finding the Main Idea

1. Drawing Generalizations

One of the most important skills tested in the SAT is the ability to generalize. Questions of this type come in a variety of forms, but the essential task in each is to draw a conclusion from ideas or incidents presented in the passage. The most common type of generalization is finding the main idea or supplying a title—covered in subsequent pages. But sometimes you are asked to generalize from a segment of the passage. Here is a sample of such question forms.

1. The author apparently feels that . . .
2. With which statement would the author probably agree?
3. Which of the following terms would the author use to describe . . . ?
4. In the last sentence of the paragraph the word ''it'' refers to . . .

Trial Test

Read the passage. Choose the answer to the question that follows it.

In Colin Wilson's science-fiction novel, *The Mind Parasites,* aliens have burrowed into human brains and are living there. To keep human beings from learning the truth, the aliens keep us functioning at about 5% of our mental capacity. That we are all underachievers is not a new idea. William James once wrote, ''There seems to be no doubt that we are each and all of us to some extent victims of habit neurosis . . . We live subject to arrest by degrees of fatigue which we have come only from habit to obey. Most of us can learn to push the barrier further off, and to live in perfect comfort on much higher levels of power.'' Wilson agrees. He is keenly interested in why we are *not* fully alive and alert all the time, why we cannot achieve all we are capable of achieving.

With which of the following statements would the author probably agree? Insert your answer, A, B, C, D, or E, on the line below.

(A) Colin Wilson is unduly critical of William James.
(B) *The Mind Parasites,* though science-fiction, is a frightening glimpse of the future.
(C) The human mind ordinarily operates at a fraction of its capacity.
(D) Fatigue is a stimulus to achievement rather than a barrier.
(E) Wilson's point of view is a creative breakthrough, novel and ingenious.

———

Study a reading question and then analyze the possible answers.

Problem

If people are asked to name dangerous animals, they suggest tigers, rhinos, wolves, leopards, and bears. Yet a far more dangerous creature is the insignifi-
5 cant mosquito, carrier of discomfort, disease, and sometimes death. Most people know about malaria-carrying mosquitoes, but few realize that some mosquitoes in the United States carry
10 the dreaded encephalitis. This disease, usually associated with the tropics, is found even in cold areas of the country, like LaCrosse, Wisconsin. It is transmitted by a nasty little fellow called the
15 "tree-hole mosquito." This woodland dweller tends to bite in the late afternoon rather than the evening hours. But whenever it bites, the results can be painful, even deadly. It's just one repre-
20 sentative of a dangerous family.

Throughout the world the lowly mosquito is a vicious enemy of human beings.

With which of the following statements would the author probably agree?

(A) Tigers are more dangerous than leopards, wolves, or bears.
(B) Most disease-bearing mosquitoes are found in Wisconsin.
(C) In classifying our natural enemies, we must realize that size is not proportional to the danger involved.
(D) Mosquito-control efforts are a waste of time, but public moneys are nevertheless spent in the quest.
(E) Encephalitis is almost always fatal, but malaria has several cures.

Strategy. No judgment is made about the relative threat posed by leopards, wolves, or bears. *(A)* is incorrect. The passage admits that mosquitoes are found in Wisconsin but says nothing about comparative percentages of disease-bearing mosquitoes found in Wisconsin and elsewhere. *(B)* is incorrect. There is no mention of mosquito-control efforts and their relative effectiveness. *(D)* is incorrect. Encephalitis is called *dreaded* but not labeled "almost always fatal." Malaria is not mentioned. *(E)* is incorrect. That leaves *(C)*. The major clue to this answer is the word *insignificant*. (Lines 4–5 of the passage.) This tiny creature is called "far more dangerous" than the larger mammals. The conclusion to be drawn is clear: size is not proportional to danger in classifying dangerous beasts. *(C)* is correct.

Review

Try your skill. The passage below is followed by questions based on its content. Use the preceding example to help you find the answers.

Arts and crafts fairs of recent years have displayed many unfamiliar skills, from the artistic arrangement of found objects and "junk" to the almost-for-
5 gotten handicrafts of colonial America. One increasingly common newcomer is the Japanese bonsai, the miniature tree.

The bonsai combines the skill of artist and gardener, of sculptor and archi-
10 tect. Potted in a shallow dish, the young tree or shrub may be carefully shaped to resemble an ancient tree on a windswept mountain. For the creator of a bonsai garden, patience is the essential
15 ingredient. The miniature trees are trained, not tortured. Though in the wild, the effects of nature may weather and dwarf trees naturally, in a cultivated plant, the artist must duplicate the ef-
20 fects of nature.

Essential procedures include pruning, repotting, and wiring. Roots, trunk, branches, and foliage are all shaped in the process. Pruning is essential to keep the plant from outgrowing its root system. Repotting is necessary to trim the roots and to provide new soil. Copper wiring is needed to shape the plant in desired forms.

Bonsai artists say their major purpose is to evoke the spirit of nature. Through "constant yet relaxed attention" they create a microcosm of serenity. If they are successful, they create a masterpiece that is a joy to behold. Their major goal is to achieve, through much direction and intelligent effort, a feeling of spontaneity, of natural beauty. Bob Kataoka, bonsai master, says, "Viewing bonsai is restful, a brief contact with nature's calmness."

1. The author of the selection apparently feels that _____.
   (A) learning to create bonsai requires little experience
   (B) repotting the bonsai is an aesthetic rather than a practical necessity
   (C) bonsai have long been popular in American craft shows
   (D) bonsai trees are younger than they look
   (E) the best bonsai appear carefully planned

   1 __

2. "Microcosm" in line 33 refers to a _____.
   (A) painting   (D) replica
   (B) herb garden   (E) model
   (C) bonsai

   2 __

3. Which of the following terms would the author probably use to describe Bob Kataoka?
   (A) artisan   (D) nurseryman
   (B) landscaper   (E) forester
   (C) artist

   3 __

SUMMARY

1. Drawing Generalizations

When drawing generalizations, first reread the passage carefully. Then get the feel of the passage as a whole.

Ordinarily the generalization grows out of that total evaluation. With that awareness of the total message, you can readily draw the generalization that is called for.

---

2. Finding the Main Idea

A common device for testing the ability to generalize is asking the candidate to find the main idea. This kind of question focuses on the entire selection, not a section of it. If there are several ideas developed, you must weigh them all and determine the *main* idea. Here is a sample of question forms.

1. The major subject of the passage is . . .
2. The chief focus of the passage is on which of the following?

3. The main point of the passage is to . . .
4. The author apparently feels that . . .
5. Which of the following best describes the main idea of the passage?

Trial Test

Take the following trial test to evaluate your skill. Read the passage and choose the answer to the question that follows it. Write the letter for your answer.

One man's meat is another man's poison. Tadpoles thrive in situations that would be impossible for other species. Spring ponds that thrive for only 5 a few months of the year before drying up are ideal habitats for tadpoles. Even puddles formed by a heavy spring rain bring forth a batch of tadpoles struggling for survival. Most other species quickly 10 perish in such circumstances, but not the tadpoles.

Like busy Americans, the tadpoles are lovers of fast-food. Called "highly efficient, specialized feeding ma- 15 chines," tadpoles eat constantly in almost any aquatic habitat. In some species newly swallowed food may account for 50% of their body weight. They eat and eat—and grow and grow. They 20 thrive on uncertainty and instability. Their life cycles are tied to rapid changes in their environment.

Would tadpoles succeed in larger bodies of water that provide some sta- 25 bility? Oddly enough, the answer is *no*. The young creatures would probably succeed in their eating goals, though they'd be competing with other species for the organic food on which they de- 30 pend. The real problem would be hun-

gry fish, which would soon gobble up the defenseless tadpoles. In fact, tadpoles and fish rarely occur together. Thus, what seems like a happy, serene, 35 nurturing environment is, for the tadpoles, a source of greatest danger.

When they grow in inhospitable conditions like the temporary pond or puddle, the tadpoles have the opportunity 40 to eat constantly in relative safety. These "safe" conditions are not guaranteed, however. If a pond or a puddle dries up too quickly, the tadpoles may starve to death or die from desiccation.

45 The tadpoles are creatures of insecurity, taking advantage of short periods and apparently impossible living conditions. They are creatures of the seasons, appearing suddenly, feeding 50 on the chance organic matter in a spring puddle, and then metamorphosing into frogs—if they are lucky.

Which of the following best describes the main idea of the passage?

(A) The life cycle of the tadpole resembles that of the fish.
(B) Tadpoles flourish in spring puddles.
(C) If a spring pond dries up, tadpoles perish.
(D) Tadpoles survive under conditions that seem unlikely and inhospitable.
(E) Tadpoles in large ponds or lakes have an excellent chance of survival.

———

Problem

Hungarians are sometimes considered a sad and serious people, but the Hungarian sense of humor is delightful and unexpected. Hungarians say, "Dis- 5 aster is a natural state in Hungary. Every situation there is hopeless—but not serious."

The Hungarian playwright Ferenc Molnar was once asked, "What was the 10 first sentence you learned in English?"

Molnar replied. "Separate checks, please."

Hungarians love their great twin city, Budapest. They say the Danube is

the bluest there, the sunshine brighter
and more pervasive than anywhere else
in Hungary. "Even the midgets there
are taller." Budapest has two million
people and all of Hungary ten million.
But all Hungarians insist they were born
in Budapest.

The spice paprika is the national
treasure. Someone asked, "Why do
Arabs have oil and Hungarians paprika?"

The reply: "When God gave out the
goodies, the Hungarians were pushier."

Which of the following best expresses the
main idea of the passage?

(A) Hungarians are a sad and serious people.
(B) Ferenc Molnar is both witty and perceptive.
(C) To a true Hungarian, paprika is more
valuable than oil.
(D) The Hungarian sense of humor is keen
and enjoyable.
(E) Hungarians are unusually proud of their
capital city, Budapest.

—

Strategy.   Though all five answers have at least partial validity in one
sense or another, only one expresses the *main* idea. The comment that Hungarians are sad and serious *(A)* is listed as a common idea, albeit a partial
misconception. At best it is a detail and therefore unacceptable. Ferenc Molnar's wit *(B)* is suggested, but again the point is a small detail. The tongue-
in-cheek comment about paprika and oil *(C)* is used to bolster the main point.
It is not the main point. Hungarians are very proud of Budapest *(E),* but their
pride is used as a humorous illustration of their sense of humor. All points
reinforce the central point: Hungarians have a good sense of humor *(D).*

Review

Try your skill. The passage below is followed by questions based on its contents.
Use the preceding example to help you find
the correct answers.

Dangerous drivers account for a dis-
proportionately large number of traffic
fatalities. Some drivers are multiple offenders. Keeping such drivers off the
roads is a desirable goal, but there are
difficulties in enforcing such a plan. Up
till now it has been possible for a driver
with a suspended or revoked license in
one state to get a license in another
state. Some of these licensees had been
involved in several tragic accidents.
The National Driver Register, which attempts to keep a nationwide, up-to-date
file on drivers, has not, until recently,
been especially prompt or effective in
providing essential information to states
requesting information. Now a bill
passed by Congress provides more
funds and puts more clout into the entire
program. A California study has shown
that license sanctions are the most effective means of reducing accidents
caused by problem drivers. This device
is at least 30% more effective than jail
terms, fines, driver-improvement
classes, or alcohol-treatment centers.
Proponents of the Register feel certain
that cooperation by the states and
greater efficiency at the national level
will reduce traffic deaths on tomorrow's
highways.

1. Which of the following expresses the main idea of the passage?
   (A) Most dangerous drivers are multiple offenders.
   (B) The National Driver Register will help states to screen prospective applicants for a license.
   (C) Curbing the dangers posed by problem drivers is a problem disregarded by Congress.
   (D) Denying or limiting the issuance of drivers' licenses is a more effective means of driver control than jail terms or fines.
   (E) A loophole of past procedures is the ability of a problem driver to get a license in a state that does not know his or her record.

   1 ___

2. With which statement would the author probably agree?
   (A) More active law enforcement is needed to protect the lives of innocent drivers.
   (B) The principle of the "second chance" should be a major consideration in handling the licenses of drivers who have had accidents.
   (C) Drivers who are at fault in serious accident cases should be jailed.
   (D) Though desirable, the National Driver Register presents a possible infringement on the rights of sovereign states.
   (E) Congress should play a purely advisory role in considering the problem driver.

   2 ___

SUMMARY

2. Finding the Main Idea

There is a common expression, "You can't see the forest for the trees." To find the main idea, you must see the forest *as well as* the trees. You must be able to see larger issues (the forest) concealed in smaller ones (the trees) and get to the heart of a reading passage.

---

3. Providing a Title

A variation of stating the main idea is choosing the best title for the selection. Like the preceding type of question, this focuses on the entire selection. The major difference is that choices are not put into statement form but into headline form. Here is a common question requiring you to provide a good title:

Which of the following titles best summarizes the content of the passage?

Trial Test

Take the following trial test to evaluate your skill. Read the passage and choose the answer for the question that follows it.

Before 1883, local communities had their own time. Each town figured noon when the sun was at the zenith. Clocks in New York City, for example, were 10 minutes and 27 seconds ahead of those in Baltimore. Railroad schedules were a nightmare. Then, an unsung hero, William F. Allen, suggested that the country be divided into four time zones, eliminating those hundreds of different local times. November 18, 1883, was called "The Day of Two Noons," for on that day Washington, D.C., gained four minutes as "local noon" was replaced by "standard noon." Some major cities resisted change. Cincinnati held out for seven years, but gradually the entire country went on Eastern, Central, Mountain, or Pacific Time. This idea, so obviously good and so universally accepted today, was an idea whose time had come, but the coming did not come easily.

Which of the following titles best summarizes the content of the passage?

(A) William F. Allen: A Man for All Seasons
(B) A History of the Calendar
(C) A Day to Remember in Washington
(D) The Introduction of Standard Time
(E) How Time Was Determined Before 1883

____

Look at a question and then analyze the possible answers.

Problem

Are you taking part in the Birkie this year?

This cryptic question would be no mystery to most active cross-country skiers. The Birkie, or *Birkebeiner* as it is correctly called, is North America's largest cross-country ski race. Held every February 25 in Cable, Wisconsin, it brings 10,000 skiers to a sleepy town of several hundred people. The race itself covers the 34 miles from Hayward, Wisconsin, to Cable. During the week before the race, Cable has ice-sculpture contests, skydivers, hot-air balloons, dancing, dozens of bands, ski clinics, a parade of nations and states, and good old Scandinavian smorgasbords. Incredible traffic jams develop. Housing facilities are stretched to the utmost. A thousand racers, for example, sleep in sleeping bags at the Hayward Middle School. The race must accommodate all these eager skiers. The starting area is a quarter-mile wide. Since top long-distance racers from around the world compete, the finishing time of the winning skier may be four hours ahead of the last skier. Yet all have a good time. Finishing the race is in itself a victory.

Which of the following titles best summarizes the content of the passage?

(A) America's Greatest Cross-Country Ski Race
(B) Fun in the Snow
(C) From Hayward to Cable, the Trip of a Lifetime
(D) The Comforts and Discomforts of Cross-Country Skiing
(E) The Race: A Victory Over Self

____

Strategy. There are several pitfalls in choosing titles.

1. Do not choose a title that is too broad. In this question *(B)* is much too broad. It says nothing about skiing. It could apply equally well to a great many other activities.
2. Do not choose a title that is too narrow. *(C)* focuses on an element of the selection, the start and finish.

3. Do not choose a title that sounds profound but is really off the topic. *(E)* sounds good, but there is nothing in the passage to suggest the philosophical implications in *(E)*.
4. Do not choose a title just because it strikes a responsive chord in your memory. *(D)* looks like the kind of title you'd expect in a passage about skiing. If you did not read the paragraph carefully, you might choose *(D)*.
5. Choose a title that fits, that is neither too broad nor too narrow, that is on the topic and generalizes about the entire passage. *(A)* is such a title. It encompasses the race and all the activities associated with the race. In any consideration about the race, the planners would have to take into account all the subsidiary activities, as well as the housing problems and traffic jams. *(A)* covers the entire passage effectively. The other alternatives do not.

Review

Try your skill. The passage below is followed by questions based on its content. Use the preceding example to help you find the right answers.

The paradox of Gilbert and Sullivan continues to amaze music lovers. The two men, utterly different in temperament and personality, somehow man-
5 aged to collaborate on more than a dozen operettas of enduring charm. Both men were told they were wasting their talents on the inconsequential Gilbert and Sullivan operettas, but some-
10 how they stayed together, through stormy years and occasional unpleasant sessions, to create immortal songs like "Tell me, pretty maiden" from *Patience,* songs that were a fortuitous
15 blend of lyric and melody.

William Schwenck Gilbert, who wrote the lyrics and generally determined the plot and direction of the operettas, was a rather stern Victorian, in-
20 tolerant of laziness, indifference, or lack of talent. His guiding hand in the actual production guaranteed the qual-

ity of the production and the integrity of the performances. His witty, often
25 satirical, lyrics punctured Victorian pomposity and inefficiency and, it is said, even ruffled the feathers of Queen Victoria.

Arthur Sullivan, who composed the
30 lovely music for Gilbert's words, was a contrast to Gilbert. Sullivan was a rather gentle person, aristocratic, fond of the good life, often melancholy. Awed by titles, he loved to hobnob with
35 the great. Seldom robustly healthy, he created some of the most beautiful music while racked with pain.

On many occasions, Sullivan said, "I don't want to do another operetta,"
40 but after each refusal, Gilbert would tempt Sullivan with plots, snatches of dialog, production ideas. In the background, Richard D'Oyly Carte acted as impresario and referee, bringing the two
45 men back together again and again, despite the apparent refusal of Sullivan to go on. Somehow, despite altercations, disagreements, and misunderstandings the two men created 14 operettas, 11 of
50 which are still frequently played.

1. Which of the following titles best summarizes the content of the passage?
   (A) Operettas of Victorian England
   (B) The Preeminence of Gilbert in the Gilbert and Sullivan Operettas
   (C) A Happy Collaboration
   (D) The Many Sides of Genius
   (E) Gilbert and Sullivan: A Study in Contrasts

   1 ___

2. With which statement would the author probably agree?
   (A) Richard D'Oyly Carte was an incompetent go-between, irritating both men.
   (B) Of the two men, Gilbert and Sullivan, Sullivan seemed more easygoing.
   (C) William Schwenck Gilbert was basically warm and forgiving.
   (D) *Patience* is probably the most popular of all Gilbert and Sullivan operettas.
   (E) If Gilbert and Sullivan had channeled their energies into other areas, their achievements would have been greater.

   2 ___

SUMMARY

3. Providing a Title

Choosing a title is very similar to finding the main idea. The major difference lies in the way the alternatives are phrased.

---

4. Providing a Summary

This is another variation of finding the main idea, but the phrasing is somewhat different. Note the following sample question:

The passage as a whole is best described as . . .

Trial Test

Take the trial test to evaluate your skill. Read the passage and choose the answer for the question that follows it.

"Because it is there!" George Mallory's explanation of why he kept trying to scale Mt. Everest is not a satisfying answer to a nonclimber. But a true
5 climber understands. In an exciting report on his mountain adventures, *Savage Arena*, Joe Tasker attempts to add his explanation to Mallory's. Tasker endured terrible hardships on the Ei-
10 gerwand in Switzerland, K2 in Kashmir, Dunagiri in India, and Everest in Nepal-Tibet. With fellow climbers he experienced hope and despair in a desperate ascent after an avalanche had

covered their tents. In a climb on the
15 West Face of K2 he lost Nich Estcourt,
a beloved comrade. Yet he always went
back—at last to his death in May 1982
not far from the summit of Everest it-
20 self, the ultimate challenge. In the book
written shortly before his death, he con-
fessed, "In some ways, going to the
mountains is incomprehensible to many
people and inexplicable to those who
25 go. The reasons are difficult to unearth
and only with those who are similarly

drawn is there no need to try to explain."

The passage as a whole principally deals
with _____.

(A) the mysterious appeal of mountain
climbing
(B) the heroism of Joe Tasker
(C) the highest peaks in Europe and Asia
(D) the dangers of rock climbing
(E) the waste of life in mountain climbing

____

Problem

The migration of the monarch butterfly is one of nature's profoundest
mysteries and most incredible stories.
Each fall the monarchs set forth on
5 the dangerous trip to their winter
homes—principally in California and
Mexico. They come from diverse areas,
fly different routes, and bivouac along
the way, often with tens of thousands
10 of their fellows. They are buffeted by
winds, threatened by long stretches of
water, and soaked by downpours. Yet
somehow or other they make their way
to "butterfly trees" on the Monterey
15 Peninsula, in the mountains near Mexico City, and in other less-well-known
sites. Each spring they mate and head
north. Most of the original migrants die
on the return journey. Their offspring
20 somehow pick up the journey and fly to
areas they have never seen before, only

to repeat the process in the fall. No
other insects migrate so predictably,
very much like birds. The monarch mi-
25 gration has been called "one of the
world's great natural events, compara-
ble to the immense mammal movements
on Africa's Serengeti Plain."

The passage as a whole is best described as
a _____.

(A) plea for protection of the monarch's
nesting sites
(B) comparison of monarch migration with
the migration of other insects
(C) description of a beautiful and mysterious
natural phenomenon
(D) testament of courage
(E) scientific evaluation of an event known
to everyone

____

Strategy. Which alternative should you choose? Note that this question
asks you to find the main idea, but instead of expressing the idea in statement
form, it provides a label (plea, comparison, etc.) with qualifying phrases.
Remember that you are seeking the main idea. You are dealing with "the
passage as a whole." *(A)* might well be a follow-up to the ideas expressed
in the paragraph, but it is not the expressed *main* idea. *(B)* is too narrow.
There is a brief comparison with the migration of other insects, but this is a
detail. *(D)* is too broad. Then, too, whether to call the instinctive reaction
of the monarch "courage" is debatable. It is certainly so in human terms but
not necessarily in scientific terms. *(E)* could fit a myriad of other paragraphs.
It's too broad. *(C)* is accurate. The paragraph is devoted to the migration
(the mysterious phenomenon) and each sentence emphasizes its mystery.

Review

The following selections test your ability to draw conclusions in a variety of formats.

1. How large a part will solar energy play in the future? When will the nonreplaceable petroleum begin to run out? How large a role will coal play in the
5 energy program of the future? Is nuclear energy a feasible alternative? Can we depend upon minihydroelectric systems to produce electricity in small but economical chunks? Questions like these
10 are bandied back and forth in television discussions, news reports, and newspaper articles. There is, however, another possibility, little considered but strategically important. We can create tiny
15 habitats that conserve energy.

Experts estimate that energy-minded landscaping can cut home energy needs by 30%. Early societies knew the value of creative plantings to
20 help people keep cool in summer and warm in winter. Much of today's architecture, however, overlooks creative possibilities for energy conservation, wasting precious resources through in-
25 efficient planning. Trees, shrubs, vines, and ground covers can be planted to protect against the summer's blazing sun. These plants are living air conditioners, evaporating water and cooling
30 the air. Planting windbreaks can help keep out wintry blasts. Even small windbreaks around a foundation reduce heat loss by providing a wall of insulating air around the house. Winter and
35 summer, living plants can work for us and save us energy dollars.

The passage as a whole is best described as a _____.

(A) warning against the depletion of coal resources
(B) comparison of today's architecture with that of another day
(C) suggestion for handling the cold of winter
(D) call for a partnership with nature in energy conservation
(E) criticism of nuclear energy as a solution to current energy problems

———

2. Would you like to grow your own vegetables without cultivation, weeding, or soil preparation? Would you like to avoid problems of ground insects,
5 moles, rabbits, or other animals? You may find hydroponic gardening your solution. This branch of gardening uses no soil. Vegetables grow in a nutrient solution in any place convenient to the gar-
10 dener. Large tracts of land are not required, for plants grow rather close together in perfect harmony. Joe Corso of Altamonte Springs, Florida, hasn't bought a vegetable in 15 years. He
15 grows several varieties of lettuce, tomatoes, cucumbers, green peppers, zucchini, broccoli, basil, scallions, and escarole. He insists a complete garden can be set up for $20–$35 as a one-time cost.
20 The nutrients will cost $15–$20 a year for a complete garden. Soilless gardening has many possibilities. Principles of hydroponic gardening, for example, are used for desert gardens where sand con-
25 tains little or no natural nutrients.

Which of the following titles best summarizes the content of the passage?

(A) Growing Vegetables the Easy Way: Without Soil
(B) A Florida Experiment That Paid Off
(C) Desert Gardens: Using the World's Barren Lands
(D) A New Product for Attacking World Hunger
(E) A Backyard Garden with a Different Approach

———

3. Until relatively recently the exploitation of the vast Amazon Basin was minimal. Extensive clearing of forests and overfishing of rivers was unknown. The primitive dwellers in the region harvested the resources conservatively and thus preserved, until recently, the tremendous natural wealth of the entire area. A restraining influence, not altogether lost on the little farmers and hunters of today, was a belief in supernatural game wardens and forest demons. These creatures, the forest dwellers believed, punish those who abuse nature's generosity. Some of these spirits watch over game. Others harass those who venture too far into the jungle. These deterrents averted the greedy, mindless destruction that has characterized man's treatment of nature in other parts of the world. Though the rise in population and new economic pressures are now threatening the entire basin, there are still signs of primitive beliefs held by the rural population of Amazonia.

Which of the following expresses the main idea of the passage?

(A) A belief in supernatural game wardens and forest demons is a sign of ignorance.
(B) Too often man has exploited the natural resources around him.
(C) A tremendous population explosion has upset the balance of nature in Amazonia.
(D) Primitive dwellers are in reality more sophisticated than urban residents.
(E) A belief in spirits kept men from exploiting the Amazon basin.

———

SUMMARY

4. Providing a Summary

The ability to summarize the essential point of a paragraph is closely related to the ability to choose the correct title and express the main idea. Be sure you are not sidetracked by details, or by generalizations broad enough to cover an article, not a reading passage.

Section I Summary: Drawing Generalizations and Finding the Main Idea

The ability to generalize takes many forms: You may be asked to generalize about a portion of the reading passage: a paragraph or even an important sentence. Or you may have to find the central point of the paragraph in a variety of question formats. The ability to extract main ideas is a crucial skill in note-taking and in study.

The strategies for drawing generalizations and finding the main idea will help you prepare for the SAT.

PART 1. Drawing Generalizations (p. 184)

A. Read the question carefully so that you are sure of the generalization asked for.
B. Find and reread the portion of the passage that has the information for making the generalization.
C. Draw the generalization asked for. Base it on the portion you reread.

PART 2. Finding the Main Idea (p. 186)

A. Reread the entire passage.
B. Get a feel for the *whole passage,* not just a part of it.
C. If several ideas are developed, weigh them all. Then decide on the main idea.

PART 3. Providing a Title (p. 189)

Choosing a title is similar to finding the main idea.

A. Get a feel for the whole passage, not just a part of it.
B. Notice that the title choices are in headline form, not sentence form.
C. Choose the "headline" that best covers the whole "story."

PART 4. Providing a Summary (p. 192)

Choosing a summary is similar to finding the main idea and choosing a title.

A. Keep the whole passage in mind; reread it if you are unsure.
B. Don't be sidetracked by details; on the other hand, don't go beyond the limits of the passage.
C. Choose the statement that sums up the whole passage and that does not go beyond it.

Section II: Drawing Inferences

1. Identifying Inferences

"Sue just sneezed. She must have a cold."

These two statements that sound alike are quite different. The first is a factual observation. The second is an inference. The first is based on a verifiable observation. The second is a judgment that may or may not accord with the facts. Sue may have an allergy. The room may be dusty.

There is nothing wrong with drawing inferences. We often run our lives on the basis of inference. We see people bundled up outside our window and prepare for a cold day. The danger arises when we take an inference for a fact. If we understand the difference between fact and inference, we manage our lives intelligently.

There are good, reasonable inferences; there are poor, irrational ones. When we hear the teakettle whistling, we reasonably infer the water is boiling. When a friend fails to appear for a meeting, we should not infer he or she is rejecting us. There may be dozens of good reasons for his or her failure to come.

Inference plays an important role in SAT reading questions. The following words and phrases are often used to test your ability to draw inferences.

assume	presume	apparently believes
convey	presuppose	can be inferred
emphasize	refer	can best be described as
exemplify	serve to	judging by
hint	suggest	may be interpreted
imply	supported by	used to illustrate
indicate	suppose	

Trial Test

For the following test question select the best inference.

The barometric pressure dropped rapidly. The wind, formerly at calm, suddenly began to whip up. The harbor flag, which had been flapping listlessly, stood out with the force of the wind. Owners of boats in the marina dashed about, fastening boat covers securely and checking all mooring ropes. A few drops of rain splattered the pavement.

The sun had already disappeared, and the world was dark.

The part of the storm being described is _____.

(A) the warning
(B) the beginning
(C) the height
(D) the end
(E) the aftermath

Problem

There is one creature perfectly adapted and temperamentally suited to some of the most inhospitable areas of the world: the camel. In the ecology of
5 the Sahara Desert, the nomad and the camel live in a mutually satisfactory dependence on each other. The nomad provides the camel with water and food. The camel provides the nomad with
10 milk, wool, transportation, and meat. Above all, the camel provides work and gives meaning to the lives of the tribes that crisscross the Sahara. The camel provides the only means by which
15 human beings can constructively utilize the desert. Camel herding, combined with nomadism to take advantage of seasonal rains and recurrent scattered vegetation, is the only feasible solution
20 to surviving in the desert. The camel is at the heart of all efforts to live in harmony with the desert.

1. The passage implies that _____.
   (A) human beings should give up the challenge of living in the desert
   (B) no other creature can replace the camel
   (C) nomads unfairly exploit their camels
   (D) the Sahara Desert is less hospitable than any other desert
   (E) camels are less satisfactory than cattle in many ways

                                        1 ___

2. The essential point made about nomads is that they are _____.
   (A) kindly toward their camels
   (B) essentially traders and merchants
   (C) experts on camel wool
   (D) wanderers
   (E) poets in harmony with life

                                        2 ___

Strategy. 1. Nowhere does the writer suggest that human beings should give up the challenge of living in the desert. Instead, the author commends survival under difficult conditions. *(A)* is incorrect. The first sentence, on the other hand, does suggest that the camel is one of a kind. The rest of the paragraph supports that suggestion. *(B)* sounds right. There is no mention of unfair treatment of camels. Reject *(C)*. There is no comparison of the Sahara with other deserts. Reject *(D)*. Cattle are nowhere mentioned or implied. Reject *(E)*.

2. There are two clues to *(D)* as the correct answer: crisscrossing the Sahara and movement to take advantage of rains and scattered vegetation. *(A)*, *(B)*, and *(C)* are nowhere suggested. *(E)* is much too grandiose, out of keeping with the straightforward, serious note of the passage. Note that this question is allied to "drawing generalizations," as outlined in Section 1 (pages 184–185). The *essential* point is a kind of generalization.

Review

Try your skill. Use the preceding example to help you find the right answers.

Amateur photographers constantly seek more complete cameras, with faster and faster lenses. They want cameras that focus automatically, deter-
5 mine the correct exposure, provide flash when needed—all to produce the perfect picture. Some photographers,

ENGLISH FOR THE COLLEGE BOARDS

however, think automation has taken some of the fun out of photography. For these photographers, a return to basics can be fun.

There is nothing more basic than a pinhole camera. Pinhole photography depends on the passage of light through a small hole in an opaque screen. The pinhole acts like a lens. The light falls on film to construct the image, as in a lens camera. Aristotle mentioned images from pinholes. Leonardo da Vinci explained the principle involved. Lord Rayleigh formally analyzed the process. The pinhole camera has an ancient history, but it has some modern appeals.

The major advantage of the pinhole camera is simplicity. Pictures made with the pinhole camera do have a special quality. But the fun is the challenge of deciding how large the pinhole is to be and how the picture is to be taken. The pinhole camera will never replace the lens camera, but for the amateur enthusiast, it can provide hours of challenge and experimentation.

1. It may be inferred that _____.
   (A) a pinhole camera is a true camera
   (B) automation in cameras should be discarded
   (C) Aristotle used a lens camera
   (D) the size of the pinhole is not important in pinhole photography
   (E) images from a pinhole camera are not inverted
   1 ___

2. The passage implies that _____.
   (A) the pinhole camera may replace the lens camera in years to come
   (B) Leonardo took pictures with a pinhole camera
   (C) light passes through a pinhole in much the same way it passes through a lens
   (D) vast numbers of amateur photographers have temporarily given up lens photography for pinhole photography
   (E) pictures taken with the pinhole camera are superior to those taken with the lens camera
   2 ___

SUMMARY

1. Identifying Inferences

An inference differs from a factual statement, but a good inference is an educated guess that is closely tied to the facts.

For an SAT answer, read between the lines and make your inference a reasonable one.

2. Supplying an Interpretation

"Joe said he won't play football this Sunday under any circumstances."

"What he really meant was that he wouldn't play unless he could start as quarterback."

Life is filled with situations in which one person interprets the words of another. Doing so requires drawing inferences. SAT questions sometimes ask for interpretations using wording like this.

Trial Test

Read the following and choose the answer for the question that follows it.

Most people are aware that ammonia, bleach, and household cleaners are poison, but few people realize that cosmetics, shampoos, shaving creams, and
5 lipstick can be deadly if swallowed by small children. The list of dangerous substances is surprisingly large, including hair spray, toothpaste, nail polish and nail polish remover, makeup, and
10 deodorants. Of course, these substances are used by adults only in small quantities and are not swallowed. Thus, many parents fail to realize that since small children put almost anything into
15 their mouths, they may swallow dangerous amounts of what are usually considered "perfectly safe" substances. Eternal vigilance is the price of safety as well as liberty.

Which of the following best expresses the meaning of the sentence, "Eternal vigilance is the price of safety as well as liberty"?

(A) Parents should probably keep hair spray out of the house.
(B) Young children should never be left unsupervised.
(C) Children should assume a share of responsibility for dangerous substances.
(D) Safety and liberty always go together.
(E) Parents need to be constantly aware of dangers in the home.

———

Problem

"Prairie fire!" The words struck terror into the hearts of many settlers. Dry grass burns rapidly. Out of control, a prairie fire can be an awesome sight.
5 Yet today controlled fires are set to help the grasslands survive. Without occasional fire, undesirable intruders like red cedar begin to take over the land. Unwelcome smaller plants, like Ken-
10 tucky bluegrass, soon replace native grasses and change the character of prairie islands preserved as examples of the American natural heritage. Litter on the prairie floor also changes the ecol-
15 ogy of an area and permits aggressive exotic plants to move in. Fire removes litter and provides the opportunity for native grasslands to be preserved for generations to come. But the fires must
20 be set only after extensive study and analysis of wind, wind speed, relative humidity, temperature, and the physical factors of the vegetation to be burned.

1. Which of the following best expresses the meaning of the phrase "changes the ecology of an area and permits aggressive exotic plants to move in?"
   (A) upsets the natural balance in favor of nonnative species
   (B) evaluates natural conditions and restrains newcomers
   (C) introduces nonproductive changes and start fires
   (D) accelerates proper soil management by allowing diversification
   (E) expresses admiration for the forces of nature and survival of the fittest

   1 ___

2. A "controlled fire" is set _____.
   (A) when the native grasses need burning
   (B) after a summer storm
   (C) as soon as a red cedar appears on the grassland
   (D) when environmental factors are right
   (E) on a consistent and regular basis

   2 ___

Strategy. 1. On first reading (A) seems to be the best answer, but let's check the others just to be sure. Litter changes the ecology but doesn't evaluate it. (B) is incorrect. Litter may permit nonproductive changes, but of itself it does not start fires. (C) is incorrect. (D) has the wrong meaning altogether. The selection speaks against diversification with exotic plants. (E) is also contrary to the idea of the passage. The passage is concerned with the survival of native plants, not necessarily with the survival of the fittest.

2. We may infer that a "controlled fire," by definition, is set when conditions can be controlled. (D) provides the right suggestion. The fire is not set when native grasses need burning (A), but when total conditions suggest the need for a fire. A summer storm (B) might provide one of the safety conditions for the fire, but it is not the determining factor. The removal of a single red cedar (C) does not require a fire. There is no indication anywhere that fires are set (E) on a regular basis. (D) is indeed the correct answer.

Review

Try your skill. The passage below is followed by four questions based on its content. Use the preceding example to help you find the right answers.

Patan is the oldest of the "Three cities of the ancient Kathmandu Valley," whose origins are lost in the mists of history. Visitors to Nepal can take a taxi
5 from the capital, Kathmandu, and find themselves transported to a mystical past, where shrines of Hindu and Buddhist deities rub elbows. On the facades of ancient temples are ornate
10 carvings with religious and historical significance. Most of these temples

have been built in a superb architectural style.
Durbar Square, in the center of the
15 city, is a colorful blend of architectural inspirations and historical associations. Along the cobble-lined streets are the houses of skilled craftsmen, whose arts, processes, and designs have been
20 passed from father to son. Here three generations of a family sit side by side, creating art of exquisite beauty. The imposing Krishna Mandir, temple of the Lord Krishna, dominates the picturesque
25 esque square, which is always vibrant with life.

1. Which of the following best expresses the meaning of the phrase "a colorful blend of architectural inspirations and historical associations"?
   (A) a subtle attempt to sway the religious beliefs of observers
   (B) a center for folk art and the treasures of another day
   (C) a picturesque mixture of modern and historical arts and crafts
   (D) brilliantly conceived architecture with historical significance
   (E) a number of functional buildings created for long-forgotten deities

   1 ___

2. Which word best summarizes the work of Nepalese craftsmen?
   (A) fatigue   (D) indifference
   (B) continuity   (E) rigidity
   (C) improvi-
       sation   2 ___

3. Which of the following titles best summarizes the content of the passage?
   (A) Durbar Square: Heart of Patan
   (B) From Kathmandu to Patan: A Royal Road
   (C) Nepalese Temples: History in Stone
   (D) Patan: A Many-Splendored City
   (E) Architecture in Nepal

   3 ___

4. An excellent adjective to describe Patan is _____.
   (A) huge   (D) sparkling
   (B) financially   (E) grim
       sound
   (C) unvaried   4 ___

SUMMARY

2. Supplying an Interpretation

An interpretation calls for drawing inferences about actions, statements, or events. Watch for interpretation questions on the SAT. You will be asked to supply another way of saying something. If you restate the phrase or sentence in your own words, you can then find the answer closest to your own.

---

3. Providing a Paraphrase

Sometimes you will be asked to provide an interpretation slightly longer than that called for in the previous part. Such an extended interpretation is a **paraphrase.** You might tend to consider such a lengthy interpretation a summary, as in Section I, Part 4, page 192. There is, however, a great difference between a summary and a paraphrase. A summary condenses, provides the gist of a selection in far fewer words. A paraphrase, on the other hand, gives the sense of a given segment in different words, but roughly in the same number of words. A good paraphrase calls for comprehension and the drawing of sound inferences. On the SAT you may meet a question with wording like the following.

Which of the following is the best interpretation of lines _____?

Trial Test

Choose the best answer for the question at the end of the selection.

The Information Explosion adds knowledge at an incredible rate. Some say that knowledge has been doubling every ten years. Others agree and add
5   that the rate is increasing. The new industries spawned by computers alone are increasing at a phenomenal rate. What is behind this breathtaking growth? What spurs people on to new
10 inventions and broader applications of existing technology? Ralph Hinton, an American anthropologist, had an unusual answer: "The human capacity for

being bored, rather than man's social or
15 natural needs, lies at the root of man's cultural advance."

Which is the best interpretation of the quotation by Ralph Hinton?
(A) A man's reach should always exceed his grasp.
(B) The Information Explosion is not necessarily a desirable thing.
(C) Man's restless spirit, not his needs, brings advances.
(D) Boredom takes time away from caring for people's needs.
(E) To be bored is to be creative; to be happy is to be lazy.

_____

Problem

"I like my football players agile, mobile, and hostile." Coach Tom Burrows' successful philosophy was summed up in that favorite statement.
5   Not an exponent of trick plays, strange formations, and razzle-dazzle, Burrows concentrated upon fundamentals: clean, hard tackling; crisp, sure blocking; thorough preparation; and a me-
10 thodical, consistent game plan. He didn't depend upon surprise. If his opponents knew his next play was a plunge off right tackle, Burrows didn't care. He depended upon complete co-
15 operation of all his players, superb execution, split-second timing, and the will to win. Burrows would have agreed with Austin O'Malley, who said, "In dealing with a foolish or stubborn adver-
20 sary, remember your own mood constitutes half the force opposing you." Other coaches belittled Burrows'

coaching philosophy and mentally put him back in the Dark Ages, but they
25 could not fault his incredible string of victories.

1. Which is the best interpretation of the quotation by Austin O'Malley?
   (A) In a close game your opponent may foolishly or stubbornly refuse to play your game.
   (B) In any sport emotion is as important an ingredient as thought and preparation.
   (C) Your opponent may defeat you by doubling his efforts while you halve yours.
   (D) In a hard game you may be your own worst enemy.
   (E) If your players do not play hard, emotions may help your opponents win.

1 ____

2. The attitude of other coaches toward
Burrows might be considered _____.
   (A) condescending but respectful
   (B) baffled but cheerful
   (C) inconsistent and terrified
   (D) hostile and uncooperative
   (E) curious and imitative

2 ___

3. Burrows probably did not rely on trick
plays because _____.
   (A) he preferred razzle-dazzle
   (B) he thought they weren't necessary
   (C) other coaches liked them
   (D) they made his players careless
   (E) they need too much planning

3 ___

Strategy.   1. The answer which best paraphrases the quotation is *(D)*.
The quotation says that "your own mood constitutes half the force opposing
you." If that mood is negative, you help to defeat yourself. *(A)* is off the
topic. Nothing is said about the opponents' game. For the same reason *(C)*
is incorrect. *(B)* is too broad. *(E)* seems plausible, but there is no suggestion
about whether or not the players play hard.

   2. The final sentence is the clue to this answer: *(A)*. "Belittled" suggests
condescension, but the victories suggest respect.

   3. The selection says that Burrows concentrated on fundamentals instead
of relying on trick plays. The answer is *(B)*.

Review

Try your skill. The passage below is followed by questions based on its content. Use
the preceding example to help you find the
right answers.

Grandpa was a monument to sanity
in a crazy world. He never set the world
on fire or put his name up in lights. He
had a modest job at the post office all
5 his working life and retired to hobbies,
crafts, and volunteer work. It was his
personality that endeared him to all who
knew him. It was his philosophy of life
that enriched the lives of his friends and
10 relatives. He embodied Reinhold Niebuhr's prayer never to worry about
what could not be changed and to concentrate only on what could be changed.
He lived today and let those two impos-
15 tors, yesterday and tomorrow, worry

about themselves. He was bright,
sunny, jovial, optimistic, and a joy to
be with. He often quoted a common
quotation to sum up his own beliefs:
20 "Inch by inch, life is a cinch. Yard by
yard, life is hard."

1. Which is the best interpretation of the
quotation in the selection?
   (A) Life can be measured in inches or
in yards.
   (B) Life is tragic if we stop to think
about it too much.
   (C) Life is easy or hard depending on
your point of view.
   (D) To avoid worry and stress, take
life a small step at a time.
   (E) If you don't plan for the future,
you won't have one.

1 ___

2. The best word to describe Grandpa is _____.
   (A) skilled
   (B) cautious
   (C) sensible
   (D) anxious
   (E) ambitious

2 __

3. Yesterday and tomorrow are called "impostors" because _____.
   (A) the future is uncertain and the past is gone
   (B) worry is always destructive
   (C) fortune-tellers take advantage of gullible people
   (D) we truly live in thinking about the future
   (E) they contradict Reinhold Niebuhr's prayer

3 __

SUMMARY

3. Providing a Paraphrase

A paraphrase is a restatement of a sentence or a selection, not a summary. A paraphrase presents the essential point in other words. It parallels the material; it doesn't condense it.

---

4. Making a Comparison

Inferences come in many forms. Sometimes on the SAT you will be asked to compare two ideas, persons, expressions, or arguments. Comparisons like these require you to draw several inferences. One SAT question used this phrasing:

In the second paragraph, the author's chief distinction is between which of the following?

Trial Test

Read the following. Then choose the answer to the question at the end.

Stamp collectors sometimes have to make a key decision: whether to concentrate on stamps that have been postally used or to collect only clean, pure,
5 unused stamps, often direct from the printing presses. Postally used stamps are not as pretty as mint stamps. Portions of their designs have been obliterated by cancellation marks. Mint
10 stamps, on the other hand, are sparkling and clear, with every design detail clearly visible. But used stamps have something extra: actual use in the mails. Often their cancellations provide infor-

15 mation about date and place of use. They often demonstrate the romance of the mails. Collectors of only used stamps call stamps *mere labels* until they perform their function in the mails.
20 Postally used stamps may conveniently be put into an album with stamp hinges, without any concern about a loss in value. On the other hand, mint stamps that have been hinged lose part of their
25 value in the marketplace. They must thus be encased in transparent envelopes and pockets that show the stamps without sticking hinges to them. Mounting mint stamps thus takes more time,
30 energy, and money. There is something

to be said for both decisions, and some collectors collect both kinds of stamps. But usually a collector has a secret preference.

In this selection the author's chief distinction is between which of the following?

(A) used stamps and mint stamps
(B) the arguments for collecting two types of stamps
(C) good stamps and worthless stamps
(D) the market values of two different types of stamps
(E) the aesthetic value of a used stamp as contrasted with that of a mint stamp

———

Now look at a question and analyze the possible answers.

Problem

Distinguishing between the speaker and his argument is difficult but essential. We tend to accept the statements of those we like and reject the state-
5 ments of those we dislike. Yet our friends may be speaking nonsense and our enemies, the truth. An obnoxious person may have something valuable to say. A major task is focusing attention
10 on what is said and not on who is saying it. There are four possible reactions. We may accept the speaker and accept his argument. We may reject the speaker and reject his argument. We may accept
15 the speaker and reject his argument. We may reject the speaker and accept his

argument. The first two are easy. A person with a closed mind finds no problem here. The person with an open mind
20 must, however, be able to have all four reactions. To focus on the argument and not be swayed unduly by the personality of the speaker is true maturity.

In this selection the writer's chief distinction is between which of the following?

(A) personality and maturity
(B) speakers and their points of view
(C) acceptance and rejection
(D) inductive and deductive reasoning
(E) the open mind and the closed mind

———

Strategy. Personality *(A)* is mentioned as an influence on reaction to argument. It is not contrasted with maturity. Speakers *(B)* do have different points of view, but the major point deals with listeners' reactions to speakers' arguments. As an answer, *acceptance* and *rejection (C)* is much too broad for this paragraph. Inductive and deductive reasoning *(D)* are neither mentioned nor implied. The basic contrast is between the open mind, which accepts all four possibilities, and the closed mind, which accepts only the first two. *(E)* is correct.

Review

Try your skill. The passage below is followed by four questions based on its content. Use the preceding example to help you find the right answers.

"The left hand is the dreamer; the right hand is the doer."

Scientists often discover wisdom in folk sayings. There has been much re-
5 cent speculation about the hemispheres of the brain and their various functions. The right hemisphere of the brain controls the left side of the body. The left hemisphere controls the right side. But
10 there is more to the division. In most people language and language-related abilities are located in the left hemisphere. Because language is so closely related to thinking and reasoning, the
15 left hemisphere is concerned with conscious thought processes and problem solving. It was once considered the major hemisphere. But recent investigations have shown that the right hemi-
20 sphere also plays an important role in the total functioning of the personality. This hemisphere provides nonverbal skills and a different mode of thinking. Whereas the left hemisphere tends to be
25 verbal and analytic, the right hemisphere tends to be nonverbal and global. The right hemisphere is not inferior to the left. It processes information differently, often providing creative leaps and
30 sudden insights not available to the left hemisphere. The left hand, controlled by the right hemisphere, is "the dreamer," but the label should not suggest inferiority or incapacity. Both hemi-
35 spheres play an equivalent, though different, role in the functioning of the personality.

1. Which of the following titles best summarizes the content of the passage?
   (A) Creativity and the Human Brain
   (B) Poetry: A Left-Brain Function
   (C) The Brain: A Two-Part Mechanism
   (D) Personality Types
   (E) Language and the Human Brain

   1 ___

2. The article suggests that _____.
   (A) the left brain controls left-handedness
   (B) the left brain is the major hemisphere
   (C) a left-handed person is at a disadvantage in a right-handed world
   (D) both hemispheres are important for a complete personality
   (E) scientists have discredited the theory that there are two hemispheres

   2 ___

3. Of the following skills, which would probably belong to the right hemisphere?
   (A) writing a summary
   (B) creating music
   (C) classifying objects
   (D) translating an article
   (E) criticizing a movie

   3 ___

4. In this selection the writer's chief distinction is between which of the following?
   (A) the left hand and the right hand
   (B) dreamers and doers
   (C) the functions of two brain hemispheres
   (D) nonverbal skills and analytic abilities
   (E) applied science and folk wisdom

   4 ___

SUMMARY

4. Making a Comparison

When asked to evaluate comparisons, be sure to isolate the two important things being compared. Don't hit upon a minor comparison. Alternative *4A*, p. 207, singles out a minor illustration though the question calls for the *chief distinction*.

Section II Summary: Drawing Inferences

An inference is an educated guess. Though it is based on facts, it goes beyond facts. It reads between the lines and makes a judgment. Often many inferences can be drawn from a single statement or situation. Always choose the most reasonable one, the one most consistent with the facts.

Review the strategies for drawing inferences often as you prepare for the SAT.

PART 1. Identifying Inferences (p. 197)

A. Recognize an inference question. Look for such words as: *imply, assume, suggest, apparently believes.*
B. Look for the facts related to the inference question.
C. Base your inference (your "educated guess") on the facts.
D. Remember, a fact is an observation you can prove. An inference is a guess or a judgment. Don't confuse the two.

PART 2. Supplying an Interpretation (p. 200)

A. Recognize an interpretation question, asking you to say something in another way. Look for such wording as:
    Which best expresses the meaning of . . .
    An excellent adjective to describe _____ is . . .
B. Find the word or phrase in question.
C. Use your own word or phrase to say the same thing.
D. Choose the answer that corresponds most closely to what you have said in your own words.

PART 3. Providing a Paraphrase (p. 202)

A. A paraphrase question asks for a restatement (or "interpretation") of an entire sentence or paragraph or more.

B. Find the material to be paraphrased.
C. Put it in your own words; be sure you are saying the same thing. Restate; don't summarize.
D. Choose the answer that corresponds most closely to what you have said in your own words.

PART 4. Making a Comparison (p. 205)

A. A comparison question asks you to compare two ideas, persons, expressions, or arguments.
B. Look for comparison words such as *difference between* or *distinction between*.
C. Be sure you know what is being compared.
D. Focus on the *important* things being compared.

Section III: Finding Details

1. Spotting Details in the Text

In reading tests, you must be able to find more than generalizations. You'll need to pick out details, specific items in the text. These test items occur in a variety of forms. Here's a skeleton sample.

1. The author refers to . . . as an example of . . .
2. The author bases the answer to the question . . . on . . .
3. According to the passage what happens to . . . ?
4. Sousa's work is "practical" in the sense that it is . . .
5. According to the passage, one of the cultural lessons taught by African art is that art should be . . .
6. The author mentions fluorescent lamps and transistors as examples of . . .
7. According to the passage a cohort study is one that . . .
8. The author cites . . . for their . . .
9. The author mentions which of the following as experiences common to . . . ?
10. According to the passage, a true work of art can be the product of all the following EXCEPT . . .

Again, despite the variety of formats, the essential task is straightforward. With these questions you must comb the selection for *specific* phrases and sentences being asked for.

Trial Test

For the following test questions write the letter for the best answer.

The long association of Joseph Duveen and Henry E. Huntington resulted in an art collection of unquestioned excellence. Like many other wealthy men
5 of his time, Huntington distrusted his own judgment, relying instead upon the impeccable taste of an art dealer who had the knack of matching millionaire and painting. It was Joseph Duveen who
10 bought for Huntington and his wife Arabella the two famous paintings often paired in the eyes of the public: Gainsborough's *The Blue Boy* and Lawrence's *Pinkie*. Without prodding
15 from Duveen, Huntington would never have bought Turner's *The Grand Canal*. Over the protest of Arabella Huntington, Duveen persuaded Huntington to buy Reynolds' masterpiece, *Sarah Sid-*
20 *dons as the Tragic Muse*. Arabella had at first objected to having a picture of an actress in her home. Another Reynolds gem, *Georgiana, Duchess of Devonshire*, was added to the Huntington col-
25 lection. One painting that Arabella Huntington bought, with Duveen's help, is the priceless painting, Rogier van der Weyden's *The Virgin and Christ Child*. Visitors to the Huntington Gallery in
30 San Marino, California, owe a debt to Henry E. Huntington, who accumulated the art now available to the public.

But it was Joseph Duveen who made it all possible.

1. The painting Arabella was reluctant to buy was _____.
   (A) *The Grand Canal*
   (B) *Georgiana, Duchess of Devonshire*
   (C) *Sarah Siddons as the Tragic Muse*
   (D) *The Blue Boy*
   (E) *The Virgin and Christ Child*

   1 ___

2. Two paintings often paired by the public are _____.
   (A) *The Grand Canal* and *Pinkie*
   (B) *Sarah Siddons as the Tragic Muse* and *Pinkie*
   (C) *The Virgin and Christ Child* and *The Blue Boy*
   (D) *Pinkie* and *The Blue Boy*
   (E) *Georgiana, Duchess of Devonshire* and *Sarah Siddons as the Tragic Muse*

   2 ___

Problem

In June, 1981, Jay Johnson started out on an incredible journey—a self-propelled trip around the United States. At no time did Johnson rely on any mo-
5 torized transportation, though he used a variety of methods. He started in northern Maine and backpacked south along the Appalachian Trail to Georgia. Still on foot, he reached Montgomery,
10 Alabama. He picked up a 15-foot dory in Montgomery and rowed down the wild Alabama River to the Gulf of Mexico. Rowing 1200 miles along the Gulf coast, he reached Brownsville, Texas.
15 Then he chose a bicycle for his 3000 mile trip through the Southwest. He gave up the bicycle in southern California and backpacked north on the Pacific Coast Trail all the way to British Colum-
20 bia, arriving in late September, 1982. His trip had lasted 16 months and covered nearly 10,000 miles. To help him along his unusual journey, he estimated his needs in advance and then used the
25 Postal Service for delivery of supplies to prearranged points. He plotted his journey like a military campaign, with a thorough evaluation of his abilities and needs. This was a magical experience,
30 but there was no magic behind its success.

1. The bicycle portion of the journey took place _____.
   (A) in Montgomery, Alabama
   (B) at the very end
   (C) in British Columbia
   (D) Before the arrival in Brownsville
   (E) in the Southwest

   1 ___

2. As used in the selection "self-propelled" means _____.
   (A) highly motivated
   (B) carrying a backpack
   (C) without motorized help
   (D) well planned
   (E) using the Postal Service

   2 ___

3. Jay Johnson used each of the following methods EXCEPT _____.
   (A) bicycle
   (B) dory
   (C) backpack
   (D) mule
   (E) rowing

   3 ___

Strategy. This is a fairly easy selection to get you started and help you see various strategies used in testing for details.

1. Often the answer is found in a single sentence: "Then he chose a bicycle for his 3000 mile trip through the Southwest." Go no further. *(E)* is correct.

2. All five answers relate to the passage, but only *(C)* is responsive to the question. Sentence 2, following immediately after Sentence 1, provides a ready definition of "self-propelled." *(C)* is correct.

3. This type of question is sometimes confusing because of *except*. Under stress and in haste, sometimes candidates fail to read carefully. They see *bicycle* and say, "He used a bicycle." But the *except*, of course, excludes *bicycle, backpack,* and *dory*. Note, too, that *rowing* and *dory* are essentially the same. There is no mention of using a mule. Therefore *(D)* is correct.

Review

Try your skill. The passage below is followed by questions based on its content. Use the preceding example to help you find the right answers.

What happens when a climate change occurs swiftly? When living conditions change almost overnight, how do various species react to the sud-
5 den demands upon them? The appearance of El Niño in 1982–83 helped scientists to study, in a short period, effects that normally take much longer to appear. El Niño—a stream
10 of unusually warm western Pacific water—had a far-reaching impact on all fish, bird, and mammalian life in an area from Chile to southern Alaska and west as far as the central Pacific.
15 The unusually warm water upset the balance, starting a chain of events that did incalculable damage. The normally cold water off the coast of Peru is rich in nutrients. These nutrients support
20 microscopic plants called *phytoplankton,* the base of the food chain. When the phytoplankton population dropped to 5% of normal, anchovies, sardines, jack mackerel, and other fish began to
25 disappear. Then the species depending upon fish had to look elsewhere. Cormorants and boobies headed north for food. Penguins and seals headed south. Though adults tended to survive, the
30 young birds and animals could not be fed and were abandoned. Even seal mothers, normally the most maternal of animals, abandoned their pups to star-

vation. Whole colonies of nesting birds
35 disappeared. Even ecosystems far from El Niño were affected by the climatic changes and disappearance of food in the normally bountiful Pacific. Yet, scientists say, there have been drastic
40 swings before, appearances of unpredictable El Niño in past history. Without additional pollution or overfishing by man, species will recover in time. There is one good result despite the dif-
45 ficulties: scientists appreciate the natural laboratory provided by the unwelcome visitor.

1. To support marine life along the coast of Peru, which of the following is most important?
   (A) abundant sunshine
   (B) an occasional tropical storm
   (C) a large school of sardines
   (D) El Niño
   (E) cold water

1 ___

2. One positive contribution of El Niño is ___.
   (A) the natural laboratory it supplied
   (B) the improvement in bathing facilities along the coast of South America
   (C) the possibility of new tourist resorts in Alaska
   (D) an indication that the conditions will never be repeated
   (E) a great increase in phytoplankton

2 ___

3. The most serious damage done by El Niño was _____.
   (A) hurricanes as far away as the Caribbean
   (B) an imbalance between mackerel and anchovies
   (C) a threat by the activities of man
   (D) a drought over the deserts of Chile
   (E) the death of young animals

   3 ___

4. Which of the following titles best summarizes the content of the passage?
   (A) Bird Life Under Stress
   (B) El Niño: A Devastating Visitor
   (C) A Study in Climate
   (D) Weather in the Western Pacific
   (E) Fish Migration and Polluted Water

   4 ___

5. Apparently contradictory behavior was exhibited by _____.
   (A) anchovies   (D) seals
   (B) phy-   (E) jack
       toplankton   mackerel
   (C) penguins   5 ___

6. In terms of species survival, the abandonment of the young by seal mothers was _____.
   (A) prudent
   (B) cruel
   (C) an indication of indifference
   (D) ill-advised
   (E) characteristic

   6 ___

7. The effects of El Niño can best be described as _____.
   (A) far-reaching
   (B) beneficent
   (C) largely unobserved
   (D) minimal
   (E) of little scientific interest

   7 ___

SUMMARY

1. Spotting Details in the Text

When checking for details in a reading passage, look for specific phrases and sentences to support your choice. If more than one answer applies to the passage, be sure you choose the answer that is responsive to the question.

2. Finding Details in Combination

Sometimes the test question will call for a combination of possibilities. Your answer must include all details called for and no details not in the selection.

Trial Test

For the following test question select the best answer.

Oats, wheat, rye, and other grains are well known and often used in America. Barley, however, has been neglected. As Raymond Sokolov has observed, "In this country, today, few people cook barley at all. Most of us taste it rarely and almost exclusively in soup." Though known from Biblical days, barley is "the all-but-forgotten grain, orphan among staples." It deserves to be better known and more often used.

Barley is a superbly hardy grass, growing everywhere from Egypt to Norway and Tibet. It thrives in climates too cold for wheat. It is a versatile grain. Bread made from barley is dark and tasty. It keeps well and is still pleasantly edible when dry. Barley can be used for cakes, breads, pancakes. It is a subtle flavoring when used in combination with other grains. Why, then, has barley done so poorly in modern America?

Wheat is the culprit in the story of barley's retreat. Though less sturdy than barley, wheat can, with modern methods, be transported and preserved more easily than in the past. Wheat has more gluten, thus allowing bread from wheat to rise. Barley bread, by contrast, is flat. Barley cannot replace wheat, but it has a niche to fill.

How can we take advantage of this neglected grain? We can combine barley with wheat for a tasty, nutritious bread. We can, of course, use it in soup, where its delicate flavor is a plus. We can eat barley as a side dish with most main courses. We can bake it with mushrooms in a pie crust. We can, like the Koreans, serve it with rice. We can also brew a tea from roasted barley, as the Japanese do. However we use it, we ought to rescue this overlooked grain from its undeserved oblivion.

Which of the following statements may be accurately derived from the selection?

I. Barley makes a bread superior to wheat bread.
II. Barley has an adaptability unsuspected by most Americans.
III. Barley is a member of the grass family.
IV. Barley combines with other grains for tasty foods.
V. Oats and wheat grow in Tibet.
(A) I only
(B) IV only
(C) II, III, and IV
(D) I, III, and V
(E) I and IV

———

Problem

The Mayan Empire once stretched from the Yucatan to western Honduras. Its power and extent are constantly being restudied as new discoveries rescue important Mayan sites from the jungle. Sites like Uxmal and Chichen-Itza in Yucatan, Tikal in Guatemala, and Copán in Honduras reveal the awesome achievements of the civilization that flourished many centuries ago. The latter two, discovered in the 1840s, "rank in archaeological importance with the pyramids of Egypt."

A more recent discovery is causing a complete reappraisal of the Mayan influence and the duration of the Mayan Empire. It had previously been thought that the Mayan civilization did not mature before 300 A.D. Then in 1978 Bruce Dahlin uncovered bits of pottery dating from 400 B.C. There, in the lost city called *El Mirador*, not far from Tikal, a civilization flourished centuries before the date usually assigned to its arrival.

The architecture at El Mirador reveals the sophistication of its artisans:

master builders, stonecutters, and
sculptors. The various structures also
suggest a high level of social organization. Here, too, are beautiful carvings
with hieroglyphics as yet undeciphered.
This graphic style of writing provided
much of the communication upon which
a civilization ultimately rests.

The new discoveries suggest that the
Mayan Empire lasted not 500 or so
years but 1500 years or more. John Gra-
ham of Berkeley flatly states, "Mayan
civilization represents the longest sus-
tained civilization in the New World."
Further explorations at El Mirador suggest that we have just scratched the surface of our knowledge about the Maya.

Which of the following statements may be
accurately derived from the selection?

I. Writing is crucial to the success of a civilization.
II. Mayan sites are predominantly in Yucatan.
III. The duration of Mayan civilization is
under reappraisal and revision.
IV. The buildings at El Mirador are contemporary with the pyramids of Egypt.
V. Hieroglyphics are associated with, and
restricted to, Egypt.

(A) III only   (D) II and IV
(B) IV only   (E) I and III
(C) I and V

____

Strategy. Statements II, IV, and V are false. Therefore any answer containing one of these statements is wrong; that is, (B), (C), and (D). Statement
III is true, but (A) is wrong because it suggests that only III applies. The
correct answer, (E), lists both correct statements: I and III.

Review

Try your skill. The passage below is followed by questions based on its content. Use
the preceding example to help you find the
right answers.

American folklore is filled with tales
of hoboes, wanderers who rode the rails
and traveled the country as uninvited
guests of the railroads. But there is another group of rail-riders, whose presence is never felt by the train but whose
journey is made possible by the Iron
Horse: weeds! These courageous adventurers establish themselves on sites
that look forbidding, even deadly, to living things. The cinders along the railbed
and the borders seem an impossible
nursery for any living organism. Yet
many plants survive in the hostile environment.

Seeds are carried by trains and dispersed along the right of way. Queen
Anne's lace, ragweed, and wild parsnip
flourish where a railroad intersects with
a road. Clovers, horseweed, and wood
sorrels do well at railroad crossings in
farm country. Some plants seem to
thrive especially well along the forbidding tracks. Dwarf snapdragon, for example, grows more abundantly along
railroad tracks than anywhere else.

It's hard to think of a more inhospitable environment than the land along
the railroad tracks. The cinders contain
little if any humus. The area is dry, sun-
baked, and often sprayed with weed
killers. Speeding trains lop off the heads
of taller species. Even smaller plants
are subjected to the air stresses created
by passing trains. Yet persistent plant
life struggles and often perpetuates its
kind, despite the odds against survival.
The track area may not be a luxurious
garden, but it nurtures many train-borne
weeds.

1. Which of the following statements may be accurately derived from the selection?
   I. A railbed is a better place to grow plants than a city garden.
   II. Different plants thrive in different conditions.
   III. The dwarf snapdragon thrives especially well along a railroad line.
   IV. Ragweed and Queen Anne's lace seem to grow well in similar environments.
   V. American folklore features the vitality and dispersion of native weeds.

   (A) II only
   (B) IV only
   (C) II, III, and IV
   (D) III and V
   (E) I, II, and III

   1 ___

2. The "courageous adventurers" referred to in lines 8–9 are ___.
   (A) hoboes
   (B) trains
   (C) dwarf snapdragons
   (D) smaller plants
   (E) weeds

   2 ___

3. Which two are compared in the selection?
   (A) hoboes and weed killers
   (B) luxurious garden and a railbed
   (C) the Iron Horse and the tracks
   (D) impossible nursery and hostile environment
   (E) railroads and automobiles

   3 ___

4. Which of the following titles best summarizes the content of the passage?
   (A) Weeds and Their Ways
   (B) Railroads: Preservers of American Wildlife
   (C) Those Unlikely Railroad "Gardens"
   (D) Endangered Species: Railroad Weeds
   (E) Weeds: The Railroads' Persistent Problem

   4 ___

5. It is reasonable to infer that ___.
   (A) some weeds can store moisture for survival
   (B) the wood sorrel is more adaptable than the dwarf snapdragon
   (C) hoboes paid a small railroad fare
   (D) cinders have hidden pockets of soil
   (E) the wild parsnip is sturdier than the ragweed

   5 ___

SUMMARY

2. Finding Details in Combination

When checking for a combination of details in a reading passage, be complete. Include only those details actually included—but don't leave any out.

3. Combining Skills

The reading skills tested are rarely pure examples of only one skill. Frequently two or more skills are needed to ferret out an answer.

An inference, for example, is frequently built upon a key detail in the selection, even though it is not, itself, a detail. You have to do two things: find the detail and make the inference. A title is frequently based on a conclusion that balances various inferences. You have to do three things: make the inferences, form a conclusion, and choose a title.

Some SAT questions require you to figure out details and then make judgments about the details. Note that the wording of the following SAT-type question does more than call for identification of details. It also calls for an inference based on details.

1. In which of the following lines is an appeal made to curiosity?

    (A) 1–5
    (B) 6–10
    (C) 11–15
    (D) 16–20
    (E) 21–25

Here's a combination in which you are not expected to state the main idea but to identify the lines in the passage which contain the main idea.

The same skills may be tested in different forms.

2. During which ten-year period was there the greatest unrest in the United States?

    (A) 1896–1905
    (B) 1905–1914
    (C) 1920–1929
    (D) 1945–1954
    (E) 1962–1971

3. The central thought of the passage is most clearly expressed in which of the following lines?

    (A) 1–5
    (B) 6–10
    (C) 11–15
    (D) 16–20
    (E) 21–25

Trial Test

Select the best answer for the following test question.

You can have your own drugstore right on your windowsill. The aloe vera plant, which is often grown as a pot plant, has some remarkable medicinal properties. The fresh leaf juice of the plant contains the drug aloin, which has many soothing properties when it is used externally.

The roster of the skin problems helped by aloe is impressive. The juice has healing properties for insect bites, minor burns, poison ivy, and athlete's foot. It can also relieve summer sunburn and dry skin.

For minor burns, victims may break off the largest leaf of the aloe plant and squeeze it gently, like a tube of toothpaste or ointment. The sticky clear gel is applied directly to the burn.

Aloe is not a recent newcomer to medication. The ancient Greeks and Egyptians knew of its medicinal proper-

ties. Cleopatra used aloe as part of her beauty treatments and medications.

The plant itself is inexpensive. It makes a beautiful pot plant. Because it is a succulent, it requires little watering. It does, however, need good drainage and lots of sun. Some people may have a mild allergy to aloe vera, but for most people, the plant can be a multipurpose medicine shelf—and a compact, decorative one besides.

In which of the following paragraphs is a possible drawback to the use of aloe mentioned?

(A) 1
(B) 2
(C) 3
(D) 4
(E) 5

Problem

Accidents will happen—but many needn't. Among the most common type of automobile accidents are rear-end collisions. In a ranking of types of automobile road accidents, these collisions rank second. Over 3½ million drivers are involved each year in this particular road hazard. Yet much can be done to cut down the number of such accidents.

The best way to reduce rear-end collisions is to improve visibility. One experimental device was the installation of a third brake light on the back of cars. In an experimental study this minor addition resulted in a drop of 50% in the number of rear-end collisions. Placing the new light centrally on the trunk, just below the rear window, provides certain new advantages. It is not used as a directional signal, nor is it used to illuminate the back of the car at night. It stays dark until the driver brakes. This is a clear signal that the car is slowing or stopping. Because it is about at eye level of the driver in the car behind, it is easily visible.

Installation of such a light is inexpensive—generally under $30. Wires go directly into the car trunk and are connected to the existing brake lights. The average motorist can install the light himself. This brake light is now standard on new cars.

The second method for avoiding rear-end collisions is to drive a light-colored car. When visibility is poor, accidents often occur because a driver doesn't see the other vehicle until it's too late. According to safety tests, drivers can see light, bright cars from a distance of up to four times farther away than they can see cars in darker tones. A white car is the most visible of all.

1. The advantage of placing the third light just below the rear window is mentioned in which of the following lines?
(A) 1–6   (D) 27–30
(B) 8–16   (E) 39–42
(C) 21–26
                              1 ___

2. The central thought of the passage is most clearly expressed in which of the following lines?
(A) 1–5   (D) 30–33
(B) 10–13   (E) 34–39
(C) 24–26
                              2 ___

Strategy.   1. The advantage of placing the light just below the rear window is mentioned in lines 10–16. Since answer *(B)* includes lines 10–16, *(B)* is the correct answer. The rest of the selection does not deal with that particular detail.

2. The central idea of the entire selection is stated in lines 10–11.

"The best way to reduce rear-end collisions is to improve visibility." The entire passage is devoted to the question of visibility, with the third light discussed at length and the color of the car discussed in the last paragraph. Since lines 10–11 are in 10–13, *(B)* is the correct answer.

Review

Try your skill. The passage below is followed by questions based on its content. Use the preceding example to help you find the right answers.

"Why bother saving wild and endangered species? It is the fate of species to become extinct someday anyway. Why bother with snail darters and wild
5 grains? Let's spend more time on more important problems."

These arguments have a specious reasonableness, but they couldn't be more wrong. We have a selfish interest
10 in wild species. We need to protect them for our own survival.

As Norman Myers has pointed out, "We use hundreds of products each day that owe their existence to plants and
15 animals. The ways in which wild species support our daily welfare fall under three main headings: agriculture, medicine, and industry."

In agriculture, for example, we need
20 a constant infusion of new genetic material from wild plants. Plant geneticists have done more to improve crop yields than artificial additives like fertilizers and pesticides. Natural immunities to
25 pests and extremes of climates are bred into native plants with the help of wild stock. Blight-resistant genes from a wild Mexican plant helped preserve the threatened American corn crop. A wild
30 wheat strain from Turkey is resistant to several diseases afflicting domestic grain. Its introduction saved the farm industry millions of dollars worth of crops each year.

35 The same situation is true in medicine. Wild organisms continue to contribute remedies for many of our ills. A child suffering from leukemia once had only a 20% chance of remission. With
40 the help of rosy periwinkle, a tropical forest plant, the child now has an 80% chance. Other anticancer drugs may well be found in the vast jungles of the Amazon basin.

45 The seas provide other medicinal materials. A Caribbean sponge may be an important antiviral agent. Menhaden, a marine fish, provides an oil that may help in treating atherosclero-
50 sis. Sea snakes can yield an anticoagulant. Extracts from the toxin of the octopus may be used as an anesthetic in modern surgery. Potential anticancer drugs may come from corals, sea anem-
55 ones, mollusks, sponges, sea squirts, and even clams.

Industry also depends upon wild species for many products. Seaweeds, for example, contribute to hundreds of
60 products, including waxes, detergents, soaps, shampoos, paints, lubricants, and dyes. Land plants like the jojoba play a large part in industrial production. The liquid wax from the jojoba is
65 a brilliantly efficient lubricant. The expansion of the chemical industry suggests that we'll need many more supplies of organic industrial chemicals. As yet untapped or undiscovered species
70 can make major contributions to industry.

The wild species of the world are not

merely decorative at best or essentially useless at worst. They are a storehouse
75 of genetic material and products that can help us improve our lives—even survive. An investment in the survival of wild species is an investment in the survival of another species—our own.

1. Genetic experimentation with plants is discussed in which of the following lines?
   (A) 1–11
   (B) 12–15
   (C) 19–34
   (D) 35–44
   (E) 57–65

   1 ___

2. From the selection, it may be inferred that _____.
   (A) wild plants are always superior to domestic plants
   (B) a cure for cancer will come from the blight-resistant Mexican wheat
   (C) domestic plants often have limited resistance to ills
   (D) we need not be concerned about the extinction of wild species
   (E) industry is blindly reluctant to accept the products derived from wild species

   2 ___

3. A wild species that contributes hundreds of products is _____.
   (A) jojoba
   (B) rosy periwinkle
   (C) seaweed
   (D) octopus
   (E) sea snake

   3 ___

4. The central thought of the passage is most clearly expressed in which of the following statements?
   (A) In agriculture, for example, we need a constant infusion of new genetic material from wild plants.
   (B) It is the fate of species to become extinct someday anyway.
   (C) The seas provide other medicinal materials.
   (D) As yet untapped or undiscovered species can make major contributions to industry.
   (E) An investment in the survival of wild species is an investment in the survival of another species—our own.

   4 ___

5. To save wild species we must _____.
   (A) preserve their natural habitats
   (B) cultivate them in our gardens
   (C) carefully monitor climate
   (D) stop using their genetic material
   (E) experiment with changing their genetic structure

   5 ___

6. Which of the following pairs is correctly matched?
   (A) seaweed-anticancer
   (B) jojoba-anesthetic
   (C) sea snake-detergent
   (D) mollusk-leukemia
   (E) menhaden-atherosclerosis

   6 ___

Section III Summary: Finding Details

Although you cannot ordinarily point specifically to a sentence or section in the text to prove an inferred answer, you can usually find in the text itself the answer to a question turning upon a detail in the selection.

Review the strategies for finding details as you prepare for the SAT.

PART 1. Spotting Details in the Text (p. 210)

A. Look for specific phrases and sentences with the details you want.
B. When you find details for *more than one* answer, do the following:
1. Reread the question to be sure you understand it.
2. Choose the answer with the details that specifically answer the question.

PART 2. Finding Details in Combination (p. 213)

When a question calls for two or more details together:

A. Read the passage carefully.
B. Choose the answer with *only* the details that you have read.
C. Be sure you don't leave out any of the details.

PART 3. Combining Skills (p. 217)

When a question asks you to combine skills, usually making an inference or judgment based on details:

A. Find the details you need.
B. Use the details to make the inference or judgment called for.
C. Make any more choices as needed (such as choosing a title or a central idea) based on what you have found and decided.

Section IV: Understanding the Author's Role

1. Evaluating the Author's Tone

When we speak, we indicate the tone of the message by our tone of voice. When we write, we indicate tone in other ways. SAT questions frequently ask candidates to describe the tone of a passage. The following are some typical adjectives and nouns to describe tone.

"TONE" ADJECTIVES

aggressive and dogmatic	indifferent
argumentative	inquisitive
conciliatory and apologetic	inspirational
honest and straightforward	instructional and explanatory
humble	ironic
objective	scholarly
reflective	sensational and melodramatic

"TONE" NOUNS

apprehension	hope	resignation
deference	indifference	reverence
despair	irrationality	sarcasm
disdain	mistrust	self-pity
enthusiasm	relief	urgency

To answer questions about tone, you must get the "feel" of the passage. You must "read between the lines" and determine what mood is suggested.

Trial Test

The morning dawned cold and gray. The freezing winter rain had stripped all but a few tenacious oak leaves from the trees outside the study window. The
5 colors were muted, with shades of gray and brown predominating in a Rembrandtesque landscape. The autumn distractions of brilliant color were gone, and the tree trunks stood stark and aus-
10 tere a few feet from the window. The corrugations of the bark were clear and distinct. The tiny patches of moss and lichen here and there accentuated the grooves rather than diminished them.
15 Through the tree silhouettes could be discerned the olive-green needles of young Southern pine, struggling for survival in the oak forest. The ground was littered with brown oak leaves, whose
20 otherwise monochromatic appearance was challenged by their curl and twist on the forest floor. Here and there,

fallen gray twigs punctuated the rust
mattress, adding a pleasant break in the
superficial uniformity. This was a subtle
scene, a scene demanding close observation to find the beauty of color and
form that was everywhere.

25

The tone of the passage can best be described
as _____.

(A) self-satisfied   (D) argumentative
(B) conciliatory   (E) apprehensive
(C) reflective

_____

Problem

OLD IRONSIDES

Ay, tear her tattered ensign down!
  Long has it waved on high,
And many an eye has danced to see
  That banner in the sky;
5 Beneath it rung the battle shout,
    And burst the cannon's roar;—
The meteor of the ocean air
  Shall sweep the clouds no more.
Her deck, once red with heroes'
    blood,
10 Where knelt the vanquished foe,
When winds were hurrying o'er the
    floods,
And waves were white below,
No more shall feel the victor's tread,
  Or know the conquered knee;—
15 The harpies of the shore shall pluck
  The eagle of the sea!

Oh, better that her shattered hulk
  Should sink beneath the wave;
Her thunders shook the mighty deep,
20 And there should be her grave;
Nail to the mast her holy flag,

Set every threadbare sail,
And give her to the god of storms,
  The lightning and the gale!

1. The tone of the poem as a whole can
best be described as _____.
(A) amiable   (D) indifferent
(B) doubtful   (E) angry
(C) acquiescent
                    1 ____

2. Lines 3–4 convey a sense of _____.
(A) humor   (D) delight
(B) pride   (E) worry
(C) uncertainty
                    2 ____

3. Which of the following lines can best
be described as *sarcastic?*
(A) 1   (D) 19
(B) 9–10   (E) 21
(C) 12–13
                    3 ____

4. The "harpies of the shore" (line 15)
are treated with _____.
(A) suspicion   (D) anticipation
(B) contempt   (E) resignation
(C) fear
                    4 ____

Strategy.   1. The poet resents the fact that the historic ship is going to
be scrapped ("tear her tattered ensign down"). This attack is angry, as other
lines confirm. The answer is *(E), angry.*

   2. If an eye "dances" to see the banner in the sky, the emotion described
is pride: *(B).*

   3. From the rest of the passage, it is clear that the poet does not want
the "tattered ensign" torn down. Quite the opposite. Since sarcasm seems
to say one thing while clearly implying the other, the answer is *(A).* The other
alternatives are straightforward and positive.

   4. Contrasting the "harpies of the shore" with "the eagle of the sea"
clearly suggests the poet's venomous attitude toward the harpies. Contempt,
(B), is an accurate word to suggest the tone of the lines.

Review

Try your skill. The passage below is followed by questions based on its content. Use the preceding example to help you find the right answers.

"Who Cares Who Killed Roger Ackroyd?" The title of Edmund Wilson's 1945 essay clearly indicates the writer's bias. Wilson called detective stories 5 "wasteful of time and degrading to the intellect." Since that time other critics have sneered, condescended, and scorned the whodunit, but its popularity has rarely faltered. The detective story 10 and related types like the spy story, the horror tale, and the Dashiell Hammett type of thriller are often lumped under the general heading *Mystery* and earn a special shelf in most libraries. The mys- 15 tery shelf is one of the most popular in every library. The books on these shelves have been worn with use. Novels by old favorite writers like John Dickson Carr vie with current favorites 20 like those by Ruth Rendell. Why do mysteries, and especially detective stories, often outlast their critics?

In an era when much modern fiction is plotless and loosely structured, the 25 detective story, with its solid plot, tells a story that appeals to the child in everyone. The detective story begins somewhere and ends somewhere. In between, readers are treated to twists of 30 plot, surprises in characterization, and challenging puzzles.

Detective stories and other mysteries, though often maligned, have influenced other current fiction. Even "liter- 35 ary" fiction has been affected by the mystery and its close relatives. Paul Theroux's *Family Arsenal,* Robert Stone's *A Flag for Sunrise,* and Margaret Atwood's *Bodily Harm* all use the 40 conventions of the thriller.

Some writers have gone further. Michiko Kakutani has pointed out that some prestigious writers "have used the conventions of the mystery to make 45 philosophical points about the nature of storytelling itself." Joyce Carol Oates in *Mysteries of Winterthurn,* Alain Robbe-Grillet in *The Erasers,* and Jorge Luis Borges in *Death and the Compass* 50 have added a dimension to the possibilities inherent in the mystery form.

1. The tone of the selection as a whole can best be described as _____.
   (A) instructional and explanatory
   (B) inquisitive and investigatory
   (C) sensational and dogmatic
   (D) biased and poorly represented
   (E) careless and unconcerned

   1 ___

2. The tone of the title "Who Cares Who Killed Roger Ackroyd?" is intended to be _____.
   (A) sympathetic and curious
   (B) wittily negative
   (C) brutally callous
   (D) straightforwardly informative
   (E) earnest and prudent

   2 ___

3. We may reasonably infer that Roger Ackroyd is _____.
   (A) a mystery writer
   (B) a book reviewer
   (C) a real-life crime victim
   (D) a character in a famous mystery
   (E) an imaginary name invented by Robert Stone

   3 ___

4. It may be assumed that the writer of this selection considers Paul Theroux's *Family Arsenal* as _____.
   (A) a true detective story
   (B) a philosophical novel
   (C) "literary" fiction
   (D) a book to be grouped with *The Erasers*
   (E) a book for the mystery shelf

   4 ___

5. The main point of the passage is
to _____.
   (A) give the mystery its rightful due in
       current fiction
   (B) explain why Dashiell Hammett's
       novels have had ups and downs
   (C) present Michiko Kakutani's point
       of view about spy stories
   (D) answer the critics of John Dickson
       Carr and Ruth Rendell
   (E) explore the origins of the whodunit
                                    5 ___

6. As a category name, *mystery* can be
   best labeled _____.
   (A) inaccurate   (D) worthless
   (B) humorous   (E) noteworthy
   (C) broad
                                    6 ___

7. The major strength of the detective
   story is its _____.
   (A) philosophical content
   (B) sense of direction
   (C) imitation of the best writing of
       Joyce Carol Oates
   (D) conventional characterization
   (E) use of exotic settings
                                    7 ___

8. The sentence "Why do mysteries, and
   especially detective stories, often out-
   last their critics?" can be interpreted
   as _____.
   (A) an unanswerable question
   (B) a petty swipe at mysteries
   (C) a baffling comment on "literary"
       fiction
   (D) an apologetic defense of literary
       critics
   (E) a commendation of the detective
       story
                                    8 ___

9. The word "literary" in "'literary' fic-
   tion" is in quotation marks be-
   cause _____.
   (A) it is quoted from a novel by Paul
       Theroux
   (B) it exposes a critical snobbish at-
       titude
   (C) here it means exactly the opposite
       of its usual meaning
   (D) it suggests that the novels men-
       tioned are largely biographical
   (E) mystery writers lack true narrative
       gifts
                                    9 ___

SUMMARY

1. Evaluating the Author's Tone

The tone of a passage cannot be found in a detail of the selection. It
can "be found only in the overall impression created by the combination of
descriptive and connotative words." (See connotation and denotation, pages
46–50.) Most SAT selections tend to have a fairly neutral tone, with emphasis
upon the presentation of information. Others, like "Old Ironsides," crackle
with a special life of their own, a mood that colors the piece.

---

2. Evaluating the Author's Attitude

Closely related to the tone of a reading passage is the attitude displayed
or suggested. A typical SAT question requires you to discover the author's

attitude toward someone or something. The following are examples of questions of this type.

1. Which of the following best expressed the author's attitude toward . . . ?
2. The attitude toward . . . is one of . . .
3. It can be inferred from the passage that the author's attitude toward the . . . is one of . . .
4. The author's attitude toward . . . is primarily one of . . .
5. The attitude toward . . . conveyed by the author's use of the words . . . is best described as one of . . .
6. The author's attitude toward the . . . mentioned in lines 1–20 is best described as . . .

Here is a brief cross-section of typical attitudes tested.

admiration	disdain
ambivalence	exasperation
anxiety	nostalgia
apathy	puzzlement
disbelief	skepticism

Sometimes the attitudes are more narrowly and specifically labeled.

delighted amazement	clear distaste
growing anger	apologetic embarrassment
reluctant approval	cold objectivity
mild condescension	admiring support
veiled disdain	detached sympathy

Other questions display a slightly different phraseology which requires a different type of answer.

The author's attitude toward . . . is that of a . . .

A correctly completed statement might look something like this:

The author's attitude toward the absentee employees is that of a parent correcting a misbehaving child.

Note that all these questions are quite different from those for tone. Questions about tone are usually general. Questions about attitude are more specific. In these questions you must uncover the author's attitude *toward someone or something*. Though the phraseology varies from question to question, the essential requirement is the same.

There is no substitute for trying your hand at a typical question.

Trial Test

Take the following trial test to evaluate your skill.

Those who see professional football on television are missing half the fun and half the show: the fans. Though the television cameraman occasionally provides tantalizing shots of oddball enthusiasts, the glimpses are not enough. Through the years there have been colorful characters on the field with pictur-esque names like "Crazylegs," "The Catawba Claw," "the Juice" and "the Fun Bunch." But the real characters are in the stands.

The Pittsburgh Steelers once numbered among their stalwart fans "Franco's Italian Army" and "Gerela's Gorillas." The "Gorillas" came, appropriately enough, dressed in gorilla suits. "Cowboys," "Indians," "Pirates," and "Vikings" regularly appear in the stands to root their teams on. Entire sections join in the fun, wearing orange sweaters and waving orange banners or singing "Hail to the Redskins." There's *active* fun in the stands, too. Stadium hijinks at halftime include passing play footballs in the stands to the roaring approval of the crowd. There is much to see and hear at a football game—and much of that is not on the field.

The author's attitude toward football fans is one of _____.

(A) righteous indignation
(B) concealed intolerance
(C) vigorous denunciation
(D) amused affection
(E) calculated indifference

_____

Problem

"The redwing blackbirds are back!" This cry in February or March reassures a winter-weary land that spring will come again. Migrating birds bring song, color, and joy into our lives. Their migrations have been cheered, observed, and analyzed for many years, but the mysteries remain.

Most birds apparently migrate to follow the food chain. When insects start to become abundant in northern meadows, migrating insect-eaters return. The appearance of flowers entices the hummingbirds. Food requirements of all species are relatively specialized and keyed to the environment.

There are many hazards, however, in migration. Storms may blow birds far off course over open water, an often fatal accident. Flying at night, birds crash into towers and tall buildings. They may arrive at their usual destination only to find a shopping center where their territories once were.

Birds make these incredible journeys each year, but the how and the why are often obscure. Why does the Arctic tern spend eight months each year migrating from the Arctic to the Antarctic and back again? How can this tiny creature successfully navigate vast areas of open seas? Though migration has been studied since the time of Aristotle, we are still in the dark. We can, however, make a contribution by protecting breeding habitats and protecting the way stations the long-distance travelers frequent on their hazardous trips.

1. The author's attitude toward migrating birds is one of _____.
   (A) satisfied curiosity
   (B) cautious skepticism
   (C) mild irritation
   (D) affectionate respect
   (E) unfeeling analysis

   1 _____

2. The author's attitude toward the flight of the Arctic tern can best be characterized by the word _____.
   (A) wonder
   (B) disbelief
   (C) approval
   (D) indifference
   (E) anxiety

   2 _____

Strategy. 1. Eliminate some of the alternatives and see what is left. Curiosity about bird migration has not been satisfied; *(A)* is incorrect. *Skepticism* is not the word needed. Skepticism implies doubt about the truth or falsity of a statement or belief. Uncertainty does not generate skepticism; dogma does. *(B)* is incorrect. There is no hint of irritation; *(C), mild irritation,* is incorrect. The author is emotionally but positively involved. *Unfeeling* tells us *(E)* is wrong. That leaves *(D), affectionate respect,* clearly the attitude of the author.

2. The author takes no direct stand about the flight of the tern *(C)*, but he or she is not indifferent *(D)*. There is no question of disbelief *(B)*. That leaves us with *(A)* and *(E)*. The use of *incredible* (line 25) and the sentences following tell us the correct answer is *wonder, (A)*.

Review

Try your skill. The passage below is followed by questions based on its content. Use the preceding example to help you find the right answers.

Though often taught as merely a pretty decoration in poetry, metaphor is in reality a basic element in language, transcending mere ornamentation. Sim-
5 ply defined as "an implied comparison between unlike objects," metaphor is really a flash of insight, a leap of imagination, a poetic explosion. When the poet Alfred Noyes in "The Highway-
10 man" calls the road "a ribbon of moonlight," he is superficially comparing a road and a ribbon, but he is really going farther. He is investing the road with the emotional, imaginative qualities as-
15 sociated with moonlight. He is pouring into that solid, substantial road all the ethereal qualities of moonlight.

Our entire language is metaphorical. Many of our commonest expressions
20 are overlooked metaphors. Think, for a moment, of the actual images concealed in "run out of patience," "a cutting remark," "drop the subject," "fly into a rage," "pull strings," "turn down a
25 suggestion," and "pick up the threads of a story."

Metaphor enlarges language. It takes commonplace building blocks and by combining them creates new and
30 beautiful meanings. Shakespeare says, "Life's but a walking shadow, a poor player that struts and frets his hour upon the stage and then is heard no more." The individual words are com-
35 mon, but the extended comparison—of life and an actor—is uncommon.

Metaphor is concealed in many common words. By derivation, a *coherent* story "sticks together." A *subliminal*
40 impulse lies "below the threshold" of consciousness. A *chrysanthemum* is "a flower of gold." *Planets* are "wanderers." Most words travel far from their original, narrow, literal meanings. In
45 the process they acquire metaphorical meanings.

Metaphor is everywhere—in sports telecasts, on the editorial pages, on the stage, in our everyday speaking and
50 writing. Even the word *metaphor* contains a hidden metaphor—from the Greek words to "carry beyond." Metaphor indeed *carries* meaning *beyond* the narrow and literal.

1. The author's attitude toward the subject of metaphor is one of _____.
   (A) amused boredom
   (B) scholarly debate
   (C) mandatory approbation
   (D) excessive enthusiasm
   (E) alert interest

1 ___

2. The author's attitude toward Shakespeare is _____.
   (A) flattering
   (B) appreciative
   (C) curious
   (D) uncritical
   (E) contradictory

2 ___

ENGLISH FOR THE COLLEGE BOARDS

3. We may reasonably infer that "The Highwayman" is a(n) _____.
   (A) essay
   (B) article
   (C) historical memoir
   (D) novel
   (E) poem

   3 ___

4. The quotation from Shakespeare is called an "extended comparison" because _____.
   (A) it contains several images
   (B) it compares life and an actor
   (C) it is more literal than metaphorical
   (D) Shakespeare rarely created simple metaphors
   (E) it is a better image than that created by Noyes

   4 ___

5. Two words that are intentionally paired and opposed are _____.
   (A) road and moonlight
   (B) struts and frets
   (C) substantial and ethereal
   (D) chrysanthemum and planets
   (E) life and actor

   5 ___

6. According to the selection a concealed metaphor is contained in the word _____.
   (A) comparison
   (B) literal
   (C) coherent
   (D) derivation
   (E) beautiful

   6 ___

7. The writer would probably classify the expression "leap of imagination" as a(n) _____.
   (A) ribbon of moonlight
   (B) metaphor
   (C) decoration
   (D) poem
   (E) extended comparison

   7 ___

8. The paragraph devoted exclusively to the physical imagery of the metaphor is _____.
   (A) 1   (D) 4
   (B) 2   (E) 5
   (C) 3   8 ___

9. Using clues from the selection, we might guess that the original meaning of *eliminate* was _____.
   (A) cast over the threshold
   (B) discard abruptly
   (C) wander from the truth
   (D) carry beyond
   (E) strut upon the stage

   9 ___

10. The main point of the passage is to _____.
    (A) extol the art of poetry
    (B) compare Noyes and Shakespeare as poets
    (C) encourage the more extensive use of metaphor
    (D) give metaphor its due as a crucial element in language
    (E) provide an implied comparison of metaphor and simile

    10 ___

SUMMARY

2. Evaluating the Author's Attitude

Searching out the author's attitude requires rereading of the selection as a whole. If you read the selection quietly to yourself, you will begin to sense the author's feeling toward her or his material. Individual words may provide clues, but you must get a feeling for the selection in its entirety. Think of the author as speaking to you. What feeling is he or she trying to convey?

3. Evaluating the Author's Purpose

As we have seen, in a reading passage the author's attitude and the tone of the selection are often linked closely together. A third ingredient, the author's purpose, also influences a reading selection. SAT questions frequently challenge you to decide just what the author is trying to achieve.

The following are examples of questions designed to uncover and probe the author's purpose:

1. Which of the following best describes the purpose of the passage?
2. The primary purpose of the passage appears to be to . . .
3. The author includes statistical information specifically to . . .
4. The author's primary purpose in this passage is to . . .
5. The author quotes . . . in order to . . .

Trial Test

Take this trial test to evaluate your skill.

"You smash and slapdash the idea while it's red hot with you. Get it down on paper." This advice by Bergen Evans should be engraved in every
5 writer's memory. Every author experiences writer's block at some time or other. Just looking at an empty paper waiting to be filled is enough to paralyze the will and freeze determination. But
10 Evan's advice can help break down the barriers.

When you have a writing assignment of any kind, don't sit numbly waiting for the perfect outline to suggest itself. Try
15 brainstorming. Jot down everything on a topic that occurs to you. Don't be critical at this stage. Capitalize on those free associations, those creative if unformed ideas, those many images that
20 float to the surface. Don't be inhibited. Don't say, "Oh, that won't work." *Put it down.* Later, after you have poured forth all those ideas, organize your jottings. Decide what belongs and what
25 doesn't. Form the related ideas into a helpful outline.

Letting your mind roam freely is excellent procedure for any creative project. It is especially useful in writing.

The author's primary purpose in this passage is to _____.

(A) extol the critical faculties in writing
(B) introduce Bergen Evans as a useful guide
(C) stress that writer's block is a trivial problem
(D) suggest a sound pre-writing technique
(E) recommend self-criticism in preparing to write

Problem

The explosive growth of racquetball as a sport is traceable in part to an increased interest in physical fitness. Instead of engaging in sedentary pursuits,
5 many people have learned to enjoy the demanding activity of jogging, bodybuilding, and other fitness sports. While it is true that racquetball enthusiasts have been lured away from tennis,
10 handball, squash, and other related activities, the racquetball ranks have also been swelled by newcomers to strenuous physical activity.

What is the appeal of this relatively
15 new sport? The key word is *action*. Racquetball is played inside a box, an en-

closed court with six playing surfaces: the four walls, the floor, and the ceiling. A close relative to squash or four-wall handball, racquetball is a flurry of incredibly swift action. Even beginners soon learn to hit the ball at speeds exceeding 80 miles an hour. Split-second decisions require reflexes that astound spectators. The ball ricochets off all surfaces with apparently little rhyme or reason, but competent players swoop balls out of corners, hit balls falling to within a few inches off the floor, and "kill" a smash without possibility of return. Quickness of response is the heart of the game.

Why has racquetball won converts from other sports? It requires little equipment: a sturdy racquet, a ball,

and, desirably, protective eye covering. It requires relatively little time for a thorough workout. Busy people can squeeze in an exciting match during a lunch hour. It requires only one opponent for a rousing game. Racquetball seems to be an idea whose time has come.

The primary purpose of the passage appears to be _____.

(A) a comparison of squash and racquetball
(B) an explanation of racquetball's recent popularity
(C) a plea for physical fitness
(D) promotion of racquetball as a spectator sport
(E) condemnation of sedentary pursuits

_____

Strategy. The key to this question is the word *primary*. While it is true, for example, that the selection contains an implied plea for physical fitness, this thrust is not the primary purpose of the passage. We can eliminate *(C)*. We can also eliminate *(E)*, for though the author apparently approves of physical activity as opposed to sedentary pursuits, this point is by no means the primary purpose. Squash and racquetball come into comparison slightly, since some squash players have turned to racquetball, but this is a minor detail. Similarly, the appeal of racquetball to spectators takes up a sentence. We can thus reject *(A)* and *(D)*. The remaining possibility, *(B)*, is clearly the answer. The expression *explosive growth* in the opening sentence is a clue to the emphasis in the selection. This question might have been rephrased as one testing generalization.

A good title for this selection is . . . Racquetball: A Popular New Sport.

Review

Try your skill. The passage below is followed by questions based on its content. Use the preceding example to help you find the right answers.

In too many performances of *Hamlet*, Polonius is depicted as a doddering old man, tottering shakily on the edge of senility. In productions like these, Polonius is often played strictly for laughs. His advice to Laertes, though not out of keeping for a typical courtier, is ridiculed by the player's exaggerated infirmity of speech and decrepitude of

action. His advice to Ophelia, though reasonable in the context of the times, is made to seem arbitrarily absurd. His admitted garrulity is overemphasized, and his interference in the action is made the work of a clown.

Unfortunately for Polonius, there is some justification for laughing at his expense now and then. Hamlet derides Polonius at every opportunity, drawing a laugh from the courtier's eagerness to please at any cost. The King often wishes Polonius would get to the point in breaking important news or giving ad-

vice on matters concerning Hamlet.
Even the generally kindly Queen says
at one time, "More matter with less
art." Yet these points are not decisive
in any full appraisal of Polonius.

Despite the audience's occasional
laughter at Polonius's expense, certain
facts remain indisputably true. Till his
death Polonius remains a respected
member of the court. Throughout the
play he has been assigned positions of
respect. The King seems to value Polonius's judgment and advice. Though
Polonius's advice has proved faulty, the
King does not object when Polonius
volunteers to spy on Hamlet and his
mother. Then in her room, the Queen
takes Polonius's ill-fated advice to "be
round" with Hamlet. That proves to be
the wrong tack.

Polonius meets his fate on an errand
he interprets as serving his king, and his
death precipitates the final tragedy. Polonius is not a nonentity, not a character
provided for comic relief. He is not a
pitiful dotard. He supplies some of the
humor, to be sure, but a sound case can
be made for playing him as a reasonably
typical courtier—not a mental or spiritual giant, but at least a respectable and
generally honored member of the court
at Elsinore.

1. The author's primary purpose in this
passage is to _____.
   (A) suggest Hamlet's unfairness to-
       ward Polonius
   (B) criticize a little-tried interpretation
       of the part of Polonius
   (C) recommend playing Polonius with
       respect
   (D) suggest Shakespeare's uncertainty
       about the characterization of Po-
       lonius
   (E) recommend playing Polonius with
       relieved seriousness

1 ___

2. The purpose of paragraph 2 is
to _____.
   (A) concede that Polonius can be
       laughed at
   (B) criticize the Queen's hypocrisy to-
       ward Polonius
   (C) suggest that a courtier should occa-
       sionally disagree with the King
   (D) present some of Polonius's strong-
       est character traits
   (E) imply that Polonius is second to
       Hamlet in importance

2 ___

3. According to the selection, which of the
following adjectives may reasonably be
applied to Polonius? _____
    I. cruel
   II. long-winded
  III. senile
   IV. loyal
    V. brilliant
   (A) II only
   (B) III only
   (C) V only
   (D) I, II, and V
   (E) II and IV

3 ___

4. The author points out typical errors in
the portrayal of Polonius in
lines _____.
   (A) 1–6
   (B) 31–36
   (C) 36–40
   (D) 44–46
   (E) 48–55

4 ___

5. The death of Polonius is _____.
   (A) not explained in the selection
   (B) well merited
   (C) by order of the King
   (D) sometimes played for laughs
   (E) not expected

5 ___

6. Which of the following titles best summarizes the content of the passage?
   (A) Hamlet and Polonius: A Study in Contrasts
   (B) Polonius: An Often-Misunderstood Character
   (C) The Dangers of Meddling
   (D) The Courtier's Role in *Hamlet*
   (E) Minor Characters with Major Impacts

   6 ___

7. The meaning of the quotation "More matter with less art" can probably be expressed as _____.
   (A) "Come to the point."
   (B) "Start from the beginning."
   (C) "Speak more slowly."
   (D) "Repeat your last sentence."
   (E) "Don't breathe a word of this to anyone."

   7 ___

8. The advice to "be round" with Hamlet proved to be _____.
   (A) generally sound
   (B) thoughtlessly blunt
   (C) ill-advised
   (D) well-planned
   (E) immediately disregarded

   8 ___

9. The author's attitude toward Polonius is generally _____.
   (A) bitter
   (B) puzzled
   (C) favorable
   (D) unpredictable
   (E) indifferent

   9 ___

SUMMARY

3. Evaluating the Author's Purpose

Determining the author's purpose calls for a special kind of inference. Some questions require you to discover the purpose of the passage as a whole. Others require you to identify the purpose of a portion of the selection, perhaps a single sentence. When in doubt, use the process of elimination to isolate the correct answer.

4. Evaluating the Author's Style

The author's purpose influences the tone of a passage. His or her attitude affects the purpose. All three are interrelated: purpose, tone, attitude. A fourth element belongs with this group: the author's style. SAT questions sometimes ask you to evaluate an author's style. Questions about style may be general or specific.

Note the difference in phraseology between the following two question types:

1. The style of the passage can best be described as . . .

This general question can be followed by single-adjective alternatives like *light, argumentative,* or *wordy.*

2. Which of the following best describes the author's technique in this passage?

This more specific question can be followed by more extended phrases like *trying to justify the use of force in certain circumstances.*

Since an author's technique is an ingredient in his or her special style, both questions ask you to appraise the author's effectiveness and the special flavor of the writing.

Trial Test

Take the following trial test to evaluate your skill.

When a forest is ravaged by fire, cut down to make way for a parking lot, or harvested for timber, there is the esthetic loss of something beautiful. A
5 complete ecosystem is destroyed, and the habitats of forest creatures are laid waste. There is an even more serious long-range problem, however: the effect upon the balance of oxygen and car-
10 bon dioxide in the atmosphere. On the one hand, the ever-expanding use of fossil fuels has liberated into the atmosphere tremendous quantities of carbon dioxide. On the other hand, deforesta-
15 tion has reduced the vegetation needed to recycle the carbon dioxide, store the carbon, and release essential oxygen for the world's living things. Too much release of stored carbon can also po-
20 tentially raise the temperature of the atmosphere through the "greenhouse effect."

Forest vegetation stores 90% of the carbon held in terrestrial ecosystems. In
25 eastern North America there has been some improvement in recent years through reforestation. But gains in the temperate zone have been offset by losses in the tropics. Wholesale destruc-
30 tion of tropical forests is the greatest single threat, since most of the world's arboreal vegetation is found in the vast forest of the Amazon and other tropical areas. Global awareness of the problem
35 is needed to provide a basis for sound management of forests, the crucial agents in the carbon cycle.

The style of this passage can best be described as: _____.

(A) self-conscious   (D) repetitious
(B) lyrical   (E) frivolous
(C) expository

_____

Problem

Saving money takes odd forms. Comparison shoppers visit half a dozen supermarkets, save a total of $1.73, and spend $1.48 for gasoline. Anglers spend
5 a fortune on fishing gear, bait, boat charges—and catch three small floun-
ders. Writers save odd pieces of string, worn rubber bands, rusty paper clips—and then throw out the lot at one
10 time. Coupon clippers save 30¢ by buying a product when an equally good competing product can be bought for

50¢ less without a coupon. Amateur carpenters buy cheap nuts, bolts, and screws and find them stripping under pressure. Is all this economizing foolish? Not at all.

The comparison shopper has enjoyed the challenge and the pursuit. The angler has had a day on the water getting sunburned and happy. The writer has eased his soul, cleaned the slate, and stimulated his genius to start again. The coupon clipper has had the satisfaction of getting "something for nothing." As for the amateur carpenter—well eventually he is going to call in a professional anyway. For his sake and the sake of his homestead, the sooner the better.

1. The style of this passage can best be described as _____.
   (A) serious but astute
   (B) light and cheerful
   (C) perceptive and rhetorical
   (D) critical and unfavorable
   (E) argumentative but good-natured

1 ___

2. The passage "For his sake and the sake of his homestead, the sooner the better" can best be described as _____.
   (A) humorous   (D) coarse
   (B) bitter   (E) rigid
   (C) calculated

2 ___

3. "Something for nothing" is put in quotation marks because _____.
   (A) it suggests the purchaser's buying fantasies
   (B) these are the actual words used in the advertising
   (C) this is an actual quotation by the purchaser
   (D) the quotation is literally true
   (E) the writer believes the purchase is a bargain

3 ___

Strategy. 1. The topic, "saving money," is not taken seriously. The examples are lighthearted. The mock-serious explanation in paragraph 2 provides another clue to the answer. An expression like "getting sunburned and happy" suggests the writer is not really dealing with a subject seriously. Since the selection is not serious, *(A)* is incorrect. There is no real argument here: the purpose is to provide a chuckle. *(E)* is incorrect. *Rhetorical* eliminates *(C)*. *Unfavorable* eliminates *(D)*. *(B)*, the remaining answer, is an accurate description.

2. The author looks upon the amateur carpenter with amused affection, but doesn't have much faith in his ability. The suggestion to call in a professional "for his sake and the sake of his homestead" is not serious. *(A)* is the answer.

3. There is no indication that anyone or anything is being quoted specifically. *(B)* and *(C)* are incorrect. If the saying were literally true, business would go out of business! *(D)* is incorrect. The writer's revelation that another product just as good could be bought for less proves he or she does not consider this purchase a bargain. The quotation marks suggest the buyer's dream is to get the best bargain for the money. The ultimate bargain is "something for nothing," a will-o'-the-wisp. *(A)* is the answer.

Review

Try your skill. The passage below is followed by questions based on its content. Use the preceding example to help you find the right answers.

Our language is a magnificent achievement, but there are pitfalls built into it—snares that catch the unwary. One of the trickiest problems arises
5 from the fact that the structure of the language does not distinguish between *fact* and *opinion*. *Walter Payton is a member of the Chicago Bears* is a factual statement. *Walter Payton is the*
10 *greatest running back of all time* is a statement of opinion. Both sentences *look* the same. Both sentences have the same grammatical structure: *subject, being verb, predicate nominative*. But
15 the difference between the two statements is astronomical. Many of the world's problems could be averted if all people—and especially those in positions of power—could recognize the
20 difference and employ the difference honestly in their speeches.

There is an essential difference between a statement of fact and a statement of opinion. "This room is 20 ×
25 24" is a factual statement. We can take out a ruler and check the dimensions. We cannot check the statement "This room is cozy (dreary, small, large, impressive, depressing)."
30 What's wrong? We all have opinions and express them. There's nothing wrong with having and stating opinions. The danger lies in confusing opinions with facts. If we make opinionated pro-
35 nouncements and believe they are factual, we are muddying our thought processes and confusing our messages. If we read someone else's opinionated pronouncements and believe they are
40 factual, we are clogging our brains with error.

Statements in factual form may be inaccurate, but at least they can be checked. That room may actually be
45 only 20 × 22. Statements in opinion

form are neither *wrong* nor *right* in any test of truth. They are merely expressions of a point of view—interesting, perhaps, but not to be taken as Truth.
50 Statements of opinion tend to tell us more about the speaker or writer than about the subject matter of the statement.

Learning to distinguish between fact
55 and opinion is a test of linguistic sophistication and emotional maturity.

1. The author's style can best be described as _____.
   (A) impassive   (D) persuasive
   (B) sportive   (E) formal
   (C) ironic
                                    1 ___

2. Which of the following best describes the author's technique in this passage?
   (A) Emphasizing the essential weakness of the English language
   (B) Deriding the use of opinion to make any statement
   (C) Presenting a viewpoint without recommending any action
   (D) Using examples to make an important point
   (E) Minimizing the crucial difference between fact and opinion
                                    2 ___

3. Which of the following sentences best expresses the central idea of the selection?
   (A) "The danger lies in confusing opinions with facts."
   (B) "The difference between the two statements is astronomical."
   (C) "If we read someone else's opinionated pronouncements and believe they are factual, we are clogging our brains with error."
   (D) "The former can be checked."
   (E) "Both sentences have the same grammatical structure: *subject, being verb, predicate nominative*."
                                    3 ___

ENGLISH FOR THE COLLEGE BOARDS

4. From the selection we may infer that _____.
   - (A) it is worse to state an opinion than to make a factual statement, no matter how erroneous the latter may be
   - (B) to call a 20 × 24 room "large" is to make a factual statement
   - (C) most speakers intentionally use statements of opinion to mislead
   - (D) statements of fact and of opinion are sometimes difficult to tell apart
   - (E) a knowledge of grammar will guarantee the ability to distinguish between fact and opinion

   4 ___

5. The writer obviously believes that _____.
   - (A) Walter Payton is the greatest running back of all time
   - (B) the same room may be classified as *large* and *small*
   - (C) a ruler can settle all arguments of fact
   - (D) most people do indeed distinguish sharply between fact and opinion
   - (E) a viewpoint is different from an opinion

   5 ___

6. From the passage it may be inferred that _____.
   - (A) statements of fact cannot tell us anything about the speaker or writer
   - (B) emotions play a larger role in expressions of opinion than in statements of fact
   - (C) speakers who avoid statements of opinion are the most respected debaters
   - (D) having a point of view is risky
   - (E) people in positions of power tend to rely heavily on factual arguments

   6 ___

7. *Truth* is capitalized in line 49 because it represents _____.
   - (A) substantiated opinion
   - (B) verifiable fact
   - (C) fundamental reality
   - (D) modified skepticism
   - (E) idiosyncratic viewpoint

   7 ___

8. The author's purpose in the last paragraph is to _____.
   - (A) provide another example of his or her basic thesis
   - (B) urge readers to be on guard
   - (C) recommend further studies in semantic evaluation
   - (D) suggest overtly contesting the opinion of others
   - (E) reveal hitherto unsuspected similarities between fact and opinion

   8 ___

SUMMARY

4. Evaluating the Author's Style

If the style is the man (or woman), then writers put themselves into every page they write. When evaluating the author's style for an SAT question, read the passage through to get the flavor of it. If you are uncertain, read it again. Be on the lookout for certain clues: humorous contradictions, angry pronouncements, subtle suggestions.

Section IV Summary: Understanding the Author's Role

The author's role reveals itself throughout an entire passage.

The *tone* and *attitude* can "be found in the overall impression created by the combination of descriptive and connotative words."

The *purpose* can be discovered by drawing an inference based upon the whole passage (unless, of course, a smaller portion is asked for).

The *style* reveals itself throughout the passage—in humorous touches, angered comments, criticisms, compliments, informal remarks, or formal statements.

The *tone, attitude, purpose,* and *style* are all ingredients calling for an examination of the flavor of the passage, the total impact.

PART 1. Evaluating the Author's Tone (p. 222)

A. Questions that ask about the author's tone provide answer choices of adjectives (*argumentative, ironic, reflective,* etc.) or sometimes nouns (*despair, indifference, sarcasm,* etc.).
B. Get an overall impression of the *whole* passage. Don't worry about details.
C. Think of words that describe its tone. Then choose the answer that best agrees with your description.
D. Most SAT passages are neutral in tone, but a few are not. If a question asks about the tone, it is probably *not* neutral.

PART 2. Evaluating the Author's Attitude (p. 225)

A. Questions ask for such attitudes as admiration, disdain, nostalgia, apathy, and skepticism.
B. Questions about attitude are often quite specific. They ask about the author's attitude *toward someone or something.*
C. Read the question and be sure you understand exactly whom or what it asks about.
D. Look for the persons or things asked for.
E. If you are unsure about specifics, reread the whole passage. Get a sense of the author's feeling toward the entire subject.

PART 3. Evaluating the Author's Purpose (p. 230)

A. Because the author's purpose usually is not stated, you must draw an inference based on the information, tone, and attitude in the passage.
B. Some questions ask about the purpose of the whole passage; others ask about a portion or a detail.
C. Read the question carefully. Be sure you understand what it asks about.
D. Reread what is asked about—the whole passage or a portion—to draw your inference about the purpose.

PART 4. Evaluating the Author's Style (p. 233)

A. Some questions about style are general; they ask for overall judgments of style, offering such word choices as *ironic, persuasive,* and *formal*.

B. Some questions about style are more specific; they ask for certain judgments of technique, offering detailed phrase choices such as *deriding the use of opinion to make any statement*.

C. Read the whole passage to get the flavor of it, the total impact. If you are unsure, reread it.

D. Look for evidence of humor, anger, cleverness, formality, persuasiveness, etc., to form your judgment.

Section V: Understanding Language in Action

1. Evaluating the Author's Diction

SAT questions occasionally ask you to evaluate the use of an author's diction: its aptness or effectiveness. Words acquire special meanings in various contexts. A word's connotation (pages 48–50) is often determined by its neighbors on the printed page. We cannot tell what most words "mean" until they are used. *Old* means one thing when it applies to a joke and quite another when it applies to a person.

This aspect of words is tested in questions like these:

The word . . . as used in line . . . means . . .
The narrator suggests that . . . speaks of her husband as if he were . . .
The word . . . is meant to suggest . . .

Note that the skill being tested is basically the same skill tested in "Context Clues," pages 14–43. If you have mastered the material on those pages, you should do well with questions of meaning.

Trial Test

Take the trial test to review your skill.

California's Silicon Valley is creating a new language, and some people are objecting. Words like *input* and *interface* have already invaded the lan-
5 guage but these are relatively conservative additions. Some computer babble is like a foreign language. If people say, "I'm interrupt driven," they are complaining about their hectic schedule. If
10 other people are labeled with a "read-only memory," they are being charged with never learning anything, always saying the same thing over and over. A "gating event" is a turning point.
15 "Bandwidth" is the amount of information exchanged in a conversation.

John A. Barry, columnist for *Info-World* magazine, attacks computer illiteracy as a failure to grasp the English
20 language. Though change and growth are inevitable in language, Barry considers these linguistic extravagances self-defeating and confusing. He feels that proliferation of such excesses can
25 only serve to pollute the language.

The word *proliferation* as used in the last sentence means _____.

(A) approval
(B) reporting
(C) increase
(D) condemnation
(E) allocation

Problem

The annals of our time are filled with horror stories, of beautiful rivers converted to sewers, of lakes destroyed by acid rain, of forests ruthlessly and thoughtlessly laid waste. There are, fortunately, a growing number of success stories also, tales of people who rolled up their sleeves and refused to be defeated.

For some blasé city dwellers, there is nothing novel under the sun, but New Yorkers have something new to cheer about. In the very backyard of New York City, in the shadow of skyscrapers and right next to busy Kennedy airport, a miracle has taken place. Jamaica Bay Wildlife Refuge, covering 13,000 acres of marsh and woodland, is now a naturalist's paradise. It is home to more than 300 species of birds—nesting not far from the heart of the city.

The refuge did not come into existence overnight. Between World Wars I and II, Jamaica Bay became a disaster area, a dumping ground for sewage and industrial waste. It was an ecologist's nightmare. After World War II the city took steps to clean up the mess. Dikes were built to create two freshwater ponds. Then, in 1953, Herbert Johnson, who was appointed superintendent of the new refuge, planned the gathering and planting of the shrubs, trees, and grasses that make the area a haven for wildlife—for rare birds like the white pelican, the cinnamon teal, and the red-wing thrush.

Now a part of Gateway National Recreation Area, Jamaica Bay Wildlife Refuge has become a mecca for bird-watchers, an idyllic retreat for citizens overwhelmed by city tensions, and a model for other cities to emulate. It is unique. It is probably the "world's only wildlife sanctuary reachable by subway."

1. The word *blasé* in the second paragraph is meant to suggest _____.
(A) charm   (D) indifference
(B) enthusiasm (E) commitment
(C) anger

1 ___

2. The word *idyllic* in the last paragraph means _____.
(A) happy and peaceful
(B) elusive and uncertain
(C) calm but taut
(D) spiritual and religious
(E) slow and unchallenging

2 ___

3. The word *emulate* in the last paragraph adds to imitation the suggestion of _____.
(A) failing   (D) planning
(B) striving   (E) envying
(C) studying

3 ___

Strategy.   1. The phrase *nothing much new under the sun* suggests boredom. If *blasé* means "bored," then it suggests *indifference, (D).*

2. The contrast of the refuge with city noises and tensions provides the clue: *happy and peaceful, (A).*

3. The use of the word *model* suggests that other cities might try *(strive)* to imitate the refuge. *(B) is correct.*

Review

Try your skill. The passage below is followed by questions based on its content. Use the preceding example to help you find the right answers.

"Nothing is the way we thought it was, and whatever we think we understand today will be changed to something else when looked at more closely tomorrow."

As we look outward from our island in the solar system, space probes and improved technology have changed our

view of the cosmos we inhabit. As we
10 direct our study inward, toward the
very small, experimentation in subatomic physics is changing our understanding of the microcosm. Now Lewis
Thomas, author of the quotation above,
15 suggests that biologists also are crossing
a new threshold in their study of life
forms. Until recently, experts have held
some hard-and-fast opinions about the
conditions needed for life. Those opin-
20 ions have now been turned upside
down. We have discovered a set of creatures that violate all the rules about life
and life-support systems.

At the bottom of certain oceanic
25 abysses, there are, from interior
sources, chimneys that heat the sea
water to temperatures exceeding 660
degrees Fahrenheit. We know that
water turns into steam at 212 degrees at
30 sea level. At 660 degrees water remains
a liquid only because it is under enormous pressure. Everything we thought
we knew suggested that life could not
survive in this superheated water under
35 265 atmospheres of pressure. But it
does.

In 1979, John Baross and some fellow oceanographers scooped up water
from a depth of 2,600 meters and dis-
40 covered living bacteria flourishing in the
superheated liquid. Later, Baross and
Jody Deming of Johns Hopkins University proceeded to duplicate these extreme conditions and grow these incred-
45 ible life forms. They were amazed to
discover that at 482 degrees Fahrenheit
the bacteria increased a thousandfold in
six hours. If "chilled" just below boiling, the bacteria would not grow at all.
50 Their joint discovery has opened up
vast new vistas. These bacteria produce
methane, hydrogen, and carbon monoxide. There is a possibility these tiny
creatures might play a role in long-range
55 geologic change. They might become a
valuable source of a new natural gas industry. Their enzymes might be useful
in industrial processes that involve high
temperatures and pressures.

60 When we think we have closed a
door on one corridor of science, another
door swings wide open. Fixed ideas and
closed minds have no place in science.
The world is truly the home of miracles.

1. The word *microcosm* in line 13
means _____.
(A) little world
(B) scientific method
(C) galaxy
(D) scientific instrument
(E) exploration
1 ___

2. The word *abysses* in line 25 is meant
to suggest _____.
(A) extreme heat
(B) submarine peaks
(C) underwater vegetation
(D) great depths
(E) submerged continents
2 ___

3. The word *chilled* in line 48 is enclosed
in quotation marks because _____.
(A) it is taken directly from Lewis
Thomas' article
(B) the writer intended to use a better
word
(C) the water was hot
(D) Lewis Thomas disagrees with John
Baross
(E) the experiment was essentially
inexact

3 ___

4. The author's purpose is to _____.
(A) amuse and entertain while enlight-
ening the reader
(B) suggest a sense of wonder at re-
cent discoveries
(C) engage in a subtle debate over the
value of "pure research"
(D) discredit any experimentation that
cannot be repeated
(E) criticize biologists of the past

4 ___

5. The bacteria grew a thousandfold at
temperatures of _____.
(A) 212 degrees
(B) 265 degrees
(C) 482 degrees
(D) 660 degrees
(E) 2,650 degrees

5 ___

6. Which of the following best expresses the main idea of the selection?
   (A) Bacteria are remarkably adaptable organisms.
   (B) Baross and Deming are pioneers in an unexplored area.
   (C) Scientists must be ready to accept and explore new ideas.
   (D) The oceans may solve most of our problems.
   (E) Life can survive in inhospitable environments.

   6 ___

7. The passage suggests that _____.
   (A) we have barely scratched the surface of knowledge
   (B) oceanographers, as a group, are superior to physicists
   (C) life is certain to be found on the moon
   (D) there are no miracles in science
   (E) the various ice ages are attributable to the deep-sea bacteria

   7 ___

8. One effect of putting water under great pressure is to _____.
   (A) prevent instruments from probing it
   (B) kill all life forms
   (C) change its subatomic structure
   (D) release enzymes useful for industry
   (E) prevent heated water from turning into steam

   8 ___

SUMMARY

1. Evaluating the Author's Diction

Questions about diction on the SAT rely heavily upon context (page 14). When you answer such questions, carefully study the surrounding words. Use the various clues—contrast, pairing, signal words, direct explanation—to help you identify the correct alternative. All the words in a reading selection directly or indirectly affect the total context. Identifying one element in the fabric often requires understanding of the whole.

---

2. Understanding Figurative Language

Your ability to interpret a figurative expression may be tested on the SAT. You will most likely be asked to identify the hidden comparison in a metaphor, but other figures of speech may also be tested.

This aspect of words is tested in a question like this:

The author uses the phrase *towering battlements* to describe . . .

In that particular question the *towering battlements* are skyscrapers. In another context they might apply to cliffs, tall trees, or castles.

Note that the skill being tested is basically the same skill tested in "Figurative Language," pages 51–55. If you have mastered the material on these pages, you should do well with questions involving figurative language.

Trial Test

Take the trial test to review your skills.

The victim explained from his hospital bed, "I had the right-of-way at the intersection."

Nearly half of all accidents occur at
5 intersections, especially intersections with traffic lights. Good preventive driving practice requires caution at all times. "Expect the worst" is one expert's advice. Writing in the *AAA* maga-
10 zine, Deborah Allen says, "Even if you think you have the right-of-way, don't assume that cross-traffic is going to stop for you. Check both ways to make sure the intersection is clear of both vehicles
15 and pedestrians before you move out into it. If you're approaching an intersection as the light turns green, take your foot off the gas pedal and be pre-
pared to brake if necessary. Look first
20 to the left and then to the right—*then to the left again*—to make sure the intersection is clear." Whether you brake or accelerate depends upon the traffic pattern. If a lumbering juggernaut heads
25 for you, accelerating and proper steering, rather than braking, may avert an accident. If you expect the worst, you'll be prepared.

The author uses the phrase "lumbering juggernaut" to mean a _____.

(A) heavy vehicle   (D) construction
(B) speeding   truck
     ambulance   (E) trailer
(C) school bus

___

Problem

We left our houseboat and stepped into a shikara, that all-purpose floating store, post office, florist shop, supply vessel, water taxi, and suburban bus.
5 Not unlike a Venetian gondola, the shikara is easily and effectively maneuverable by one person, sometimes poling, sometimes paddling. Because power boats would pollute beautiful Dal Lake,
10 the jewel of the Vale of Kashmir, the shikara reigns supreme, darting back and forth across the surface with charm and grace.

Soon we left the open charms of Dal
15 Lake for a tributary of the River Jhelum. A hand-operated lock regulates the water level of the lake and prevents river pollutants from flowing back into the lake. Through narrow passageways
20 lined with houseboats in every stage of repair and disrepair, we floated noiselessly along, observing the everyday life of the Kashmiri, waving to happy children and nodding gravely to older mem-
25 bers of the river community. Here was poverty but not ugliness. Beautiful pewter implements graced the shelves of even the poorest houseboat. Washed clothes hung to dry from every home,
30 no matter how modest.

After 45 minutes and another lock, we were carried into the broad expanse of the River Jhelum. Instead of simple houseboats, tall multiple dwellings lined
35 the river on both sides. A five-story apartment house, at a Pisa-like angle, clung to the hillside with Kashmiri tenacity. Old and decrepit, this aged skel-

eton still housed families glad for some shelter in a crowded land. By contrast, the crumbling palace of a former maharajah, a ghostly sepulcher, showed no signs of life.

The vitality of the Kashmiri, their will to survive, is epitomized in the river and the vitality along the river banks. If life is a river, each Kashmiri has a shikara to carry him along.

1. The "suburban bus" in the first sentence is _____.
(A) a front-wheel-drive vehicle
(B) an official car
(C) a boat
(D) a tractor
(E) a houseboat

1 ___

2. The "skeleton" referred to in the third paragraph is _____.
(A) a former palace
(B) a sinking houseboat
(C) a condominium
(D) a temple
(E) an apartment house

2 ___

3. The phrase "ghostly sepulcher" in the third paragraph suggests _____.
(A) lifelessness
(B) a supernatural tale
(C) plague
(D) limited vitality
(E) a legend

3 ___

4. The expression "Pisa-like angle" suggests that the house _____.
(A) has collapsed
(B) is basically sound
(C) has a holy aura
(D) is leaning
(E) is being rebuilt

4 ___

5. The shikara in the last sentence is _____.
(A) a gondola
(B) a native ferry
(C) a canoe
(D) a government steamship
(E) not a boat

5 ___

Strategy. 1. Like the five other functions, *suburban* bus is a function of the shikara. *(C)* is the correct answer.

2. The context tells us this "aged skeleton" still housed families. It is clearly the apartment house, *(E)*.

3. *Ghostly sepulcher* is contrasted with the lively apartment house, with all its people and vitality. It does not have even limited vitality, *(D)*. *(A)*, *lifelessness*, is correct.

4. One of Pisa's claims to fame is the Leaning Tower. If the angle is Pisa-like, the building is leaning, *(D)*.

5. The meaning of boat and river shifts here. Life is compared with a river. Then shikara must refer to the strength each Kashmiri has to carry him along that difficult river. In any event, shikara does not mean a boat here. *(E)*, *not a boat*, is correct.

Review

Try your skill. The passage below is followed by questions based on its content. Use the preceding examples to help you find the right answers.

The Extraordinary is easy. And the more extraordinary the Extraordinary is, the easier it is: "easy" in the sense that we can almost always recognize
5 it . . . . The Extraordinary does not let you shrug your shoulders and walk away.

But the Ordinary is a much harder case. In the first place, by making itself
10 so noticeable—it is around us all the time—the Ordinary has got itself in a bad fix with us: we hardly ever notice it. The Ordinary, simply by *being* so ordinary, tends to make us ignorant or
15 neglectful; when something does not insist on being noticed, when we aren't grabbed by the collar or struck on the skull by a presence or an event, we take for granted the very things that most de-
20 serve our gratitude.

And this is the chief vein and deepest point concerning the Ordinary: that it *does* deserve our gratitude. The Ordinary lets us live out our humanity; it
25 doesn't scare us, it doesn't excite us, it doesn't distract us . . . . Ordinariness can be defined as a breathing-space: the breathing-space between getting born and dying, perhaps, or else the breath-
30 ing-space between rapture and rapture; or, more usually, the breathing-space between one disaster and the next. Ordinariness is sometimes the *status quo,* sometimes the slow, unseen movement
35 of a subtle but ineluctable cycle, like a ride on the hour hand of the clock; in any case the Ordinary is above all *what is expected.*

And what is expected is not often
40 thought of as a gift.

1. The author uses the phrase "struck on the skull" in lines 17–18 to mean _____.
   (A) seriously injured
   (B) mildly irritated
   (C) overwhelmed
   (D) physically confronted
   (E) overlooked

1 ___

2. A "breathing-space between rapture and rapture" in lines 29–30 could be described as _____.
   (A) an uneventful period
   (B) a preparation for excitement
   (C) a reliving of an exciting past
   (D) an unsuspected tension
   (E) a crucial training regimen

2 ___

3. The important characteristic of "a ride on the hour hand of the clock" in lines 35–36 is that it is _____.
   (A) slow and boring
   (B) depressingly time-consuming
   (C) subtle but unavoidable
   (D) characterized by staccato leaps
   (E) not always welcome

3 ___

4. Ordinariness may be _____.
   (A) cyclical or unchanging
   (B) cyclical and unexpected
   (C) cyclical and upsetting
   (D) unchanging or revolutionary
   (E) unexpected or rapturous

4 ___

5. The author implies that you can shrug your shoulders and walk away from _____.
   (A) the Extraordinary
   (B) the rapturous
   (C) the unexpected
   (D) the Ordinary
   (E) the neglectful

5 ___

6. This selection is basically _____.
   (A) a snide comment on pretense
   (B) an attack on boredom
   (C) a praise of the predictable
   (D) an exposé of the "average"
   (E) a paean to excitement

6 ___

7. The author thinks that we take too much for granted those things that are _____.
   (A) noticeable
   (B) ordinary
   (C) critical
   (D) cyclical
   (E) unexpected

7 ___

ENGLISH FOR THE COLLEGE BOARDS

3. Evaluating Degree and Exclusion

Sometimes the phraseology of SAT questions requires a reversal of familiar techniques. Questions of this type are usually phrased as follows:

1. With which of the following statements would the author be LEAST likely to agree?

2. In the passage, the author exhibits all of the following attitudes toward the surroundings EXCEPT . . . .

3. It can be inferred from the passage that all of the following might explain why the author describes the EARTH as "presumably lifeless" (line _____) EXCEPT . . . .

These questions are the reverse of most questions. Ordinarily you are asked to choose the main idea or the most likely statement. In question 1 you do the opposite. You choose the *least* likely statement. Similarly, questions like 2 or 3 list a majority of items that are included and ask you to choose the one that is *not* included. These test many skills already touched upon, even though the phraseology is different.

Trial Test

Take the trial test to evaluate your skill.

When an insect army marches on trees, the old warriors are not without their own defenses. Scientists once thought that insect populations were 5 controlled only by the weather and by natural predators, like birds. New findings, however, show that trees and other plants are not passive victims. 10 They fight back with an arsenal of deadly chemicals to thwart the insect hordes. What is even more amazing is that trees under siege may warn their neighbors to get ready to fight!

Apparently when insects begin to
15 ravage a tree, the tree sends poisonous chemicals into its leaves to discourage or kill the invader. What is more, the tree sets off a silent alarm. An airborne chemical from the infested tree is car-
20 ried to neighboring trees. Forewarned, the neighboring trees increase the concentration of chemicals in *their* leaves to protect themselves from the rampaging horde.

25 Different plants create different chemicals. A short-lived wildflower often has extremely powerful toxins ready to repel any insect invader before it strikes. Since it has little time to grow
30 and reproduce, it cannot waste any time. Long-lived trees, on the other hand, have a more elaborate strategy. Some of their chemicals merely interfere with an insect's digestion. Others
35 are more deadly. In the continuing battle between insect and plant life, the stationary, exposed plants are not entirely defenseless, even without man's intervention.

1. With which of the following statements would the author be LEAST likely to agree?
   (A) Without man's help, the great forests of the Northeast would be almost entirely denuded.
   (B) Insects avoid plants with toxic chemicals as their first line of defense.
   (C) In some way or other, trees transmit crucial messages to other trees.
   (D) Insect populations are not entirely controlled by birds and weather.
   (E) Plants vary in their ability to fight infestation.

   1 ___

2. In the struggle against insect infestations, the author mentions all of the following defenses EXCEPT _____.
   (A) chemicals that interfere with digestion
   (B) powerful toxins
   (C) messages from one tree to another
   (D) other insects
   (E) concentration of chemicals

   2 ___

Problem

There is nothing more alone in the universe than man. He is alone because he has the intellectual capacity to know that he is separated by a vast gulf of
5 social memory and experiment from the lives of his animal associates. He has entered into the strange world of history, of social and intellectual change, while his brothers of the field and forest
10 remain subject to the invisible laws of biological evolution. Animals are molded by natural forces they do not comprehend. To their minds there is no past and no future. There is only the ev-
15 erlasting present of a single generation—its trails in the forest, its hidden pathways of the air and in the sea.

Man, by contrast, is alone with the knowledge of his history until the day
20 of his death. When we were children we wanted to talk to animals and struggled to understand why this was impossible. Slowly we gave up the attempt as we grew into the solitary world of human
25 adulthood; the rabbit was left on the lawn, the dog was relegated to his kennel. Only in acts of inarticulate compassion, in rare and hidden moments of communion with nature, does man
30 briefly escape his solitary destiny. Frequently in science fiction he dreams of worlds with creatures whose communicative power is the equivalent of his own.

1. With which of the following statements would the author be LEAST likely to agree?
   (A) In reality, children would like a closer communion with animals.
   (B) Man's solitary destiny is sometimes escaped, but only for brief moments.
   (C) Animals intuitively understand more than does man.
   (D) Social and intellectual change has molded man.
   (E) Science fiction may be a kind of wish fulfillment.

   1 ___

2. All the following are mentioned as characteristic of man EXCEPT _____.
   (A) social memory
   (B) living completely in the present
   (C) knowledge of history
   (D) hidden moments of communion
   (E) acts of compassion

   2 ___

Strategy. 1. Man's peculiar and unique destiny is awareness—of past and future. The first sentence in the second paragraph specifically says that man is *alone*. The animals cannot share his experience. *(C)*, which gives animals a greater awareness, is in contradiction to the sense of the passage. *(C)* is correct.

2. Animals, rather than man, are able to live in *the everlasting present of a single generation*. *(B)* is correct.

Review

Try your skill. The passage below is followed by questions based on its content.

Few manifestations of natural forces are as terrifying as the tsunami, the tidal wave that begins as a disturbance in the sea because of an earthquake and ends
5 as a devastating wall of water inundating an unprotected shore. As the tsunami strikes the shore, it may exceed 100 feet in height. Its power and destructiveness are awesome. A tsunami
10 arising from the explosion of the volcano Krakatoa, west of Java, killed more than 36,000 people 100 years ago. In 1896, on the northeast coast of Honshu in Japan, a tsunami killed more than
15 27,000 people. Modern detection and warning systems have greatly reduced the loss of life from these deadly waves, but as recently as 1983 a tsunami raised havoc on the northwest coast of Hon-
20 shu. Human error delayed the warning and many children lost their lives.

Some readers picture tsunamis as towers of water, rushing across the surface of the ocean, causing ships to rise
25 and fall a hundred feet in a few seconds. Nothing could be further from the truth. Storm waves may indeed rise to mountainous heights at sea and toss ships about like corks. Not tsunamis. If a tsu-
30 nami passes beneath a boat in the open ocean, the passengers may be unaware of the gentle rise and fall of water, so slight it seems. These mild swells become deadly as the tsunami approaches
35 land. The ocean becomes shallower. Friction builds up. The sea bottom near shore is exposed as the tsunami seems to draw in its breath before striking. Fish and other sea creatures flop about
40 on the hitherto unexposed sea bottom. Then the tsunami strikes with devastating effect, crushing buildings near shore, tossing about ships in the harbor, washing out to sea any curious, unlucky
45 bystanders.

The basic difference between a tsunami and other sea waves is in the length of the wave, between crest and crest. Tsunamis, generated by a dis-
50 placement in the land beneath the sea, have extraordinarily long wavelengths. William Van Dorn of the Scripps Institution of Oceanography in La Jolla, California, says, "A big wave is generated
55 when you move a big piece of real estate perhaps the size of Indiana a couple of meters." This tremendous displacement causes a huge bulge on the water that races out in all directions. These
60 waves may move out with jet-plane speeds—as high as 600 m.p.h. Since the Pacific area is marked by geologic instability, most tsunamis occur in that area, with Japan particularly vulnerable to
65 their deadly arrival.

These seismic sea waves appropriately have the Japanese name, *tsunami;* Japan, located on the Ring of Fire, is particularly vulnerable. The Pacific is
70 encircled by a zone of earthquake and volcanic activity. Seismic activities anywhere in the vast area may have consequences thousands of miles away.

There have been destructive tsuna-
75 mis in other areas, however. About 1450 B.C. the volcano on the island of Thera in the Aegean Sea exploded. The resulting tsunami seriously crippled the Minoan civilization. More than 3000 years
80 later, a catastrophic earthquake struck Lisbon on November 1, 1755. The re-. sulting waves and earthquakes killed 60,000 people.

The Pacific Tsunami Warning Cen-
85 ter in Hawaii monitors potential tsunami activity and sends out warnings of the impending arrival of a tsunami, along with its strength and probable arrival time. These warnings do not pre-
90 vent destruction of property but they do save lives.

1. With which of the following statements would the author be LEAST likely to agree?
(A) The tsunami can have severe economic and social effects.
(B) A tsunami is immediately recognizable at the point of origin because of the great height of water generated above it.
(C) The excitement of watching a tsunami approach a shore outweighs any slight danger attendant upon the observation.
(D) Tsunamis are quite different from storm waves, both in origin and in appearances.
(E) An area with much volcanic activity is more likely to generate a tsunami than a more stable area.

1 ___

2. All of the following are characteristic of the tsunami EXCEPT _____.
(A) tie-in with earthquakes
(B) great height at the shore
(C) slow speed of dispersal
(D) shallow height at sea
(E) prevalence in the Pacific area

2 ___

3. If faced by an approaching tsunami on the open sea, the best procedure for a ship's captain to protect the ship is to _____.
(A) turn the prow of the ship into the wave
(B) steam in the same direction as the tsunami
(C) alert all passengers to stand by for lifeboat drill
(D) radio for help as a precautionary measure
(E) take no unusual steps

3 ___

4. The author uses the phrase "draw in its breath" to mean _____.
(A) pull water away from the shore
(B) send jets of water forward
(C) completely squander its strength
(D) generate a strong wind
(E) meet resistance on the beach

4 ___

5. The author uses the phrase "seismic activities" to indicate _____.
(A) waves
(B) wavelengths
(C) friction
(D) detection
(E) earthquakes

5 ___

6. In the grip of a storm, ships are compared with _____.
(A) walls
(B) sea creatures
(C) corks
(D) crushed buildings
(E) mild swells

6 ___

7. The best example of figurative language is the expression _____.
(A) earthquake zone
(B) deadly waves
(C) Ring of Fire
(D) warning systems
(E) unprotected shore

7 ___

8. Which of the following titles best summarizes the content of this passage?
(A) Earthquakes: The Unexpected Enemy
(B) The Ring of Fire
(C) The Killer Waves
(D) Detecting Tsunamis
(E) Nature at Its Deadliest

8 ___

SUMMARY

3. Evaluating Degree and Exclusion

Least and *except* questions are merely variations of questions already discussed and tested. A *least* question calls for the opposite of a main idea. An *except* question asks you to identify a missing item. The key to success with these questions is reading the directions carefully.

Section V Summary: Understanding Language in Action

How the author uses language is a legitimate testing area for the SAT. When asked to supply a meaning for a word in a reading passage, examine the context carefully. The question will not ordinarily ask for a strict dictionary definition. It will ask you to consider how the word is being used in the text selection (Connotation and Denotation, pages 46–50). It may also ask you to consider whether or not there are figurative meanings concealed in the text (pages 51–55). When reading LEAST and EXCEPT questions, be especially careful.

Review these strategies for understanding language in action as you prepare for the SAT.

PART 1. Evaluating the Author's Diction (p. 240)

A. Questions on diction ask about the meaning and usage of specific words in the context of a passage.
B. Deciding on a word's meaning is the same skill as using context clues.
C. Read at least the whole sentence to decide on a word meaning.
D. Use your "Context Clues" (pages 14–43): the entire sentence, pairing, direct explanation, comparison, contrast, sequence, signal words.

PART 2. Understanding Figurative Language (p. 243)

A. Giving the meaning for a figurative expression is the same skill explained in "Figurative Language" (pages 51–55).
B. Most such questions ask for the meaning of a metaphor, such as *lumbering juggernaut* for a *heavy vehicle*.
C. Find the expression and read at least the whole sentence in which it occurs. Then decide on the meaning.
D. Use your knowledge of "Figurative Language": metaphor, simile, personification, metonymy, synecdoche, hyperbole, understatement, irony.

PART 3. Evaluating Degree and Exclusion (p. 247)

A. "Least" and "except" questions are the reverse of most SAT questions.
B. A "least" question asks for a statement with which the author would be *least* likely to agree.
C. An "except" question presents information or statements, all of which the author would agree with *except* one.
D. Read "least" or "except" questions *very* carefully. Remember, they are the reverse of most questions.
E. Check back through the passage for information as needed.

Section VI: Looking Beyond the Passage

1. Predicting Outcomes

SAT questions occasionally ask you to take a step beyond the selection, to predict what will happen next. The required skill is an extension of drawing an inference—with one difference. Instead of inferring something about an idea or event in the selection, you must decide what the future consequences of an idea or event will be.

Questions of this type may be phrased as follows:

1. The final statement in the passage suggests which of the following outcomes?
2. Which of the following is likely to happen next?

Though the answer is not spelled out in the reading selection, there are clues to help you. If an anxious lawyer candidate receives notice he or she has passed the bar exam, his or her likely reaction is exuberance. Read between the lines and take one step further. Though other answers may be possible, the most probable answer is the one to choose.

Trial Test

Take the trial test to evaluate your skill.

Ted glanced across the net at his opponent, Frank Gilbert, number one seed in the tournament. Coolly waiting for Ted to serve, Frank danced lightly on
5 his toes and smiled. Through dogged determination, Ted had stayed close in this final match and had kept the score respectable. But having lost the first set, 6–3, and dropped behind, 5–1, in
10 the second set, Ted knew that the match was nearly over.

Frank was living up to his reputation as a hard hitter with control and finesse. With a backhand as good as his fore-
15 hand, Frank moved to either side easily to return the balls with grace and authority. In desperation Ted had tried lobbing over the head of his opponent, but Frank reached up and showed an
20 overhead shot as strong as his forehand.

Ted searched his memory for advice from friends and coaches. "When in trouble, change your game. Whatever you've been doing—drop it. Do some-
25 thing different. Instead of angling your shots, hit back toward your opponent's belt buckle. What have you got to lose?"

Ted served. Frank returned the ball
30 with apparent ease. The rally continued. Then Ted tried a drop shot from midcourt. It was a beauty, falling two feet from the net. Frank rushed in, scooped it up and gently lobbed the ball
35 over Ted's head. The first point went to Frank. Ted served to Frank's backhand. The ball came back to Ted's forehand. "I've got to change," thought Ted as he moved toward the ball.

1. The final statement in the passage suggests which of the following outcomes?
   (A) Ted hits a smashing drive to Frank's backhand.
   (B) Ted tries a deep lob over Frank's head.
   (C) Frank unexpectedly rushes the net.
   (D) Ted hits the ball directly at Frank.
   (E) Ted glances up into the stands and gets a secret signal from his coach.

   1 ___

2. Which of the following suggests the most probable outcome of the tennis match?
   (A) Ted turns the match around and wins in three sets.
   (B) After Frank has won in two sets, the two boys shake hands.
   (C) After losing in two sets, Ted refuses to shake hands with Frank.
   (D) Ted wins the second set, but Frank comes back to win the third.
   (E) In exasperation, Ted walks off the court and defaults.

   2 ___

Problem

On a quiet St. Valentine's Day in 1981, 12-year-old Todd Domboski ran across his grandmother's yard in Centralia, Pennsylvania. Suddenly a 100-foot pit opened beneath his feet and he tumbled in. Fortunately a tree root broke his fall, and his cousin was able to pull him safely to the surface. This frightening episode symbolizes the troubles of Centralia, a once-prosperous mining town in the heart of some of the richest anthracite regions in the world.

Centralia has a devastating problem. Beneath the streets and houses of this community, a coal-fire has been burning for decades. No one knows just how long. Each year increases the danger as the fire spreads through rich coal seams and old mine tunnels.

Many efforts have been made to drown, smother, or in some other way contain the blaze, but every effort has failed. There is just not enough water for drowning it. There are too many natural vents to smother it. The fire could take a hundred years to burn out—or a thousand. It could spread to an additional 3,500 acres with potential for even greater havoc.

What have been the results of the fire thus far? Carbon monoxide seeps into houses, posing serious threats to health and life. Basement walls crack. Lawns sink several feet into the ground. Steam vents make the area seem like the thermal display of Yellowstone National Park.

Some residents have already left. Many are reluctant to leave their homesteads, hoping against hope that the fire will burn itself out. Most, however, have reached the conclusion that the situation is hopeless and are asking the federal government for financial assistance in relocating. The financial burden would be enormous, and officials are seeking solutions that would not harm the residents.

In Calamity Hollow, Pennsylvania, a smaller mine fire turned out to be a blessing. A new technique called *controlled burning* did not attack the fire, attempting fruitlessly to put it out. Instead this innovation used the underground fire to produce natural energy in this huge natural furnace. Controlled burning can actually produce heat and electricity at a profit.

There are two additional advantages to controlled burning. First, it utilizes coal that would otherwise be wasted. Even an abandoned mine retains at least half its coal. Secondly, by fanning the flames this method could end mine fires much sooner than they would die out on their own.

The history of humankind is filled with disasters that turned out to have many beneficial results. War, the ultimate horror, has accelerated medical and surgical improvements. Citywide fires have encouraged inhabitants to rebuild—and improve. To be sure, no one recommends encouraging disasters so that we might be tested and thus make far-reaching discoveries. But sometimes misfortunes may open doors to new achievements.

1. Which of the following suggests the most probable outcome of the Centralia problem?
   (A) Most former inhabitants will be encouraged to return.
   (B) Profit from controlled burning will finance the relocation of Centralians.
   (C) Controlled burning will be found to be impractical for Centralia.
   (D) The government will make one last concerted attempt to put the underground fire out.
   (E) The Centralia fire will influence the price of coal on the open market.
   1 ___

2. The future of controlled burning as a solution to underground fires can best be described as _____.
   (A) dubious   (D) unecomical
   (B) hopeless   nomical
   (C) encouraging   (E) unpopular
   2 ___

Strategy. 1. Since all efforts at putting out the fire have failed miserably, it is unlikely the government will try again. *(D)* is incorrect. For the same reasons, it is unlikely that most inhabitants will return. *(A)* is incorrect. There is no indication that this fire in a small area of the United States could influence the price of coal. *(E)* is incorrect. There is no suggestion that the controlled burnout technique would not be successful in Centralia. Its inclusion in this excerpt clearly suggests it is a likely solution for the Centralia problem. *(C)* is incorrect. Since the selection mentions the profit from controlled burning, *(B)* is the most likely answer.

2. The excerpt is clearly enthusiastic about the future of controlled burning. The two advantages listed are specific clues. *(C)* is the most likely answer.

Review

Try your skill. The passage below is followed by questions based on its content. Use the preceding example to help you find the right answer.

Half a billion books have been published since Gutenberg printed his first Bible. Each year about 30,000 books are published in America alone. Each year about the same number go out of print. Thousands and thousands and thousands of books! What happens to them?

Most books disappear from public notice within a few years. They are stored in dusty attics, damp basements, and back rooms. They are discarded in paper drives. They find their way to church fairs, old bookstores, and library book sales. The bright promise of their publication fades, and they land in ignominious heaps on the tables of discount dealers, sold at a fraction of their publication price.

Many are physically destroyed. Fire and flood take a heavy toll. The deterioration of cheap paper consigns many to the dustheap prematurely. A great many titles disappear utterly.

Despite the hazards of existence, many titles do survive in odd and unusual places. There are some clever book detectives who make their living hunting up wanted out-of-print books and selling them at a high enough markup to provide a living. These bookfinders are ingenious, resourceful, persistent, and often lucky!

Donald Dryfoos is a successful book detective. As he describes his business, "One, you find the people who want to find books; two, you find the books." Both steps require time and effort.

Dryfoos has built up a list of regular customers. Some are individuals. Some are publishers. Some are other booksellers. When he is given a title to find, he checks his own stock and then goes hunting elsewhere. He makes no charge for the search, but the price he gets for the book must cover his expenses. Profits from individual sale are not tremendous, but the thrill of the search keeps Dryfoos ever on the trail.

What kind of people send out lists of books they want to find? Dryfoos calls them *uncategorizable*. They're all different. They all want different books. A bookstore specializing in bestsellers sells hundreds of copies of the same book. "To me that would be boring," insists Dryfoos.

Although customers vary, there are a few discernible trends. One group seeks books with happy childhood associations. These people want their children or grandchildren to share their remembered joys. Another group specializes in medicine, science, music, or another field. These people want to build up a specialized library, sometimes to provide a bibliography for a doctoral degree. Still another group has discovered an author, like Dorothy Miles Disney, whose works strike a responsive chord. These people will buy anything by the favorite author.

Dryfoos has extensive sources beyond his own stock. Like all bookfinders, he frequents book fairs, hastily checking the books donated by retirees, house redesigners, people moving out of state, legatees who don't want to be bothered with the impedimenta of an uncle's life. The competition between bookfinders is keen, and the pace is swift.

He has frequented the stores of all his competitors and knows where many titles can be found. He confesses, "I can't remember what I had for breakfast, but I remember the location of those books." As he says, it's a lot of fun just to meander through bookstores, even though it cannot provide a reasonable financial result for time spent.

Dryfoos has also built up contacts with many book suppliers throughout the country—bookstores and private libraries. Dealers who specialize in a particular field send him their catalogs. The magazine *AB Bookman's Weekly* provides advertising space for dealers on the prowl for certain titles.

How successful is the search? "We find very close to exactly 50 percent of the books we look for," says Dryfoos. If the book is to be found, it will probably be located within six weeks. As time goes on, hope dims, though occasionally a book will unexpectedly turn up late in the search.

A true book detective is a lover of books. The same amount of skill, intelligence, and persistence when applied in another field might bring more lucrative results. But a true book lover picks up a book with affection, understanding, and anticipation. Every book is a key to a world beyond its pages.

1. If Donald Dryfoos found a book re-
   quested by one of his clients, he would
   probably _____.
   (A) send it out immediately to the cus-
       tomer
   (B) send the customer a description of
       the book's condition, together with
       its price
   (C) arrange to have the book cleaned
       up and rebound if it were discov-
       ered in imperfect condition
   (D) keep it temporarily for himself and
       the next customer, while looking
       for another copy of the book
   (E) contact another customer to set up
       a competitive bidding situation

                                    1 ___

2. The word *ignominious* in the second
   paragraph is meant to suggest
   the _____.
   (A) author's   (D) editor's em-
       crushed   barrassment
       hope   (E) advertiser's
   (B) publisher's   loss of
       anger   revenue
   (C) bookfinder's
       irritation   2 ___

3. The primary purpose of the passage ap-
   pears to be to _____.
   (A) explain   (D) irritate
   (B) amuse   (E) challenge
   (C) persuade   3 ___

4. The word *uncategorizable* (seventh par-
   agraph) is applied to _____.
   (A) remaindered   (D) bookfinders
       books   (E) book fair
   (B) professional   sponsors
       magazines   4 ___
   (C) buyers of
       used books

5. The legatees in the ninth paragraph
   may best be characterized as _____.
   (A) prudent   (D) disloyal
   (B) cruel   (E) impatient
   (C) antagonistic   5 ___

6. All the following are mentioned as book-
   finding methods EXCEPT _____.
   (A) attending book fairs
   (B) tapping competitors' stocks
   (C) advertising in a magazine
   (D) getting in touch with private li-
       braries
   (E) dealing directly with the original
       publishers

                                    6 ___

7. Which of the following best expresses
   the main idea of the passage?
   (A) Publishers are missing out on a
       profitable sideline.
   (B) Finding specific old books is an al-
       most hopeless task.
   (C) Book detectives, on average, are
       wealthy individuals.
   (D) Looking for out-of-print books can
       be an exciting search.
   (E) Library book fairs are excellent
       sources for wanted books.

                                    7 ___

8. Dorothy Miles Disney is mentioned as
   an author _____.
   (A) of children's books
   (B) of professional books
   (C) in demand
   (D) for candidates of doctoral degrees
   (E) who is never remaindered

                                    8 ___

9. From this selection we may infer
   that _____.
   (A) more books are published in sci-
       ence than in literature
   (B) book dealers never cooperate with
       each other
   (C) Dryfoos stays in his business pri-
       marily for monetary reasons
   (D) many books in recent years have
       been printed on rapidly deteriorat-
       ing paper
   (E) there are no original Gutenberg Bi-
       bles in existence

                                    9 ___

1. Predicting Outcomes

When asked to predict outcomes, read the passage carefully for clues that point the way to future activity. Your answer should be consistent with the elements in the passage. It should reasonably be inferred from the salient points in the selection itself. Keep in mind that though all suggested answers may be possible, you will be asked to choose the most probable.

2. Providing an Application

Another skill that takes you beyond the passage itself is providing applications of ideas in the reading passage. Like predicting outcomes, this skill requires that you carefully analyze the content of the passage and then take a step beyond. From a general principle in the passage, you might be asked to make a specific application. If, for example, the selection discussed the advantages of speed reading as a general skill, you might be asked to decide whether a light novel, an editorial, a math textbook, an article on quantum physics, or a legal contract should be read rapidly.

Here, for example, are two application questions taken directly from the SAT.

1. According to the information in the passage, an artist inspired by the basic principles of African art would most likely have produced which of the following?
2. The author believes that an "ordinary" person (lines 17 and 31) would be most likely to agree with which of the following statements about art?

Trial Test

Take the trial test to evaluate your skill.

Logical reasoning is usually classified as one of two kinds: inductive and deductive. People use both types often without knowing their names. Inductive 5 reasoning proceeds from the particular to the general. Deductive reasoning proceeds from the general to the particular. Children begin using a kind of induc- tive reasoning at an early age. A child 10 may touch a hot radiator on a number of occasions and conclude that all radia- tors are hot. He has reasoned from the particular experiences—touching radia- tors—to the generalization—all radia- 15 tors are hot. Though the conclusion may be faulty because of insufficient and un- characteristic examples, the process is still inductive.

Deductive reasoning proceeds in re-
20 verse. A child may be told by a parent
not to touch radiators because radiators
are hot. Then he may test the generalization by touching a radiator. If the generalization is sound, the specific exam-
25 ples should follow. In this example, the
generalization is unsound because it is
incomplete. Radiators are hot only at
certain times. The example demonstrates the method, however.
30 Inductive reasoning is commonly
used in science. On the basis of observation and experiment, general principles or laws may be derived. These conclusions are subject to review as
35 additional information becomes available, but they serve as useful guides in
the meantime.
Deductive reasoning is commonly
used in argumentation and persuasion.
40 From a presumably accepted generalization, debaters derive arguments in
favor of their positions. If the statement
that smoking is harmful to health is accepted, an editorial writer can plead for
45 more restrictions on smoking in public
places. Deductive arguments can often
be put in the form of syllogisms, with

major and minor premises and conclusions.
50 Both forms of reasoning are useful.
Once their limitations are understood,
they provide useful tools for handling
the problems of everyday living.

According to the information in the passage,
which of the following would be an example
of deductive reasoning?

(A) A visitor to Mexico tastes several dishes
with jalapeño peppers and decides that
such dishes are too hot for his taste.
(B) On Saturday afternoon in a small city on
his route, a traveler looks in vain for an
open hardware store. He concludes
stores in this city close Saturday after-
noons.
(C) A chocolate enthusiast finds that he gets
a headache after every bout of chocolate
indulgence. He decides to give up chocolate because he may be allergic to it.
(D) Because Labrador retrievers have the
reputation of being good with children,
a father buys one for his young family.
(E) After finding a dozen strawberries in the
basket utterly tasteless despite their lus-
cious appearance, a cook throws away
the rest of the box.

Problem

If wheels are the most efficient form
of land transport ever invented by
human beings, why did nature not develop creatures with some kind of
5 wheels instead of feet, paddles, or flip-
pers? The question is not so frivolous
as it sounds. Nature anticipated the invention of the submarine, glider, airplane, and jet-propelled vehicles. Why
10 not wheels?
Some animals use their whole bodies
as wheels. The pangolin of Southeast
Asia curls into a ball and rolls down
steep hills to avoid predators. Rolling
15 spiders and somersaulting shrimps use
the principle of the wheel. Even rolling
plants, like the western tumbleweed,
demonstrate the wheel in action. But
none of these has wheels in place of ap-
20 pendages.

Some writers conjecture that the
joint problem proved an insuperable obstacle for the development of a living
wheel. A rotating joint of living tissue
25 might be a biological impossibility.
Other writers dispute this explanation,
pointing out that nature has devised un-
believably sophisticated solutions to all
kinds of problems. These scientists be-
30 lieve nature did not provide wheeled animals for sound reasons of survival.
Michael LaBarbera of the University of Chicago has suggested three reasons why animals are better off without
35 wheels. As a preface, he pointed out
that human beings use wheels only
under special conditions, for longer
rather than shorter trips.
First, wheels are efficient only on
40 hard surfaces. The heavier the wheeled

vehicle, the more difficult it is to move on a soft surface. The use of oversized tires reduces the problem but does not eliminate it.

45 Secondly, wheels are not too useful when confronted with vertical obstructions. A wheeled vehicle with a rigid chassis cannot climb a curb higher than half the wheel radius.

50 Finally, wheels do not permit quick turning in a space cluttered with obstacles. Nor can wheeled vehicles turn efficiently in a small space. The switchbacks on mountain roads, for example,
55 test the limits of the maneuverability of wheeled vehicles.

The efficiency of the wheel under certain conditions is more than offset by its inefficiency under other conditions.
60 Certainly, under suitable conditions the wheel is incredibly more efficient than walking or running. In the Boston Marathon a wheelchair athlete finished the course 22 minutes faster than the best
65 runner. The bicycle, a common example of a wheeled vehicle, is 15 times as efficient as a running dog.

When conditions are right, the wheel is indeed unexcelled for quick, clean,
70 efficient locomotion. But since conditions are rarely "right" in the animal's natural domain, "wheeled animals" are an unlikely development in the scheme of things.

1. According to the point of view of the passage, which of the following statements is most likely true?
   (A) If the earth's surface were relatively flat and hard, creatures with wheels might have evolved.
   (B) The form of the wheel does not appear anywhere in natural design.
   (C) The adaptability of living tissue is severely limited.
   (D) Wheels would be particularly useful in woodlands.
   (E) The principle of jet propulsion in animals is quite different from the principle of jet propulsion in aviation.

1 __

2. With which of the following statements would the writer of this passage agree?
   (A) Wheeled prey animals would more easily escape their predators than four-footed ones.
   (B) Camels are more efficient in deserts than bicycles.
   (C) Any speculation about wheeled animals is a ridiculous waste of time.
   (D) Roller skates will eventually be used almost universally to save time and energy during shopping.
   (E) It is difficult to understand why animals have not developed wheels for locomotion.

2 __

Strategy. 1. Since the passage emphasizes the adaptability of animals, it suggests three reasons why wheels were not developed. A surface relatively flat and hard would have removed the three obstacles. Theoretically, then, wheeled animals might have developed. *(A)* is correct. The passage says the form of the wheel appears in ways other than as appendages. Therefore, *(B)* is incorrect. The passage emphasizes the adaptability of living tissue. *(C)* is incorrect. Since woodland surfaces are not flat and hard, *(D)* is incorrect. Though the fuels are different, animals and man both use the same principle of jet propulsion. *(E)* is incorrect.

2. Since soft surfaces are difficult for wheeled vehicles, *(B)* is correct. Since prey animals do not live in conditions suitable for wheels. *(A)* is incorrect. The entire passage is devoted to speculation about wheeled animals. *(C)* is incorrect. There is no indication that roller skates will take over for

legs during short walking trips. The passage emphasizes the value of wheels for longer trips, not shorter ones. *(D)* is incorrect. Since the passage gives three reasons why animals have not developed wheels, *(E)* is incorrect.

Review

Try your skill. The passage below is followed by questions based on its content.

Jules Verne is credited with anticipating many technological and scientific achievements of the 20th century, but 400 years earlier another prophet fore-
5 saw the world of the future with even more uncanny accuracy. Verne embodied his prophecies in a series of enchanting science-fiction novels. Leonardo da Vinci sketched his prophetic visions in
10 great detail. His sketches are so clear and informative that working models have been constructed. A traveling IBM exhibit encourages young people to turn cranks, pull levers, and push buttons to
15 demonstrate mechanically how brilliant were the conceptions of this artist-scientist-inventor.

Leonardo's notebooks contain the fruits of his fertile imagination. Written
20 in tiny but accurate left-handed mirror writing, the notebooks are filled with sketches of innovations, creative ideas, inventions, and improvements of already existing devices. Designs for air
25 conditioners, two-level highways for pedestrians and vehicles, parachutes, and rotating hoists poured from his inventive brain.

Leonardo devised an airplane that
30 modern engineers say is technically sound. He defined a key aerodynamic principle 200 years before Newton. He foresaw the helicopter and devised an aerial screw to lift it. His analysis of
35 gears anticipated their use in modern-day machines. He even designed the first mechanical car.

He was a truly scientific mapmaker, devising an instrument for measuring
40 the radius of the earth accurately to within a few miles—all of this while Co-

lumbus was making his voyage of discovery to the New World. He invented a printing press that could be run by one
45 man, a vast improvement over the more cumbersome Gutenberg press. He devised a tank for warfare centuries before the British unveiled the first tank on the Western Front in World War I.

50 What kept all his inventions from revolutionizing world technology? He was too soon. His genius outstripped the facilities of his time. He needed a compact power unit and a metal hard
55 enough for his needs. Though these were far in the future, his free-ranging mind had an impact on progress to come.

His studies in other branches of sci-
60 ence were far-ranging and perceptive. He described ring patterns of trees as a key to their growth. He systematically and individually pursued scientific studies of anatomy—of plants and the
65 human body. He became interested in the laws of optics. He studied meteorology and geology.

The breadth and the depth of Leonardo's genius are emphasized by his
70 success in nonscientific areas. He was an artist of renown, painter of the "Mona Lisa," "The Last Supper," "Virgin and Child with St. Anne," and other masterpieces. He had a powerful
75 impact on the young Raphael and Michelangelo. Sometimes his paintings suggest the fusion of his scientific and artistic interests.

This restless genius, turning from
80 one field to another and interpreting the world with unimpaired vision, is the prototype of that many faceted personality sometimes called "Renaissance Man."

1. Which of the following persons most closely approaches the "Renaissance Man" qualities of Leonardo as outlined in the passage?
   (A) H. G. Wells, who wrote science fiction dealing with time machines and interplanetary travel
   (B) Emily Dickinson, who wrote poems of outstanding sensitivity from her self-imposed isolation
   (C) Samuel F. B. Morse, who was a painter of great renown before pioneering work in electric telegraphy
   (D) Ludwig van Beethoven, whose musical achievements were a triumph over deafness
   (E) Claude Monet, whose paintings helped to launch the Impressionist movement in art

   1 ___

2. The word *cumbersome* (fourth paragraph) suggests _____.
   (A) inefficiency   (D) compactness
   (B) speed   (E) streamlining
   (C) plodding
       effcctiveness   2 ___

3. In the fourth paragraph Columbus is mentioned for which of the following reasons?
   (A) Leonardo measured the size of the earth, while some people (though not Columbus) still believed in the flat-earth theory.
   (B) Columbus as an active adventurer, physically exploring, is contrasted favorably with Leonardo as an armchair scientist.
   (C) Columbus probably had worked closely with Leonardo in determining his strategy for exploring the New World.
   (D) Neither Columbus nor Leonardo could possibly anticipate the profound results of the opening up of the New World.
   (E) Columbus and Leonardo were both Italians, citizens of regions in social and political ferment.

   3 ___

4. All the following inventions of Leonardo are mentioned in the selection EXCEPT _____.
   (A) parachute   (D) machine gun
   (B) two-level   (E) printing
       highway   press
   (C) mechanical
       car   4 ___

5. The author's attitude toward Leonardo is one of _____.
   (A) skepticism   (D) awe
   (B) envy   (E) acceptance
   (C) disbelief
                              5 ___

6. From this passage we may infer that _____.
   (A) Leonardo at first accepted the idea of a flat earth but later rejected it.
   (B) Leonardo provided Columbus with a map for his first voyage to the New World.
   (C) Working models can teach mechanical principles more effectively than can mere sketches.
   (D) Jules Verne consulted the notebooks of Leonardo before beginning a novel.
   (E) Leonardo's airplane could not have flown, even with modern energy sources and materials.

   6 ___

7. For which of the following reasons does the writer mention Jules Verne?
   (A) Jules Verne is the best prophet of the future in all of history.
   (B) The popular mind associates Jules Verne with prophecy, but Leonardo is more deserving of the reputation.
   (C) Jules Verne and Leonardo were essentially alike as personalities.
   (D) Both Jules Verne and Leonardo were painters as well as prophets.
   (E) Leonardo's time machine anticipated Jules Verne's by four centuries.

   7 ___

8. Which of the following titles best summarizes the content of the passage?
   (A) Science in the 15th Century
   (B) Jules Verne and Leonardo da Vinci: A Study in Contrasts
   (C) Leonardo as a Key Renaissance Painter
   (D) Leonardo da Vinci: Renaissance Man
   (E) Unrecognized Genius: A Study in Failure

   8 —

SUMMARY

2. Providing an Application

Though providing applications requires you to go beyond the facts and statements in the passage, you will find in the passage sufficient hints and clues to guide you in your selection. The extraordinary virtuosity of Leonardo in the preceding passage provides clues for the application question, as well as for other questions.

Section VI Summary: Looking Beyond the Passage

Predicting outcomes and providing applications are further extensions of one major skill: *drawing inferences*.

The inferences analyzed in this section are more specialized and often more challenging because they ask you to bring experience to bear on the answers. In one form or another, you have been predicting outcomes and providing applications all your life. In this section you will put those experiences and skills to work.

Review these strategies for looking beyond the passage when you are preparing for the SAT.

PART 1. Predicting Outcomes (p. 253)

A. Predicting an outcome is drawing an inference about a *probable* event based on information in the selection.

B. Look for clues that suggest what may happen in the future. (Sometimes you must "read between the lines.")

C. Many answers may be *possible*. Choose the most *probable* one.

D. Remember, information *in the passage* (not information you already know) should lead you to your answer.

PART 2. Providing an Application (p. 258)

A. Providing an application is predicting a specific outcome. It is another special kind of inference.

B. Look for clues in the passage that can suggest the application.

C. Choose the most probable (not just possible) application.

D. Although you must move beyond the passage for the application, the reasons for it are in the passage itself.

Section VII: Understanding Narrative

1. Characterization

Narrative depends upon the depiction of characters in challenging situations. The characters may be human beings, aliens, robots, inanimate objects, or cartoon characters. The many Disney films suggest the range of possibilities. All narrative characters have traits that may be identified by defining labels.

A SAMPLE OF DESCRIPTIVE ADJECTIVES

even-tempered	callous
exuberant	cantankerous
friendly	domineering
fun loving	flighty
generous	melancholy
humorous	overbearing
kindly	pugnacious
likable	self-indulgent
reliable	smug
upright	stingy
vivacious	temperamental
witty	vindictive

Trial Test

The following brief passage from *Look Homeward, Angel,* by Thomas Wolfe, suggests the essence of a colorful character. Your decision about Gant's character will be based on his actions, his dialogue, and how others react to him.

Seated before a roast or a fowl, Gant began a heavy clangor on his steel and carving knife, distributing thereafter Gargantuan portions to each plate. Eu-
5 gene feasted from a high chair by his father's side, filled his distending belly until it was drumtight, and was permitted to stop eating by his watchful sire only when his stomach was impregnable
10 to the heavy prod of Gant's big finger. "There's a soft place there," he would roar, and he would cover the scoured plate of his infant son with another heavy slab of beef. That their ma-
15 chinery withstood this hammerhanded treatment was a tribute to their vitality and Eliza's cookery.

Gant ate ravenously and without caution. He was immoderately fond of
20 fish, and he invariably choked upon a bone while eating it. This happened hundreds of times, but each time he would look up suddenly with a howl of agony and terror, groaning and crying
25 out strongly while a half-dozen hands pounded violently on his back.

"Merciful God!" he would gasp finally, "I thought I was done for that time."

30 "I'll vow, Mr. Gant," Eliza was vexed. "Why on earth don't you watch what you're doing? If you didn't eat so fast you wouldn't always get choked."

35 The children, staring, but relieved, settled slowly back in their places.

1. The chief focus of the passage is on which of the following?
   (A) Describing a typical meal in a middle-class family
   (B) Portraying the character of Gant
   (C) Sermonizing on the dangers of eating rapidly
   (D) Praising moderation in all things
   (E) Suggesting that a roast is a better meal than fish

1 ___

2. Of Gant it might reasonably be said that _____.
   (A) he was a devoted father and husband
   (B) he believed in moderation in all things
   (C) he was cruel to Eliza
   (D) he didn't learn from experience
   (E) he was careful not to make the children nervous

2 ___

3. The author's attitude toward Gant's table behavior is one of _____.
   (A) awe
   (B) endorsement
   (C) fury
   (D) envy
   (E) disapproval

3 ___

4. Gant prodded Eugene's belly to _____.
   (A) make sure Eugene was completely stuffed
   (B) keep the baby awake
   (C) irritate Eliza
   (D) keep the children in line
   (E) show his favoritism for the youngest child

4 ___

5. As used in this selection, *Gargantuan* (line 4) means _____.
   (A) modest
   (B) thrifty
   (C) huge
   (D) tasty
   (E) rationed

5 ___

Look at a typical question and analyze the possible answers. In this selection, Prince Florizel is ready for more adventures.

Problem

During his residence in London, the accomplished Prince Florizel of Bohemia gained the affection of all classes by the seduction of his manner and by 5 a well-considered generosity. He was a remarkable man even by what was known of him; and that was but a small part of what he actually did. Although of a placid temper in ordinary circum-10 stances, and accustomed to take the world with as much philosophy as any ploughman, the Prince of Bohemia was not without a taste for ways of life more adventurous and eccentric than that to 15 which he was destined by his birth.

Now and then, when he fell into a low humour, when there was no laughable play to witness in any of the London theatres, and when the season of the 20 year was unsuitable to those field sports in which he excelled all competitors, he would summon his confidant and Master of the Horse, Colonel Geraldine, and bid him prepare himself against an eve-25 ning ramble. The Master of the Horse was a young officer of a brave and even temerarious disposition. He greeted the news with delight, and hastened to make ready. Long practice and a varied 30 acquaintance of life had given him a sin-

266

gular faculty in disguise; he could adapt not only his face and bearing, but his voice and almost his thoughts, to those of any rank, character, or nation; and in this way he diverted attention from the Prince, and sometimes gained admission for the pair into strange societies. The civil authorities were never taken into the secret of these adventures; the imperturbable courage of the men and the ready invention and chivalrous devotion to each other had brought them through a score of dangerous passes; and they grew in confidence as time went on.

One evening in March they were driven by a sharp fall of sleet into an Oyster Bar in the immediate neighborhood of Leicester Square. Colonel Geraldine was dressed and painted to represent a person connected with the Press in reduced circumstances; while the Prince had, as usual, travestied his appearance by the addition of false whiskers and a pair of large adhesive eyebrows. These lent him a shaggy and weather-beaten air, which, for one of his urbanity, formed the most impenetrable disguise. Thus equipped, the commander and his satellite sipped their brandy and soda in security.

1. The context suggests that *temerarious* (line 27) probably means _____.
   (A) rash and daring
   (B) impatient and nasty
   (C) reserved and thoughtful
   (D) proud but shy
   (E) rebellious and cruel

   1 ___

2. Lines 9–14 suggest that the Prince's personality is _____.
   (A) essentially agreeable and loving
   (B) complex and somewhat contradictory
   (C) unruffled and consistent
   (D) predictable but interesting
   (E) unpleasant if superficially charming

   2 ___

3. Which of the following best describes the main idea of the selection?
   (A) Prince Florizel is well liked by his friends and associates.
   (B) Disguise is a deceitful, disagreeable device with little justification for its use.
   (C) The Prince of Bohemia is basically an industrious, hardworking individual.
   (D) The Prince and the Colonel seek new adventures and unusual experiences.
   (E) Colonel Geraldine is the motivator of the disguised friends.

   3 ___

4. Which of the following is likely to happen next?
   (A) The Colonel is greeted by an old, forgotten friend.
   (B) The Prince tires of the masquerade and returns home.
   (C) The Prince and the Colonel have an unusual adventure.
   (D) The disguised pair are unmasked by the press.
   (E) The storm gets worse, and the men find lodgings.

   4 ___

5. As used in the selection *in reduced circumstances* (line 52) means _____.
   (A) on a restricted assignment
   (B) in a state of uncertainty
   (C) attached to a newspaper
   (D) in a shabby suit
   (E) somewhat low in money

   5 ___

Strategy 1. The word *brave* suggests courage, and the word *even* implies that *temerarious* is *brave* to a greater degree. "Rash and daring" (A) suggest an extension of *brave*. The other alternatives are either obviously incorrect, like (E), or not covered, like (C).

2. The Prince has a "placid temper" and takes life as it comes, but he has a "taste for ways of life more adventurous and eccentric." He is "complex" in his interests and "contradictory" in his mood swings (B).

3. Though statement (A) is true, it does not represent the *main* idea. It is an important detail. (B) is nowhere implied. (C) suggests boredom and avoidance of adventure. (E) is obviously false. Only (D) accurately describes the attitudes and personalities of the two men.

4. The stage is set for something unusual to happen. The men are disguised. The weather is bad. The adventurers are in a strange place. There's certainly an adventure to come (C).

5. "In reduced circumstances" (line 52) suggests a shortage of money (E).

Review

In the following excerpt, Rosemary picks up a street person and brings her home to tea.

"Rosemary, may I come in?" It was Philip.

"Of course."

He came in. "Oh, I'm sorry," he 5 said, and stopped and stared.

"It's quite all right," said Rosemary smiling. "This is my friend, Miss —"

"Smith, madam," said the languid figure, who was strangely still and un- 10 afraid.

"Smith," said Rosemary. "We are going to have a little talk."

"Oh, yes," said Philip. "Quite." And his eye caught sight of the coat and 15 hat on the floor. He came over to the fire and turned his back to it. "It's a beastly afternoon," he said curiously, still looking at that listless figure, looking at its hands and boots, and then at 20 Rosemary again.

"Yes, isn't it?" said Rosemary enthusiastically. "Vile."

Philip smiled his charming smile. "As a matter of fact," said he, "I 25 wanted you to come into the library for a moment. Would you? Will Miss Smith excuse us?"

The big eyes were raised to him but 30 Rosemary answered for her. "Of course she will." And they went out of the room together.

"I say," said Philip, when they were alone. "Explain. Who is she? What does it all mean?"

35 Rosemary, laughing, leaned against the door and said: "I picked her up in Curzon Street. Really. She's a real pick-up. She asked me for the price of a cup of tea, and I brought her home with 40 me."

"But what on earth are you going to do with her?" cried Philip.

"Be nice to her," said Rosemary quickly. "Be frightfully nice to her. 45 Look after her. I don't know how. We haven't talked yet. But show her—treat her—make her feel—"

"My darling girl," said Philip, "You're quite mad, you know. It simply 50 can't be done."

"I knew you'd say that," retorted Rosemary. "Why not? I want to. Isn't that a reason? and besides, one's always reading about these things. I de- 55 cided—"

"But," said Philip slowly, and he

268   **ENGLISH FOR THE COLLEGE BOARDS**

cut the end of a cigar, "she's so astonishingly pretty."

"Pretty?" Rosemary was so sur-
60 prised that she blushed. "Do you think
so? I—I hadn't thought about it."

"Good Lord!" Philip struck a
match. "She's absolutely lovely. Look
again, my child. I was bowled over
65 when I came into your room just now.
However . . . I think you're making a
ghastly mistake. Sorry, darling, if I'm
crude and all that. But let me know if
Miss Smith is going to dine with us in
70 time for me to look up *The Milliner's
Gazette*."

"You absurd creature!" said Rosemary, and she went out of the library,
but not back to her bedroom. She went
75 to her writing-room and sat down at
her desk. Pretty! Absolutely lovely!
Bowled over! Her heart beat like a
heavy bell. Pretty! Lovely! She drew
her cheque book towards her. But no,
80 cheques would be no use, of course.
She opened a drawer and took out five
pound notes, looked at them, put two
back, and holding the three squeezed in
her hand, she went back to her
85 bedroom.

1. The author's primary purpose in this
   passage is to _____.
   (A) expose Philip as a cruel cynic
   (B) analyze, through conversation
       alone, the character of Rosemary
   (C) suggest some of the dangers in old
       relationships
   (D) reveal aspects of a bitter class
       struggle
   (E) show how some people recognize
       beauty where others are blind

   1 ___

2. Rosemary's purpose in bringing the
   stranger home was to _____.
   (A) make a friend of Miss Smith
   (B) provide a dinner guest
   (C) indulge a whim
   (D) hire her as a personal maid
   (E) make amends for a previous slight

   2 ___

3. The word *languid* in line 8 is meant to
   suggest _____.
   (A) Miss Smith's fatigue
   (B) Rosemary's lack of perception
   (C) Philip's curiosity
   (D) Philip and Rosemary's essential
       malice
   (E) repressed anger

   3 ___

4. Although she speaks only two words,
   Miss Smith maintains a certain _____.
   (A) irritation   (D) amiability
   (B) composure   (E) anxiety
   (C) coquet-
       tishness   4 ___

5. Rosemary's answering for Miss Smith
   (lines 29–30) suggests Rose-
   mary's _____.
   (A) real interest in Miss Smith's
       welfare
   (B) repressed dislike for Philip
   (C) unselfish generosity
   (D) curiosity about Miss Smith's back-
       ground
   (E) snobbishness

   5 ___

6. "One's always reading about these
   things. . ." (lines 53–54) suggests
   that _____.
   (A) Rosemary is a keen student of
       human motivation
   (B) Miss Smith is responsible for her
       own plight
   (C) Rosemary is playing out a fantasy
   (D) Philip is an unkind husband
   (E) money isn't everything

   6 ___

7. The sentence "Her heart beat like a
   heavy bell" suggests that Rose-
   mary _____.
   (A) has a physical weakness
   (B) finds she is running low on funds
   (C) is about to scream at Miss Smith
   (D) is jealous
   (E) realizes some money has been
       stolen

   7 ___

8. The turning point of the episode comes with which quotation?
   (A) "Be nice to her."
   (B) "Will Miss Smith excuse us?"
   (C) "She's a real pick-up."
   (D) "It's a beastly afternoon."
   (E) "But she's so astonishingly pretty."

   8 —

9. The most significant key to Rosemary's character is found in the word(s) _____.
   (A) "Vile" (line 22)
   (B) "laughing" (line 35)
   (C) "nice" (line 43)
   (D) "frightfully" (line 44)
   (E) "haven't talked yet" (line 46)

   9 —

10. It might reasonably be said that Philip _____.
    (A) has fallen in love with Miss Smith
    (B) is surprisingly cruel in his attitude toward Miss Smith
    (C) understands his wife better than she knows
    (D) really hopes that Miss Smith will stay on
    (E) is ready to indulge his wife's every impulse

    10 —

11. Which of the following is likely to happen next?
    (A) Philip leaves in an angry mood.
    (B) Miss Smith speaks at length with Philip.
    (C) Philip and Rosemary take Miss Smith to dinner.
    (D) Philip and Rosemary argue about Miss Smith's presence.
    (E) Rosemary sends Miss Smith away promptly.

    11 —

12. A word that might reasonably be applied to Rosemary is _____.
    (A) insightful
    (B) nasty
    (C) secure
    (D) unfashionable
    (E) pampered

    12 —

13. The end of the episode _____.
    (A) was planned and anticipated by Philip
    (B) came as a surprise to Philip
    (C) showed Rosemary's deep concern for Miss Smith
    (D) ran counter to Rosemary's real wishes
    (E) showed Miss Smith's ability to forecast events

    13 —

SUMMARY

1. Characterization

Characterization is a major element in narration. Characters most frequently are human, but nonhuman, even inanimate, characters can arouse emotional responses in readers or listeners. Characters usually exhibit specific traits, which are revealed in challenging situations.

2. Plot

"What happened next?" If you have ever asked this question, you have been interested in plot, in what happened. Plot is the essence of storytelling. Some plots are relatively simple—succession of incidents without much conflict. Confrontation, however, is an important element of a good story.

The skeleton of a typical plot is found in the simplest plot outline of all.

1. Boy meets girl. The opening situation sets the stage for later events.
2. Boy loses girl. There is conflict, opposition, a stirring up of the earlier serene waters.
3. Boy wins girl. Despite the problems, there is a resolution.

This spare outline, though oversimplified, is not entirely out of place in a good story. There is almost always a static situation which is destroyed by conflict. The final solution ties threads together. Though not always happy, the usual story ending wraps up the plot elements.

Some stories are open-ended, with conclusions that are not neatly wrapped up. Perhaps the most famous of this type is "The Lady or the Tiger?" which leaves the ending entirely to the reader. Still, it does contain other plot elements like conflict. Character, of course, plays a major role in plot. Character affects plot; plot affects character.

Another influence on plot and character is setting. Characters are tested by harsh environments. Challenging environments help shape what happens. Robert Louis Stevenson wrote, "Some places speak distinctly. Certain dank gardens cry out for a murder; certain old houses demand to be haunted; certain coasts are set apart for shipwreck."

The following passage from *The Great Railway Bazaar* by Paul Theroux suggests, in a brief excerpt, the elements of a longer literary selection. It contains conflict, an essential ingredient in plot. The conflict shows how character and plot can be interrelated. In this excerpt the conflict reveals character, and character influences incident. Setting is an all-important element in the story.

Trial Test

At Trieste, Molesworth discovered that the Italian conductor had mistakenly torn out all the tickets from his Cook's wallet. The Italian conductor 5 was in Venice, leaving Molesworth no ticket for Istanbul, or, for that matter, Yugoslavia. But Molesworth stayed calm. He said his strategy in such a situation was to say he had no money and 10 knew only English: "That puts the ball in their court."

But the new conductor was persistent. He hung by the door of Molesworth's compartment. He said, 15 "You no ticket." Molesworth didn't reply. He poured himself a glass of wine and sipped it. "You no ticket."

"Your mistake, George."

"You," said the conductor. He 20 waved a ticket at Molesworth. "You *no* ticket."

"Sorry, George," said Molesworth,

still drinking. "You'll have to phone Cook's."

25   "You no ticket. You pay."

"I no pay. No money." Molesworth frowned and said to me, "I do wish he'd go away."

"You cannot go."

30   "I go."

"No ticket! No go!"

"Good God," said Molesworth. This argument went on for some time. Molesworth was persuaded to go into
35 Trieste Station. The conductor began to perspire. He explained the situation to the stationmaster, who stood up and left his office; he did not return. Another official was found. "Look at the uni-
40 form," said Molesworth. "Absolutely wretched." That official tried to phone Venice. He rattled the pins with a stumpy finger and said, *"Pronto! Pronto!"* But the phone was out of
45 order.

Finally Molesworth said, "I give up. Here—here's some money." He flourished a handful of 10,000 lire notes. "I buy a new ticket."

50   The conductor reached for the money. Molesworth withdrew it as the conductor snatched.

"Now look, George," said Molesworth. "You get me a ticket, but
55 before you do that, you sit down and write me an endorsement so I can get my money back. Is that clear?"

But all Molesworth said when we were again under way was, "I think
60 they're all very naughty."

1. Which of the following statements can reasonably be made?
   (A) Molesworth's ticket was in Venice, but he was in Trieste.
   (B) The conductor was acting vindictively in asking for a ticket.
   (C) Molesworth stuck to his guns and never paid for a ticket.
   (D) The telephone call proved that Molesworth was right.
   (E) The narrator of the story was embarrassed by Molesworth's actions.
   1 __

2. Molesworth's strategy can best be described by the word _____.
   (A) *sympathetic*   (D) *responsive*
   (B) *indifferent*   (E) *humorous*
   (C) *stonewalling*
   2 __

3. The essential conflict in this excerpt is between _____.
   (A) Yugoslavs and Italians
   (B) official regulations and human error
   (C) Molesworth and the narrator
   (D) Istanbul and Trieste
   (E) the laws of one country and the laws of another
   3 __

4. Molesworth's attitude toward the conductor is revealed by his _____.
   (A) sympathetic understanding of the conductor's plight
   (B) willingness to speak the conductor's language
   (C) payment of a handful of 10,000 lira notes
   (D) use of the name *George*
   (E) acceptance of local train procedures
   4 __

5. The conductor's attitude toward Molesworth can best be described as one of _____.
   (A) murderous rage
   (B) sweet reasonableness
   (C) patience
   (D) soothing persuasion
   (E) exasperation
   5 __

Problem

I was on the point of slinking off, to think how I had best proceed, when there came out of the house a lady with a handkerchief tied over her cap, and a pair of gardening gloves on her hands, wearing a gardening-pocket like a toll-man's apron, and carrying a great knife. I knew her immediately to be Miss Betsey, for she came stalking out of the house exactly as my poor mother had so often described her stalking up our garden at Blunderstone Rookery.

"Go away!" said Miss Betsey, shaking her head, and making a distant chop in the air with her knife. "Go along! No boys here!"

I watched her, with my heart at my lips, as she marched to a corner of her garden, and stopped to dig up some little root there. Then, without a scrap of courage, but with a great deal of desperation, I went softly in and stood beside her, touching her with my finger.

"If you please, ma'am," I began.

She started and looked up.

"If you please, aunt."

"Eh?" exclaimed Miss Betsey, in a tone of amazement I had never heard approached.

"If you please, aunt, I am your nephew."

"Oh, Lord!" said my aunt. And sat flat down in the garden path.

"I am David Copperfield, of Blunderstone, in Suffolk—where you came, on the night when I was born, and saw my dear mamma. I have been very unhappy since she died. I have been slighted, and taught nothing, and thrown upon myself, and put to work not fit for me. It made me run away to you. I was robbed at first setting out, and have walked all the way, and have never slept in a bed since I began the journey." Here my self support gave way all at once; and with a movement of my hands intended to show her my ragged state, and call it to witness that I had suffered something, I broke into a passion of crying, which I suppose had been pent up within me all the week.

My aunt, with every sort of expression but wonder discharged from her countenance, sat on the gravel staring at me, until I began to cry; when she got up in a great hurry, collared me, and took me into the parlour. Her first proceeding there was to unlock a tall press, bring out several bottles, and pour some of the contents of each into my mouth. I think they must have been taken out at random, for I am sure I tasted aniseed water, anchovy sauce, and salad dressing. When she had administered these restoratives, as I was still quite hysterical, and unable to control my sobs, she put me on the sofa, with a shawl under my head, and the handkerchief from her own head under my feet, lest I should sully the cover; and then, sitting herself down behind the green fan or screen I have already mentioned, so that I could not see her face, cried out at intervals, "Mercy on us!" letting those exclamations off like minute-guns.

1. Complication as a typical element in plot development is here demonstrated by _____.
   (A) David's beginning uncertainty
   (B) the appearance of Miss Betsey
   (C) the shyness of David Copperfield
   (D) David's identifying himself
   (E) David's crying spell

   1 ___

2. The word that quickly got Miss Betsey's attention was _____.
   (A) "please"
   (B) "ma'am"
   (C) "aunt"
   (D) "Suffolk"
   (E) "robbed"

   2 ___

3. The author's mention of "aniseed water, anchovy sauce, and salad dressing" is intended to _____.
   (A) suggest Miss Betsey's basic indifference
   (B) add a touch of humor
   (C) reveal the manners and mores of the time
   (D) show how David would react to an unusual drink
   (E) display a mastery of prose rhythms

   3 ——

4. In line 65 "restoratives" most nearly means _____.
   (A) "health aids"
   (B) "bitter pills"
   (C) "vegetable oils"
   (D) "sound foods"
   (E) "helpful suggestions"

   4 ——

5. The expression "Mercy on us" is meant to suggest Miss Betsey's _____.
   (A) sense of humor
   (B) deeply religious nature
   (C) control of the unexpected situation
   (D) love for her newly arrived nephew
   (E) agitation

   5 ——

6. The passage implies that _____.
   (A) David is a cruel boy, about to take advantage of a relative
   (B) Miss Betsey is, at best, an inefficient gardener
   (C) Miss Betsey is not really disturbed by David's arrival
   (D) Miss Betsey has a prejudice against boys
   (E) David's hysteria is feigned

   6 ——

7. From her actions we may infer that Miss Betsey _____.
   (A) despised David immediately and intensely
   (B) felt a house should be lived in, not preserved as a museum piece
   (C) was gruff but not unkind
   (D) kept in close communication with David's mother
   (E) welcomed the newcomer without reservations

   7 ——

8. At the close of the passage, Miss Betsey probably _____.
   (A) disclaimed all responsibility for David
   (B) called the local welfare office
   (C) fell into a deep faint
   (D) helped David
   (E) wrote a letter to Blunderstone

   8 ——

9. Which of the following titles best summarizes the content of the passage?
   (A) David Meets Miss Betsey
   (B) A Sad Story
   (C) How I Traveled from Blunderstone to Miss Betsey's
   (D) The Practical Uses of Hysteria
   (E) A Frightened Little Boy

   9 ——

Strategy. 1. Miss Betsey seems quite self-sufficient by her initial appearance and actions, but then her calm is shaken by David's revelation of his relationship to her. His arrival (D) introduces a complication.

2. When David uses the word *aunt,* (C), Miss Betsey reacts "in a tone of amazement I had never heard before." The other words produce no emotional response.

3. Since the subjects mentioned are ill-assorted and not medicinal, we may assume that they have been introduced for a touch of humor (B).

4. The restoratives have been administered to David so that he will recover his composure. We may assume they are health aids (A). The basic word *restore* provides an additional clue.

5. The previous context suggests that Miss Betsey has been upset by David's arrival. The emotional exclamation, "Mercy on us," suggests agitation (E). Miss Betsy has not demonstrated a sense of humor (A). The context suggests that the exclamation is not religious (B). Miss Betsey has not yet exhibited control over the situation (C). It is much too soon for Miss Betsey to have developed love for her nephew (D).

6. When Miss Betsey tells David, "Go away! No boys here!" we may assume she has a prejudice against boys (D). She doesn't say, "No children here," suggesting that boys may be a particularly unwelcome sight. David is pathetic, not cruel (A). Miss Betsey's actions with gloves and gardening knife suggest that she is an efficient gardener (B). Her agitation reveals her disturbance at David's arrival (C). David reveals that his crying is uncontrolled, not feigned (E).

7. Miss Betsey's immediate attempts to help David in his impassioned crying suggests that she has a good heart. Her actions have shown her to be gruff, but she doesn't turn David away heartlessly. She is gruff but not unkind (C).

8. Since Miss Betsey has apparently assumed some responsibility for David because she is his aunt, we may assume that she helped David (D). Her hasty efforts at restoratives show that she has his welfare at heart.

9. A process of elimination helps to determine the title. (B) is much too general. It could apply to many passages. (C), by contrast, is too specific. Besides it omits mention of the meeting between David and Miss Betsey. (D) is quite off the subject. There is nothing to suggest that David tried to manipulate his aunt by crying. (E) presumes to say more than is implied. Perhaps later events will prove the truth of this statement, but there is not enough in the passage itself to justify the broad comment. The simple title, (A), is a good title for the passage.

Review

In this excerpt from a short story, Elaine, a divorced mother, has charge of her two sons for a brief time. At the time of the divorce, nine-year-old Jesse and eleven-year-old Matthew had both chosen to live with their father, Peter, who was as surprised as Elaine by the boys' decision. Elaine and her children are staying at her parents' condominium in Florida.

Ignoring her mother's warning and her father's dire predictions, Elaine took the boys everywhere they wanted to go: Monkey Jungle, Parrot Jungle, 5 and the Seaquarium. The boys seemed excited and happy, though often they would run ahead of her, too impatient to stay by her side. Once, from a distance, 10 Elaine saw Jesse casually rest his arm on his brother's shoulder as the two of

them stood watching a pair of orangutans groom each other; she kept waiting for Matthew to shake Jesse off, but it never happened. Two nights in a row,
15 they went to see the movie *Airplane!* A couple of nights, they played miniature golf. At the end of each day, Jesse and Matthew told Elaine they had had "the best time." She supposed that this
20 meant the trip was a success, that they would have nothing to complain about to their father when they went back home. She had kept them entertained, which was all they seemed to have
25 wanted from her. She might have been anyone—a camp counsellor, a teacher leading them on class trips, a friend of the family put in charge while their parents were on vacation. There was plenty
30 of time to talk, and they told her a lot—long, involved stories about the fight Jesse had recently had with his best friend, the rock concert Matthew had gone to with two thirteen-year-olds,
35 the pair of Siamese fighting fish with beautiful flowing fins they'd bought for the new fish tank in their bedroom—all about the things that had happened to them in the four months they had been
40 out of touch. But she still didn't know if they were really all right, if they loved their father, loved her. You couldn't ask questions like that. When, several years ago, her brother had started seeing a
45 shrink, he'd complained that his parents were always asking him if he was happy. It's none of their business, the shrink told him—if you don't feel you want to give them an answer, don't. As
50 simple as that.

It was nearly midnight; the boys had just gone to bed. Elaine went into her parents' room, where her mother and father were sitting up in their king-size
55 bed watching *Columbo* on a small color TV. Dick Van Dyke was tying his wife to a chair. He took two Polaroid pictures of her and then he picked up a gun. His wife insisted he was never going to
60 get away with it; he aimed the gun at her and pulled the trigger.

"Wait a minute," Elaine's mother said. "Is this the one where Columbo tricks him into identifying his camera at
65 the—"

"Thanks a lot," her father said. "You know how I love Peter Falk."

"Who knows, maybe I'm wrong."

"You're not," Elaine said. "I saw
70 this one, too."

"Well, it's nice to be right about something."

Elaine lay down on her stomach at the foot of the bed, facing the TV set.
75 She yawned and said, "Excuse me."

"All that running around," her mother said. "Who wouldn't be tired?"

"It's not necessary to run like that all day long," her father said. "Didn't
80 those two kids ever hear of sleeping around the pool, or picking up a book or a newspaper? Maybe they're hyperactive or something."

"They're kids on vacation. What do
85 they want to read the newspaper for?" her mother said.

Elaine sat up and swung her legs over the side of the bed. "It's my fault," she said. "I couldn't bring myself to say
90 no to them about anything."

"Did you accomplish anything all those hours you were running?" her mother asked. "Do you feel like you made any headway?"

95 Elaine was watching an overweight woman on TV dance the cha-cha with her cat along a shining kitchen floor. "What?" she said.

"Of course, if they really are just
100 fine there with Peter and his sleep-over girlfriends, that's another story," her father said.

"Quiet," her mother said. "Look who's here."

105 Jesse stood in the doorway, blinking his eyes. "There's a funny noise in my ears that keeps waking me up," he said. He sat down on the floor next to the bed and put his head in Elaine's lap. "You
110 know," he said, "like someone's whistling in there."

Elaine hesitated, then kissed each ear. "Better?"

"A little."

115 "More kisses?"
Jesse shook his head.
"Let me take you back to bed."
Elaine walked him to the little den at
the other end of the apartment, where
120 Matthew was asleep on his side of the
convertible couch. Jesse got onto the
bed. On his knees, he sat up and looked
out the window. "I can't go to sleep
right now," he said quietly. Beneath
125 them the water was black; above, the
palest of moons appeared to drift by.
There were clouds everywhere, and just
a few dim stars.
"Did you want to tell me some-
130 thing?" Elaine waited; she focused on
the sign lit up on top of the Holiday Inn
across the Waterway.
"We're getting a new car. A silver
BMW," Jesse said dreamily. "We saw
135 it in the showroom." He moved away
from the window and slipped down on
the bed. "We might drive it over to Fort
Lee and come and see you. And when
Matthew has his license, the two of us
140 will pick you up every day and take you
anywhere you want to go."
Elaine still faced the window; she
did not turn around. "To the moon,"
she said. "Will you do that for me?"
145 Jesse didn't answer for a long time.
"We can do that," he said finally, and
when she turned to look at him he was
asleep.

1. Tension is an important element in plot
   complication. Part of Elaine's tension
   is generated by her desire to _____.
   (A) help her parents' marriage
   (B) belittle the boys' father
   (C) make the boys' visit as perfect as
       possible
   (D) play one son against the other
   (E) find out from the boys what went
       wrong

   1 __

2. The probable follow-up to the passage
   is _____.
   (A) the boys' changed decision to live
       with their mother
   (B) a bitter exchange of letters be-
       tween Peter and Elaine
   (C) a decision by Elaine to remain
       with her parents
   (D) a bold action by Elaine's father to
       keep the children
   (E) a return to the situation as before

   2 __

3. The author introduces lines 8–14 to
   show that _____.
   (A) Jesse is more mature than
       Matthew
   (B) the boys have been deeply dis-
       turbed by the divorce
   (C) the boys have bonded together
   (D) the boys are unhappy in Elaine's
       presence
   (E) the boys have no love for either
       parent

   3 __

4. A sentence that captures Elaine's es-
   sential heartbreak is _____.
   (A) "At the end of each day, Jesse
       and Matthew told Elaine they had
       had 'the best time.'"
   (B) "She might have been anyone—a
       camp counsellor, a teacher leading
       them on class trips, a friend of the
       family put in charge while their
       parents were on vacation."
   (C) "I couldn't bring myself to say no
       to them about anything."
   (D) "It's not necessary to run like that
       all day long,' her father said."
   (E) "Elaine walked him to the little
       den on the other side of the apart-
       ment, where Jesse was asleep on
       the convertible couch."

   4 __

5. The experience of Elaine's brother suggests that _____.
   (A) his childhood may have been unhappy
   (B) he'd probably have made a poor husband
   (C) Elaine's parents were excellent role models
   (D) he and Elaine never got along well
   (E) he understood Jesse and Matthew very well

   5 ___

6. The author introduces the *Columbo* episode (lines 55–72) to _____.
   (A) explore the parents' addiction to television
   (B) bring Elaine and her parents closer together
   (C) show the father's enjoyment of Peter Falk
   (D) paint a pleasant picture of a family evening
   (E) point up a flaw in the parents' relationship with each other

   6 ___

7. The "headway" Elaine's mother refers to in lines 93–94 is _____.
   (A) physical stamina for the excursions
   (B) an effort to win back the children
   (C) an improvement in Elaine's financial situation
   (D) a desire to learn more about Peter's current lifestyle
   (E) an attempt to establish Elaine's Florida residency

   7 ___

8. The author mentions the woman doing the cha-cha with the cat (lines 95–97) to _____.
   (A) introduce an ironic trivial note in a tense situation
   (B) show the diversity of television's offerings
   (C) make a negative comment about the mother's taste
   (D) distract the reader momentarily
   (E) suggest that Elaine was not really concerned about her sons

   8 ___

9. The father's comments in lines 99–102 are an example of _____.
   (A) compassion
   (B) broad-mindedness
   (C) acceptance
   (D) sarcasm
   (E) deception

   9 ___

10. When, at the end, Elaine asks, "Did you want to tell me something?" she probably hopes that Jesse will _____.
    (A) mention again the good time they had all had
    (B) tell her about the new car
    (C) fall asleep before answering
    (D) tell her how much he liked Florida
    (E) express his love and need for her

    10 ___

11. Elaine's answer, "To the moon" (lines 142–144) expresses her _____.
    (A) jubilation
    (B) sadness
    (C) indifference
    (D) curiosity
    (E) hatred

    11 ___

12. Elaine can take some comfort in the knowledge that _____.
(A) her ex-husband is having his problems, too
(B) Matthew has been relatively indifferent to her
(C) her parents deeply understand her feelings
(D) Jesse shows signs of missing his mother
(E) the children will soon return to their father

12 ___

13. An essential truth demonstrated in this passage is that _____.
(A) divorce is easier on wives than on husbands
(B) older people cannot relate successfully to the young
(C) material things are obstacles to happiness
(D) innermost thoughts are hard to verbalize
(E) children are intentionally cruel

13 ___

14. The author seems to be saying that in unfortunate divorce situations, _____.
(A) the husband is to blame
(B) unfeeling children may bring about the split
(C) there may be no villains
(D) mothers-in-law may play negative roles
(E) the wife is an unfit mother

14 ___

15. The setting plays a role in the story because _____.
(A) the heat makes the boys inactive
(B) it suggests that Elaine's parents are poor
(C) the children and their father cannot get in touch with each other
(D) the apartment accommodations throw the characters closely together
(E) there are relatively few things for the boys to do in the area

15 ___

SUMMARY

2. Plot

The ancient art of storytelling is alive and well. The thread of the narrative, *plot*, is a crucial element in most fiction. As in life, character, incident, and setting interact. Character may influence plot or be influenced by setting. All three tend to play a role in narrative.

Section VII Summary: Understanding Narrative

Most people find narrative easy to read, but appreciation of a good story is heightened by an awareness of the ingredients, especially plot, character, and setting.

PART 1. Characterization (p. 265)

A. When you read a story, think about the characters. What special traits do they display? How do they interact with each other?

B. Get a general impression of each character. Are the actions consistent? Are the characters self-aware or do they act blindly?

C. As a person outside the action, how do you picture each character? Do you identify with one of the characters?

PART 2. Plot (p. 271)

A. As you read, note the opening situation. Get an impression of each character as the plot is set in motion.

B. Note how some kind of conflict or confrontation sets the wheels rolling.

C. Follow the conflict to its conclusion. Is the ending satisfactory? Does it grow reasonably out of the previous events?

D. What role does characterization play in the resolution? Do the characters change the direction of the plot? How? How do the incidents impact upon the characters, influencing their actions?

E. What role does setting play? Could the events have taken place in a quite different setting? Why or why not?

Section VIII: Studying the Longer Passage

1. The Single Selection

In its 1994 revision of the SAT, the College Boards introduced a critical reading section with longer and more challenging selections than before. All the skills you have been developing in this book will stand you in good stead when you meet a difficult longer passage. This section will provide some additional practice, using examples of the type you will face on the test itself.

Because the new reading passages run much longer than those used in the past, each selection can test a great many skills. A *single* selection can test a majority of such skills as these:

> Generalizations and Main Ideas
> The Author's Purpose, Style, Method, and Tone
> Vocabulary and the Interpretation of Phrases
> Figurative Language
> Inferences
> Outcomes and Applications
> Sequence
> Awareness of Skills Being Used

The new reading passages signal a shift in emphasis from the literal understanding of text information, like finding details. The College Board notes that the new passages measure "students' ability to make inferences; to relate parts of the text to each other or to the whole; to follow the logic of an argument; to synthesize meaning; to identify the author's purpose, attitude, or tone, etc."

Trial Test

The following passage, written during the Bosnian-Serb conflict in the last decade of the twentieth century, discusses a disturbing trend with dangerous implications for the future.

When George Orwell published his provocative novel *1984,* in 1948, the world seemed to be going in one inevitable direction. As Orwell looked 36 years into the future, he projected then-current trends and envisioned a world of three superpowers: Oceania, Eurasia, and Eastasia. Each dominated completely its own people and spheres of influence, using technology for complete mind manipulation. Rulers of the three superpowers maintained power by waging perpetual limited warfare, not for the usual territorial or political reasons but principally for internal social control. How accurate was the prophecy of the division of the world into three monolithic geographical areas?

20   Thirty years earlier, another prophecy had been made. During World War I, President Woodrow Wilson argued for the self-determination of all peoples, but his own Secretary of State, Robert
25 Lansing, was worried by the sweeping declaration. He wrote, "Will it not breed discontent, disorder, and rebellion? The phrase is simply loaded with dynamite. It will raise hopes which can
30 never be realized. It will, I fear, cost thousands of lives.

    "What a calamity that the phrase was ever uttered! What misery it will cause!"

35   After 1984 rolled around, there were significant indications that Lansing, rather than Orwell, was in one way the better prophet. The concept of the superpower was being eroded. The most
40 significant events in this trend were the fall of the Berlin Wall, the end of the Cold War, and the disintegration of the Soviet empire. As states broke away from that union, other areas picked up
45 the battle cry of self-determination.

    Self-determination is a worthy ideal. Reasonable persons uphold the principle. It often works well. Some "new" nations, like the Baltic republics—Lat-
50 via, Lithuania, and Estonia—had already demonstrated a capacity for nationhood in the years between World Wars I and II. But other new nations suffered violent disruptions at their
55 birth, with serious continuing problems.

    The roots of the problem lie in history, in the invasions and suppressions in the long, unhappy tale of war and conquest. The collapse of the Yugosla-
60 vian Republic in the late twentieth century and the consequent troubles provided a sense of déjà vu. It had all happened before. Sarajevo, scene of bitter fighting in the Bosnian-Serb con-
65 flict, was the city where the assassination of Archduke Ferdinand provided the spark that ignited World War I. When the Austro-Hungarian and Otto-

man empires dissolved early in the
70 twentieth century, the nationalistic components of these empires had their sights set on independence, but there were conflicting claims. At the Treaty of Versailles, an attempt was made to
75 integrate smaller groups into larger units, like Czechoslovakia and Yugoslavia, but those experiments were ultimately doomed.

    Upon what bases are claims for na-
80 tional sovereignty made? Religious, ethnic, racial, and political differences fuel sectional fires. The problem is aggravated by the simple reality that the groups are often intermingled, as with
85 Muslim enclaves in largely orthodox communities and ethnic minorities inside ethnic majorities. Differences in language and culture play a role, too. Adolf Hitler annexed the Czechoslova-
90 kian Sudetenland in 1938 with the excuse that the peoples of that area were largely of German origin, language, and culture.

    By 1919, the word *Balkanize* had appeared: "to break up a region into smaller, ineffectual, and often hostile units." By 1990, the word had taken on new and dangerous applications. The process was being demonstrated, not
100 only in a corner of Europe, the Balkans; it had applications around the world.

    During the Bosnian-Serb crisis, the *New York Times* printed a map of the world, identifying 45 actual and poten-
105 tial trouble spots. Europe, Asia, and Africa showed the most danger signals, but even traditional paradises like Indonesia, Fiji, and Papua New Guinea were not exempt from the violence. Nearly
110 all dissident groups called for the creation of new states composed of disaffected minorities.

    New states are not always born in violence. Czechs and Slovaks, for ex-
115 ample, agreed to go their separate ways, and the Republic of Czechoslovakia disappeared in 1993, without bloodshed. Elsewhere the transitions were not so peaceful. Bloody civil war in the former
120 Yugoslavia pointed up the hazards of

creating new states by carving them out of the bodies of former larger nations.

The creation of new states often encourages further splintering, as dissidents within these new nations attempt to break away into still smaller units. The eastern region of Moldova, for example, declared independence in 1990, but western Moldova sought closer ties with Romania. Other former Soviet republics, like Georgia and Azerbaijan, slipped into near anarchy.

The principle of self-determination, long a tenet of the United States, was incorporated into the charter of the United Nations. Sometimes good principles clash. The principle of human rights is *also* a cornerstone of U.N. policy. Unfortunately, when new nations are formed, human rights are often trampled upon. When minorities become majorities, they sometimes persecute new minorities.

In the *Times* article, the list of trouble spots was long: Northern Ireland, Romania, and Spain in Europe; Iraq, Turkey, and the Sudan in the Middle East and North Africa; Liberia, Togo, Angola, Kenya, and Senegal in Africa; Afghanistan, Pakistan, India, and Sri Lanka in Asia; Guatemala, Colombia, Peru, and Brazil in South America. The list goes on and on. And the article didn't even mention less dangerous but troublesome problems like the Quebec separatist movement in Canada.

The U.N. was presented with problems that had far-reaching consequences. No one could predict the future.

1. The author believes that George Orwell and Robert Lansing _____.
   (A) were clear-sighted prophets with uncanny ability to foresee the future
   (B) gained their expertise through actually being involved in the running of government
   (C) looked at the world around them and developed somewhat different views about future events
   (D) were contemporaries who had arrived at similar, but incorrect, conclusions based on current trends
   (E) both played a role in the development of the novel *1984*

   1 ___

2. In line 18, the word *monolithic* most nearly means _____.
   (A) permanently nonsectarian
   (B) unexpectedly heterogeneous
   (C) narrowly defined
   (D) rigidly uniform
   (E) carelessly created

   2 ___

3. At the moment of writing, the author of the passage felt that _____.
   (A) there was danger that the Cold War would reappear on the world scene
   (B) the disintegration of the Soviet Union had few dangerous results
   (C) the Baltic republics had a promising future
   (D) the coming years would bring a significant reduction in the number of danger spots
   (E) the Czechs and Slovaks would eventually reunite

   3 ___

4. Orwell probably intended to show that waging "perpetual limited warfare" (line 13) helped to maintain internal social control by _____.
   (A) increasing farm production for military purposes
   (B) supplying an "enemy" against which all citizens could rally
   (C) training low-level citizen leaders in the armies of the superpowers
   (D) demonstrating the legitimacy of the cause for which each superpower fought
   (E) encouraging freedom of thought and expression

   4 ___

5. The meaning of *déjà vu* in line 62 can best be captured by the expression _____
   (A) "I've seen it all before."
   (B) "Let sleeping dogs lie."
   (C) "Don't trouble trouble or trouble will trouble you."
   (D) "Birds of a feather stick together."
   (E) "Nothing happens the same way twice."

   5 ___

6. The author's attitude toward the principle of self-determination is one of _____.
   (A) undiluted support
   (B) approval with some concerns
   (C) disagreement with Lansing but not Orwell
   (D) unreserved disapproval
   (E) objection to its being included in the U.N. charter

   6 ___

7. The "larger units" mentioned in lines 75–76 were doomed because of _____.
   (A) disputes over the wording of the Treaty of Versailles
   (B) the powerful and negative influence of the Soviet Union
   (C) the conflicting positions of the Austro-Hungarian and Ottoman Empires
   (D) positive models of independence provided by the United States
   (E) reviving nationalist ambitions

   7 ___

8. In line 85, the word *enclaves* means _____.
   (A) distinct units enclosed within larger units
   (B) restless and potentially dangerous groups
   (C) cultural majorities
   (D) democratically elected local governments
   (E) peaceful areas in the midst of violence

   8 ___

9. The author probably mentions Hitler's annexation of the Sudetenland to show that _____.
   (A) World War II would not have started if Hitler had not entered Czechoslovakia
   (B) irresponsibly exploited self-determination can have tragic consequences
   (C) language and culture are stronger unifying elements than religion
   (D) the Western Allies were inattentive to the just needs of a people
   (E) Hitler was more concerned with the well-being of Sudeten Germans than of his own people

   9 ___

10. A sharp contrast is pointed up in the author's comparison of _____.
   (A) Estonia and Czechoslovakia
   (B) Georgia and Yugoslavia
   (C) India and Turkey
   (D) Yugoslavia and Czechoslovakia
   (E) Liberia and Senegal

   10 ___

11. The basic problem for the U.N. is the conflict between two good principles: _____.
   (A) economic security and political independence
   (B) education and self-determination
   (C) self-determination and human rights
   (D) human rights and economic security
   (E) political independence and education

   11 ___

12. With which of the following statements would the author probably agree?
   (A) Once Yugoslavia is quiet, the rest of the world will also quickly quiet down.
   (B) The world would be better off with 1,500 nations in the U.N. than with 150.
   (C) The United States should send troops to all the world's trouble spots.
   (D) Force is the only way to settle problems of self-determination.
   (E) The future will see additional demands for the creation of new nations.

   12 ___

Problem

The following longer selection will provide practice in critical reading. Take the test before reading "Strategy," the analysis of the questions (pages 289–291). Try to uncover any weak areas in your reading. Then review helpful sections of the text itself.

How healthy is dieting? The following passage addresses some of the questions raised by dieters.

Among the topics of table conversation in the United States, diet holds an important place. So many people are future dieters, current dieters, or back-
5 sliders that nearly everyone has something to say about dieting. On the surface, the problem is simple. *Eat less and lose weight.* While this statement is partly true, its simplicity is deceptive.
10 As the title of one article states, "Weight regulation may start in our cells, not psyches."

Some weight loss is always possible. Diets like those proposed by Weight
15 Watchers have an understandable rationale, allowing for reasonably nutritious and balanced meals throughout the dieting process. Others may be fad
20 diets that recommend excessive consumption of single foods like bananas or grapefruit, good in themselves but likely to result in a neglect of some important food groups. Since the number of diet books is astronomical, the number of
25 persons trying diets must be surprisingly large.

The body is a self-repairing, self-perpetuating machine. All diets must fight the body's natural desire to protect it-
30 self, to retain the status quo. If there is a deviation, the body begins to fight against the change. In general, if the body feels it is being starved, it takes protective measures that make continu-
35 ing weight loss difficult—and often agonizing. This defensive strategy of the

body explains the high failure rate of dieters, most of whom relapse after a strenuous effort to lose weight and thus to become fashionably slim. The percentage of recidivists, those who relapse and regain their former weight, is estimated at two thirds. For those who are far above their ideal weights, the failure rate is higher. The body's tendency to retain a state of equilibrium is called *homeostasis*—"staying the same."

Diets begin with enthusiasm. Initial success disguises the difficulties ahead. Losing weight is only part of the problem. Maintaining the weight loss is the major hurdle. Many persons go on and off diets, the so-called yo-yo effect. These persons are chagrined to discover that it's harder to lose weight on the second time around than on the first time. The situation gets worse on the third, fourth, and fifth attempts.

Recent studies have overturned some favorite explanations of obesity. Though it was once thought that emotional disorders cause obesity by overeating, a research group at the University of Pennsylvania thinks that obesity causes emotional disorders. In societies that accept, even admire, obesity, the overweight person does not feel guilt, envy, or rejection. Being excessively overweight does present some health hazards, but the condition is not helped by acute anxiety and self-condemnation.

Extreme concern for trendy slenderness, especially in young women, may result in bulimia or anorexia. With bulimia, defined as "an abnormally voracious appetite," victims overeat and then purge themselves. With anorexia, defined as "a pathological fear of weight gain," victims starve themselves until malnutrition causes severe health damage, even death. Their gaunt appearance is anything but attractive.

In their constant depiction of the so-called "ideal woman," the media saturate the minds of young women with images of extremely slender models and actresses. As a result, the self-esteem of young girls is eroded. In one study, 60% of elementary-school girls said, "I'm happy the way I am." By high school, only 29% of the girls made the same statement. There is much less uneasiness reported for boys than for girls. Part of the upset can be traceable to the glandular turbulence of adolescence. But a major part of the damage can be laid at the door of faddish appearance. Healthy, lovely girls starve themselves, seek cosmetic surgery, attempt to emulate the models whose genetic makeup is largely responsible for that thin, sometimes gaunt, appearance. The girls' efforts may be in a losing struggle. The genetic component cannot be underestimated. Thin people tend to come from "thin families."

At Rockefeller University, three obesity researchers have come to the conclusion that one's weight has something to do with the fat cells in the body. A major problem is how large these fat cells become. Generally the fat cells tend to stay constant in size in animals and even in human beings. There is a subtle regulation in effect. When this regulation is disturbed, the fat cells may increase in size. When scientists destroyed the part of a rat's brain that regulates its eating behavior, the rat became grossly obese. Fat cells grew to four or five times their normal size. Probably, in obese people, the signals that regulate fat-cell size may be somehow disturbed.

What about the problem with human beings? Two of the researchers selected a group of women and one man, all of whom belonged to Overeaters Anonymous. These people are formerly obese people. They are now of normal weight, but their body chemistries have been disturbed. They have tiny fat cells, but the dieters look gaunt and starved. They have low blood pressure and below-normal pulse rates. They are always cold. They constantly think about food because they survive on a very low-calorie diet.

Would people of normal weight have similar biochemical changes if they lost weight? The researchers studied a volunteer for a year and concluded that the body constantly fights to adjust its metabolism to retain its ideal weight. They also found that people have problem fat cells in specific areas. Women tend to have such fat cells on their hips and thighs. Different people have different distributions of fat cells. One man complained, "Everything I eat goes to waist." Dieters sometimes find that weight loss is uneven. A desirable loss of 20 pounds may come not from the paunch but from elsewhere.

There is much research to be done before any hard-and-fast conclusions can be drawn. What, then, is an overweight person to do? The first bit of advice is to make only small changes in the lifestyle, at least at first. A drastic change is often self-defeating. This realization leads to the second bit of advice: don't be a yo-yo dieter. Your body will work against you. Finally, monitor your eating by restricting calories in a reasonable way. Don't seek to become someone you were never, by nature, intended to be. Exercise more. Above all, don't develop a habit of self-recrimination. Accept yourself. Realize that the problem is difficult and pervasive. You are not alone. Work on the attainable—and eliminate that anxiety.

1. The author's general attitude toward dieting can best be characterized as _____.
   (A) strongly approving
   (B) fervently dogmatic
   (C) unalterably opposed
   (D) somewhat skeptical
   (E) generally recommended

   1 ___

2. The author thinks that the "simple problem" (line 7) is _____.
   (A) best disregarded
   (B) poorly stated
   (C) tried and true
   (D) not accepted by most dieters
   (E) quite complex

   2 ___

3. "Weight regulation may start in our cells, not psyches" (lines 11–12), can best be matched with which statement from the passage?
   (A) "Emotional disorders cause obesity by overeating." (lines 62–64)
   (B) "Make only small changes in the lifestyle." (lines 161–162)
   (C) "The number of persons trying diets must be surprisingly large." (lines 24–26)
   (D) "Exercise more." (line 170)
   (E) "If the body feels it is being starved, it takes protective measures." (lines 32–34)

   3 ___

4. As used in line 12, "psyches" means _____.
   (A) minds
   (B) genes
   (C) cultural backgrounds
   (D) early training
   (E) good intentions

   4 ___

5. As used in lines 15–16, "rationale" means _____.
   (A) underlying reason
   (B) weak excuse
   (C) graphic chart
   (D) alternative plan
   (E) rallying cry

   5 ___

6. As used in line 24, the word "astronomical" is an example of _____.
   (A) simile
   (B) hyperbole
   (C) personification
   (D) alliteration
   (E) innovation

   6 ___

7. Yo-yo dieting can best be characterized as _____.
   (A) ultimately rewarding
   (B) entertaining
   (C) self-defeating
   (D) constantly encouraging
   (E) often fatal

   7 ___

8. All the following are mentioned as eating problems EXCEPT _____.
   (A) anorexia
   (B) yo-yo dieting
   (C) bulimia
   (D) fad diets
   (E) cholesterol

   8 ___

9. In answering question 8, which of the following skills would you use? _____
   (A) determining the author's purpose
   (B) looking for significant generalizations
   (C) intensive rereading of the selection
   (D) skimming for words mentioned
   (E) drawing inferences

   9 ___

10. The quotation marks around the expression following the word "homeostasis" in lines 47–48 suggest that the expression _____.
    (A) is a quotation from one of the research articles
    (B) is an interesting, though somewhat inaccurate, statement
    (C) provides the etymological definition
    (D) is too farfetched for acceptance
    (E) provides an alternative interpretation of homeostasis

    10 ___

11. A major problem leading to diets, with their consequent failure, is _____.
    (A) a person's self-image
    (B) business disagreements
    (C) anorexia
    (D) eating more than 1,000 calories daily
    (E) broken engagements

    11 ___

12. The power of the media is probably best reflected in the word _____.
    (A) "exercise" (line 170)
    (B) "trendy" (line 74)
    (C) "backsliders" (lines 4–5)
    (D) "turbulence" (line 97)
    (E) "relapse" (line 38)

    12 ___

13. In line 102, "emulate" means _____.
    (A) outdo   (D) imitate
    (B) analyze   (E) photograph
    (C) report

    13 ___

14. That anorexic persons starve themselves to look better is an example of _____.
    (A) indifference
    (B) common sense
    (C) metaphor
    (D) irony
    (E) good health

    14 ___

15. In lines 102–103, "genetic" means _____.
    (A) unclassifiable
    (B) irrational
    (C) manageable
    (D) nonspecific
    (E) inherited

    15 ___

16. From current research, it seems apparent that _____.
    (A) the body may actually encourage obesity
    (B) fat cells increase in size and number entirely on their own
    (C) some persons have no fat cells
    (D) definitive answers about curing obesity have now been found
    (E) obesity results from eating too much of one kind of food

    16 ___

17. "Everything I eat goes to waist" (lines 152–153) is intended to be _____.
    (A) gritty   (D) humorous
    (B) self-pitying   (E) solemn
    (C) untrue

    17 ___

18. In line 173, "pervasive" means _____.
    (A) discouraging
    (B) widespread
    (C) pessimistic
    (D) trivial
    (E) time-consuming

    18 ___

19. The last paragraph in the passage is intended to _____.
   (A) reassure as well as inform
   (B) say the last word about dieting
   (C) condemn all attempts at losing weight
   (D) frighten the reader
   (E) provide a humorous summary

19 ___

20. The following outline of the structure of the passage is scrambled. Choose the sequence that best suggests the order of treatment.
   a. Challenges to Conventional Thinking About Diet
   b. Popularity of Dieting
   c. Advice to Dieters
   d. Dangers of Dieting
   e. Problems of Dieting
   f. The Part Played by Fat Cells
   (A) a, d, c, b, e, f
   (B) d, a, f, b, e, c
   (C) b, e, a, d, f, c
   (D) e, f, d, c, b, a
   (E) c, d, f, b, a, e

20 ___

21. The tone and style of the author can best be characterized as _____.
   (A) strongly reproachful
   (B) quietly informative
   (C) characteristically bitter
   (D) pungently witty
   (E) consistently argumentative

21 ___

22. The author's attitude toward crash diets is basically _____.
   (A) disapproving
   (B) apathetic
   (C) accepting under controlled situations
   (D) unequivocally favorable
   (E) not implied in the passage

22 ___

23. Young women are especially vulnerable to anorexia because _____.
   (A) they are more likely to have the spirit of adventure than young men
   (B) there are inherited tendencies toward the disease
   (C) they are more likely to catch an infection from friends
   (D) they are subject to more pressure than men to look slender
   (E) many movie stars have exhibited signs of the disease

23 ___

24. After reading this passage, a reader is likely to feel _____.
   (A) impelled to disagree strongly with the author
   (B) a little more secure about himself or herself
   (C) free to eat anything and everything formerly considered harmful
   (D) that nothing works in weight control
   (E) motivated to enter a weight-loss contest

24 ___

Strategy. 1. The *general* tone of the passage is skeptical about diets, but lines 157–159 *specifically* indicate reserved judgment. The answer is (D) somewhat skeptical.

2. The passage repeatedly discusses the complexities of diet. The answer is (E) quite complex.

3. Taking protective measures (lines 32–34) is equivalent to regulating weight. Therefore (E) is the best answer.

4. The wording of the sentences suggests that the answer is contrasted with *cells*. Genes are part of cells, so this answer (B) may be eliminated. Only (A) suggests a reasonable contrast: *cells* not *minds*.

5. Context provides the answer, not only in the whole sentence but also in the use of *reasonably* and *balanced* in lines 16–17. The answer is (A) underlying reason.

6. Astronomy deals with billions and multibillions. The number of diet books, though large in comparison with books on other topics, is tiny when compared with the immensities of space. This is exaggeration or (B) hyperbole.

7. After the author mentions yo-yo dieting in line 54, he tells how dieters usually cannot keep their weight down, suggesting that the yo-yo diet is (C) self-defeating.

8. The answer to this question requires skimming. A process of elimination reveals that cholesterol has nowhere been mentioned (E).

9. See question 8. The answer is (D).

10. The pairing of the word and the quoted expression following suggests that the author is defining an unfamiliar word for the reader (C). The other possibilities are irrelevant.

11. Lines 100–102 deal specifically with self-image and its effect on eating habits. Unrealistic goals bring unrealistic diets and unhealthy bodies. The answer is (A) a person's self-image.

12. Lines 85–89 detail the power of the media in shaping the images and goals of young women. Line 99 introduces the word faddish, a clue to the answer (B) trendy.

13. Obviously the girls are trying to be like the models, suggesting that the answer is (D) imitate.

14. Irony (D) is a contrast of opposites. Anorexic persons hope to look better, but they actually have a "gaunt appearance" (lines 83–84). The intended purpose is beauty, but the result is its opposite.

15. In lines 107–108, the author writes that "thin people tend to come from 'thin families'" Thus the answer is (E) inherited.

16. By fighting against weight loss and by striving to maintain the status quo, the body may actually encourage (A) obesity. The other answers are in no way suggested.

17. The pun on *waist* and *waste* suggests that the statement is intended to be (D) humorous.

18. If "you are not alone," the problem is (B) widespread.

19. After all the discouraging statements, the final paragraph provides a brief blueprint for effective action. An overweight person *can* do something, even if only in a modest way. The author is thus reassuring as well as informing the reader (A).

20. The opening paragraph immediately comments about the popularity of dieting. Thus (C) jumps out at once as having the best opening topic. For purposes of answering this question, this recognition is all that is needed, but

further check will reveal that the sequence of topics is popularity, problems, challenges, dangers, fat cells, and advice. (C) is the confirmed answer.

21. Though (B) seems obvious, it is sometimes prudent to eliminate the other possibilities. The author is nowhere reproachful (A). He is positive, rather than bitter (C). There is one small pun, not enough to characterize the passage as a whole (D). The author is modest, balanced, and understated, if anything, not argumentative (E).

22. The author suggests his disapproval (A) throughout the passage. He talks about the body's protective measures, the high percentage of dieters who relapse, the dangers of yo-yo dieting, the threat of anorexia, and other problems of dieting.

23. In line 75, the author uses the expression *especially in young women*, a clue to (D).

24. The passage is upbeat about the possibilities for modest success in dieting. It also disapproves the media's efforts to make all women clones of a few unusual types. It shows the futility of yo-yo dieting. It says, "Work on the attainable—and eliminate that anxiety." This is a reassuring message that should make readers feel more secure (B)

Review

The authorship of Shakespeare's plays is a perennial source of controversy, as this passage points out.

Who wrote the plays of Shakespeare? Nearly all scholars logically and reasonably answer, "William Shakespeare," but for the past 200 years,
5 there have been attempts to "prove" that someone else wrote the plays. Sir Francis Bacon, English philosopher and statesman, was the first to be considered seriously. He was a slightly older
10 contemporary of Shakespeare and had a busy but not-altogether-successful career in politics.

Bacon, however, was only the first of many candidates. Some others pro-
15 posed for the honor include the Earl of Essex, John Donne, Ben Jonson, Sir Walter Raleigh, the Earl of Southampton, and even Cardinal Wolsey. There is no limit to the absurdities. Among the
20 proposed creators were Mary, Queen of Scots; Queen Elizabeth; and an Irish nun.

Why did all these candidates gain any credence at all? One argument is
25 heard over and over. How could a simple country boy become so brilliant, so knowledgeable, so sophisticated, so wise in the ways of the world? The answer, like that to the opening question,
30 is obvious. Shakespeare was not a "simple country boy."

There is little doubt that Shakespeare had a good education. The fact that there is no record of his schooling
35 is irrelevant. There is no record of the schooling of most of Shakespeare's contemporaries. School records are generally not permanent documents. Indeed, there are even such gaps in the bio-
40 graphies of recent writers. Shakespeare's knowledge of history and the classics may well have come from the commonly used schoolbooks of the time. Since his father was a prominent
45 town official, it is likely that Shakespeare was given a suitable education. In *The Merry Wives of Windsor*, Shakespeare parodies a typical Latin lesson

of the kind he was probably subjected to.

There are other equally baseless objections to Shakespeare's claim to authorship of the plays, but one calm and measured voice relies on a very subtle reading of the plays themselves. More than half a century ago, Caroline Spurgeon published a study that forever settled the matter of Shakespeare's authorship, at least to the satisfaction of most scholars. *Shakespeare's Imagery* is a seminal book of great insight and impressive erudition. Shakespeare's use of figurative language, the author claims, is idiosyncratic, unique to the playwright. His use of various images reflects his personality and provides insight into his mind.

In *Orlando*, the novelist Virginia Woolf writes, "Every secret of a writer's soul, every experience of his life, every quality of his mind, is written large in his works, yet we require critics to explain the one and biographers to expound the other."

Since no two persons have exactly the same experiences, personalities inevitably vary. People develop individual ways of speaking, of expressing an idea, of using figurative language. The specialized experiences of childhood and adulthood inevitably determine the images we use. The moon has been variously called a "ghostly galleon," a "feather," a "silver pinhead," an "arrant thief," an "orbed maiden with white fire laden," the "hostess of the sky," even the "sweet surprise of heaven." At this very moment, perhaps, a lover is writing a love poem with still another image for the journeying moon.

Shakespeare's imagery, the author points out, is quite different from that of Francis Bacon or any other contemporary. More significantly, a great many of Shakespeare's images can be traced to specific incidents and experiences in his life. As a boy, Shakespeare undoubtedly dreamed on the Stratford bridge as he watched the current beneath. The peculiar ebb and flow of the River Avon at that point appears in an image in a play

Images often arise unbidden from the unconscious; yet Shakespeare channels these bursting images and furthers the dramatic qualities of his plays by their use. The images almost explode. In *Troilus and Cressida*, Ulysses tries to lure Achilles back into the fight against the Trojans. In a speech of 36 lines, Shakespeare pours forth more than 25 images, tumbling and cascading over each other, showing Achilles that fame and honor are, at best, transient and must be attended to constantly.

Spurgeon has analyzed plays individually to show how a specific constellation of images dominates certain plays. *Othello*, for example, has many sea images. Images of sickness in *Hamlet* reinforce the thought that something is "rotten in Denmark." *The Tempest* abounds in sound imagery. *As You Like It* includes a great many country images. Sleep and the lack of it have a prominent place in *Macbeth*. And so it goes. The number is astounding—for example, 204 images in *Romeo and Juliet* and 279 in *Hamlet*.

Spurgeon does more than analyze Shakespeare's plays. She also studies the writing of his contemporaries, especially those who have been put forth as claimants to the authorship of the plays. She finds vast differences, for example, between the images of Shakespeare and those of Christopher Marlowe. Marlowe's imagery is bookish, chiefly classical. Animals and nature come second, with most nature images confined to celestial bodies. With Shakespeare, nature and animals lead. Learning is in fourth place. Marlowe's images tend to be imaginative, chiefly personifications. Shakespeare's nature images are drawn from daily life.

There is one last rebuttal to the arguments that Shakespeare did not, could not write the plays. Shakespeare's contemporaries—fellow actors and playwrights alike—respected him enough to

preserve his plays. By contrast, most of the vast play production of his fellow
155 playwrights has been lost forever. When all is said and done, Shakespeare is really Shakespeare!

Wearying of the fruitless controversy, a scholar once wrote, "William
160 Shakespeare didn't write the plays. It was another person of the same name."

1. The use of quotation marks around the word "prove" in line 5 suggests _____.

    (A) that an authority is being quoted
    (B) the author's skepticism
    (C) a conviction that Shakespeare was not the author of the plays
    (D) a subtle tribute to Sir Franics Bacon
    (E) a linkage with the later discussion of *Shakespeare's Imagery*

1 ___

2. The use of "even" in line 18 suggests that the author considers Cardinal Wolsey _____.
    (A) a more likely candidate than the Earl of Essex
    (B) a possible associate of the Irish nun
    (C) the leading contender for the title of Shakespearean author
    (D) a most unlikely candidate
    (E) a secret author

2 ___

3. In line 24, "credence" means _____.
    (A) unreliable report
    (B) criticism
    (C) advantages
    (D) misfortune
    (E) believability

3 ___

4. The author dismisses the no-education argument because _____.
    (A) school records confirm Shakespeare's attendance at a common school
    (B) Shakespeare probably attended Oxford or Cambridge University
    (C) school records are ordinarily not preserved
    (D) Francis Bacon attested to Shakespeare's education
    (E) all records were probably destroyed in the great London fire

4 ___

5. In line 35, "irrelevant" means _____.
    (A) impossible
    (B) immaterial
    (C) irreproachable
    (D) irremediable
    (E) inexplicable

5 ___

6. Shakespeare's knowledge of history, unlike his knowledge of nature, probably came from _____.
    (A) his early experiences in and around Stratford
    (B) his school textbooks
    (C) his father's prominence as a local dignitary
    (D) a special course in the classics
    (E) his friendly association with Ben Jonson and the Earl of Southampton

6 ___

7. The gaps in the biographies of recent authors suggest that _____.
    (A) we should cease to worry about Shakespeare's attendance at a Stratford school
    (B) keepers of records are incredibly remiss and worthy of reproach
    (C) those authors probably had some skeletons in their closets
    (D) modern record keeping is probably worse than that of Shakespeare's time
    (E) biographies are inherently more difficult to write than novels

7 ___

8. The "calm and measured voice" mentioned in lines 53–54 belongs to _____.
   (A) Caroline Spurgeon
   (B) Virginia Woolf
   (C) a critic of *Shakespeare's Imagery*
   (D) an unnamed scholar
   (E) Shakespeare himself

   8 ___

9. In line 62, "erudition" means _____.
   (A) conjecture
   (B) length
   (C) credentials
   (D) writing style
   (E) scholarship

   9 ___

10. In line 64, "idiosyncratic" means _____.
    (A) overwhelming
    (B) individualistic
    (C) unexpected
    (D) untamed
    (E) unwise

    10 ___

11. In line 72, "yet" suggests that Virginia Woolf _____.
    (A) concludes that Shakespeare wrote the plays
    (B) considers most critics biased and unreliable
    (C) has a surprising unfamiliarity with the writing of biography
    (D) deplores the excessive use of imagery in a writer's work
    (E) thinks the writer's secrets should be clear to all readers

    11 ___

12. The labels attached to the moon (lines 82–88) are all _____.
    (A) in poor taste
    (B) images
    (C) examples of personification
    (D) used by young poets writing to their lovers
    (E) similes

    12 ___

13. In lines 90–91, "the journeying moon" is an example of _____.
    (A) simile
    (B) irony
    (C) exaggeration
    (D) metaphor
    (E) understatement

    13 ___

14. If a specific image relating to the River Avon appears in a Shakespeare play, we may assume that _____.
    (A) Shakespeare probably wrote that play
    (B) a great many other writers saw the same ebb and flow
    (C) Francis Bacon could never have used a nature image
    (D) Shakespeare probably lived within sight of the bridge
    (E) he probably used the same image over and over

    14 ___

15. In lines 105–106, "channels" suggests _____.
    (A) ineptness
    (B) exploitation
    (C) destruction
    (D) control
    (E) repression

    15 ___

16. In line 113, "cascading" suggests comparison with _____.
    (A) water
    (B) fireworks
    (C) volcanic ash
    (D) athletics
    (E) storms

    16 ___

17. The author obviously considers Ulysses' speech in *Troilus and Cressida* _____.
    (A) an ineffective argument to present to Achilles
    (B) a digression from the dramatic action
    (C) an amazing achievement
    (D) an excessive use of simile
    (E) an indication that Shakespeare probably did not write the play

    17 ___

18. In line 115, "transient" means _____.
    (A) fleeting
    (B) confusing
    (C) contradictory
    (D) useless
    (E) common

    18 ___

19. In lines 118–119, "constellation" suggests a _____.
    (A) burst of creativity
    (B) predominance of astronomical images
    (C) study
    (D) slight scattering
    (E) special grouping

    19 ___

20. In the discussion of images, the author mentions all the following plays EXCEPT _____.
    (A) *Hamlet*
    (B) *Macbeth*
    (C) *The Tempest*
    (D) *The Merry Wives of Windsor*
    (E) *As You Like It*

    20 ___

21. In line 138, the name of Christopher Marlowe _____.
    (A) bolsters the claims of other candidates
    (B) is put forth for the first time in the passage
    (C) suggests a preeminent master of nature images
    (D) is brought in almost as an afterthought
    (E) has often been linked to *As You Like It*

    21 ___

22. The comparison of Marlowe and Shakespeare suggests that _____.
    (A) Marlowe, at least in his early years, was probably superior to Shakespeare
    (B) Marlowe drew more on personal experience than Shakespeare did
    (C) Marlowe probably had more formal education than Shakespeare
    (D) the two men probably disliked each other intensely
    (E) Spurgeon may have actually liked Marlowe's plays better than Shakespeare's

    22 ___

23. The last paragraph is an attempt at _____.
    (A) mild humor
    (B) scholarly pretense
    (C) self-glorification
    (D) bitter anger
    (E) timid uncertainty

    23 ___

Review

Like the preceding passage, this dialogue is a longer exercise to challenge your critical reading abilities. It tests a variety of skills, but your experiences with previous chapters will help you meet the challenge.

When is a screwdriver not a screwdriver? The following passage presents some surprising answers.

I was putting up storm windows. My neighbor, Alfred Nansen, loves to supervise a job, any job.

"Hey! Need any help?"

5   Knowing the quality of the "help" he was offering, I declined graciously, but Al came over anyway. Besides being a nondoer of any physical work, Al is a homespun philosopher. No, he 10 never worked as a stevedore, but his work as a bridge tender on the Mathers Bridge gives him plenty of time to read—and think.

I was having trouble. "This window 15 is sticking. I need to chisel a small section off the corner, but I can't find my wood chisel. Got one?"

"No. Use your screwdriver," he suggested. He handed it to me, and I 20 nicked just enough off the frame to ease the window back into place.

"You know," he said, "if you understand the screwdriver, you can understand what language is all about."

25   "What's to understand? A screwdriver is a screwdriver."

"Ah, but there you're wrong. *You* say a screwdriver is a screwdriver. *I* say it breaks through those simple boundaries. 30 A screwdriver can be a chisel, a scriber, a wedge, a lever for prying open can tops, a knife, a letter opener, a . . ."

"Whoa," I interrupted. "A screwdriver was designed for a specific purpose. 35 Why burden it with other chores?"

"Why not? It can be the core of a puppet, a doorstop, a hammer, a post in croquet, a boundary marker, a plumb 40 bob, a splint, the gnomon of a sundial, a . . ."

"But what's the point?" I again interrupted a bit peevishly. "What is this catalogue of yours proving? What's so 45 great about using a screwdriver as a hammer? Why not get a hammer?"

"Ah, but suppose you don't have a hammer handy? Also, suppose you need a tool that hasn't been invented 50 yet, like a skrillion. How can you get a skrillion if there isn't any to be had?"

"What's a skrillion?" I asked a bit testily.

"I don't know," Al replied, "but 55 you certainly could use one. A skrillion would be useful for retrieving items that have fallen beneath heavy objects like stoves and refrigerators. I know. I've used a screwdriver for the job, but a 60 skrillion would have been better. But if it hasn't been invented yet, what can you do?"

"Well," I said, getting into the spirit of things, "maybe you don't need a 65 skrillion. Besides the screwdriver you could use a dowel, a piece of lath, a poker, a marshmallow fork, a coathanger, a cane, a walking stick, a sword, a javelin, a sickle, a boomerang, 70 a . . ."

"*Now* you're getting it," Al chuckled.

"But you said I'd understand what language is all about. How does that 75 screwdriver provide such magnificent enlightenment? You've convinced me I can use a screwdriver for many different things. So what?"

"So what!" Al echoed. "Don't you 80 see what we've just been doing?"

"Yes, we've been talking about different uses of tools for different jobs. I don't get any special enlightenment from that information."

85   "We have been crossing boundaries and breaking boxes. Like most people," Al told me, "you live in boxes. No, I'm not insulting the shape of your lovely house. I'm talking about the 90 boxes you can't see."

"What are these mysterious boxes?" I asked. "Four dimensional boxes? Tesseracts?"

"No, no, no. These are the boxes of 95 language, the names we give things, the classifications we make, the generalizations we derive every day of our lives."

"What's wrong?" I protested. "We need names and classifications. How 100 could we communicate if we didn't agree on various word meanings and classifications? Language is the greatest achievement of humankind, and you're criticizing it.''

105 "Not at all. Language is indeed a miracle, but miracles are dynamite. We have to know what we're dealing with. We have to set up these boxes to live in society, but we must not be over-
110 whelmed by them. The boxes were made for us; we were not made for the boxes.''

"What's all this got to do with screwdrivers?'' I asked mischievously.
115 "Everything! If you say a screw-driver is a screwdriver, period, you are being controlled by your boxes. A screwdriver isn't really anything until it is used. When you use it to attach a fix-
120 ture to the wall, you are indeed using it as a screwdriver. But when you use it to open a can of paint, you are breaking out of a box. The screwdriver is now a 'can opener.'''

125 "It's still a screwdriver to me!'' I in-sisted.

"OK, if it makes you feel better, just as long as you know you can break out of that box. Breaking out of the box
130 once frees you for other little victories. I had trouble opening a jar of wheat germ, which is vacuum-packed. I couldn't turn the cover. I didn't have a jar clamp. What to do? Aha, my 'screwdriver.' I
135 gently placed the blade under the cover and twisted. Success! The vacuum was broken. My screwdriver was now a 'jar opener.'''

"Very clever,'' I noted grudgingly,
140 "but I'm still a little unsure of your point about boxes.''

In a nutshell this is it: we have to have boxes but we have to understand their limitations. We have to create
145 boxes and then we must break out of them.''

"Why is breaking out so im-portant?''

"Because we are straitjacketed by
150 the boxes. The major characteristic of the creative person is a willingness to break out of the boxes, an ability to go beyond the classifications. The artist

155 creates patterns that open our eyes to new ways of seeing. The poet links un-likely words to create unique combina-tions and 'new boxes.' The inventor looks at a need and creates a clothespin, a safety pin, a zipper. After the inven-
160 tion, everything looks simple. But how many people stayed in the boxes before the geniuses broke through?''

"Hmmm,'' I mused. "But aren't some boxes fixed? Aren't some classifi-
165 cations tied so close to nature they can't be attacked or shifted? How about the classification for *dog*? Isn't there some-thing out there that always and forever matches our word *dog*?''

170 "*All* our classifications are made by us. A dog doesn't know it's a dog. We have decided to lump all of a certain type of animal in a box we label *dog*. But the label is ours. We could have
175 used other bases of classification. Even the word *dog* becomes a little fuzzy when wolves breed with dogs. There's a huge something we label 'reality.' To handle this huge whatever, we slice it up
180 into convenient pieces. This piece we'll label 'dog.' That piece we'll label 'tree' and so on. But the slices are our own! All ours!''

"Those slices are helpful,'' I inter-
185 posed. "No, not just helpful; they're es-sential.''

"Agreed,'' Al said. "A marvelous achievement all right. But it sometimes gives us the feeling we know more than
190 we know. Reality is unknowable. The mystery of life is beyond us. Like New-ton, we are playing with pebbles on the shores of knowledge. I often think of a quotation attributed to Ralph Sockman:
200 'The larger the island of knowledge, the longer the shoreline of wonder.' But in everyday life we must play with those pebbles and build roads with them. Lan-guage certainly helps.''

205 Al had me thinking. I picked up the screwdriver and looked at it thought-fully. Finally, I said to Al, "You know what I'm going to do? I'm going out and invent a skrillion.''

1. The selection is essentially about _____.
   (A) the handyman's approach to tasks
   (B) the many uses of a screwdriver
   (C) the genius vs. the common man
   (D) language at work
   (E) the meaning of friendship

   1 ___

2. Skrillion is introduced as _____.
   (A) a practical solution to a problem
   (B) a new tool
   (C) an alternative to a screwdriver
   (D) a power tool as opposed to a manual tool
   (E) an example

   2 ___

3. "We are straitjacketed by boxes" suggests that _____.
   (A) we are limited by language
   (B) our lives are cluttered by material things
   (C) creative people are especially confined
   (D) the accumulation of goods is self-defeating
   (E) we are trapped, without escape

   3 ___

4. The writer is using narrative essentially to _____.
   (A) depict two interesting friends
   (B) make a point
   (C) demonstrate an ability to write dialogue
   (D) entertain
   (E) mislead the reader

   4 ___

5. Of the following quotations from the article, the most important is _____.
   (A) "I need to chisel a small section off the corner, but I can't find my wood chisel."
   (B) "What's to understand? A screwdriver is a screwdriver."
   (C) "A screwdriver isn't really anything until it is used."
   (D) "A screwdriver was designed for a specific purpose."
   (E) "What's so great about using a screwdriver as a hammer?"

   5 ___

6. The boxes mentioned throughout the article are _____.
   (A) in the mind only
   (B) easily understood and easily handled
   (C) essentially areas where tools are kept
   (D) animal pens, especially for dogs
   (E) labels for social position

   6 ___

7. Which of the following comments by baseball umpires accurately reflects the point of view of Al Nansen?
   (A) "Some are strikes and some are balls, and I try my best to call them."
   (B) "Some are strikes and some are balls, but I occasionally miss a call."
   (C) "Some are strikes and some are balls, and I call them as they are."
   (D) "Some are strikes and some are balls, and I call them as I see them."
   (E) "Some are strikes and some are balls, but they aren't anything till I call them."

   7 ___

8. Of the two neighbors, we may say that _____.
   (A) Al is a better carpenter
   (B) the writer is a more astute student
   (C) Al is a good teacher
   (D) there is considerable animosity between them
   (E) Al is less sympathetic

   8 ___

9. The writer uses conversation to _____.
   (A) make abstract ideas concrete
   (B) reveal Al's superficiality
   (C) dramatize the battle of wits between the neighbors
   (D) make the appearance of the page more interesting
   (E) compare a box of cereal with a toolbox

   9 ___

10. In his attitude toward the screwdriver, Al is _____.
    (A) dogmatic and limited
    (B) unconsciously funny
    (C) free and unrestricted
    (D) grossly in error
    (E) incongruously reverent

    10 ___

11. Al Nansen would probably be most critical of _____.
    (A) directions for assembling a kite
    (B) a television sitcom
    (C) the weather report
    (D) campaign speeches
    (E) lovers' conversations

    11 ___

12. The expression "pebbles on the shores of knowledge" is an example of _____.
    (A) simile
    (B) irony
    (C) exaggeration
    (D) a literal statement
    (E) metaphor

    12 ___

13. The style of the dialogue is _____.
    (A) interesting but ponderous
    (B) dull and argumentative
    (C) repetitious and self-conscious
    (D) light and breezy
    (E) deceptively unpleasant

    13 ___

14. A tesseract (line 93) is probably _____.
    (A) a screwdriver
    (B) a box with more than six sides
    (C) a fourth-dimension concept
    (D) another name for *skrillion*
    (E) something Al made up

    14 ___

15. At the conclusion of the dialogue, the author probably _____.
    (A) invented a skrillion
    (B) invited Al in for a three-dimensional tea
    (C) understood language a little better
    (D) found a chisel in his toolbox
    (E) thought things over and disagreed with Al

    15 ___

SUMMARY

1. Studying the Longer Passage

Beginning in 1994, the SAT included longer and more challenging critical reading selections. Each selection tested a greater variety of skills than was possible with shorter selections. Readers had to hold on to a point of view for a longer period. The skills tested, however, are those developed working with shorter passages. For greater teaching effectiveness, the preceding chapters in this book isolate the reading skills being reviewed. Longer passages provide the opportunity for readers to flex their critical muscles, to call upon their skills to handle new and more complex combinations.

2. Studying Paired Passages

An additional innovation beginning with the 1994 SAT is the introduction of paired passages. The passages may agree with each other, disagree, or complement each other, thereby enriching the point of view presented. The College Board notes, "Some of the questions on the paired passages will assess students' ability to compare or contrast the two passages, to use information from one to interpret information in the other, and to identify assumptions they share or pivotal differences between them." Paired passages provide greater challenges but also arouse greater interest in the subject matter. Readers welcome different viewpoints on the same or similar topics. The paired passages provide those viewpoints.

Trial Test

The following two passages talk about a common tendency that may have deeper implications than we realize.

Passage 1

In my previous talk, "On a Certain Blindness," I tried to make you feel how soaked and shot-through life is with values and meanings which we fail to realize because of
5 our external and insensible point of view. The meanings are there for the others, but they are not there for us. There lies more than a mere interest of curious speculation in understanding this. It has the most tremen-
10 dous practical importance. I wish that I could convince you of it as I feel it myself. It is the basis of all our tolerance, social, religious, and political. The forgetting of it lies at the root of every stupid and sanguinary mistake
15 that rulers over subject-peoples make. The first thing to learn in intercourse with others is non-interference with their own peculiar ways of being happy, provided those ways do not assume to interfere by violence with
20 ours. No one has insight into all the ideals. No one should presume to judge them off-hand. The pretension to dogmatize about them in each other is the root of most human injustices and cruelties, and the trait in
25 human character most likely to make the angels weep.

Passage 2

She was, moreover, one of those few persons—for they are very few—who are contented to go on with their existence without making themselves the center of any special 30 outward circle. To the ordinary run of minds it is impossible not to do this. A man's own dinner is to himself so important that he cannot bring himself to believe that it is a matter utterly indifferent to everyone else. A lady's 35 collection of baby clothes, in early years, and of house linen and curtain fringes in later life, is so very interesting to her own eyes that she cannot believe but that other people will rejoice to behold it. I would not, however, 40 be held as regarding this tendency as evil. It leads to conversation of some sort among people, and perhaps to a kind of sympathy. Mrs. Jones will look at Mrs. White's linen chest, hoping that Mrs. White may be in- 45 duced to look at hers. One can only pour out of a jug that which is in it. For the most of us, if we do not talk of ourselves, or at any rate of the individual circles of which we are the centers, we can talk of nothing. 50

1. A common proverb that sums up the philosophy of the author of Passage 1 is _____.
   (A) "Never leave till tomorrow what you can do today."
   (B) "Live and let live."
   (C) "A good name is rather to be chosen than great riches."
   (D) "A soft answer turneth away wrath."
   (E) "Look before you leap."

   1 ___

2. The author feels that "a mere interest of curious speculation" _____.
   (A) may fail to realize the deeper significance
   (B) may lead to rigidity and inflexibility
   (C) interferes with the rights of others
   (D) inevitably leads to deeper awareness
   (E) is a waste of time

   2 ___

3. The rights we take for granted are _____.
   (A) seldom appreciated
   (B) gained at the expense of others
   (C) given up too easily to authority figures
   (D) basically deceptive and unreal
   (E) limited by the rights of others

   3 ___

4. When the author says, "No one has insight into all the ideals," he is calling for _____.
   (A) his own particular insights and ideas
   (B) strong leaders
   (C) reviewers who judge film through their own special insights
   (D) higher education
   (E) an open mind

   4 ___

5. In line 22, the word "dogmatize" most nearly means _____.
   (A) express a rigid opinion
   (B) talk sympathetically
   (C) research extensively
   (D) speak loudly
   (E) seek revenge

   5 ___

6. Throughout, the author's approach is one of _____.
   (A) anxious pleading
   (B) measured reasonableness
   (C) strong denunciation
   (D) feigned indifference
   (E) subtle humor

   6 ___

7. Both Passage 1 and Passage 2 deal with _____.
   (A) personal ill will
   (B) self-centeredness
   (C) deep-seated prejudice
   (D) human injustices and cruelties
   (E) attempts to convert others politically

   7 ___

8. In comparison with the basic premise of Passage 1, Passage 2 is more concerned with _____.
   (A) the evils brought on by monopolizing conversations
   (B) generally unselfish behavior
   (C) the pointlessness of human communication
   (D) harmless human weaknesses
   (E) the dangers of misleading others

   8 ___

9. The author suggests that many speakers _____.
   (A) have uninterested listeners
   (B) seek to dominate their listeners
   (C) would rather listen to others than speak
   (D) have much of interest to speak about
   (E) are rather shy with strangers

   9 ___

10. One way of suggesting the central idea of Passage 2 is the expression _____.
   (A) Talk is the lubricant of friendship.
   (B) Dinner conversation makes dining pleasant.
   (C) Talking about the experiences of childhood may not be interesting to others.
   (D) Excellent conversationalists are born, not made.
   (E) Every person is the hero of his/her own life.

   10 __

11. The author introduces the jug metaphor (lines 46–47) to suggest the _____.
   (A) dangers of alcoholism
   (B) limitations of human conversation
   (C) techniques of interpersonal relationships
   (D) need for communication
   (E) source of conversational ideas

   11 __

Let's analyze together another paired selection.

Problem

When social scientists talk about the future of the world and population growth, they tend to divide into two groups, popularly called the *Cassandras* and the *Pollyannas*. Authorities in the former group take a negative position, foretelling global disaster. They tend to be biologists. Authorities in the latter group take a positive position, suggesting that the world will somehow solve its problems. They tend to be economists. The first passage below takes the Cassandra position; the second passage, the Pollyanna.

Passage 1

Concern about the dangers of overpopulation is not new. In 1589, Giovanni Botero, an Italian scholar, warned of the dangerous maladjustment
5 of population and resources. These two, he said, were on a collision course. Two centuries later, in 1798, Robert Thomas Malthus warned, in his "Essay on Population," that the world faced a terrible
10 problem. He wrote, "The power of population is indefinitely greater than the power in the earth to provide subsistence for man." Population grows faster than the means to feed all the new
15 mouths.

Although Malthus did not know or use the term *ecology*, modern scientists point out the environmental catastro-
20 phes created by unchecked population growth. There are ecological limits beyond which land cannot support life. Nature is ruthless. When wild creatures expand beyond the carrying capacity of their habitat, disaster occurs, whether
25 they be deer in Michigan or lemmings in Norway.

Every year, the earth is adding a hundred million people. At current rates, by the year 2100, the earth will
30 have to support 10 to 12 billion people. They will not only have to be fed. They'll have to be provided living space, jobs, cars, recreation, material goods and services. How can the global
35 economy provide all the necessary elements? The traffic of life will be in perpetual gridlock.

In sub-Saharan Africa, overpopulation has led to desertification, the de-
40 struction of land. Overgrazing, deforestation, and erosion make the land less habitable, but meanwhile the population soars. In the Himalayas, the destruction of mountain forests has led to
45 soil erosion and subsequent floods in the populous cities of India. Today's firewood is used at the expense of tomorrow's flood control. Again, population pressures result in ecological night-
50 mares.

In some instances, population tensions have led to civil strife and famine, as in Somalia in the last decade of the twentieth century. Even when food is available, civil repression often prevents its distribution. Laboratory rats kept in too close confinement exhibit serious personality disorders. Perhaps people do, too.

Overpopulation is felt in many related ways. To feed growing populations, fishing fleets exhaust fisheries. Tropical rain forests are destroyed to provide farmlands, often abandoned because of infertile soil. The ozone layer becomes more and more punctured, opening the world's populations to new dangers. Some authorities believe the greenhouse effect, the result of the combustion of fossil fuels, may cause a rise in the world's temperatures, with some significant negative results all too possible.

Some writers emphasize a decline in the quality of life as population increases so rapidly. The demands upon health organizations become more difficult to meet. Overcrowding leads to frazzled tempers, ill health, and civil explosions. In the United States, three states—Florida, Texas, and California—will feel the brunt of the pressure most keenly. All three states already have problems. California has a perennial water problem. Texas, the giant among states, has an "unsteady economy," as the writer Charles C. Mann has pointed out. Florida's fragile ecosystem has had too many demands upon it. Greed and indifference have irreparably damaged many areas.

Rich countries can ameliorate many of the growing problems. Americans have forced petroleum companies to phase out leaded gas. Twenty-three industrialized countries have drastically reduced the rate of release of the most dangerous compounds that destroy the ozone. But poorer countries, caught in the vicious cycle of ever-increasing population, cannot do the same. All human beings want a piece of the pie, but the future may find the pie divided into shreds.

Somehow the world's governments must devise ways to check the disastrous growth of population. At this writing, the future looks bleak.

Passage 2

The "authorities" have been predicting catastrophes for 400 years. So far, none have arrived. The world has had its share of troubles, of course, but the horrible apocalypse so often predicted has not materialized. No one denies the dangers of unchecked population growth. Nature's incredible fertility has led many wild creatures to starvation, as resources dwindle. But nature also institutes a system of balances. When the arctic hare diminishes in numbers, the arctic fox has fewer offspring.

Of course, humankind has no such system. Wars, famines, and plagues have kept populations in check in the past. To some extent they still do, with war, starvation, and diseases like AIDS checking to some slight degree the increases in population. The word is *slight,* for despite these terrible checks, population continues to grow.

There is, of course, a major difference between human beings and gypsy moths. People have shown an amazing resiliency and flexibility in dealing with seemingly insuperable problems. Malthus was right. Given the productivity of the world's farmlands at his time, we'd already be starving now. But even though population has grown, food is still plentiful. Tons of food were shipped to Somalia to pull the inhabitants back from the brink of starvation. These tons of food represent food surpluses elsewhere in the world. The ability to increase food production has been phenomenal. Ansley Coale of Princeton says, "If you had asked someone in 1890 about today's population, he'd say, "There's no way the United States can support two hundred and fifty million people. Where are they going to pasture all their horses?' "

In 1949, Paul Ehrlich wrote *The Population Bomb,* a depressing scenario for the future. As Mann writes, "Twenty-five years ago 3.4 billion people lived on earth. Now the United Nations estimates that 5.3 billion do—the biggest, fastest increase in history. But food production increased faster still. The per capita food production rose more than 10% from 1968 to 1990. The number of chronically malnourished people fell by more than 16 percent." Though some authorities declare that the good days are ending, others insist that by using modern agricultural methods, Third World countries could keep that favorable trend going.

Pessimists overlook the fact that trends can be reversed. Many former forests were cut down for farms only to return to forests when the farms were abandoned. In 1875, six counties in the lower Hudson Valley contained 573,003 acres of forest. In 1980, the forests covered an area three times as large. American forests as a whole are bigger and healthier now than they were at the turn of the century. Salmon are returning to American rivers. White-tailed deer, once hunted to the point of near-extinction, are now more numerous than ever. Wild turkeys now enjoy a greater range than they did 300 years ago. All these happy events occurred while the population was growing.

Some think that the problem we are concerned with is less population growth than political incompetence and corruption. Pressures upon governmental agencies increase as population grows, but foresight and intelligent management can often minimize the resulting problems and even take advantage of new conditions. Increases in local populations, for example, can open the way to better health facilities, more varied shopping possibilities, and improved educational opportunities.

No one denies that population growth brings with it new challenges and new dangers, but many of the threats repeated by the doomsayers are overstated and inaccurate projections, or excuses for gloomy apathy. One reliable survey has pointed out that fertility in poor countries actually dropped 30 percent in the period between 1965–1970 and 1980–1985. The problem is admittedly complex, but the peoples of the world have the potential of meeting the challenge of population growth while avoiding the wholesale collapse of civilization sometimes prophesied.

1. The author of Passage 1 mentions Botero and Malthus to _____.
   (A) contrast their respective positions
   (B) quote their statistics on the modern growth of population
   (C) show that population concerns are not new
   (D) make use of their studies of explosive growth in wild populations
   (E) suggest that they may have overstated their case

   1 ___

2. A word that graphically suggests the meaning of *gridlock* (line 37) is _____.
   (A) disappointment
   (B) anger
   (C) mobility
   (D) strangulation
   (E) indifference

   2 ___

3. The author suggests that tropical rain forests _____.
   (A) have relatively infertile soil
   (B) play a minor role in the world's ecology
   (C) can be explored for lifesaving new drugs
   (D) will return in a generation after wholesale timbering
   (E) can provide a home for some of the world's excess population

   3 ___

4. The author's attitude toward tree cutting by Himalayan peoples is one of _____.
   (A) unrestrained rejection
   (B) sympathetic disapproval
   (C) limited admiration
   (D) studied indifference
   (E) complete bafflement

   4 ___

5. In lines 51 to 59, the author _____.
   (A) deplores the actions of callous researchers
   (B) suggests that Somali fighters are motivated by survival
   (C) indicates that rats in the wild do not have the same personality disorders as laboratory rats
   (D) approves of laboratory research with animals
   (E) compares the world to a laboratory

   5 ___

6. Throughout, the author uses figurative language to make a point. All the following are examples of figurative language EXCEPT _____.
   (A) The traffic of life will be in perpetual gridlock
   (B) Again, population pressures result in ecological nightmares
   (C) The ozone layer becomes more and more punctured
   (D) Every year, the earth is adding a hundred million people
   (E) The future may find the pie divided into shreds

   6 ___

7. In line 92, "ameliorate" most nearly means _____.
   (A) overlook
   (B) relieve
   (C) explore
   (D) uncover
   (E) deplore

   7 ___

8. The opening sentence of Passage 2 conveys a sense of _____.
   (A) wry humor
   (B) perverse hostility
   (C) sympathetic agreement
   (D) puzzled research
   (E) understated disagreement

   8 ___

9. Though "apocalypse" has several meanings, the synonym closest in meaning in line 113 is _____.
   (A) prophecy
   (B) mismanagement
   (C) devastation
   (D) war
   (E) drought

   9 ___

10. The author of Passage 2 places his hopes for human survival on _____.
    (A) zero population growth
    (B) research into social forces that encourage increases
    (C) persuading the Cassandras to accept his blueprint for the future
    (D) studying closely the natural cycles of Norwegian lemmings
    (E) human ingenuity and flexibility

    10 ___

11. The same author says, "Malthus was right" in his _____.
    (A) essentially hopeless picture of the world's future
    (B) estimates of the world's potential for growing enough food
    (C) warning about deforestation and the dangers of desertification
    (D) projections into the future based on then-current situations
    (E) friendly disagreement with the previous prophet, Giovanni Botero

    11 ___

12. Ansley Coale says, "Where are they going to pasture all their horses?" to show how _____.
    (A) changing conditions modify the truth or falsity of prophecies
    (B) an agrarian economy can effectively handle population growth
    (C) the horse has become superfluous in today's world
    (D) the prediction was incorrect in details but essentially correct in general
    (E) people were stupid in 1890

    12 ___

13. Salmon, turkeys, and deer are mentioned as examples of _____.
    (A) endangered species
    (B) food sources for the future
    (C) trend reversal
    (D) game animals
    (E) successful adjustment to urban life

    13 ___

14. The mythical Cassandra was probably noted for _____.
    (A) cheerful evaluations that were usually incorrect
    (B) steadfastness and loyalty toward those she admired
    (C) superficial skepticism tinged with basic optimism
    (D) gloomy prophecies that no one believed
    (E) a willingness to accept varying points of view

    14 ___

15. Both authors are similar in their _____.
    (A) long-term projections of population growth
    (B) desire to limit the number of children in a family
    (C) acceptance of the views of Malthus
    (D) emphasis upon trend reversal as a possible solution
    (E) acceptance of the point that population growth *is* a problem

    15 ___

16. When confronted with negative news about drought, famine, and war, the author of Passage 2 would probably use which of the following well-known quotations?
    (A) "Figures don't lie, but liars figure."
    (B) "We shall overcome."
    (C) "Every dog will have his day."
    (D) "The times are out of joint."
    (E) "This is a day of infamy."

    16 ___

Strategy   1. The author of Passage 1 introduces his arguments by pointing out that population problems were predicted centuries ago. Since Botero and Malthus essentially agree, (A) is wrong. The two men generalize about the future but do not provide statistics (B). Wild populations are not mentioned by the writers (D). Since the author generally agrees with Botero and Malthus, (E) is wrong. The author of Passage 1 is generally in agreement with the two writers' position. The answer is (C).

2. The strain placed on all elements of life as population grows will cause breakdowns. The global economy will fail to provide needed elements. The author uses figurative language—traffic, gridlock—to suggest that life will be poorer in the years to come. Gridlock is to traffic as strangulation is to the normal flow. (D) is the answer.

3. Line 65 mentions the infertile soil of rain forests. (A) is the answer.

4. Tree cutting for firewood is an understandable human need, but short-term gains result in long-term disasters. (A) is too strong. The author cannot admire the destruction of forests (C). The author's concern rules out (D). The author isn't baffled (E). He understands why trees are cut but deplores the actions. The answer is (B) sympathetic disapproval.

5. The author compares the personality disorders of laboratory rats kept in close confinement with similar manifestations of violence among humans in too close contact. The answer is (E).

6. (D) is a straightforward, literal statement. The figurative expressions include *traffic* and *gridlock* (A), *pressures* and *nightmares* (B), *punctured* (C), and *pie* and *shreds* (E).

7. In lines 92–99, the author provides two examples of environmental improvement through the efforts of rich countries. The context suggests that (B) is the answer.

8. The author puts quotation marks around "authorities" to suggest that the authorities are not good prophets. His dig at authorities is intended to be ironic. The answer is (A).

9. The context clearly links "catastrophes" in line 110 with "apocalypse" in line 113. Prophecy (A) is irrelevant. Mismanagement (B) is too mild. War (D) is too specific, as is drought (E). The answer is (C) devastation.

10. Lines 211–216 clearly state the author's faith in human ingenuity and flexibility (E).

11. The clue to the answer is "then-current." Lines 137–139 note that the productivity of Malthus's time would be inadequate now. Productivity has soared. Malthus's projections were adequate for his time but inadequate now. The answer is (D).

12. In 1890 horses were a mainstay of commerce, transportation, agriculture, and recreation. A hundred years later in the United States, the number of horses has greatly diminished even though the population has greatly increased. Worrying about pasturing horses has become a minor problem. The answer is (A).

13. Lines 181–188 point out that species once endangered have now become numerous, even though population has grown. The answer is (C).

14. The contrast between Cassandras and Pollyannas in the introduction stresses that Cassandras take a negative view. "Cheerful" eliminates (A). "Optimism" rules out (C). Cassandra's open-mindedness or lack thereof is nowhere mentioned or implied. (E) is wrong. There is no indication about Cassandra's steadfastness and loyalty, eliminating (B). "Gloomy prophecies" accords with the adjective *negative* applied to the pessimists. (D) is correct.

15. The projections of population growth are specific and alarming in Passage 1. They are less specific and alarming in Passage 2. Thus (A) is wrong. (B)

isn't mentioned. The two authors look upon Malthus differently. The author of Passage 1 believes that Malthus's predictions are more likely to happen than not. The author of Passage 2 is more optimistic. (C) is wrong. Although Passage 2 suggests trend reversal as a possible solution, Passage 1 doesn't rely upon it. Elimination of the others leaves (E). Passage 1 is devoted almost entirely to the dangers of population growth. Passage 2 agrees that population growth is a serious problem (lines 202–204), but it takes a more optimistic view of the world's prospects.

16. The concluding lines, 211–216, state the author's belief that the peoples of the world can successfully meet the challenges and dangers that lie ahead. The answer is (B).

Review

Will robots ever be able to act and think like human beings? What limits exist? The following two excerpts by philosophers, one American and one
5 French, discuss the differences between living things and nonliving things. William James (Passage 1) published *The Principles of Psychology* in 1890. René Descartes (Passage 2) published
10 *Discourse on Method* 250 years earlier, in 1637. Yet both philosophers address a problem very much in current science news. The debate about artificial intelligence continues.

Passage 1

15 If some iron filings be sprinkled on a table and a magnet brought near them, they will fly through the air for a certain distance and stick to its surface. A savage seeing the phenomenon explains it
20 as the result of an attraction or love between the magnet and the filings. But let a card cover the poles of the magnet, and the filings will press forever against its surface without its ever occurring to
25 them to pass around its sides and thus come into more direct contact with the object of their love. Blow bubbles through a tube into the bottom of a pail of water, they will rise to the surface
30 and mingle with the air. Their action may again be poetically interpreted as due to a longing to recombine with the mother-atmosphere above the surface.

But if you invert a jar full of water over
35 the pail, they will rise and remain lodged beneath its bottom, shut in from the outer air, although a slight deflection from their course at the outset, or a re-descent towards the rim of the jar
40 when they found their upward course impeded, would easily have set them free.

If now we pass from such actions as these to those of living things, we notice
45 a striking difference. Romeo wants Juliet as the filings want the magnet; and if no obstacles intervene, he moves toward her by as straight a line as they. But Romeo and Juliet, if a wall be built
50 between them, do not remain idiotically pressing their faces against its opposite sides like the magnet and the filings with the card. Romeo soon finds a circuitous way, by scaling the wall or otherwise,
55 of touching Juliet's lips directly. With the filings the path is fixed; whether it reaches the end depends on accidents. With the lover it is the end which is fixed; the path may be modified indefi-
60 nitely.

Passage 2

If there were machines which bore a resemblance to our body and imitated our actions as far as it was morally possible to do so, we should always have
65 two very certain tests by which to recognise that, for all that, they were not

real men. The first is, that they could never use speech or other signs as we do when placing our thoughts on record
70 for the benefit of others. For we can easily understand a machine's being constituted so that it can utter words, and even emit some responses to action on it of a corporeal kind, which brings
75 about a change in its organs; for instance, if it is touched in a particular part it may ask what we wish to say to it; if in another part it may exclaim that it is being hurt, and so on. But it never
80 happens that it arranges its speech in various ways, in order to reply appropriately to everything that may be said in its presence, as even the lowest type of man can do. And the second difference
85 ence is, that although machines can perform certain things as well as or perhaps better than any of us can do, they infallibly fall short in others, by which means we may discover that they did not act
90 from knowledge, but only from the disposition of their organs. For while reason is a universal instrument which can serve for all contingencies, these organs have need of some special adaptation for every particular action. From this it follows that it is morally impossible that there should be sufficient diversity in any machine to allow it to act in all the events of life in the same way as our
100 reason causes us to act.

1. The author uses "its ever occurring to them . . ." in lines 24–25 to suggest _____.
   (A) the flexibility of magnetic attraction
   (B) the limitations of nonliving things
   (C) that bubbles act differently from iron filings
   (D) the way a savage interprets natural events
   (E) the poetic union of filings and magnet

   1 ___

2. The word "phenomenon" in line 19 means _____.
   (A) unexpected surprise
   (B) colorful demonstration
   (C) source of confusion
   (D) observable fact
   (E) apparent contradiction

   2 ___

3. In line 25, the pronoun "them" refers to _____.
   (A) savages
   (B) magnets
   (C) cards
   (D) objects
   (E) filings

   3 ___

4. It may be inferred that the bubble example is used to _____.
   (A) reinforce the point of the magnet example
   (B) contrast the way in which nonliving things act
   (C) compare it with the following example of Romeo and Juliet
   (D) demonstrate the illogicality of all three examples
   (E) demonstrate the force of hydraulic pressure

   4 ___

5. In line 33, "mother-atmosphere" is an example of _____.
   (A) simile
   (B) understatement
   (C) literal language
   (D) metaphor
   (E) exaggeration

   5 ___

6. The word "impeded" in line 41 means _____.
   (A) facilitated
   (B) hindered
   (C) demonstrated
   (D) misdirected
   (E) uncovered

   6 ___

7. In line 53, "circuitous" means _____.
   (A) effective
   (B) surprising
   (C) roundabout
   (D) inferior
   (E) mechanical

   7 ___

8. The author uses the example of Romeo and Juliet to _____.
   (A) pay a special tribute to William Shakespeare
   (B) emphasize the unpredictability of life
   (C) show differences between living and nonliving things
   (D) suggest the importance of romance in life
   (E) add a note of sadness at their ultimate tragedy

   8 ___

9. The word "want" in line 46 _____.
   (A) strikes a note of subtle humor
   (B) is a literal representation of the filings' desires
   (C) is meant to irritate the reader
   (D) suggests that inanimate objects may have feelings
   (E) is so extreme as to be confusing

   9 ___

10. The word "idiotically" in line 50 suggests _____.
    (A) the impetuosity of Romeo
    (B) the imprudence of the romance
    (C) the power of a wall
    (D) the inflexibility of nonliving things
    (E) the rule of natural law

    10 ___

11. "The end" in line 57 refers to _____.
    (A) a meeting of lovers
    (B) an inevitable tragedy
    (C) union with the magnet
    (D) the means
    (E) the lovers' final breakup

    11 ___

12. The two "certain tests" mentioned in line 65 are _____.
    (A) hesitant speech and limited mobility
    (B) organic composition and brisk responsiveness
    (C) steadfast reliability and flawless speech
    (D) responsive speech and reasoning ability
    (E) self-repair and alert awareness

    12 ___

13. The word "infallibly" in lines 87–88 means _____.
    (A) infrequently
    (B) certainly
    (C) unwittingly
    (D) flawlessly
    (E) disappointingly

    13 ___

14. In line 93, the word "contingencies" means _____.
    (A) failures
    (B) successes
    (C) organic requirements
    (D) personal contracts
    (E) possibilities

    14 ___

15. The word "morally" in line 96 suggests that machines _____.
    (A) cannot reason from knowledge
    (B) are superior to human beings in certain essentials
    (C) are incapable of making mistakes
    (D) have a weakly developed moral sense
    (E) might induce weak human beings to act immorally

    15 ___

16. In line 98, "diversity" means _____.
    (A) compatibility
    (B) intelligence
    (C) comprehensiveness
    (D) variety
    (E) resilience

    16 ___

17. If the author of Passage 2 were con-
fronted with a current computer that
asks and answers questions, his re-
sponse would probably be one
of _____.
(A) relief
(B) fatigue
(C) boredom
(D) disbelief
(E) irritation

17 ___

18. Passages 1 and 2 are alike in
their _____.
(A) emphasis upon a machine's capabil-
ities
(B) use of magnet and filings as illus-
trations
(C) tribute to human reason
(D) use of a literary example
(E) chatty, colloquial style

18 ___

19. Passage 2 differs from Passage 1 in
its _____.
(A) emphasis on machines rather than
natural processes
(B) downplaying the role of human
knowledge
(C) disdain for uncomplicated procedures
(D) rejection of any mechanical capabilities
(E) suggestion that machines might
someday replace human beings

19 ___

20. Compared to the tone of Passage 2, the
tone of Passage 1 is more _____.
(A) argumentative
(B) humble
(C) inspirational
(D) humorous
(E) scholarly

20 ___

21. Which assumption does the author of
Passage 2 make?
(A) Machines could be made to speak
as humans do.
(B) Machines could be made to act as
flexibly as humans do.
(C) Machines could never perform
tasks better than humans do.
(D) Machines could never be made
with the infinite responsiveness of
humans.
(E) Machines could be made that
could not be distinguished from
humans.

21 ___

22. In lines 49–60, to make his point, the
author uses _____.
(A) obvious humor
(B) balanced contrast
(C) dull repetition
(D) subtle understatement
(E) exaggerated explanation

22 ___

Section VIII Summary: Studying the Longer Passage

The longer passage provides unique challenges, possible only with a more complex selection or paired selection.

PART 1. The Single Selection (p. 281)

A. Read the passage carefully. Before answering any questions, determine the author's general point of view. What position does he or she take with respect to the topic discussed?
B. Take the sample test before analyzing the answers.
C. Check your answers against those given in the text.
D. If your answer disagrees with one given in the text, carefully go back over the passage. Try a process of elimination to see whether this procedure provides the accepted answer. If not, look again. In a test situation, if a choice must be made between two possible answers, you must select the BEST. Do you feel you have as acceptable an answer as the one provided? If possible, talk things over with classmates. Although not common, an alternative possibility will sometimes slip by the test constructors. The important part of the test is your close evaluation, your reasons for deciding on an answer. The book provides acceptable reasons. Does your answer do so?

E. The ultimate purpose of test taking is sharpening critical perceptions, not just writing letters on a test answer sheet. Take advantage of Problem and Strategy to fine-tune your own reading skills.

PART 2. Studying Paired Passages (p. 300)

A. Everything said about the single selection above holds especially strongly for this section. Review A–E.
B. The paired selections add an extra challenge: critically reading two somewhat related passages and trying to ferret out the relationships. This challenge invites more rereading than does the single selection.
C. The test usually includes questions about the first passage, questions about the second, and then questions relating to the two passages. These combining questions send you back to both selections.
D. Keep in mind that the paired passages have been chosen for a reason. When you discover the reason (agreement, disagreement, comparison, contrast, enrichment), you will find the questions easier to answer.

Practice Tests

How well have you developed skill in extracting the meaning from reading passages? Take the following practice tests for additional drill.

A

In this segment from a story by Edith Wharton, a woman proposes to her husband that they adopt a baby. The conversation opens.

Lethbury, surveying his wife across the dinner table, found his transient glance arrested by an indefinable change in her appearance.

5 'How smart you look! Is that a new gown?' he asked.

Her answering look seemed to deprecate his charging her with the extravagance of wasting a new gown on him, 10 and he now perceived that the change lay deeper than any accident of dress. At the same time, he noticed that she betrayed her consciousness of it by a delicate, almost frightened blush. It was 15 one of the compensations of Mrs. Lethbury's protracted childishness that she still blushed as prettily as at eighteen. Her body had been privileged not to outstrip her mind, and the two, as it 20 seemed to Lethbury, were destined to travel together through an eternity of girlishness.

'I don't know what you mean,' she said.

25 Since she never did, he always wondered at her bringing this out as a fresh grievance against him; but his wonder was unresentful, and he said good-humoredly: 'You sparkle so that I thought 30 you had on your diamonds.'

She sighed and blushed again.

'It must be,' he continued, 'that you've been to a dressmaker's opening. You're absolutely brimming with illicit 35 enjoyment.'

She stared again, this time at the adjective. His adjectives always embarrassed her; their unintelligibleness savored of impropriety.

40 'In short,' he summed up, 'you've been doing something that you're thoroughly ashamed of.'

To his surprise she retorted: 'I don't see why I should be ashamed of it!'

45 Lethbury leaned back with a smile of enjoyment. When there was nothing better going he always liked to listen to her explanations.

'Well—?' he said.

50 She was becoming breathless and emotional. 'Of course you'll laugh—you laugh at everything!'

'That rather blunts the point of my derision, doesn't it?' he interjected; but 55 she pushed on without noticing.

'It's so easy to laugh at things.'

'Ah,' murmured Lethbury with relish, 'that's Aunt Sophronia's, isn't it?'

Most of his wife's opinions were 60 heirlooms, and he took a quaint pleasure in tracing their descent. She was proud of their age, and saw no reason for discarding them while they were still serviceable. Some, of course, were so 65 fine that she kept them for state occasions, like her great-grandmother's Crown Derby; but from the lady known as Aunt Sophronia she had inherited a stout set of everyday prejudices that 70 were practically as good as new; whereas her husband's, as she noticed, were always having to be replaced. In the early days she had fancied there might be a certain satisfaction in taxing 75 him with the fact; but she had long since been silenced by the reply: 'My dear, I'm not a rich man, but I never use an opinion twice if I can help it.'

She was reduced, therefore, to 80 dwelling on his moral deficiencies; and

314   ENGLISH FOR THE COLLEGE BOARDS

one of the most obvious of these was his refusal to take things seriously. On this occasion, however, some ulterior purpose kept her from taking up his taunt.

'I'm not in the least ashamed!' she repeated, with the air of shaking a banner to the wind; but the domestic atmosphere being calm, the banner drooped unheroically.

'That,' said Lethbury judicially, 'encourages me to infer that you ought to be, and that, consequently, you've been giving yourself the unusual pleasure of doing something I shouldn't approve of.'

She met this with an almost solemn directness.

'No,' she said. 'You won't approve of it. I've allowed for that.'

'Ah,' he exclaimed, setting down his liqueur glass. 'You've worked out the whole problem, eh?'

'I believe so.'

'That's uncommonly interesting. And what is it?''

She looked at him quietly. 'A baby.'

If it was seldom given her to surprise him, she had attained the distinction for once.

'A baby?'

'Yes.'

'A—human baby?'

'Of course!' she cried, with the virtuous resentment of the woman who has never allowed dogs in the house.

Lethbury's puzzled stare broke into a fresh smile. 'A baby I shan't approve of? Well, in the abstract I don't think much of them, I admit. Is this an abstract baby?'

Again she frowned at the adjective, but she had reached a pitch of exaltation at which such obstacles could not deter her.

'It's the loveliest baby—' she murmured.

'Ah, then it's concrete. It exists. In this harsh world it draws its breath in pain—'

'It's the healthiest child I ever saw!' she indignantly corrected.

'You've seen it, then?'

Again the accusing blush suffused her. 'Yes—I've seen it.'

'And to whom does this paragon belong?'

And here indeed she confounded him. 'To me—I hope,' she declared.

He pushed his chair back with an articulate murmur. 'To you—?'

'To *us*,' she corrected.

'Good Lord!' he said. If there had been the least hint of hallucination in her transparent gaze—but no; it was as clear, as shallow, as easily fathomable as when he had first suffered the sharp surprise of striking bottom in it.

It occurred to him that perhaps she was trying to be funny: he knew that there is nothing more cryptic than the humor of the unhumorous.

'Is it a joke?' he faltered.

'Oh, I hope not. I want it so much to be a reality—'

He paused to smile at the limitations of a world in which jokes were not realities, and continued gently: 'But since it is one already—'

'To us, I mean: to you and me. I want—' her voice wavered, and her eyes with it. 'I have always wanted so dreadfully . . . it has been such a disappointment . . . not to . . .'

'I see,' said Lethbury slowly.

But he had not seen before. It seemed curious now that he had never thought of her taking it in that way, had never surmised any hidden depths beneath her outspread obviousness. He felt as though he had touched a secret spring in her mind.

There was a moment's silence, moist and tremulous on her part, awkward and slightly irritated on his.

'You've been lonely, I suppose?' he began. It was odd, having suddenly to reckon with the stranger who gazed at him out of her trivial eyes.

'At times,' she said.

'I'm sorry.'

'It was not your fault. A man has so many occupations; and women who are clever—or very handsome—I suppose

185 that's an occupation too. Sometimes
I've felt that when dinner was ordered
I had nothing to do till the next day.'
        'Oh,' he groaned.
        'It wasn't your fault,' she insisted. 'I
190 never told you—but when I chose that
rosebud paper for the front room upstairs, I always thought—'
        'Well—?'
        'It would be such a pretty pa-
200 per—for a baby—to wake up in. That
was years ago, of course; but it was
rather an expensive paper . . . and it
hasn't faded in the least . . .' she broke
off incoherently.
205   'It hasn't faded?'
        'No—and so I thought . . . as we
don't use the room for anything . . . now
that Aunt Sophronia is dead . . . I
thought I might . . . you might . . . oh,
210 Julian, if you could only have seen it
just waking up in its crib!'
        'Seen what—where? You haven't
got a baby upstairs?'
        'Oh, no—not *yet*,' she said, with her
215 rare laugh—the girlish bubbling of merriment that had seemed one of her chief
graces in the early days. It occurred to
him that he had not given her enough
things to laugh about lately. But then
220 she needed such very elementary
things: she was as difficult to amuse as
a savage. He concluded that he was not
sufficiently simple.
        'Alice,' he said almost solemnly,
225 'what *do* you mean?'
        She hesitated a moment: he saw her
gather her courage for a supreme effort.
Then she said slowly, gravely, as
though she were pronouncing a sacra-
230 mental phrase:
        'I'm so lonely without a little
child—and I thought perhaps you'd let
me adopt one. . . . It's at the hospital . . .
its mother is dead . . . and I could . . . pet
235 it, and dress it, and do things for it . . .
and it's such a good baby . . . you can ask
any of the nurses . . . it would never,
never bother you by crying. . . .'

1. In lines 7–8, ''deprecate''
   means _____.
   (A) misunderstand   (D) encourage
   (B) belittle   (E) reinforce
   (C) emphasize

                              1 ___

2. The best word to apply to Lethbury's
   treatment of his wife at the beginning
   of the passage is _____.
   (A) cruel   (D) patronizing
   (B) understanding   (E) intolerant
   (C) violent

                              2 ___

3. In essence, the sentence ''Her
   body . . . girlishness'' (lines 18–22)
   means that _____.
   (A) maturity characterized the wife's
       appearance and behavior
   (B) the wife's travels had not broad-
       ened her mind
   (C) the wife's appearance gave a more
       mature impression than her mind
   (D) though the wife's body had not ma-
       tured, her mind had
   (E) immaturity characterized the
       wife's appearance and behavior

                              3 ___

4. Lethbury probably spoke as he did to
   his wife to _____.
   (A) keep asserting his own sense of su-
       periority
   (B) remember constantly her beloved
       Aunt Sophronia
   (C) remind her of their early married
       years
   (D) enjoy conversation with his intel-
       lectual equal
   (E) complain about her spendthrift
       ways

                              4 ___

5. Which of the following pairs is incor-
   rectly matched?
   (A) (line 16) protracted—drawn out
   (B) (line 34) illicit—improper
   (C) (line 39) impropriety—unkindness
   (D) (line 43) retorted—replied
   (E) (line 54) derision—ridicule

                              5 ___

316

6. The "heirlooms" mentioned in line 60 were _____.
   (A) of considerable monetary value
   (B) jewels
   (C) convictions
   (D) her great-grandmother's
   (E) frequently changed

   6 ___

7. In comparison with his wife, Lethbury might be said to be less _____.
   (A) skilled in give-and-take
   (B) prejudiced
   (C) self-satisfied
   (D) intelligent
   (E) attractive in appearance

   7 ___

8. Lethbury's intent in the reply "My dear . . . . help it" (lines 76–78) can be characterized as _____.
   (A) wry humor
   (B) cruel deception
   (C) agreement with his wife
   (D) prejudice
   (E) confession of evil thoughts

   8 ___

9. In the wife's eyes, one of Lethbury's most grievous faults was his _____.
   (A) wife abuse
   (B) careless attire
   (C) unfaithfulness
   (D) quick temper
   (E) taunting humor

   9 ___

10. Which of the following pairs is incorrectly matched?
    (A) (line 83) ulterior—hidden
    (B) (line 85) taunt—mockery
    (C) (line 91) judicially—repetitively
    (D) (line 134) suffused—spread over
    (E) (line 136) paragon—standard of excellence

    10 ___

11. In lines 89–90, the "banner drooped unheroically" because _____.
    (A) the storm had abated
    (B) the wife stumbled as she walked
    (C) Lethbury decided to change the subject
    (D) the wife raised her voice
    (E) there was no loud argument

    11 ___

12. What will probably happen next is that Mrs. Lethbury will _____.
    (A) win over Lethbury immediately
    (B) come to her senses and give up the idea of adoption
    (C) be judged incompetent and not be given the baby
    (D) stick to her guns and get the baby
    (E) ask a friend to adopt the child for her

    12 ___

13. In line 124, "deter" means _____.
    (A) restrain
    (B) inform
    (C) distract
    (D) reveal
    (E) insult

    13 ___

14. "The virtuous resentment of the woman who has never allowed dogs in the house" (lines 114–115) suggests _____.
    (A) an animal hater
    (B) an orderly housekeeper
    (C) an ill-tempered hag
    (D) a relaxed servant
    (E) a frustrated veterinarian

    14 ___

15. In line 138, "confounded" means _____.
    (A) soothed
    (B) provoked
    (C) ridiculed
    (D) baffled
    (E) humored

    15 ___

B

The following article discusses two challenging concepts: irony and paradox. It seeks to explain both.

That's not his bag is a current slang expression which can be approximately translated as "That's not his forte." The original metaphor is a vigorous one, however, and a more honest description than the milder formal version. It helps lay bare the linguistic obsession with classification, a necessary obsession, but an obsession nonetheless. Each one of us has a great many bags, or boxes, into which we neatly put our experiences, our reactions, our environment, and our fellow human beings. Sometimes these boxes confuse us and mislead us.

Many puzzling elements disappear, however, when we take a closer look at the boxes we habitually employ, these nets for attempting to catch the elusive "Reality" that is ultimately uncommunicable and unmanageable. Analyzing the classification practice clarifies two devices, seemingly disparate but all related to the "boxing" habit: irony and paradox.

Irony is usually defined as a confrontation of opposites. John Glenn returns safely from a hazardous trip through space to injure himself in a bathroom fall. The irony involves the confrontation of what *is* and what *appears to be,* between reality (whatever that is) and appearance. The appearance assigned "danger" to space and "safety" to home. The reality proved quite the opposite.

Irony implies an observer who can see the contradiction. Unless there is someone to evaluate appearance and reality, there is no irony. In *Oedipus Tyrannus* the audience knows the reality and notes the discrepancy between Oedipus's misevaluation of the situation and the situation itself. It is the observer who sees the difference between appearance and reality. He makes the classifications. Otherwise there is no irony. In "reality" the bathroom was a more dangerous place than space, at least for John Glenn in the context he found himself in. The irony, then, consists in our setting up categories which produce the contradictions.

Since we act on assumptions and extrapolations, many of our actions in retrospect seem to us "ironic" because they contrast the reality (what actually happened) with the appearances or expectations (what we assume would happen). The irony, however, is linguistic in origin. It depends upon putting things into mutually exclusive boxes (appearance and reality—or something and its opposite). Reality, which is unconcerned with linguistic classification, has nothing to do with irony.

Like irony, paradox involves contradictions, but the contradictions are more readily apparent. "I lie all the time." This paradoxical statement seems to set up irreconcilable contradictions. If in reality I lie all the time, then the verbalization must be a lie. But if the verbalization is a lie, then I cannot in reality lie all the time. This paradox, like irony, involves classification, putting things into boxes. Here we are actually setting up two boxes: one we might label "those who lie all the time" and one we might label "those who don't lie all the time." The speaker linguistically cannot fit into both boxes. The paradox is clarified when the classification is cleared up. If "I lie all the time," I set up a linguistic box that excludes the possibility of telling the truth. But there are really two different boxes: (1) "lying all the time" and (2) "lying some of the time." Obviously the statement is an indication that the second box is the one we might use here.

Paradox is a favorite literary device. Authors sometimes employ it to illuminate a truth by suggesting the apparent but superficial absurdity of the statement. The works of G. K. Chesterton abound in paradox.

1. The closest metaphor to the images in the first paragraph suggests that the mind is a kind of _____.
(A) desktop computer
(B) seamless quilt
(C) filing cabinet
(D) steam turbine
(E) rainbow

1 ___

2. In line 20, the author put "reality" in quotation marks because he or she _____.
(A) is quoting from another article
(B) thinks that no one knows what reality is
(C) believes that reality yields to concentration
(D) considers it the most important word in the sentence
(E) feels that so doing improves the rhythm of the sentence

2 ___

3. The author suggests that irony _____.
(A) exists in the mind of an observer
(B) is another word for metaphor
(C) is the same as paradox
(D) destroys a person's faith in ultimate goodness
(E) is always associated with bad luck

3 ___

4. The word which does NOT belong with the others is _____.
(A) bags
(B) classifications
(C) categories
(D) appearances
(E) boxes

4 ___

5. In lines 54–55, the word "extrapolations" most closely suggests _____.
(A) thoughts and ideas that surface during discussions
(B) classifications based on previous positive experiences
(C) projections into the future based on current information
(D) dream states that promote positive actions
(E) vigorous denunciations of counterproductive activities

5 ___

6. Using the paragraph beginning line 67 as a guide, decide which of the following may be considered a paradox.
(A) Toby is a friend of mine. She is also a good friend of Annette's.
(B) Terry lies all the time.
(C) An irresistible force met an immovable object.
(D) A friend in need is a friend indeed.
(E) April showers bring May flowers.

6 ___

7. "All generalizations are untrue, including this one." This is an example of paradox because _____.
(A) generalizations are usually true
(B) the statement is itself a generalization
(C) the author is trying to be funny
(D) the author successfully avoids generalizations
(E) it is also ironic

7 ___

8. The author probably believes that _____.
(A) classifications should be avoided in everyday conversation
(B) the less frequently irony is used, the better
(C) G. K. Chesterton weakened his writing by using paradox
(D) classifications are necessary, but we must be wary when setting them up
(E) irony and paradox are interchangeable terms

8 ___

9. *Oedipus Tyrannus* is introduced into the passage to _____.
   (A) provide an illustration of irony
   (B) arouse the readers' sense of pity
   (C) show how insensitive some theater-goers can become
   (D) approve of the punishment received by Oedipus
   (E) demonstrate a basic difference between John Glenn and *Oedipus*

   9 ___

10. All the following are correctly paired EXCEPT _____.
    (A) (line 7) obsession—overpowering idea
    (B) (line 71) irreconcilable—incompatible
    (C) (line 42) discrepancy—inconsistency
    (D) (lines 55–56) retrospect—a look back
    (E) (line 23) disparate—anxious

    10 ___

11. The author apparently believes that _____.
    (A) irony is essential to provide color to every kind of writing
    (B) Greek tragedies, though relevant for their own time, have little to say to us today
    (C) most people are aware of the many boxes and classifications they set up
    (D) figures don't lie, but liars figure
    (E) to a great extent, language controls our actions

    11 ___

12. With which of the following quotations would the author probably agree?
    (A) "He who does not know the force of words cannot know men." Confucius
    (B) "Women are always on the defensive." John C. Collins
    (C) "I often quote myself. It adds spice to my conversation." George Bernard Shaw
    (D) "It is certain that more people speak English correctly in the United States than in Britain." Ralph Waldo Emerson
    (E) "Words are feminine; deeds are masculine." Baltasar Gracian

    12 ___

C

Below are two excerpts from books by English philosophers of the past. Both passages deal with education: its advantages and purposes. Passage 1, by Adam Smith, appeared in 1776, the year of the Declaration of Independence. Passage 2, by John Locke, appeared almost a century earlier, in 1690. Both address themselves to the issue of education and its place in life.

Passage 1

A man without the proper use of the intellectual faculties of a man, is, if possible, more contemptible than even a coward, and seems to be mutilated and
5 deformed in a still more essential part of the character of human nature. Though the state was to derive no advantage from the instruction of the inferior ranks of people, it would still de-
10 serve its attention that they should not be altogether uninstructed. The state, however, derives no inconsiderable advantage from their instruction. The more they are instructed the less liable

they are to the delusions of enthusiasm
and superstition, which, among ignorant nations, frequently occasion the
most dreadful disorders. An instructed
and intelligent people, besides, are always more decent and orderly than an
ignorant and stupid one. They feel
themselves, each individually, more respectable and more likely to obtain the
respect of their lawful superiors, and
they are therefore more disposed to respect those superiors. They are more
disposed to examine, and more capable
of seeing through, the interested com-
plaints of faction and sedition, and they
are, upon that account, less apt to be
misled into any wanton or unnecessary
opposition to the measures of government. In free countries, where the
safety of government depends very
much upon the favourable judgment
which the people may form of its conduct, it must surely be of the highest
importance that they should not be disposed to judge rashly or capriciously
concerning it.

Passage 2

A sound mind in a sound body is a
short but full description of a happy
state in this world. He that has these
two has little more to wish for; and he
that wants either of them will be but little the better for anything else. Men's
happiness or misery is most part of their
own making. He whose mind directs not
wisely will never take the right way; and
he whose body is crazy and feeble will
never be able to advance in it. I confess
there are some men's constitutions of
body and mind so vigorous and well
framed by nature that they need not
much assistance from others; but by the
strength of their natural genius they are
from their cradles carried towards what
is excellent; and by the privilege of their
happy constitutions are able to do won-
ders. But examples of this kind are but
few; and I think I may say that of all
the men we meet with, nine parts of
ten are what they are, good or evil,

useful or not, by their education. 'Tis
that which makes the great difference in
mankind.

1. The word "even" (line 3) suggests that
Adam Smith uses "coward" to _____.
   (A) label the coward the most frightened of all persons
   (B) deepen the guilt of a person who
   lives in constant fear
   (C) absolve a coward of all personal responsibility
   (D) strongly emphasize the importance
   of using the intellect properly
   (E) comment in passing on the many
   ways in which talented persons
   can fail

   1 ___

2. "Should not be altogether uninstructed" (lines 10–11) can be interpreted as _____.
   (A) a plea for universal education
   (B) an aristocratic argument for selec-
   tive education
   (C) a counterproposal for managing
   the educational budget
   (D) an exploration of the need for
   teacher education and selection
   (E) a cool, unemotional appraisal of
   current educational practices

   2 ___

3. The expression "no inconsiderable ad-
vantage" (lines 12–13) suggests that
the state will _____.
   (A) be indifferent
   (B) muddle through
   (C) benefit
   (D) object strenuously
   (E) waste resources

   3 ___

4. The word "delusions" in line 15
means _____.
   (A) misconceptions
   (B) instances
   (C) applications
   (D) interpretations
   (E) clarifications

   4 ___

5. Adam Smith feels that education _____.
   (A) helps individuals to accept their place in the social order
   (B) spreads unrest among those most highly trained
   (C) helps every person to reach a level of total equality
   (D) is often wasteful and ineffective
   (E) guarantees every person economic security

   5 ___

6. *Always* in lines 19–20 can best be characterized as a(n) _____.
   (A) misguided falsehood
   (B) oratorical pronouncement
   (C) concerned benevolence
   (D) optimistic generalization
   (E) unvarying truth

   6 ___

7. The word "capriciously" in line 39 means _____.
   (A) venomously
   (B) vigorously
   (C) slyly
   (D) mournfully
   (E) impulsively

   7 ___

8. If we were to put Adam Smith's opinion of education into a metaphor, we might call it _____.
   (A) a gadfly
   (B) a lighted fuse
   (C) an island of serenity
   (D) a safety valve
   (E) a pot of gold

   8 ___

9. The tone of Passage 1 is _____.
   (A) aggressive and dogmatic
   (B) inspirational, though illogical
   (C) measured and reasonable
   (D) bitter and sarcastic
   (E) concerned and uneasy

   9 ___

10. According to Passage 1, a good reason for the state's support of education is _____.
    (A) thought control
    (B) financial solvency
    (C) pure altruism
    (D) military training
    (E) informed citizens

    10 ___

11. Both Passage 1 and Passage 2 are alike in their _____.
    (A) emphasis upon good health as well as intellect
    (B) suggestion that the state benefits little by its educational system
    (C) celebration of the naturally brilliant individual
    (D) tribute to the benefits of education
    (E) fear of popular uprisings

    11 ___

12. Passage 2 differs from Passage 1 in its _____.
    (A) concentration upon the individual rather than the state
    (B) concern for the stability of government
    (C) indifference to the excesses of ignorance
    (D) glorification of parental guidance
    (E) equating terrorism with poverty

    12 ___

13. As contrasted with Passage 2, Passage 1 is more _____.
    (A) accepting of class differences
    (B) critical of sex differences
    (C) interested in child welfare
    (D) concerned with health and sanitation
    (E) convinced that people determine their own happiness

    13 ___

14. "The privilege of their happy constitutions" in lines 58–59 is a reference to _____.
    (A) home nurture
    (B) specialized educational techniques
    (C) genetic advantages
    (D) governmental protection by a social contract
    (E) inequality before the law

    14 ___

15. Which of the following statements may reasonably be made about Passage 2?
    (A) A sound mind is more important than a sound body.
    (B) A sound body is more important than a sound mind.
    (C) Man's misery comes from external sources.
    (D) In the nature-nurture controversy, it supports nurture as more important.
    (E) Natural geniuses always have excellent constitutions as well as keen minds.

    15 ___

16. What irony does the publication date of *Wealth of Nations* suggest?
    (A) Rebellion and revolution may come even with education.
    (B) Sound reasoning can avert bloodshed.
    (C) Violence is always an offshoot of excessive education.
    (D) Adam Smith was a leader of the American Revolution.
    (E) Luck plays a major role in human affairs.

    16 ___

17. The use of the masculine pronoun *he* throughout both passages suggests that _____.
    (A) it was a convention to use the masculine pronoun for both men and women
    (B) both Smith and Locke were essentially opposed to providing any education for women
    (C) men generally make the best educators, though some women achieve extraordinary teaching skill
    (D) the apparently greater strength of men is a matter of nurture, not nature
    (E) even untutored men are likely to have keen intellects when sufficiently stimulated

    17 ___

D

Seeing is a difficult and complicated task, as the author of the following passage makes clear.

I chanced on a wonderful book by Marius von Senden, called *Space and Sight*. When Western surgeons discovered how to perform safe cataract operations, they ranged across Europe and America operating on dozens of men and women of all ages who had been blinded by cataracts since birth. Von Senden collected accounts of such cases; the histories are fascinating. Many doctors had tested their patients' sense perceptions and ideas of space both before and after the operations. The vast majority of patients, of both sexes and all ages, had, in von Senden's opinion, no idea of space whatsoever. Form, distance, and size were so many meaningless syllables. A patient "had no idea of depth, confusing it with roundness." Before the operation a doctor would give a blind patient a cube and a sphere; the patient would tongue it or feel it with his hands, and name it correctly. After the operation the doctor would show the same objects to the patient without letting him touch them; now he had no clue whatsoever what he was seeing. One patient called lemonade "square" because it pricked on his tongue as a square shape pricked on the touch of his hands. Of another postoperative patient, the doctor writes, "I have found in her no notion of size, for example, not even within the narrow limits which she might have encompassed with the aid of touch. Thus when I asked her to show me how big her mother was, she did not stretch out her hands, but set her two index-fingers a few inches apart." Other doctors reported their patients' own statements to similar effect. "The room he was in . . . he knew to be but part of the house, yet he could not conceive that the whole house could look bigger"; "Those who are blind from birth . . . have no real conception of height or distance. A house that is a mile away is thought of as nearby, but requiring the taking of a lot of steps. . . . The elevator that whizzes him up and down gives no more sense of vertical distance than does the train of horizontal."

For the newly sighted, vision is pure sensation unencumbered by meaning: "The girl went through the experience that we all go through and forget, the moment we are born. She saw, but it did not mean anything but a lot of different kinds of brightness." Again, "I asked the patient what he could see; he answered that he saw an extensive field of light, in which everything appeared dull, confused, and in motion. He could not distinguish objects." Another patient saw "nothing but a confusion of forms and colours." When a newly sighted girl saw photographs and paintings, she asked, "'Why do they put those dark marks all over them?' 'Those aren't dark marks,' her mother explained, 'those are shadows. That is one of the ways the eye knows that things have shape. If it were not for shadows many things would look flat.' 'Well, that's how things do look,' Joan answered. 'Everything looks flat with dark patches.'"

But it is the patients' concepts of space that are most revealing. One patient, according to his doctor, "practiced his vision in a strange fashion; thus he takes off one of his boots, throws it some way off in front of him, and then attempts to gauge the distance at which it lies; he takes a few steps towards the boot and tries to grasp it; on failing to reach it, he moves on a step or two and gropes for the boot until he finally gets hold of it." "But even at this stage, after three weeks' experience of seeing," von Senden goes on, "'space,' as he conceives it, ends with visual space, i.e. with colour-patches that happen to bound his view. He does not yet have the notion that a larger object (a chair) can mask a smaller one (a dog), or that the latter can still be present even though it is not directly seen."

In general the newly sighted see the world as a dazzle of color-patches. They are pleased by the sensation of color, and learn quickly to name the colors, but the rest of seeing is tormentingly difficult. Soon after his operation a patient "generally bumps into one of these colour-patches and observes them to be substantial, since they resist him as tactual objects do. In walking about it also strikes him—or can if he pays attention—that he is continually passing in between the colours he sees, that he can go past a visual object, that a part of it then steadily disappears from view; and that in spite of this, however he twists and turns—whether entering the room from the door, for example, or returning back to it—he always has a visual space in front of him. Thus he gradually comes to realize that there is also a space behind him, which he does not see."

1. With which of the following statements would the author of the passage probably agree?
   (A) A suddenly blinded sighted person would soon be as competent in moving about as a person blind at birth.
   (B) In their impact, cataract operations generally do more harm than good.
   (C) Though newly sighted persons are puzzled by color, they quickly learn to manipulate shapes and forms.
   (D) Because of their long years of experience, newly sighted older persons adapt more readily to the new sensations.
   (E) Sight is an obvious physical gift, but seeing is a process that takes a long time to achieve.

   1 ___

2. Which of the following statements suggests a parallel with the feelings of many newly sighted persons?
   (A) Becoming suddenly sighted immediately opens a new world of familiar objects given an exciting new dimension.
   (B) Some hearing impaired persons have regretted the insertion of cochlear implants, preferring the impairment to the confusion of sound.
   (C) The removal of a cataract from a sighted person does not have results different from those of a person blind from birth.
   (D) Cataract surgery has experienced many improvements in the past decade, rendering the surgery almost routine.
   (E) The reactions of newly sighted persons are quite similar, whether the persons be young or old, men or women, children or adults.

   2 ___

3. A person's conceptions of space are apparently ___.
   (A) inborn, part of the genetic makeup that determines a person's physical characteristics
   (B) learned instantaneously inasmuch as the physical world surrounds a person at birth
   (C) a factor of intelligence as determined by the ability of a person to function effectively in a social environment
   (D) dependent upon the visual keenness of both parents
   (E) mastered only after a considerable period of time with many setbacks

   3 ___

4. In lines 35–36, "encompassed" most nearly means ___.
   (A) surrounded
   (B) comprehended
   (C) surmised
   (D) expanded
   (E) appreciated

   4 ___

5. The phrase "pure sensation unencumbered by meaning" (lines 54–55) suggests ___.
   (A) a significant glow of brilliant light
   (B) a joyous sensory experience
   (C) a confusing blur
   (D) a reference to all five senses
   (E) the most meaningful experience of a lifetime

   5 ___

6. From the passage we may infer that a child at birth ___.
   (A) recognizes his mother's face immediately
   (B) has none of the problems that a newly sighted person experiences
   (C) has more acute sight than hearing
   (D) takes a while to learn to differentiate objects visually
   (E) prefers a brightly lighted room to one less brilliantly lit

   6 ___

7. Lemonade was called "square" by _____.
   (A) a person with limited mental ability
   (B) a writer of humorous essays
   (C) a person dependent upon touch
   (D) Marius von Senden in *Space and Sight*
   (E) a child with no experience of lemonade

   7 ___

8. For spatial problems, blind persons generally depend upon _____.
   (A) the sense of touch
   (B) information picked up by Braille reading
   (C) a kind of sonar, developed through trial and error
   (D) sighted partners who explain problems to them
   (E) the uncertain guidance of other blind persons

   8 ___

9. The author's writing style may be best characterized as _____.
   (A) heavy but informative
   (B) smooth and flowing
   (C) interesting though somewhat disconnected
   (D) breathless and a bit jerky
   (E) plodding and monotonous

   9 ___

10. The author quotes von Senden (lines 90–99) to _____.
    (A) undercut, by providing poorly expressed explanations, his central thesis
    (B) provide a break in sentence structure and rhythm
    (C) suggest the author's incredulity at the astounding cases being reported
    (D) point out that even after three weeks a newly sighted patient has difficulties with space and distance
    (E) provide an insight into the kinds of small-muscle tension that interfere with seeing

    10 ___

11. In lines 108–109, the word "tactual" most nearly means _____.
    (A) in accord with the facts
    (B) verifiable
    (C) showing sensitivity
    (D) pertaining to touch
    (E) obvious to sight

    11 ___

12. As we read the author's description of the experiences of newly sighted persons, we may detect a sense of _____.
    (A) interest coupled with amazement
    (B) fatigue in trying to explain
    (C) dissatisfaction with the reports
    (D) light humor in the guise of scientific reporting
    (E) personal interest in each case history

    12 ___

13. In one example, a patient _____.
    (A) threw a boot in front of him to capitalize on his keen sense of hearing
    (B) equated shadows with dark patches
    (C) correctly judged how big her mother was
    (D) correctly identified a cube and a sphere with purely visual help
    (E) had a keen sense of vertical distance while riding in an elevator

    13 ___

14. We may infer that to a newly sighted person the visual world seems _____.
    (A) a continuing delight because of the new experience
    (B) basically of one color
    (C) a friendly combination of sight and sound
    (D) a familiar and secure place
    (E) two dimensional

    14 ___

E

This first chapter of a classic novel suggests the theme of the novel and introduces interesting characters.

It is a truth universally acknowledged that a single man in possession of a good fortune must be in want of a wife.

5 However little known the feelings or views of such a man may be on his first entering a neighborhood, this truth is so well fixed in the minds of the surrounding families, that he is considered as the rightful property of some one or other

10 of their daughters.

"My dear Mr. Bennet," said his lady to him one day, "have you heard that Netherfield Park is let at last?"

Mr. Bennet replied that he had not.

15 "But it is," returned she; "for Mrs. Long has just been here, and she told me all about it."

Mr. Bennet made no answer.

"Do not you want to know who has

20 taken it?" cried his wife impatiently.

"*You* want to tell me, and I have no objection to hearing it."

This was invitation enough.

"Why, my dear, you must know,

25 Mrs. Long says that Netherfield is taken by a young man of large fortune from the north of England; that he came down on Monday in a chaise and four to see the place and was so much delighted

30 with it that he agreed with Mr. Morris immediately; that he is to take possession before Michaelmas, and some of his servants are to be in the house by the end of next week."

35 "What is his name?"

"Bingley."

"Is he married or single?"

"Oh! single, my dear, to be sure! A single man of large fortune; four or five

40 thousand a year. What a fine thing for our girls!"

"How so? How can it affect them?"

"My dear Mr. Bennet," replied his wife, "how can you be so tiresome! You

45 must know that I am thinking of his marrying one of them."

"Is that his design in settling here?"

"Design! Nonsense, how can you talk so! But it is very likely that he *may*

50 fall in love with one of them, and therefore you must visit him as soon as he comes."

"I see no occasion for that. You and the girls may go, or you may send them

55 by themselves, which perhaps will be still better, for as you are as handsome as any of them, Mr. Bingley might like you the best of the party."

"My dear, you flatter me. I certainly

60 *have* had my share of beauty, but I do not pretend to be anything extraordinary now. When a woman has five grown-up daughters, she ought to give over thinking of her own beauty."

65 "In such cases, a woman has not often much beauty to think of."

"But, my dear, you must indeed go and see Mr. Bingley when he comes into the neighborhood."

70 "It is more than I engage for, I assure you."

"But consider your daughters. Only think what an establishment it would be for one of them. Sir William and Lady

75 Lucas are determined to go, merely on that account, for in general, you know, they visit no newcomers. Indeed you must go, for it will be impossible for *us* to visit him if you do not."

80 "You are over-scrupulous, surely. I dare say Mr. Bingley will be very glad to see you; and I will send a few lines by you to assure him of my hearty consent to his marrying whichever he

85 chooses of the girls: though I must throw in a good word for my little Lizzy."

"I desire you will do no such thing. Lizzy is not a bit better than the others;

90 and I am sure she is not half so handsome as Jane, nor half so good-humored as Lydia. But you are always giving *her* the preference."

"They have none of them much to

recommend them," replied he; "they are all silly and ignorant, like other girls; but Lizzy has something more of quickness than her sisters."

100 "Mr. Bennet, how can you abuse your own children in such a way? You take delight in vexing me. You have no compassion of my poor nerves."

"You mistake me, my dear. I have a high respect for your nerves. They are
105 my old friends. I have heard you mention them with consideration these twenty years at least."

"Ah! You do not know what I suffer."

110 "But I hope you will get over it, and live to see many young men of four thousand a year come into the neighborhood."

"It will be no use to us, if twenty
115 such should come, since you will not visit them."

"Depend upon it, my dear, that when there are twenty, I will visit them all."

120 Mr. Bennet was so odd a mixture of quick parts, sarcastic humor, reserve, and caprice, that the experience of three-and-twenty years had been insufficient to make his wife understand his
125 character. *Her* mind was less difficult to develop. She was a woman of mean understanding, little information, and uncertain temper. When she was discontented, she fancied herself nervous.
130 The business of her life was to get her daughters married; its solace was visiting and news.

1. The author's intent in the first sentence is to achieve _____.
   (A) sly humor
   (B) profound philosophy
   (C) subtle argument
   (D) economic protest
   (E) deep character analysis

   1 __

2. Mrs. Bennet's manner of addressing her husband suggests _____.
   (A) an ill-concealed dislike
   (B) a confidence in her ability to control him
   (C) the formality of an earlier time
   (D) a self-assuredness superior to her husband's
   (E) a pixie sense of humor

   2 __

3. When Mr. Bennet makes no answer (line 18) his reason is _____.
   (A) complete inattention to what his wife has been saying
   (B) anger at her raising the subject of marriage for his daughter
   (C) a slight defect that occasionally impairs his hearing
   (D) his awareness that he'll hear about the matter anyway
   (E) an inner turmoil at the complexities of everyday living

   3 __

4. Mrs. Bennet considers the new occupant of Netherfield _____.
   (A) somewhat pretentious because of his arrival in a chaise and four
   (B) an interesting young man born in the nearby vicinity
   (C) an insensitive, impetuous aristocrat with several faults
   (D) a person to be manipulated according to her design
   (E) a landowner considerate of his servants and tenant farmers

   4 __

5. When Mr. Bennet delivers the line "Is that his design in settling here" (line (47), he is being _____.
   (A) moderately curious
   (B) gently sarcastic
   (C) in full support of his wife
   (D) favorably disposed toward Mr. Bingley
   (E) suitably impressed

   5 __

ENGLISH FOR THE COLLEGE BOARDS

6. The dialogue between husband and wife suggests that Mrs. Bennet _____.
   (A) has somewhat of a one-track mind
   (B) is quick thinking and excellent at repartee
   (C) has unselfish motives in making a stranger welcome
   (D) understands her husband only too well
   (E) has a clear favorite among her daughters

   6 ___

7. The coming visit of the Lucases to Mr. Bingley has convinced Mrs. Bennet that _____.
   (A) the Bennets should do more charity work on their own
   (B) the family should visit Bingley as a group
   (C) one can count on friends when times are difficult
   (D) Bingley might be a very good catch
   (E) friends must stick together

   7 ___

8. In talking about his children, Mr. Bennet shows that he _____.
   (A) apparently prefers Jane to Lizzy
   (B) has no inflated ideas of their capabilities
   (C) thinks that his wife has been a cruel mother
   (D) becomes uncharacteristically serious
   (E) would like to get all daughters married quickly

   8 ___

9. The paragraph beginning "You mistake me, my dear" (line 103) suggests that _____.
   (A) Mr. Bennet misses certain old friends
   (B) Mrs. Bennet often forgets old friends
   (C) Mr. Bennet is a bit weary of certain conversations
   (D) Mr. Bennet is here expressing his love in a subtle way
   (E) Mrs. Bennet's worries are principally financial

   9 ___

10. The author's appraisal of Mrs. Bennet is that she is essentially _____.
    (A) relaxed
    (B) inconsiderate
    (C) impolite
    (D) beautiful
    (E) shallow

    10 ___

11. The character of Mr. Bennet, as suggested in the last paragraph, can best be characterized as _____.
    (A) transparent
    (B) vulgar
    (C) complex
    (D) bitter
    (E) unreliable

    11 ___

12. In line 122, the word "caprice" most nearly means _____.
    (A) judgment
    (B) whim
    (C) sincerity
    (D) fascination
    (E) agreeableness

    12 ___

13. In line 131, the word "solace" most nearly means _____.
    (A) tiring exercise
    (B) vocation
    (C) humorous action
    (D) revenge
    (E) comfort

    13 ___

14. The tone of the passage can best be characterized as _____.
    (A) pretentious
    (B) lighthearted
    (C) humorless
    (D) disdainful
    (E) inspirational

    14 ___

15. If we may judge by the conversation, it is reasonable to assume that in later pages _____.
    (A) Mrs. Bennet will come to love Lizzy best
    (B) Mr. Bennet will leave his family
    (C) Mrs. Bennet will change and become less nervous
    (D) Mr. Bennet will visit Mr. Bingley
    (E) Mr. Bingley won't move to Netherfield

    15 ___

F

How does a novel come into being? What impulses and forces drive an author to create a special world of his own? The following passage, part of a long explanation, suggests some of the challenges.

I am not so pretentious as to imagine that it is possible for me to account completely for my own book, *Native Son*. But I am going to try to account for as 5 much of it as I can, the sources of it, the material that went into it, and my own years' long changing attitude toward that material.

In a fundamental sense, an imagina-10 tive novel represents the merging of two extremes; it is an intensely intimate expression on the part of a consciousness couched in terms of the most objective and commonly known events. It 15 is at once something private and public by its very nature and texture. Confounding the author who is trying to lay his cards on the table is the dogging knowledge that his imagination is a kind 20 of community medium of exchange: what he has read, felt, thought, seen, and remembered is translated into extensions as impersonal as a worn dollar bill.

25 The more closely the author thinks of why he wrote, the more he comes to regard his imagination as a kind of self-generating cement which glued his facts together, and his emotions as a kind of 30 dark and obscure designer of those facts. Always there is something that is just beyond the tip of the tongue that could explain it all. Usually, he ends up by discussing something far afield, an 35 act which incites skepticism and suspicion in those anxious for a straight-out explanation.

Yet the author is eager to explain. But the moment he makes the attempt 40 his words falter, for he is confronted and defied by the inexplicable array of his own emotions. Emotions are subjective and he can communicate them only when he clothes them in objective guise; 45 and how can he ever be so arrogant as to know when he is dressing up the right emotion in the right Sunday suit? He is always left with the uneasy notion that maybe *any* objective drapery is as good 50 as *any* other for any emotion.

And the moment he does dress up an emotion, his mind is confronted with the riddle of that "dressed up" emotion, and he is left peering with eager dismay back into the dim reaches of his own incommunicable life. Reluctantly, he comes to the conclusion that to account for his book is to account for his life, and he knows that that is impossible. Yet, some curious, wayward motive urges him to supply the answer, for there is the feeling that his dignity as a living being is challenged by something within him that is not understood.

So, at the outset, I say frankly that there are phases of *Native Son* which I shall make no attempt to account for. There are meanings in my book of which I was not aware until they literally spilled out upon the paper. I shall sketch the outline of how I *consciously* came into possession of the materials that went into *Native Son,* but there will be many things I shall omit, not because I want to, but simply because I don't know them.

The birth of Bigger Thomas goes back my childhood, and there was not just one Bigger, but many of them, more than I could count and more than you suspect. But let me start with the first Bigger, whom I shall call Bigger No. 1.

When I was a bareheaded, barefoot kid in Jackson, Mississippi, there was a boy who terrorized me and all of the boys I played with. If we were playing games, he would saunter up and snatch from us our balls, bats, spinning tops, and marbles. We would stand around pouting, sniffling, trying to keep back our tears, begging for our playthings. But Bigger would refuse. We never demanded that he give them back; we were afraid, and Bigger was bad. We had seen him clout boys when he was angry and we did not want to run that risk. We never recovered our toys unless we flattered him and made him feel that he was superior to us. Then, perhaps, if he felt like it, he condescended, threw them at us and then gave each of us a swift kick in the bargain, just to make us feel his utter contempt.

That was the way Bigger No. 1 lived. His life was a continuous challenge to others. At all times he *took* his way, right or wrong, and those who contradicted him had him to fight. And never was he happier than when he had someone cornered and at his mercy; it seemed that the deepest meaning of his squalid life was in him at such times.

I don't know what the fate of Bigger No. 1 was. His swaggering personality is swallowed up somewhere in the amnesia of my childhood. But I suspect that his end was violent. Anyway, he left a marked impression upon me; maybe it was because I longed secretly to be like him and was afraid. I don't know.

1. In line 1, "pretentious" suggests _____.
   (A) being bright and alert
   (B) winning without concern for others
   (C) doing things for show
   (D) having a winning manner
   (E) justifying wrong actions

   1 ___

2. The writer looks upon the imaginative novel as _____.
   (A) a conflict between the author and the blank page
   (B) a transformation of the subjective into the objective
   (C) the result of many attempts to sample reader opinion
   (D) a cooperative effort involving publisher, editor, author, and, ultimately, reader
   (E) an attempt to avoid laying cards on the table

   2 ___

3. The author introduces the example of a dollar bill as _____.
   (A) a subtle attack upon greed as a writer's motivation
   (B) a metaphor for unrecognized creativity in an increasingly indifferent world
   (C) a sad expression of the writer's dependence upon financial success
   (D) a medium through which authors express observations, thoughts, and feelings
   (E) an image emphasizing the impersonality of the actual writing result

   3 ___

4. According to the author, the "community medium of exchange" is _____.
   (A) the ever-present dollar bill
   (B) objectively known events
   (C) the emotions
   (D) the imagination
   (E) the merging of two extremes

   4 ___

5. In his search of the source and origin of his novel, the author _____.
   (A) is not altogether sure about the creative process
   (B) considers emotions "a kind of self-generating cement"
   (C) calls upon literary authorities for an answer
   (D) considers his childhood experiences of little value
   (E) proclaims his opposition to novels without emotion

   5 ___

6. In line 41, the word "inexplicable" _____.
   (A) is opposed to the phrase "eager to explain"
   (B) emphasizes the objectivity of the imaginative novel
   (C) suggests a confrontation between fact and fiction
   (D) has the meaning "unjustified"
   (E) labels the author's creative efforts as futile

   6 ___

7. All the following are examples of figurative language EXCEPT _____.
   (A) "glued his facts together"
   (B) "beyond the tip of the tongue"
   (C) "dressing up the right emotion"
   (D) "he knows that that is impossible"
   (E) "peering with eager dismay"

   7 ___

8. "They literally spilled out upon the paper" is _____.
   (A) an attempt to present an interrupted flow of words
   (B) actually a contradiction between *literal* and *figurative*
   (C) the author's excuse for hasty, slipshod writing
   (D) a reference to notes jotted down by the author over a period of years
   (E) an unsuccessfully repressed attempt at self-concealment

   8 ___

9. In line 60, the word "wayward" most nearly means _____.
   (A) unintentional
   (B) incomprehensible
   (C) vigorous
   (D) pressing
   (E) erratic

   9 ___

10. When the author examines the challenge to "account for the book," his reaction may be paraphrased in the following way:
    (A) "I plan to omit long sections as being too private."
    (B) "An outsider could possibly do a better job."
    (C) "I can't really explain but I'll try."
    (D) "I'll explain all emotional impulses as they appear in the book."
    (E) "I regret the experience as being too painful."

    10 ___

332

11. The passage suggests that a novelist _____.
    (A) may include meanings he's unaware of
    (B) needs a bitter childhood to succeed
    (C) enjoys proofreading his own novel, not others
    (D) finds his best material in the news media
    (E) is usually a wide and perceptive reader

    11 ___

12. Throughout, the attitude of the author seems _____.
    (A) reflective but inhibited
    (B) self-satisfied and glib
    (C) intentionally obscure
    (D) open and honest
    (E) weak and hesitant

    12 ___

13. Bigger Thomas is apparently _____.
    (A) the author of *Native Son*
    (B) based on the author's own physical prowess
    (C) a character in *Native Son*
    (D) a particular bully in Jackson, Mississippi
    (E) the pen name of the writer

    13 ___

14. The author in describing his experiences with the bully makes clear that at the time he _____.
    (A) resolved to use the experience in a novel some day
    (B) felt degraded in having to flatter the bully
    (C) formed a group with other boys to defeat the bully
    (D) felt that the bully would be a success some day
    (E) did not allow the troubles to make him depressed

    14 ___

15. When the bully "condescended," he _____.
    (A) apologized for his actions but then continued
    (B) walked down the stairs to abuse the other boys
    (C) yelled horrible names at the boys
    (D) became violent and broke the other boys' toys
    (E) dealt with the boys as inferiors

    15 ___

16. In line 113, the word "squalid" means _____.
    (A) violent and uproarious
    (B) mean and unclean
    (C) poor but understated
    (D) thoughtless and unfriendly
    (E) depressing and uncertain

    16 ___

17. "The amnesia of my childhood" is in all probability _____.
    (A) a disease that the author outgrew in maturity
    (B) the sights, sounds, and other sensations of childhood
    (C) a protective mechanism against the early troubles
    (D) an inability to defeat the bully of early years
    (E) the uncluttered recollections of an observant writer

    17 ___

18. The last two sentences suggest that the author _____.
    (A) really had a warm spot in his heart for Bigger No. 1
    (B) didn't want to reveal the real identity of Bigger No. 1
    (C) is discounting the importance of his early childhood
    (D) is being honest in evaluating his own motivations
    (E) considered himself a coward for not striking Bigger No. 1

    18 ___

G

The following description captures for the reader a moment in time at the shore.

At noon white wings sailed over the sand dunes and a snowy egret swung down long black legs. The bird alighted at the margin of a pond that lay, half
5 encircled by marsh, between the eastern end of the dunes and the inlet beach. The pond was called Mullet Pond, a name given to it years before when it had been larger and mullet had some-
10 times come into it from the sea. Every day the small white heron came to fish the pond, seeking the killifish and other minnows that darted in its shallows. Sometimes, too, he found the young of
15 larger fishes, for the highest tides of each month cut through the beach on the ocean side and brought in fish from the sea.

The pond slept in noonday quiet.
20 Against the green of the marsh grass the heron was a snow-white figure on slim black stilts, tense and motionless. Not a ripple nor the shadow of a ripple passed beneath his sharp eyes. Then eight pale
25 minnows swam single file above the muddy bottom, and eight black shadows moved beneath them.

With a snakelike contortion of its neck, the heron jabbed violently, but
30 missed the leader of the solemn little parade of fish. The minnows scattered in sudden panic as the clear water was churned to muddy chaos by the feet of the heron, who darted one way and an-
35 other, skipping and flapping his wings in excitement. In spite of his efforts, he captured only one of the minnows.

The heron had been fishing for an hour and the sanderlings, sandpipers,
40 and plovers had been sleeping for three hours when a boat's bottom grated on the sound beach near the point. Two men jumped out into the water and made ready to drag a haul seine through
45 the shallows on the rising tide. The heron lifted his head and listened. Through the fringe of sea oats on the sound side of the pond he saw a man walking down the beach toward the
50 inlet. Alarmed, he thrust his feet hard against the mud and with a flapping of wings took off over the dunes toward the heron rookery in the cedar thickets a mile away. Some of the shore birds
55 ran twittering across the beach toward the sea. Already the terns were milling about overhead in a noisy cloud, like hundreds of scraps of paper flung to the wind. The sanderlings took flight and
60 crossed the point, wheeling and turning almost as one bird, and passed down the ocean beach about a mile.

The ghost crab, still at his hunting of beach fleas, was alarmed by the tur-
65 moil of birds overhead, by the many racing shadows that sped over the sand. By now he was far from his own burrow. When he saw the fisherman walking across the beach he dashed into the
70 surf, preferring this refuge to flight. But a large channel bass was lurking nearby, and in a twinkling the crab was seized and eaten. Later in the same day, the bass was attacked by sharks and what
75 was left of it was cast up by the tide onto the sand. There the beach fleas, scavengers of the shore, swarmed over it and devoured it.

1. A recurring contrast in the selection is the difference between _____.
   (A) the cruelty of the heron and the nonaggressiveness of the minnows
   (B) the apparent serenity of the beach scene and the tumultuous events occurring all around
   (C) the wastefulness of the fishermen and the economy of the heron
   (D) the colorful nature of the pond and the dullness of the surrounding sea
   (E) the gentleness of nature and the violence of human beings

1 ____

2. The variety of fish in Mullet Pond depends upon _____.
   (A) a temporary inlet
   (B) restocking by fishermen
   (C) the efforts of herons and other shore birds
   (D) patternless weather conditions
   (E) dredging by local contractors

   2 ___

3. From the passage we may infer that _____.
   (A) killifish are not minnows
   (B) the name *Mullet Pond* is no longer an accurate description
   (C) the heron is rarely disturbed by the arrival of humans
   (D) plovers do not rest during the day
   (E) the heron perches on tall black posts

   3 ___

4. In line 44, "seine" most nearly means a _____.
   (A) narrow rowboat
   (B) baited line
   (C) block and tackle
   (D) kind of net
   (E) clam rake

   4 ___

5. From the selection we may infer that _____.
   (A) herons are more at home in deeper water than in shallow
   (B) sandpipers are more efficient at fishing than sanderlings
   (C) the lack of maneuvering by minnows makes them easy targets
   (D) channel bass subsist for the most part on sea oats
   (E) herons and plovers have different times for activity

   5 ___

6. The author makes an ironic and powerful comment on life by pointing out that _____.
   (A) in a sense, beach fleas are at the bottom of the food chain and at the top
   (B) the channel bass, though larger than the ghost crab, is also its prey
   (C) fishermen are working at the rising tide, perhaps a poor time to fish
   (D) though basically nonsocial birds, herons frequently flock with sandpipers
   (E) the men are spoiling the beach habitat

   6 ___

7. All the following are examples of figurative language EXCEPT _____.
   (A) "the pond slept" (19)
   (B) "figure on slim black stilts" (21–22)
   (C) "the minnows scattered" (31)
   (D) "milling about overhead in a noisy cloud" (56–57)
   (E) "hundreds of scraps of paper" (58)

   7 ___

8. The heron may have been largely unsuccessful in his fishing because of _____.
   (A) a lack of concentration on the task at hand
   (B) his own efforts that stirred up the water
   (C) an individual ineptitude uncharacteristic of herons
   (D) too intense competition between the heron and the other shore birds
   (E) turbulence caused by tides

   8 ___

9. The attitude of the author towards the events described can best be characterized as _____.
   (A) horror at the cruelty displayed
   (B) bored reporting of essentially repetitive actions
   (C) alert interest in the workings of nature
   (D) protest at the wastefulness of natural processes
   (E) sensitivity to the humor beneath the surface

9 ___

10. The "white wings" mentioned in line 1 belong to a _____.
    (A) tern   (D) sandpiper
    (B) sanderling   (E) heron
    (C) plover

10 ___

11. The author's purpose in introducing the episode of the ghost crab is to _____.
    (A) deplore the arrival of the fishermen
    (B) demonstrate the courage of this lowly creature
    (C) contrast its behavior with that of the heron
    (D) show how the food chain operates
    (E) underscore the voraciousness of the channel bass

11 ___

12. The *eight black shadows* belong to _____.
    (A) terns
    (B) herons
    (C) egrets
    (D) ghost crabs
    (E) minnows

12 ___

13. It might be said of scavengers (line 77) that they will _____.
    (A) eat all kinds of food
    (B) survive long after the herons have disappeared
    (C) litter the shore with their carcasses
    (D) provide nourishing food for egrets
    (E) become an endangered species

13 ___

14. Which of the following quotations is closest in spirit to that of the passage?
    (A) "Nature I loved, and next to nature, art." W. S. Landor
    (B) "Those things are better which are perfected by nature than those which are finished by art." Cicero
    (C) "Nothing which we can imagine about Nature is incredible." Pliny the Elder
    (D) "Nature is visible thought." Heinrich Heine
    (E) "Art quickens nature." Robert Herrick

14 ___

H

The following passage describes a new method of mining that may bring changes in mining techniques.

The recovery of copper from the drainage water of mines was probably a widespread practice in the Mediterranean basin as early as 1000 B.C. Although such mining operations are diffi-
5 cult to document, it is known that the leaching of copper on a large scale was well established at the Río Tinto mines in Spain by the 18th century. What none
10 of the miners engaged in this traditional method of mineral extraction realized until about 25 years ago is that bacteria take an active part in the leaching process. They help to convert the copper
15 into a water-soluble form that can be carried off by the leach water. Today bacteria are being deliberately exploited to recover millions of pounds of copper from billions of tons of low-grade ore.
20 Copper obtained in this way accounts

for more than 10 percent of the total U.S. production. In recent years bacterial leaching has also been applied to the recovery of another nonferrous metal:
25 uranium.

"Recent progress in the genetic manipulation of microorganisms for industrial purposes promises to revitalize not only the bacterial leaching of metal-
30 bearing ores but also the microbiological treatment of metal-contaminated waste water. The enthusiasm of the microbiologists working on the development of the new "biomining" tech-
35 niques is matched by a need in the minerals industry to find alternatives to conventional methods of mining, ore processing and waste-water treatment. The need arises from recent trends in
40 the industry: the continued depletion of high-grade mineral resources, the resulting tendency for mining to be extended deeper underground, the growing awareness of environmental
45 problems associated with the smelting of sulfide minerals and the burning of sulfur-rich fossil fuels and the rising cost of the prodigious amounts of energy required in the conventional recovery
50 methods. The current methods will surely prevail for many years to come, but biological processes are generally less energy-intensive and less polluting than most nonbiological technology in
55 mining ore processing, and waste-water treatment is likely to become increasingly important.

1. All the following are mentioned as stimulating the need for biomining EXCEPT _____.
   (A) depletion of high-grade mineral resources
   (B) environmental problems
   (C) intensive foreign competition
   (D) need for ever deeper mining
   (E) energy considerations

1 ___

2. Microorganisms are playing a greater role in industrial technology as a result of _____.
   (A) presidential decree
   (B) historical study
   (C) genetic manipulation
   (D) innovation by Spanish miners
   (E) underground exploration

2 ___

3. As used in the passage, *leaching* refers to _____.
   (A) bleaching discolored elements
   (B) chemically destroying pollutants
   (C) smelting sulfide minerals
   (D) separating components
   (E) depleting high-grade mineral resources

3 ___

4. Which of the following best describes the main idea of the passage?
   (A) Copper obtained from drainage water is superior to that directly mined.
   (B) Microbiologists decry the exploitation of genetics for industrial purposes.
   (C) The role of biological technology in mining and related areas is growing.
   (D) Waste-water treatment is undergoing major changes in technology.
   (E) Biological processes tend to be more polluting than nonbiological ones.

4 ___

5. *Biomining* is put in quotation marks because _____.
   (A) biomining is an unnatural procedure
   (B) it should really be *bioleaching*
   (C) it is a newly coined word
   (D) no scientist believes in its efficacy
   (E) the word was first used in the 18th century and revived

5 ___

6. The leaching process is apparently most economically feasible with _____.
   (A) low-grade ore
   (B) sulfide minerals
   (C) burning of fossil fuels
   (D) rich veins of ore
   (E) agriculture

   6 ___

7. The recovery of copper from the waste water of mines _____.
   (A) began in the Río Tinto mines of Spain
   (B) is an attractive plan but a will-o'-the-wisp in practice
   (C) relies basically on sulfur-rich fossil fuels during the processing
   (D) probably goes back 3,000 years
   (E) accounts for most copper produced in the United States

   7 ___

8. The passage admits which of the following are being exploited in the copper-recovery process?
   (A) miners
   (B) waste-water processors
   (C) microbiologists
   (D) bacteria
   (E) biochemical engineers

   8 ___

9. In line 17, "exploited" most nearly means _____.
   (A) disregarded
   (B) utilized
   (C) changed
   (D) advertised
   (E) transported

   9 ___

10. In line 40, the word "depletion" most nearly means _____.
    (A) increasing
    (B) neglecting
    (C) scattering
    (D) revitalizing
    (E) draining

    10 ___

11. The author's attitude toward new methods of mining is one of _____.
    (A) skepticism
    (B) approval
    (C) antagonism
    (D) tolerance
    (E) indifference

    11 ___

I

The following passage discusses the difficulties that computers face when tackling a problem in language. Of the five problem areas, four are analyzed here.

Computers stand up well to a grand master when it comes to the logic of chess, but they can't match the skills of a 7-year-old when it comes to language.

5 The reason for the glacial pace of progress in MT (machine translation) over the past four decades can be found in one factor: the intractable ambiguities of natural language. An MT system

10 must peel away at least five layers of ambiguity before it is able to map sentences from one language to another with any degree of accuracy. If you understand how MT copes with these difficulties,

15 you will have a clear idea of just how these systems work and why they do not work better.

Step inside an MT system and see how it handles the following simple sentence:

20 tence: *The heavy-duty truck turned into a driveway.* As you follow this sentence through the system, notice how nearly every other word poses a challenge—and an opportunity for error.

When the system looks in the dictionary for the word *truck,* it immediately encounters ambiguity: The word is encoded in the dictionary as both a noun and a verb. The system's dictionary can tell you only that *truck* can take the form of two parts of speech. It can't tell you which form it takes in this sentence.

To make that determination, you must move further into the system and view the word in the context of the sentence. At this point, the system still has no idea what the sentence means and sees it only as a syntactic string containing elements that have more than one interpretation.

To operate at the sentence level of the syntactic stage, you must have some kind of grammar—typically stored as a set of rules. One of these rules will determine that, in the given sentence, without violating grammatical rules, *truck* cannot be anything but a noun. So far, so good—although it is not always going to be that easy.

Now that you know that *heavy-duty truck* is a noun phrase, a second layer of ambiguity comes to light. The system still sees your noun phrase purely syntactically, as the string Adj N1 N2. It has no idea, for example, whether the adjective *heavy* modifies *duty* or *truck.* The system has to resolve this ambiguity if it's to get the agreement right. Therefore, you have to go beyond syntax into lexical semantics.

At this deeper stage, more intelligent rules come into play and use the semantic properties that were retrieved for the words earlier in your sentence during the dictionary lookup stage. These semantic-property codes are designed to resolve ambiguities such as that posed by *heavy-duty truck.* Now you're going to run into some rough going.

The majority of low-end MT systems don't get into semantics—or they do so only in trivial ways. These systems generally are weak, but even high-end systems will have trouble trying to figure out which noun *heavy* modifies.

The issues are subtle. At this point, most developers will resort to brute force by storing the phrase as a unit in the dictionary.

Slightly more tractable examples of this kind of ambiguity would be *old people and children* and *smart girls and boys.* If a smart rule uses a test for semantic symmetry (or lack thereof) among the noun pairs, it could figure out that the adjective *old* modifies only *people* and that *smart* modifies both *boys* and *girls.* Clearly, getting a machine to cope with this challenge isn't easy.

Processing at the lexical semantic stage introduces its own kind of confusion—the third layer—having to do with multiple meanings of words. For example, the verb *turn into* has at least two lexical meanings: One is the sense of motion, and the other is the sense of becoming. To decide which meaning applies in your sentence, you have to move to sentence-level semantics, where the verb *turn into* can be examined in its semantic context.

A semantic rule associated with the words *turn into* would know that the meaning of this verb is going to be a function of the verb's direct object. So, in this sentence, the rule has to test only the semantic-property code for *driveway* to determine the verb's meaning: If *driveway* were given a semantic-property code signifying a path, the rule would know to select the verb's motional sense. Such a rule would work with Cinderella, too, if her carriage turned into a driveway rather than a pumpkin.

A fourth layer of difficulty has to do with ambiguities introduced at the sentence level of the semantic stage. Unfortunately (or fortunately), the sample sentence doesn't illustrate this kind of complexity. But to get the idea, consider the meaning of the preposition *for* in the following sentences: Check the newspapers for errors. Check the newspapers for dates.

In the first sentence, the preposition *for* signifies *for the presence of,* and in

the second sentence, it means *for infor-*
130 *mation about*. As used in this example, in a language like Vietnamese, the preposition *for* would be expressed differently in each case.

Thus, the system has to determine
135 which case applies if it's to translate the meaning correctly. You can see that the meanings of the word *for* are a function of the sentence as a whole; you won't find them in any dictionary. Also, notice
140 how the sentence as a whole affects the meaning of the verb *check*. In the first sentence, *check* means to examine. In the second, *check* means to consult.

1. In lines 8–9, "intractable ambiguities" suggests _____.
   (A) a difficulty brought on by fallacies in logic
   (B) the logical organization and structure of natural language
   (C) an ornery problem with two or more meanings
   (D) a double dose of crystal-clear prose
   (E) an inferior example of circular reasoning

   1 ____

2. The language skills of a seven-year-old are superior to those of the finest computer because _____.
   (A) the child's brain is a superior machine for translation
   (B) computer skills in chess are no better than those in language
   (C) a computer is an inanimate object without logical skills
   (D) the complexities of even a simple sentence baffle the computer
   (E) seven is the age at which children begin to speak standard English

   2 ____

3. The author implies that the sentence "The heavy-duty truck turned into the driveway" _____.
   (A) poses only two difficulties for a computer
   (B) is simple enough for certain types of computers to translate
   (C) is not a good example of English sentence structure
   (D) would be extremely difficult to translate into Vietnamese
   (E) would not be a problem for a seven-year-old

   3 ____

4. When determining whether *truck* is a noun or a verb, a person or computer would _____.
   (A) have to look at the rest of the sentence
   (B) check the dictionary or built-in word list
   (C) first assume that it is a verb
   (D) instantaneously sift through the rules of grammar
   (E) have to make a guess

   4 ____

5. From the selection, we may assume that semantics deals principally with _____.
   (A) word order
   (B) meaning
   (C) spelling
   (D) literature
   (E) metaphor

   5 ____

6. In line 96, "lexical" most nearly means _____.
   (A) linked to computers
   (B) literate
   (C) open-ended
   (D) pertaining to words
   (E) challenging

6 ___

7. Which of the following methods would make it easier for the computer to handle the "truck" sentence?
   (A) Change "driveway" to "roadway."
   (B) Rearrange the word order of the sentence.
   (C) Insert into its dictionary "heavy-duty" as one unit.
   (D) Change "into" to "from."
   (E) Anticipate the sentence by putting it into the system beforehand.

7 ___

8. In the two quoted sentences (lines 124–126), the major difficulty is _____.
   (A) similar to a difficulty found in Vietnamese
   (B) deciding on the meaning of the preposition "for"
   (C) determining the part of speech of "for"
   (D) the rather slipshod word order
   (E) determining the motive of the speaker of each sentence

8 ___

9. In the quoted sentences mentioned in 8, an added difficulty is _____.
   (A) differences in the meaning of "check"
   (B) a deceptive difference in word order
   (C) use of the imperative rather than the declarative
   (D) the placement of the two prepositional phrases
   (E) the subtle difference between "newspapers" in sentences 1 and 2

9 ___

10. The author uses a fairly simple English sentence, "The heavy-duty truck turned into the driveway," to _____.
    (A) critically evaluate different types of computers
    (B) show, step by step, how a computer successfully manages the difficulties of translation
    (C) demonstrate his own complete mastery of English sentence structure
    (D) contrast the sentence with "Check the newspaper for errors"
    (E) point out some of the critical difficulties in translating even a simple sentence

10 ___

11. All the following are examples of figurative language EXCEPT _____.
    (A) "peel away" (10)
    (B) "some kind of grammar" (43–44)
    (C) "system still sees" (53–54)
    (D) "run into some tough going" (70)
    (E) "brute force" (78–79)

11 ___

12. The author's style may best be described as _____.
    (A) flowery
    (B) halting
    (C) methodical
    (D) pompous
    (E) flamboyant

12 ___

13. The author intends the opening sentence _____.
    (A) as a shocker to get the reader's attention
    (B) to belittle the much-vaunted powers of computers
    (C) to glorify humanity at the expense of the inanimate computer
    (D) to emphasize that the days of human superiority in chess are dying
    (E) as an indication that both chess and language are to be discussed in the passage

13 ___

Reading Diagnostic Tests

First take Test A, below, and Test B on page 345. Referring to pages 461–463, check your answers, and go over the analysis. In the analysis you will find the page numbers where to turn in this book for additional help and strategy.

Find your weaknesses well in advance of the SAT testing date so that you will have ample time to work on the types of test items that you find most difficult. Remember you are building your personal power to take the SAT with confidence.

Reading Diagnostic Test A

Each passage below is followed by questions based on its content. Answer all questions following a passage on the basis of what is *stated* or *implied* in that passage.

The character of the prince who now ascended the throne of England and became lord of Normandy, Anjou, Touraine, and Maine, claimant to Brittany
5 and heir to Queen Eleanor's Aquitaine, was already well known. Richard had embodied the virtues which men admire in the lion, but there is no animal in nature that combines the contradictory
10 qualities of John. He united the ruthlessness of a hardened warrior with the craft and sublety of a Machiavellian. Although from time to time he gave way to furious rages, in which "his eyes darted
15 fire and his countenance became livid," his cruelties were conceived and executed with a cold, inhuman intelligence. Monkish chroniclers have emphasized his violence, greed, malice, treachery,
20 and lust. But other records show that he was often judicious, always extremely capable, and on occasions even generous. He possessed an original and inquiring mind, and to the end of his life
25 treasured his library of books. In him the restless energy of the Plantagenet race was raised to a furious pitch of instability. A French writer, it is true, has tried to throw the sombre cloak of mad-
30 ness over his moral deformities, but a study of his actions shows John gifted with a deep and persistent sagacity, of patience and artifice, and with an unshakable resolve, which he fulfilled, to
35 maintain himself upon the throne while the breath was in his body. The difficulties with which he contended, on the whole with remarkable success, deserve cool and attentive study. More-
40 over, when the long tally is added it will be seen that the British nation and the English-speaking world owe far more to the vices of John than to the labours of virtuous sovereigns; for it was through
45 the union of many forces against him that the most famous milestone of our rights and freedom was in fact set up.

1. The selection focuses its major attention upon _____.
   (A) the virtues of Richard
   (B) the progeny of Queen Eleanor
   (C) the energy of the Plantagenets
   (D) the contradictory nature of John
   (E) the deviousness of the Normans

1 ___

2. Which of the following pairs of adjectives may be applied to John?
   (A) gentle and mad
   (B) cruel and intelligent
   (C) handsome and ruthless
   (D) patient and weak
   (E) greedy and stupid

   2 ___

3. Monkish chroniclers _____.
   (A) tended to report John's worst qualities
   (B) glorified John
   (C) praised him for supporting freedom
   (D) called him a *Machiavellian*
   (E) commented on his fine library

   3 ___

4. A generalization that may be drawn from the passage is that _____.
   (A) you can't tell a book by its cover
   (B) violence begets violence
   (C) evil actions may bring good results
   (D) restless energy leads to virtuous action
   (E) the concept of kingship is obsolete

   4 ___

Kentucky-born John Stark was fifty-eight years old when he first heard Joplin play the piece that was the patrons' favorite at Sedalia's Maple Leaf Club.
5 Disregarding warnings that no market existed for black composers' works, Stark agreed to have Joplin's piece printed and to sell it in his music store. Published in September 1899, "Maple
10 Leaf Rag" did not sell well at first. But it gained popularity in the fall of 1900, boosted by the sudden eruption of a national ragtime craze. Stark and his son moved to St. Louis, where they printed
15 ten thousand copies of Joplin's piece on a small hand press and hung up a sign reading "John Stark and Son, Music Publishers." Orders for "Maple Leaf Rag" came in from all over the country.
20 Stark hired a staff, exchanged his work clothes for a business suit, and prepared to face life as a successful publisher. Soon he had a fine house in St. Louis

and a thriving business whose principal
25 product was the works of a previously unknown composer named Scott Joplin.

Joplin followed Stark to St. Louis in 1901. He bought a house there,
30 equipped it with a piano, and settled down to his chosen work of serious composing. The compositions that Joplin produced in the next ten years are still remembered as classics of ragtime.
35 They were appealing pieces with flowing melodies, intricate syncopations, and expressive themes. They bore such names as "The Entertainer," "Peacherine Rag," "The Easy Winners,"
40 "Elite Syncopations," and "The Strenuous Life." He also wrote songs, marches, waltzes, and an elegant tango called "Solace." For several years, he appeared on vaudeville stages, billed as
45 "King of Ragtime Composers—Author of 'Maple Leaf Rag.'" But his ambitions transcended the confines of popular dance and show music. He longed to adapt the rhythms of ragtime to more
50 ambitious musical forms, to show that characteristic black syncopation was capable of expressing enduring musical ideas.

5. Which of the following titles best summarizes the content of the passage?
   (A) John Stark, Entrepreneur
   (B) St. Louis, Home of Ragtime
   (C) The Problems of Music Publishing
   (D) Famous Composers of Ragtime
   (E) The King of Ragtime

   5 ___

6. "Maple Leaf Rag" took its name from _____.
   (A) a club in Sedalia
   (B) a sign in John Stark's office
   (C) Canada
   (D) a tree in Joplin's garden
   (E) a previous composition

   6 ___

7. All the following types of musical composition are mentioned in the passage EXCEPT _____.
   (A) waltz
   (B) tango
   (C) march
   (D) opera
   (E) song

   7 ___

8. Scott Joplin had to earn his living as _____.
   (A) an assistant to John Stark
   (B) a dance instructor
   (C) a vaudeville entertainer
   (D) a printer
   (E) a distributor of his own work

   8 ___

On a global basis, it has been estimated that the annual net loss of soil from cropland is some 23 billion tons in excess of soil formation. As world pop-
5 ulation expands, demand for food and fiber expands. Driven by economic and social pressures, more of the world's marginal cropland is put to the plow each year—only to be abandoned as
10 soils are depleted after a short period of production. Mining of the world's arable soils is an ongoing and accelerating process, the inevitable consequences of which must be obvious to any thinking
15 person. It may come to pass that sustaining this nation's food and fiber-producing capacity may become our most potent deterrent to international conflict.
20 To blame farmers for abandoning well-known soil-conservation practices is akin to denouncing one who is drowning for futilely clutching at straws. In far too many cases, the
25 farmer is fighting for survival; when he is reduced to choosing between bankruptcy now or later, his choice is obvious. Long-term conservation practices suffer under the harsh demands of
30 economic survival. But there are others who are farming the subsidy/tax-incentives system for a quick profit at the expense of family farmers, consumers, and taxpayers alike.

9. As used in the selection *marginal* is equivalent to _____.
   (A) bordering   (D) terminal
   (B) arable   (E) poor
   (C) desert

   9 ___

10. The author uses the phrase "futilely clutching at straws" to suggest _____.
    (A) promising survival strategies
    (B) measures of desperation
    (C) short-term ineffectiveness, long-term success
    (D) taking advantage of the incentives system
    (E) compromises with reality

    10 ___

11. A major deterrent to global war may be America's _____.
    (A) new, improved mining techniques
    (B) food-producing capacity
    (C) intelligent use of tax incentives
    (D) current treatment of farm problems
    (E) arsenal of military might

    11 ___

In 1644, the Manchus, a tribal people on the northeastern frontier of the Ming empire, captured Peking, overthrew the Ming and established the
5 Ch'ing dynasty, which lasted until the founding of the Chinese Republic in 1911. Under the K'ang-hsi emperor (reigned 1662–1722), the early Ch'ing world was one of reconstruction after
10 late Ming fragmentation. Orthodox painters aimed to recapture the former glories of traditional painting by studying and copying ancient models. By infusing old conventions with renewed
15 energy, painters attempted to achieve a true correspondence *(ho)* to ancient models. On the other hand, some artists scorned the new orthodox conservatism. The so-called individualist mas-
20 ters often painted in a free, emotion-filled calligraphic manner. Because of their loyalty to the fallen Ming dynasty, they expressed a strong sense of dislocation and alienation in their works.

ENGLISH FOR THE COLLEGE BOARDS

25 Avoiding the rationalism and methodology of the orthodox painters, the individualists preferred to derive their art directly from nature and to express it through more personal artistic means.

12. Which of the following is the best characterization of the K'ang-hsi emperor?
    (A) He was the last of the Ming emperors; with him the Ming dynasty ended.
    (B) He was a painter who mastered the calligraphic style.
    (C) He was the spiritual forerunner of the Chinese republic.
    (D) He was an early emperor of the Ch'ing dynasty.
    (E) He was a master of the emotion-filled calligraphic manner.

                                    12 ___

13. Those who "preferred to derive their art directly from nature" are described in the selection as _____.
    (A) orthodox painters and new conservatives
    (B) a tribal people on the frontier of the Ming empire
    (C) concentrating on the correspondence (ho) to ancient models
    (D) former warriors forced to become artists in peacetime
    (E) alienated because of loyalty to the Ming empire

                                    13 ___

14. The primary purpose of the passage appears to be to _____.
    (A) compare the Ch'ing paintings unfavorably with those of the Ming
    (B) explain the failure of the 17th century artists to paint from nature
    (C) explain the two major schools of painting in the Ch'ing period
    (D) show how orthodox painters expressed nature through personal means
    (E) slyly suggest the inferior simplicity of Ming paintings

                                    14 ___

15. Toward the end of the Ming dynasty the "former glories of traditional painting" were _____.
    (A) fragmented   (D) forgotten
    (B) overthrown   (E) improved
    (C) despised
                                    15 ___

Reading Diagnostic Test B

Each passage below is followed by questions based on its content. Answer all questions following a passage on the basis of what is *stated* or *implied* in that passage.

In the following passage, Mark Twain engages a native Egyptian in a strange activity.

The traditional Arab proposed, in the traditional way, to run down Cheops, cross the eighth of a mile of sand intervening between it and the tall
5 pyramid of Cephren, ascend to Cephren's summit and return to us on the top of Cheops—all in nine minutes by the watch, and the whole service to be rendered for a single dollar. In the
10 first flush of irritation, I said let the Arab

and his exploits go to the mischief. But stay. The upper third of Cephren was coated with dress marble, smooth as glass. A blessed thought entered my brain. He must infallibly break his neck. Close the contract with dispatch, I said, and let him go. He started. We watched. He went bounding down the vast broadside, spring after spring, like an ibex. He grew smaller and smaller till he became a bobbing pygmy, away down toward the bottom—then disappeared. We turned and peered over the other side—forty seconds—eighty seconds—a hundred—happiness, he is dead already?—two minutes—and a quarter—"There he goes!" Too true— it was too true. He was very small, now. Gradually, but surely, he overcame the level ground. He began to spring and climb again. Up, up, up—at last he reached the smooth coating—now for it. But he clung to it with toes and fingers, like a fly. He crawled this way and that—away to the right, slanting upward—away to the left, still slanting upward—and stood at last, a black peg on the summit, and waved his pygmy scarf! Then he crept downward to the raw steps again, then picked up his agile heels and flew. We lost him presently. But presently again we saw him under us, mounting with undiminished energy. Shortly he bounded into our midst with a gallant war-whoop. Time, eight minutes, forty-one seconds. He had won. His bones were intact. It was a failure. I reflected. I said to myself, he is tired, and must grow dizzy. I will risk another dollar on him.

He started again. Made the trip again. Slipped on the smooth coating—I almost had him. But an infamous crevice saved him. He was with us once more—perfectly sound. Time, eight minutes, forty-six seconds.

I said to Dan, "Lend me a dollar—I can beat this game, yet."

Worse and worse. He won again. Time, eight minutes, forty-eight seconds. I was out of all patience now. I was desperate. Money was no longer of any consequence. I said, "Sirrah, I will give you a hundred dollars to jump off this pyramid head first. If you do not like the terms, name your bet. I scorn to stand on expenses now. I will stay right here and risk money on you as long as Dan has got a cent."

1. The purpose of the author is to _____.
   (A) horrify   (D) persuade
   (B) enlighten   (E) preach
   (C) entertain
                                      1 ___

2. Dan is probably playing the role of _____.
   (A) knowledgeable go-between
   (B) skilled interpreter
   (C) angry friend
   (D) weary athlete
   (E) unwilling banker
                                      2 ___

3. What is likely to happen next?
   (A) The climber agrees to jump off the pyramid.
   (B) The author grumpily gives up his plan to win the bet.
   (C) Dan says he hasn't enjoyed himself so much in years.
   (D) The author is arrested by police for encouraging a criminal act.
   (E) The author determines to outdo the climber by performing the feat himself.
                                      3 ___

4. The *black peg* on the summit is actually _____.
   (A) the apex of the pyramid
   (B) a pygmy scarf
   (C) an ibex
   (D) the climber
   (E) the author
                                      4 ___

5. The author of the selection can best be characterized as _____.
   (A) humorously irascible
   (B) benevolently charitable
   (C) single-mindedly serious
   (D) unrelievedly vicious
   (E) unashamedly greedy
                                      5 ___

The following passage suggests some of the difficulties in using language to interpret the real world.

Anyone who has sincerely tried to describe some genuine experience exactly, no matter how small and insignificant it may have been, to someone who
5 did not share that experience with some degree of similarity, probably became keenly aware of the discrepancy between experience and words. And yet, the problems of knowing and under-
10 standing others—and, to some extent, ourselves—centers around the relationship of language to reality or experience. The problem with using language to talk about and represent knowledge
15 of the world is that the structure of language does not correspond to the structure of reality. Although it seems obvious that a word itself is not the same as the object to which it refers, this type
20 of structural difference is commonly forgotten. Such structural differences are simple in themselves, but can be critically important to each of us in our daily lives, as well as to the scientist in
25 her or his pursuit of scientific knowledge. Simple examples of these structural differences include such facts as: 1) there is not one word for each object, 2) the same word refers to many differ-
30 ent things, and 3) many words can be used to describe any single aspect of one thing.

Another discrepancy between language and reality centers around the
35 "process nature" of reality. Language, used in a certain way, can give the impression that reality itself is static. While we cannot do without generalizations, classes, categories, and names,
40 we should realize that things change; generalizations are not always dependable or useful; classifications should not become rigid. To different degrees, we are all guilty of identifying the generali-
45 zation, category, or name with the object it describes and in doing so, we limit our own experiences and decrease our effectiveness in dealing with the real world.

50 Korzybski uses the analogy of a map's relation to the territory it depicts to describe the relation of language to reality. His point is that the usefulness of a map depends precisely on the de-
55 gree to which it corresponds to the territory. As differences arise between the map and the territory, we must quickly be able to separate the two of them and recognize that it is the map that needs
60 changing.

6. Which of the following titles best summarizes the content of the passage?
(A) Words, Not Things
(B) Limiting Our Experiences
(C) Problems of Understanding Others
(D) Differences Between Language and Reality
(E) Korzybski: Language Pioneer

6 ___

7. Which of the following pairings is most accurate?
(A) language—territory
(B) map—reality
(C) language—map
(D) map—territory
(E) territory—categories

7 ___

8. The "process nature" of reality can best be characterized as _____.
(A) static   (D) generalizing
(B) changing   (E) dependable
(C) analogous
8 ___

9. A map is valuable if _____.
(A) it corresponds to the territory
(B) its language is creative
(C) it is not static
(D) it is scientifically explainable
(E) it clarifies the discrepancies in language

9 ___

10. The author points out that generalizations _____.
(A) are avoidable
(B) describe reality accurately
(C) are constantly changing
(D) cannot be described in words
(E) are essential

10 ___

The planet itself is a sojourner in airless space, a wet ball flung across nowhere. The few objects in the universe scatter. The coherence of matter dwindles and crumbles toward stillness. I have read, and repeated, that our solar system as a whole is careering through space toward a point east of Hercules. Now I wonder: what could that possibly mean, east of Hercules? Isn't space curved? When we get "there," how will our course change, and why? Will we slide down the universe's inside arc like mud slung at a wall? Or what sort of welcoming shore is this east of Hercules? Surely we don't anchor there, and disembark, and sweep into dinner with our host. Does someone cry, "Last stop, last stop"? At any rate, east of Hercules, like east of Eden, isn't a place to call home. It is a course without direction; it is "out." And we are cast.

11. The expression "a wet ball flung across nowhere" is meant to suggest _____.
    (A) hilarity
    (B) condescension
    (C) insignificance
    (D) purpose
    (E) courage

    11 ___

12. The author's appraisal of the future of earth is _____.
    (A) confident   (D) angry
    (B) sad   (E) imitative
    (C) hopeful
                                    12 ___

13. As used in the selection, *careering* means _____.
    (A) vibrating   (D) sliding
    (B) speeding   (E) anticipating
    (C) pulsating
                                    13 ___

14. According to the writer of this passage, the earth _____.
    (A) has destination and a mission in space
    (B) is inextricably linked with every object in the universe
    (C) will slide down the universe's inside arc
    (D) is a homeless wanderer in space
    (E) will come to rest east of Hercules

                                    14 ___

15. The tone of the passage can best be described as _____.
    (A) perky and optimistic
    (B) coldly logical
    (C) assured and happy
    (D) vigorously antiscientific
    (E) wryly humorous

                                    15 ___

Division C
Facsimile Tests

A Strategy for the Facsimile Tests

■ You have come a long way and are ready for the moment of truth. The tests that follow approximate the SAT you will be taking, but they are practice tests only.

■ Review the Introduction, pages 1–8.

■ Before you begin, be sure you have the appropriate amount of time to spend on the test. Try to approximate test conditions as much as possible.

■ Have a watch with you to check your timing. Don't spend too much time on any one question. If you waste time on a question, you may not reach questions that are easy for you. If you have trouble with a question, put a check mark next to it so that you can find it quickly again, and go right on. If you have time later, go back and try again.

■ Read the questions carefully. Following directions is an important part of the test.

■ If you are unsure of an answer, don't panic. You won't know all the answers, but do the best you can. By now you have discovered that you have unexpected resources if you stay calm and build upon what you already know.

■ You will find complete explanations for the correct answers for Facsimile Tests 1, 2, and 3 beginning on page 441. These answers will help you analyze your responses. The page reference before each question tells you where to look in this book for help.

Organization

■ The new SAT is divided into six sections. Sections 1, 3, and 5 are devoted to the verbal questions: sentence completions, analogies, and reading questions. Sections 2, 4, and 6 are devoted to mathematics. The SAT section numbers are retained in the five facsimile tests that follow, but you must remember that Sections 2, 4, and 6 would be included in the full tests.

Directions

■ In general, you will find typical SAT directions in the Facsimile Tests. However, the final question, Section 5, has a slightly different form on the SAT, as explained on page 8.

A Final Word on the Reading Passages

Keep in mind that a bulletin of the College Board says, "A much smaller number of questions will assess students' literal understanding of significant information in the text." The basic, bread-and-butter skills are still, and always will be, important, for they help with more challenging questions. The SAT assumes that you have these skills.

The bulletin also declares, "Most questions based on the reading selections will be analytical and evaluative, measuring students' ability to make inferences, to relate parts of the text to each other or to the whole; to follow the logic of an argument; to synthesize meaning; to identify the author's purpose, attitude, or tone, etc."

The four reading selections will have 6–13 questions apiece. "One of the selections will consist of a *pair* of related passages, the second of which will oppose, support, or in some other way complement the point of view expressed in the first. Some of the questions on the paired passages will assess students' ability to compare or contrast the two passages, to use information from one to interpret information in the other, and to identify assumptions they share or pivotal differences between them."

The test will draw upon four general categories: narratives, humanities, natural sciences, and social sciences. All of these categories are well represented in the teaching text (pages 183–348). Each Facsimile Test (353–439) contains a passage from each category, one of which is a paired passage. There is practice aplenty in the pages that follow.

Facsimile Test 1

Section 1   **1**

Time-30 Minutes—For each question in this section, select the best answer
  30 Questions   from among the choices given.

Each sentence below has one or two blanks, each blank indicating that
something has been omitted. Beneath the sentence are five lettered words
or sets of words labeled A through E. Choose the word or set of words that
best fits the meaning of the sentence as a whole.

EXAMPLE

Although its publicity has been _____,
the film itself is intelligent, well-acted,
handsomely produced, and altogether _____.

(A) tasteless . . respectable
(B) extensive . . moderate
(C) sophisticated . . spectacular
(D) risqué . . crude
(E) perfect . . spectacular

A

(pages 35–38)

1. Denny's _____ behavior may lead
him from the conventional to
the _____ in a few brief moments.
(A) erratic . . outrageous
(B) smooth . . uninspired
(C) snobbish . . orthodox
(D) atrocious . . solicitous
(E) consistent . . theatrical

1 __

(pages 24–27)

2. Some endangered creatures may sur-
vive by transfer of populations, _____
species in areas where they no longer
occur.
(A) commemorating
(B) reestablishing
(C) studying
(D) uniting
(E) popularizing

2 __

(pages 31–35)

3. The arbitrator remained _____ de-
spite efforts of the press to anticipate
his decision.
(A) sluggish
(B) prejudiced
(C) irritated
(D) insensitive
(E) noncommittal

3 __

(pages 14–20)

4. If a patient's hospital room has a win-
dow overlooking a scenic stand of
trees, _____ tends to be _____.
(A) boredom . . manifest
(B) interest . . dispersed
(C) convalescence . . inflexible
(D) recuperation . . accelerated
(E) mobility . . minimal

4 __

(pages 24–27)

5. Newborn infants are little Buddhas, ob-
serving life with _____ glances and
impressive _____.
(A) inattentive . . comprehension
(B) compassionate . . condescension
(C) penetrating . . equanimity
(D) competent . . indifference
(E) stolen . . magnanimity

5 __

(pages 14–20, 84)

6. The poet Emily Dickinson was such a(n) _____ that she would not meet her guests but speak to them from another room.
   (A) raconteur
   (B) ogre
   (C) chatterbox
   (D) recluse
   (E) observer

6 ___

(pages 31–35)

7. After the _____ review of his novel *Jude the Obscure,* Thomas Hardy gave up writing novels and turned to poetry for the rest of his life.
   (A) elaborate
   (B) laudatory
   (C) mandatory
   (D) derogatory
   (E) illusory

7 ___

(pages 14–20)

8. It is with a sense of _____ that Henry Jekyll began to realize that his evil "twin," Edward Hyde, was beginning to take control of his life.
   (A) ennui
   (B) elation
   (C) foreboding
   (D) approbation
   (E) recollection

8 ___

(pages 14–20, 94)

9. The chance that a man and his wife may have the same first name is _____; yet the Marquis de Lafayette and his wife did have the same first name: *Marie*.
   (A) minuscule
   (B) predetermined
   (C) irregular
   (D) trite
   (E) unpopular

9 ___

Each question below consists of a related pair of words followed by five lettered pairs of words labeled A through E. Select the lettered pair that *best* expresses a relationship similar to that expressed in the original pair.

+-----------------------------------+
| **EXAMPLE** |
| YAWN : BOREDOM :: |
| (A) anger : madness |
| (B) dream : sleep |
| (C) smile : amusement |
| (D) face : expression |
| (E) impatience : rebellion |
| |
| C |
+-----------------------------------+

(pages 154, 157)

10. CHISEL : CARPENTRY ::
    (A) chain : bicycle
    (B) mainsail : schooner
    (C) scale : weight
    (D) blowtorch : welding
    (E) music : tuning fork

10 ___

(pages 165–166, 170)

11. INFLUENCE : DOMINATION ::
    (A) worship : admiration
    (B) budget : plan
    (C) subscriber : underwriter
    (D) blossom : flower
    (E) cooperation : sabotage

11 ___

(pages 156, 157)

12. MANUSCRIPT : EDIT ::
    (A) lemonade : consume
    (B) evidence : destroy
    (C) account : audit
    (D) peruse : newspaper
    (E) dress : injury

12 ___

(page 171)

13. SWAN : CYGNET ::
    (A) fawn : deer
    (B) goose : gosling
    (C) goose : gander
    (D) sheep : kid
    (E) antelope : cub

13 ___

ENGLISH FOR THE COLLEGE BOARDS

(pages 147–149)
14. EXCESS : SCANT ::
    (A) actor : incompetent
    (B) true : hallucination
    (C) deterioration : worse
    (D) delegation : authorized
    (E) delirium : logical

(pages 161–162, 163)
15. THERAPIST : REHABILITATION ::
    (A) direction : pilot
    (B) physicist : atom
    (C) lumberjack : cabinetmaking
    (D) pharmacist : diagnosis
    (E) jester : entertainment

14 ___   15 ___

Each passage below is followed by questions based on its content. Answer the questions following each passage on the basis of what is <u>stated</u> or <u>implied</u> in that passage and in any introductory material that may be provided.

A brief story can suggest, in a few lines, a setting, character interrelationships, and a simple plot.

Marge . . . Day's work is an education! Well, I mean workin' in different homes you learn much more than if you was steady in one place. . . . I tell you, it really keeps your mind sharp tryin' to watch for what folks will put over on you.

5   What? . . . No, Marge, I do not want to help shell no beans, but I'd be more than glad to stay and have supper with you, and I'll wash the dishes after. Is that all right? . . .

Who put anything over on who? . . . Oh yes! It's like this. . . . I been working for Mrs. E . . . one day a week for several months and I
10   notice that she has some peculiar ways. Well, there was only one thing that really bothered me and that was her pocketbook habit. . . . No, not those little novels. . . . I mean her purse—her handbag.

Marge, she's got a big old pocketbook with two long straps on it . . . and whenever I'd go there, she'd be propped up in a chair with her
15   handbag double wrapped tight around her wrist, and from room to room she'd roam with that purse hugged to her bosom . . . yes, girl! This happens every time! No, there's nobody there but me and her. . . . Marge, I couldn't say nothin' to her! It's her purse, ain't it? She can hold onto it if she wants to!

20   I held my peace for months, tryin' to figure out how I'd make my point. . . . Well, bless Bess! Today was the day! . . . Please, Marge, keep shellin' the beans so we can eat! I know you're listenin', but you listen with your ears, not your hands. . . . Well, anyway, I was almost ready to go home when she steps in the room hangin' onto her bag as
25   usual and says, "Mildred, will you ask the super to come up and fix the kitchen faucet?" "Yes, Mrs. E . . ." I says, "as soon as I leave." "Oh, no," she says, "he may be gone by then. Please go now." "All right," I says, and out the door I went, still wearin' my Hoover apron.

I just went down the hall and stood there a few minutes . . . and
30   then I rushed back to the door and knocked on it as hard and frantic as I could. She flung open the door sayin', "What's the matter? Did you see the super?" . . . "No," I says, gaspin' hard for breath, "I was almost downstairs when I remembered . . . I left my pocketbook!"

With that I dashed in, grabbed my purse and then went down to get
35 the super! Later, when I was leavin' she says real timid-like, "Mildred,
I hope that you don't think I distrust you because . . ." I cut her off
real quick. . . . "That's all right, Mrs. E . . . , I understand, 'Cause if
I paid anybody as little as you pay me, I'd hold my pocketbook too!"
Marge, you fool . . . lookout! . . . You gonna drop the beans on the
40 floor!

(pages 197–199)

16. The "pocketbook habit" (line 11) both-
ered the narrator because it demon-
strated
(A) mean-spirited cruelty
(B) a sick sense of humor
(C) potential senility
(D) bitter anger
(E) a lack of trust

16 ___

(pages 247–251)

17. Marge probably asked all the following
questions EXCEPT _____.
(A) "Would you shell the beans?"
(B) "Would you have supper with
me?"
(C) "Does she read a lot?"
(D) "Are you fond of her?"
(E) "Is there anyone else there be-
sides you?"

17 ___

(pages 197–199)

18. When the narrator said, "You listen
with your ears, not your hands,"
she _____.
(A) probably broke into a loud laugh
(B) was telling Marge to keep working
(C) suggested Marge's laziness
(D) paused for a minute to gather her
thoughts
(E) was referring directly to Mrs. E

18 ___

(pages 200–202)

19. The narrator's final comment to Mrs.
E is an example of _____.
(A) unjustified cruelty
(B) an expression of despair
(C) an undignified plea
(D) a bitter lament
(E) an appropriate retort

19 ___

(pages 265–270)

20. Throughout, the author stresses
Mildred's _____.
(A) deep-seated anger
(B) sense of dignity
(C) love of her job
(D) fondness for food
(E) lack of understanding

20 ___

(pages 271–279)

21. When the narrator talks about knock-
ing "hard and frantic," _____.
(A) it reveals an inner upset
(B) she's putting on an act
(C) she hopes to catch Mrs. E before
she leaves
(D) she hopes to get the super's at-
tention
(E) she's afraid she'll be too late for
the super

21 ___

As children, we soon discover how things work. Fire burns. A well-hit
tennis ball zips across the net. In winter, the days are shorter and colder
than in the summer. But of all these perceptions we form a picture of the
world, a *paradigm* as the philosopher Thomas Kuhn has said. If we discovered that our paradigm didn't work, we'd be upset. In the following selection,
a brilliant scientist, Lynn Margulis, challenges familiar scientific paradigms.

ENGLISH FOR THE COLLEGE BOARDS

Despite her success, Margulis' work remains controversial. Hers is not the kind of work with which the scientific community can simply agree to disagree. "It's a question of changing your religion," she says. Academia rewards its brightest stars with a specially funded teaching position called a named chair. A few years ago, Margulis was on the verge of being appointed to a named chair at a major university but was not offered the position, though the possibility still remains. The antagonism stems, in part, from Margulis' collaboration with British chemist James Lovelock on Gaia, the hypothesis that the Earth acts as a self-regulating, self-maintaining system (*Phenomena,* May 1988). Gaia's most vocal supporters are ecoactivists, church groups, and science-fiction writers. To some establishment scientists, these countercultural associations make the ideas behind Gaia suspect. Ironically, Margulis is hard on Gaia's popular supporters. "Lynn is ferocious about going after mysticism," says Stewart Brand, founder of the *Whole Earth Catalog.* "New Age types are drawn to her and then she busts them high, low, and center for being softheaded."

In a sense, Margulis challenges the American myth of the rugged individual—alone, self-contained and able to survive. "Our concept of the individual is totally warped," she says. "All of us are walking communities of microbes. Plants are sedentary communities. Every plant and animal on Earth today is a symbiont, living in close contact with others."

Consider one species of desert termite. Living in its hindgut are millions of single-celled, lemon-shaped organisms called *Trichonympha ampla.* Attached to the surface of one *T. ampla* live thousands of whip-like bacteria known as spirochetes. Inside live still other kinds of bacteria. If not for these microbial symbionts (in some wood-eating insects, the symbionts are too numerous to count), the termite, unable to digest wood, would starve.

But, the termite itself is only one element in a planetary set of interlocking, mutual interactions—which Lovelock's neighbor, novelist William Golding, dubbed Gaia, for the Greek goddess of the Earth. After digesting wood, the termite expels the gas methane into the air. (In fact, the world's species of termites, cows, elephants and other animals harboring methane-producing bacteria account for a significant portion of Earth's atmospheric methane.) Methane performs the vital task of regulating the amount of oxygen in Earth's atmosphere. If there were too much oxygen, fires would burn continuously; too little, and animals, plants and many other live beings would suffocate. Earth's atmospheric oxygen is maintained, altered and regulated by the breathing activities of living creatures, such as those of the methane-makers in the microcosmos. Life does not passively "adapt." Rather, it actively, though "unknowingly," modifies its own environment.

When NASA sponsored a search for life on Mars, in the early 1970s, Lovelock looked for ways that life might have modified the Martian atmosphere. Finding no particular modification attributable to microbes or any other form of life, he and Margulis predicted that the Viking

probe would find a dead Mars. They turned out to be right. "Gaia is
50 more a point of view than a theory," says Margulis. "It is a manifestation
of the organization of the planet."

That organization resembles those hollow Russian dolls that nest one
inside another. "For example, some bacteria in the hindgut of a termite
cannot survive outside that microbial community," explains Gail
55 Fleischaker, Boston University philosopher of science and a former
graduate student of Margulis'. "The community of termites, in turn,
requires a larger ecological nest. And so it expands. You will never find
life in isolation. Life, if it exists at all, is globe-covering."

Although Margulis provided the "biological ammunition" for Gaia
60 and remains its staunch advocate, she does little work on it directly.
"I've concentrated all my life on the cell," she says. The ideas that she
has championed were once "too fantastic for mention in polite biological
society," as one scientific observer described them in the 1920s. As
recently as 20 years ago, these ideas were so much at odds with the
65 established point of view that, according to another observer, they
"could not be discussed at respectable scientific meetings." Although
aspects of the symbiotic theory of cell evolution still provoke hostility,
the theory is now taught to high school students. "This quiet revolution
in microbiological thought is primarily due to the insight and enthusiasm
70 of Lynn Margulis," states Yale ecologist G. Evelyn Hutchinson. "Hers
is one of the most constructively speculative minds, immensely learned,
highly imaginative, and occasionally a little naughty."

(pages 210–213)

22. The author believes that Lynn Margulis _____.
    (A) has some good ideas and many wrong ones
    (B) is opposed to the views of James Lovelock
    (C) was wrong about life on Mars
    (D) spends too much time on the microcosm
    (E) was not treated fairly by a university

22 ___

(pages 24–27, 103–116)

23. In line 22, "symbiont" means _____.
    (A) a consumer of methane
    (B) an interdependent organism
    (C) an organism that can live without oxygen
    (D) a self-contained organism
    (E) a microbiologist

23 ___

(pages 184–186)

24. According to Margulis, life has survived on earth because of _____.
    (A) the survival of the fittest
    (B) modified competition
    (C) adaptations to climate
    (D) interlocking associations
    (E) pure chance

24 ___

(pages 192–197)

25. A way of expressing Margulis's viewpoint is _____.
    (A) "We're all in this together."
    (B) "Self-interest is the highest good."
    (C) "Throughout nature, the female is the stronger sex."
    (D) "Fair-weather friends are not true friends."
    (E) "Every species has a chance to become dominant."

25 ___

(pages 197–199)
26. Margulis's attitude toward "New Age Types" is one of _____.
   (A) warm enthusiasm
   (B) complete indifference
   (C) strong disapproval
   (D) friendly assistance
   (E) genuine rapport

   26 ___

(pages 247–251)
27. "The American myth of the rugged individual" _____.
   (A) has been blasted by Hollywood
   (B) is the major tenet of Margulis's philosophy
   (C) is counter to the views of Lynn Margulis
   (D) has sparked Margulis's career
   (E) is a helpful guide to living

   27 ___

(pages 210–213)
28. The quotation "You will never find life in isolation" was made by _____.
   (A) James Lovelock
   (B) William Golding
   (C) Lynn Margulis
   (D) Gail Fleischaker
   (E) G. Evelyn Hutchinson

   28 ___

(pages 210–213)
29. To find the answer to question 28, the best technique is to _____.
   (A) carefully reread each paragraph
   (B) skim for the quotation
   (C) stop for each name mentioned and check for the quotation
   (D) try to think which person would have been likely to use the quotation
   (E) check just the topic sentence of each paragraph

   29 ___

(pages 192–197)
30. The author of the article makes the point that _____.
   (A) James Lovelock is wrong, even though Margulis works with him
   (B) scientific research into the cell is a tedious process
   (C) methane plays a minor role in the health of the planet
   (D) the rejected theory of yesterday may be accepted today
   (E) true genius is recognized almost immediately

   30 ___

Section 3

3 3 3

Time-30 Minutes—For each question in this section, select the best answer.
35 Questions

Each sentence below has one or two blanks, each blank indicating that something has been omitted. Beneath the sentence are five lettered words or sets of words labeled A through E. Choose the word or set of words that *best* fits the meaning of the sentence as a whole.

(pages 31–35)
1. In his autobiography Simenon does not spare himself, recounting his _____ failures as well as his many _____ successes.
(A) incredible . . undeserved
(B) tolerable . . conspicuous
(C) ludicrous . . peevish
(D) personal . . professional
(E) cinematic . . ecclesiastical

1 ___

(pages 35–38)
2. As the favorable election results poured from the television screen, the candidate went from quiet _____ to expressive _____.
(A) uneasiness . . contentment
(B) curiosity . . concern
(C) statement . . exaggeration
(D) confusion . . preeminence
(E) pleasure . . jubilation

2 ___

(pages 14–20)
3. In the _____ view of some critics, the only _____ goal of television is not to inform or even entertain but to sell goods.
(A) positive . . overlooked
(B) jaundiced . . unrealized
(C) cynical . . serious
(D) tiresome . . illusory
(E) blatant . . unacknowledged

3 ___

(pages 31–35)
4. Although some ecosystems are _____ and able to adjust, others are too _____ to survive much tampering.
(A) dependable . . accommodating
(B) resilient . . fragile
(C) prodigal . . incompetent
(D) inflammable . . arid
(E) inexhaustible . . self-contained

4 ___

(pages 14–20)
5. Formerly accepted _____ of the proper roles of men and women have _____ the fate of the mastodon and the sabre-toothed tiger.
(A) stereotypes . . experienced
(B) assignments . . retold
(C) depictions . . broadcast
(D) critiques . . elucidated
(E) reprimands . . analyzed

5 ___

(pages 24–27, 137)
6. The word *chortle* was devised by Lewis Carroll, _____ the two words *chuckle* and *snort*.
(A) destroying   (D) dissecting
(B) accepting   (E) telescoping
(C) transporting

6 ___

(pages 24–27)
7. The Tower of London has had a(n) _____ career, for it has served as a mint, a prison, the royal palace, an observatory, and the home of the British Crown jewels.
(A) humdrum   (D) checkered
(B) irksome   (E) prophetic
(C) prosaic

7 ___

(pages 14–20)
8. An inspirational book about the _____ of Marco Polo accompanied Christopher Columbus on his first voyage to the New World.
(A) eccentricities   (D) odyssey
(B) dogma   (E) proficiency
(C) spleen

8 ___

360

(pages 20–23)
9. *Charlotte Temple,* by America's first best-selling woman novelist Susanna Rowson, may have had wooden characters and a(n) _____ plot, but it went through 200 editions.
   (A) superlative
   (B) original
   (C) hackneyed
   (D) scintillating
   (E) coherent

9 ___

(pages 14–20)
10. In 1844, New York policemen staged a strike against the wearing of blue uniforms, considered by the men to be a symbol of _____.
    (A) perturbation
    (B) squalor
    (C) servitude
    (D) ambiguity
    (E) decorum

10 ___

Each question below consists of a related pair of words, followed by five lettered pairs of words labeled A through E. Select the lettered pair that *best* expresses a relationship similar to that expressed in the original pair.

EXAMPLE

YAWN : BOREDOM ::
   (A) dream : sleep
   (B) anger : madness
   (C) smile : amusement
   (D) face : expression
   (E) impatience : rebellion

C

(pages 158–159, 163)
11. DISCIPLE : FOLLOWS ::
    (A) amphibian : slides
    (B) cries : infant
    (C) candidate : vote
    (D) courier : writes
    (E) trustee : administers

11 ___

(pages 150–151, 153)
12. MOUTHPIECE : OBOE ::
    (A) clock : cape
    (B) cannon : ammunition
    (C) eyepiece : telescope
    (D) warp : woof
    (E) drill : bit

12 ___

(pages 155–157)
13. PAMPHLET : TOME ::
    (A) turnip : radish
    (B) oration : election
    (C) butterfly : caterpillar
    (D) hill : mountain
    (E) shout : cry

13 ___

(pages 164–165, 170)
14. HIBERNATION : INACTIVITY ::
    (A) disorder : entropy
    (B) devastation : ruin
    (C) deterioration : growth
    (D) embargo : trade
    (E) bafflement : tardiness

14 ___

(pages 168–170)
15. PATHOLOGY : SICKNESS ::
    (A) paleontology : fossils
    (B) psychology : education
    (C) archaeology : plant life
    (D) geology : gasoline
    (E) psychiatry : medicine

15 ___

(pages 162, 163)
16. ARTIST : PALETTE ::
    (A) conductor : baton
    (B) saber : fencer
    (C) soldier : boot
    (D) typewriter : stenographer
    (E) nurseryman : cradle

16 ___

(pages 166–168, 170)
17. STEAK : BROIL ::
    (A) baste : turkey
    (B) lawn : mow
    (C) book : overlook
    (D) roll : call
    (E) neurotic : calm

17 ___

(pages 152, 153)
18. CASKET : JEWEL ::
  (A) doctrine : philosophy
  (B) page : cover
  (C) vase : flower
  (D) water : kettle
  (E) receptacle : ticket

18 ___

(pages 155–156, 157)
19. FABLE : STORY ::
  (A) factor : teacher
  (B) sale : fair
  (C) charter : mortgage
  (D) senator : legislator
  (E) wholesaler : retailer

19 ___

(pages 159–160, 163)
20. NEUTRALITY : MEDIATOR ::
  (A) humor : physician
  (B) fairness : pitcher
  (C) hero : courage
  (D) horse : patience
  (E) skill : athlete

20 ___

(pages 151–152, 153)
21. EXPOSURE : CHILL ::
  (A) impertinence : flippancy
  (B) obstruction : frustration
  (C) abandonment : solidarity
  (D) thrift : poverty
  (E) frivolity : irritability

21 ___

(pages 160–161, 163)
22. LIBRETTIST : OPERA ::
  (A) circus : clown
  (B) angler : regatta
  (C) mountaineer : rock face
  (D) ornithologist : aquarium
  (E) museum : curator

22 ___

(pages 149–151, 153)
23. ELUDE : CUNNING ::
  (A) embezzle : upright
  (B) discriminating : criticize
  (C) beautify : wealthy
  (D) fumble : clumsy
  (E) stubborn : endure

23 ___

The passage below is followed by questions on its content. Answer the questions on the basis of what is <u>stated</u> or <u>implied</u> in the passage and in any introductory material that may be provided.

The following passage talks about a special aspect of language, the use of *is* and other linking verbs. It suggests a more disciplined approach to communication.

In 1923, the philosopher George Santayana wrote, "The little word *is* has its tragedies. It names and identifies different things with the greatest innocence; and yet no two are ever identical, and if therein lies the charm of wedding them and calling them one, therein, too, lies the
5 danger."
   Surprisingly, Santayana uses the word *are* in the passage above, even as he decried the use of such linking verbs!
   Philosophers have been concerned with *is* since the 17th century. Why? Why denounce this most useful word, a common element in seri-
10 ous essays as well as in everyday conversation? How can anyone object to its use?
   Words like *is* suggest deceptive couplings. A moment's consideration can detect the vast difference between "Inez is a student" and "Inez is insufferably conceited." Both use the same verb, but the second doesn't
15 express the same relationship as the first. Irresponsible use of *is* can

damage friendships, mislead correspondents, and cause havoc with communication.

Students of general semantics concern themselves with language in action. Language attempts to interpret the "real world," but reality resists easy capture in words. Calling Inez *conceited* does an injustice to her, for it conceals the fact that someone's subjective judgment masquerades as objective truth.

The preceding two examples of the use of *is* barely scratch the surface. Many such statements defy reasoning while assuming the mask of reason. An expression like "As is well known" assumes a dubious truth. The word *is* makes everything neat and orderly, but the real world resists such tidiness.

In recent years, semanticists have concerned themselves with a new and challenging idea. In the late 1940s, D. David Bourland, Jr., decided to eliminate all forms of *is* in his own writing. He called his writing system "E-Prime." From that time on, he wrote everything in E-Prime, but for a while no one noticed. In 1965, he went public with his idea in an article written for *General Semantics Bulletin*. Since then, other semanticists have supported the cause.

Complete agreement about the use of E-Prime has eluded language philosophers. Some writers take a strict position. They eliminate *is* and its relatives in all forms. They even try to eliminate absolute words like *always* and *never*. Others take a more lenient position, allowing the *is* of existence, helping verbs in passives and *is*es of identity, like "Iron is a mineral."

E-Prime tends to make writing more objective, though not entirely so. E-Prime reflects a subjective judgment in "Juliana sang poorly," but it avoids subjective judgments like "Juliana is a busybody."

Does a listener or reader recognize E-Prime as something strange and exotic? Does the elimination of verbs like *is, was,* and *seem* create a noticeable gap? Perhaps E-Prime doesn't call attention to itself. It retains normal rhythm and expressions. It does require a great deal of discipline, particularly for those trying it for the first time. Despite the appeal, however, E-Prime has a formidable adversary: Convenience. It will probably not eliminate linking verbs from the language. But occasionally trying to write and speak in E-Prime sharpens perceptions and gives users additional awareness of the ways in which language can mislead us.

Except for quoted examples, this passage provides an example of E-Prime. Did you notice?

(pages 31–35)
24. In line 7, "decried" means _____.
    (A) explained
    (B) promoted
    (C) evaluated
    (D) condemned
    (E) uncovered

    24 ___

(pages 230–233)
25. The author quotes Santayana
    to _____.
    (A) express the basic problem attacked
        by E-Prime
    (B) present a point of view later dis-
        credited
    (C) provide a sample of a paragraph
        written in E-Prime
    (D) point out that Santayana would dis-
        agree with Bourland
    (E) discredit the widespread practice
        of E-Prime

    25 ___

(pages 46–50)
26. The phrase *cause havoc with communi-
    cation* suggests _____.
    (A) sabotage
    (B) deception
    (C) explanation
    (D) hatred
    (E) vitality

    26 ___

(pages 247–251)
27. All the following sentences are written
    in E-Prime EXCEPT _____.
    (A) Some semanticists have reserva-
        tions about E-Prime.
    (B) E-Prime had its beginnings in the
        1940s.
    (C) George Santayana possibly used a
        linking verb unconsciously.
    (D) E-Prime is an excellent new tech-
        nique for writing clearly.
    (E) General semantics concentrates on
        language in action.

    27 ___

(pages 197–199)
28. In line 19, "real world" is put in quota-
    tion marks because _____.
    (A) George Santayana referred to it in
        his paragraph
    (B) the author is poking gentle fun at
        semanticists
    (C) no one is sure just what the real
        world is
    (D) semanticists are self-promoting in
        their description of reality
    (E) E-Prime is further from reality
        than is traditional communication

    28 ___

(pages 253–257)
29. E-Prime doesn't call attention to itself
    because _____.
    (A) listeners don't pay attention
    (B) Bourland has always been modest
        about his creation
    (C) the majority of speakers intention-
        ally use E-Prime for greater clarity
    (D) the sentence structure of E-Prime
        is that of traditional communi-
        cation
    (E) most television shows are boring
        and forgettable

    29 ___

(pages 20–23)
30. In line 51, "perceptions"
    means _____.
    (A) insights
    (B) prejudices
    (C) language skills
    (D) conversations
    (E) sympathies

    30 ___

(pages 233–237)
31. The author's style may best be charac-
    terized as _____.
    (A) self-conscious and artificial
    (B) light and informative
    (C) humorous and frivolous
    (D) critical and unfavorable
    (E) dull and repetitious

    31 ___

(pages 247–251)
32. To a student of E-Prime, the LEAST objectionable of the following sentences would probably be _____.
    (A) Juanita is self-sufficient and intelligent
    (B) Juanita seems modest
    (C) Juanita is captain of the field-hockey team
    (D) Juanita was irritable yesterday
    (E) Juanita is a poor leader but a good player

    32 ___

(pages 51–55)
33. The strict interpretation of E-Prime would eliminate a metaphor like _____.
    (A) In his sly maneuvering, Elliot resembles a snake
    (B) Margot was president of the junior class last year
    (C) On the basketball court, Maria is a tiger
    (D) Dogs give love without expecting anything in return
    (E) The Super Bowl is always a lavish spectacle

    33 ___

(pages 197–199)
34. Some users of E-Prime avoid using words like *always* and *never* because _____.
    (A) these words inevitably destroy sentence rhythms
    (B) life is open-ended and the next moment may provide exceptions
    (C) they want to show how clever they can be
    (D) Santayana implies that these words are dangerous
    (E) meanings of the two words cancel each other out

    34 ___

(pages 46–50)
35. An example of a subjective statement is _____.
    (A) Jennifer completed her first marathon last spring
    (B) E-Prime was introduced by D. David Bourland, Jr.
    (C) In winter, the United States imports fresh fruits from Chile
    (D) Chad spoke boringly about his prowess on the football field
    (E) Hurricane Andrew struck Homestead, just south of Miami

    35 ___

Section 5   5 5 5 5 5

Time-15 Minutes—For each question in this section, select the best answer
  13 Questions   from among the choices given.

The two passages below are followed by questions based on their content and on the relationship between the two passages. Answer the questions on the basis of what is <u>stated</u> or <u>implied</u> in the passages and in any introductory material that may be provided.

The following passages celebrate two brilliant historical periods centuries apart. The two periods share many resemblances.

PASSAGE 1

There have been times in the history of man when the earth seems suddenly to have grown warmer or more radioactive . . . I don't put that forward as a scientific proposition, but the fact remains that three or four times in history man has made a leap forward that would have been
5 unthinkable under ordinary evolutionary conditions. One such time was about the year 3000 B.C., when quite suddenly civilization appeared, not only in Egypt and Mesopotamia but in the Indus valley; another was in the late sixth century B.C., when there was not only the miracle of Ionia and Greece—philosophy, science, art, poetry, all reaching a
10 point that wasn't reached again for 2000 years—but also in India a spiritual enlightment that has perhaps never been equalled. Another was round about the year 1100. It seems to have affected the whole world; but its strongest and most dramatic effect was in Western Europe—where it was most needed. It was like a Russian spring. In every branch of
15 life—action, philosophy, organization, technology—there was an extraordinary outpouring of energy, an intensification of existence. Popes, emperors, kings, bishops, saints, scholars, philosophers were all larger than life, and the incidents of history—Henry II at Canossa, Pope Urban announcing the First Crusade, Heloise and Abelard, the martyrdom of
20 St. Thomas à Becket—are great heroic dramas, or symbolic acts, that still stir our hearts.

The evidence of this heroic energy, this confidence, this strength of will and intellect, is still visible to us. In spite of all our mechanical aids and the inflated scale of modern materialism, Durham Cathedral remains
25 a formidable construction, and the east end of Canterbury still looks very large and very complex. And these great orderly mountains of stone at first rose out of a small cluster of wooden houses; everyone with the least historical imagination has thought of that. But what people don't always realize is that it all happened quite suddenly—in a single lifetime.
30 An even more astonishing change took place in sculpture. Tournus is one of the very few churches of any size to have survived from before the dreaded year 1000, and the architecture is rather grand in a primitive way. But its sculpture is miserably crude, without even the vitality of barbarism. Only fifty years later sculpture has the style and rhythmic
35 assurance of the greatest epochs of art. The skill and dramatic invention that had been confined to small portable objects—goldsmith work or ivory carving—suddenly appear on a monumental scale.

PASSAGE 2

The men who had made Florence the richest city in Europe, the bankers and wool-merchants, the pious realists, lived in grim defensive houses
40 strong enough to withstand party feuds and popular riots. They don't foreshadow in any way the extraordinary episode in the history of civilization known as the Renaissance. There seems to be no reason why suddenly out of the dark, narrow streets there arose these light, sunny arcades with their round arches 'running races in their mirth' under
45 their straight cornices. By their rhythms and proportions and their open, welcoming character they totally contradict the dark Gothic style that preceded, and, to some extent, still surrounds them. What has happened? The answer is contained in one sentence by the Greek philosopher Protagoras, 'Man is the measure of all things'. The Pazzi Chapel,
50 built by the great Florentine Brunellesco in about 1430, is in a style that has been called the architecture of humanism. His friend and fellow-architect, Leon Battista Alberti, addressed man in these words: 'To you is given a body more graceful than other animals, to you power of apt and various movements, to you most sharp and delicate senses, to you
55 wit, reason, memory like an immortal god.' Well, it is certainly incorrect to say that we are more graceful than other animals, and we don't feel much like immortal gods at the moment. But in 1400 the Florentines did. There is no better instance of how a burst of civilization depends on confidence than the Florentine state of mind in the early fifteenth
60 century. For thirty years the fortunes of the republic, which in a material sense had declined, were directed by a group of the most intelligent individuals who have ever been elected to power by a democratic government. From Salutati onwards the Florentine chancellors were scholars, believers in the *studia humanitatis,* in which learning could be used
65 to achieve a happy life, believers in the application of free intelligence to public affairs, and believers, above all, in Florence.

(pages 184–186)
1. When the author of Passage 1 contemplates the year 1100, he is _____.
   (A) convinced that a moderation in climate had produced a sensational change
   (B) overcome by awe at the unexpected achievements of the period
   (C) certain that perhaps only half a dozen great leaders brought on the surprising upheavals
   (D) more impressed by the achievements in drama than in architecture
   (E) convinced that such a spectacular experience happens only once a century

(pages 210–213)
2. The author makes the point that these remarkable leaps forward were _____.
   (A) cyclical in nature
   (B) anticipated by outstanding philosophers
   (C) more widespread than local
   (D) strong in philosophy, weak in art
   (E) criticized by large clusters of the population

2 ___

1 ___

(pages 205–208)

3. The birth date of Buddha is estimated to be about 563 B.C. The birth date of Lao-tzu is estimated to be about 604 B.C. The author would agree that these are _____.
   (A) linked with "the miracle of Ionia and Greece"
   (B) almost supernatural coincidences
   (C) not uncommon in the history of mankind
   (D) sources of the civilization that arose in the Indus Valley
   (E) dates with little significance for the major point of the passage

3 ___

(pages 184–186)

4. To call historical personages "larger than life" is to _____.
   (A) suggest, through irony, their essential weaknesses
   (B) wonder at the secret of their incredible longevity
   (C) highlight the spiritual nature of their achievements
   (D) be amazed that persons of average ability were raised to such heights
   (E) emphasize the dramatic nature of their lives and achievements

4 ___

(pages 210–213)

5. Durham Cathedral and the east end of Canterbury are singled out as _____.
   (A) prime examples of the flourishing of art that took place in a brief period
   (B) cathedrals of great architectural skill but poor sculpture
   (C) mirror images of the church at Tournus
   (D) cathedrals that stack up poorly against the churches that preceded them
   (E) cathedrals from which Pope Urban announced the First Crusade

5 ___

(pages 197–199)

6. We may assume that fine goldsmith work and ivory carving were _____.
   (A) neglected after 1100
   (B) considered during the Middle Ages to be more important than architecture
   (C) practiced before 1100
   (D) not essentially products of "skill and dramatic invention"
   (E) artworks dominated by vitality of barbarism

6 ___

(pages 31–35)

7. In line 37, "monumental" most nearly means _____.
   (A) made of stone
   (B) surprising and unexpected
   (C) continuing on a smaller scale
   (D) religious and spiritual
   (E) massive and enduring

7 ___

(pages 230–233)

8. The opening sentence of Passage 2 is intended to _____.
   (A) give a picture of Florence during the Renaissance
   (B) belittle the achievement of the money grubbers
   (C) explain why the Renaissance began in Florence
   (D) contrast with the years after 1400
   (E) exemplify the philosophy of the Greek philosopher Pythagoras

8 ___

(pages 205–208)

9. In Passage 2, the "dark Gothic style" of architecture is _____.
   (A) essentially the architecture of the Italian Renaissance
   (B) criticized as ugly and ever debasing
   (C) the style of architecture used in the Pazzi Chapel
   (D) contrasted with the architecture that followed it
   (E) the crowning achievement of Leon Battista Alberti

9 ___

(pages 197–199)
10. According to the Florentines, the happy life could be achieved through _____.
    (A) access to power
    (B) a reasonable amount of wealth
    (C) art, especially architecture
    (D) learning
    (E) luck

    10 ___

(pages 205–208)
11. The events described in Passage 2 are different from those in Passage 1 in that _____.
    (A) no great leaders are mentioned
    (B) a discerning person could have predicted them
    (C) architecture is not mentioned
    (D) no important work of art is mentioned
    (E) they are more localized

    11 ___

(pages 205–208)
12. Passage 2 is similar to Passage 1 in its _____.
    (A) emphasis upon sudden bursts of glory
    (B) main idea that architecture reflects material, not spiritual, goals
    (C) stress on the importance of democratic leadership
    (D) exaltation of modern technology over older inferior skills
    (E) assertion that the cycles of history make predictions relatively routine

    12 ___

(pages 258–263)
13. To find out more about the subject of the second passage, it would be most efficient to find a book on _____.
    (A) Gothic architecture in Florence
    (B) the beginnings of the Renaissance
    (C) Italian history
    (D) the life of Leon Battista Alberti
    (E) a history of democracy

    13 ___

Facsimile Test 2

Section 1   1

Time-30 Minutes—For each question in this section, select the best answer
30 Questions   from among the choices given.

Each sentence below has one or two blanks, each blank indicating that
something has been omitted. Beneath the sentence are five lettered words
or sets of words labeled A through E. Choose the word or set of words that
best fits the meaning of the sentence as a whole.

EXAMPLE

Although its publicity has been _____,
the film itself is intelligent, well-acted,
handsomely produced, and alto-
gether _____.
- (A) tasteless . . respectable
- (B) extensive . . moderate
- (C) sophisticated . . spectacular
- (D) risqué . . crude
- (E) perfect . . spectacular

A

(pages 39–43)
1. The dependence of public television
   upon public contributions for _____ is
   a sad but _____ fact of life.
   - (A) expansion . . harrowing
   - (B) survival . . inescapable
   - (C) news . . humdrum
   - (D) ratings . . captivating
   - (E) audiences . . general

   1 ___

(pages 20–23)
2. The great horned owl, one of the most
   efficient and _____ of all _____, oc-
   casionally kills more prey than it can
   eat.
   - (A) docile . . birds
   - (B) casual . . fliers
   - (C) inept . . hunters
   - (D) ruthless . . predators
   - (E) amusing . . parents

   2 ___

(pages 20–23, 24–27)
3. The _____ celebration of the Metro-
   politan Opera recalled a hundred years
   of great artists, innovative directors,
   and _____ designers.
   - (A) centennial . . creative
   - (B) showy . . headstrong
   - (C) recent . . inept
   - (D) halfhearted . . indifferent
   - (E) biennial . . avant-garde

   3 ___

(pages 35–38)
4. As the day wore on, New Delhi, at
   first uncomfortably warm, be-
   came _____ hot and _____.
   - (A) somewhat . . annoying
   - (B) cloudlessly . . quiet
   - (C) unbearably . . stifling
   - (D) unexpectedly . . torrential
   - (E) sleepily . . cheery

   4 ___

(pages 14–20)
5. First _____ in 1865 by a group of
   French Republicans, Liberty was fi-
   nally unveiled in New York Harbor in
   1886.
   - (A) advertised
   - (B) completed
   - (C) photographed
   - (D) engineered
   - (E) conceived

   5 ___

(pages 31–35)

6. Because of the tremendous potential for good or ill, recent progress in the field of genetic engineering has raised both _____ and _____ for the future.
   (A) hopes . . fears
   (B) challenges . . disappointments
   (C) energy . . concern
   (D) faith . . disbelief
   (E) concerns . . anxieties

   6 ___

(pages 35–38)

7. At the antique car rally an ancient Franklin began slowly and _____ then accelerated and _____ by the judges' stand, to the delight of all spectators.
   (A) grotesquely . . wheezed
   (B) steadily . . inched
   (C) noisily . . crept
   (D) uncertainly . . whizzed
   (E) sadly . . went

   7 ___

(pages 14–20)

8. After the _____ reception of his early paintings, Picasso sometimes kept warm by burning his drawings.
   (A) frenzied
   (B) diminutive
   (C) insatiable
   (D) long-delayed
   (E) lackluster

   8 ___

(pages 31–35)

9. Although a bottom quark has a lifetime of only 1.5 trillionths of a second, this period is much _____ than scientists had anticipated.
   (A) shorter
   (B) longer
   (C) more dramatic
   (D) less important
   (E) more informative

   9 ___

Each question below consists of a related pair of words followed by five lettered pairs of words labeled A through E. Select the lettered pair that *best* expresses a relationship similar to that expressed in the original pair.

EXAMPLE
YAWN : BOREDOM ::
   (A) anger : madness
   (B) dream : sleep
   (C) smile : amusement
   (D) face : expression
   (E) impatience : rebellion

   C

(pages 164–165, 170)

10. NEGLIGENCE : LAX ::
   (A) leisure : energetic
   (B) density : repetitive
   (C) coincidence : skeptical
   (D) novelty : fresh
   (E) guile : candid

   10 ___

(pages 162, 163)

11. SCULPTOR : CHISEL ::
   (A) carpenter : square
   (B) wrench : plumber
   (C) pilot : airplane
   (D) surveyor : mortgage
   (E) lawyer : automobile

   11 ___

(pages 158–159, 163)

12. PEDIATRICIAN : CHILD ::
   (A) ophthalmologist : eyes
   (B) neurologist : criminals
   (C) radiologist : mass media
   (D) geologist : novas
   (E) philosopher : sculpture

   12 ___

(pages 169, 170)
13. TIME : MILLENNIA ::
   (A) work : salary
   (B) pain : aches
   (C) distance : light-years
   (D) weight : liters
   (E) joys : laughter

13 ___

(pages 154–155, 157)
14. PAIN : AGONY ::
   (A) drowsiness : laziness
   (B) exploration : ramble
   (C) industry : weakness
   (D) plenty : adequacy
   (E) fun : hilarity

14 ___

(pages 152–153)
15. SUGAR : CANISTER ::
   (A) barrel : oil
   (B) table : dishes
   (C) pig : sty
   (D) horse : racetrack
   (E) sheep : shepherd

15 ___

Each passage below is followed by questions based on its content. Answer the questions following each passage on the basis of what is stated or implied in that passage and in any introductory material that may be provided.

Has humankind progressed beyond the Age of Superstition? The following passage presents a challenging point of view.

Those who speak of the various "ages" of man, such as the Age of Belief, the Age of Discovery, the Age of Reason, the Atomic Age, and so forth, may be responsible for the nonsensical belief, widely held today, that humankind has become sophisticated, that we are less super-
5 stitious than the species used to be, less susceptible to hoaxes and irrational fears; that our minds, in short, are far from the primitive.

Perhaps the matter can never be fully resolved, since a scientific poll cannot be taken of the human being of other ages to learn just how superstitious he was. Certainly some of his superstitions have been ex-
10 ploded by modern science, and certainly there are hundreds of thousands of people today, able to read, who can be aware of such exposés. But we accept new superstitions as we discard old ones; intellectual development does not necessarily reform our mental behavior and habits even when we know better. A scientist may develop a most complicated
15 computer, and still toss some salt over his left shoulder if he spills it at the table, or walk around a black cat, or refuse the third light on a match, or whatever it is he harbors in the way of superstitious hangover. For, no matter how far advanced our intellectual development, we still have no control over the autonomic nervous system: we cannot prevent the
20 hair from "standing on end" when we are suddenly frightened in the dark.

So, while we have every right to point out the nonsense which humankind accepts, and indeed by which we direct our lives, we would do well to temper our merriment with the realization that at bottom our
25 own thinking is just as solidly based upon the primitive mentality as was

that of the serf, the ancient Roman, or the tribesman in awe of the Umbundu chant. As the French philosopher Lévy-Bruhl put it: "Dans tout esprit humain, quel qu'en soît le développement intellectuel, subsiste un fond indéracinable de mentalité primitive." (In all humankind,
30 whatever its intellectual attainments, an ineradicable basis exists of primitive mentality.) And Nilsson said: "Primitive mentality is a fairly good description of the mental behavior of most people today except in their technical or consciously intellectual activities."

(pages 186–189)
16. Which of the following best describes the main idea of the passage?
 (A) The mind of modern man is far from the primitive.
 (B) The Atomic Age is the latest in a list of famous "ages."
 (C) The autonomic nervous system sometimes makes our hair stand on end.
 (D) For all their sophistication, people today have their primitive superstitions.
 (E) Lévy-Bruhl and Nilsson share a particular point of view.

16 ____

(pages 247–251)
17. All the following are mentioned as examples of superstition or primitive mentality EXCEPT ____.
 (A) walking around a black cat
 (B) being in awe of the Umbundu chant
 (C) refusing the third light on a match
 (D) throwing salt over the left shoulder
 (E) breaking a mirror and worrying about bad luck

17 ____

(pages 225–229)
18. The author believes that mental behavior and habits ____.
 (A) often run counter to intellectual development
 (B) are directly correlated with the degree of sophistication
 (C) are usually life-enhancing
 (D) block the impact of irrational thought
 (E) are fairly similar in persons of similar intellectual development

18 ____

(pages 31–35)
19. In line 24, "temper" most nearly means ____.
 (A) increase
 (B) understand
 (C) reduce
 (D) moderate
 (E) advertise

19 ____

(pages 258–263)
20. Which of the following proverbs best expresses a point of view in the passage?
 (A) "A rolling stone gathers no moss."
 (B) "People in glass houses shouldn't throw stones."
 (C) "A stitch in time saves nine."
 (D) "He who hesitates is lost."
 (E) "A friend in need is a friend indeed."

20 ____

(pages 65–67)
21. In line 30, "ineradicable" most nearly means "not able to be. . . ." ____.
 (A) comprehended
 (B) uprooted
 (C) matched or equaled
 (D) taught
 (E) repeated

21 ____

The following excerpt from a short story suggests the impact of a new family's arrival in a neighborhood.

"It certainly feels good to sit down," Mrs. Harris said. She sighed. "Sometimes I feel that moving is the most terrible thing I have to do."

"You were lucky to get that house," Mrs. Tylor said, and Mrs. Harris nodded. "We'll be glad to get nice neighbors," Mrs. Tylor went
5 on. "There's something so nice about congenial people right next door. I'll be running over to borrow cups of sugar," she finished roguishly.

"I certainly hope you will," Mrs. Harris said. "We had such disagreeable people next door to us in our old house. Small things, you know, and they do irritate you so." Mrs. Tylor sighed sympathetically.
10 "The radio, for instance," Mrs. Harris continued, "all day long, and so *loud*."

Mrs. Tylor caught her breath for a minute. "You must be sure and tell us if ours is ever too loud."

"Mr. Harris cannot bear the radio," Mrs. Harris said. "We do not
15 own one, of course."

"Of course," Mrs. Tylor said. "No radio."

Mrs. Harris looked at her and laughed uncomfortably. "You'll be thinking my husband is crazy."

"Of course not," Mrs. Tylor said. "After all, lots of people don't
20 like radios; my oldest nephew, now, he's just the *other* way—"

"Well," Mrs. Harris said, "newspapers, too."

Mrs. Tylor recognized finally the faint nervous feeling that was tagging her; it was the way she felt when she was irrevocably connected with something dangerously out of control: her car, for instance, on an
25 icy street, or the time on Virginia's roller skates. . . . Mrs. Harris was staring absent-mindedly at the movers going in and out, and she was saying, "It isn't as though we hadn't ever *seen* a newspaper, not like the movies at all; Mr. Harris just feels that the newspapers are a mass degradation of taste. You really never *need* to read a newspaper, you
30 know," she said, looking around anxiously at Mrs. Tylor.

"I never read anything but the—"

"And we took *The New Republic* for a *number* of years," Mrs. Harris said. "When we were first married, of course. Before James was born."

"What is your husband's business?" Mrs. Tylor asked timidly.
35 Mrs. Harris lifted her head proudly. "He's a scholar," she said. "He writes monographs."

Mrs. Tylor opened her mouth to speak, but Mrs. Harris leaned over and put her hand out and said, "It's *terribly* hard for people to understand the desire for a really peaceful life."
40 "What," Mrs. Tylor said, "what does your husband do for relaxation?"

"He reads plays," Mrs. Harris said. She looked doubtfully over at James. "Pre-Elizabethan, of course."

"Of course," Mrs. Tylor said, and looked nervously at James, who
45 was shoveling sand into a pail.

"People are really very unkind," Mrs. Harris said. "Those people

I was telling you about, next door. It wasn't only the radio, you see. Three times they *deliberately* left their *New York Times* on our doorstep. Once James nearly got it."

50 "Good Lord," Mrs. Tylor said. She stood up. "Carol," she called emphatically, "don't go away. It's nearly time for lunch, dear."

"Well," Mrs. Harris said. "I must go and see if the movers have done anything right."

Feeling as though she had been rude, Mrs. Tylor said, "Where is 55 Mr. Harris now?"

"At his mother's," Mrs. Harris said. "He always stays there when we move."

"Of course," Mrs. Tylor said, feeling as though she had been saying nothing else all morning.

60 "They don't turn the radio on while he's there," Mrs. Harris explained.

"Of course," Mrs. Tylor said.

Mrs. Harris held out her hand and Mrs. Tylor took it. "I do so hope we'll be friends," Mrs. Harris said. "As you said, it means such a lot 65 to have really thoughtful neighbors. And we've been so unlucky."

"Of course," Mrs. Tylor said, and then came back to herself abruptly. "Perhaps one evening soon we can get together for a game of bridge?" She saw Mrs. Harris's face and said, "No. Well, anyway, we must all get together some evening soon." They both laughed.

70 "It does sound silly, doesn't it," Mrs. Harris said. "Thanks so much for all your kindness this morning."

"Anything we can do," Mrs. Tylor said. "If you want to send James over this afternoon."

"Perhaps I shall," Mrs. Harris said. "If you really don't mind."

75 "Of course," Mrs. Tylor said. "Carol, dear."

With her arm around Carol she walked out to the front of the house and stood watching Mrs. Harris and James go into their house. They both stopped in the doorway and waved, and Mrs. Tylor and Carol waved back.

80 "Can't I go to the movies," Carol said, "*please,* Mother?"

"I'll go with you, dear," Mrs. Tylor said.

(pages 53, 55)

22. Mrs. Tylor's comment, "We'll be glad to get nice neighbors," turns out to be ironic because _____.
   (A) the two families will fight bitterly
   (B) the Harrises will probably stay only a month or two
   (C) the children will never speak to each other
   (D) the new neighbors are not "nice" in the usual way Mrs. Tylor expects
   (E) Mrs. Harris is an evil person

(pages 265–270)

23. When Mrs. Tylor "sighed sympathetically" (line 9), she _____.
   (A) tried to catch Mrs. Harris off guard
   (B) had no idea what was coming
   (C) already had the radio on too loud
   (D) suggested her puzzlement
   (E) revealed her basic cunning

23 ___

22 ___

(pages 65–67, 78, 89)
24. In line 23, "irrevocably" suggests _____.
    (A) no possibility of escape
    (B) excitement
    (C) many possibilities of action
    (D) a not unpleasant depression
    (E) a host of alternatives

    24 ___

(pages 184–186)
25. The most appropriate word to apply to Mr. Harris is _____.
    (A) brutish
    (B) agreeable
    (C) antisocial
    (D) extroverted
    (E) companionable

    25 ___

(pages 200–202)
26. In the paragraph beginning line 22, Mrs. Harris is saying that _____.
    (A) the movers aren't doing a good job
    (B) most newspapers are bad, though not all
    (C) she herself thinks that newspapers are necessary
    (D) the Harrises never go to the movies
    (E) she really agrees with Mrs. Tylor's statements thus far

    26 ___

(pages 265–270)
27. The repetition of the phrase "of course" suggests _____.
    (A) Mrs. Tylor's inability to have two consecutive coherent thoughts
    (B) Mrs. Tylor's growing desperation at the way the conversation is going
    (C) an author's device for making short, readable paragraphs
    (D) Mrs. Tylor's complete agreement with everything that Mrs. Harris has said
    (E) unfriendliness on the part of Mrs. Tylor

    27 ___

(pages 65–67, 265–270)
28. In line 29, "degradation" most nearly means _____.
    (A) elevation
    (B) corruption
    (C) advertisement
    (D) expansion
    (E) exclusion

    28 ___

(pages 197–199)
29. Mrs. Harris classifies the leaving of a *New York Times* on the doorstep as a(n) _____.
    (A) cruel deed
    (B) act of kindness
    (C) mistake
    (D) attempt to upset James
    (E) insane action

    29 ___

(pages 253–257)
30. Mrs. Tylor decides to go to the movies because _____.
    (A) she feels she hasn't been paying enough attention to Carol
    (B) by providing an example, she may help Mrs. Harris out of her isolation
    (C) she wants to shake off the depressing conversation she has been having
    (D) she is a movie enthusiast and is looking forward to a favorite star
    (E) she wants to demonstrate to Mrs. Harris that she is a modern, up-to-date person

    30 ___

Time-30 Minutes—For each question in this section, select the best answer
35 Questions   from among the choices given.

Each sentence below has one or two blanks, each blank indicating that
something has been omitted. Beneath the sentence are five lettered words
or sets of words labeled A through E. Choose the word or set of words that
best fits the meaning of the sentence as a whole.

EXAMPLE

Although its publicity has been _____,
the film itself is intelligent, well-acted,
handsomely produced, and altogether _____.

  (A) tasteless . . respectable
  (B) extensive . . moderate
  (C) sophisticated . . spectacular
  (D) risqué . . crude
  (E) perfect . . spectacular

                      A

(pages 31–35)

1. The more the insect tried to disentan-
gle itself from the spider's web, the
more _____ it became.
  (A) wary   (D) angry
  (B) formidable   (E) enmeshed
  (C) careless
                    1 __

(pages 31–35)

2. Although most people consider ci-
ties _____ wildlife, birds and even
mammals _____ in even the most un-
likely urban areas.
  (A) favorable toward . . thrive
  (B) devoid of . . deteriorate
  (C) receptive toward . . appear
  (D) alien to . . abound
  (E) unconcerned with . . dart

                  2 __

(pages 14–20)

3. The book *The Evening Stars* presents a
history of television's evening news
programs, with _____ those news an-
chors who came to _____ the news.
  (A) disregard for . . lead
  (B) minor attention to . . enjoy
  (C) description of . . study
  (D) emphasis upon . . dominate
  (E) affection for . . represent

                  3 __

(pages 35–38)

4. Plentiful and crystal-clear at its source,
the Arkansas River becomes less and
less _____ as it flows east, finally dis-
appearing on the _____ Kansas
plains.
  (A) abundant . . dry
  (B) powerful . . fruitful
  (C) beautiful . . moisture-laden
  (D) polluted . . unplowed
  (E) available . . hilly

                  4 __

(pages 28–31)

5. Initial reserve soon disappeared, and
the gathering of bird-watchers soon became as _____ as a congregation of
first-graders on the school playground.
  (A) dignified   (D) subtle
  (B) exuberant   (E) impressive
  (C) mischievous
                  5 __

(pages 35–38)
6. In 1789, George Washington urged Congress to use its "best endeavors to improve the education and manners of a people to accelerate the progress of art and science; to _____ works of genius, to confer rewards for inventions of utility and to cherish institutions favorable to humanity."
   (A) support
   (B) advertise
   (C) admire
   (D) confirm
   (E) study

6 ___

(pages 31–35)
7. Vincent van Gogh, whose _____ reputation has helped sell his works for millions of dollars, is known to have sold only one painting during his lifetime.
   (A) fanciful
   (B) posthumous
   (C) erratic
   (D) stolid
   (E) faded

7 ___

(pages 31–35)
8. In an attempt to become an upwardly mobile English gentleman, the teenage Gandhi spent hours practicing how to arrange his tie and hair, a far cry from the _____ tendencies of his maturity.
   (A) ascetic   (D) antagonistic
   (B) egotistical   (E) acquiescent
   (C) bashful

8 ___

(pages 14–20)
9. Though blind, Bill Irwin walked the 2100-mile Appalachian Trail, _____ by his faithful dog Orient.
   (A) followed   (D) encumbered
   (B) revitalized   (E) accompanied
   (C) driven

9 ___

(pages 14–20)
10. When Juanita, after much searching, discovered the elusive Mouse King for her nutcracker collection, she was in a state of _____ for days.
   (A) lethargy   (D) euphoria
   (B) elasticity   (E) disgruntlement
   (C) consternation

10 ___

Each question below consists of a related pair of words followed by five lettered pairs of words labeled A through E. Select the lettered pair that *best* expresses a relationship similar to that expressed in the original pair.

EXAMPLE
YAWN : BOREDOM ::
   (A) anger : madness
   (B) dream : sleep
   (C) smile : amusement
   (D) face : expression
   (E) impatience : rebellion

C

(pages 151–152, 153)
11. GERMINATE : GROWTH ::
   (A) chuckle : humor
   (B) drop : chair
   (C) try : failure
   (D) harden : brittleness
   (E) combine : mixture

11 ___

ENGLISH FOR THE COLLEGE BOARDS

(pages 166–168, 170)
12. AGRICULTURE : WEATHER ::
 (A) prices : demand
 (B) wool : sheep
 (C) enthusiasm : lubrication
 (D) sincerity : radiation
 (E) wealth : formality

12 ___

(pages 150–151, 153)
13. SOLAR SYSTEM : EARTH ::
 (A) nebula : galaxy
 (B) comet : meteor
 (C) planet : satellite
 (D) sun : sunspots
 (E) asteroid : moon

13 ___

(pages 161–162, 163)
14. PIONEER : TRAILBLAZING ::
 (A) typesetter : authorship
 (B) novelist : censure
 (C) pirate : theft
 (D) flight : fugitive
 (E) usher : entertainment

14 ___

(pages 154–155, 157)
15. INCONVENIENCE : CALAMITY ::
 (A) colorless : dull
 (B) fear : terror
 (C) fault : blame
 (D) diplomacy : tact
 (E) hysteria : reassurance

15 ___

(pages 155–156, 157)
16. YEAR : DECADE ::
 (A) comma : period
 (B) sapling : tree
 (C) hawk : falcon
 (D) anniversary : party
 (E) university : college

16 ___

(pages 168, 170)
17. ETYMOLOGY : DERIVATIONS ::
 (A) archaeology : rivers
 (B) entomology : primates
 (C) cosmology : decoration
 (D) ornithology : birds
 (E) analogy : argumentation

17 ___

(pages 154, 157)
18. ROD : FISHING ::
 (A) ski : bobsledding
 (B) football : volleyball
 (C) javelin : shot put
 (D) sailing : oar
 (E) bow : archery

18 ___

(pages 160–161, 163)
19. SHIP : NAVIGATOR ::
 (A) angler : lake
 (B) stage : actor
 (C) bookkeeper : studio
 (D) office : puppeteer
 (E) fire engine : nurse

19 ___

(pages 156, 157)
20. ENGRAVE : PLATE ::
 (A) purchase : presentation
 (B) strike : clock
 (C) find : excuses
 (D) bind : book
 (E) try : plan

20 ___

(pages 155–156, 157)
21. FLOWER : SNAPDRAGON ::
 (A) flounder : perch
 (B) bread : doughnut
 (C) collie : spaniel
 (D) oak : elm
 (E) mineral : iron

21 ___

(pages 149–150, 153)
22. HIGH : AERIE ::
 (A) puzzling : dishonesty
 (B) faithful : heretic
 (C) exaggerated : caricature
 (D) timid : swashbuckler
 (E) picturesque : idol

22 ___

(pages 147–149, 153)
23. HARMLESS : SCOUNDREL ::
 (A) ingenious : milliner
 (B) brilliant : moron
 (C) agent : condescending
 (D) literate : editor
 (E) studious : scholar

23 ___

The two passages below are followed by questions based on their content and on the relationship between the two passages. Answer the questions on the basis of what is <u>stated</u> or <u>implied</u> in the passages and in any introductory material that may be provided.

Passage 1 is the opening section of the Constitution of the United States. Passage 2 is the opening section of the Charter of the United Nations.

PASSAGE 1

We the People of the United States, in Order to form a more perfect Union, establish Justice, insure domestic Tranquillity, provide for the common defence, promote the general Welfare, and secure the Blessings of Liberty to ourselves and our Posterity, do ordain and establish this
5 Constitution for the United States of America.

ARTICLE. I.

SECTION. 1. All legislative Powers herein granted shall be vested in a Congress of the United States, which shall consist of a Senate and House of Representatives.

SECTION. 2. The House of Representatives shall be composed of
10 Members chosen every second Year by the People of the several States, and the Electors in each State shall have the Qualifications requisite for Electors of the most numerous Branch of the State Legislature.

No Person shall be a Representative who shall not have attained to the age of twenty five Years, and been seven Years a Citizen of the
15 United States, and who shall not, when elected, be an Inhabitant of that State in which he shall be chosen.

Representatives and direct Taxes shall be apportioned among the several States which may be included within this Union, according to their respective Numbers, which shall be determined by adding to the
20 whole Number of free Persons, including those bound to Service for a Term of Years, and excluding Indians not taxed, three fifths of all other Persons. The actual Enumeration shall be made within three Years after the first Meeting of the Congress of the United States, and within every subsequent Term of ten Years, in such Manner as they shall by Law
25 direct. The Number of Representatives shall not exceed one for every thirty Thousand, but each State shall have at Least one Representative; and until such enumeration shall be made, the State of New Hampshire shall be entitled to choose three, Massachusetts eight, Rhode-Island and Providence Plantations one, Connecticut five, New-York six, New
30 Jersey four, Pennsylvania eight, Delaware one, Maryland six, Virginia ten, North Carolina five, South Carolina five, and Georgia three.

When vacancies happen in the Representation from any State, the Executive Authority thereof shall issue Writs of Election to fill such Vacancies.
35 The House of Representatives shall choose their Speaker and other Officers; and shall have the sole Power of Impeachment.

We the peoples of the United Nations determined

to save succeeding generations from the scourge of war which twice in
our lifetime has brought untold sorrow to mankind, and

40 to reaffirm faith in fundamental human rights, in the dignity and worth
of the human person, in the equal rights of men and women and of
nations large and small, and

to establish conditions under which justice and respect for the obligations arising from treaties and other sources of international law can be
45 maintained, and

to promote social progress and better standards of life in larger freedom.

and for these ends

to practice tolerance and live together in peace with one another as good
neighbors, and

50 to unite our strength to maintain international peace and security, and

to ensure, by the acceptance of principles and the institution of methods,
that armed force shall not be used, save in the common interest, and

to employ international machinery for the promotion of the economic
and social advancement of all peoples,

55 **have resolved to combine our efforts to accomplish these aims.**

Accordingly, our respective Governments, through representatives assembled in the city of San Francisco, who have exhibited their full powers found to be in good and due form, have agreed to the present Charter
of the United Nations and do hereby establish an international organiza-
60 tion to be known as the United Nations.

CHAPTER I

Purposes and Principles

Article 1

The Purposes of the United Nations are:

1. To maintain international peace and security, and to that end: to
take effective collective measures for the prevention and removal of
threats to the peace, and for the suppression of acts of aggression or
65 other breaches of the peace, and to bring about by peaceful means,
and in conformity with the principles of justice and international law,
adjustment or settlement of international disputes or situations which
might lead to a breach of the peace;

2. To develop friendly relations among nations based on respect for
70 the principle of equal rights and self-determination of peoples, and to
take other appropriate measures to strengthen universal peace;

3. To achieve international cooperation in solving international problems of an economic, social, cultural, or humanitarian character, and in

promoting and encouraging respect for human rights and for fundamental
75 freedoms for all without distinction as to race, sex, language, or religion;
and

4. To be a center for harmonizing the actions of nations in the attainment of these common ends.

(pages 210–213)
24. This section of the Constitution is concerned principally with _____.
  (A) the election of the President
  (B) impeachment procedures for the removal of a federal officer
  (C) determining the number of Representatives
  (D) eligibility rules for Presidential candidates
  (E) electing members of the Senate

24 ___

(pages 14–20)
25. In line 11, "requisite" most nearly means _____.
  (A) essential
  (B) voted upon
  (C) suggested
  (D) developed
  (E) discovered

25 ___

(pages 14–20)
26. The expression "bound to Service" in line 20 probably refers to _____.
  (A) the perennially unemployed
  (B) slaves
  (C) members of the new Congress
  (D) indentured servants
  (E) newly elected Representatives

26 ___

(pages 197–199)
27. In Section 2, the suggested numbers of Representatives are based on _____.
  (A) the first national census
  (B) statistics supplied by the new Senate
  (C) the states' contributions to the American Revolution
  (D) the number of delegates to the convention
  (E) temporary estimates

27 ___

(pages 197–199)
28. By a process of elimination, we may infer that the three-fifths figure refers to _____.
  (A) civil servants
  (B) native Americans
  (C) slaves
  (D) electors in each state
  (E) senators

28 ___

(pages 210–213)
29. *Providence Plantations* is obviously linked with _____.
  (A) Connecticut
  (B) New Jersey
  (C) New York
  (D) Rhode Island
  (E) Massachusetts

29 ___

(pages 24–27)
30. In line 38, "scourge" most nearly means _____.
  (A) occurrence
  (B) affliction
  (C) challenge
  (D) threat
  (E) unexpectedness

30 ___

(pages 205–208)
31. The similarity between the opening words of the Constitution and the United Nations Charter is probably _____.
  (A) coincidental
  (B) a cause of present difficulties in the U.N.
  (C) intentional
  (D) accidental
  (E) an indication of unfair domination by the U.S.

31 ___

(pages 205–208)

32. The U.N. Charter is different from the Constitution in its emphasis upon _____.
    (A) proper representation
    (B) monetary agreements between nations
    (C) the election of delegates
    (D) the creation of larger national units
    (E) international peace

    32 ___

(pages 205–208)

33. The Charter and the Constitution resemble each other in their emphasis on _____.
    (A) securing freedom and liberty
    (B) concern for the elimination of world tensions
    (C) the role of the executive
    (D) the importance of economics
    (E) social and cultural differences between peoples

    33 ___

(pages 247–251)

34. The Charter does NOT _____.
    (A) eliminate the possible use of force
    (B) concern itself with both self-determination and human rights
    (C) support equal rights for women
    (D) approve the signing of new treaties between nations
    (E) mention universal law

    34 ___

(pages 184–186)

35. If a single word were chosen to express the essential spirit of the Charter, the word would be _____.
    (A) *culture*
    (B) *cooperation*
    (C) *principles*
    (D) *sadness*
    (E) *joy*

    35 ___

Section 5   5 5 5 5 5

Time-15 Minutes—For each question in this section, select the best answer
13 Questions   from among the choices given.

In the perennial battle against insect pests, certain names stand out. The following selection discusses the work of an outstanding African scientist.

A famous cartoon shows a dinosaur stepping on a cockroach. The dinosaur says, ''That's the end of the cockroach!'' The dinosaurs have long since disappeared, but the hardy cockroach, now 300 million years old as a species, is still with us. Insects have survived and flourished,
5 sometimes for the benefit of human beings, but often to their detriment. An estimated 30 million different species inhabit the planet, but only a million have been discovered. Insects outweigh the human population at least 12 times and account for about 85% of all animal life.
In Africa, insects have dominated human life. Termites and ants
10 outweigh elephants, rhinos, and all other mammals put together. Two insects especially have influenced how and where human beings live: the mosquito and the tsetse fly. The mosquito carries malaria and yellow fever; the tsetse fly, sleeping sickness. These two insects did put a limit on colonial settlements, but they have also devastated the Africans
15 themselves.

Thomas Odhiambo, a Kenyan entomologist, vowed to do something about the insect depredations. In the early seventies he founded ICIPE in a Nairobi garage. The International Center of Insect Physiology and Ecology has grown into a major research center with many world-class scientists, graduate students, and postdoctoral students at work.

The tsetse fly's deadly bite has spread sleeping sickness across a vast area, larger than that of the United States. Another deadly disease, malaria, carried by mosquitoes, kills great numbers of children every year. But the diseases of Africa are not limited to those that make a direct assault on human beings. The farmer's livelihood and the people's food are threatened by crop pests and cattle infestations. Weevils, mites, and stem-borers destroy crops. Diseases carried by ticks destroy cattle. Though ticks and mites are technically arachnids, not insects, ICIPE is concerned with all threats. It attempts to attack all of them.

Thomas Risley Odhiambo is a tireless visionary. Called "the smartest man in East Africa," he is a dynamo of energy and planning. Ralph Waldo Emerson said, "An institution is the lengthened shadow of one man." ICIPE is the lengthened shadow of Thomas Odhiambo.

In the control of insects, poisonous chemicals have been shown to have limitations. There is always the threat to pets, livestock, birds, and human beings. More serious, though, is the insects' ability to overcome pesticides. If a few insects are naturally immune to the pesticide, they will survive and breed other immune insects.

Odhiambo believes that we can find more ways to use insects positively. "There are obvious cases, like honey from bees. But did you know that termites make excellent chicken food? It seems sensible to incorporate insects into our livestock-production systems." To a chicken in a farmyard, eating insects is nothing new, but large-scale use of insects as food may provide two benefits at once.

Odhiambo earned his graduate degrees at Cambridge University. On returning to Africa, he established the entomology department at the University of Nairobi. He began organizing "centers of excellence" in Africa. He attracted many outstanding research scientists. With help from American scientific academies, he set up an international center. Other nations, the World Bank, and OPEC also contributed.

Odhiambo faces powerful and pitiless adversaries. Among these terrifying enemies, the tsetse fly has been especially dangerous. The fly may give a painful bite, but the serious damage is done by a blood parasite transmitted by the bite. If the fly is infected, the victim of the bite develops sleeping sickness, so called because the victim sinks into a lethal doze. On the shores of Lake Victoria alone, 200,000 people died after being bitten by the infected fly. The disease has also spread to animals, reducing Africa's cattle crop by 85%.

Many methods, including a drastic scorched-earth policy, have temporarily halted the spread of the fly, or even, in a few instances, caused a retreat. But the victories have always been temporary. Odhiambo's plan is more strategically sound: to "make sure the blood parasite and the tsetse are not in the same place at the same time." New and better

traps have been introduced and have reduced the tsetse population by
65 half over a 62-square-mile area.

While experimentation is concerned with the tsetse fly, research into
other insect pests goes on apace. Stem-boring moths, other biting flies,
mosquitoes, even seemingly innocuous sandflies—host to a deadly parasite—are being studied by some of the best minds in entomological re-
70 search. In a *Smithsonian* magazine article for August, 1988, Thomas
Bass examines in some detail many of the projects under the general
direction of Thomas Risley Odhiambo, ecologist extraordinary.

(pages 53, 55)
1. "That's the end of the cockroach" is
   introduced as an example of _____.
   (A) metaphor
   (B) irony
   (C) literal language
   (D) euphemism
   (E) hyperbole

1 ___

(pages 184–186)
2. From the various contexts, we may
   infer that entomology is the study
   of _____.
   (A) the higher mammals
   (B) African geology
   (C) insects
   (D) word origins
   (E) human behavior

2 ___

(pages 210–213)
3. Honey is mentioned as a _____.
   (A) medicine used in fighting sleeping
       sickness
   (B) major ingredient in Odhiambo's ex-
       perimentation
   (C) carrier of dangerous parasites
   (D) positive contribution of insects
   (E) major West African crop

3 ___

(pages 200–202)
4. Ralph Waldo Emerson is
   quoted _____.
   (A) as an amateur authority on insects
   (B) to pay tribute to Odhiambo
   (C) to add sophistication to the
       passage
   (D) for his courageous stand on the en-
       vironment
   (E) because he is Odhiambo's favorite
       author

4 ___

(pages 31–35)
5. In line 68, *innocuous* means _____.
   (A) gaudily colored
   (B) poisonous
   (C) tiny
   (D) unpredictable
   (E) harmless

5 ___

(pages 184–197)
6. The scorched-earth policy may be eval-
   uated as _____.
   (A) helpful in the long run
   (B) creatively designed
   (C) ultimately unsuccessful
   (D) the answer to one insect only
   (E) a mistake by Odhiambo

6 ___

(pages 247–251)
7. All the following insects have been mentioned EXCEPT _____.
   (A) sandflies
   (B) moths
   (C) tsetse flies
   (D) mosquitoes
   (E) butterflies

   7 ___

(pages 14–20)
8. *Depredations* in line 17 means _____.
   (A) savage attacks
   (B) peaceful interactions
   (C) strengths and weaknesses
   (D) manifestations
   (E) retreats

   8 ___

(pages 225–229)
9. The writer's attitude toward Odhiambo and his work is one of _____.
   (A) watchful waiting
   (B) excessive amazement
   (C) idle curiosity
   (D) sincere admiration
   (E) professional jealousy

   9 ___

(pages 197–199)
10. Odhiambo's attack on the insect problem may best be characterized as _____.
    (A) enthusiastic but doomed
    (B) all-embracing
    (C) tediously slow
    (D) ill-balanced
    (E) based on intuition, not research

    10 ___

(pages 210–213)
11. A method mentioned as having good results is _____.
    (A) pesticides
    (B) sending out infertile males
    (C) genetic engineering
    (D) trapping
    (E) scorched-earth

    11 ___

(pages 258–263)
12. When Odhiambo finds a problem he can't solve, he probably _____.
    (A) checks the encyclopedia of insect pests
    (B) turns to another problem, to save time
    (C) calls on the researchers at ICIPE
    (D) sends a telegram to colleagues at OPEC
    (E) solves it within a day

    12 ___

(pages 222–225)
13. The tone of the passage may be characterized as _____.
    (A) quietly informational
    (B) breathlessly enthusiastic
    (C) vigorously critical
    (D) lukewarm
    (E) somewhat indifferent

    13 ___

Facsimile Test 3

Section 1   1

Time-30 Minutes—For each question in this section, select the best answer
  30 Questions   from among the choices given.

Each sentence below has one or two blanks, each blank indicating that
something has been omitted. Beneath the sentence are five lettered words
or sets of words labeled A through E. Choose the word or set of words that
best fits the meaning of the sentence as a whole.

EXAMPLE

Although its publicity has been _____,
the film itself is intelligent, well-acted,
handsomely produced, and alto-
gether _____.
  (A) tasteless . . respectable
  (B) extensive . . moderate
  (C) sophisticated . . spectacular
  (D) risqué . . crude
  (E) perfect . . spectacular

                                    A

(pages 28–31)
1. Like an airplane in a steep power dive,
   the falcon _____ down upon
   the _____ sparrows and captured a
   terrified victim.
   (A) swooped . . scattering
   (B) lunged . . assembled
   (C) flew . . disinterested
   (D) looked . . sluggish
   (E) circled . . courageous

                           1 ___

(pages 31–35)
2. Though playwrights can usually man-
   age a good first act, by the middle of
   the last act, _____ often re-
   places _____.
   (A) consternation . . contemplation
   (B) desperation . . inspiration
   (C) deliberation . . commendation
   (D) cancellation . . alteration
   (E) stagnation . . disorganization

                           2 ___

(pages 14–20)
3. The _____ of many coastal plains and
   moors for housing and other develop-
   ment has _____ many fine ecological
   habitats.
   (A) inaccessibility . . uncovered
   (B) analysis . . displayed
   (C) suitability . . doomed
   (D) advertisement . . enhanced
   (E) exclusion . . emphasized

                           3 ___

(pages 31–35)
4. On our Spaceship, Earth, recycling is not a _____ to be _____ but a necessity to guide our actions.
   (A) concept . . followed
   (B) plant . . adapted
   (C) dream . . fantasized
   (D) luxury . . indulged
   (E) discipline . . fostered

4 ___

(pages 31–35)
5. The _____ heat at midday was briefly relieved by a thunderstorm, but a short time later the temperatures again began to climb.
   (A) anticipated
   (B) moderate
   (C) timely
   (D) dappled
   (E) oppressive

5 ___

(pages 14–20)
6. The name *United Nations,* suggested by Winston Churchill from a poem by Lord Byron, _____ the original name: *Associated Powers*.
   (A) refurbished
   (B) galvanized
   (C) acknowledged
   (D) divulged
   (E) supplanted

6 ___

(pages 14–20, 68)
7. To be ready for the ballet tryouts, Marie followed a(n) _____ diet for several months.
   (A) copious
   (B) Spartan
   (C) carnivorous
   (D) condiment
   (E) alternative

7 ___

(pages 14–20, 105)
8. Because of their continuing search for perfection, experts are likely to be _____ in judging the work done in their special area.
   (A) lackadaisical
   (B) generous
   (C) therapeutic
   (D) hypercritical
   (E) fretful

8 ___

(pages 20–23)
9. Indiana Jones seemed to have a _____ love of danger, inherited, no doubt, from some swashbuckling adventurer in Francis Drake's navy.
   (A) tiresome
   (B) negative
   (C) congenital
   (D) grisly
   (E) rational

9 ___

Each question below consists of a related pair of words followed by five lettered pairs of words labeled A through E. Select the lettered pair that *best* expresses a relationship similar to that expressed in the original pair.

EXAMPLE
YAWN : BOREDOM ::
   (A) anger : madness
   (B) dream : sleep
   (C) smile : amusement
   (D) face : expression
   (E) impatience : rebellion

___C

(pages 158–159, 163)
10. WIZARD : MAGIC ::
   (A) embezzler : money
   (B) computer programmer : calculator
   (C) linguist : language
   (D) dreamer : confusion
   (E) cyclist : handlebars

10 ___

(pages 155–156, 157)
11. BUS : VEHICLE ::
   (A) squash : spinach
   (B) child : infant
   (C) time : tide
   (D) waterfall : canyon
   (E) hammer : tool

11 ___

(pages 154–155, 157)
12. CHESS : KNIGHT ::
   (A) swimming : diving
   (B) croquet : mallet
   (C) golf : fairway
   (D) football : goalposts
   (E) softball : pitcher

12 ___

(pages 150–151, 153)
13. ATOM : MOLECULE ::
   (A) neutron : atom
   (B) cell : nucleus
   (C) electron : kilowatt
   (D) amoeba : protozoa
   (E) yard : inch

13 ___

(pages 164–165, 170)
14. SPECULATION : RISK ::
   (A) compromise : conciliation
   (B) travel : research
   (C) communication : telephone
   (D) skiing : skis
   (E) reading : pamphlet

14 ___

(pages 149–150, 153)
15. AMAZE : ASTONISHMENT ::
   (A) designate : veto
   (B) interfere : interchange
   (C) merge : coalition
   (D) intensify : inspire
   (E) entwine : weave

15 ___

The two passages below are followed by questions based on their content and on the relationship between the two passages. Answer the questions on the basis of what is stated or implied in the passages and in any introductory material that may be provided.

What dangers do nations face? How can a democracy be destroyed? The following two passages, both written many years ago, discuss the dangers and offer warnings to a free people.

PASSAGE 1

Democracy's Danger

To turn a republican government into a despotism the basest and most brutal, it is not necessary formally to change its constitution or abandon popular elections. It was centuries after Caesar before the absolute master of the Roman world pretended to rule other than by authority
5 of a Senate that trembled before him.

But forms are nothing when substance is gone, and the forms of popular government are those from which the substance of freedom may most easily go. Extremes meet, and a government of universal suffrage and theoretical equality may, under conditions which impel the change,
10 most readily become a despotism. For there despotism advances in the name and with the might of the people. The single source of power once

secured, everything is secured. There is no unfranchised class to whom appeal may be made, no privileged orders who in defending their rights may defend those of all. No bulwark remains to stay the flood, no emin-
15 ence to rise above it. They were belted barons led by a mitered arch-bishop who curbed the Plantagenet with Magna Charta; it was the middle classes who broke the pride of the Stuarts; but a mere aristocracy of wealth will never struggle while it can hope to bribe a tyrant.

And when the disparity of condition increases, so does universal
20 suffrage make it easy to seize the source of power. . . . Given a commu-nity with republican institutions, in which one class is too rich to be shorn of its luxuries, no matter how public affairs are administered, and another so poor that a few dollars on election day will seem more than any abstract consideration; in which the few roll in wealth and the many
25 seethe with discontent as a condition of things they know not how to remedy, and power must pass into the hands of jobbers who will buy and sell it as the Praetorians sold the Roman purple, or into the hands of demagogues who will seize and wield it for a time, only to be displaced by worse demagogues.

PASSAGE 2

The Deadliest Enemies of Nations

30 The deadliest enemies of nations are not their foreign foes; they al-ways dwell within their own borders. And from these internal enemies civilization is always in need of being saved. The nation blest above all nations is she in whom the civic genius of the people does the saving day by day, by acts without external picturesqueness; by speaking, writing,
35 voting reasonably; by smiting corruption swiftly; by good temper be-tween parties; by the people knowing true men when they see them, and preferring them as leaders to rabid partisans or empty quacks. Such nations have no need of wars to save them. Their accounts with right-eousness are always even; and God's judgments do not have to overtake
40 them fitfully in bloody spasms and convulsions of the race.

(pages 184–186)
16. According to the author of Passage 1, having popular elections _____.
   (A) insures that freedom may not be lost
   (B) provides a check against cor-ruption
   (C) tends to equalize the distribution of wealth
   (D) tends to take care of the poorest citizens
   (E) may still lead to despotism

16 ___

(pages 210–213)
17. For centuries after Caesar, the Roman emperors _____.
   (A) consulted the Senate on all impor-tant decisions
   (B) acted as model rulers during their early years
   (C) were intimidated by the Roman Senate
   (D) concealed the source of true au-thority
   (E) were lawful descendants of the pre-ceding emperors

17 ___

(pages 197–199)
18. In the discussion of form and sub-
    stance, substance is represented
    by _____.
    (A) a constitution
    (B) the privilege of voting
    (C) freedom
    (D) popular elections
    (E) republican institutions

                                    18 ___

(pages 14–20)
19. In line 14, the word "bulwark" most
    nearly means _____.
    (A) strong leader
    (B) constitutional restraint
    (C) diversion
    (D) creative idea
    (E) barrier

                                    19 ___

(pages 184–186)
20. The author of Passage 2 suggests that
    nations are most vulnerable to _____.
    (A) foreign aggressors
    (B) mercenary ideals
    (C) depletion of natural resources
    (D) incompetent military leaders
    (E) internal weakness

                                    20 ___

(pages 258–263)
21. The authors of both passages would
    most probably subscribe to which of
    the following quotations?
    (A) "It is my certain conviction that
        no man loses his freedom except
        through his own weakness."
        Gandhi
    (B) "Nothing is so weak and unstable
        as a reputation for power not
        based on force." Tacitus
    (C) "A shortcut to riches is to sub-
        tract from our desires." Petrarch
    (D) "There is no worse torture than
        the torture of laws." Francis
        Bacon
    (E) "Honour sinks where commerce
        long prevails." Oliver Goldsmith

                                    21 ___

The passage below is followed by questions based on its content. Answer
the questions on the basis of what is <u>stated</u> or <u>implied</u> in the passage and in
any introductory material that may be provided.

This introduction to the stories of Edith Wharton evaluates her work and
personality.

        Edith Wharton's autobiography, *A Backward Glance,* is a brilliant
exercise in both worldliness and concealment. Both of these qualities
are completely authentic: no cover-up is intended. For she was both the
great lady she so pleasingly describes and that secret inward-looking
5 creature to whom she only briefly alludes. The writing of fiction—and
she was tirelessly prolific, combining her work with an extensive social
life—proceeds from the hidden self, a self which exists only on the
borders of consciousness. Edith Wharton's outer life was spent in the
public gaze. She was *mondaine* in every sense of the word, born into a
10 rigidly stratified society of accepted families, married young to a suitable
husband, owner of many beautiful houses, and tirelessly available to a
host of friends. She was also a great traveller, a great expatriate, and a

great worker: indeed her efforts in the First World War earned her a
Légion d'Honneur from the French government. As she tells the story,
there would not seem to be either the time or the place for a writer of
fiction to emerge and to blossom. Indeed the world in which she grew
up saw her literary activity as a sort of aberration or solecism, and only
one of her numerous relations ever read her books. Her easy sophistication enables her to dismiss this as she seems to have dismissed every
other obstacle in her path.

And yet she was that awkward thing, a born writer. When she was
a very small child, before she could read or write, she was subject to
compulsive episodes of 'making up'. When one of these came upon her
she would seize a book, walk up and down, and chant stories of her
own invention, turning the pages at intervals which an adult reader might
observe. She was even known to abandon a children's tea party when
visited by a sudden desire to 'make up'. Perhaps this is not surprising
in a child, but then few children go on to write forty books. The same
magic impulse that went into the making-up episodes seems to have
stayed with her throughout her career, for, as she tells it, she never had
to search for a theme or a subject, and even the names of her characters
arrived of their own accord, sometimes long in advance of the characters
themselves.

Those who seek for a sober explanation for these phenomena would
no doubt point to the excellence of her education, the sort of education
not enjoyed by anyone today. The young Edith Wharton was allowed
to read only the finest works in any language. As she spoke French,
German, and Italian from an early age she grew up acquainted with the
masterpieces of four languages. At the same time she was introduced
to the pleasures of Europe, which was to become her second home, in
an age when such pleasures had to be pursued over unmade roads and
in occasionally dubious hotels. Although she never went to school, she
seems to have had the best and kindest of governesses. And of course
agreeable company was assured from the start, the society of old New
York reinforcing what her own extensive family habitually provided.

This brilliant education had excellent results. A gracious manner and
an inspired way with friends might be qualities one would expect from
such an upbringing, but in addition to these qualities Edith Wharton had
a characteristic which can only be described as zest. She was zestful in
the decoration of her houses, zestful in her long and audacious travels,
zestful in the delight and enthusiasm which she felt for her work. She
seems not to have known fear or discouragement or everyday depression, but perhaps her innate moral and social code forbade her ever to
refer to such moods.

That she was aware of the tensions and restrictions of life lived among
others is evident in her writing, particularly in her masterpieces, *The
House of Mirth, The Custom of the Country, The Reef,* and *The Age of
Innocence.* These novels have to do with the doomed attempts to challenge the social code, but at the same time they establish the very real
validity of the Dionysiac impulse at work in the challenger. Lily Bart

and Undine Spragg are far stronger than those among whom they attempt to establish themselves, just as the exquisite Anna Leath is weaker than the coarse beings to whom it is her lot to be superior. Yet if society wins every time, it is a society of vaguely disappointed and disappointing people, idle, rigid, without ambition. Although not as nerveless as the heroes of her great friend Henry James, Edith Wharton's men are no match for her women.

(pages 197–199)

22. In reporting the two sides of her personality, Edith Wharton _____.
   (A) concentrates on her innermost thoughts and feelings
   (B) tells how her childhood experiences had no effect on her fiction
   (C) reveals a life plagued by unhappiness and self-disgust
   (D) underplays her innermost feelings
   (E) presents a woman almost completely withdrawn from the world

   22 ___

(pages 247–251)

23. All the following are correctly paired EXCEPT _____.
   (A) (5) alludes—refers
   (B) (6) prolific—productive
   (C) (10) stratified—layered
   (D) (12) expatriate—former political leader
   (E) (50) audacious—bold

   23 ___

(pages 184–186)

24. Edith Wharton's behavior in childhood might be characterized as _____.
   (A) unhappy
   (B) traditional
   (C) disrupted by family
   (D) aimless
   (E) unusual

   24 ___

(pages 20–23)

25. In line 17, the context suggests that a "solecism" is _____.
   (A) an excess of overweening pride
   (B) a revelation of basic uncertainty
   (C) a departure from the normal
   (D) an indication of inner turmoil
   (E) an intolerant attack on the establishment

   25 ___

(pages 197–199)

26. When Edith Wharton realized that only one of her relations read her books, she was
   (A) saddened
   (B) furious
   (C) vengeful
   (D) indifferent
   (E) amused

   26 ___

(pages 197–199)

27. A thread running throughout the four novels mentioned in lines 57–58 is _____.
   (A) the loss of innocence in a sophisticated society
   (B) the inevitable victory of culture
   (C) a rebellion against society
   (D) the greater happiness of the upper crust
   (E) the foolish impetuosity of youth

   27 ___

(pages 14–20)

28. In line 60, "validity" most nearly means _____.
   (A) soundness
   (B) strangeness
   (C) contradiction
   (D) explanation
   (E) wonder

   28 ___

(pages 51–55, 247–251)

29. Each of the following is an example of figurative language EXCEPT _____.
   (A) "no cover-up is intended" (3)
   (B) "the borders of consciousness" (8)
   (C) "fiction to emerge and blossom" (16)
   (D) "a very small child" (22)
   (E) "visited by a sudden desire" (27)

   29 ___

(pages 258–263)
30. The author would probably maintain that Edith Wharton is suitable for modern readers. One reason might be that _____.
   - (A) her characters are two-dimensional but the plots are artfully conceived
   - (B) her picture of her own childhood can present models of parenting
   - (C) she presents women characters who are modern in their attitude toward men and society
   - (D) her experiences during the war have a modern ring when placed alongside modern war stories
   - (E) the picture of her contemporary society, though essentially untrue, does provide some colorful hints of life many years ago

30 ____

Section 3

3 3 3

Time-30 Minutes—For each question in this section, select the best answer
35 Questions   from among the choices given.

Each sentence below has one or two blanks, each blank indicating that something has been omitted. Beneath the sentence are five lettered words or sets of words labeled A through E. Choose the word or set of words that *best* fits the meaning of the sentence as a whole.

EXAMPLE

Although its publicity has been _____, the film itself is intelligent, well-acted, handsomely produced, and altogether _____.
   - (A) tasteless . . respectable
   - (B) extensive . . moderate
   - (C) sophisticated . . spectacular
   - (D) risqué . . crude
   - (E) perfect . . spectacular

A

(pages 31–35)
1. Events in the Olympics are not _____, for many events once popular have been dropped and, _____, many new events have been added.
   - (A) dull . . certainly
   - (B) controlled . . surprisingly
   - (C) changeable . . similarly
   - (D) unvarying . . conversely
   - (E) historical . . advantageously

1 ____

(pages 14–20)
2. In an attempt to stop the _____ filibuster, some senators mapped strategy to _____ the cloture rule.
   - (A) interminable . . enforce
   - (B) amusing . . dramatize
   - (C) unexpected . . discuss
   - (D) simple . . research
   - (E) enlightening . . evaluate

2 ____

(pages 14–20)
3. Tour groups in the South Pacific _____ seem to find that explorer Captain James Cook _____ them, whether the scene is Hawaii, Tahiti, or New Caledonia.
   - (A) doggedly . . outdid
   - (B) inevitably . . preceded
   - (C) breathlessly . . foresaw
   - (D) irritably . . missed
   - (E) complacently . . avoided

3 ____

(pages 31–35)
4. Though perpetual motion has long been classified as an impossible dream, _____ inventors still try to patent machines that are supposed to run forever.
(A) informed
(B) callous
(C) biased
(D) candid
(E) undaunted

4 ___

(pages 14–20)
5. The ranger explained, to our _____, that there is no typical "sled dog," that many breeds have proved suitable for the _____ demands of exertion in temperatures below zero.
(A) consternation . . delicate
(B) horror . . occasional
(C) surprise . . rigorous
(D) amusement . . unfair
(E) satisfaction . . expected

5 ___

(pages 20–23)
6. Many tennis experts suggest that the difference between the greats in tennis and the nearly greats is more a matter of _____ and single-mindedness of purpose rather than raw ability.
(A) talent
(B) dexterity
(C) egotism
(D) concentration
(E) guile

6 ___

(pages 31–35)
7. The All-Star game is a(n) _____ affair, offering the opportunity of making a great play and becoming a hero or committing a serious error and becoming an object of _____.
(A) breathless . . wonderment
(B) typical . . scorn
(C) one-shot . . criticism
(D) well-publicized . . analysis
(E) nightmare . . approval

7 ___

(pages 31–35)
8. _____ gas furnaces may run at 65 percent efficiency or less, but a _____ breakthrough now offers furnaces with efficiency ratings of 96 percent or more.
(A) Conventional . . technological
(B) Rejected . . former
(C) Natural . . modest
(D) Ancient . . well-documented
(E) Unpopular . . costly

8 ___

(pages 39–43)
9. The vice-presidency is widely considered a do-nothing office with little or no _____; yet there is never a shortage of applicants for that _____ lowly position.
(A) money . . truly
(B) regrets . . apparently
(C) clout . . disgracefully
(D) reward . . historically
(E) prestige . . supposedly

9 ___

(pages 14–20)
10. Looking like something out of _____, a new X-ray machine can explore the body from every angle without putting a scalpel to the patient and making _____.
(A) mystery stories . . an enquiry
(B) science fiction . . an incision
(C) motion pictures . . a fuss
(D) westerns . . a diagnosis
(E) fantasy . . a disturbance

10 ___

Each question below consists of a related pair of words followed by five lettered pairs of words labeled A through E. Select the lettered pair that *best* expresses a relationship similar to that expressed in the original pair.

EXAMPLE
YAWN : BOREDOM ::
- (A) anger : madness
- (B) dream : sleep
- (C) smile : amusement
- (D) face : expression
- (E) impatience : rebellion

_C_

(pages 166–168, 170)
11. WEED : GARDEN ::
- (A) trim : hedge
- (B) describe : scene
- (C) enjoy : concert
- (D) soar : sailplane
- (E) add : numbers

11 ___

(pages 149–150, 153)
12. NURTURE : SUPPORTIVE ::
- (A) object : rude
- (B) save : frugal
- (C) fret : funny
- (D) judge : argumentative
- (E) reprimand : sorrowful

12 ___

(pages 159–160, 163)
13. ARBITER : IMPARTIALITY ::
- (A) angler : ingenuity
- (B) gardener : diversity
- (C) artist : creativity
- (D) hunter : compassion
- (E) musician : serenity

13 ___

(pages 151–152, 153)
14. TRIP : STUMBLE ::
- (A) weep : shout
- (B) dominate : befriend
- (C) try : err
- (D) amuse : laugh
- (E) eject : recall

14 ___

(pages 169, 170)
15. FOOT-POUND : WORK ::
- (A) kilowatt-hour : electricity
- (B) land : acre
- (C) dollar : gold
- (D) sigh : sadness
- (E) pound : liquid

15 ___

(pages 164–165, 170)
16. STEAM : SCALD ::
- (A) mist : reveal
- (B) telescope : photograph
- (C) ice : chill
- (D) waterfall : display
- (E) tree : leaf

16 ___

(pages 147–149, 153)
17. EXCESSIVE : SCARCITY ::
- (A) cruel : joy
- (B) energetic : fatigue
- (C) curious : vigor
- (D) numerous : quantity
- (E) serious : play

17 ___

(pages 162, 163)
18. AERIALIST : TRAPEZE ::
- (A) makeup : clown
- (B) score : singer
- (C) jogger : routine
- (D) circus : ringmaster
- (E) pathfinder : compass

18 ___

(pages 147–149, 153)
19. MALICE : HUMANE ::
- (A) crusade : evangelical
- (B) health : painstaking
- (C) accord : agreeable
- (D) accident : incidental
- (E) farce : serious

19 ___

(pages 156, 157)
20. MOON : TIDES ::
  (A) pen : pencil
  (B) dog : kennel
  (C) friend : acquaintance
  (D) weather : crops
  (E) telephone : message

20 ___

(pages 159–160, 163)
21. PHILANTHROPIST :
    GENEROSITY ::
  (A) nomad : stability
  (B) knight : chivalry
  (C) computer : programmer
  (D) hockey : puck
  (E) despot : amnesty

21 ___

(pages 150–151, 153)
22. SUBHEAD : OUTLINE ::
  (A) song : recitation
  (B) lamp : light
  (C) clock : chime
  (D) lion : paw
  (E) sole : shoe

22 ___

(pages 155–156, 157)
23. BEAGLE : DOG ::
  (A) sapphire : gem
  (B) cheetah : leopard
  (C) salamander : snake
  (D) beech : oak
  (E) insect : spider

23 ___

The following selection analyzes causes of severe floods and suggests possible preventive measures.

"For too long, we've been trying to adjust rivers to human needs, and then we wonder why our rivers are messed up and why we continue to get flooded; it's not a mystery." Larry Larson, director of the Association of State Floodplain Managers, then went on to say, "We need to
5 adjust human behavior to river systems."
The Midwest floods of 1993 were the worst since records were first kept. For some experts, the disaster was not a surprise. In the previous twenty years, there had been four serious floods. The new situation was a catastrophe just waiting to happen. Property and crop damage ran into
10 the billions of dollars, not millions. The cost in human suffering was incalculable, with many deaths directly attributable to the raging waters.
The questions asked by many victims were "Why? Why didn't our flood-control measures protect us? Could we have foreseen the breaks in the levees? Are we at the mercy of a capricious weather system wholly
15 beyond our control?"
Flood experts agree that weather is unpredictable, that excessive rainfall and drought alternate in unanticipated ways. But before people arrived on the scene, nature had ways of handling such extremes. Natural floodplains were safety valves that let off pressure, reducing the
20 quantity and intensity of flow downstream. Many of these natural balances yielded to commercial, industrial, and residential developments.
People like to build near the seashore. The views are magnificent; the air is cool and clear; the living is pleasurable. But recent northeasters, tropical storms, and hurricanes have shown how tenuous is our
25 grip upon the seashore. Houses are washed away. Beaches are eroded. The sea covers tennis courts, swimming pools, hotel sites. Living at

dune line is chancy at best. Attempts to protect the shore—by building barrier jetties, for example—often exacerbate the problem.

Rivers present similar dangers. It's pleasant to live on the shore of
30 a lovely river, even within walking distance. There is a risk, however. Unsuspecting residents are sometimes washed away by a stream that held a trickle of water the day before. In like manner but on a grander scale, the areas bordering the Missouri—Ohio—Mississippi basin are also at risk.

35 In an attempt to tame the wild rivers, engineers have prevented the floodplain from performing its basic natural function: flood control. The plain stores and slows flood waters, reducing the force and height of the water. The situation has a parallel in a common household experience. When a nozzle isn't available, a gardener can partially block with
40 fingers the end of the hose, increasing its force and reach. The levee system squeezes the river water in the same way, increasing the force of the water. Such water is concentrated, not allowed to dissipate its strength and volume in a floodplain. When the levees fail to hold, as so often happens, the water rushes through with ferocious intensity and
45 forms a floodplain not always convenient for those who live in the flooded areas.

"Cooperate with nature; don't fight it." The new approach to flood control doesn't try to subdue natural forces but to work with them. It tries to restore natural ecosystems, permitting natural flood-control
50 systems to work.

New methods are being devised. Communities are acquiring wetlands to serve as natural flood basins. Throughout the plain, they are creating natural detention areas for flood waters. Stretches of natural floodplain are being used as parks, ball fields, and green belts. When
55 these are flooded the problem is temporary. Many communities are discouraging development of areas that are prime targets for flooding. Soldiers Grove in Wisconsin has moved the entire business district to higher ground. Littleton, Colorado, has established a 625-acre park in its floodplain to relieve the flood pressures of the South Platte River.

60 "We can't pick Des Moines up and put it on a hill," an army engineer, Harry Fitch, declared. Existing cities in the floodplain present continuing difficulties. Long-range planning, combining some structural methods along with natural ones, holds some hope for the future. One thing is certain. Sometime in the future, the rains in the great river watershed
65 will again be excessive. Rampaging waters will roar down the narrow river corridors. Will the people again be subjected to communities without water, power, or sewage? Will they watch the waters rise to the top floors of their houses? How quickly and effectively can we take measures that take the sting out of abnormal weather conditions?

70 Mankind continues to learn, at its peril, that tampering with natural ecosystems can be fatal.

(pages 186–189)
24. The overriding message of the selection is that _____.
(A) the 1993 floods were the worst in history
(B) some communities are making progress in flood control
(C) floods are a continuing nightmare for people of the Midwest
(D) cooperation with nature makes more sense than fighting it
(E) flood plains are safety valves

24 ___

(pages 24–27)
25. In line 14, "capricious" most nearly means _____.
(A) cruel
(B) overloaded with moisture
(C) erratic
(D) regularly cyclical
(E) nourishing

25 ___

(pages 197–199)
26. The author asks two questions in lines 13–15: "Could . . . control?" His two answers would be _____:
(A) No. Yes.
(B) No. No.
(C) No. Not entirely.
(D) Yes. Not entirely.
(E) Yes. Yes.

26 ___

(pages 205–208)
27. The author brings in the seashore example to _____.
(A) contrast the problems of seashore dwellers with those who live near rivers
(B) provide an example of how well people have coped with problems at the shore
(C) provide a light change of pace in the development of his idea
(D) show how a floodplain also exists at the shore
(E) compare two areas with somewhat similar problems

27 ___

(pages 205–208)
28. The two items that are most similar in intended function are _____.
(A) levees and town parks
(B) jetties and levees
(C) jetties and floodplains
(D) levees and floodplains
(E) jetties and green belts

28 ___

(pages 14–20)
29. In line 24, "tenuous" most nearly means _____.
(A) recent
(B) sharp
(C) slight
(D) firm
(E) well-intended

29 ___

(pages 51–55, 247–251)
30. All the following are examples of figurative language EXCEPT _____.
(A) "there had been four serious floods" (8)
(B) "catastrophe just waiting to happen" (9)
(C) "floodplains were safety valves" (19)
(D) "waters will roar" (65)
(E) "measures that take the sting out" (69)

30 ___

(pages 31–35)
31. In line 42, "dissipate" most nearly means _____.
(A) intensify
(B) scatter
(C) pollute
(D) gather
(E) discover

31 ___

(pages 247–251)
32. The following are all mentioned as remedies for flood control EXCEPT _____.
    (A) acquiring wetlands
    (B) using parks
    (C) discouraging development
    (D) moving to higher ground
    (E) reinforcing levees

    32 ___

(pages 225–229)
33. Which of the following quotations best expresses the viewpoint of the author?
    (A) "Let us permit nature to have her way: she understands her business better than we do." Montaigne
    (B) "Nature, like us, is sometimes caught without her diadem." Emily Dickinson
    (C) "Nature, red in tooth and claw." Tennyson
    (D) "In nature's infinite book of secrecy
        A little I can read." Shakespeare
    (E) "Nature is visible thought." Heinrich Heine

    33 ___

(pages 210–213)
34. The most serious difficulty in controlling the floods is _____.
    (A) trying to guess when the next bad weather will occur
    (B) stated by Harry Kitch
    (C) overlooked by citizens of Soldiers Grove
    (D) overlooked by Larry Larson
    (E) obvious to all riverside dwellers

    34 ___

(pages 184–186)
35. The key problem in flood control is _____.
    (A) the lack of neighborliness among townspeople
    (B) insufficient levees
    (C) unawareness of solutions by any engineer
    (D) failure to warn areas of impending floods
    (E) shortsightedness

    35 ___

Section 5

5 5 5 5 5

Time-15 Minutes—For each question in this section, select the best answer
   13 Questions   from among the choices given.

The passage below is followed by questions based on its content. Answer the questions on the basis of what is <u>stated</u> or <u>implied</u> in the passage and in any introductory material that may be provided.

In this excerpt from a detective novel set in the American Southwest, two Navajo police officers are at odds over the place of witchcraft in the Navajo culture. A bone bead begins the confrontation.

Still, Leaphorn had kept the bone bead.
"I'll see about it," he'd said. "Send it to the lab. Find out if it is bone, and what kind of bone." He'd torn a page from his notebook, wrapped the bead in it, and placed it in the coin compartment of his
5 billfold. Then he'd looked at Chee for a moment in silence. "Any idea how it got in here?"

"Sounds strange," Chee had said. "But you know you could pry out the end of a shotgun shell and pull out the wadding and stick a bead like this in with the pellets."

10 Leaphorn's expression became almost a smile. Was it contempt? "Like a witch shooting in the bone?" he asked. "They're supposed to do that through a little tube." He made a puffing shape with his lips.

Chee had nodded, flushing just a little.

Now, remembering it, he was angry again. Well, to hell with Leap-
15 horn. Let him believe whatever he wanted to believe. The origin story of the Navajos explained witchcraft clearly enough, and it was a logical part of the philosophy on which the Dinee had founded their culture. If there was good, and harmony, and beauty on the east side of reality, then there must be evil, chaos, and ugliness to the west. Like a nonfunda-
20 mentalist Christian, Chee believed in the poetic metaphor of the Navajo story of human genesis. Without believing in the specific Adam's rib, or the size of the reed through which the Holy People emerged to the Earth Surface World, he believed in the lessons such imagery was intended to teach. To hell with Leaphorn and what he didn't believe. Chee
25 started the engine and jolted back down the slope to the road. He wanted to get to Badwater Wash before noon.

But he couldn't quite get Leaphorn out of his mind. Leaphorn posed a problem. "One more thing," the lieutenant had said. "We've got a complaint about you." And he'd told Chee what the doctor at the Bad-
30 water Clinic had said about him. "Yellowhorse claims you've been interfering with his practice of his religion," Leaphorn said. And while the lieutenant's expression said he didn't take the complaint as anything critically important, the very fact that he'd mentioned it implied that Chee should desist.

35 "I have been telling people that Yellowhorse is a fake," Chee said stiffly. "I have told people every chance I get that the doctor pretends to be a crystal gazer just to get them into his clinic."

"I hope you're not doing that on company time," Leaphorn said. "Not while you're on duty."

40 "I probably have," Chee said. "Why not?"

"Because it violates regulations," Leaphorn said, his expression no longer even mildly amused.

"How?"

"I think you can see how," Leaphorn had said. "We don't have any
45 way to license our shamans, no more than the federal government can license preachers. If Yellowhorse says he's a medicine man, or a hand trembler, or a road chief of the Native American Church, or the Pope, it is no business of the Navajo Tribal Police. No rule against it. No law."

"I'm a Navajo," Chee said. "I see somebody cynically using our
50 religion . . . somebody who doesn't believe in our religion using it in that cynical way. . ."

"What harm is he doing?" Leaphorn asked. "The way I understand it, he recommends they go to a *yataalii* if they need a ceremonial sing. And he points them at the white man's hospital only if they have a white
55 man's problem. Diabetes, for example."

Chee had made no response to that. If Leaphorn couldn't see the problem, the sacrilege involved, then Leaphorn was blind. But that wasn't the trouble. Leaphorn was as cynical as Yellowhorse.

"You, yourself, have declared yourself to be a *yataalii,* I hear,"
60 Leaphorn said. "I heard you performed a Blessing Way."

Chee had nodded. He said nothing.

Leaphorn had looked at him a moment, and sighed. "I'll talk to Largo about it," he said.

And that meant that one of these days Chee would have an argument
65 with the captain about it and if he wasn't lucky, Largo would give him a flat, unequivocal order to say nothing more about Yellowhorse as shaman. When that happened, he would cope as best he could. Now the road to Badwater had changed from bad to worse. Chee concentrated on driving.

(pages 197–199)
1. The officers are apparently concerned with the bone bead because it is some kind of _____.
   (A) ornamentation
   (B) shotgun shell
   (C) writing
   (D) evidence
   (E) food

1 ___

(pages 265–270)
2. When Leaphorn says, "They're supposed to do that through a little tube," he is being _____.
   (A) cruel
   (B) witty
   (C) sarcastic
   (D) sympathetic
   (E) alarmed

2 ___

(pages 265–270)
3. The relationship between Chee and Leaphorn can best be described as _____.
   (A) comradely
   (B) prickly
   (C) indifferent
   (D) satisfying
   (E) dangerous

3 ___

(pages 197–199)
4. We might infer that Chee's attitude toward his religion is basically _____.
   (A) reverent   (D) negative
   (B) confused   (E) depressing
   (C) belligerent

4 ___

(pages 200–202)
5. The best description of Yellowhorse is that he _____.
   (A) is a Navajo doctor who scorns Western medicine
   (B) is an undercover member of the Navajo Tribal Police
   (C) has set himself up as some kind of medicine man
   (D) once did Leaphorn a favor and is now protected by him
   (E) proposes to cure all diseases himself

5 ___

(pages 14–20)
6. On line 57, "sacrilege" suggests _____.
   (A) a disrespect for sacred things
   (B) a religious rite performed by a priest
   (C) unintentional humor
   (D) active participation in religion
   (E) a sacred activity

6 ___

(pages 210–213)
7. Yellowhorse's practices cannot be stopped because _____.
   (A) he is a member of another Native American tribe
   (B) he has somehow bribed persons in high authority
   (C) he is doing a wonderful job
   (D) there is no law against his activities
   (E) his intentions are honorable

7 ___

(pages 24–27)
8. In line 51, "cynical" most nearly means _____.
   (A) optimistic
   (B) sneering
   (C) naive
   (D) well-informed
   (E) enthusiastic

8 ___

(pages 210–213)
9. Largo is identified as _____.
   (A) Leaphorn's subordinate
   (B) Chee's detective partner
   (C) a doctor supplied by the federal government
   (D) a Tribal Police captain
   (E) a relative of Yellowhorse's

9 ___

(pages 75–91)
10. In line 66, the word "unequivocal" most nearly means _____.
    (A) unique
    (B) confusing
    (C) double-barreled
    (D) clear
    (E) improper

10 ___

(pages 210–213)
11. The best way to find the answer to question 9 is to _____.
    (A) reread the first sentence of each paragraph for topic-sentence clues
    (B) skim through rapidly, looking for the word *Largo*
    (C) read the entire article carefully
    (D) search your memory for possible recall
    (E) examine carefully the first two paragraphs for early clues

11 ___

(pages 265–270)
12. Lieutenant Leaphorn may best be characterized as _____.
    (A) a world-weary man of keen intelligence
    (B) a rather gullible believer in the status quo
    (C) a hot-headed irrational bully
    (D) an enthusiastic newcomer to tribal matters
    (E) a person willing to scrap the rules for a cause

12 ___

(pages 230–233)
13. The central character of the story seems to be Chee, but Leaphorn is introduced by the author to provide essential _____.
    (A) local color
    (B) humorous episodes
    (C) conflict and give-and-take
    (D) tragic overtones
    (E) suspects for the mystery

13 ___

Facsimile Test 4

Time-30 Minutes—For each question in this section, select the best answer
   30 Questions   from among the choices given.

Each sentence below has one or two blanks, each blank indicating that
something has been omitted. Beneath the sentence are five lettered words
or sets of words labeled A through E. Choose the word or set of words that
best fits the meaning of the sentence as a whole.

EXAMPLE

Although its publicity has been _____,
the film itself is intelligent, well-acted,
handsomely produced, and altogether _____.

  (A) tasteless . . respectable
  (B) extensive . . moderate
  (C) sophisticated . . spectacular
  (D) risqué . . crude
  (E) perfect . . spectacular

                        A

(pages 35–38)

1. Strenuous exercise can be _____ and
   sometimes _____, especially for those
   in the middle years and later.
  (A) easygoing . . overwhelming
  (B) physical . . unpleasant
  (C) addictive . . excessive
  (D) habitual . . occasional
  (E) comical . . austere

                        1 __

(pages 31–35)

2. Although the _____ of many a Renais-
   sance painting is a portrait, the artist
   managed to insert a lovely landscape
   into the _____.
  (A) foreground . . framework
  (B) description . . setting
  (C) basis . . altarpiece
  (D) ground . . border
  (E) subject . . background

                        2 __

(pages 20–23)

3. In the desert a severe storm fifty miles
   away may cause _____ flooding,
   drowning _____ travelers.
  (A) deep . . arrogant
  (B) surprising . . eastern
  (C) alpine . . mountain-climbing
  (D) catastrophic . . unwary
  (E) monumental . . lackadaisical

                        3 __

(pages 20–23, 89, 92)

4. When asked about his stand on the
   civil rights issue, the shrewd candi-
   date _____ and then _____, leaving
   considerable doubt as to his real po-
   sition.
  (A) stammered . . shouted
  (B) hesitated . . equivocated
  (C) rose . . explained
  (D) sighed . . babbled
  (E) shouted . . apologized

                        4 __

(pages 39–43)

5. The continuing success of "Radio
   Reader" on National Public Radio
   proves _____ that even adults like to
   be read to, if the material is _____.
  (A) humorously . . outrageous
  (B) paradoxically . . personal
  (C) vigorously . . abstruse
  (D) conclusively . . interesting
  (E) brilliantly . . prerecorded

                        5 __

(pages 20–23)
6. Believing that the story of Jason and the Golden Fleece has a basis in historical fact, a British author duplicated the voyage of the *Argo,* using a _____ of a Bronze Age boat for the _____.
   (A) replica . . venture
   (B) representative . . trip
   (C) photograph . . routing
   (D) pilot . . production
   (E) hull . . safari

6 ___

(pages 20–23)
7. Though never accepted by society and the military, Eva Peron, wife of Argentinian president Juan Peron, won _____ and emotional support from the masses of people.
   (A) contempt
   (B) interest
   (C) adoration
   (D) appeasement
   (E) acquaintanceship

7 ___

(pages 31–35)
8. Exhausted but not _____, the climbers gazed at the peak of Everest and resolved to make a run for the _____ the next day.
   (A) elated . . camp
   (B) defeated . . summit
   (C) incapacitated . . slope
   (D) foolish . . sanctuary
   (E) indifferent . . flag

8 ___

(pages 31–35)
9. Casey Stengel, whose _____ prose often concealed a great deal of baseball sense, found new ways of making a simple idea _____.
   (A) brilliant . . crystal clear
   (B) recorded . . emphatic
   (C) straightforward . . incomprehensible
   (D) vigorous . . unimportant
   (E) tortured . . complicated

9 ___

Each question below consists of a related pair of words followed by five lettered pairs of words labeled A through E. Select the lettered pair that *best* expresses a relationship similar to that expressed in the original pair.

```
EXAMPLE
YAWN : BOREDOM ::
  (A) anger : madness
  (B) dream : sleep
  (C) smile : amusement
  (D) face : expression
  (E) impatience : rebellion
                            C
```

(pages 160–161, 163)
10. COACH : ATHLETE ::
    (A) criminal : victim
    (B) teacher : student
    (C) hunter : angler
    (D) writer : editor
    (E) child : doll

10 ___

(pages 164–165, 170)
11. UTOPIA : PERFECTION ::
    (A) anesthesia : activity
    (B) uproar : noise
    (C) impudence : attention
    (D) contract : contribution
    (E) authority : commendation

11 ___

(pages 149–150, 153)
12. INFINITY : BOUNDLESS ::
    (A) emotion : satisfying
    (B) gullibility : credulous
    (C) distinction : similarity
    (D) aptness : dexterity
    (E) deviation : repetition

12 ___

(pages 155–157)
13. STREAM : RIVER ::
   (A) bridge : span
   (B) automobile : motorcycle
   (C) pamphlet : correspondence
   (D) highway : road
   (E) sapling : tree

13 ___

(pages 161–162, 163)
15. APPRENTICE : LEARN ::
   (A) penitent : rejoice
   (B) humanitarian : observe
   (C) devotee : fear
   (D) blackguard : reclaim
   (E) charlatan : deceive

15 ___

(pages 147–149, 153)
14. PSEUDONYM : AUTHENTIC ::
   (A) flicker : flame
   (B) deliberation : reasonable
   (C) writer : anonymity
   (D) delay : punctual
   (E) measure : proportional

14 ___

Each passage below is followed by questions based on its content. Answer the questions following each passage on the basis of what is stated or implied in that passage and in any introductory material that may be provided.

The following selection, from a chapter on French Gothic architecture, presents an individual point of view about certain cathedrals.

Nothing could be more typical of its age than that both Notre-Dame de Paris and the Sainte-Chapelle should be situated on the Île de la Cité in the middle of Paris, with that again as the heart or kernel of the Île de France, and the two buildings in question embodying in themselves
5 so much of the national character and genius. The exterior of Notre-Dame is as typically, as irrevocably French as a French railway engine, but this is of course until the impersonal introduction of the diesel engine when even trains lost their character and nationality. The idiom and idiosyncrasy of the outside of Notre-Dame is in the flying buttresses,
10 and it is ever an experience to walk round the sides and back of Notre-Dame in order to look at them.
   The flying buttresses are in every sense the stresses of the building: there, of necessity, and as implicit to the whole as sails to a sailing ship. Or they are more nearly equivalent to the tie ropes that prevent the
15 whole vessel of stone from keeling over, as, indeed, could happen in a heavy gale. Soon it is apparent that the nave of Notre-Dame could not stand up without them. Yet they come out of the walls, thicken in their downward descent, and join into free-standing pinnacles or tie posts that are firmly planted in the ground, and now seem to us for a moment
20 like the claws, whiskers, antennae, of some crustacean animal coming toward us slowly, purposefully, but with uncoordinated walk along the seabed.
   Have they, as well, an ornamental purpose? Are they like the curlers in a woman's hair?—which make the best of necessity when they are

25   in position and leave things the better when they are removed away.
But the flying buttresses are no temporary measure. They are not there
to be taken down at an appointed time. And it is not the flying buttresses
that are in danger, unless the building they are propping up collapses
on them. It would fall in on itself while they stand out of the way. At
30   Notre-Dame the flying buttresses are solid like stalks or limbs of stone.
At Amiens, which may be a few years later in date, they have arches
of varying size with little trefoil heads worked into them so that they
resemble one side only, over and over again, of a Gothic Bridge of Sighs.
And what will happen at Notre-Dame when the tie ropes are cut and the
35   stone vessel runs down the slip-way and is launched with a big splash? It
suddenly becomes clear to our eyes that the flying buttresses of Notre-
Dame are absurd as well as necessary; that they are in some degree a
confession of failure, of undertaking a building that they lacked the skill
to make stand of its own strength and had perforce to leave the stays
40   and the scaffolding permanently in place; that the flying buttresses are
the props or crutches, not the wings and crest. But not for anything
would one have them otherwise or not be there.

The front of Notre-Dame I find less inspiring, for most of the great
iconographical schemes of sculpture on its three portals were seriously
45   damaged during the Revolution. The ironwork of the doors is better
preserved than the stone carvings, while the gallery of the Kings of
Israel and Judah, mythical ancestors of the Kings of France, are nineteenth-century replacements and proclaim that at the first glance. For
the lover of rose windows like the present writer, there is a simple and
50   beautiful specimen of its kind above them. But it is above the gallery
that forms the third story of the façade of Notre-Dame, at the base of
its two towers, that there runs the balustrade or parapet on which are
perched the strange beasts and birds, the hobgoblins and chimaeras that
lean out, looking down over Paris.

(pages 197–199)

16. Though "Flying buttresses" are nowhere defined exactly, the reader may
infer that they are a special kind of support characterized by _____.

(A) slanting braces attached to the
walls and ending on tops of posts
(B) additional heavy posts supporting
the roof in the wall of the building
(C) light and airy wall structures en-
closing stained-glass windows
(D) religious decorations apparent to
every worshiper who enters the
building
(E) S-shaped elements that help support the walls

16 ___

(pages 78, 89)

17. In line 6, "irrevocably" most nearly
means _____.

(A) dubiously
(B) certainly
(C) irresponsibly
(D) in an undistinguished manner
(E) uncommonly

17 ___

(pages 247–251)
18. Each of the following is correctly paired EXCEPT _____.
   (A) (line 8) idiom—special kind of expression
   (B) (9) idiosyncrasy—personal peculiarity
   (C) (13) implicit—natural
   (D) (20) crustacean—absurdly designed
   (E) (32) trefoil—three-leafed decoration

18 ___

(pages 197–199)
19. The author apparently feels that the nineteenth-century replacements of original statues are _____.
   (A) noticeably inferior to the imagined originals
   (B) needed in the structure of the building
   (C) cleaner, fresher, hence slightly superior
   (D) placed too high for adequate study and appreciation
   (E) likely to interfere with the view of the rose window

19 ___

(pages 247–251)
20. Each of the following terms as applied to a church are mentioned EXCEPT _____.
   (A) nave—main aisle
   (B) façade—front
   (C) balustrade—railing
   (D) parapet—low wall
   (E) transept—crossing aisle

20 ___

(pages 51–55, 247–251)
21. All the following are examples of figurative language EXCEPT _____.
   (A) "the heart or kernel" (line 3)
   (B) "an experience to walk round the sides and back" (10)
   (C) "vessel of stone from keeling over" (15)
   (D) "like the claws, whiskers, antennae" (20)
   (E) "the props or crutches" (41)

21 ___

The excerpt below is a short short story. Two young people are discussing a project the woman has in mind.

Today she tells me that it is her ambition to walk the Appalachian Trail, from Maine to Georgia. I ask how far it is. She says, "Some two thousand miles."

"No, no," I reply, "you must mean two hundred, not two
5 thousand."

"I mean two thousand," she says, "more or less, two thousand miles long. I've done some reading too, about people who've completed the journey. It's amazing."

"Well, you've read the wrong stuff," I say. "You should've read
10 about the ones that didn't make it. Those stories are more important. Why they gave up is probably why you shouldn't be going."

"I don't care about that, I'm going," she says with a determined look. "My mind is made up."

"Listen," I say, reaching for words to crush her dream. "Figure it
15 out, figure out the time. How long will it take to walk two thousand miles?" I leap up to get a pen and paper. Her eyes follow me, like a cat that is ready to pounce.

"Here now," I say, pen working, setting numbers deep into the paper. "Let's say you walk, on average, some twenty miles a day. That's
20 twenty into two thousand, right? It goes one hundred times. And so, one hundred equals exactly one hundred years. It'll take you one hundred years!"

"Don't be stupid," she says. "One hundred *days,* not years."

"Oh, yeah, okay, days," I mumble. I was never good at math. I feel
25 as if someone has suddenly twisted an elastic band around my forehead. I crumple the paper, turn to her and say, "So if it's one hundred days, what is that? How many months?"

"A little over three." She calculates so fast that I agree without thinking. "Fine, but call it four months," I say, "because there's bound
30 to be some delay: weather, shopping for supplies, maybe first-aid treatments. You never know, you have to make allowances."

"All right, I make allowances, four months."

What have I done? It sounds as if all of this nonsense is still in full swing. *Say more about the time.* "Okay," I say, "so where do we get
35 the time to go? What about my job? What about my responsibilities, *your* responsibilities too? What about—?"

"What about I send you a postcard when I finish the trip," she says, leaving the room.

I sit there mouthing my pen. I hear her going down the basement
40 steps. Pouting now, I think. Sulking. She knows she's wrong about this one.

"Seen my backpack?" she calls from below. God, she's really going to do it. "Next to mine," I say, "On the shelf beside the freezer."

I am angry with myself. She has had her way, won without even
45 trying. "Take mine down too," I blurt out. "You can't expect to walk the Appalachian Trail all alone." I stare at my feet. "Sorry," I say to them both, "I'm really sorry about all of this."

(pages 225–229)
22. The narrator's attitude toward the woman's project may be characterized as _____.
(A) bitter   (D) skeptical
(B) enthusiastic (E) devious
(C) curious

22 ___

(pages 51–55)
23. An example of figurative language is _____.
(A) "like a cat that is ready to pounce . . ."
(B) "What about my responsibilities?"
(C) "I crumple the paper."
(D) "one hundred days . . ."
(E) "A little over three . . ."

23 ___

(pages 271–279)
24. From the dialogue we may reasonably assume that _____.
(A) the woman is a scatterbrain
(B) the man loves the woman
(C) the Appalachian Trail is easy to complete
(D) the couple do not get along
(E) the couple will not attempt the hike

24 ___

(pages 265–270)
25. In getting the man to come with her, the woman was _____.
(A) heavy-handed   (D) argumentative
(B) fearful   (E) slow-witted
(C) clever

25 ___

(pages 265–270)
26. The words "Say more about the time" in line 34 are in *italic* type to indicate that _____.
   - (A) the narrator is speaking directly to the woman
   - (B) the narrator is thinking to himself
   - (C) the narrator has written down a note
   - (D) the woman is about to explain at considerable length
   - (E) the clock has probably just struck

   26 ____

(pages 271–279)
27. When the woman mentions the postcard (line 37), he _____.
   - (A) rages out of control
   - (B) sees the vision through her eyes
   - (C) knows he has lost
   - (D) decides to get a map
   - (E) finishes the sentence she had interrupted

   27 ____

(pages 197–199)
28. From the dialogue we may infer that _____.
   - (A) the man is an unfeeling bully
   - (B) the woman is a shrew
   - (C) there are barriers of communication between them
   - (D) there is essentially good rapport between them
   - (E) the man has no sense of humor

   28 ____

(pages 222–225)
29. The ending has been planned to _____.
   - (A) suggest the man's sudden refusal to go
   - (B) increase the tension
   - (C) add a touch of humor
   - (D) leave the reader wondering
   - (E) resolve the problem about job responsibilities

   29 ____

(pages 197–199)
30. Though the story is short, the dialogue succeeds in _____.
   - (A) arousing the reader's interest in hiking the Appalachian Trail
   - (B) suggesting a relationship between a man and a woman
   - (C) emphasizing the irrational element in a man's life
   - (D) declaring the natural superiority of women
   - (E) irritating the unsuspecting reader

   30 ____

Section 3

3 3 3

Time-30 Minutes—For each question in this section, select the best answer
35 Questions   from among the choices given.

Each sentence below has one or two blanks, each blank indicating that something has been omitted. Beneath the sentence are five lettered words or sets of words labeled A through E. Choose the word or set of words that *best* fits the meaning of the sentence as a whole.

(pages 31–35)
1. Within the borders of Nepal are some
of the highest mountains in the world,
but the southern portion of the country
contains the Terai, a _____ region of
swamps, forests, and cultivable land.
(A) barren   (D) friendly
(B) low-lying   (E) historic
(C) steep
1 ___

(pages 20–23)
2. It is a hard fact of economics that
some of the most boring, _____, repetitive jobs bring the lowest financial _____.
(A) tedious . . remuneration
(B) challenging . . reward
(C) unnecessary . . recognition
(D) weary . . productivity
(E) life-threatening . . contracts
2 ___

(pages 24–27)
3. Brad knocks over glasses and bumps
into things with the cheerful _____ of
a month-old puppy.
(A) vigor
(B) premeditation
(C) friendliness
(D) malice
(E) clumsiness
3 ___

(pages 20–23)
4. Because the field of computers encourages creative _____, many young
computer wizards have made significant _____ and have become million-
aires.
(A) duplication . . contributions
(B) experimentation . . failures
(C) imitation . . modifications
(D) innovation . . breakthroughs
(E) communication . . miniatures
4 ___

(pages 20–23)
5. When there is stiff competition, air-
lines offer all kinds of bonuses
and _____ that _____ passengers to
choose one airline rather than another.
(A) tickets . . impel
(B) meals . . compel
(C) incentives . . induce
(D) awards . . allow
(E) theories . . provoke
5 ___

(pages 24–27)
6. In *Puzzles from Other Worlds,* the au-
thor-wizard Martin Gardner provides _____ brainteasers, with one
puzzle leading to another and another,
all written in _____ prose that carries
the reader effortlessly along.
(A) numerous . . adequate
(B) several . . flowery
(C) challenging . . spritely
(D) repetitive . . pedestrian
(E) transparent . . humdrum
6 ___

(pages 28–31)
7. To the _____ visitors, the dome of
the Taj Mahal, like a silver bowl floating on a shadowy sea, had a(n) _____
glow in the moonlight.
(A) casual . . incandescent
(B) awestruck . . otherworldly
(C) numerous . . ineffectual
(D) critical . . obscure
(E) assembled . . unimaginable
7 ___

(pages 20–23, 31–35)

8. _____ old Boston belies its reputation as a(n) _____ city, for it surprisingly celebrates Bastille Day, on July 14, with dancing and feasting on Marlborough Street.
(A) Unruffled . . backwoods
(B) Wily . . New England
(C) Flighty . . down-to-earth
(D) Exuberant . . tempestuous
(E) Staid . . proper

8 ___

(pages 31–35)

9. The golden tan, now a _____ symbol suggesting affluence and a carefree lifestyle, once was _____ avoided by all Victorian ladies.
(A) familiar . . seldom
(B) cheerful . . sullenly
(C) variable . . unintentionally
(D) prestige . . earnestly
(E) hard-won . . unconsciously

9 ___

(pages 14–20)

10. The _____ rain of tropical rain forests may deprive the soil of precious nutrients and leave it ecologically _____ for other uses.
(A) constant . . unsuitable
(B) warm . . overheated
(C) occasional . . arid
(D) well-publicized . . ready
(E) moisture-laden . . accommodating

10 ___

Each question below consists of a related pair of words followed by five lettered pairs of words labeled A through E. Select the lettered pair that *best* expresses a relationship similar to that expressed in the original pair.

EXAMPLE
YAWN : BOREDOM ::
(A) anger : madness
(B) dream : sleep
(C) smile : amusement
(D) face : expression
(E) impatience : rebellion

C

(pages 149–150, 153)

11. BLASÉ : APATHY ::
(A) lacking : deficiency
(B) defense : armored
(C) convex : microscopic
(D) argumentative : conundrum
(E) pagan : religious

11 ___

(pages 154–155, 157)

12. NICK : GOUGE ::
(A) niche : chip
(B) crater : lava
(C) dislike : detest
(D) lethal : deadly
(E) correction : fact

12 ___

(pages 164–165, 170)

13. HEAT : CONVECTION ::
(A) freeze : cold
(B) loss : anxiety
(C) thermometer : degrees
(D) oration : rebuttal
(E) poison : antidote

13 ___

(pages 160–161, 163)
14. NOMAD : WANDERING ::
   (A) laborer : humor
   (B) invalid : health
   (C) gymnast : curiosity
   (D) surgeon : dexterity
   (E) peasant : wealth

14 ___

(pages 158–159, 163)
15. SOOTHSAYER : FORETELLS ::
   (A) whimpers : puppy
   (B) soloist : animates
   (C) accountant : calculates
   (D) amateur : personifies
   (E) welder : glows

15 ___

(pages 152, 153)
16. FILE : CORRESPONDENCE ::
   (A) drawer : desk
   (B) stream : brook
   (C) book : concept
   (D) closet : clothing
   (E) room : window

16 ___

(pages 154–155, 157)
17. ALARM : TERRIFY ::
   (A) revive : alert
   (B) scatter : clutter
   (C) look : see
   (D) reveal : disclose
   (E) reprimand : denounce

17 ___

(pages 164–165)
18. MARATHON : ENDURANCE ::
   (A) track : field
   (B) gardening : strength
   (C) nightmare : dream
   (D) fever : temperature
   (E) impetuosity : patience

18 ___

(pages 164–165, 170)
19. BRAZEN : BOLDNESS ::
   (A) brassy : iron
   (B) freezing : heat
   (C) breathless : patient
   (D) cramped : congestion
   (E) competitive : victory

19 ___

(pages 147–149, 153)
20. CHILDLIKE : SOPHISTICATION ::
   (A) tardy : punctuality
   (B) purposeful : goal
   (C) cowardly : foolishness
   (D) critical : rebuke
   (E) reliable : recompense

20 ___

(pages 166–168, 170)
21. KITCHEN : COOKING ::
   (A) cabinetmaker : carpentry
   (B) pebble : gardening
   (C) barn : refrigeration
   (D) office : weaving
   (E) theater : acting

21 ___

(pages 161–162, 163)
22. SUPERVISES : DIRECTOR ::
   (A) swimmer : dives
   (B) sketches : orator
   (C) disrupts : troublemaker
   (D) provokes : acquaintance
   (E) recalls : astronaut

22 ___

(pages 166–168, 170)
23. EQUATOR : EARTH ::
   (A) circumference : circle
   (B) latitude : longitude
   (C) degree : minute
   (D) skin : pear
   (E) pencil : eraser

23 ___

The passage below is followed by questions based on its content. Answer the questions on the basis of what is stated or implied in the passage and in any introductory material.

The following passage discusses various national days, each with its own "festivities, speeches, celebrations." How did these arise?

Islam as a religion is more overtly historical than either Christianity or Judaism, and its birth is a more explicitly defined sequence of historical events. The founder of Judaism is difficult to name; the founder of Christianity suffered and died on the cross, and his followers remained
5 a persecuted minority for centuries. The founder of Islam became a sovereign in his lifetime, governing a community, administering justice, and commanding armies, and history of the conventional type begins with his own career. Perhaps for this very reason, the major Muslim festivals are not primarily historical. The birthday of the Prophet Mu-
10 hammad is, however, celebrated as a minor festival, and the birthdays of numerous local holy men are also commemorated by feasts and fairs in much the same way as the lesser saints of Christendom. The Muslims also seem to have adopted from the Jews the practice of compiling historical calendars, known as *taqwīm*, setting forth the anniversaries of major
15 events in the past. The purpose of these is partly to help commemoration, partly to assist in predicting the future.

Until modern times such commemorations were almost exclusively religious; even the foundation of Rome, ostensibly a secular event, was celebrated by priests and with sacrifices. The modern series of commem-
20 orative anniversaries seems to have begun with the American July 4 and it is noteworthy that American historians who have tackled this problem critically have been unable to agree on the precise significance of this date. What if anything did happen on the Fourth of July and was it that day anyway? The popular memory, however, is unconcerned with such
25 scholarly niceties. The winning of American independence was a long-drawn-out and complex process, but the popular imagination, as so often, telescoped it into a single dramatic event on a single date suitable for annual celebration. In the same way, a few years later, the storming of the Bastille on July 14 provided the peg on which to hang the annual
30 celebration of that long series of changes and upheavals, the French Revolution.

The pattern set by the United States and France was followed by many other nations, each establishing some national day to provide an occasion for festivities, speeches, celebrations, and other methods of
35 restoring and revitalizing the nationalist or revolutionary energy, as the case may be, of the nation concerned. Even the older nations which have undergone the rigors neither of liberation nor of revolution have felt obliged to conform to the pattern and have chosen, rather arbitrarily, some saint's day or historical event as a national day. In England, where
40 the doctrine of the ancient constitution and immemorial liberties of Englishmen precluded the ascribing of a foundation date to either, the monarch's birthday, officially and permanently fixed in early June, provides the formal occasion for celebration, while the popular fancy fastened on Guy Fawkes, a Catholic conspirator whose failure to blow up Parlia-
45 ment in 1605 is still celebrated with fireworks and effigies—called guys—every November 5. There are now more than a hundred embassies and legations in Washington, each of them with at least one national celebration to which officials must be invited every year, and the grow-

414

ing burden of commemoration is a serious impediment to the conduct
50 of public affairs.

Sometimes the authorities who seek to commemorate some major
historical event in which they are the prime movers are not content with
merely setting an anniversary, but seek to establish a new era. In most
parts of the world it was usual in antiquity to date events from the
55 beginning of a new reign or dynasty. This custom still survives in some
parts. The foundation of Rome and the career of Alexander provided
the starting points of calendars of more general and extensive usage.
Judaism, as a religion which has no specific starting point, had no specific calendar, but used several, finally settling on the present era pur-
60 porting to date from the creation of the world. Christianity and Islam
each envisaged themselves as starting a new era and began new calendars, the one dating from the birth of Christ, the other from the migration
of Muhammad from Mecca to Medina or, more precisely, from the beginning of the Arab year in which that event took place. In more modern
65 times both the French revolutionaries and the Italian fascisti attempted
to demonstrate the importance of their achievements and the momentous
significance of their advent by starting new calendars. Neither was of
long duration.

Another form of remembered history, of more significance in some
70 societies than in others, is surviving custom and law—the living past
which is still part of our everyday life. The English Common Law, like
the Jewish *Halakha* and the Muslim *Sunna,* is essentially case law, based
on old custom as modified by judicial ruling and precedent. In societies
governed by this kind of law the role of lawyers—a term which for this
75 purpose includes rabbis and '*ulemā* as well as attorneys-at-law—is of
considerable importance in conserving the memory of the past as embodied in the laws they administer and the institutions through which they
administer them.

(pages 28–31)

24. In line 1, the word "overtly"
means _____.
  (A) somewhat
  (B) openly
  (C) negatively
  (D) supposedly
  (E) precisely

24 ___

(pages 197–199)

25. Though Islam has a historical origin,
its festivals are not primarily historical.
This may be cited as an example
of _____.
  (A) metaphor
  (B) analogy
  (C) euphemism
  (D) paradox
  (E) irony

25 ___

(pages 184–186)

26. In citing his examples, the author is
suggesting that _____.
  (A) each group or nation has an impulse toward the celebration of a
person or incident
  (B) the Jews borrowed from the Muslims the practice of compiling historical calendars
  (C) England can point specifically to
the date when it might be said the
modern nation came into existence
  (D) there were uncanny parallels between the events of the French
Revolution and the American Revolution
  (E) the Fourth of July is a precise date
to signal the declaration of American Independence.

26 ___

(pages 247–251)

27. All the following words are correctly paired with their synonyms EXCEPT _____.
    (A) (18) ostensibly—seemingly
    (B) (35) revitalizing—restoring vigor
    (C) (37) rigors—difficulties
    (D) (38) arbitrarily—conveniently
    (E) (45) effigies—images

    27 ___

(pages 225–229)

28. The author's attitude toward the establishment of so many national celebrations is one of _____.
    (A) enthusiastic promotion
    (B) lukewarm indifference
    (C) bitter disagreement
    (D) tacit understanding
    (E) moderate disapproval

    28 ___

(pages 210–213)

29. The word "guy" is associated with _____.
    (A) a Parliamentary leader
    (B) an ambassador noted for informality
    (C) a failed conspirator
    (D) an attacker of the Bastille
    (E) an Italian fascist

    29 ___

(pages 210–213)

30. The best way to answer question 29 is to _____.
    (A) carefully reread the selection paragraph by paragraph
    (B) skim the selection for the word *guy*
    (C) check the initial sentence of each paragraph to seek a possible clue to the word
    (D) look first for a Parliamentary leader, then an ambassador, and so on down through the alternatives
    (E) rely on memory, asking the question, "Now where did I see the word?"

    30 ___

(pages 53–55)

31. The author's statement (67–68), "Neither was of long duration," _____.
    (A) is an ironic commentary on the way in which history passes judgment on men and movements
    (B) implies a sense of loss at the disappearance of what might have been colorful
    (C) though it suggests failure of sorts, is really a song in praise of human daring and innovation
    (D) should probably have been omitted, since it adds a negative note
    (E) might have been better placed as the topic sentence of the next paragraph

    31 ___

(pages 205–208)

32. According to the author, "the living past" consists of _____.
    (A) concise biographies of leaders who have inspired their people to greatness
    (B) contemporary celebrations that mirror festival days in the past
    (C) calendars that have their starting dates at some dramatic moment in the past
    (D) laws and customs that still help govern our actions and guide our procedures
    (E) bards and poets, whose oral traditions have persisted even in an age of writing and printing

    32 ___

416

(pages 184–186)
33. In one respect, the English, Jewish, and Muslim customs come together in _____.
   (A) celebration of two or three common festivals each year
   (B) honoring the founders of all religions, even the pagan
   (C) restricting the role of lawyers by holding them to rigid constitutional procedures
   (D) the ways in which religious persons are expected to behave in their various houses of worship
   (E) using laws based primarily upon customs and precedents

33 ___

(pages 20–23)
34. In line 49, the word "impediment" means _____.
   (A) thrust
   (B) commentary
   (C) obstruction
   (D) explanation
   (E) destruction

34 ___

(pages 230–233)
35. The author's major purpose in writing this passage was to _____.
   (A) show the superiority of American customs
   (B) glorify the achievements of the prophet Muhammed
   (C) restore the reputation of Guy Fawkes
   (D) contrast some customs of contemporary religions
   (E) point out the futility of seeking permanent fame

35 ___

Section 5   5 5 5 5 5

Time-15 Minutes—For each question in this section, select the best answer
   13 Questions   from among the choices given.

The two passages below are followed by questions based on their content and on the relationship between the two passages. Answer the questions on the basis of what is stated or implied in the passages and in any introductory material that may be provided.

In Passage 1, the author supports the use of captive dolphins in marine parks for educational and entertainment purposes. In Passage 2, the author takes a contrary view, arguing against the use of captive dolphins for any reason.

PASSAGE 1

The sight of graceful dolphins swimming powerfully and freely in a marine pool has delighted millions of visitors. Introducing visitors to the ways of this magnificent creature has stimulated interest in marine ecology. People all over the world have a sympathetic attitude toward dolphins because of their firsthand acquaintance with them in marine parks.

Dolphins are treated well in captivity, enjoying their friendly association with people. Once, when an activist cut the cage wires for the dolphin Charlie Brown to escape, he stayed in his cage, refusing to leave. In captivity, dolphins live 30–40 years, with the best of food, medical care, and freedom from predation.

Visits to parks where dolphins display their intelligence and beauty stir a new concern for ocean life. Public outcry against catching dolphins in tuna nets has had a positive effect. Since dolphins are mammals, not fish, they must come to the air at intervals to breathe. Being trapped in a tuna net drowns the unfortunate victims.

Marine parks perform many positive tasks. Their first duty is to attend to the well-being of their dolphins, but they also engage in research and conservation activities. They sponsor educational programs. They rescue stranded animals on the shore and nurse them back to health, usually returning them to the sea when they are able to survive on their own. They have sponsored studies of dolphin intelligence, which many scientists equate with that of the chimpanzee.

Activists against the use of captive dolphins emphasize the occasional fatality in captivity. There are only about 500 in captivity. Yet 25,000 dolphins were killed in 1991 alone by tuna-fishing fleets. It is estimated that half a million die annually at sea from man-made causes like pollution.

The dolphin has a large and complex brain. It enjoys the challenges of performing. It does what it wants to do. When a dolphin doesn't feel like performing, it just refuses. This is not the action of a miserable slave but of a willing partner. The impression most visitors receive is that dolphins are having a wonderful time showing off.

An objection is sometimes raised against the capture of dolphins in the open sea. As more and more dolphins are bred in captivity, even that objection will lose its force.

If we balance all the positive gains from the use of dolphins in clean, adequate surroundings against the activist arguments, we must vote in favor of the parks. Just as modern zoos try to provide natural habitats for their animal groups, so marine parks try to provide an environment favorable for the well-being of dolphins.

PASSAGE 2

In the open sea, a dolphin can swim 100 miles a day. How can a dolphin in a man-made enclosure experience its birthright of freedom? True, it may come to love its chains, but is this submission fair to a creature that can roam the oceans? Activist Richard O'Barry describes the life of a free dolphin like this: "Happiness in life is the journey itself, not some place you arrive at. Dolphins live that way every day,"

O'Barry would like to see the use of captive dolphins ended. He has made personal efforts to free those now in captivity.

Dolphins are sensitive creatures, easy prey to mismanagement or
50 careless handling. During 1975–77, a study was made of dolphins captured in that period. Within the first two years, 30% had died. No one knows quite why many dolphins languish in captivity and die. Jacques Cousteau, famous oceanographer, has been against capturing dolphins since a 1958 incident when he observed two captive dolphins kill them-
55 selves by swimming headfirst into the tank walls.

In the mid-1980s, resorts built enclosed lagoons where visitors, for a price, could swim with dolphins. Conditions were ideal; yet some dolphins died without adequate explanation. Proponents of the swim-with-dolphins idea claim it had a profound positive effect on those who
60 participated. Is the trade-off worth it?

Although most marine parks do their best to maintain good standards, some are inferior. *Ocean World* in Fort Lauderdale, for example, was fined for neglect and cruelty. A dolphin named Shadow died after an attempt was made to put her into a pen against her will. Consider
65 how artificial the park environment is. Even those parks of generous size cannot begin to approximate conditions in the open sea. There, dolphins can easily dive hundreds of feet beneath the surface. They travel in large herds, perhaps with as many as 100 individuals. Within the larger group, they form smaller groups. When they breed, the gestation
70 period lasts 12 months. The young dolphins nurse for a period up to 20 months. During birth and after, other females may act as midwives or caring "aunts." These conditions can never be duplicated in captivity.

The much-touted" educational values" can be duplicated without subjecting wild, free creatures to captivity. Ocean Park in Paris is a
75 marine museum without captive animals. Technologically sophisticated displays recreate reality for the many visitors. The Monterey Bay Aquarium has no captive dolphins or whales. Yet it attracts nearly two million visitors a year. Recently opened aquariums follow this lead, doing without the display of captive sea mammals.

80 Certainly there are arguments on both sides, but when the constraints of captivity are balanced against the joys of freedom, who can vote for captivity? Dolphins were born free. Let us not keep them in chains.

(pages 197–199)
1. When presented with the argument dealing with the occasional dolphin fatality in captivity, the author of Passage 1 _____.
   (A) responds indirectly by mentioning the many dolphin deaths in the sea
   (B) attacks the statistics as being examples of a stacked deck against the interests of the marine parks
   (C) challenges the activists to provide better care and show a greater concern for captive animals
   (D) blames those fatalities on the uncharacteristic carelessness of a few marine parks
   (E) questions the motives of those who would sacrifice the happiness of many for the benefit of a few

   1 ___

(pages 247–251)
2. In making his pitch for captive dolphins, the author uses all the following elements EXCEPT _____.
   (A) public education
   (B) esthetic satisfaction
   (C) well-being of dolphins
   (D) helpful research
   (E) financial considerations

   2 ___

(pages 230–233)
3. The author uses modern zoos to _____.
   (A) contrast them with marine parks
   (B) stress the evolution of animals as servants of mankind
   (C) make a helpful analogy
   (D) disguise his central point
   (E) point out that activists favor zoos

   3 ___

(pages 14–20)
4. In line 10, "predation" most nearly means _____.
   (A) starvation
   (B) plague
   (C) pollution
   (D) preying
   (E) elimination

   4 ___

(pages 197–199)
5. Charlie Brown probably refused to move because _____.
   (A) he feared the stranger
   (B) he had been injured
   (C) he was used to current conditions
   (D) he would have starved in the open sea
   (E) he had become attached to the dolphin Shadow

   5 ___

(pages 205–208)
6. Both passages profess to be deeply concerned about _____.
   (A) the ecological impact of removing dolphins from their habitat
   (B) the well-being of dolphins
   (C) the way in which modern zoos set up natural habitats
   (D) methods of training dolphins for performances
   (E) the way in which museums display marine life

   6 ___

(pages 222–225)
7. The opening paragraph of Passage 2 can best be characterized as _____.
   (A) misleading
   (B) irrational
   (C) cut-and-dried
   (D) emotional
   (E) unsympathetic

   7 ___

(pages 14–20, 115, 117)
8. Both authors have been perceived as using anthropomorphism. In this sense, "anthropomorphism" probably means _____.
   (A) ascribing human traits to animals
   (B) using arguments insincerely and glibly
   (C) comparing dolphins to chimpanzees
   (D) changing the arguments in the middle of their presentations
   (E) rationalizing, finding reasons for emotional arguments

   8 ___

420   ENGLISH FOR THE COLLEGE BOARDS

(pages 222–225)
9. In line 73, the phrase "educational values" is enclosed in quotation marks to _____.
   (A) express the words of Jacques Cousteau exactly
   (B) emphasize the importance of the phrase
   (C) support the author's acceptance of the values mentioned
   (D) provide an alternative suggestion for training dolphins
   (E) suggest the author's disagreement with it

9 ___

(pages 31–35)
10. In line 80, "constraints" most nearly means _____.
   (A) pleasures
   (B) appeals
   (C) restrictions
   (D) surprises
   (E) cruelties

10 ___

(pages 230–233)
11. The second author's purpose in mentioning the Monterey Bay Aquarium is to show that _____.
   (A) America has taken the leadership in museum displays
   (B) the effect of captivity on dolphins depends on the facilities they enjoy
   (C) there are two sides to every discussion
   (D) dolphins are happiest in huge saltwater pools
   (E) the success of an aquarium does not depend upon the display of dolphins and whales

11 ___

(pages 205–208)
12. In comparing Passages 1 and 2, we might say that _____.
   (A) Passage 1 is based substantially on the words of Jacques Cousteau; Passage 2 is based upon the words of Richard O'Barry
   (B) Passage 1 is more concerned with the public's interests; Passage 2 is more concerned with the individual dolphin
   (C) both passages are sympathetic with the interests of commercial fisher fleets as well as with the welfare of dolphins
   (D) neither passage is concerned with the management of museums, only marine parks
   (E) Passage 1 is more compassionate than Passage 2

12 ___

(pages 197–199)
13. We can be reasonably sure that Jacques Cousteau _____.
   (A) agrees with the author of Passage 1
   (B) has made a film about his capture of dolphins
   (C) is directly opposed to the views of Richard O'Barry
   (D) approves the way in which Paris's Ocean Park is presented
   (E) has spent a portion of his life training and caring for dolphins

13 ___

Facsimile Test 5

Time-30 Minutes—For each question in this section, select the best answer
  30 Questions   from among the choices given.

Each sentence below has one or two blanks, each blank indicating that something has been omitted. Beneath the sentence are five lettered words or sets of words labeled A through E. Choose the word or set of words that *best* fits the meaning of the sentence as a whole.

EXAMPLE

Although its publicity has been _____, the film itself is intelligent, well-acted, handsomely produced, and altogether _____.

(A) tasteless . . respectable
(B) extensive . . moderate
(C) sophisticated . . amateur
(D) risqué . . crude
(E) perfect . . spectacular

A

(pages 28–31)
1. Like expressing a taste for certain kinds of food, movie criticism tends to be _____, reflecting the _____ and prejudices of the reviewer rather than absolute truths.
   (A) objective . . faults
   (B) petty . . profundities
   (C) exaggerated . . anecdotes
   (D) subjective . . whims
   (E) deceptive . . pride

1 ___

(pages 20–23)
2. Costa Rica, a country with more volcanoes per capita than any other nation, has, _____, a quiet political and social scene, reflecting the maturity and _____ of its people.
   (A) by contrast . . stability
   (B) correspondingly . . uncertainty
   (C) for example . . concern
   (D) repressively . . alertness
   (E) proudly . . excitability

2 ___

(pages 14–20)
3. Fluctuating interest rates encourage a _____ game involving borrowers and lenders, impelling some borrowers to take on disastrous obligations and putting some _____ thrift organizations in peril.
   (A) rational . . conservative
   (B) lively . . well-balanced
   (C) stylish . . extraordinary
   (D) sophisticated . . stubborn
   (E) guessing . . imprudent

3 ___

(pages 24–27)

4. Human _____ is nowhere better demonstrated than in collectibles, for people will _____ anything enthusiastically, from barbed wire to used oil rags.
   (A) discretion . . purchase
   (B) eccentricity . . hoard
   (C) irritability . . trade
   (D) envy . . peddle
   (E) sensitivity . . advertise

4 ___

(pages 35–38)

5. In *Buddenbrooks* Thomas Mann shows how a merchant family's overemphasis upon _____ values and appearances ultimately leads to disintegration and _____.
   (A) unanticipated . . surprise
   (B) inviolate . . indifference
   (C) glamorous . . fulfillment
   (D) spiritual . . disappointment
   (E) material . . tragedy

5 ___

(pages 31–35)

6. Despite the disappearance of the great mass-market magazines, specialized magazines in a _____ variety of subjects and fields have testified to the _____ of magazine publishing in America.
   (A) limited . . decline
   (B) bewildering . . vitality
   (C) colorful . . perils
   (D) nonexistent . . unimportance
   (E) diminishing . . contraction

6 ___

(pages 14–20)

7. Hal's cruel _____ of his old friend Falstaff in *Henry IV, Part Two*, was _____ in Hal's transformation from playboy to king.
   (A) recognition . . understated
   (B) promotion . . perplexing
   (C) rejection . . inevitable
   (D) ridicule . . ludicrous
   (E) deliverance . . superficial

7 ___

(pages 35–38)

8. Though an underdog at the Democratic convention in 1912, Woodrow Wilson _____ held on through 46 ballots and _____ won the nomination from a disappointed "Champ" Clark.
   (A) nervously . . predictably
   (B) cheerfully . . easily
   (C) unintentionally . . casually
   (D) doggedly . . finally
   (E) unexpectedly . . dejectedly

8 ___

(pages 20–23)

9. In the sad history of species extinction, the story of the great auk provides one of the most _____ chapters.
   (A) depressing   (D) agreeable
   (B) rewarding   (E) awe-inspiring
   (C) profound

9 ___

Each question below consists of a related pair of words or phrases, followed by five lettered pairs of words or phrases labeled A through E. Select the lettered pair that *best* expresses a relationship similar to that expressed in the original pair.

EXAMPLE

YAWN : BOREDOM ::
- (A) dream : sleep
- (B) anger : madness
- (C) smile : amusement
- (D) face : expression
- (E) impatience : rebellion

C

(pages 155–156, 157)

10. LILAC : SHRUB ::
- (A) beagle : terrier
- (B) watch : timepiece
- (C) marigold : chrysanthemum
- (D) motorcycle : bus
- (E) color : blue

10 ___

(pages 147–149, 153)

11. DIVERSIFY : SIMILARITY ::
- (A) admire : contempt
- (B) detrimental : harm
- (C) memorable : monument
- (D) verify : testify
- (E) offend : aggression

11 ___

(pages 152–153)

12. CHURN : BUTTER ::
- (A) barber : hair
- (B) cultivation : flour
- (C) needle : thread
- (D) pot : stew
- (E) trap : mouse

12 ___

(pages 154, 157)

13. RAZOR : BEARD ::
- (A) tree : pruning hook
- (B) fork : knife
- (C) pencil : inventory
- (D) bow : violin
- (E) lamp : illumination

13 ___

(pages 150–151, 153)

14. FLOOR: ROOM ::
- (A) arm : leg
- (B) orange : pit
- (C) television : video recorder
- (D) sole : shoe
- (E) pot : frying pan

14 ___

(pages 156, 157)

15. GRAFT : TWIG ::
- (A) animal : train
- (B) destroy : evidence
- (C) assail : argument
- (D) reserve : judgment
- (E) plant : cuttings

15 ___

Each passage below is followed by questions based on its content. Answer the questions following each passage on the basis of what is <u>stated</u> or <u>implied</u> in that passage and in any introductory material that may be provided.

Did aliens visit Earth during the distant past and leave their mark? The following passage expresses a strong point of view on the subject.

And if extraterrestrial civilizations have visited Earth and have, on principle, left us to develop freely and undisturbed, might they have visited Earth so recently that human beings had come into existence and were aware of them?

5   All cultures, after all, have tales of beings with supernormal powers who created and guided human beings in primitive days and who taught them various aspects of technology. Can such tales of gods have arisen from the dim memory of visits of extraterrestrials to Earth in ages not too long past? Instead of life having been seeded on the planet from

10   outer space, could technology have been planted here? Might the extraterrestrials not merely have allowed civilization to develop here, but actually helped it?

It is an intriguing thought, but there is no evidence in its favor that is in the least convincing.

15   Certainly, human beings need no visitors from outer space in order to be inspired to create legends. Elaborate legends with only the dimmest kernels of truth have been based on such people as Alexander the Great and Charlemagne, who were completely human actors in the historical drama.

20   For that matter, even a fictional character such as Sherlock Holmes has been invested with life and reality by millions over the world, and an endless flood of tales is still invented concerning him.

Second, the thought that any form of technology sprang up suddenly in human history, or that any artifact was too complex for the humans

25   of the time, so that the intervention of a more sophisticated culture must be assumed is about as surely wrong as anything can be.

This dramatic supposition has received its most recent reincarnation in the books of Eric von Däniken. He finds all sorts of ancient works either too enormous (like the pyramids of Egypt) or too mysterious (like

30   markings in the sands of Peru) to be of human manufacture.

Archaeologists, however, are quite convinced that even the pyramids could be built with not more than the techniques available in 2500 B.C., plus human ingenuity and muscle. It is a mistake to believe that the ancients were not every bit as intelligent as we. Their technology was

35   more primitive, but their brains were not.

(pages 213–216)
16. Which of the following statements may be accurately derived from the selection?
    I. Though supposedly a fictional character, Sherlock Holmes actually existed.
    II. The great pyramids of Egypt could have been created by people with the technology of the times.
    III. The belief in extraterrestrial visitors springs from motivating yearnings in all cultures.
    IV. Though slight, the evidence for visits by extraterrestrials in recent years is convincing.
    V. The ancients had qualities modern people do not have, but their intelligence was not as great as ours.
       (A) I, III, V   (D) I, IV
       (B) II, IV, V   (E) II only
       (C) II, III

                                    16 ___

(pages 197–199)
17. Stories about Alexander the Great and Charlemagne demonstrate _____.
    (A) a completely fictional source
    (B) the gullibility of Eric von Däniken
    (C) a tie-in with visits by extraterrestrials
    (D) the influence of primitive technology
    (E) the legend-making abilities of human beings

                                    17 ___

(pages 247–251)
18. All the following are examples of figurative language EXCEPT _____.
    (A) "life having been seeded" (9)
    (B) "dimmest kernels of truth" (16–17)
    (C) "endless flood of tales" (22)
    (D) "any form of technology sprang up" (23)
    (E) "technology was more primitive" (34–35)

                                    18 ___

(pages 225–229)
19. Of the author, it might be said that he or she _____.
    (A) has an optimistic view of the capabilities of mankind
    (B) detests the thought that aliens might have visited Earth
    (C) doesn't think the Peruvian markings will ever be explained
    (D) accepts the bulk of von Däniken's books while rejecting portions
    (E) suggests that Alexander the Great may be a purely fictional character

                                    19 ___

(pages 14–20)
20. In line 21, "invested" most nearly means _____.
    (A) put money into
    (B) endowed
    (C) brimming
    (D) overcome
    (E) enriched

                                    20 ___

(pages 222–225)
21. The tone of the passage may best be characterized as _____.
    (A) excited and enthusiastic
    (B) hopeful but wavering
    (C) aggressive and dogmatic
    (D) reasonable and measured
    (E) sarcastic and bitter

                                    21 ___

ENGLISH FOR THE COLLEGE BOARDS

Is there, securely lodged within his or her work, the personality and identity of a writer? The writer of the following selection believes that Shakespeare has left a signature imprinted on his work.

I know I am talking of a trite and threadbare theme—namely, figures of speech. But the trite we fight shy of because it *is* trite, is sometimes more shining than the upstart new, if we will but brush off the dust.

Convention and Revolt in Poetry, John Livingston Lowes.

When Polonius instructs his man Reynaldo how best to find out what kind of life his son is leading in Paris, he suggests various circuitous ways of extracting information from Laertes' friends, such as hinting that he games or drinks, and noting how they receive such hints, and
5 so by the judicious use of these indirect methods to draw forth the truth.

He illustrates his meaning by a metaphor from bowls; a game Shakespeare was interested in, and in which the curious fact that the player does not aim directly at the jack, but sends his ball in a curve, trusting to the bias to bring it round again, greatly appealed to him.

10 Thus, says Polonius, characteristically, do we men of wisdom and capacity, with winding ways

and with assays of bias,

By indirections find directions out.

These lines describe so exactly what I propose to try and do in this
15 book, that 'assays of bias' might well have served as title for it, could these words have been more easily understood by modern readers. I venture moreover to say I believe the game would have appealed to Shakespeare, for just as he was attracted by the subtle element in bowls, and the measure of skill and judgment needed to turn an indirect aim
20 into a good and true hit, so would he have been interested in the working of the same method in the sphere of literature and psychology.

I believe it to be profoundly true that the real revelation of the writer's personality, temperament, and quality of mind is to be found in his works, whether he be dramatist or novelist, describing other people's
25 thoughts or putting down his own directly.

In the case of a poet, I suggest it is chiefly through his images that he, to some extent unconsciously, 'gives himself away'. He may be, and in Shakespeare's case is, almost entirely objective in his dramatic characters and their views and opinions, yet, like the man who under
30 stress of emotion will show no sign of it in eye or face, but will reveal it in some muscular tension, the poet unwittingly lays bare his own innermost likes and dislikes, observations and interests, associations of thought, attitudes of mind and beliefs, in and through the images, the verbal pictures he draws to illuminate something quite different in the
35 speech and thought of his characters.

The imagery he instinctively uses is thus a revelation, largely unconscious, given at a moment of heightened feeling, of the furniture of his mind, the channels of his thought, the qualities of things, the objects and incidents he observes and remembers, and perhaps most significant
40 of all, those which he does not observe or remember.

My experience is that this works out more reliably in drama than in pure poetry, because in a poem the writer is more definitely and consciously seeking the images; whereas in the drama, and especially drama written red-hot as was the Elizabethan, images tumble out of the mouths
45 of the characters in the heat of the writer's feeling or passion, as they naturally surge up into his mind.

The greater and richer the work the more valuable and suggestive become the images, so that in the case of Shakespeare I believe one can scarcely overrate the possibilities of what may be discovered through
50 a systematic examination of them. It was my conviction of this which led me to assemble and classify all his images, so as to have in orderly and easily accessible form the material upon which to base my deductions and conclusions.

I use the term 'image' here as the only available word to cover every
55 kind of simile, as well as every kind of what is really compressed simile—metaphor. I suggest that we divest our minds of the hint the term carries with it of visual image only, and think of it, for the present purpose, as connoting any and every imaginative picture or other experience, drawn in every kind of way, which may have come to the poet,
60 not only through any of his senses, but through his mind and emotions as well, and which he uses, in the forms of simile and metaphor in their widest sense, for purposes of analogy.

(pages 197–199)

22. Shakespeare uses the game of bowls to _____.
   (A) provide Polonius with a metaphor
   (B) suggest a major interest of Reynaldo
   (C) suggest a major interest of Laertes
   (D) demonstrate his knowledge of Elizabethan sports
   (E) provide a challenging puzzle for the audience

   22 ___

(pages 197–199)

23. The expression ''assays of bias'' is meant to suggest _____.
   (A) extreme snobbery
   (B) slanted literary work
   (C) indirect analysis
   (D) failed attempts
   (E) detailed directions

   23 ___

(pages 51–55, 247–251)

24. All the following are examples of figurative language EXCEPT _____.
   (A) ''unwittingly lays bare'' (31)
   (B) ''the furniture of his mind'' (37–38)
   (C) ''assays of bias'' (12)
   (D) ''the channels of his thought'' (38)
   (E) ''incidents he observes'' (39)

   24 ___

(pages 197–199)

25. The author would not feel so secure in analyzing the imagery of pure poetry because poets _____.
   (A) tend to write more diffusely than others
   (B) tend to be superior to dramatists in the creative impulse
   (C) turn out their work ''red-hot''
   (D) are conscious of the images they create
   (E) reveal themselves coldly and analytically

   25 ___

(pages 51–55)

26. The image that comes closest to the image in lines 44–46 is _____.
    (A) the flow of a glacier
    (B) the bursting open of buds in spring
    (C) a boiling cauldron
    (D) the swinging open of gates
    (E) the flow of the tides

                                        26 ___

(pages 205–208)

27. The author contrasts the objectivity of Shakespeare's characterizations with _____.
    (A) Shakespeare's muscular tension
    (B) the self-revelation of Shakespeare's imagery
    (C) the opinions the characters express
    (D) the temperament of pure poets
    (E) the subjectivity of novelists

                                        27 ___

(pages 184–186)

28. The author's appraisal of Shakespeare's ability is best summed up in the phrase _____.
    (A) "attracted by the subtle element in bowls" (18)
    (B) "real revelation of the writer's personality" (22–23)
    (C) "innermost likes and dislikes" (32)
    (D) "those which he does not observe or remember" (40)
    (E) "greater and richer the work the more valuable and suggestive become the images" (47–48)

                                        28 ___

(pages 197–199)

29. We may assume that when the author has assembled and classified Shakespeare's images, they will _____.
    (A) consist mostly of simile and metaphor
    (B) all be visual in nature
    (C) reveal personality and temperament but not quality of mind
    (D) have limited value in revealing the inner Shakespeare
    (E) reveal only what Shakespeare wants to reveal

                                        29 ___

(pages 14–20, 46)

30. In line 58, "connoting" means _____.
    (A) writing down
    (B) revealing directly
    (C) implying
    (D) enhancing
    (E) supporting

                                        30 ___

Section 3   3 3 3

Time-30 Minutes—For each question in this section, select the best answer
   35 Questions   from among the choices given.

Each sentence below has one or two blanks, each blank indicating that something has been omitted. Beneath the sentence are five lettered words or sets of words labeled A through E. Choose the word or set of words that *best* fits the meaning of the sentence as a whole.

EXAMPLE

Although its publicity has been _____, the film itself is intelligent, well-acted, handsomely produced, and altogether _____.

(A) tasteless . . respectable
(B) extensive . . moderate
(C) sophisticated . . spectacular
(D) risqué . . crude
(E) perfect . . spectacular

<u>   A   </u>

(pages 31–35)
1. Combining the symbols for woman and child, the Chinese ideograph for *good*, though somewhat _____ at first, makes sense on maturer reflection.
   (A) provocative
   (B) emphatic
   (C) cryptic
   (D) droll
   (E) objectionable

   1 ___

(pages 39–43)
2. Contrary to common beliefs about the effectiveness of a loud, _____ voice, young children are more likely to obey if they are directed in a(n) _____ voice.
   (A) discreet . . low
   (B) sensitive . . colorless
   (C) authoritative . . soft
   (D) piercing . . high
   (E) pleasing . . wavering

   2 ___

(pages 14–20)
3. Improvements in _____ and transportation have converted the entire world into a(n) _____ village.
   (A) housing . . leaderless
   (B) finance . . modern
   (C) negotiation . . noisy
   (D) individuality . . disorganized
   (E) communication . . global

   3 ___

(pages 28–31)
4. Like expressing a taste for certain kinds of food, movie criticism tends to be _____, reflecting the _____ and prejudices of the reviewer rather than absolute truths.
   (A) objective . . faults
   (B) petty . . profundities
   (C) exaggerated . . anecdotes
   (D) subjective . . whims
   (E) deceptive . . pride

   4 ___

(pages 31–35)
5. Costa Rica, a country with more volcanoes per capita than any other nation, has, _____, a quiet political and social scene, reflecting the maturity and _____ of its people.
   (A) by contrast . . stability
   (B) correspondingly . . uncertainty
   (C) for example . . concern
   (D) repressively . . alertness
   (E) proudly . . excitability

   5 ___

(pages 35–38)
6. Martha's Vineyard, once a sleepy vacation spot for _____ visitors, has now become a(n) _____ mecca for hordes of sun-worshiping tourists.
   (A) myriad . . quiet
   (B) impoverished . . weary
   (C) discriminating . . bustling
   (D) impetuous . . depressing
   (E) curious . . pensive

   6 ___

(pages 14–20)
7. Louis Braille, blind from the age of three, cunningly devised an alphabet consisting of _____ letters.
   (A) etched
   (B) heavily inked
   (C) phonic
   (D) embossed
   (E) multicolored

   7 ___

(pages 14–20)
8. Fluctuating interest rates encourage a _____ game involving borrowers and lenders, impelling some borrowers to take on disastrous obligations and putting some _____ thrift organizations in peril.
   (A) rational . . conservative
   (B) lively . . well-balanced
   (C) stylish . . extraordinary
   (D) sophisticated . . stubborn
   (E) guessing . . imprudent

8 ___

(pages 24–27)
9. Human _____ is nowhere better demonstrated than in collectibles, for people will _____ anything enthusiastically, from barbed wire to used oil rags.
   (A) discretion . . purchase
   (B) eccentricity . . hoard
   (C) irritability . . trade
   (D) envy . . peddle
   (E) sensitivity . . advertise

9 ___

(pages 35–38)
10. At first _____ by the British escalation of taxation, the American colonists became indignant and then _____ to the point of rebellion.
    (A) irked . . enraged
    (B) amused . . motivated
    (C) compelled . . irritated
    (D) unmoved . . enlivened
    (E) untouched . . nudged

10 ___

Each question below consists of a related pair of words followed by five lettered pairs of words labeled A through E. Select the lettered pair that *best* expresses a relationship similar to that expressed in the original pair.

EXAMPLE
YAWN : BOREDOM ::
   (A) anger : madness
   (B) dream : sleep
   (C) smile : amusement
   (D) face : expression
   (E) impatience : rebellion

C

(pages 166–168, 170)
11. LOOM : WEAVING ::
    (A) engraving : stylus
    (B) parallel bar : gymnasium
    (C) quarterback : football
    (D) easel : painting
    (E) swimming : pool

11 ___

(pages 147–149, 153)
12. INVOLUNTARY : PREMEDITATION ::
    (A) exaggerated : understatement
    (B) fundamental : reality
    (C) critical : review
    (D) circumstantial : evidence
    (E) circular : hole

12 ___

(pages 164–165, 170)
13. CANDLE : LIGHT ::
    (A) physique : stature
    (B) magic : charm
    (C) countersign : password
    (D) sword : saber
    (E) perfume : scent

13 ___

(pages 149–150, 153)
14. NUPTIAL : WEDDING ::
   (A) obvious : nuance
   (B) everlasting : eternity
   (C) legacy : contribution
   (D) civil : disrespect
   (E) beauty : attractive

14 ____

(pages 149–150, 153)
15. AROUSE : INFLAME ::
   (A) interfere : promote
   (B) flinch : trifle
   (C) bulge : bubble
   (D) jar : jolt
   (E) acquit : denounce

15 ____

(pages 166–168, 170)
16. MILLER : GRAIN ::
   (A) jogger : track
   (B) chef : menu
   (C) baker : dough
   (D) veterinarian : kennel
   (E) umpire : baseball

16 ____

(pages 152, 153)
17. VASE : BUD ::
   (A) crate : orange
   (B) barrel : basket
   (C) seed : sunflower
   (D) band : wedding
   (E) ailment : cure

17 ____

(pages 147–149, 153)
18. GARRULOUS : SILENCE ::
   (A) simultaneous : different
   (B) inflatable : mute
   (C) infirm : strength
   (D) deliberate : composure
   (E) heedful : attention

18 ____

(pages 155, 157)
19. DOWNPOUR : DRIZZLE ::
   (A) whisper : shout
   (B) fact : fiction
   (C) conflagration : glow
   (D) game : contest
   (E) carrot : motivation

19 ____

(pages 147–149, 153)
20. LAVISH : STINGINESS ::
   (A) positive : confidence
   (B) plentiful : profusion
   (C) evasive : stupidity
   (D) disorganized : comfort
   (E) rash : caution

20 ____

(pages 152, 153)
21. CRADLE : INFANT ::
   (A) pouch : knapsack
   (B) wallet : leather
   (C) pigeonhole : papers
   (D) bucket : pail
   (E) food : platter

21 ____

(pages 169, 170)
22. MILLIMETER : CENTIMETER ::
   (A) booklet : book
   (B) mansion : cottage
   (C) mile : kilometer
   (D) spider : beetle
   (E) liter : gram

22 ____

(pages 162, 163)
23. MASON : TROWEL ::
   (A) clay : potter
   (B) whaler : harpoon
   (C) mechanic : automobile
   (D) meteorologist : weather
   (E) plasterer : wall

23 ____

432

The passage below is followed by questions based on its content. Answer the questions on the basis of what is <u>stated</u> or <u>implied</u> in the passage and in any introductory material that may be supplied.

In the following excerpt from a short story, a mother brings home a girl who has been paroled in the mother's custody. Her son has just received the news.

Thomas rose from his Morris chair, dropping the review he had been reading. His large bland face contracted in anticipated pain. "You are not," he said, "going to bring that girl here!"

"No, no," she said, "calm yourself, Thomas." She had managed
5 with difficulty to get the girl a job in a pet shop in town and a place to board with a crotchety old lady of her acquaintance. People were not kind. They did not put themselves in the place of someone like Star who had everything against her..

Thomas sat down again and retrieved his review. He seemed just to
10 have escaped some danger which he did not care to make clear to himself. "Nobody can tell you anything," he said, "but in a few days that girl will have left town, having got what she could out of you. You'll never hear from her again."

Two nights later he came home and opened the parlor door and was
15 speared by a shrill, depthless laugh. His mother and the girl sat close to the fireplace where the gas logs were lit. The girl gave the immediate impression of being physically crooked. Her hair was cut like a dog's or an elf's and she was dressed in the latest fashion. She was training on him a long, familiar, sparkling stare that turned after a second into
20 an intimate grin.

"Thomas!" his mother said, her voice firm with the injunction not to bolt, "this is Star you've heard so much about. Star is going to have supper with us."

The girl called herself Star Drake. The lawyer had found that her
25 real name was Sarah Ham.

Thomas neither moved nor spoke but hung in the door in what seemed a savage perplexity. Finally he said, "How do you do, Sarah," in a tone of such loathing that he was shocked at the sound of it. He reddened, feeling it beneath him to show contempt for any creature so
30 pathetic. He advanced into the room, determined at least on a decent politeness and sat down heavily in a straight chair.

"Thomas writes history," his mother said with a threatening look at him. "He's president of the local Historical Society this year."

The girl leaned forward and gave Thomas an even more pointed
35 attention. "Fabulous!" she said in a throaty voice.

"Right now Thomas is writing about the first settlers in this county," his mother said.

"Fabulous!" the girl repeated.

Thomas by an effort of will managed to look as if he were alone in
40 the room.

"Say, you know who he looks like?" Star asked, her head on one side, taking him in at an angle.

"Oh someone very distinguished!" his mother said archly.

"This cop I saw in the movie I went to last night," Star said.

45 "Star," his mother said, "I think you ought to be careful about the kind of movies you go to. I think you ought to see only the best ones. I don't think crime stories would be good for you."

"Oh this was a crime-does-not-pay," Star said, "and I swear this cop looked exactly like him. They were always putting something over 50 on the guy. He would look like he couldn't stand it a minute longer or he would blow up. He was a riot. And not bad looking," she added with an appreciative leer at Thomas.

"Star," his mother said, "I think it would be grand if you developed a taste for music."

55 Thomas sighed. His mother rattled on and the girl, paying no attention to her, let her eyes play over him. The quality of her look was such that it might have been her hands, resting now on his knees, now on his neck. Her eyes had a mocking glitter and he knew that she was well aware he could not stand the sight of her. He needed nothing to tell him 60 he was in the presence of the very stuff of corruption, but blameless corruption because there was no responsible faculty behind it. He was looking at the most unendurable form of innocence. Absently he asked himself what the attitude of God was to this, meaning if possible to adopt it.

65 His mother's behavior throughout the meal was so idiotic that he could barely stand to look at her and since he could less stand to look at Sarah Ham, he fixed on the sideboard across the room a continuous gaze of disapproval and disgust. Every remark of the girl's his mother met as if it deserved serious attention. She advanced several plans for 70 the wholesome use of Star's spare time. Sarah Ham paid no more attention to this advice than if it came from a parrot. Once when Thomas inadvertently looked in her direction, she winked. As soon as he had swallowed the last spoonful of dessert, he rose and muttered, "I have to go, I have a meeting."

75 "Thomas," his mother said, "I want you to take Star home on your way. I don't want her riding in taxis by herself at night."

For a moment Thomas remained furiously silent. Then he turned and left the room. Presently he came back with a look of obscure determination on his face. The girl was ready, meekly waiting at the parlor door. 80 She cast up at him a great look of admiration and confidence. Thomas did not offer his arm but she took it anyway and moved out of the house and down the steps, attached to what might have been a miraculously moving monument.

"Be good!" his mother called.

85 Sarah Ham snickered and poked him in the ribs.

(pages 271–279)
24. In line 2, Thomas's "anticipated pain" suggests that _____.
   - (A) his bland face is a source of intended deception
   - (B) the review he'd been reading has upset him
   - (C) he has a fondness for the girl, a fondness unshared by his mother
   - (D) he and his mother have discussed the problem before
   - (E) he had hoped to get the girl a job in another city

   24 ___

(pages 14–20)
25. In line 6, "crotchety" most nearly means _____.
   - (A) boorish
   - (B) cranky
   - (C) lovable
   - (D) wrinkled
   - (E) ancient

   25 ___

(pages 225–229)
26. The author's attitude toward Sarah Ham is _____.
   - (A) compassionate, with a deep understanding of her problem
   - (B) consistently disapproving despite the problems Sarah has faced
   - (C) concealed beneath a number of descriptive passages
   - (D) basically baffled but willing to give Sarah the benefit of any doubt
   - (E) indifferent, without any sense of judging

   26 ___

(pages 205–208)
27. Two elements intentionally contrasted in the excerpt are _____.
   - (A) Thomas's stiffness and Sarah's relaxedness
   - (B) the mother's attitude toward Sarah at the beginning of the excerpt and at the end
   - (C) Thomas's inward anger and his consistent attempt to make a good impression
   - (D) Sarah's outwardly flip manner and her inner sensitivity
   - (E) Sarah's goodness and Thomas's evil

   27 ___

(pages 265–270)
28. In line 20 the "intimate grin" undoubtedly _____.
   - (A) angers the mother
   - (B) shows the softer side of Sarah
   - (C) is really intended for the mother
   - (D) reflects favorably on Sarah
   - (E) embarrasses Thomas

   28 ___

(pages 271–279)
29. The mother's firm voice in line 21 suggests that she is _____.
   - (A) pleased that Thomas agrees with her
   - (B) trying to get Sarah to stay
   - (C) merely announcing supper in the usual way
   - (D) afraid Thomas will disappear
   - (E) hoping that Thomas is attracted to Sarah

   29 ___

(pages 265–270)
30. The author intentionally has Sarah repeat "Fabulous" (line 38) to suggest _____.
   - (A) an admirable youthful enthusiasm
   - (B) an exercise in vocabulary building
   - (C) an attempt to impress the mother
   - (D) a warm and sincere tribute
   - (E) a superficial and glib mentality

   30 ___

(pages 265–270)
31. Thomas's reaction to "Fabulous" (question 30) can be characterized as _____.
    (A) curious but uncertain
    (B) mildly interested, though not over-whelmed
    (C) icily unresponsive
    (D) warmly receptive
    (E) deeply appreciative

    31 ___

(pages 265–270)
32. Sarah's motive in changing her name was undoubtedly to _____.
    (A) conceal her parentage
    (B) choose a name similar to Thomas's
    (C) make herself more glamorous
    (D) elude the police
    (E) confuse Thomas's mother

    32 ___

(pages 265–270)
33. A good phrase to describe the relation-ship between Sarah and Thomas is _____.
    (A) deep-seated tenderness
    (B) humorous acceptance
    (C) willful misunderstanding
    (D) joyous fellowship
    (E) basic incompatibility

    33 ___

(pages 230–233)
34. The two sentences (lines 69–71) "She advanced . . . a parrot" use both "Star" and "Sarah Ham." Why does the author use both names?
    (A) Thomas is unaware that "Sarah" is really "Star."
    (B) Despite superficial appearances, the girl actually prefers the name "Sarah."
    (C) The mother has an idealized image of the girl that is unrelated to reality.
    (D) Thomas changes his attitude to-ward the girl when he thinks of her as "Star."
    (E) The mother would probably like to adopt "Star" into her own family.

    34 ___

(pages 253–257)
35. The pages following this selection prob-ably show that _____.
    (A) Thomas and Star fall in love
    (B) Thomas's mother urges Thomas to marry the girl
    (C) Star completely changes and be-comes an admirable person
    (D) Star continues to get on Thomas's nerves
    (E) Star tells Thomas that she has loved him from afar for years

    35 ___

Section 5

5 5 5 5 5

Time-15 Minutes—For each question in this section, select the best answer
    13 Questions   from among the choices given.

The two passages below are followed by questions based on their content and on the relationship between the two passages. Answer the questions on the basis of what is <u>stated</u> or <u>implied</u> in the passages and in any introductory material that may be provided.

We are told that life should be lived fully . . .but how? The following two passages have some specific advice to offer. The first passage, written more than a century ago, uses the masculine pronoun for the common gender, a practice frowned upon by some modern authorities.

PASSAGE 1

Above all, we cannot afford not to live in the present. He is blessed over all mortals who loses no moment of the passing life in remembering the past. Unless our philosophy hears the cock crow in every barnyard within our horizon, it is belated. That sound commonly reminds us that
5 we are growing rusty and antique in our employments and habits of thought. His philosophy comes down to a more recent time than ours. There is something suggested by it that is a newer testament—the gospel according to this moment. He has not fallen astern; he has got up early and kept up early, and to be where he is is to be in season, in the foremost
10 rank of time. It is an expression of the health and soundness of nature, a brag for all the world—healthiness as of a spring burst forth, a new fountain of the Muses, to celebrate this last instant of time. Where he lives no fugitive slave laws are passed. Who has not betrayed his master many times since last he heard that note?
15 The merit of this bird's strain is in its freedom from all plaintiveness. The singer can easily move us to tears or to laughter, but where is he who can excite in us a pure morning joy? When, in doleful dumps, breaking the awful stillness of our wooden sidewalk on a Sunday, or, perchance, a watcher in the house of mourning, I hear a cockerel crow far
20 or near, I think to myself, 'There is one of us well, at any rate,'—and with a sudden gush return to my senses.—

PASSAGE 2

Every moment some form grows perfect in hand or face; some tone on the hills or the sea is choicer than the rest; some mood of passion or insight or intellectual excitement is irresistibly real and attractive for
25 us—for that moment only. Not the fruits of experience, but experience itself, is the end. A counted number of pulses only is given to us of a variegated, dramatic life. How may we see in them all that is to be seen in them by the finest senses? How shall we pass most swiftly from point to point and be present always at the focus where the greatest number
30 of vital forces unite in their purest energy? To burn always with this hard, gemlike flame, to maintain this ecstasy, is success in life. In a sense it might even be said that our failure is to form habits: for, after all, habit is relative to a stereotyped world and meantime it is only the roughness of the eye that makes any two persons, things, situations,
35 seem alike. While all melts under our feet we may well catch at any exquisite passion or any contribution to knowledge that seems by a lifted horizon to set the spirit free for a moment, or any stirring of the senses, strange dyes, strange colors and curious odors, or work of the artist's hands, or the face of one's friend. Not to discriminate every moment
40 some passionate attitude in those about us and in the brilliancy of their gifts some tragic dividing of forces on their ways, is, on this short day of frost and sun, the sleep before evening.

(pages 184–186)
1. The author of Passage 1 suggests that happiness _____.
   (A) is an illusion
   (B) depends upon material things
   (C) is found in the present moment
   (D) depends upon a demanding philosophy of life
   (E) is particularly accessible on a Sunday

1 ___

(pages 230–233)
2. The author introduces the cock crow _____.
   (A) as a sound rich in complicated harmonies
   (B) to recall happy experiences with friends
   (C) as an extraneous irrelevant example
   (D) to illustrate the diversity of nature
   (E) as a symbolic example of a universal truth

2 ___

(pages 200–202)
3. The sentence, "Where he lives no fugitive slave laws are passed," (lines 12–13) suggests that _____.
   (A) the fugitive slave law has caused the author some concern
   (B) the author is merely using a contemporary illustration of no particular consequence
   (C) the nation has successfully fought off attempts to pass a fugitive slave law
   (D) singers have sung not always effectively, of the evils of slavery
   (E) many people are indifferent to the shame of slavery legislation

3 ___

(pages 14–20)
4. In line 15, "plaintiveness" most nearly means _____.
   (A) expression   (D) sadness
   (B) insincerity   (E) discord
   (C) irritation

4 ___

(pages 210–213)
5. When the author mentions the singer in line 16, he is probably _____.
   (A) suggesting that one of the Muses can move him to "a pure morning joy"
   (B) contrasting human song with the joyous message of the cock's crow
   (C) recalling a Sunday church meeting and a many-talented choir singer
   (D) recalling how he has at times been prompted to song by sheer inner gladness
   (E) using the word with no particular person in mind

5 ___

(pages 205–208)
6. In comparison with the author of Passage 1, the author of Passage 2 _____.
   (A) does not emphasize the importance of the present moment
   (B) has a more complicated prose style
   (C) is less intellectual in his presentation
   (D) is more concerned with hearing than seeing
   (E) doesn't observe with discrimination

6 ___

(pages 20–23)
7. In line 27, "variegated" most nearly means _____.
   (A) intense   (D) many-colored
   (B) amusing   (E) uneven
   (C) thoughtful

7 ___

438

(pages 51–55)
8. The image "the focus where the greatest number of vital forces unite in their purest energy" (29–30) suggests a _____.
   (A) blast furnace
   (B) crossroads
   (C) convex lens
   (D) collision of material objects
   (E) spider's intricate web

   8 ___

(pages 51–55)
9. The author uses the image of "a hard, gemlike flame" to suggest _____.
   (A) a persistent alertness that keeps an individual keenly aware of uniquely beautiful moments
   (B) a dogged persistence in studying, researching, and finally mastering the artist's technique
   (C) a growing awareness of the ways in which the beauties of jewelry are duplicated in the experiences of nature
   (D) a fierce loyalty to the principles of the fine arts as revealed in the hills and the sea
   (E) an extension of a humanitarian love for the earth and all its creatures

   9 ___

(pages 184–186)
10. If we would follow the suggestions of the author of Passage 2, we need to _____.
   (A) take a course in art history to familiarize ourselves with what has gone before
   (B) move to the country, which has a monopoly of beautiful scenery
   (C) learn to see differences, since no two moments are ever the same
   (D) become immersed in craft work as a union of perception and creativity
   (E) take a course in color, in dyes and paints, to improve our seeing eye

   10 ___

(pages 197–199)
11. If two persons, things, or situations seem alike, _____.
   (A) we are to be commended for seeing similar elements in dissimilar things
   (B) we may be breaking the mold of a stereotyped world
   (C) they are, to all intents and purposes, alike
   (D) the fault may be in our perceptions
   (E) we may be increasing our store of knowledge in the process

   11 ___

(pages 51–55)
12. When the author uses the extended metaphor, "on this short day of frost and sun, to sleep before evening," he is referring to _____.
   (A) the joys of winter: the cold and then the pleasant aftermath indoors
   (B) his belief that pleasure is varied, with beauty often found in the apparently commonplace
   (C) the brevity of life and the tragedy of dying too soon
   (D) a particular day that has lived on in the author's memory
   (E) a day so busy that fatigue set in happily and sleep came early

   12 ___

(pages 258–263)
13. The best way to apply the suggestions in Passage 2 would be to _____.
   (A) read extensively in the works of nature writers
   (B) doze beneath the shade of a spreading oak tree
   (C) notice how the colors of a sunset change almost imperceptibly
   (D) telephone a distant friend after a long lapse in communication
   (E) write a letter to the editor extolling a new conservation program

   13 ___

Division D
Answers

Answers to Trial Tests
for Division A, Vocabulary

Pages 15–16

1. *(B)* Since binoculars are being used, the answer must have something to do with seeing. The only answer that deals with seeing is *see clearly*.
2. *(D)* If the explorers put the plan into operation, the answer must show that the plan is practical. The only answer that deals with this point is *workable*.
3. *(A)* If "calm settled over the city," hostilities must have stopped. The correct answer is *stopping*.
4. *(E)* If Charles was permitted "a few hours of sleep," the pain must have lessened. The correct answer is *lessened*.
5. *(C)* Since vinegar is sharp and sour, Bonnie's expression must have shown her unhappy surprise. The correct answer is *distorted face*.
6. *(E)* The back-and-forth nature of a tennis match provides the clue here. Linda returned the volley. The correct answer is *returned like for like*.
7. *(A)* If Mel "tripped awkwardly in front of Betty," he must have been embarrassed. The correct answer is *embarrassment*.
8. *(B)* Robins announce the coming of spring. Therefore a *harbinger* must be some kind of early messenger. The word that best suggests this definition is *forerunner*.
9. *(D)* If Pru worked throughout the night and finished her report in time, she must have worked hard. The correct answer is *industriously*.
10. *(A)* Jesse James is a famous outlaw who was involved in only one side of the battle against crime: the wrong side. The correct answer is *committed*.

Page 21

1. *(B)* The word **flamboyant** is paired with "colorful." The word closest in meaning to both words in the pair is *showy*.
2. *(D)* **Acclamation** is paired with "obvious approval." The correct answer is *applause*.

3. *(E)* **Despicable** is paired with "mean." The correct answer is *unkind*.
4. *(A)* **Demurred** is paired with "disapproving." To demur is to disapprove. The correct answer is *objected*.
5. *(C)* **Reveries** is paired with "daydreams." Daydreams are *fantasies*.
6. *(D)* **Concise** is paired with "to the point." Something to the point is *brief*, not wordy.
7. *(B)* **Arduous** and "difficult" are paired. *Strenuous* means about the same.
8. *(A)* **Malign** is paired with "to tell an evil lie." The idea of evil suggests that the correct answer is *wrong*.
9. *(B)* **Privation** and "hardship" are paired. The correct answer is *want*. Here *want* is used as a noun.
10. *(E)* **Morose** and "ill-tempered" are paired. The word closest to describing such a state of mind is *gloomy*.

Pages 24–25

1. *(D)* "Rarely engaging in exercise" provides a definition of **sedentary.** Therefore the correct answer is *inactive*.
2. *(A)* **Subside** is explained by its appositive, "settle down." The correct answer is *calm down*.
3. *(B)* "Hitting a finger" and "sawing a crooked line" are given as examples of **ineptitude.** Since those activities show a lack of skill, the correct answer is *clumsiness*.
4. *(E)* **Velocity** is explained by its appositive, "speed." The correct answer is *rapidity*.
5. *(D)* **Predilection** is explained by its appositive, "taste." The correct answer is *preference*.
6. *(A)* **Harangue** is explained by its appositive, "endless lecture." The correct answer is *long, ranting speech*.
7. *(B)* If the **derisive** members "hooted and howled," we can assume the correct answer is *scornful*.
8. *(D)* "Presenting an obstacle" explains **protrudes.** The correct answer is *sticks out*.

9. *(C)* "Making unavoidable the mass slaughter" tells us that **precluded** means "made a peaceful solution impossible." The correct answer is *prevented*.
10. *(C)* "Miserly and thrifty to the point of excess" tells us what **parsimonious** means. The correct answer is *stingy*.

Pages 28–29

1. *(C)* "A wasp whose nest has been disturbed" is not likely to be happy. The comparison suggests that **irascibility** means *quickness to anger*.
2. *(E)* "A hammer smashing an eggshell" shows no "subtlety." Therefore Frank overwhelmed everyone. The correct answer is *bullied*.
3. *(C)* "Winter twilight" and "overcast sky" suggest darkness and gloominess. The correct answer is *gloomy*.
4. *(C)* "Endless drops from a leaky faucet" suggest a steady, annoying sound. The correct answer is *continuing*.
5. *(A)* "A startled lizard" moves rapidly. Therefore **alacrity** must mean *quick motion*.
6. *(C)* "An evening dress" is out of place "at a picnic." Therefore **incongruous** must mean *unsuitable*.
7. *(A)* "A corrosive acid" eats away substances. **Caustic** means *biting*.
8. *(E)* "A snake's trail" winds. Therefore **sinuous** means *winding*.
9. *(B)* "Scolding" is disapproving speech. Therefore **tirade** must mean *denunciation*.
10. *(C)* "A tiger on a starvation diet" would be very hungry. Therefore **ravenous** must mean *hungry*.

Pages 32–33

1. *(B)* The opposite of "harmonious" is *conflicting*.
2. *(A)* When all participants share in decision making, the decision is not **unilateral** or *one-sided*.
3. *(C)* **Ludicrous** is opposed to "taking the proposal seriously." Therefore **ludicrous** must mean *laughable*.
4. *(E)* If "weak" and "changing" are opposites of **tenacious,** the correct answer is *persistent*.

5. *(B)* "Generous" is opposed to **penurious.** The alternative which means the opposite of "generous" is *stingy*.
6. *(A)* The word "not" attached to **infallible** tells us that **infallible** means "the opposite of making many errors." The correct answer is *always right*.
7. *(B)* "Active" is contrasted with **dormant.** Therefore the correct answer must be the opposite of "active" or *quiet*.
8. *(C)* **Ephemeral** is contrasted with "lasting." Therefore the correct answer must be the opposite of "lasting" or *short-lived*.
9. *(D)* The wording shows that **cacophony** is contrasted with "blissful blending." Therefore the correct answer must be the opposite of "blissful blending" or *harsh sounds*.
10. *(E)* **Placate** is contrasted with "angered." Therefore the correct answer must be the opposite of "angered" or *soothe*.

Page 36

1. *(D)* The wording suggests a change in degree from "slow" to **obtuse.** It even tells us that **obtuse** is like "slow"—only more so. The correct answer is *dull*.
2. *(C)* The change from **improvise** to "revise" suggests that improvise is freer, more spontaneous. The correct answer is *compose offhand*.
3. *(C)* "Steep" is high, but **exorbitant** is higher. The correct answer is *excessive*.
4. *(A)* The change from "irritating" to **obnoxious** suggests a downward trend. **Obnoxious** must mean "worse than irritating." The correct answer is *offensive*.
5. *(B)* The sequence suggests that **arduous** is harder than "challenging." The correct answer is *strenuous*.
6. *(E)* **Stereotyped** is obviously worse than "dull." The correct answer is *stamped from a mold*.
7. *(A)* **Irksome** is a lesser degree of "unbearable." **Irksome** is unpleasant but not unendurable. The correct answer is *annoying*.
8. *(D)* The wording, with "frightening," suggests that **gruesome** is a stronger word than frightening. *Unpleasant* and *bitter* are negative words, but we need a very strong word here. The correct answer is *hideous*.

9. *(B)* The wording suggests that **unparalleled** is not merely "magnificent." It is something greater, without any possible comparison. The correct answer is *incomparable*.
10. *(B)* The progression is from "wild" to something more wild. The correct answer is *frantic*.

Pages 40–41

1. *(E)* "Because" suggests the reason for the children's rebellion. The first four alternatives suggest no reason for rebellion, but the fifth does. The correct answer is *strongly controlling*.
2. *(B)* "If" suggests the reason for next year's dues increase. If the funds are inadequate, dues must be raised. *(A)*, *(C)*, and *(D)* make little sense. *(E)* is a remote possibility but unlikely. *Decrease* is the best answer.
3. *(D)* "But" tells us the drought was reversed. The rains *refilled* the reservoir with water.
4. *(C)* "Because" is the clue. Ted's friends "like to tell him wild stories" because he believes everything. The correct answer is *believing*.
5. *(A)* The words "in an attempt to" tell us the editor is trying to change the tired words and expressions, to make the report less *commonplace*.
6. *(D)* The key word "unless" shows a way out of the difficulty: "giving more help." If the speaker is uncertain about "the right course," he or she must be in a *state of uncertainty*.
7. *(C)* "Although" tells us we have contrasting ideas: *meticulous* and "careless." We need an alternative that is opposed to "careless." The correct answer is *very careful*.
8. *(C)* "Since" ties up the idea of the downpour with Beth's appearance. Rain does spoil peoples' appearances. The correct answer is *untidy*.
9. *(A)* "Until" suggests that the stables had been clean before rainwater leaked onto the dirt floor. The correct answer is *spotless*.
10. *(B)* The wording suggests that the speaker would like to correct a mistake or else resign as president. The correct answer is *correct*.

Pages 47–48

1. *(B)* *Flabby* is a word applied to weak muscles. The alternatives are unsuitable. *Delicate* may be applied to an aroma. *Flimsy* may be applied to the construction of a house. *Limp* may be applied to the way hair hangs. *Loose* is a general word with many applications. None of these words can appropriately be applied to muscles.
2. *(C)* The five alternatives are rough synonyms and may generally be applied to a word like "speaking." When camera shots are mentioned, however, the correct word is *candid*.
3. *(E)* All the alternatives have something to do with "make-believe," but the term used for characters in a novel is *fictitious*.
4. *(A)* All the alternatives can be said of winds, but the word "mild" limits the possibilities. Only a *breeze* is mild.
5. *(D)* All the alternatives have to do with *copying*, but they all have different applications. *Copying* is a general word that covers many situations. *Mocking* and *aping* are unflattering words, unsuitable here. *Imitating* and *matching* do not describe the writing process. The only possibility is *copying*.
6. *(B)* The word "stricken" tells us that the spectators acted from terror. All the alternatives but one are inadequate to express their actions. The correct answer is *panic*.
7. *(E)* The word "unreasonable" suggests that the owner expected *perfection*, which is not a reasonable expectation. The correct answer is *perfection*.
8. *(C)* The alternatives are rough synonyms, but only *familiar* suggests the appearance of a place we might return to. The correct answer is *familiar*.
9. *(A)* All the alternatives suggest a weakened hiker. The extent of his deprivation—a week without food and with very little water—calls for the strongest word among the alternatives. The correct answer is *haggard*.
10. *(E)* When three blocks of houses burn, ordinary words for fire are inadequate. The correct answer is *conflagration*.

Pages 53–54

1. (A) Jean's quick action is compared with the action of a terrified mouse. Since the comparison uses **like,** this is a simile.
2. (B) The buds of the potato are compared with "eyes," but no comparison word is used. Metaphor.
3. (G) Obviously rainy weather and mosquitoes are not fun. Irony.
4. (E) Mr. Acton may have been angry, but he didn't hit the roof. This exaggeration is hyperbole.
5. (D) "Nose" is being used for the entire dog. Synecdoche.
6. (C) "Gloom" is here given human qualities. Personification.
7. (B) The error in reading is compared with actual stumbling in walking. Metaphor.
8. (A) This is an extended comparison with **as.** Simile.
9. (F) Six weeks of hospital stay is much more than an inconvenience. Understatement.
10. (C) "Love" is given human traits. Personification.

Pages 57–58

1. (B) *Constructed* is usually used for structures. *Created* is a general word applied to a wide variety of abstractions like ideas and fusses. *Prepared* is a general word for anything from arguments to meals. *Produced* is another general word, often applied to words like masterpieces or films. The word especially applied to music is *composed*.
2. (D) All the words suggest something long lasting, but the word reserved for flowers that last more than a season is *perennial*.
3. (B) All the words suggest opposition, but the word association with justice is *obstruct*.
4. (D) *Glut, cloy, cram*, and *gorge* suggest excess. Since the words "very little" are used, the correct answer is a milder word, *satisfy*.
5. (C) *Catalog* is too comprehensive for something brief. *Enumeration, inscription*, and *register* are too grand. The correct answer is *memorandum*.
6. (A) All words suggest inner qualities, but the word for athletic ability is *native*.
7. (B) All alternatives deal with frequent activities, but the word for a special, repeated activity is *routine*.

8. (D) All alternatives suggest a coming together, but the word reserved for roads that come together at one point is *merged*.
9. (A) All alternatives deal with duplication. When books are exactly reproduced, the correct word is *facsimile*.
10. (C) All words suggest cockiness and self-assurance. The key word "charming" tells us we need a word with pleasant connotations. The only word that qualifies is *pert*.

Page 62

1. (C) *Song, rhapsody, hymn*, and *chant* are all musical forms. The word not associated with the others is **struggle.**
2. (D) *Dwell, lodge, reside*, and *occupy* have to do with living in a place. The word out of place is **support.**
3. (E) *Dye, stain, tint*, and *paint* all have to do with applying color to something. Though **sketch** might involve applying color, the basic meaning does not include that process. The correct answer is **sketch.**
4. (A) All the alternatives but **aid** have the idea of listening to someone.
5. (D) All the alternatives but **ballad** have the idea of a mixture.
6. (C) All the alternatives but **nervous** suggest boldness. **Nervous** is actually opposed in meaning.
7. (E) All the words but **violet** refer to parts of a tree.
8. (C) All the alternatives but **agree** suggest differences. **Agree** is the opposite, not associated with the others.
9. (B) *Majesty, grandeur, greatness*, and *splendor* are words suggesting magnificence. **Queen** and *majesty* may be associated, but this association does not account for the other three.
10. (C) All the alternatives but **scratch** have to do with drawing back.

Page 66

3	hope	4	tasty
6	clearness	5	understanding
1	efficiency	8	unequal
2	certain	10	criticism
9	normality	7	thrifty

Pages 69–70

1. *(A)* There would be *noise and confusion* in such a hospital.
2. *(C)* A general would be associated with military *discipline*.
3. *(E)* If Machiavelli believed in possible deceit, *crafty* is the best answer.
4. *(E)* "Impossible feats" suggests Don Quixote was *impractical*.
5. *(B)* The unprotected heel was a *source of weakness*.
6. *(E)* Berserkers *raged violently*.
7. *(B)* "Strict rotation" eliminates the possibility of choice.
8. *(C)* The twisting, turning river suggests *wandering aimlessly*.
9. *(B)* Mesmer's powers suggest *hypnotic fascination*.
10. *(D)* Proteus's ability to change his shape suggests that **protean** means *extremely changeable*.

Pages 79–80

1. super	4. contra	7. retro	10. ante
2. ambi	5. dis	8. se	
3. post	6. ex	9. ab	

Page 81

1. tri	4. bi	7. omni	10. mill
2. oct	5. semi	8. tri	
3. multi	6. uni	9. cent	

Pages 85–86

1. cresc	6. flu	11. ag	16. cant
2. cogn	7. fer	12. fus	17. doc
3. dict	8. duc	13. gen	18. don
4. fac	9. dorm	14. curs	19. fug
5. fract	10. clam	15. ceed	20. cid

Pages 87–88

1. mit	6. pos	11. mand	16. prehend
2. junct	7. ques	12. mers	17. puls
3. jud	8. port	13. mut	18. plaud
4. ject	9. lect	14. nasc	19. plac
5. grad	10. loqu	15. neg	20. pet

Page 89

1. tort	6. scrib	11. Tens	16. vol
2. strict	7. Sed	12. spect	17. vok
3. sta	8. tain	13. sequ	18. verg
4. vis	9. sect	14. volut	19. ven
5. vinc	10. rupt	15. turb	20. trus

Pages 92–93

1. digit	8. dent	14. corp	20. domin
2. Brev	9. ego	15. capit	21. ev
3. anim	10. equ	16. Centr	22. aqu
4. al	11. fid	17. dia	23. cur
5. culp	12. civ	18. ferv	24. arm
6. ann	13. cor	19. equ	25. cruc
7. ben			

Page 95

1. ment	8. man	14. mort	20. liter
2. labor	9. fin	15. liber	21. miser
3. Ign	10. fort	16. Grav	22. fum
4. Leg	11. loc	17. greg	23. grat
5. lev	12. mal	18. herb	24. flor
6. Mar	13. mater	19. min	25. foli
7. Magn			

Pages 97–98

1. nov	8. vok	14. Somn	20. vac
2. nox	9. par	15. son	21. termin
3. temp	10. plus	16. optim	22. sanct
4. norm	11. ped	17. terr	23. ocul
5. popul	12. sol	18. umbr	24. ver
6. reg	13. numer	19. Urb	25. verb
7. prim			

Pages 104–105

1. C	4. B	7. D	9. C
2. B	5. A	8. B	10. A
3. D	6. B		

Pages 106–107

1. mis	6. pseudo	11. para	16. ana
2. iso	7. poly	12. peri	17. amphi
3. mega	8. an	13. micro	18. syn
4. cata	9. anti	14. neo	19. Hypo
5. auto	10. Hyper	15. pan	20. eu

Page 108

1. kilo	4. Tri	7. di	9. hexa
2. penta	5. tetra	8. deca	10. octa
3. mono	6. Proto		

Pages 110–111

1. Hydr	8. heli	14. hetero	20. iatr
2. geo	9. cycl	15. lith	21. chron
3. Derm	10. bibli	16. graph	22. crat
4. erg	11. chiro	17. homo	23. crypt
5. arch	12. alg	18. Chrom	24. gam
6. bar	13. Anthrop	19. dem	25. Hem
7. dynam			

Pages 113–114

1. thes	8. Ortho	15. Tele
2. the	9. pyr	16. trop
3. zo	10. Phil	17. typ
4. tom	11. Soph	18. phan
5. neur	12. scop	19. path
6. morph	13. Tax	20. meter
7. onym	14. pod	

Page 118

1. A	4. C	7. D	9. B
2. B	5. D	8. A	10. C
3. B	6. A		

Page 120

1. be	4. fore	7. Off	9. on
2. over	5. for	8. under	10. up
3. out	6. un		

Page 127

A   **B**

A	B
4	*make* systematic, arrange
9	*smallest* speck
6	*science* of production, distribution, and consumption of wealth
1	*place where* birds are kept
3	*having quality of* happiness
7	manual *skill*
8	*related to* light, clear
2	*one who* does good deeds
10	*in the manner of* a statue
5	*not able to* be reformed

Page 129

A   **B**

A	B
10	*having quality of* being annoying
6	*inflammation* of the stomach
3	*little* slice
2	*one who* is in charge of a museum or a library
5	*make* a speech of praise
7	*in the manner of* a greedy person
8	*place where* people work and experiment
4	*like* a horse
9	*diseased condition* of the mind
1	*quality of* unselfishness

Pages 132–133

A

1. American Indian	plants for food
2. French	fashion
3. Dutch	seafaring skills
4. German	science, chemistry
5. Arabic	science, mathematics
6. Spanish	opening up of the West
7. Persian	fruits and flowers
8. Italian	music
9. African	strange and new animals
10. American	technology and invention

B

10	China
15	England
5	England and Scotland
2	France
8	Germany
6	Hungary
3	India
4	Italy
9	Mesopotamia
13	Mexico
14	Morocco
11	Persia
12	Poland
1	Russia
7	Syria

1. abridged   5. severed   8. zealously
2. tenuous   6. naive   9. count
3. frisky   7. aptitude   10. borne
4. florid

Page 147

1. *(A)* Since **exhaust** and **fatigue** are synonyms, we need synonyms in our answer. *Plunge* and *swim* are neither synonyms nor antonyms. *Exertion* and *slumber* are opposed in meaning. An *officer* may be part of a *confederation*, but the words are not synonymous. *Generosity* and *greed* are opposed in meaning. The correct pair of words is *(A)*, *utensil : implement*.

2. *(C)* **Frankness** and **trickery** are antonyms. We need antonyms in our answer. *Radical* and *tasty* are not related. *Bankruptcy* and *insolvency* are close in meaning. *Memory* and *recollection* are synonyms. *Mercy* and *commentary* are unrelated. The correct pair of words is *(C)*, *benefit : harm*.

3. *(E)* **Affirm** and **deny** are antonyms. *Converse* and *declare* are loosely related. *Follow* and *pursue* are synonyms. *Check* and *inhibit* are synonyms, as are *endeavor* and *attempt*. *(E)*, *prosper* and *fail* are the antonyms we need.

4. *(E)* **Misfortune** and **tribulation** are synonyms. *Affliction* and *sanitation* are opposed in meaning. Fluid may be a food, but *fluid* and *food* are not synonyms. *Repute* and *uncertainty* are not related. *Suggestion* and *denunciation* are not related closely enough. *(E)*, *injustice* and *unfairness* are the synonyms we need.

Answers and Analysis for Vocabulary Diagnostic Test A

Part 1, Page 173

1. *(C)* The entire sentence (pages 14–20) suggests a barrier in the climbers' attempt to reach the summit. The climbers are stuck during the period of the blizzard. We need a verb that suggests the climbers are facing a difficulty. *Impeded,* meaning "faced with a hindrance," fits the slot nicely. *Seriously* conflicts with *motivated (A)*. *Embittered* would be a possibility if *impeded* had not been included. You must choose the *best* answer. There is nothing to suggest that the climbers were physically *impaired (D)*. *Revolted (E)*, with its suggestion of disgust, is nowhere implied.

2. *(E)* The conjunction *but* (40) signals a contrast between what the clay was like before the sculptor began to work and what it was like afterwards. Since the sculptor is obviously artistically competent, we need a suitable word for the second blank. *Stubby (A)* is unlikely. The writer probably would not introduce a word like *stubby* to describe the sculptor's fingers. However, just to make sure, look at the first word in the pair. *Sodden* is not a good description of clay that is ready to be worked. This rather lengthy explanation intends to show that (a) one word of the pair may reject the alternative or (b) the two words in conjunction may fail to complete the picture obviously intended by the writer. The first word in *(B)* is obviously incorrect, as is the second word in *(C)*. The elimination of *(A)*, *(B)*, and *(C)* leaves us with two possibilities. If the sculptor has to shape the clay, it is probably not shapely when he first sees it. *(D)* can be eliminated, even though the second word in the pair is excellent. That leaves us with *(E)*. Here, both words fit. For extra satisfaction, you'll recognize the Greek root *morph* (112) in *amorphous*.

3. *(A)* Allusions of one kind or other (67–71) often help in getting the sense of a sentence. Hitler and Mussolini were notorious dictators, presumably known to every person who takes this test. There is another, confirming clue: *sweep democracy away*. That one clue immediately eliminates *(C)*, *(D)*, and *(E)* because of the faulty second word in the pair. A choice must be made between *(A)* and *(B)*. Upon reflection, we must reject *namesakes*. The likelihood of a great many people named *Hitler* and *Mussolini* is slim. *(A)* fits the slot nicely. *Clones*, originally a word from biology, can be applied to any imitation.

4. *(D)* A plan that guaranteed benefits that could never be taken away must be comprehensive *(D)*, "all inclusive." Again the context of the entire sentence (14–20) is a clue to meaning. *(A)* is obviously absurd. *(B)* suggests permanence. *(C)* would not do much for health benefits. *(E)* suggests poor planning. Common sense dictates the right answer. *Comprehensive* is also covered in the section on Latin verbs (87).

5. *(B)* This is a vocabulary question that requires you to know the meaning of the key word. Sometimes all alternatives may be unknown to you. Then you must look to the words themselves. The context provides a clue. The key word must mean something like "lighten," "lessen," or "remove." Your memory of Latin roots (pages 83–103) recalls that *lev* means "light." *Alleviate* then must mean something like "lighten, lessen, partially remove."

6. *(D)* The sentence as a whole provides the clues (14–20). The answers are keyed to the clause "When it is time to return home." The best choice is *(D)*. Students achieve competence and then balk at returning. The phrasing suggests that the students are expected to return home to provide services in their homeland. That expectation is frustrated. The other choices fail to catch this point.

7. *(A)* Contrast provides the essential clue (31–35). *Merest* conflicts with *impressive*. The word modified by *merest* must contrast with *impressive*. *Quibble*, a "trivial objection," provides that contrast *(A)*. If you are uncertain about *quib-*

ble, you can still get the right answer by concentrating upon the second word in the pair. *Impressive philosophical structure* calls for a strong negative word in the blank. *Topple* meets the need. A strong structure can be *toppled*. The other choices make little sense.

8. *(B)* The answer relies upon comparison (28–31). Modern and ancient athletes are compared. *Triumphant (B)* best fits the sense for the first slot and *exploited* best fits the sense for the second. In the other choices, one or both words are unsuitable.

9. *(E)* A comparison is suggested between the schooling of Japanese schoolchildren and American schoolchildren (28–31). Students are paired (20–23) to sharpen the comparison. If Japanese schoolchildren go to school "240 challenging days a year," we may infer that their training is harder—more *intensive (E)*. The other choices do not concern themselves with that inference

10. *(B)* This is a sentence in which all five first choices fit the first slot and all five second choices fit the second slot. But only one *pair* fits. *Casual*, for example, would fit with *communication*, but *strategy*, the other word in the pair, doesn't make sense in the completed sentence. On the other hand, *strategy* might fit in the second slot, but the completed sentence would need a word other than *casual* to make good sense. The context of the sentence (14–20) requires the words in *(B)*. If *tactile* is unfamiliar, remember the *tact* root (88), meaning "touch."

11. *(E)* "Despite" warns us immediately that a contrast (pages 31–35), lies ahead. Something is being contrasted with the total success of the opening performance. The director did not expect the success. Therefore, he must have been worried. *Foreboding (E)* is the best choice. Note that in this type of question, many answers fit. The director might have been *excited* after the disastrous dress rehearsal. He might have shown *vigor* to bolster his morale. Choices *(A)* and *(D)* are not, however, as good as *(E)*. You are asked not merely to supply an answer that fits. You are asked to supply the answer that *best* fits

the meaning of the sentence as a whole. In this sentence the likelihood is that the director was worried. If *foreboding* is unfamiliar, you might reach it by a process of elimination or by analyzing the parts. **Bode** in "bodes no good" suggests bad possibilities. **Fore** obviously means "beforehand." *Foreboding* is thus a feeling that things will not turn out well. There are often many approaches to the right answer.

12. *(A)* Often, a key word will provide an essential clue. Here the key word is *inspiration*. The word is positive, suggesting a person worthy of being imitated, *emulated*, with the aim of equaling or surpassing the original. *(E)* makes a weak kind of sense, but it misses the essential tone of the statement. *(D)* is strong but inappropriate. Lionizing a former Senator is pointless. *(B)* and *(C)* make even less sense.

13. *(B)* The sentence describes an unusual achievement: the creation of a written language by one person. *(A)* is incorrect; no comparison is made. *(C)* is opposed to the sense of the sentence. *(E)* is not relevant. *(B)* and *(D)* are possible, but when listed with *(B)*, *(D)* is faulty. Singular, "unique," perfectly completes the sentence.

14. *(B)* Though it might seem more difficult to supply two words instead of one, actually supplying two words is often easier. Note how having two words, one of which is clearly wrong, helps us choose the right one. Choice *(A)* doesn't make sense. *Attentiveness* would have prevented the accident. Choice *(C)* provides a possible answer in *accepted*, but *boredom* does not fit the context. The word "although" clearly suggests a contrast (31–35), eliminating *boredom*. If "although" had been "because," the choices might have worked. *Dexterity* in *(D)* eliminates that possibility. The choices in *(E)* are farfetched and inappropriate. Choice *(B)* fits perfectly. The jury did not accept Mandy's disclaimer and decided she had been negligent.

15. *(C)* Comparison and contrast often provide clues (28–35). If Gorky, Smith, and Pollock died tragic deaths and De Kooning is unlike them, we may assume he *survived (C)*.

Part 2, Page 175

16. *(D)* The relationship tested here is that of a word and an opposed word (prob. 1: pages 147–149). We must therefore find among the choices two words opposed to each other. The first word in the pair must be an adjective and the second a noun. An excellent device is putting the relationship in the form of a statement (148). The statement for this analogy would look like this.
The statement:

A **hypocrite** is never **candid**.

The correct choice:

(D) A *fiend* is never *angelic*.

17. *(E)* The relationship is that of container and something contained (prob. 5: page 152).
The statement:

A **guppy** is kept in an **aquarium**.

The correct choice:

(E) *Jewelry* is kept in a *safe*.

What's wrong with *(B)* and *(C)*? Isn't a *letter* kept in a *file* and isn't a *dog* kept in a *kennel*? Careful! The categories have been reversed. The container comes first in the original pair.

18. *(C)* The relationship is that of tool or implement and activity (prob. 6: page 154).
The statement:

A **putter** is used in **golf**.

The correct choice:

(C) A *needle* is used in *knitting*.

Note that *(A)* and *(B)* have been reversed and are therefore not acceptable. A *line judge* is used in *football (D)* and an *onion* is used in *cooking (E)*. Why aren't these acceptable? Neither a *line judge* nor an *onion* can qualify as a tool.

19. *(B)* The relationship is that of the smaller to larger (prob. 8: page 155).
The statement:

A **pound** is smaller than a **kilogram**.

The correct choice:

(B) A *foot* is smaller than a *yard*.

A *century* is larger than a *year*. Therefore *(A)* is incorrect. A *liter* is larger than a *quart*. Therefore *(C)* is incorrect. A *centimeter* measures length and a *gram* measures weight. They cannot be compared. Therefore *(D)* is incorrect. *Calorie* is a measure of *heat;* it isn't larger than heat. Therefore *(E)* is incorrect.

20. *(C)* The relationship is that of a person to a quality associated with the person (prob. 12: pages 159–160).
The statement:

> An essential quality of the **referee** is **impartiality.**

The correct choice:

> *(C)* An essential quality of the *counselor* is *understanding.*

A *chef* does not need *strength*. *(A)* is incorrect. A *winner* does not tend to *regret*. *(B)* is incorrect. Though a *pessimist* may be *certain* about the terrible state of the world, *certainty* is not a crucial quality. *(D)* is incorrect. Though an *archer* needs *arrows* as a referee needs impartiality, the arrows cannot be considered a quality. When two or more choices seem to fit, go further. Refine the statement.

21. *(A)* The relationship is that of general term to specific term (prob. 9: page 155).
The statement:

> A **beetle** is a kind of **insect.**

The correct choice:

> *(A)* A *cobra* is a kind of *reptile.*

Choices *(C)*, *(D)*, and *(E)* are incorrect because one of the choices is not a general classification which contains the other. A *porpoise* is a kind of *mammal*. Therefore why not *(B)* also? Note that the terms have been reversed.

22. *(A)* The relationship is that of something and its associated quality (prob. 16: pages 164–165).
The statement:

> **Confusion** is characteristic of (or associated with) **chaos.**

The correct choice:

> *(A) Poise* is associated with *serenity.*

Choices *(B)*, *(C)*, and *(E)* are inappropriate. A *headache (D)* may be brought on by *noise*, but it is not necessarily linked with *noise*. *Noise* may even be a happy sound.

23. *(E)* The relationship is that of cause and effect (prob. 4: pages 151–152).
The statement:

> **Infection** may bring on **illness.**

The correct choice:

> *(E)* A *cloudburst* may bring on *flooding.*

An *explosion* may bring on *destruction (A)*, but note that the terms are reversed. There is no cause-and-effect relationship between an *eclipse* and *disaster (B)*, though ancient peoples may have thought so. *Bark* and *howl (C)* are similar, not causally related. There is no relationship between *sentimentality* and *ingenuity (D)*.

24. *(B)* The relationship is that of a lesser and a greater degree of intensity (prob. 7: pages 154–155).
The statement:

> **Fondness** is less intense than **infatuation.**

The correct choice:

> *(B) Enjoyment* is less intense than *rapture.*

Irritation is less intense than *rage (A)*, but the terms are reversed. *Excitement* and *indifference (C)* are antonyms. *(D)* and *(E)* have unrelated pairs.

25. *(D)* The relationship is that of a person to what he or she does (prob. 11: pages 158–159).
The statement:

> An **athlete competes.**

The correct choice:

> *(D)* A *matador kills.*

The function of the matador in the bullring is to kill the bull. The other choices do not show basic functions. The *meteorologist* doesn't *plant*. The *potter* doesn't *plow*. And so on for the others.

Answers and Analysis for Vocabulary Diagnostic Test B

Part 1, Page 176

1. *(D)* Though *cajoled* may be unfamiliar to you, a process of elimination suggests the answer. As often happens, a key bit of information provides a clue to a missing word (24). If Johnson sought party harmony, he wouldn't have done anything to alienate the Kennedy aides. On this basis alone, *(A)*, *(B)*, and *(C)* can be eliminated. *Distracted* doesn't sound much better. What would be the point? That leaves us with *cajoled*, "persuaded." *Cajoled* also has the suggestion of using flattery to win over a person.

2. *(A)* The entire sentence (14–20) provides essential clues to the correct answer. These are clues: the two months' delay and the successful result. One must be played against the other. Thus the blank must be filled with a word having negative connotations (46–50). *(B)*, *(D)*, and *(E)* may be eliminated because they are positive or neutral. We are left with *(A)* and *(C)*. *Sabotage (C)* has a negative connotation. Not only is there no hint of sabotage, but the nature of sabotage makes two months of it unlikely. Sabotage is usually an isolated action. Continuing sabotage on a program as heavily guarded as the shuttle flights would be unlikely. *Tribulations*, "distressful experiences," perfectly fits the slot.

3. *(E)* A quilting expert would not put down the very practice she is engaged in. This insight eliminates both *(A)* and *(B)*. Take the next step. Look at the second word in each pair and note the identical situation. The expert would not suggest that lap quilting is in any way out of step with American life-styles. With this realization, we can eliminate *(C)* and *(D)*. If you know the meaning of *espouses*, "supports," you might have used the process of elimination just to prove that you had chosen properly. If you did not know the meaning of *espouses*, you could still have solved the problem by the process of elimination explained above. Context (14–20) is a powerful ally.

4. *(B)* Knowing what *irony* (53) is supplies a quick answer to this problem. Irony suggests that reality is quite different from appearances. The passengers thought that planes were more dangerous than trains. In this situation, the opposite proved to be true. *Wistfully (A)* is sentimental and inappropriate. *Prematurely (C)* makes little sense. *Realistically (D)* runs counter to the point of the passage. *Contradictorily (E)* has a general application, but *ironically* catches the nuances of the sentence as well as its literal meaning.

5. *(C)* The sentence context suggests (14–20) that if the protection of human rights had been missing from the Constitution, the slot must mean something like "clear," "obvious," "definite." The only word that carries this meaning is *explicit*, "clearly stated," "definite."

6. *(D)* The key to the sentence is *wasteful*. We are most concerned about waste when resources cannot be replaced. **Profligate** means *wasteful*, but even if the word is unfamiliar to you, the second word of the pair will help you choose the right pair.

7. *(C)* Be especially aware of function words that provide essential clues (pages 39–43). The word *though* tells us that a contrast is coming. We'd expect anything abnormal to be bad, but *though* tells us to expect the unexpected. Some **deviations** from abnormality may not be bad but **benign.**

8. *(E)* Though occasionally a word in a pair makes sense, only **native** and **extinction** both fit into the sentence. These are obviously correct, but an examination of all the other alternatives shows their unsuitability.

9. *(A)* If the signals are being scrambled, the static must be **disruptive.** The first word in the pair, **intermittent,** also fits perfectly into the sentence.

10. *(B)* If new world records have come about because of changes in swimming

strokes, then the correct pair must complete a positive statement. Only **subtle** and **obsolete** make sense in this context.

11. *(B)* The pairing of "dead laboratory specimens" with "living creatures in the field" tells us contrast (pages 31–35) is a major clue. We can pinpoint the meaning by filling the first blank or the second. Since "dead" is being contrasted with "living," find a word that appropriately describes living creatures. We can immediately eliminate *(A)* since *stodgy* is completely inappropriate. *Vibrant* and *active* seem the best possibilities. The other word along with *vibrant* is *scrutiny*. This word fits perfectly, but to be sure see whether the word with *active* fits: *carelessness*. This doesn't fit. The only pair that fits perfectly is *scrutiny* and *vibrant (B)*. Frequently one word in the pair will fit but not the other, as in *(E)*.

12. *(E)* The sequence of ideas (35–38) and the function words **from** and **to** (39–43) provide the clues here. In addition, there is a contrast (31–35) of "realism" and "abstract design." Trying the possibilities suggests that *(E)* is the correct answer. *Literal* provides a sound contrast with *abstract*. With such contrast, the diversity may well be *incredible*.

13. *(B)* **Although** tells us a contrast (31–35) is a clue. In addition, the blank before "intelligence" is paired with "outer space." This is intelligence from outer space. A word linked with "outer space" is *extraterrestrial (B)*. The prefix **extra,** meaning "beyond" (78) and the root **terr,** meaning "earth" (96), tell us *extraterrestrial* means "beyond the earth," another expression for "outer space." Though words like *superior* and *galactic* may seem to fit also, their paired words do not fit. Neither *transfer* nor *broadcast* makes sense in the context. This sentence demonstrates that there are often many ways to ferret out the answer.

14. *(D)* The sentence as a whole (14–20) provides the needed clues here, but there is another, the pairing of "mysterious" and the blank. The only suggested word that can be reasonably paired with "mysterious" is *miraculous (D)*. Trying *limitless* in the first blank verifies our choice.

15. *(A)* What is the characteristic of a "meteor on an August night"? The trail is bright . . and brief. Here a comparison (28–31) provides the clues. The only word that fits the first blank is *blazed (A)*. *Faded* fits neatly into the second blank. All the other possibilities have one or both inappropriate choices.

Part 2, Page 178

16. *(D)* The relationship tested is that of a person and an important tool (15: 162).
The statement:

> The **gardener** uses a **trowel.**

The correct choice:

> *(D)* The *angler* uses a *rod*.

The *aviator* may use a *signal (A),* but the *signal* is not a tool.

Though all the other pairs are related, the relationship is not the same as that of the test words.

17. *(A)* The relationship is that of part to the whole (3: 150–151).
The statement:

> The **filament** is part of the **bulb.**

The correct choice:

> *(A)* The *stamen* is part of the *flower*.

Check the other choices. *Bark* is part of the *tree (B),* but the words are reversed. *Warmth* is associated with a *blanket (C),* but *warmth* is not a physical part. Besides, the words are reversed. A *character* may appear in a *novel (D),* but he or she is not a physical part of a novel. Again, the words are reversed. A *telephone* may carry a *message,* but the *message* is not a physical part of the *telephone (E)*.

18. *(B)* The relationship is that of a unit of measurement and something to be measured (20: 169).
The statement:

> A **milligram** is a measure of **weight.**

The correct choice:

> *(B)* An *acre* is a measure of *area*.

Choices (A) and (C) show correct relationships—but in reverse. *Ecstasy* and *happiness* are roughly synonymous (D), but neither is a unit of measurement. Both *meter* and *foot (E)* are units of measurement, but neither is something to be measured.

19. (C) The relationship is that of a person and the place associated with him or her (13: 160–161).
    The statement:

    An **astronaut** functions in a (space) **shuttle.**

    The correct choice:

    (C) The *cook* functions in a *galley*.

    Choices (A) and (B) would be possible, but they are presented in reverse. A *canary* does not function in a *kennel* (D). A *senator* does not function in the *White House* (E).

20. (E) The relationship is that of an action and the object acted upon (10: 156).
    The statement:

    Someone can **chisel marble.**

    The correct choice:

    (E) Someone can *mold clay*.

    Sometimes, as here, you have to carry the statement a bit farther. Every choice makes sense according to the simple statement:
    Someone can *burn* a *field*.
    Someone can *grow asparagus*.
    Someone can *read* an *article*.
    Some can *buy* a *newspaper*.

    What makes (E) better than the others? When an artist **chisels marble,** he or she is seeking an artistic creation. This goal is not true of the four incorrect choices, but it is true of (E). A person *molds clay* to create a work of art. After you have analyzed all the choices, if you like, you can rephrase your original statement to make it more specific.
    Someone can **chisel marble** to create a work of art.

    Then (E) becomes more obvious as the correct choice.

21. (E) The relationship is that of a word and a word similar in connotation, though not necessarily in part of speech (2: 149–150).

The statement:

    If someone **eulogizes,** he or she is complimentary.

The correct choice:

    (E) If someone *economizes,* he or she is *prudent*.

Note that the first word in the pair is a verb and the second an adjective. Your correct choice should show the same parts of speech in the same order.

22. (D) The relationship is that of a person and his or her purpose (14: 161–162).
    The statement:

    A **mentor guides.**

    The correct choice:

    (D) An *impostor deceives*.

    The other choices do not show an essential relationship.

23. (B) The relationship again is that of an action and the object acted upon (10: 156), but there is a difference between 20 above and this question. The purpose is not to create a work of art but to pen an animal.
    The statement:

    Someone can **corral** a **mustang.**

    The correct choice:

    (B) Someone can *cage* an *antelope*.

    The other choices seem plausible at first, for someone can *train* a *tiger* (A) or *herd sheep* (E), but only (B) suggests the essential purpose: to put an animal into some kind of pen.

24. (A) The relationship is that of the symbol and the thing symbolized (25: 171).
    The statement:

    The **rainbow** is a symbol of **hope.**

    The correct choice:

    (A) The *flag* is a symbol of *patriotism*.

    The *diploma* is a symbol of *graduation* (D) and the *skeleton* is a symbol of *Halloween* (C), but the pairs are reversed. *Food* might, in some instances, be considered a symbol of *sustenance*, but the words are reversed (B). The *crown (E)* is really a symbol of *royalty* rather than *wealth*.

25. *(A)* The relationship is that of a science and the subject of study (19: 168).

The statement:

Genetics is the study of **heredity.**

The correct choice:

(A) Seismology is the study of *earthquakes.*

Vulcanology is the study of *volcanoes (C),* but the words in the pair are reversed. *Meteorology* is the study of *weather,* not *asteroids (D). Aerodynamics* is not the study of *air pollution (B). Metaphysics* has nothing to do with *subatomic particles, (E).*

Answers to Trial Tests for Division B, Reading Comprehension

Page 184

(C) The human mind ordinarily operates at a fraction of its capacity. Examine each of the statements in turn. Since William James' quote supports the Wilson point of view, *(A)* is incorrect. There is no suggestion in the paragraph that *The Mind Parasites* is other than an ingenious bit of fantasy, with no relation to the future. Therefore, we can discard *(B)*. That the human mind is idling most of the time is the point of view of the paragraph. Therefore, *(C)* is sound. Look at the other alternatives, just to be sure. Fatigue *(D)* inhibits achievement. It does not stimulate it. Wilson's point of view *(E)* was anticipated by James and others. The paragraph flatly says, "That we are all underachievers is not a new idea." The generalization stated in *(C)* is the only correct one.

Page 187

(D) Tadpoles survive under conditions that seem unlikely and inhospitable. The life cycles of fish and tadpole are not compared. *(A)* is incorrect. *(B)* and *(C)* are correct statements, but they are details, not main ideas. They can be eliminated. *(E)* is incorrect. The passage specifically says that tadpoles could eat in ponds but could also be eaten. The paradoxical nature of tadpole survival is the theme of the passage. *(D)* is the correct answer.

Pages 189–190

William F. Allen *(A)* was indeed a man for all seasons, but the paragraph is about time. His contribution, while important, is not the whole story. *(B)* is irrelevant, off the topic. The paragraph deals with time, not with the calendar. *(C)* deals with a single sentence in the paragraph and is a detail. The same objection holds for *(E)*. *(D)* tells what the paragraph is about. All sentences deal with this topic, beginning with a brief description of timekeeping before 1883. The central section deals with the transition from the old time keeping methods to the new. The final section mentions the final victory of the four-zone agreement and comments on the importance of the change. Only *(D)* includes all three of these major sections.

Pages 192–193

(A) the mysterious appeal of mountain climbing. The pitfalls in answering this question resemble the pitfalls discussed in choosing titles. *(B)* is too narrow. Of course, the heroism of Joe Tasker is an important element in the passage, but it does not deal with the passage as a whole. *(E)* is an inference based on a detail. It does not deal with the passage as a whole. In a sense, *(D)* is much too broad. It also fails to address itself to the major point of the passage. *(C)* is irrelevant to the point of the passage. Only *(A)* adequately sums up the point of the passage.

Page 197

(B) The entire passage suggests the beginning of a storm, but there are more specific clues, too: the sudden whipping of the wind, the frantic activity of boat owners, the beginning of the rain. The full force of the storm has not yet struck, but its impact is beginning to be felt. We can infer from the clues that the worst is yet to come.

Page 200

(E) The major thrust of the paragraph is the danger in many common household substances. The summarizing statement suggests that the dangers require constant vigilance on the part of parents. This is the idea contained in *(E)*. The statement parallels a famous quotation: "Eternal vigilance is the price of liberty." Knowing the quotation adds interest to the question, but such knowledge is not necessary for the correct answer.

Page 203

(C) The last sentence of the selection gives the central idea. The best paraphrase of the idea is *(C)*: "Man's restless spirit, not his needs, brings

advances." Note that both the original statement and the paraphrase say essentially the same thing.

Pages 205–206

(B) The selection is an extended comparison of the arguments for collecting two types of stamps: mint and used. Though all five choices suggest comparisons, only (B) states the essential comparison: the *arguments* for collecting the two types of stamps. (A) is incomplete. (C) and (D) are not touched upon. (E) is a detail only partially covered.

Pages 210–211

1. (C) The selection specifically says, "Over the protest of Arabella Huntington, Duveen persuaded Huntington to buy Reynolds' masterpiece, *Sarah Siddons as the Tragic Muse*."

2. (D) The selection talks about "the two famous paintings often paired in the eyes of the public: Gainsborough's *The Blue Boy* and Lawrence's *Pinkie*."

Page 214

(C) Statements I and V are nowhere stated or implied. Any answer with either of these can be dismissed at once. We can thus eliminate (A), (D), and (E). (B) contains a correct statement, but since it says "IV only" it cannot be the desired answer.

Pages 217–218

(E) The last paragraph specifically says, "Some people may have a mild allergy to aloe vera." The statement goes on to say that most people find aloe beneficial. Yet this one drawback tells us that (E) is the right answer. No other paragraph mentions a disadvantage.

Pages 222–223

(C) This is a quiet sketch of a natural scene, emphasizing the subtle elements frequently overlooked in a cursory glance. This invites the reader to stand still a moment and recreate in imagination the stillness of a winter morning. The tone is *reflective*.

Pages 226–227

(D) This is by no means a negative appraisal. Therefore, (A), (B), and (C) can be immediately rejected. It is positive, amused, interested in the behavior of the fans. It is not indifferent. Eliminate (E). It does write with amused affection of the unusual characters who cheer on their football teams.

Page 230

(D) Since the selection deals exclusively with the activity *before* writing, the word *pre-writing* provides an immediate clue. The author plays down the critical faculties and self-criticism at the pre-writing stage. (A) and (E) are incorrect. Evans is introduced to make an opening point, but the purpose goes beyond Evans. (B) is incorrect. Phrases like *paralyze the will* and *freeze determination* suggest that writer's block is not trivial.

Page 224

(C) This is a down-to-earth explanation of the importance of trees in the carbon cycle. It is strictly *expository*. It is too serious for (E), too objective for (A), too matter-of-fact for (B). There is no indication of repetition (D).

Page 240

(C) Since John A. Barry is objecting to computer illiteracy, he would naturally object to any *increase*, since such increase would further pollute the language.

Page 244

(A) *Lumbering* suggests slowness and bulk. *Juggernaut* suggests a force that crushes every object in its path. All the answers but (A) are too specific. *Juggernaut* doesn't specify truck, bus, trailer, or ambulance.

Pages 247–248

1. (A) Since trees do not depend on birds and weather for their defense, we can eliminate (D). If the tree's chemicals "discourage or kill the invader," we can eliminate (B), since the author clearly

agrees. Trees and wildflowers handle insect infestations in different ways. We can eliminate (E). "Warn their neighbors" tells us the author agrees with (C). That leaves (A). Since trees have defenses independent of man, the author would disagree with (A). Therefore (A) is the right answer.

2. (D) The items mentioned in (A), (B), (C), and (E) are specifically mentioned in the selection. Therefore these alternatives can be discarded. Nowhere in the selection are other insects mentioned as a check on insect growth. (D) is correct.

Pages 253–254

1. (D) The only advice that has not yet been tried is hitting the ball back to the opponent, at "the belt buckle." The backhand strategy has failed. (A) is incorrect. Frank has killed overheads. (B) is incorrect. There is no discernible reason for Frank to rush the net. (C) is incorrect. No mention has been made of the coach's presence, but more important: Ted is moving toward the ball. He has no time to look up into the stands. (E) is incorrect.

2. (B) There is no logical reason to suppose that Ted can turn the match around at this point. Though turnabouts sometimes occur, the law of averages (except in fiction) tends to suggest otherwise. Ted is in trouble, only one game away from defeat. The logical outcome is (B). Thus we may eliminate (A) and (D).

Pages 258–259

(D) The father starts with a generalization—that Labrador retrievers are good with children—and then concludes that a certain Labrador will be good for his children. If put in the form of a syllogism, the argument would look like this:

Major premise—Labrador retrievers are good with children.
Minor premise—This dog is a Labrador.
Conclusion—This Labrador will be good with my children.

The other arguments are all inductive, drawing conclusions from a series of incidents.

Pages 265–266

1. (B) The unusual behavior of Gant is touched upon throughout the selection, as the family revolves about him. (A) is all wrong. (C) might be inferred, but it's not the main idea. (D) is much too broad. (E) is nowhere stated or implied.

2. (D) That he kept choking on a fish bone says little for his ability to learn from experience. In some respects he may have been a devoted father (A), but nothing is said about his credentials as a husband. He obviously didn't believe in moderation (B) and he did make the children nervous (C). (D) is not stated or implied.

3. (E) Since Gant was doing nothing to help self or family, the author clearly disapproves of Gant's table behavior. (A) and (B) are incorrect. (C) is too strong. (D) is nowhere suggested.

4. (A) "Impregnable to the heavy prod of Gant's big finger" (lines 9–10) tells us he wanted to make sure Eugene was stuffed.

5. (C) The portions had to be large to fit Eugene's distending belly. (A), (B), and (E) are opposed to the meaning of the selection. (D) is not related. *Gargantuan* is a word from a name, the hero of a work by Francois Rabelais, a French writer.

Pages 271–272

1. (A) The problem arises because Molesworth's ticket was not in Trieste, but Venice. The other alternatives are for one reason or another inappropriate. The conductor was not vindictive, merely within his rights to ask for a ticket. (B) is wrong. Molesworth finally paid for a ticket, invalidating (C). The telephone call never went through (D). The narrator may have been embarrassed, but the details are presented objectively. (E) is, in any event, a weaker answer than the objectively provable (A).

2. *(C)* Molesworth resolutely refused to take the ticket problem seriously. *(A)*, *(B)*, and *(D)* are off the mark. One might have chosen *(E)* *humorous* if the perfectly appropriate *stonewalling* had not been provided. The total effect was humorous, but Molesworth's strategy was to be unresponsive, as he clearly indicates in lines 10–11.

3. *(B)* The poor conductor is a slave of the system. Molesworth has no ticket; therefore, he can't ride. That there had been some human error did not matter. *(A)* is far too general. *(C)* is apparently untrue; the narrator and Molesworth are friends. There is no intercity conflict *(D)*. The railroad rules rather than national laws are the cause of the problem *(E)*.

4. *(D)* Molesworth is not sympathetic *(A)*, nor willing to speak the conductor's language *(B)*. He doesn't accept local train procedures *(E)*. That leaves *(C)* and *(D)*. Molesworth tends to be condescending toward the conductor. He drinks while dismissing the conductor's request, showing his contempt by his manner of speaking. The way in which Molesworth pays the 10,000 lire is a kind of put-down *(C)*, but calling the conductor by a completely inappropriate name is even more revelatory of Molesworth's scorn.

Since the conductor's first name is obviously unknown to Molesworth, we must assume that he is being snobbishly superior in using a familiar first name where none was indicated.

The episode with the lire occurs only once. It might display a momentary irritation with the conductor, but the use of the patronizing "George" three times is a continuing indication of Molesworth's attitude. Remember: when a strong case can be made for more than one answer, choose the BEST.

5. *(E)* The conductor's attitude is revealed by his reiteration of the "no ticket, no go" theme. At one point, he begins to perspire. Exasperation is clearly the answer. *Murderous rage (A)* is too strong. *(B)*, *(C)*, and *(D)* suggest a calm that the conductor obviously didn't display.

Pages 281–285

1. *(C)* Orwell, at least, failed to predict the disintegration of great states. *(A)* is incorrect. Lansing was involved in government but not Orwell. *(B)* is incorrect. The two men were not contemporaries. Lansing was of an earlier generation. *(D)* is incorrect. Lansing had nothing to do with writing *1984*. *(E)* is incorrect. Only *(C)* draws correct conclusions from the passage.

2. *(D)* The preceding sentence (lines 11–16) suggests that the three superpowers were repressive. The common prefix *mono* ("one") is another clue. The correct answer is *(D)*.

3. *(C)* In lines 47–53, the author notes that these nations had already demonstrated a capacity for nationhood in the years between World Wars I and II. *(C)* is correct.

4. *(B)* Any kind of warfare requires an enemy. *(B)* is correct.

5. *(A)* The next sentence provides the answer *(A)*.

6. *(B)* On the one hand, the author says, "Self-determination is a worthy ideal." In lines 136–137, he says, "Sometimes good principles clash." *(B)* is correct.

7. *(E)* The following paragraphs mention the disintegrating, deteriorating situation because of rampant nationalism. *(E)* is correct.

8. *(A)* The key clues are *in* (lines 85, 86–87) and *inside*. The prefix *en* (in) provides another clue. *(A)* is correct.

9. *(B)* Some of the tragic consequences of self-determination are *bloody civil war* (119), *human rights are often trampled upon* (140), *persecute new minorities* (143). *(B)* is correct.

10. *(D)* The partition of Yugoslavia was bloody (line 119 and following). The partition of Czechoslovakia was peaceful (117). *(D)* is correct.

11. *(C)* Both self-determination and human rights are excellent principles, but sometimes self-determination results in some loss of human rights (140). *(C)* is correct.

12. *(E)* The author suggests that there is a momentum that propels groups to seek nationhood. Lines 123 to 132 talk about further splintering. *(E)* is correct.

Pages 300–302

1. *(B)* In lines 15–20, the author says, "The first thing to learn . . . ours." We should not try to foist our own ideas and customs on others.

2. *(A)* "Curious speculation" is too shallow. An understanding of diversity has the most tremendous practical importance. That speculation is only a beginning. It may lead to a "deeper awareness," but there is no guarantee.

3. *(E)* The key to the answer is *non-interference*. We cannot expect our own rights to limit the rights of others.

4. *(E)* If no one has such insight, a rational solution is to keep an open mind, learning about the good ideas of others.

5. *(A)* The context clearly calls for a word with negative connotations, thus eliminating *(B)* and *(C)*. The word *pretension* suggests an assumption of superior wisdom. Such assumption would not nec-

essarily require a loud voice *(D)*. *(E)* is nowhere hinted at.

6. *(B)* The message is simply given with the expectation that readers are reasonable people. The point is made without anxious pleading *(A)*. *(C)* is too strong. *(D)* is untrue. There is no attempt at humor *(E)*.

7. *(B)* Both passages make the point that each person is essentially concerned with his or her own values and meanings. "The meaning is there for the others, but not for us." (6–7)

8. *(D)* Passage 1 takes a more serious view of human failings. It deals with larger problems than Passage 2, which is more forgiving.

9. *(A)* The author suggests that the lady's listener would not be interested in the collection of baby clothes and house linen (35–40).

10. *(E)* The final sentence emphasizes the importance of talking of ourselves or our own groups.

11. *(B)* Just as a jug cannot pour out anything that isn't in it, so a person cannot pour out, in conversation, anything not in the person.

Answers and Analysis for Reading Diagnostic Test A

Page 342

1. *(D)* The word *major* tells us we must draw a generalization (184) from the passage. Richard *(A)* is touched briefly. Queen Eleanor *(B)* is a detail. Energy *(C)* is one side of the Plantagenets. The deviousness of the Normans *(E)* is not in the passage. The contradictory personality of John is emphasized throughout—for example, his rages and his cold intelligence, his greed and his generosity. The best choice is *(D)*.

2. *(B)* A question may require us to seek out details (210) in the passage, as here.

John's cruelty is mentioned ("cruelties were conceived"), as is his intelligence ("a cold, inhuman intelligence"). *(B)* is clearly the correct choice. John was not gentle *(A)*, weak *(D)*, or stupid *(E)*. He is not called handsome *(C)* in the passage.

3. *(A)* This passage requires us to spot a detail (210) and then draw an inference (197). We read that "monkish chroniclers have emphasized his violence, greed, malice, treachery, and lust." We reasonably infer that these are "John's worst qualities" *(A)*. None of the other choices can be justified by the passage. They either state the opposite *(B)* or make a point

not mentioned in the passage at all *(C)*, *(D)*, *(E)*.

4. *(C)* The point of the selection is summarized in the last sentence: "The English-speaking world owe(s) far more to the vices of John than to the labours of virtuous sovereigns." This says the same essentially as *(C)*. Finding generalizations (184) often requires the candidate to draw inferences (197) as well.

5. *(E)* A title (189) must cover the subject, being neither too broad nor too narrow. The subject of the passage is not John Stark *(A)* but Scott Joplin. Stark is mentioned only as he plays a role in Joplin's life. *(B)* is too narrow. *(C)* is too broad—and partly off the subject. *(D)* is inaccurate. Other composers are not mentioned. *(E)* is the correct choice.

6. *(A)* The answer, a detail in the selection (210), is found in the opening sentence. The song was named after the Maple Leaf Club, where it was played *(A)*.

7. *(D)* Questions with *except* reverse the usual challenge. Check off items actually mentioned in the selection. The one left is the answer. "He also wrote *songs, marches, waltzes,* and an elegant *tango.*" *Operas* are not mentioned by name in the passage.

8 *(C)* An actual detail (43–44) in the passage provides the answer: "For several years, he appeared on vaudeville stages." The correct choice is *(C)*.

9. *(E)* Questions sometimes test your ability to define a word in context (14), as here. *Marginal* cropland is plowed but quickly abandoned because of soil depletion. We may reasonably infer (197) that such soil is poor. *(E)* is the correct choice. Note that *margin* usually means *border. Bordering* for *marginal* is an enticing choice, but it doesn't fit here.

10. *(B)* Questions sometimes test figurative language (51). Since straws are insubstantial and clutching at them quite ineffectual, we may assume that *(B)* is the correct choice.

11. *(B)* This is the key sentence: "Sustaining this nation's food and fiber-producing capacity may become our most potent deterrent to international conflict." This suggests that the world may need America for food to survive *(B)*. This detail (210) is there in the text. The other alternatives are inaccurate, opposed, or even not mentioned. Though you might be of the opinion that *(E)* is a reasonable answer, you cannot choose it, for it is nowhere mentioned in the selection.

12. *(D)* Dates are provided: 1644 for the overthrow of the Ming dynasty; 1662–1722 for the reign of K'ang-hsi. We may infer (197) from the details (210) that *(D)* is the correct choice. *(A)* is flatly incorrect. There is no justification for any of the other choices.

13. *(E)* The last sentence of the paragraph identifies those who "preferred to derive their art directly from nature" as individualists. The previous sentence tells us these same painters, "expressed a strong sense of dislocation and alienation in their works." Once again selecting details (210) and then drawing the proper inference (197) suggest that *(E)* is the correct choice.

14. *(C)* Identifying the main purpose of the author (230) is akin to finding the main idea (186). Let's evaluate each choice in turn. There is no attempt to glorify one school of painting at the expense of another. The author is quite neutral and objective. Therefore *(A)* is incorrect. There is no suggestion that "17th century artists" failed to paint from nature. Eliminate *(B)*. *(C)* expresses the central purpose of the author: to explain rather than criticize or take sides. *(C)* is correct. The individualists rather than the orthodox painters expressed nature through personal means. Eliminate *(D)*. As we have already seen in *(A)*, the author is not taking sides. Eliminate *(E)*.

15. *(A)* Sentence 2 supplies the key phrase: "after late Ming fragmentation." Spotting this detail (210) enables us to infer that *(A)* is the correct choice. The "early Ch'ing world" occurred right after the fall of the Ming dynasty. At this time orthodox painters aimed to recapture the "former glories of traditional painting." Thus we may infer that toward the end Ming art had been fragmented.

Answers and Analysis for Reading Diagnostic Test B

Page 345

1. *(C)* The episode is reported in utter seriousness, but the outrageousness of the events tells us the author's purpose (230) is to entertain *(C)*. Exaggeration, like its opposite, understatement, is often employed as a humorous device. The author's apparent hope to get the native killed is obvious exaggeration of a mild annoyance at the native's persistence.

2. *(E)* This question requires us to draw an inference (197). Though we are not told so directly, we can reasonably assume that Dan is being bothered for a silly whim. "As long as Dan has got a cent" suggests that Dan will not relish being relieved of all his money. The answer is *(E)*.

3. *(B)* This question requires us to look beyond the passage and predict outcomes (253). It also calls for an inference. Choices *(A)* and *(E)* are absurd. There is no suggestion the police are involved *(D)*. Dan hasn't said a word *(C)*. Elimination brings us to *(B)*, the most likely result.

4. *(D)* Finding details in the passages is a commonly tested skill (210). The sentence beginning "He crawled" clearly identifies the peg as the climber *(D)*.

5. *(A)* The author's attitude (225) is humorously irascible *(A)*. Note that *irascible* is related to *irate*. The other alternatives are unsuitable.

6. *(D)* Since the passage contrasts language and reality, the best title is *(D)* (189). *(A)* makes no statement about the contents of the passage or the relationship between words and things. *(B)* is too narrow. *(C)* is too broad. *(E)* is a detail.

7. *(C)* Korzybski uses an analogy that might be represented as follows:

map : territory :: language : reality

Thus *map* corresponds to *language* and *territory* to *reality*. The correct pairing is *language* and *map (C)*. Two skills are involved here: finding details (210) and drawing inferences (197).

8. *(B)* This question requires analyzing the author's use of language (240).
The first two sentences of paragraph two contrast the "process nature of reality" with the static impression sometimes given by language. If reality is not *static*, it must be *changing (B)*.

9. *(A)* The passage says, "The usefulness of a map depends precisely on the degree to which it corresponds to the territory." Spotting this sentence (210) tells us *(A)* is the best choice.

10. *(E)* The passage flatly says, "We cannot do without generalizations." (184). Therefore *(E)* is correct.

11. *(C)* Shrinking the earth to a "wet ball" emphasizes its insignificance.

12. *(B)* The last two sentences, with the suggestion "cast out," conclude the paragraph on a quietly sad note.

13. *(B)* This is a vocabulary question. If the word *careering* is unfamiliar to you, try eliminating answers. *(A)* and *(C)* suggest motions nowhere hinted at. *(D)* suggests an image inappropriately descriptive of the solar system's movement. *(E)* makes little sense.

14. *(D)* When the solar system arrives "east of Hercules," it won't be "a place to call home."

15. *(E)* The metaphor of the dinner party, so obviously inappropriate for a wandering solar system, adds a note of humor in the sad context.

Answers to Facsimile Test 1

Section 1 Pages 353–359

1. *(A)* The context tells us that *conventional* is being contrasted with another word. Both *theatrical* and **outrageous** provide such a contrast, but only **erratic** suitably completes the sentence. Though Denny's behavior may become *theatrical,* it would not then be *consistent.*

2. *(B)* If creatures are transferred to areas where they no longer occur, they are **re-established** in the new area.

3. *(E)* If the arbitrator thwarted the efforts of the press to anticipate his decision, he didn't give things away. He was **noncommittal.**

4. *(D)* A favorable setting would hasten a person's recovery. Therefore his or her **recuperation** would be **accelerated.**

5. *(C)* Newborn infants are obviously too young to show *comprehension, condescension* or *magnanimity.* Both **equanimity** and *indifference* are possible, but only **penetrating** suitably completes the sentence. A newborn infant could scarcely be called *competent.*

6. *(D)* **Recluse,** "a person who leads a solitary life," fits the context here. Again, if you're not sure of the word, try eliminating the others. (A) and (C) can be dismissed out of hand. (B) is nowhere hinted at. Since Emily Dickinson speaks, (E) is inexact.

7. *(D)* The reviews had to be **derogatory,** "unfavorable," to turn a novelist to writing a different literary type.

8. *(C)* "Began to realize" suggests that Henry Jekyll was aware that Edward Hyde would take over. The context calls for a word that suggests a deep uneasiness: **foreboding.**

9. *(A)* The likelihood of such a coincidence is so slim that the answer must address this element. Only **minuscule,** "very small," fills the slot. The *min* root is mentioned on page 94.

10. *(D)* A **chisel** is used in **carpentry.** (prob. 6, page 154) In the same way a **blowtorch** is used in **welding.** All other pairs are related, but not in the same way. A *tuning fork* is used in *music,* but the terms are reversed.

11. *(A)* **Influence** is a lesser degree of **domination.** In the same way, **admiration** is a lesser form of **worship.** (prob. 17, page 165)

12. *(C)* A **manuscript** is **edited.** In the same way an **account** is **audited.** (prob. 10, page 156)

13. *(B)* A **cygnet** is a **young swan.** (prob. 23, page 171) A **gosling** is a **young goose.** *(A)* is reversed. *(C)* differentiates between male and female. *(D)* and *(E)* have incorrect pairings of animals.

14. *(E)* Here we have a word and an opposed word. (prob. 1, page 147) **Excess** is opposed to **scant.**

15. *(E)* The goal of a **therapist** is **rehabilitation.** (prob. 14, page 161) The goal of a **jester** is **entertainment.**

16. *(E)* Mrs. E was not a cruel person, but her fussiness about the pocketbook showed an insensitivity to Mildred's feelings and a **lack of trust.**

17. *(D)* Although we hear only one side of the conversation, we can infer Marge's questions by Mildred's replies. These are the answers to Marge's questions: *(A)* "No, Marge. . . ." (5). *(B)* "I'd be more than glad . . ." (5–6). *(C)* "No, not those little novels . . ." (11–12). *(E)* "No, there's nobody there but me and her." (17) That leaves *(D),* which is nowhere mentioned or implied.

18. *(B)* Mildred tells Marge to **keep working** as she tells her that hands aren't necessary for listening (23).

464   **ENGLISH FOR THE COLLEGE BOARDS**

19. *(E)* Mrs. E has demonstrated a lack of trust, even when she and Mildred are the only ones in the house. The narrator gets in a double-barreled sting: Mrs. E's stinginess and suspicious nature.

20. *(B)* Despite her mean-spirited employer, Mildred retains a **sense of dignity,** without anger.

21. *(B)* Mildred sees an opportunity to let Mrs. E know how she has been bothered by the mistrust. That she waited a few minutes (29) indicates that she is setting up a situation to bring Mrs. E to her senses. The "gaspin' hard for breath" is part of the melodramatic act.

22. *(E)* The author mentions the *almost* appointment (6), says it "was not offered" (7), and mentions the antagonism" (8).

23. *(B)* "Every plant and animal on Earth today is a symbiont, living in close contact with others." (22). The Greek prefix *-sym* is mentioned on page 106. *Symbiont,* by derivation, means "living together."

24. *(D)* "You will never find life in isolation" (57–58). The examples of termites, spirochetes, and microbes stress the **interlocking associations.**

25. *(A)* The thrust of the passage is the interrelatedness of all things. When Margulis challenges the concept of the "rugged individual" (18–19), she is saying, in effect, **"we're all in this together."**

26. *(C)* "New Age types are drawn to her and then she busts them high, low and center for being softheaded" (16–17).

27. *(C)* "Margulis challenges the American myth of the rugged individual" (18–19). This question demonstrates the importance of basing your answer solely on the passage. Some Hollywood movies have blasted "the American myth of the rugged individual" *(A),* but such information is irrelevant here. Stick to the passage.

28. *(D)* This kind of question requires that you skim the selection to identify the speaker. Certainly, Lynn Margulis could have spoken those words, but as it happens, the speaker is Gail Fleischaker (57–58).

29. *(B)* *(A)* is a waste of time. *(C)* puts the cart before the horse. First find the quotation. Margulis *might* have used the quotation *(D)* but she didn't. *(E)* is irrelevant. Only *(B)* suggests the most efficient method.

30. *(D)* The controversy over Margulis's work suggests that recognition doesn't come easily. *(A)* is untrue. *(B)* is not mentioned. *(C)* is the opposite of what is true. *(E)* is belied by the controversy over Margulis's work.

Section 3 Pages 359–365

1. *(D)* The use of *as well as* suggests a contrast between Simenon's failures and successes. A process of elimination suggests that **personal** *failures* is being contrasted with **professional** *successes.* The other alternatives do not provide the needed contrast.

2. *(E)* The context suggests a change in degree in the candidate's reactions. *Quiet* **pleasure** gives way to *expressive* **jubilation.** *Favorable* suggests that both words must be positive. The other alternatives all contain negative elements.

3. *(C)* Since most proponents of television insist its primary purpose is to *inform* or *entertain,* the emphasis on *sell goods* is clearly a **cynical** reaction. The other alternatives make no sense or contain contradictions.

4. *(B)* **Dependable, resilient,** and **inexhaustible** could fill the first slot. Therefore the second word in the pair is crucial. If the ecosystems cannot survive much tampering, they must be **fragile.** Thus, even if *resilient* is a new word for you, the clues for choosing *resilient . . fragile* are easy to find.

5. *(A)* Once again the second word in the pair is a major clue. Both the mastodon and the sabre-toothed tiger are extinct. A

common idiom is *experience the fate.* **Experienced** fits the second slot nicely. **Stereotypes** fits into the first slot, and the modifiers *formerly accepted* make the choice certain. The stereotypes are as extinct as the animals.

6. *(E)* The parts of a collapsible telescope slide over and into each other, suggesting a condensing of its parts. In the same way, two words, *chuckle* and *snort,* were condensed to form one new word. Words like *chortle* are sometimes called "blends" or "portmanteau words." A portmanteau is a traveling case with two compartments, just as *chortle* is a word with two elements.

7. *(D)* The number and variety of uses for the Tower call for **checkered,** "diversified."

8. *(D)* A rich background and a knowledge of allusions (67–72) help here. An **odyssey,** an "extended wandering or journey," takes its name from the Greek warrior, Odysseus, who spent ten years wandering the seas in an effort to reach his native Ithaca, after the Trojan War.

9. *(C) But* tells us that the novel's success was in spite of negative qualities. Linking *wooden characters* and a(n) _____ plot suggests that the plot was not sparkling or scintillating. Of the alternatives, **hackneyed,** "trite," is the only one that logically completes the sentence.

10. *(C)* The policemen wouldn't have staged a strike against anything construed as positive or neutral. The sentence requires a word with negative connotations. **Servitude,** which implies a master-slave relationship, fits the slot.

11. *(E)* A **disciple follows.** (prob. 11, page 158) In the same way a **trustee administers.** An **infant cries,** but the words are reversed. **Amphibians** may **slide,** but sliding is not their main feature or function. A **courier carries** messages and doesn't **write** them. **Candidate : votes** seems tricky at first, but the primary function of the candidate is to be elected.

12. *(C)* A **mouthpiece** is part of an **oboe.** (prob. 3, page 150) In the same way an **eyepiece** is part of a **telescope.** The **bit** is part of a **drill,** but the words are reversed. **Ammunition** is inserted into a **cannon,** but it is not an essential part of a cannon. **Warp** and **woof** are threads used in weaving but their relationship to each other is complementary. The **warp** is not a smaller part of the **woof.**

13. *(D)* A **pamphlet** is smaller than a **tome.** In the same way a **hill** is smaller than a **mountain.** (prob. 8, page 155) The other pairs are related to each other, but do not complete the analogy. A **turnip** and a **radish** are vegetables, but a turnip is not related to a radish in size. An **oration** may be used in **election** speeches. A **caterpillar** may become a **butterfly.** A **shout** and a **cry** are roughly synonymous. Only *hill : mountain* shows the proper relationship.

14. *(B)* **Inactivity** is a quality associated with **hibernation.** (prob. 12, page 159) In the same way **ruin** is associated with **devastation. Disorder** is associated with **entropy,** but the words are reversed.

15. *(A)* **Pathology** is the study of **sickness.** (prob. 19, page 168) In the same way **paleontology** is the study of **fossils.** Words in the other pairs are associated, but not in the same way.

16. *(A)* An artist uses a palette. (prob. 15, page 162) In the same way a **conductor** uses a **baton.** The pairs in *(B)* and *(D)* are reversed. Besides, a **stenographer** may not use a **typewriter.** A **soldier** wears a **boot,** but doesn't use it as an *artist* uses a *palette.* The association of *nurseryman* and *cradle* accounts for the incorrect *(E).*

17. *(B)* A steak may be **broiled** (prob. 18, page 166) in the same way a **lawn** may be **mowed.** The other alternatives are unacceptable. The **roll** may be **called,** but there is no physical action taking place. A **book** may be **overlooked,** but there is no physical change in the book. A **neurotic** may be **calmed,** but such action is quite different from that in *broiling* and *mowing.* A **turkey** may be **basted,** but the words are reversed.

18. *(C)* A **jewel** is kept in a **casket.** (prob. 5, page 152) In the same way a **flower** is kept in a **vase.** *Water* is kept in a *kettle,* but the words are reversed. The trickiest alternative is *(E).* A *ticket* may be kept in a *receptacle,* but *receptacle* is a general word that may contain hundreds of dissimilar items of all sizes. Besides, a *receptacle* is not a primary container for a *ticket.*

466

19. *(D)* **Fable** is a kind of **story,** but it is a more specific term. (prob. 9, page 155) In the same way **senator** is a kind of **legislator,** but it too is a more specific term.

20. *(E)* **Neutrality** is the quality needed for a **mediator.** (prob. 12, page 159) In the same way, **skill** is the quality needed for an **athlete.** *Courage* is the quality needed for a *hero,* but the words are reversed. The other pairings suggest desirable qualities but not essential ones. *Humor* is not essential for a *physician,* though it might help!

21. *(B)* **Chill** is the result of **exposure.** (prob. 4, page 151) **Frustration** is the result of **obstruction.**

22. *(C)* A **librettist** is associated with the **opera.** (prob. 12, page 159) A **mountaineer** is associated with the **rock face** of a mountain. *(A)* and *(E)* are reversed.

23. *(D)* To **elude,** you must be **cunning.** Though the words are of different parts of speech, they are related. (prob. 2, page 149) To **fumble,** you must be **clumsy.** *(E)* is reversed.

24. *(D)* *Even as* suggests that Santayana disapproved of what he was doing. **Decried** means "condemned."

25. *(A)* As the opening paragraph, the Santayana quotation is intended to set the theme and tone of the passage. Interestingly, even though the paragraph espouses the principle of E-Prime, it actually uses *are* (3) in contradiction of the point of view expressed.

26. *(B)* The use of *is* can be deceptive. A statement of opinion has the same form as a statement of fact. *(A)* and *(D)* are too strong. *(C)* is opposed in meaning. *(E)* has nothing to do with the sentence.

27. *(D)* Even though *(D)* mentions E-Prime, its use of *is* disqualifies it as a sentence written in E-Prime.

28. *(C)* If "reality resists easy capture in words," no one can be sure just what the real world is, since our picture of reality is based on our verbal image, even if inadequate.

29. *(D)* Although E-Prime avoids the use of *is* and other linking verbs, it does use **traditional structure,** as in the present sentence.

30. *(A)* Looking for the smaller word within the larger (65–67) often helps on the SAT. **Perception** is the noun of the verb *perceive,* "recognize, take note of, become aware of." This method points to *insights* as the answer, but context also helps. Try out each alternative. "Sharpens insights" makes good sense.

31. *(B)* Three possibilities, all negative, may be eliminated at once: *(A), (D),* and *(E).* The passage is not frivolous. We can eliminate *(C).* It is informative, written in a readable style.

32. *(C)* All the sentences are subjective judgments except *(C).* This sentence, though using the word *is,* eliminates one objection to writing that is not in E-Prime.

33. *(C)* The only **metaphor** (51–52) is contained in *(C).*

34. *(B)* E-Prime attempts to avoid rigid classifications, especially those based on subjective judgments. Absolute words like *always* and *never* destroy this flexibility.

35. *(D)* The judgment word **boringly** makes this a subjective statement. Boring? How? According to whom? There are no objective yardsticks for measuring boredom.

Section 5 Pages 365–369

1. *(B)* Note how the wrong alternatives become quite apparent. In *(A)* no mention is made of climate. *More* than a half dozen leaders were responsible *(C).* The mention of "great heroic dramas" (20) is a red herring. It uses dramas in a sense different than those in *(D).* "Three or four times in history" rules out *(E).* Only *(B)* properly fills the slot.

2. *(C)* Mention of "the whole world" identifies *(C)* as the answer.

3. *(A)* "The late sixth-century B.C." approximates the times of Buddha and Lao-tzu,

a time described as the **"miracle of Ionia and Greece."**

4. *(E)* The author uses the phrase "larger than life" to emphasize their extraordinary impact on their period. *(A)* and *(D)* are opposed in meaning. Longevity is not mentioned *(B)*. Emphasis is not upon the spiritual nature of their achievements *(C)*. Only *(E)* captures the point of lines 17–18.

5. *(A)* The author suggests that the "heroic energy, confidence, strength of will and intellect" are visible in Durham Cathedral and the east end of Canterbury. *(B)*, *(C)*, and *(D)* run counter to the author's message. The author doesn't say *(E)* where Pope Urban announced the First Crusade (line 19).

6. *(C)* The last sentence of the first passage says that goldsmith work and ivory carving **had been practiced,** though on a small scale.

7. *(E)* The smaller word *monument* within **monumental** is a clue, but note also that **monumental** is contrasted with "small portable objects." Monuments may be made of stone *(A)*, but not necessarily.

8. *(D)* The "grim defensive houses" are contrasted with the "light, sunny arcades." It is concerned with *pre*-Renaissance Florence *(A)*. The achievement of the money grubbers is mentioned and accepted, not criticized *(B)*. Rather than explain *(C)* the Florentine origins of the Renaissance, the sentence leads to the opposite—awe at the miraculous change. *(E)* may be relevant to the rest of the paragraph, but not to the opening sentence.

9. *(D)* The key is the statement "they totally contradict the dark Gothic style that preceded . . . them" (Lines 46–47).

10. *(D)* The passage says, "**Learning** could be used to achieve a happy life" (64–65). This is a detail, not an inference.

11. *(E)* Passage 1 ranges the world; Passage 2 is devoted to Florence.

12. *(A)* The use of "suddenly" in Passage 1 (line 29) and "suddenly out of the dark" in Passage 2 (43) clearly signals the author's emphasis on the **"sudden bursts of glory."**

13. *(B)* "The extraordinary episode in the history of civilization known as the Renaissance" (lines 41–42) identifies *(B)* as the correct answer. *(A)* is too early, off the topic. *(C)* and *(E)* are much too broad. *(D)* is a minor detail. Only *(B)* satisfactorily completes the sentence.

Answers to Facsimile Test 2

Section 1 Pages 370–376

1. *(B)* If we try every pair in the sentence, only **survival . . inescapable** makes sense. *Harrowing* is much too strong a word in *(A)*. *Humdrum* in *(C)* makes little sense. *Captivating* is scarcely a word to be used with *fact (D)*. *Public contributions* wouldn't bring *audiences (E)*. *General* is a meaningless term.

2. *(D)* If the owl kills more prey than it can eat, it must be **ruthless.** When we try **predators** in the second slot, we find that it fits nicely. If you know only one word in the pair, you can often guess the pair correctly.

3. *(A)* The *hundred years* is a clue to **centennial** in the first slot. We need a positive word for the second slot, to go along with *great* and *innovative*. Only **creative** fits.

4. *(C)* *Uncomfortably warm* suggests that matters grew worse. **Unbearably** hot and **stifling** complete the expected sequence.

5. *(E)* The difference in dates, *1865* and *1886*, suggests that the project took a long time. **Conceived** suggests the beginning of the project.

6. *(A)* The use of *good or ill, both . . and* suggests we need contrasting words.

Though there is a contrast suggested in (B) and (D), only (A) makes sense.

7. (D) *Accelerated* makes nonsense of (A), (B), and (C). *Went* in (E) is too general. Besides, *sadly* makes no sense in the first blank.

8. (E) If Picasso had to use his drawings for firewood, the critical reception couldn't have been very good: **lackluster.** (A) and (C) run counter to the sense of the sentence. (B) and (D) are irrelevant.

9. (B) The clue lies in the important word *although,* which suggests a contrast. *Only 1.5 trillionths of a second* suggests an almost unimaginable brevity. The only contrasting word is **longer.**

10. (D) **Lax** is an adjective associated with **negligence.** In the same way, **fresh** is an adjective associated with **novelty** (prob. 16, pages 164–165). (A) and (E) suggest opposite qualities. (B) and (C) are scarcely related.

11. (A) A **sculptor** uses a **chisel** as an important tool in his or her work. In the same way a **carpenter** uses a **square** (prob. 15, page 162). A *plumber* uses a *wrench* as an important tool, but the words are reversed. The other selections do not relate a tool and an artisan.

12. (A) A **pediatrician** acts upon or treats a **child.** In the same way an **ophthalmologist** acts upon or treats **eyes** (prob. 11, page 158). The alternatives show no meaningful relationships.

13. (C) **Millennia** is a measure of **time.** In the same way, **light-years** are a measure of **distance** (prob. 20, page 169). *Liters* measures capacity, not *weight.* Though *salary* is related to *work,* it is not a measure of work. (B) and (E) show pairs of related words, without any suggestion of measurement.

14. (E) **Pain** is a lesser degree of **agony.** In the same way **fun** is a lesser degree of **hilarity** (prob. 17, page 165). Similar relationships occur in (B) and (D), but the words are reversed. (C) presents antonyms. *Drowsiness* and *laziness* are related, but *drowsiness* is not a degree of *laziness.*

15. (C) **Sugar** is kept in a **canister.** In the same way **pigs** are kept in a **sty** (prob. 5, page 152). *Oil* is kept in a *barrel,* but the words

are reversed. *Dishes* may be placed on, not kept in, a *table;* in any event the words are reversed. A *horse* is kept in a *stable,* not a *racetrack. Sheep* and *shepherd* are associated in a different way altogether.

16. (D) The author points out specific examples of modern **superstitions**—for example, tossing salt, walking around a black cat, or refusing the third light on a match.

17. (E) Skimming is the best strategy. (A), (C) and (D) are mentioned in lines 17–18. (B) is mentioned in lines 28–29. Only (E) is not mentioned.

18. (A) The answer is found in the last sentence.

19. (D) One of the best ways to find a vocabulary answer is to read the sentence with each alternative in place of the tested word. Doing so suggests that only **moderate** appropriately completes the sentence.

20. (B) We can laugh at man's stupidity, but we must realize that our own thinking has primitive foundations (27–28). We cannot feel superior since, in a sense, we all "live in glass houses."

21. (B) The smaller word *eradicate* suggests that *ineradicable* means "not able to be eradicated." *Eradicate* means "destroy, **tear out by the roots.**" A *radical* idea uproots current ones.

22. (D) The passage contrasts pleasant, easygoing Mrs. Tylor with worried, tense, fearful Mrs. Harris. Mrs. Tylor is expecting a no-trouble, relaxed person like herself, but in reality she's getting potentially difficult neighbors because of the lifestyle of Mr. Harris. Mrs. Harris sets down some ground rules that may cause problems. The expectation is at odds with the reality, as slowly perceived by Mrs. Tylor.

23. (B) In an effort to be neighborly and agreeable, Mrs. Tylor sighs sympathetically, but she has no idea that Mrs. Harris will zero in on the radio and other "problems." As a result, Mrs. Tylor worries about the Tylor radio habits. Then come the other phobias: newspapers, movies, bridge. Prospects for a happy association are bleak. The Harrises have always been "unlucky" in their neighbors, but perhaps it was the other way around.

24. (A) Mrs. Tylor's feelings here are compared with her feelings when her car went dangerously out of control (24–25). The alternative that catches this feeling of no escape is (A). The meaning of *irrevocably* is also derived from the sum of its parts: *in,* "not" (78), *re,* "back" (78), *voc,* "call" (89), *able* (126). Putting the parts together defines *irrevocable:* "not be able to be called back." The situation was getting out of control.

25. (C) Mr. Harris doesn't approve of neighbors' friendly gestures, the usual means of friendly communication. He's obviously a loner.

26. (D) Mrs. Harris says that the Harrises have at least *seen* a newspaper, "not like the movies at all." Apparently, the Harrises don't go to the movies.

27. (B) Mrs. Tylor, in an effort to be friendly with the new neighbor, at first is trying to be agreeable. Later she uses "of course" because she doesn't know what else to say. What Mrs. Harris is saying goes far beyond what Mrs. Tylor might consider reasonable. The phrase becomes a mechanical, knee-jerk reaction.

28. (B) Mrs. Harris's negative remarks about newspapers requires a negative answer: *corruption.* The other alternatives are neutral or positive. *Degradation* has an interesting etymology: *de,* "down" and *grad,* "walk." Because some Latin words have been in the language a long time, they acquire a metaphorical (51–52) meaning. Thus, *degradation* is a kind of "walking down," a lowering in quality, a good explanation of Mrs. Harris's appraisal of newspaper taste.

29. (A) Mrs. Harris calls the previous neighbors "unkind." Then she mentions what she considers a terrible deed: leaving the *New York Times* on the doorstep three times. Apparently, the "unkind" neighbors were trying to be neighborly, but Mrs. Harris imputed evil motives to them. When Mrs. Tylor says, "Good Lord," her astonishment is stirred, not by the "evil deed," but by Mrs. Harris's incredible reaction to it.

30. (C) This short sketch is a gem, allowing the interplay of characters. What starts out as a pleasant episode of a woman reaching out to a new neighbor turns into an increasingly neurotic explanation of the new family's antisocial quirks. The conversation, with its glimpse into a strange new world, has been a strain on Mrs. Tylor. Though she had obviously no intention of going to the movies (or even perhaps of letting Carol go), she seizes upon the movies for a return to normal behavior and a relief from Mr. Harris and his browbeaten wife.

Section 3 Pages 377–383

1. (E) A contrast is suggested between *disentanglement* and the insect's entrapment. The contrasting word here is **enmeshed.**

2. (D) The word *unlikely* is an important clue. Both *thrive* and **abound** fit the second blank, but *although* suggests that *favorable toward* (A) does not fit the first blank. **Alien to** and **abound** complete the sentence logically.

3. (D) The title, with its key word *stars,* suggests that the book is dealing with the major news anchors. Therefore **dominate** fits perfectly into the second blank. **Emphasis upon** neatly completes the sentence.

4. (A) The word *plentiful,* followed by *less and less* suggests that a contrast is called for. The essential word for the first blank is **abundant. Dry** perfectly completes the sentence.

5. (B) If the *initial reserve* disappeared, the missing word must suggest its opposite: **exuberant.** There is another clue: the activity of first-graders on a school playground.

6. (A) The quotation suggests that Congress take an active role in advancing the goals set up by Washington. Conferring rewards requires a strong word like **support.** The others are too mild, passive.

7. *(B)* If the current reputation has helped sell his works for millions of dollars, it cannot be negative, thus eliminating *(C)*, *(D)*, and *(E)*. A clue to the correct answer is the use of *lifetime*. His paintings didn't sell during his life, but they have sold well since his death. *Fanciful* is inappropriate, leaving **posthumous**, "after burial."

8. *(A)* If you know that **ascetic** means "austere, self-denying," you need go no further. If not, you still have a good chance. *Far cry* suggests a contrast between the teenage dandy and the mature leader of his people. *(B)* and *(D)* are opposite to the intended meaning. *(C)* and *(E)* make little sense.

9. *(E)* A guide dog leads a blind person, doesn't follow *(A)*. That such dogs are gentle eliminates *(C)*. They are not encumbrances *(D)*. *(B)* is much too grandiose for the situation. Only *(E)* fills the slot appropriately.

10. *(D)* The fulfillment of a search would bring joy, satisfaction. *(A)*, *(C)* and *(E)* suggest the opposite. *(B)* makes little sense. An added proof is the prefix *eu*, "good, well" (105), suggesting that **euphoria** is "feeling good."

11. *(E)* To **germinate** is to lead to **growth.** In the same way to **combine** is to lead to a **mixture.** (prob. 4, page 151) The other alternatives do not show cause and effect.

12. *(A)* **Agriculture** is affected by the **weather.** In the same way **prices** are affected by **demand.** (prob. 18, pages 166–168) None of the other pairs shows a similar relationship.

13. *(D)* The **earth** is a part of the **solar system.** In the same way **sunspots** are a part of the **sun.** (prob. 3, page 150). A *nebula* may be a *galaxy*. A *comet* and a *meteor* are different objects, as are *asteroid* and *moon*. A *satellite* may be attached to a *planet*, but it is not part of the planet.

14. *(C)* A major purpose or activity of the **pioneer** is **trailblazing.** In the same way a major purpose or activity of a **pirate** is **theft.** (prob. 14, pages 161–162) An *usher* may be present at an *entertainment*, but his or her major activity is showing people to their seats. The words in *(D)* are reversed.

15. *(B)* **Inconvenience** shows a lesser degree of intensity than **calamity.** In the same way **fear** is a lesser form of **terror.** (prob. 7, page 154) None of the other pairs shows a similar relationship.

16. *(B)* A **year** is smaller than a **decade.** In the same way a **sapling** is smaller than a **tree.** (prob. 8, page 155) *(E)* might be a possibility, but the words are reversed.

17. *(D)* **Etymology** is the study of (word) **derivations.** In the same way **ornithology** is the study of **birds.** (prob. 19, page 168) *Entomology* is the study of *insects*, not *primates*.

18. *(E)* A **rod** is used in **fishing.** In the same way a **bow** is used in **archery.** (prob. 6, page 154) *(A)*, *(B)*, and *(C)* deal with wholly different activities. An *oar* may be used in *sailing* if the wind drops down, but it is not essential to sailing. Besides, the words are reversed.

19. *(B)* A **navigator** is associated with a **ship.** In the same way an **actor** is associated with a **stage.** (prob. 12, pages 159–160). An *angler* is associated with a *lake*, but the words are reversed.

20. *(D)* To **engrave** is to perform some constructive action on a **plate.** In the same way, to **bind** is to perform some constructive action on a **book.** (prob. 10, page 156). While we may *try* a *plan*, we do not then perform the same kind of physical action as we do when we *engrave* a *plate* or *bind a book*. The other alternatives are still further afield.

21. *(E)* **Snapdragon** is a more specific term than **flower.** In the same way, **iron** is a more specific term than **mineral.** (prob. 9, page 155) *(A)*, *(C)*, and *(D)* provide specific terms only. *Doughnut* is not a specific word for *bread*.

22. *(C)* An **aerie** is **high.** In the same way, a **caricature** is **exaggerated.** (prob. 2, pages 149–150) In both pairs an essential quality is listed. Though an *idol* may be *picturesque*, picturesqueness is not an essential quality. In the same way *puzzling* is not essential to *dishonesty*. *(B)* and *(D)* show opposite qualities.

23. *(B)* A **scoundrel** is not **harmless.** In the same way, a **moron** is not **brilliant** (prob. 1, pages 147–148). The words are not anto-

nyms because one word in each pair is a noun and one an adjective. But they do suggest opposition of essential qualities. *(A), (D),* and *(E)* suggest association rather than opposition. There is no clear relationship of any kind in *(C).*

24. *(C)* This opening section of the Constitution is not concerned with *(A), (B), (D),* and *(E),* all of which are considered in later sections.

25. *(A)* The context clearly calls for a word meaning "required, **essential.**" Trying each alternative in the slot suggests *(A).*

26. *(D)* The passage specifically mentions "**free persons,**" a reference to indentured servants.

27. *(E)* Since the first national census was still in the future, "until such enumeration shall be made," the numbers of representatives had to be arbitrarily assigned.

28. *(C)* "The whole number of free persons" includes *(A), (D),* and *(E).* "Indians not taxed" takes care of *(B).* That leaves only slaves, for whom the three-fifths fraction was adopted.

29. *(D)* All are accounted for in the passage EXCEPT Rhode Island. The capital of Rhode Island, Providence, still retains the old name.

30. *(B)* The horror of war calls for a strong word here. *(A)* and *(E)* are too colorless. *(C)* and *(D)* are stronger, but still inadequate to describe war.

31. *(C)* The precisely parallel wording rules out accident, coincidence, or any other explanation. The opening was clearly based upon the much admired Constitution of the United States.

32. *(E)* The passage is not concerned with *(A), (B), (C),* or *(D).* The theme of peace predominates.

33. *(A)* The U.S. Constitution did not consider global problems. *(B)* and *(E)* are wrong. Neither *(C)* nor *(D)* is considered in either passage. The Constitution talks about "the blessings of liberty" (3–4). The Charter promotes "human rights" (40), "justice and respect" (43), and "tolerance" (48). Both point to *(A)* as the answer.

34. *(A)* The *not* is a caution sign. If you find one of the possibilities covered in the passage, eliminate it. Self-determination and human rights are mentioned in line 40. The rights of women are mentioned in 41. Treaties are mentioned in 44. International law is mentioned in 44. The Charter does allow the use of armed force "in the common interest" (52). You may find *(A)* directly or by a process of elimination. Sometimes one method works better than the other.

35. *(B)* The passage includes "unite our strength" to affirm the basic purpose of the U.N.: cooperation.

Section 5 Pages 383–386

1. *(B)* In irony, the surface meaning of a sentence is quite opposed to the deeper meaning (page 53). The dinosaur, foretelling the end of the cockroach, is long gone, but the cockroach is still with us!

2. *(C)* Since the major thrust of the passage is the control of insects, *(C)* is the only possibility. *Etymology,* the "study of word origins," is similar in appearance to *entomology* but an entirely different study.

3. *(D)* Odhiambo points to positive help, "obvious cases, like honey from bees" (40).

4. *(B)* The Emerson quotation perfectly describes Odhiambo, a person who made the ICIPE happen.

5. *(E)* The use of *seemingly* suggests that appearances are deceiving. Sandflies *seem* harmless but are "host to a deadly parasite" (68–69). Substituting each alternative in the sentence eliminates *(A),* irrelevant; *(B),* counter to the meaning; *(C),* inappropriate as a contrast to *deadly;* and *(D),* meaningless.

6. *(C)* Lines 59–61 reveal that "many methods,

including a drastic scorched-earth policy, have temporarily halted the spread of the fly, or even, in a few instances, caused a retreat." The key to the answer is the word *temporarily*.

7. *(E)* To answer a question like this, you will probably have to skim, quickly spotting and checking off the insects mentioned. Remember that on the SAT test you may write on the question pages. The passage mentions sandflies (68), moths (67), tsetse flies (66), and mosquitoes (68). Only butterflies have *not* been mentioned.

8. *(A)* Substituting each alternative in the sentence points to *(A)* as the only answer.

9. *(D)* The author emphasizes Odhiambo's brilliance, his successes, his ability to work with people, all qualities that stimulate admiration.

10. *(B)* Odhiambo has many solutions: using insects for food (41–44), keeping blood parasites away from insects (53–54), providing new and better traps (63–64). His attack is inclusive, all embracing.

11. *(D)* Although all methods may have good results, you must base the answer solely on the passage. "New and better traps have been introduced and reduced the tsetse population by half over a 62-square-mile area" (63–65).

12. *(C)* Odhiambo created ICIPE to enlarge the attack on insect pests, combining the insights and intelligence of many researchers and presenting a well-balanced approach to insect control. It is obvious that he would call upon those researchers.

13. *(A)* The attitude of the author toward Odhiambo is entirely positive. *(C)*, *(D)*, and *(E)* may be eliminated. *(B)* implies an excited passage, filled with exclamation points. Actually, the passage presents a great deal of information in an objective way.

Answers to Facsimile Test 3

Section 1 Pages 387–394

1. *(A)* The falcon's action is compared to an airplane in a steep power dive. The verb that best expresses the comparison is **swooped. Scattering** suitably completes the sentence.

2. *(B)* *Though* tells us a contrast is called for between the good first act and the middle of the last act. The first word in the pair must be negative and the second positive. *Consternation* is a possibility for the first blank, but *contemplation* makes no sense. The only suitable pair is **desperation . . inspiration.**

3. *(C)* The context suggests that ecological habitats are being threatened. The only suitable word for the second blank is **doomed. Suitability** fits nicely into the first blank.

4. *(D)* *Not* tells us the first blank is opposed to *necessity*. The opposite of *necessity* is **luxury. Indulge** suitably completes the sentence.

5. *(E)* The key word is *relieved,* which suggests the heat must have been *uncomfortable.* The second clause supports the choice of **oppressive** in the blank.

6. *(E)* If *Associated Powers* is the original, but rejected, name, the needed word is *supplanted,* "replaced."

7. *(B)* The rigors of ballet require a muscular, lean body. Preparation would require a highly disciplined diet. The people of ancient Sparta had the reputation of living austere, highly disciplined lives. *Spartan* means "stoical, frugal, austere."

8. *(D)* A "continuing search for perfection" in an imperfect world is usually doomed to disappointment. Experts will be more than critical: *hypercritical. Hyper* (105) means "above, beyond."

9. *(C)* The clue here is a pairing of ideas (20–23). The word "inherited" is paired with the missing word. If something is inherited, it is part of the personality : *congenital (C).* If *congenital* is a hard

word for you, work through Latin prefixes and roots (75–99) or through a process of elimination. The other choices just don't fit.

10. *(C)* The major interest of a wizard is magic. (prob. 11, pages 158–159) In the same way, the major interest of a linguist is language. Magic is not a physical object like money *(A),* calculator *(B),* and handlebars *(E).* A dreamer may sometimes be confused *(D),* but confusion is not his major interest.

11. *(E)* *Bus* is a more specific term than *vehicle.* (prob. 9, pages 155–156) In the same way, *hammer* is a more specific term than *tool. Squash* and *spinach* are both specific *(A). Infant* is more specific than *child (B),* but the items are reversed. *Time* and *tide* are associated in the popular phrase, but one is not a more specific term for the other *(C).* A waterfall may be a feature of a canyon *(D),* but it is not a more specific term for canyon.

12. *(B)* A knight is used in chess. (prob. 6, page 154) A mallet is used in croquet. The other alternatives, though associated, do not show the relationship of tool to activity. The closest possibility is *(D),* but goalposts are stationary markers, not objects actively moved during the activity.

13. *(A)* An atom is part of a molecule. (prob. 3, pages 150–151) A neutron is part of an atom. A nucleus is part of a cell *(B),* but the positions have been reversed. A similar reversal is *(E).* An electron is a particle; a kilowatt is a measure or unit of electrical energy *(C).* An amoeba is a protozoan, not part of one *(D).*

14. *(A)* Risk is an essential part of speculation. (prob. 16, pages 164–165) Similarly, conciliation is an essential element in compromise. *(C), (D),* and *(E)* pair associated elements, but the second element in each is a physical object, unlike the second element in the test pair. Research may be helpful in preparing to travel, but it is not an essential element.

15. *(C)* *Amaze* is related to *astonishment*, but it is a different part of speech: verb, noun. (prob. 2, pages 149–150) In the same way, *merge* is related to *coalition (C)*, but it is also a different part of speech—verb, noun. *Weave* and *entwine* are related *(E)*, but they are both verbs. None of the others show a similar relationship.

16. *(E)* Under certain conditions, universal suffrage may "make it easy to seize the source of power" (20).

17. *(D)* "The absolute master of the Roman world *pretended* to rule . . by authority of a Senate that trembled before him" (3–5).

18. *(C)* Freedom is the reality. All others mentioned are subject to abuse: constitution (A-2), the privilege of voting (B-8), popular elections (D-3), republican institutions (E-21). The substance of freedom is mentioned in line 7.

19. *(E)* Something to "stay the flood" (14) would be a *barrier*.

20. *(E)* "The deadliest enemies of nations . . . dwell within their own borders" (30–31).

21. *(A)* The first passage points out that people may vote themselves into despotism. The other passage declares that an alert citizenry can avoid despotism. Both emphasize that the people determine their fate.

22. *(D)* The key to the answer is the word *concealment* (line 2). Although "no cover-up is intended" (3), she "only briefly alludes" (5) to "that secret inward-looking creature" (4–5) that is part of her personality.

23. *(D)* The Latin elements help with a word like *expatriate*. *Ex,* meaning "out of," combines with *patr,* "father," to suggest someone who has "left the fatherland." The other alternatives are correctly paired.

24. *(E)* Children do not usually abandon parties to "make up" stories. Though children are frequently creative, Edith Wharton's childhood creativity was beyond the usual. The answer may be confirmed by a process of elimination.

25. *(C)* In the "rigidly stratified society" (10), "there would not seem to be either the time or the place for a writer of fiction to emerge and to blossom" (15–16). Thus literary activity would be a departure from the normal. Once again, the Latin elements help confirm the choice. The prefix *ab,* "away," combines with the root *err,* "wander." An *aberration* "wanders away from the normal."

26. *(D)* When she discovered the lack of interest in her books, "her easy sophistication enables her to dismiss this" (18–19). She was indifferent, shrugging it off.

27. *(C)* "These novels have to do with the doomed attempts to challenge the social code" (58–59).

28. *(A)* Trying each of the alternatives in turn suggests that *soundness* makes the best sense. Though the attempts to challenge the social code are doomed, the challengers are strong persons with sound motives.

29. *(D)* "A very small child" is a literal statement with no comparison stated or implied. All the others contain metaphors (51–52).

30. *(C)* These are strong women (61) who were not afraid to challenge the rigid social code.

Section 3 Pages 394–400

1. *(D)* If events are being dropped and added, then the events are not unvarying. *(C)* presents an opposite meaning entirely.

2. *(A)* *Stop* tells us that the filibuster is unpopular. We need a negative word for the first blank. Only **interminable** fits. **Enforce** effectively completes the sentence. *(C),* with *unexpected* in the first blank, seems possible, but *discussing* a rule wouldn't stop the filibuster; so **discuss** doesn't fit.

3. *(B)* *(C), (D),* and *(E)* refer to emotional reactions out of place with the quiet tone of the sentence. Since Captain Cook was an explorer, not a tourist, *outdid* makes

nonsense out of *(A)*. Only **inevitably . . preceded** makes sense within the sentence.

4. *(E)* Perpetual motion is an impossible dream. *Though* tells us the inventors refuse to accept this truth. The only word that makes sense is **undaunted.** The inventors are not discouraged by the cold reality.

5. *(C)* The first word of each pair in *(A)* and *(B)* is much too strong. *(D)* and *(E)* make little sense. If there is no *typical* "sled dog," we must have been surprised.

6. *(D)* The context suggests a contrast between *raw ability* and another quality. That quality is here linked with *single-mindedness of purpose. Talent* and *dexterity* are too close to *raw ability. Guile* and *egotism* are irrelevant. The only word that fits is **concentration.**

7. *(C)* The context suggests a contrast between *becoming a hero* and *becoming an object of* **criticism. Scorn** is too strong, and **typical** doesn't fit well into the first blank. Only *(C)* makes good sense.

8. *(A) But* tells us a contrast is needed. *Breakthrough* contrasts with only one word, **conventional. Technological** perfectly completes the sentence.

9. *(E) Clout, reward,* and *prestige* all fit into the first blank, but only **supposedly** suitably completes the sentence. *(D)* is the closest alternative, but when there are two possibilities, be sure to pick the better.

10. *(B)* "Putting a scalpel" suggests *cutting,* an **incision.** This new machine doesn't make an *incision.* Thus *(B)* is the correct answer. **Science fiction** fits neatly into the first blank.

11. *(A)* When we **weed** a **garden** or **trim** a **hedge,** we perform a physical action. (prob. 18, pages 167–168). The hedge and the garden are physically changed by the activity. When we *describe* a *scene, enjoy* a *concert,* or *add numbers,* we are not performing the same kind of physical activity.

12. *(B)* Those who **nurture** are **supportive.** In the same way those who **save** are **frugal.** (prob. 2, pages 149–150). The alternatives show relationships, but these are nonessential or negative relationships. Those who *object* may or may not be *rude.* Those who *fret* are not likely to be *funny.* Those who *judge* should be impartial, not *argumentative.* Those who *reprimand* may make others *sorrowful.*

13. *(C)* An essential quality of an **arbiter** is **impartiality.** In the same way an essential quality of an **artist** is **creativity.** (prob. 12, page 159) In the remaining alternatives, the qualities may be associated with the subjects, but the connection is not essential.

14. *(D)* To **stumble** results from to **trip.** In the same way, to **laugh** results from to **amuse.** Cause and effect are suggested here. (prob. 4, page 151) *(E)* suggests opposites. There is no connection between *weep* and *shout* *(A)*.

15. *(A)* **Foot-pound** is a measure of **work.** In the same way a **kilowatt-hour** is a measure of **electricity.** (prob. 20, page 169). *Acre* is a measure of *land,* but the words are reversed.

16. *(C)* **Steam scalds.** In the same way **ice chills** (prob. 16, pages 164–165). A *mist* conceals, not *reveals.* A *telescope* may be used to *photograph* celestial bodies, but the photographing is not essentially connected with the telescope.

17. *(B)* When something is **excessive,** there is no **scarcity.** In the same way, when someone is **energetic,** there is no **fatigue.** (prob. 1, pages 147–149). Note that the two pairs contain opposed words, but they are not the same part of speech. **Excessive** and **energetic** are adjectives. **Scarcity** and **fatigue** are nouns. **Play** can be a very **serious** business, eliminating *(E)*. In *(A), miserable* would be a better pairing than **cruel.**

18. *(E)* The **aerialist** uses a **trapeze** in his or her major activity. In the same way, a **pathfinder** uses a *compass.* (prob. 15, page 162) A *clown* uses *makeup,* but the words are reversed, as are *score : singer.* A *jogger* may follow a *routine,* but he or she doesn't *use* a routine.

19. *(E)* **Malice** is not **humane.** In the same way a **farce** is not **serious.** (prob. 1, pages 147–149). These are opposed words of different parts of speech. *(A)* and *(C)* show related words, not opposed.

20. *(D)* The **moon** acts upon **tides.** In the same way **weather** acts upon **crops.** (prob. 10, page 156). The alternatives fail to show a similar relationship.

21. *(B)* The essential quality of a **philanthropist** is generosity. In the same way the essential quality of a **knight** is **chivalry** (prob. 12, page 159). *(A)* and *(E)* show contrasted pairs. *(C)* and *(D)* are associated pairs, but they do not show the same relationship as does *(B)*.

22. *(E)* A **subhead** is part of an **outline.** In the same way a **sole** is part of a **shoe.** (prob. 3, pages 150–151) In *(D)* the words are reversed.

23. *(A)* **Beagle** is a more specific term for **dog.** In the same way **sapphire** is a more specific term for **gem.** (prob. 9, page 155) *(B)* and *(D)* contain specific terms only. A *salamander* is not a *snake*, just as an *insect* is not a *spider*.

24. *(D)* All the statements are true, but the question calls for the main idea. The last sentence comes to the point, establishing *(D)* as the correct answer. The quotation at the end of paragraph 1 confirms it.

25. *(C)* Despite all efforts, the weather systems are beyond control, unpredictable. *(B)* is too specific. *(E)* is too positive. *(D)* is untrue. Since weather systems bring life and moisture as well as death and destruction, *(A)* is too one-sided. The systems are erratic.

26. *(D)* Breaks in the levee have occurred and will occur. We may thus eliminate *(A)*, *(B)*, and *(C)* because a *yes* answer is required for question 1. That leaves *(D)* and *(E)*. The fact that many communities are taking steps to minimize flood damage suggests that "not entirely" is a reasonable answer to the second question, identifying *(D)* as the correct answer.

27. *(E)* The author points out that building barrier jetties at the shore often has the same negative effect as building levees on rivers. In both places, manmade barriers prove harmful.

28. *(B)* Jetties and levees have both been designed as barriers to water flow. They have similar functions.

29. *(C)* If the seashore is easily eroded, our grip upon it must be weak, *slight*.

30. *(A)* "There had been four serious floods" is a literal, straightforward statement, with no comparison stated or implied. In *(B)*, catastrophes "wait." In *(C)* flood plains are "safety valves." In *(D)* waters "roar." In *(E)* measures "take the sting out."

31. *(B)* *Not* tells us that we need a word opposed to *concentrated*. *Scattered* is a good antonym.

32. *(E)* Reinforcing levees is ultimately not the answer. The others are all mentioned as possible remedies.

33. *(A)* The first quotation, which suggests cooperation with nature, is in tune with the main idea of the passage.

34. *(B)* "We can't pick Des Moines up and put it on a hill" (60). This quotation by Harry Fitch sums up the problem, but alternative *(D)* uses the word *overlooked,* which eliminates that possibility. Riverside dwellers *(E)* accept short-term, ultimately inadequate, solutions: LEVEES.

35. *(E)* "It's not a mystery," said Larry Larson. "We need to adjust human behavior to river systems." But most solutions have been shortsighted efforts that postpone realistic solutions. There is no mention of lack of neighborliness *(A)*. Insufficient levees *(B)* are just part of the problem. They also give residents a false sense of security. The key problem is shortsighted failure to cooperate with nature.

Section 5 Pages 400–403

1. *(D)* The clue to the answer is the sentence, "Send it to the lab." (2). If Navajo police officers send in something to the lab, it must be considered evidence.

2. *(C)* The author provides a clue: "Was it contempt?" (10) In line 14, Chee is angry. Both suggest that Leaphorn was being sarcastic.

3. *(B)* The sarcasm (question 2) and Chee's embarrassment, "flushing just a little," suggest that the two officers have a prickly relationship.

4. *(A)* "Chee believed in the poetic metaphor of the Navajo story of human genesis" (20–21). "He believed in the lessons such imagery was intended to teach" (23). His attitude is positive. The other alternatives are essentially negative.

5. *(C)* Leaphorn says, "If Yellowhorse says he's a medicine man . . . . , it is no business of the Navajo Tribal Police" (46–48). This quotation points to *(C)*.

6. *(A)* Chee has been complaining about "somebody cynically using our religion" (49–50). Leaphorn has summarily dismissed Chee's religious concerns. Such lack of concern is a disregard for sacred things *(A)*, a sacrilege.

7. *(D)* A specific detail, recognizable in a passage, takes precedence over inferences. The former is objective; the latter, subjective. Of course, SAT questions test inferences, but in these test items, no detail is there to override an inference. The specific quotation here is "No rule against it. No law" (48).

8. *(B)* Chee has already sensed contempt in Leaphorn's words (10). Leaphorn lacks sensitivity to Navajo religious beliefs (56–58). He is being compared with the

rogue Yellowhorse. *Sneering* captures the disbelief in *cynical.*

9. *(D)* Largo is identified as a captain in lines 64–65.

10. *(D)* The linkage with *flat* and the rest of the context suggest that the captain's order would be forthright, frank, and clear. The Latin elements in *unequivocal* tell a relevant story. *Voc,* "voice," and *equ,* "equal" suggest "equal voice." (89, 92) If two alternatives were presented at the same time, with equal authority, the message might be unclear. So here: *un* "not," is added to the two roots to mean "not of two equal voices."

11. *(B)* If you try *(A) (C)*, and *(D)*, you will waste valuable time. Your memory may be faulty *(D)*. Skimming is the best technique here.

12. *(A)* You might infer *(A)* immediately, but you can also eliminate the wrong alternatives. Leaphorn's sharp comments identify him as far from gullible *(B)*. He is cool, not hot-headed *(C)*. He's an old-timer, not a newcomer *(D)*. He believes in following rules *(E)* (47–48).

13. *(C)* Leaphorn is a major personage, not just local color *(A)*. There are no humorous episodes in the passage *(B)*. Leaphorn is not a tragic figure *(D)*. Leaphorn, a police officer, is nowhere suggested as a suspect. The conflict (27–29) adds zest.

INDEX